Alfred Marshall (1842–1924)
and
Francis Edgeworth (1845–1926)

Pioneers in Economics

Series Editor: Mark Blaug

Professor Emeritus, University of London
Consultant Professor, University of Buckingham
Visiting Professor, University of Exeter

This important series presents critical appraisals of influential economists from the 17th century to the present day. It focuses in particular on those economists who were influential in their own time and whose work has had an impact – often inadequately recognized – on the evolution and development of economic thought. The series will be indispensable for a clear understanding of the origin and development of economic ideas and the role played by the leading protagonists of the past.

A full list of published and future titles in this series is printed at the end of this volume.

Alfred Marshall (1842–1924) and Francis Edgeworth (1845–1926)

Edited by

Mark Blaug

Professor Emeritus, University of London

An Elgar Reference Collection

Published by
Edward Elgar Publishing Limited
Gower House
Croft Road
Aldershot
Hants GU11 3HR
England

Edward Elgar Publishing Company
Old Post Road
Brookfield
Vermont 05036
USA

A CIP catalogue record for this book is available from the British Library

Library of Congress Cataloguing in Publication Data
Alfred Marshall (1842–1924) and Francis Edgeworth (1845–1926)/edited by Mark Blaug.
p. cm. – (Pioneers in economics: 29)
1. Neoclassical school of economics. 2. Edgeworth, Francis Ysidro, 1845–1926. 3. Marshall, Alfred, 1842–1924. I. Blaug, Mark. II. Series.
HB98.2.A44 1992
330.15–dc20 92–8792
CIP

ISBN 1 85278 492 X

Printed in Great Britain at the University Press, Cambridge

Contents

Acknowledgements

The editor and publishers wish to thank the following who have kindly given permission for the use of copyright material.

Academic Press, Inc. for article: Menahem E. Yaari (1981), 'Rawls, Edgeworth, Shapley, Nash: Theories of Distributive Justice Re–Examined', *Journal of Economic Theory*, **24** (1), 1–39.

American Economic Association for article: Ulrich Kohli (1986), 'Robert Giffen and the Irish Potato: Note', *American Economic Review*, **LXXVI** (3), 539–42.

American Statistical Association for article: Paul J. Fitzpatrick (1960), 'Leading British Statisticians of the Nineteenth Century', *Journal of the American Statistical Association*, **55**, 38–70.

Association of Polytechnics and Teachers in Economics for article: O.F. Hamouda (1984), 'On the Notion of Short-Run and Long-Run: Marshall, Ricardo and Equilibrium Theories', *British Review of Economic Issues*, **6** (14), 55–82.

Basil Blackwell Ltd. for articles: A.J. Nichol (1935), 'Edgeworth's Theory of Duopoly Price', *Economic Journal*, **XLV**, 51–66; Donald A. Walker (1973), 'Edgeworth's Theory of Recontract', *Economic Journal*, **83**, 138–49; David Collard (1975), 'Edgeworth's Propositions on Altruism', *Economic Journal*, **85**, 355–60; Phyllis Deane (1983), 'The Scope and Method of Economic Science', *Economic Journal*, **93**, 1–12; Stephen M. Stigler (1978), 'Francis Ysidro Edgeworth, Statistician', Series A, *Journal of the Royal Statistical Society*, **141** (3), 287–313; J. Creedy (1983), 'F.Y. Edgeworth's Mathematical Training', *Journal of the Royal Statistical Society*, Series A, **146** (2), 158–62.

Duke University Press for articles: William Jaffé (1974), 'Edgeworth's Contract Curve: Part 1. A Propaedeutic Essay in Clarification', *History of Political Economy*, **6** (3), 343–59; William Jaffé (1974), 'Edgeworth's Contract Curve: Part 2. Two Figures in its Protohistory: Aristotle and Gossen', *History of Political Economy*, **6** (3), 381–404; John Creedy (1980), 'Some Recent Interpretations of Mathematical Psychics', *History of Political Economy*, **12** (2), 267–76; Vincent J. Tarascio (1980), 'Some Recent Interpretations of *Mathematical Psychics*: A Reply', *History of Political Economy*, **12** (2), 277–81; John Creedy (1984), 'Edgeworth: Utilitarianism and Arbitration', *History of Political Economy*, **16** (4), 609–18; Bruce Larson (1987), 'Edgeworth, Samuelson and Operationally Meaningful Theorems', *History of Political Economy*, **19** (3), 351–57; Jun-Ji Shih (1989), 'Edgeworth's Contribution to the Theory of "Ramsey Pricing"', *History of Political Economy*, **21** (2), 345–9.

Eastern Economic Association for articles: Lawrence A. Boland (1982), 'Difficulties with the Element of Time and the "Principles" of Economics or Some Lies My Teacher Told Me', *Eastern Economic Journal*, **VIII** (1), 47–58; Laurence Moss (1982), 'Biological Theory and Technological Entrepreneurship in Marshall's Writings', *Eastern Economic Journal*, **VIII** (1), 3–13.

Econometric Society for article: Arthur L. Bowley (1934), 'Francis Ysidro Edgeworth', *Econometrica*, **II**, 113–24.

Hermathena for article: Sir John Hicks (1983), 'Francis Ysidro Edgeworth', *Hermathena*, **CXXXV**, 157–8, 160–74.

Oxford University Press for article: A.D. Brownlie and M.F. Lloyd Prichard (1963), 'Professor Fleeming Jenkin, 1833–1885: Pioneer in Engineering and Political Economy', *Oxford Economic Papers*, **15**, 204–16.

Western Economic Association International for article: V.J. Tarascio (1972), 'A Correction: On the Geneology of the So-Called Edgeworth-Bowley Diagram', *Western Economic Journal*, **X** (2), 193–7.

Every effort has been made to trace all the copyright holders but if any have been inadvertently overlooked the publishers will be pleased to make the necessary arrangement at the first opportunity.

In addition the publishers wish to thank the library of the London School of Economics and Political Science and The Alfred Marshall Library, Cambridge University for their assistance in obtaining these articles.

Introduction

Alfred Marshall is one of the most perplexing of all great economists. He was the dominant figure in British economics from the 1890s right up to the 1930s, and his *Principles of Economics* (1890) still has the power to fascinate and excite the reader. On the other hand, his moral zeal and Victorian piety have always repelled some commentators while on the Continent his slighting of Walras, Menger and Böhm-Bawerk was always deeply resented. He was an excellent mathematician – indeed far better than such avowedly mathematical economists as Jevons, Walras and Barone – but he hid his mathematics away in appendices and even relegated his elegant diagrams in footnotes because he hoped to be read by businessmen. He made many original contributions to static equilibrium theory and yet hankered all his life for a dynamic theory that he was unable to produce, even going so far as to proclaim that biology and not mechanics is 'the Mecca of the economist'. His one grand theme was that price is always determined by demand *and* supply (cut by both 'blades of the scissors'); he struggled against all the evidence to argue that this had of course been well understood by the great classical economists before him: the history of economic thought was a seamless web and there never had been a 'marginal revolution'. He was a firm believer in private property and the merits of a market economy and yet he discovered some of the best arguments ever against the doctrine that free markets maximize economic welfare; moreover, he always retained a sneaking sympathy for trade unions and even socialism. He never expressed an opinion, whether on pure theory or on questions of practical policy, without an almost endless list of qualifications. In short, he was a very complex, contradictory economist which perhaps is the secret of his longlasting appeal.

His life was relatively uneventful, even for an academic. He was born in London in 1842 in a modest middle-class family and brought up by an extremely stern father in the expectation that he would become a clergyman. He rebelled against this plan, however, and went to St John's College, Cambridge, to study mathematics, graduating in 1865 as 'second wrangler in the tripos', a super bachelor's degree. He was immediately elected to a fellowship in mathematics at St John's but was forced to resign the post in 1877 when he married Mary Paley, a former student of his (in those days, fellows at Oxford and Cambridge were required to be celibate like priests). He then spent five years as principal and professor of political economy at University College, Bristol (now the University of Bristol), a year as fellow of Balliol College, Oxford (the Oxbridge requirement of celibacy by then having been eliminated), returning to Cambridge in 1885 as professor of political economy. He remained at Cambridge until his retirement in 1908 when he was succeeded by his star pupil Pigou.

By the time he published *Principles of Economics* (1890), he was already 48 years of age; apart from reviews and some articles, he had published little. Two early tracts on *The Pure Theory of Foreign Trade* and *The Pure Theory of Domestic Values*, both published in 1879, reworked some of the ideas of John Stuart Mill into rigorous diagrams; they showed Marshall in possession of the essence of marginalism but without a hint of utility theory. A slender book written jointly with his wife, *The Economics of Industry* (1879), again bore little sign of the new economics. In later years, he was fond of claiming that Cournot, Dupuit and Thünen had supplied him with the discovery of marginal utility and marginal productivity in the 1860s well before the publication of the works of Jevons, Menger and Walras. This claim must be doubted. Nevertheless, by waiting so long to put the final touches to the *Principles*, he ensured its authoritative summing-up of the fruits of the 'marginal revolution', at the same time managing somehow to reconcile the old classical with the new neoclassical economics. He published two more tomes in later life, *Industry and Trade* (1919) and *Money, Credit and Commerce* (1923), but neither of these enjoyed the success of his *Principles*. Likewise, his many official memoranda and evidence given before Royal Commissions of Inquiry in the 1880s and 1890s were little known outside Cambridge.

Among many of Marshall's original contributions to economics, all of which he modestly disguised as part of the wisdom of the past, we may single out partial equilibrium analysis, the distinction between the market period, the short period and the long period, the improved discussion of demand curves, the idea of the price-elasticity of demand, the concept of consumer and producer surplus, the analysis of the conditions for stability of equilibrium, the distinction between internal and external economies of scale, the explicit recognition of the incompatibility of competition and long-run falling supply curves (culminating in the proposition that perfect competition does not maximize economic welfare because total welfare can always be increased by a fiscal policy of taxing increasing-cost industries to subsidize decreasing-cost industries), the concept of quasi-rents, the definition of the representative firm... but enough. Some of these have become the bread and butter of economic textbooks, whereas others – such as his version of consumer and producer surplus, the tax–subsidy conclusion, and the concept of the representative firm – have been almost entirely discarded. Still others, like the distinction between increasing and decreasing costs and between internal and external economies, have been absorbed in the literature but so altered and refined as to render them almost unrecognizable as Marshallian in origin.

But even saying all that, there is still so much else left in the book that is classical in both senses of the term; that is, of enduring value and of retaining the best of the classical tradition of political economy. So much of Jevons, Menger and Walras is based on the assumption that there is a fixed supply of resources in the economy, the only problem being how to allocate them among alternative uses. Marshall, however, never lost sight of the fact that resources also grow through time and that therefore the growth of population and the accumulation of capital, not to mention technical progress, are genuine economic problems. Similarly, he found space for a discussion of 'the peculiarities of labour', those dynamic forces acting on the supply of labour that lead to cumulative disadvantages in labour's bargaining position in labour markets, thus adding what is perhaps the most penetrating contribution to labour economics since *The Wealth of Nations*. It is true that he said almost nothing about monetary theory (at least in the *Principles*) or about business cycles and macroeconomics, and was therefore responsible for the pre–Keynesian view that these questions really belonged to the periphery of economics. Also the way that he interlaced his static analysis with bits and pieces of dynamics and even historical processes sowed confusions that took the best efforts of a generation of economists to resolve. That is the price, not so much of greatness, as of too much influence; indeed, Marshall had more influence, particularly in Britain, than any great economist deserves.

Francis Ysidro Edgeworth was an economists' economist: almost the whole of his literary output was addressed to his fellow economists, taking the form of elegant technical essays on taxation, monopoly and duopoly pricing, the pure theory of international trade and the theory of index numbers. He did venture one larger-scale work, *Mathematical Psychics* (1881), a quantitative application of utilitarian ethics to economic life; its flowery and slightly old-fashioned prose, full of Greek quotations and passing allusions to classical literature, suggests a wider audience. In fact, however, it was a deep and elusive work, which even went over the heads of many of his colleagues. Its use of indifference curves caught on only slowly, while its suggestion of the 'core' of an exchange economy has only recently attracted attention as a result of developments in games theory. His exposition was terse and obscure at the best of times and his personality was retiring, with the result that most of his ideas were, and still are, continually being rediscovered by those who arrive at them in their own way. Marshall, for example, was decisively influenced by Edgeworth on a number of technical points and yet Edgeworth always deferred to Marshall as the master at whose feet he sat. When the *Economic Journal* was founded in 1891 as the organ of the Royal Economic Society, Edgeworth became its editor, a task he carried on for 35 years. He was usually perfectly fair, but on a number of occasions did reject valuable articles which he thought might impugn the reputation of the Cambridge School headed by Marshall.

Edgeworth's contributions to economics are legion: he was the first to define the laws of diminishing returns in terms of the decline of the *marginal* product of a variable factor, whereas everyone before him right back to Malthus and Ricardo had always defined it in terms of the decline of the *average* product; he was the first to define a 'generalized utility function', the utility of a good depending not just on the quantity consumed of that good but on the quantities of all other goods consumed by the individual, thus bringing substitutability and complementarity between goods squarely within the purview of utility theory; he was also the first to introduce indifference curves, the loci of combinations of two goods conveying equal total utility (drawn upside down compared with the way they are drawn nowadays), as well as the 'contract curve', the locus of tangency points of the indifference curves of different individuals. But his most beautiful contribution is the theory of the core of an exchange economy. Imagine a set of traders with certain initial holdings of goods setting out to exchange goods before there is anything like a market; these traders may act alone or they may form blocs or coalitions to improve their initial situation; everything is allowed but each and every trader must agree voluntarily to any final outcome from trade. Edgeworth then shows that in the limit, as the number of traders increases, the 'core' of the final distribution of goods resulting from unanimously agreed upon trade is the same as the set of equilibrium allocations of goods that would result from a price system under perfect competition. This insight has proved valuable to modern games theorists in proving the existence of general equilibrium à la Walras.

Edgeworth was born in 1845 in Ireland and educated at home until he was old enough to enter Trinity College, Dublin. From Trinity College he went to Balliol College, Oxford, where he graduated in letters in 1865. After practising law in London and lecturing on English literature at Bedford College, London, he took up a post as lecturer in logic at King's College, London, followed by a professorship in political economy at King's in 1885. In 1891 he became Drummond Professor of Political Economy at Oxford, which then as now carried with it a non-teaching fellowship at All Souls College, Oxford. He retired in 1922 but went on editing *The Economic Journal* jointly with John Maynard Keynes until his death in 1926 at the age of 81.

Apart from *Mathematical Psychics*, he published a youthful book on ethics and a brief work on the measurement of utility, *Metrike* (1887), as well as several lectures on the economics of war during and immediately after the First World War. He collected his major essays and reviews together in a three-volume publication, *Papers Relating to Political Economy* (1925). He is one of the few great economists (apart from Bernoulli and Slutsky) to have made original contributions to mathematical statistics. In the first programme of his television series, *The Age of Uncertainty* (1981), John Kenneth Galbraith remarked that 'all races have produced notable economists, except the Irish'. Had he forgotten the names of Cantillon, Longfield, Cairnes, Leslie and particularly Edgeworth?

Note

Several paragraphs in this Introduction were borrowed from my *Great Economists Before Keynes* (Wheatsheaf Books, 1986).

[1]

FRANCIS YSIDRO EDGEWORTH

By Arthur L. Bowley

Among the pioneers of econometrics, Francis Ysidro Edgeworth must be given a very high place. Especially important are his contributions with regard to the study of the theory of economics and the theory of statistics by the help of mathematics. For actual measurement he would give place to Jevons, for the theory of measurement to no economist.

With the recent publication of J. M. Keynes's *Essays in Biography*,[1] the facts of Edgeworth's life are familiar. He was born in 1845 at Edgeworthstown, County Longford, Ireland, on the estate where his ancestors established themselves in the sixteenth century—reduced to very small value by the time he inherited it in 1911. His father (1809–1847), who appears to have spent his life in the peripatetic pursuit of knowledge, is described by Thomas Carlyle[2] as he appeared about the year 1836; Maria Edgeworth (1767–1847), the celebrated authoress, well-known in the literary circles of the early nineteenth century, was his aunt. His mother was a Spanish refugee, married after a brief acquaintance in London. One of his great-great-grandfathers was a Huguenot refugee. Francis Ysidro was the youngest of five sons and survived all his brothers. His features suggested his Spanish descent; in his knowledge of French, German, Italian, and Spanish, and in his ready acquaintance with economists of all nations, there is a suggestion of his international origin.

In 1862 he entered at Trinity College, Dublin, where it may be presumed he studied both mathematics and classics. He was never at a loss for a classical quotation. I have found no record of his graduation at Dublin, but in 1867, in his twenty-second year, he went to Oxford, and in 1868 was admitted to Balliol College. In 1869 he was awarded first class honors in Literis Humanioribus, the great school of Philosophy; but he did not actually take his degree (B.A.) till 1873.[3] He was admitted to the Bar in 1877. During the ten years after he reached Oxford his interests appear to have been philosophy, ethics and, subsequently, economics. He was immersed in the writings of Bentham and others of the utilitarian school, while in economics he was educated in the works of John Stuart Mill. In this period he probably neglected

[1] Keynes's study of Edgeworth is essentially the same as the obituary that appeared immediately after his death, *Economic Journal*, 1926.

[2] *Life of Sterling*, Part II, Chapter IV.

[3] Subsequently he took the M.A. degree in 1877 (a matter of formality), and at a later date was given an honorary D.C.L. of the University of Durham.

mathematics, for his mathematical writing indicates a want of systematic training. Though he shows great insight into the principles of mathematics, there is a want of facility and neatness in his handling of problems. Familiar as he was with the work of Laplace, Todhunter, and Clerk Maxwell, he had difficulty in elementary applications. His line of thought is often a little obscure; sometimes he labors the obvious, and at others is so brief as to be difficult to follow. He was always the victim of numerical mistakes and errors in writing and printing. Apparently he settled in London immediately after he left Oxford, and had no definite occupation.

PHILOSOPHY AND THE PHILOSOPHICAL ASPECT OF ECONOMICS

It is evident that in the first part of his life he turned his mind principally to philosophic questions and especially to the relation between ethics and economics. His first known publication is a paper on "New and Old Methods of Ethics" in 1877. He began to interpret utilitarian and economic ideas by mathematical symbols, and very early he must have realized the importance of the conception of probability. The result of this period of study and incubation was the publication of his *Mathematical Psychics* in 1881. The mathematical economics in this book he owes primarily to Cournot, Jevons, and Gossen, something to his great contemporary Marshall;[4] the ethics is developed from Mill and Sidgwick; but the whole conception and treatment are original in the highest degree. It was so original that its importance has been only very gradually realized. The circulation was limited and it was little known;[5] the number of philosophers or economists qualified to understand it was very small, but among them were Jevons and Marshall. The following extracts from *Memorials of Alfred Marshall*, edited by A. C. Pigou, are interesting from many points of view.[6]

Alfred Marshall first became for me a notable name when Jevons [in 1879 or 1880], conversing about mathematical economics, recommended as the latest contribution to that subject the now celebrated papers on the *Pure Theory of Foreign Trade and Domestic Values*. At the same time Jevons highly praised the then recently published *Economics of Industry*. Eagerly studying these writings, I discerned a new power of mathematical reasoning, not only in the Papers

[4] Cournot 1801–77, Gossen 1810–58, Jevons 1835–82, Marshall 1842–1924, Edgeworth 1845–1926, Wicksell 1851–1926.

[5] "Three days after Part II was finished, I received and saw for the first time the *Mathematical Psychics* of Professor Edgeworth." Irving Fisher in Preface to *Mathematical Researches in the Theory of Value and Prices*, dated 1892. (The phrase is re-translated from the French edition.)

[6] P. 66, *Reminiscences* by Professor F. Y. Edgeworth.

bristling with curves and symbols, but also in certain portions of the seemingly simple textbook. With reference to such passages, writing in the year 1881, I characterized the author by a phrase which he himself afterwards acknowledged to be appropriate, "bearing under the garb of literature the armour of mathematics." The phrase might be applied to many passages in the text of the *Principles of Economics.*

J. M. Keynes on Marshall (pp. 25–26):

In 1881 [Marshall], reviewing Edgeworth's *Mathematical Psychics*, after beginning "This book shows clear signs of genius, and is a promise of great things to come," adds "It will be interesting, in particular, to see how far he succeeds in preventing his mathematics from running away with him, and carrying him out of sight of the actual facts of economics."

Perhaps Marshall did not appreciate the path-breaking quality of the book, since he was already averse from the mathematical exposition of economics. The reading of it is at least essential to all who wish to understand the concepts that underly Edgeworth's later writings, and it is fortunately now easily accessible, since it has been reprinted at the London School of Economics (price 5s.).

PROBABILITY AND STATISTICS

We next find Edgeworth appointed as Lecturer in Logic at King's College, London, in 1880; in 1890 he succeeded Thorold Rogers there as Tooke Professor of Economic Science and Statistics, a chair more noticeable for the distinguished men who have held it than for its emoluments.[7]

Now begins the period of the publications on the theory of probability. In 1883–84, at least six papers appeared in this sphere, of which the first was "The Law of Error" (*Phil. Mag.* 1883). While *Mathematical Psychics* laid the foundation and showed part of the construction of the edifice of his economic theory, the paper (only 36 pages) on *Methods of Statistics*, read at the Jubilee Meeting of the Statistical Society in 1885, exhibits at once the whole plan of his statistical work. To use the kind of metaphor in which he delighted, the foundation, based on the work of Laplace, Lexis, and Venn, was laid, the first story was completed, and the frame work of the second was partly set up, partly in the process of execution. In the next forty years more stories were added, additional buttresses were erected where the structure was weak, and innumerable decorations within and without added to the amenities of the edifice in the best classical and italianate styles, while secret rooms were provided for initiates. There is little in the

[7] The professors have been Thorold Rogers, Edgeworth, Cunningham, Urwick. After the war its annual value was about £50, and it was merged in another professorship, now held by F. A. von Hayek under the original title.

subsequent work whose origin cannot be traced through this paper, but, as with *Mathematical Psychics*, it was appreciated by very few, and the development and the use of the important principles which Edgeworth was the first to introduce to English statisticians was left almost entirely to him for many years.

Edgeworth was the philosopher of statistics rather than the practitioner. We may give prominence to two of his main subjects, those in which his point of view differs from most modern statisticians.—Every judgment based on mathematical chance is related to *a priori* probability. There must be some presumption about the field in which the events take place. If an event occurs of which the chance is small, e.g., five successive throws of double-six with a pair of dice, we must choose between the alternatives that the dice were loaded and that an improbable event has taken place. If the difference between the average of two samples is greater than the three times the computed standard deviation, we have the alternatives that the samples were badly selected, that an unusual event has taken place, or that the populations from which they were drawn were essentially different. Or again we may need to assume, as in field samples in agricultural tests, the existence of an underlying normal curve of variation. Edgeworth frequently used the principle of maximum probability and deviations from it—his method of "genuine inverse probability"—but his treatment of it was essentially different from that of Professor R. A. Fisher. I understand the latter to deny the applicability of the conception of *a priori* probability and to make strenuous efforts to evade its use. Edgeworth was convinced that there was always an element of the unknown, that in the end we must fall back on unmeasured experience. But in his hands this did not mean that we could not obtain useful results, for in appropriate cases the influence of the unknown could be reduced to such small dimensions as to leave the result almost unaffected on any reasonable hypothesis. It is not certain, however, that this judgment, based principally on economic statistics, would be applicable to all physical experiments, though he traced it in the theory of atomic motion.

The second subject which Edgeworth developed from a specially distinctive view is the Law of Error. His Law of Great Numbers is usually erroneously classed as one of a species which contains the formulae of Thiele, Charlier, Karl Pearson, and others. It is true that the mathematical expression is very similar, but the fundamental conception is not the appropriateness for representing experimental results, but the determination of a form that would be derived from given hypotheses; the experimental verification is secondary. The hypotheses, based on Laplace's work, are the existence of numerous independent causes and their interplay in producing aggregates or averages. According to the number and strength of these causes, the successive terms of his law of great numbers have greater or less importance. This law is

$$z = e^{-(-1/3!k_1 D^3 + 1/4!k_2 D^4 -)} \left(e^{-x^2/c^2} / c\sqrt{\pi} \right)$$

where z is the frequency with which a deviation of x from the average of measurements occurs, and c, k_1, k_2, are constants depending on the successive moments of the curve. Qualifications are introduced when the causes are not completely independent and when successive experiments are inter-related. A development to the 'method of translation' is made, when the observed quantity is not itself distributed according to the law but is some function of a variable so distributed. The formula is extended also to two or more variables.

It was a favorite theme for Edgeworth that the normal law of error, or its generalized expression, is prevalent in nature and in the subject matter of economics, however much disguised; or, if not in the raw material, then in the play of averages. It is hardly yet realized how nearly normal is the distribution of averages, even when the number of their constituents is small. The law of small numbers is practically indistinguishable from the normal law, unless the numbers are indeed very small. This was pointed out very clearly by Edgeworth. He said, "if the Greeks had been acquainted with the Law of Error, they would have erected an altar to it," presumably alongside that to the Unknown God. His interest was rather in the fundamental prevalence of the law than in its applicability to the representation of groups; his long series of papers on the Mathematical Representation of Statistical Data (*Statistical Journal*, 1913–18) was, I think, more valuable for its by-products than for its major thesis, and Edgeworth himself expressed doubt of their use. The important applications were in measuring the accuracy of averages, and the significance of the differences between them. His study of fluctuations (*Statistical Journal*, 1885) may be compared with Professor R. A. Fisher's method of variance; the one in a cross table of death-rates in years and districts, the other in a Roman square of agricultural experiments.

A general view of the several facets of Edgeworth's intellectual interests is obtained by studying his work on Index-Numbers of Prices, beginning with his reports to a British Association Committee, 1887–1890. On the statistical side, we find the examination of the merits of various types of averages, of the effect of weights and their small importance in this problem, and of the application of the law of error for determination of precision.[8] On the economic side, there is a very care-

[8] "By rejecting the Calculus of Probabilities (Mr. Walsh) has . . . thrown away an instrument necessary for the performance of that measurement" (i.e. of the value of money). *Papers*, II, 376. (Written in 1901.)

ful and systematic analysis of the quaesitum, the quantity to be measured for particular economic purposes, and of the relation to currency problems. "Beneath the apparent unity of a single question there is discoverable upon a close view a plurality of distinct problems."[9] The logical basis of the investigation is further developed in later papers, especially those which deal with Mr. Correa Walsh's work. It may be recommended to anyone who wishes to do serious work on Index Numbers to read Professor Irving Fisher's *The Making of Index Numbers*, Mr. Walsh's *The Problem of Estimation*, and Edgeworth's series of papers, reports, and reviews. If, in consequence of inability to bring all the views expressed into a coherent body of thought, our aspirant gives up the problem, he will at least have obtained an insight into the psychology of the writers.

In 1892 Edgeworth published his first paper on Correlation. It is idle to try to determine whether he or Professor Karl Pearson can claim priority in arriving at the main ideas which have led to the now well-known methods. Both attacked the problem of joint variation at the point which Galton had reached. Edgeworth gave in 1892 the general formula for multiple correlation in essentially the same form as is now used, viz.,

$$z = Ce^{-1/D.(x_1^2R_{11}+x_2^2R_{22}+\cdots+2x_1x_2R_{12}+\cdots)}$$

where R_{11}, R_{12} $\cdots$ are the minors of the determinant

$$D = \begin{vmatrix} 1 & \rho_{12} & \rho_{13} & \cdot\cdot \\ \rho_{12} & 1 & \rho_{23} & \cdot\cdot \\ \cdot & \cdot & \cdot & \cdot\cdot \\ \cdot & \cdot & \cdot & \cdot\cdot \\ \cdot & \cdot & \cdot & \cdot\cdot \end{vmatrix}.$$

Here ρ_{12} is an average of the inverse ratios of an x_1, to that value of x_2 which is most frequently associated with it. This average was more closely investigated and defined in 1893, and an expression for it was obtained which was subsequently identified with Pearson's sum-product formula.

The numerous statistical studies published between 1893 and 1926 are to a very large extent the working out of ideas expressed or latent in the papers already named, with numerous applications to a great variety of problems and with critical and explanatory references to the work of other writers. Throughout the twoscore papers listed for these years runs the thread of the importance of sound fundamental ideas on probability in all mathematical statistics as opposed to purely empirical work. The ground deliberately chosen as central to his posi-

[9] *Papers*, I, 199.

tion is described in his Presidential Address to the Royal Statistical Society in 1912 "On the Use of the Theory of Probabilities in Statistics Relating to Society."

In writing of Edgeworth's attitude to statistics I feel that I am on fairly safe ground. When, in 1895, I was appointed to lecture on Statistics at the newly founded School of Economics, on Marshall's introduction I wrote to him for advice on the nature and literature of the subject, and he recommended principally Venn's *Logic of Chance*, Todhunter's *History of Probability* and Lexis' *Zur Theorie der Massenerscheinungen*, to which I naturally added his 1885 paper at the Jubilee meeting and his reports on Index-Numbers. From that time till his death I constantly learned from him, worked with him, and met him frequently in London and Oxford. It was with difficulty that I could turn the conversation from the nature of probabilities and the applications of the Law of Error. A trivial anecdote illustrates this. In 1904, a party of economists was bicycling out of Cambridge, and, with some danger to the traffic, Edgeworth began to discuss the method of translation or some similar topic; Professor Cannon drew up alongside and said, "Put on the pace, Bowley, he can't talk mathematics at more than 12 miles an hour."

GENERAL ECONOMICS

In Economics proper, to which I now turn, I cannot claim the same intimacy, and depend rather on the judgment of economists as shown in their quotations from his works, and especially on Pigou's very sympathetic review of Edgeworth's collected papers in the *Economic Journal*, June 1925.

Wherever economic theory called for mathematical treatment Edgeworth's interest was specially aroused, and, though this test by no means admits all the topics he treated, it is of special importance to econometricians.

It is the original analysis in *Mathematical Psychics* that has found the principal place in economic literature, namely the invention or discovery of Indifference Curves and their relation to the Contract Curve. The same analysis was applied in 1893 to the Pure Theory of International Values, and the findings of this study have been incorporated widely in treatment by later authors. Edgeworth did not seek after exceptions or paradoxes for their own sake; but in conscientious analysis he found that accepted rules were only true approximately and within limits. Thus, though convinced that free-trade was the best policy, at least for England, his analysis led to determination of the cases where an import or export duty was in part borne by the foreigner. He was greatly interested in Mr. Bickerdike's view of "incipient taxes" which were advocated as benefiting an importing country, but his final judgment was adverse, as is seen in the concluding sentences of his criticism, which may be quoted in full as typical of his style and outlook.

Thus, the direct use of the theory is likely to be small. But it is to be feared that its abuse will be considerable. It affords to unscrupulous advocates of vulgar Protection a peculiarly specious pretext for introducing the thin edge of the fiscal wedge. Mr. Bickerdike may be compared to a scientist who, by a new analysis, has discovered that strychnine may be administered in small doses with prospect of advantage in one or two more cases than was previously known; the result of this discovery may be to render the drug more easily procurable by those whose intention, or at least whose practice, is not medicinal. It was thus that the "drama of poison" perpetrated in the reign of Louis XIV was initiated by one whose baleful receipt was obtained from Glaser, a chemist of eminence, the discoverer of a new substance. Let us admire the skill of the analyist, but label the subject of his investigation *Poison*.[10]

From Cournot onwards, it has been recognized that the theory of monopoly demands essentially mathematical treatment. In this connection we find numerous studies relating to taxation, to railway rates, and other topics. The possible advantages of monopoly, in every stage from its establishment in one industry to complete socialism, are brought to light, in some cases to be condemned, in others accepted. In particular, Edgeworth discusses the possibility of discrimination, that is, rates or charges differentiated by place or class of customer, which is not inherent in pure competition but may result in net benefit to all concerned. There is very much that is important in these studies besides the often-quoted proof that in a specially devised and exceptional case a tax on one of two rival commodities may result in a lowering of the price of both. The mathematical results need for their application statistical data, such as are the proper study of econometricians—for example, questions on whether certain functions are positive or negative—and depend on the actual measurement of their elasticity.

We may agree with Pigou that the papers on the "Application of Probabilities to Economics" (*Economic Journal*, 1910, pp. 286 and 441 *seq.*) are most noticeable, and we may add, most characteristic. One of the earlier sentences in the first paper is "The theory of Probabilities lends to Economics, as to other sciences, certain premises which are evidenced, neither by pure intuition nor by formal induction, but by general impressions and what may be called mathematical common sense." We can often proceed a considerable distance with certainty by the help of accepted postulates, such that demand in

[10] *Papers*, II, 365.

general falls with an increase of price. Presently the results depend on the neglect of quantities which may be presumed to be small; such results are probably true in the light of general experience of the behavior of continuous functions. Though no numerical measurement of chance can be obtained, it may be affirmed that the probability of the failure of a theorem is very small. We may even go further and assume that in the absence of specific information a positive value of a variable is as likely to occur as a negative value, and even this meagre datum may afford definite guidance. It is to be remarked that in these papers are included not only instances of mathematical chance, but a number of applications of the conception of continuity of functions, where arguments are commonly based on unverified assumptions, not proved to be valid, but held to be reasonable or probable. Closely allied to this is the neglect of quantities presumed to be small.

Though there seems to be a cleavage between the studies on the theory of probability and those on international trade and monopoly, to Edgeworth there was an underlying unity in the fundamental conceptions and in much of the method of Economics and of Statistics; this unity found its expression in the mathematical treatment of both, and his interest was most easily aroused where mathematical ideas were involved, whether in ethics, economics, or statistics. It is in this region of fundamental similarities that we find what is most characteristic of his genius, that which distinguished him from almost all other economists and statisticians.

Neither subjective happiness nor belief can be measured, but indicators can be found in allied measurable quantities. Wealth has a relationship to welfare, belief can be connected with mathematical probability. There are scales of greater and less for incommensurable objects. The utilitarian's ideal of the greatest possible happiness is related to the mathematical economic conception of maximum utility. The best judgment or belief to be obtained from statistical data can be founded on algebraic maxima. From the fundamental expression for maximum utility and maximum probability are derived the detailed equations of exchange on the one side, and such formulae as those for 'least squares' on the other, as in Mechanics the principle of minimum potential energy leads to equations of equilibrium. While the foundations are similar, there is also interaction in the developments. Utilitarian ideas are involved in the choice of the 'best mean,' and probability justifies the conception of the representative firm, of the average man, and of the similarity of groups in relation to utility. In particular in many cases, where the solution of an economic problem depends on the determination of the direction of a curve, *a priori* probability will supply the most plausible answer.

EDITORIAL WORK

In 1891 Edgeworth succeeded Thorold Rogers[11] as Drummond Professor of Political Economy at Oxford and held that chair till he resigned in 1922 and became Emeritus Professor. During the whole of this period and till his death in 1926 he was Editor, or one of the Editors, of the *Economic Journal,* the first issue of which was in March 1891.

So far as he had a home it was, according to the time of year, two rooms at Mount Vernon, Hampstead, on the outskirts of and overlooking London, or in his Fellow's room at All Souls College, Oxford. Characteristically he had his own means of transit; from Oxford he bicycled by a route known to his friends as "Edgeworth's way" 30 miles to Great Missenden, whence he took train to Hampstead. Very few of his friends ever penetrated to his sanctum at Oxford—bachelor's rooms, for he never married—very many were entertained by him at All Souls College and at the Savile Club, London. He made no collection of books. In London he was to be found working in the rooms of the Statistical Society, and there or at Oxford he studied the books sent to the *Economic Journal* to review. He was also to be met at the sessions of the Statistical Society (President in 1912–14) at the Economics Society (that used to meet at University College, London where H. S. Foxwell was professor), and at the historic Political Economy Club, to which he was elected in 1891;[12] these three societies meet in regular sequence in the first three weeks of each winter month. He was for many years regular in attendance at the annual meetings of the British Association for the Advancement of Science, being President of the Economic Section in 1889. His name was in the first list of elected members of the British Academy in 1903. Edgeworth was thus the most accessible of the English economists. He usually spent his vacations in the Alps or near Dublin, but otherwise was not a great traveller.

The professional duties at Oxford were during his tenure of office very light. Economics till after his retirement was not a major subject in any 'School,' and in any case the custom at Oxford is to depend

[11] Thorold Rogers was Professor at Oxford 1862–68 and again from 1888 till his death in 1890. He was Tooke Professor in London from 1859 till 1890, occupying the two chairs simultaneously. Edgeworth gave up the Tooke Professorship on his appointment at Oxford. He was succeeded in London by Dr. W. Cunningham, and at Oxford by D. H. Macgregor in 1922.

[12] The first paper he read there was entitled "Under what conditions, if any, is the burden of a customs duty not borne by the consumers of the imported commodity," in 1893. The date is important in connection with his later work on tariff problems.

rather on College lecturers and tutors than on professorial teaching. Though he had great influence on many individuals, he did not organize any corporate teaching; the few courses of lectures he gave were not well attended, for indeed he had no faculty for that method of teaching. His work was in fact almost independent of his position at Oxford.

Mr. Keynes has testified to the great importance of his editorial work. It was specially marked in the organization of reviews of books. Though Edgeworth's direct writings turn on a limited number of subjects, his acquaintance with economic theory and with economists was very extensive in place and time and his memory was remarkable. In the reviews written by himself and republished, his encyclopaedic knowledge is as evident as the acuteness of his critical powers; but even these reviews are selective, for he appears to have looked critically at every book that reached the *Journal's* office. A request for a review would be accompanied by some apposite remarks on particular points in the text. Because he never developed a system of economics and never published a book except *Mathematical Psychics*, there is an erroneous impression that his sole interest was in refinements and exceptions, in mathematical curiosa rather than in the broad stream of economic thought; this impression is completely dispelled by reading his volume of reviews. Since nearly the whole edition of his *Papers* has been sold, it is to be hoped that a just view of his range has now been reached by all competent judges.

*

Readers of Edgeworth's writings[13] are often deterred by what appears to be deliberate obscurantism in the arguments. Many by-paths are followed and left with a quotation from the classics; mathematical curiosa are interspersed with poetry; elaborate metaphors are developed, where one would expect rigid deductions. But if one studies carefully a treatise as a whole, with some knowledge of Edgeworth's general lines of thought, and then reads it a second time, one finds that the whole is coherent, the arguments valid and consecutive, the theme

[13] A nearly complete study of Edgeworth's work can be made from the sources here listed:

Papers Relating to Political Economy. Three volumes. Published on behalf of the Royal Economic Society by Macmillan and Co., 1925.

Review of the above by A. C. Pigou, *Economic Journal*, June 1925.

Mathematical Psychics, 1881, reprinted by the London School of Economics, 1932.

F. Y. Edgeworth's Contributions to Mathematical Statistics. Published as a separate pamphlet by the Royal Statistical Society, 1928. This contains an annotated bibliography of seventy-four papers by him on mathematical statistics.

is made clearer and more vivid by the variations. "By steps that are neither violently abrupt nor tediously circuitous, he reaches the heights from which the mutual dependence of all economic quantities can best be contemplated. At those heights too, are observed some curiosities of theory, like Alpine flowers, found only at great altitudes." These words may surely be transferred from his review of a book by another writer and applied tc himself.

London School of Economics

[2]

EDGEWORTH'S THEORY OF DUOPOLY PRICE[1]

A NEW generation often brushes decisively aside what was once considered the final truth. This paradox is definitely, though somewhat inconspicuously illustrated in the theory of *competition among a few*. Cournot was first to perceive the problem.[2] When Cournot's work finally attracted posthumous attention, Professor F. Y. Edgeworth became his best known critic.[3] So effective was Edgeworth's counter-approach that in the very last years of his life he was still able to say, "The demolition of Cournot's theory is generally accepted." [4] But in the same way that Edgeworth disputed the departed shade of Cournot, so in our generation voices arise to contradict his own spirit.[5] In the face of a second general reversal of opinion, the present article is in part a defence of Edgeworth.

It is important to note that Edgeworth's contribution to the theory of duopoly is conditioned by the assumption of increasing cost. In his paper on "The Pure Theory of Monopoly" he

[1] This article was completed by the writer during his tenure of a Sterling research fellowship at Yale University.

[2] A. A. Cournot, *Recherches sur les principes mathématiques de la théorie des richesses* (Paris, 1838). English translation by N. T. Bacon, with Introduction and Notes by Irving Fisher (Macmillan, 1897; reprinted 1927, 1929). See also A. A. Cournot, *Principes de la théorie des richesses* (Paris, 1863); *Revue sommaire des doctrines économiques* (Paris, 1876).

Luigi Amoroso, Italian mathematical economist, was Cournot's most ardent disciple. *Lezioni di economica matematica* (Bologna, 1921), pp. 254 ff.; "La curva statica di offerta," *Giornale degli economisti*, Vol. LXX (1930), pp. 1–26.

[3] F. Y. Edgeworth, *Mathematical Psychics* (London, 1881); reprint by the London School of Economics and Political Science (1932). "La teoria pura de monopolio," *Giornale degli economisti*, July 1897, pp. 13–31; English translation in F. Y. Edgeworth, *Papers Relating to Political Economy*, Vol. I, pp. 111–42.

[4] Edgeworth, *Papers*, Vol. I, p. 111.

[5] Knut Wicksell, "Mathematische Nationalökonomie," *Archiv für Sozialwissenschaft und Sozialpolitik*, Vol. LVIII, Heft 2 (1927), pp. 252–81, especially pp. 267–75; Joseph Schumpeter, "The Instability of Capitalism," ECONOMIC JOURNAL, Vol. XXXVIII (1928), particularly pp. 369–70 n.; Harold Hotelling, "Stability of Competition," ECONOMIC JOURNAL, Vol. XXXIX (1929), pp. 41–57; E. H. Chamberlin, "Duopoly: Value when Sellers are Few," *Quarterly Journal of Economics*, Vol. XLIV (1929), pp. 81–100; Erich Schneider, "Zur Theorie des mehrfachen Monopols," *Archiv für Sozialwissenschaft und Sozialpolitik*, Vol. LXIII (1930), pp. 541–46; Erich Schneider, *Reine Theorie monopolistischer Wirtschaftsformen* (Tübingen, 1932), especially pp. 132–75; Edward Chamberlin, *The Theory of Monopolistic Competition* (Harvard University Press, 1933), pp. 30–55.

featured "an extreme case of increasing cost," one in which there were no costs at all except in the sense that production beyond a certain limit was subject to infinite cost, *i.e.* impossible. A case of gradually increasing cost is treated in mathematical language in his review of Amoroso.[1] The form in which Edgeworth's ideas are expressed, however, is not nearly so important as their content. Therefore, instead of following the unusual diagrams and symbols of his original presentation, a more conventional illustration may be considered.

Let us suppose that a certain uniform commodity is produced for a given market in twelve factories, each subject to identical conditions of increasing cost as shown in Table I. The figures in this table include transportation and selling costs as well as those of physical production. The product is sold to an extremely

TABLE I

Schedule of Costs for each Factory.

Quantity produced.*	Fixed Costs.	Total Variable Costs.	Average Variable Costs.	Marginal Costs.
0	2,000	0	0·10	0·10
2,000	2,000	300	0·15	0·20
4,000	2,000	800	0·20	0·30
6,000	2,000	1,500	0·25	0·40
8,000	2,000	2,400	0·30	0·50
10,000	2,000	3,500	0·35	0·60
12,000	2,000	4,800	0·40	0·70
14,000	2,000	6,300	0·45	0·80
16,000	2,000	8,000	0·50	0·90
18,000	2,000	9,900	0·55	1·00
20,000	2,000	12,000	0·60	1·10

* Units per interval of time. All quantities in the following tables and in the text are to be interpreted in this sense.

large number of buyers, each of whom purchases a very small part of the total. An assumed schedule representing the total demand is shown in Table II. In this particular case 0·60 may be termed the price of perfect competition, for at this price each factory can produce and sell as under perfect competition a quantity (10,000 units—see Table I) the marginal cost of which is exactly equal to price 0·60. The total production of all twelve factories, *i.e.* 120,000 units, is then exactly equal to the quantity demanded at price 0·60 (see Table II). On the other hand, if all twelve factories are combined under monopoly management,

[1] "The Mathematical Economics of Professor Amoroso," ECONOMIC JOURNAL, Vol. XXXII (1922), pp. 400–407.

it may be shown on the basis of the information in Tables I and II that the monopoly realises a maximum profit at price 1·00.

TABLE II

Demand Schedule

Price.	Quantity.
0·40	144,000
0·50	132,000
0·60	120,000
0·70	108,000
0·80	96,000
0·90	84,000
1·00	72,000
1·10	60,000
1·20	48,000

Special attention is invited, however, to the behaviour of prices when productive facilities are divided between two independent combinations. For convenience in calculation let us assume that each combination controls six factories. From Table I may be derived a schedule of costs for each group of six factories as shown in Table III. The managers of the two competing combinations may be designated *A* and *B*. When the market opens, it may be supposed that *A* offers to sell[1] at price 1·00. If *A* maintains this price, and if *A*'s customers all desert

TABLE III

Schedule of Costs for each Group of Six Factories.

Quantity produced.	Fixed Costs.	Total Variable Costs.	Average Variable Cost.	Marginal Cost.
0	12,000	0	0·10	0·10
12,000	12,000	1,800	0·15	0·20
24,000	12,000	4,800	0·20	0·30
36,000	12,000	9,000	0·25	0·40
48,000	12,000	14,400	0·30	0·50
60,000	12,000	21,000	0·35	0·60
72,000	12,000	28,800	0·40	0·70
84,000	12,000	37,800	0·45	0·80
96,000	12,000	48,000	0·50	0·90
108,000	12,000	59,400	0·55	1·00
120,000	12,000	72,000	0·60	1·10

[1] It is implicitly assumed in Edgeworth's analysis of duopoly that prices are named by sellers. Buyers have an indirect influence but no direct voice in the determination of prices. On the other hand, prices in Cournot's market depend upon competitive bidding among buyers, and sellers have no direct voice. For further analysis of this difference see A. J. Nichol, "A Re-appraisal of Cournot's Theory of Duopoly Price," *Journal of Political Economy*, Vol. XLII (1934), pp. 80–105.

him in so far as a sufficient quantity is available at any lower price, it is to *B*'s greatest advantage to sell at a price slightly lower than 1·00, taking all *A*'s business temporarily away from him. Edgeworth assumed extremely minute gradations in price, but no great violence is done to his theory if instead no gradations in price are considered less than one-hundredth of the standard monetary unit. *B* then may be expected to sell at price 0·99. With positions reversed, *A* finds it to his greatest immediate advantage to cut to price 0·98. Prices in accordance with

TABLE IV

Step.	*A*'s Price.	*B*'s Price.	*A*'s Sales.	*B*'s Sales.
1	1·00	—	72,000	0
2	1·00	0·99	0	73,200
3	0·98	0·99	74,400	0
4	0·98	0·97	0	75,600
15	0·86	0·87	88,800	0
16	0·86	0·85	0	90,000
* 17	0·84	0·85	88,800	2,368
18	0·84	0·83	4,738	87,600
19	0·82	0·83	86,400	7,108
20	0·82	0·81	9,478	85,200
21	0·80	0·81	84,000	11,850
22	0·80	0·79	14,222	82,800
23	0·78	0·79	81,600	16,595
24	0·78	0·77	18,969	80,400
29	0·72	0·73	74,400	30,845
30	0·72	0·71	33,222	73,200
31	0·70	0·71	72,000	35,600
* 32	0·70	0·69	37,978	70,800
* 33 ?	0·68	0·69	69,600	40,357

* Indicates step to which special reference is made in the text.

Edgeworth's conception continue to drop, with results as shown in Table IV.

In each of the first steps of the process the manager who has just cut his price takes up all the available business, leaving none at all for his rival. As soon as prices fall below 0·85, however, if the leader in any new price adjustment sells all that is asked at his price, he loses money on part of his sales, as may be seen by comparing Table II and the schedule of marginal costs in Table III. Consequently, in step 17 Table IV and thereafter, the price leader, whether *A* or *B*, may be expected to restrict his sales and meet only part of the demand. Thus the momentarily passive seller in each of these steps retains a part of the business. This part at first is small; but as prices continue to fall, the price leader, restricting his own sales in order to keep his marginal cost down to the level of his price, leaves more and more business to his rival. The process may continue until at price 0·60 the two competitors share the business equally.[1]

Before price 0·60 is reached, however, one or the other of the two rival managers may perceive that an increase in price has become profitable. Whenever either competitor cuts his price but fails to supply all those who are willing and able to buy from him, the other competitor, instead of offering his rival's customers a further reduction in price, may if he chooses deal only with those unable to buy from his rival, and charge them a higher price.[2] Such procedure is possible in step 17 and every step in Table IV thereafter; but at first, because of the small volume of business thus obtainable, this sort of tactics does not pay. Even when it becomes possible to make a considerable profit in this manner, further reductions in price continue for some time to be more profitable. As prices drop lower and lower, however, the advantage gained by underselling one's rival becomes less pronounced.

Buyers are repeatedly divided into two groups: (1) those who succeed in purchasing at the lower of two prices, and (2) those who do not. A change in the composition of each group may be expected with each new price adjustment, but at any given time each group tends to have at any particular price or over any given range of prices the same elasticity of demand.

[1] The price-cutting process just described creates the impression in some readers' minds that all Edgeworth described was "cut-throat competition." See, for example, the reaction of Dr. Erich Schneider, *Reine Theorie monopolistischer Wirtschaftsformen*, pp. 132–75. Edgeworth, however, anticipated and refuted this interpretation in his own summary analysis.

"The instability is due not merely to the hope of one monopolist to ruin his rival by 'cutting prices,' a case that has often been described, but also to a more fundamental though less obvious cause. The instability does not cease in cases where it is not possible for one monopolist to drive the other completely off the field." (Edgeworth, *Papers*, Vol. I, p. 136.)

[2] Edgeworth first advanced the proposition that perfect uniformity of price is not a necessary assumption in analysis of imperfect competition. See *Mathematical Psychics*, p. 47. Cournot's assumption of one and the same price for both duopolists immensely simplified his analysis, and at the same time divorced it from reality. If two sellers, subject to no external interference, always charge the same price, there can be only two explanations of the fact. Either there is a price agreement between them, or else price is determined by competitive bidding among buyers for the combined offerings of both sellers. In the first case we have monopoly but not duopoly; in the second case, a phenomenon which seldom actually occurs.

In most cases in which sellers charge different prices, buyers also pay different prices—even though offerings are exactly alike. Sales do not necessarily take place at exactly the same time. Presumably there is first a rush to buy at the cheaper price; but a sensible person, finding the article he desires all sold out in one place, does not refuse to buy it elsewhere at a higher price if it is worth that much to him.

Though there may be great variation in the nature of individual demands,[1] nevertheless, in accordance with the law of large numbers, the total demand of each group tends to have the same general characteristics as the demand of the whole body of buyers, and in particular the same elasticity.

In accordance with this tendency a turning-point is reached in the movement of prices when step 32 in Table IV has been completed. At this juncture *B* has sold 70,800 units at price 0·69. This amount is 59/91 of 109,200 units, the total quantity demanded at this price. Then to the buyers who if they could would take the remaining 32/91 at price 0·69, *A* can sell 32/91 of the total demanded at any higher price. A schedule of such amounts is shown in Table V. By interpolation in Tables III and V it may be shown that *A* obtains a maximum profit at price 0·96. At this price he obtains more profit than at any other price included in the schedule in Table V. As shown in Table VI, *A*'s profit at 0·96 is also slightly greater than he can obtain by cutting his price to 0·68. No similar condition has

TABLE V

(Derived from Table II.)

Demand Schedule for A's *Offerings at Prices above* 0·69 *when* B *is Selling* 70,800 *Units at Price* 0·69.

Price.	Quantity.
0·70	32/91 of 108,000 = 37,978
0·80	32/91 of 96,000 = 33,758
0·90	32/91 of 84,000 = 29,538
1·00	32/91 of 72,000 = 25,319
1·10	32/91 of 60,000 = 21,099
1·20	32/91 of 48,000 = 16,879

TABLE VI

Results of Two Possible Price Quotations by A *following Step* 32, *Table IV.*

Price.	Sales.	Gross Receipts.	Total Cost.	Net Profit.
0·96	27,007	25,926·72	17,739·80	8,186·92
0·68	69,600	47,328·00	39,144·00	8,184·00

[1] Edgeworth simplified his analysis by assuming all individual demands to be exactly alike. The same general results tend to follow even if there is great variety in the nature of individual demands.

previously arisen. At this point, therefore, *A* may be expected to raise his price to 0·96. It is then to *B*'s advantage to raise his price to 0·95. As soon as he does, another long series of price reductions begins; but when either *A*'s price or *B*'s price becomes equal to 0·69, the other competitor will raise his price to 0·96 again. Thus, in accordance with Edgeworth's assumptions, prices tend to fluctuate perpetually within the limits of 0·96 and 0·69.

From a superficial reading of Edgeworth's paper on "The Pure Theory of Monopoly" it is easy to gain a false impression of the range of price oscillation in his market. Edgeworth himself described in detail an initial fluctuation between the level of pure monopoly and that of unlimited competition, but in accordance with his analysis prices by no means continue to move throughout this entire range.

"And so we return to the position from which we started and are ready to begin a new cycle. This need not have exactly the same path as that which we have described. For at every stage in the fall of the price, and *long before it has reached its limiting value*, it is competent to each monopolist to deliberate whether it will pay him better to lower his price against his rival as described, or rather to raise it to a higher, *perhaps* the initial, level for the remainder of the customers of whom he cannot be deprived by his rival." [1]

If we examine closely any particular problem, the narrower range within which Edgeworthian prices tend to be confined may be at least approximately determined. It has been so determined in the problem just discussed. Any formulas to which the answer may be subject are exceedingly complicated; but it may be noted that in general the upper limit of price oscillation is lower than the price of pure monopoly, and the lower limit higher than the price of unlimited competition. Thus 0·96 is lower than 1·00, and 0·69 is higher than 0·60.

Other problems of interest and importance arise if productive facilities are divided among more than two competitors. The twelve factories under consideration may be equally divided among three, four or six independent combinations; and indeed each of the twelve factories may have its own individual management. In all these cases, if no change is assumed in the general behaviour of buyers and sellers, the limits of price oscillation may be determined by the same general arithmetic methods already exemplified. Solutions may be obtained much more

[1] Edgeworth, *Papers*, Vol. I, p. 120. Italics inserted.

quickly, however, by the use of algebra and calculus.[1] At the same time much finer gradations in price may be considered. Let N stand for the number of competing groups. The total demand represented in Table II may also be represented by either one of two equivalent equations, viz.:

(1) $D = -120{,}000\,p + 192{,}000.$

(2) $p = \frac{-D}{120{,}000} + 1{\cdot}60.$

The total cost of any quantity s produced in any factory in this problem (see Table I) may be represented by the function:

(3) $\frac{s^2}{40{,}000} + 0{\cdot}10s + 2000.$

Each manager controls $\frac{12}{N}$ factories. The total cost of $\frac{12}{N}s$ units produced in $\frac{12}{N}$ factories is:

(4) $\frac{12}{N}\left[\frac{s^2}{40{,}000} + 0{\cdot}10s + 2000\right].$

Let $\frac{12}{N}s$ be designated S. Then substituting $s = \frac{NS}{12}$ in (4), and simplifying, we have the total cost of any quantity S produced in any group of $\frac{12}{N}$ factories expressed as follows:

(5) $\frac{NS^2}{480{,}000} + 0{\cdot}10S + \frac{24{,}000}{N}.$

Corresponding marginal cost is represented by the first derivative of (5) with respect to S:

(6) $\frac{NS}{240{,}000} + 0{\cdot}10.$

$N - 1$ managers may be supposed in the process of competition to reduce their prices to a general level p_1, their individual prices differing from p_1, if at all, by negligible amounts. At this price or prices they do not satisfy the entire demand, but restrict production so that marginal cost is equal to price. Thus, if S_1 represents the production of anyone of them,

(7) $p_1 = \frac{NS_1}{240{,}000} + 0{\cdot}10.$

Solving for S_1:

(8) $S_1 = \frac{1}{N}\,24{,}000\,(10p_1 - 1).$

[1] Those not interested in the mathematical analysis following may perhaps be interested in its results shown in Table VII, p. 60 below. The symbols, D for amount demanded, and p for price, are adapted from Cournot.

The total amount produced and sold by $N - 1$ competitors is :

$$(9)\ \frac{N-1}{N}\ 24{,}000\ (10p_1 - 1).$$

The total demand at price p_1 conforms with the equation :

$$(10)\ D = -\ 120{,}000\ p_1 + 192{,}000.$$

The unfulfilled demand is equal to the difference between (9) and the right-hand member of (10). This difference may be expressed as follows :

$$(11)\ \frac{1}{N} 24{,}000[(-\ 15N + 10)p_1 + 9N - 1].$$

Dividing (11) by the right-hand member of (10), we obtain the proportion of the demand unfulfilled :

$$(12)\ \frac{(-\ 15N + 10)p_1 + 9N - 1}{N(-\ 5p_1 + 8)}.$$

With $N - 1$ competitors selling the quantity indicated in (9) at price p_1, it is assumed that the other competitor can fulfill the unsatisfied portion of the demand at any higher price such as p_2. By (1) and (12) his sales S_2 at price p_2 conform with the equation :

$$(13)\ S_2 = \frac{(-\ 15N + 10)p_1 + 9N - 1}{N(-\ 5p_1 + 8)} (-\ 120{,}000p_2 + 192{,}000).$$

Solving for p_2 :

$$(14)\ p_2 = \frac{N(-\ 5p_1 + 8)S_2}{-\ 120{,}000[(-\ 15N + 10)p_1 + 9N - 1]} + 1{\cdot}60.$$

If profits at price p_2 are to be a maximum, marginal revenue equals marginal cost. Thus :

$$(15)\ \frac{N(-\ 5p_1 + 8)S_2}{-60{,}000[(-15N+10)p_1+9N-1]} + 1{\cdot}60 = \frac{NS_2}{240{,}000} + 0{\cdot}10.$$

Now if the manager who raises his price does so at the point where a further slight reduction in price would bring him a slightly smaller profit, we may disregard the extremely small differences involved and set the two possible profits equal. Thus :

$$(16)\ p_1S_1 - \frac{NS_1{}^2}{480{,}000} - 0{\cdot}10S - \frac{24{,}000}{N} =$$

$$p_2S_2 - \frac{NS_2{}^2}{480{,}000} - 0{\cdot}10S_2 - \frac{24{,}000}{N}.$$

To find the particular values of p_1, p_2, S_1, and S_2, we have four equations, viz. (7), (13), (15), and (16). Solving simultaneously :

$$(17)\ p_1 = \frac{5 + 3\sqrt{4N^2 + 1}}{2(3N - 2)} - 0{\cdot}40.$$

$$(18)\ p_2 = \frac{(10p_1 - 1)^2}{300} + 0{\cdot}85.$$

Solutions may also be obtained for S_1 and S_2, but are of no particular importance in present discussion. By assigning to N in (17) particular values 2, 3, 4, 6, and 12 respectively, corresponding values of p_1 may be obtained. These are shown in Table VII together with the corresponding values of p_2.

TABLE VII.

Ranges of Price Oscillation when Twelve Factories are Equally Divided among Different Numbers of Competitors.

Number of competitors .	N	2	3	4	6	12
Factories controlled by each . . .	$\frac{12}{N}$	6	4	3	2	1
Upper limit of price oscillation . . .	p_2	0·964+	0·953+	0·948+	0·943−	0·938+
Lower limit of price oscillation . . .	p_1	0·686−	0·657−	0·642+	0·628+	0·614−
Total range of oscillation	$p_2 - p_1$	0·278	0·296	0·306	0·315	0·324

The surprising feature of price oscillation according to Table VII is that the range of oscillation increases with each increase in the number of competitors. Thus when there are only two competitors, prices tend to fluctuate between 0·686 − and 0·964 + ; but when there are twelve, between 0·614 − and 0·938 +. If productive facilities are assumed to be divided among still larger and larger numbers of competitors without any change in the general cost situation or the other assumptions of the problem, the lower limit of price movements approaches the freely competitive level of 0·60, but the upper limit descends only towards $0{\cdot}93\frac{1}{3}$. At first sight, then, Edgeworth's theory of competition among a few does not appear to merge, as does Cournot's theory, into an acceptable theory of competition among many. With any increase in the number of competitors, prices, instead of fluctuating less, fluctuate more.[1] In *Mathematical*

[1] Cf. Edward Chamberlin, *Theory of Monopolistic Competition*, pp. 40 ff. Professor Chamberlin believes the continued instability of Edgeworth's prices to be explained by an inconsistent monopolistic condition, viz. the division of the market into parts at the lower limit of price fluctuation. Edgeworth's market, however, is repeatedly and consistently divided into parts. Before the lower limit of price oscillation is reached, each competitor, dissatisfied with the number of customers his rival leaves him, brings about a new division in the market by an additional price cut. At the lower limit of price oscillation, one competitor, accepting the customers whom his rival leaves, charges them a higher price. This difference arises logically out of past events, and involves no contradiction or inconsistency.

In an attempt to better Edgeworth's theory Professor Chamberlin falls into the same sort of inconsistency of which he accuses the original author. At the lower limit of price fluctuation he introduces competitive bidding among buyers —though elsewhere in his own revised version of the story no such bidding occurs.

Psychics Edgeworth analysed transactions between a few sellers and a few buyers, and advanced the proposition that any increase in the number of either made "contract" less indeterminate.[1] In his paper on "The Pure Theory of Monopoly" he considered dealings between a few sellers and many buyers, but in this case any increase in the number of sellers seems to make "contract" more indeterminate.

In actual practice the increasing range of price fluctuation may apply to a smaller and smaller proportion of the market. With productive facilities divided among numerous competitors, only the most alert and the most venturesome may raise their prices much above the lower level of oscillation; but if all competitors are equally alert, all of the market is equally unstable in accordance with Edgeworth's assumptions.[2]

The speed of Edgeworthian price movements may be expected to change with any increase in the number of competitors. Any downward movement of prices tends to be swifter the more competitors there are. On the other hand, under the same conditions any upward price movement tends to be retarded. Thus, though prices fluctuate more widely when competitors are numerous, prices tend also to fluctuate more infrequently, and when they rise, fall back again more rapidly to a lower level. Upon this basis alone it is possible to reconcile Edgeworth's theory of duopoly with the theory of perfect competition. If prices fluctuate more infrequently with any increase in the number of competitors, eventually they tend towards stable equilibrium.

Fortunately there is still another explanation of the apparent discrepancy. Edgeworth's analysis of competition between two involves an assumption which, though at least partially justifiable under the original circumstances, certainly requires modification when the number of competitors is moderately increased, and must be entirely discarded when the number of competitors is unlimited. When there are only two competitors, and one raises his price above the other's, it is comparatively easy for him to sell to all or almost all buyers who do not succeed in purchasing from his rival, provided his new price does not exceed these buyers' demand prices. Edgeworth assumed full realisation of this possibility by one or the other of his two competitors. As the number of sellers increases, however, it becomes more and more difficult for any one of them to perform a similar feat.

[1] *Mathematical Psychics*, p. 20.
[2] Cf. Chamberlin, *Theory of Monopolistic Competition*, p. 41 n.

Potential customers at any price above the general level are more easily lost in the crowd. Any seller who tries to do business at a higher price has himself more difficulty in being seen or heard. Even if possible buyers come in contact with him, before they pay him his price, they call on other sellers to find out if their offerings have really been exhausted. When there is only one other seller, the temporary exhaustion of other offerings is readily verified; not so when other sellers are many. In the meantime the seller who considers an increase in price is led to reverse his intentions and make further reductions in price. When any seller does increase his price, it is profitable to do so by a more moderate amount. Thus the increasing difficulty of actually transacting all potential business at any higher price narrows the range of price fluctuation, and brings it much nearer the level of perfect competition. No account has been taken of this practical consideration in previous mathematical analysis.

When the number of competitors is unlimited, it becomes impossible for any individual among them to resist successfully a downward movement of price towards the equilibrium level, or to initiate by his own unaided efforts an upward movement from that level. This ultimate elimination of an initial possibility does not lessen the significance of Edgeworth's analysis. In fact it brings out more clearly one of the outstanding differences between competition among many and competition among few. When an unlimited number compete in the sale of the same product, each one to do business must keep his price down to the prevailing market level. On the other hand, when only a few sell the same product, each competitor enjoys a greater degree of liberty in the determination of his own price.

A rising school of young economists is evolving theories of imperfect competition quite different from Edgeworth's.[1] A harvest of new ideas has already been gathered, some of them very unsound. When two or more competitors sell the same general type of product, and one cuts his price slightly below the rest, it has been directly or indirectly assumed that none of the

[1] R. F. Harrod, "Notes on Supply," ECONOMIC JOURNAL, Vol. XL (1930); Joan Robinson, "Imperfect Competition and Falling Supply Price," *ibid.*, Vol. XLII (1932); Edward Chamberlin, *The Theory of Monopolistic Competition*; Joan Robinson, *The Economics of Imperfect Competition*; R. F. Harrod, "The Equilibrium of Duopoly," ECONOMIC JOURNAL, Vol. XLIV (1934); R. F. Harrod, "Doctrines of Imperfect Competition," *Quarterly Journal of Economics*, Vol. XLVIII (1934).

See also Piero Sraffa, "The Laws of Return under Competitive Conditions," ECONOMIC JOURNAL, Vol. XXXVI (1926); Harold Hotelling, "Stability of Competition," *ibid.*, Vol. XXXIX (1929).

other competitors loses many customers.[1] Sellers would be happy indeed if this were always true. Each individual competitor may build up through salesmanship, advertising, location, minor peculiarities of product, personal relationships, and type of service a following not easily estranged; but in addition most markets contain buyers of indeterminate allegiance. To them one brand is not much better than others; one location only a little more convenient; one type of service about the same as the rest. Some buyers have no preference at all for any individual seller or any individual offering. The presence of these *marginal buyers* prevents the practical fulfilment of more than one current theory of imperfect competition. Doubtless Edgeworth's assumption that all buyers are swayed by small reductions in price does not apply to many real situations; but even if a small minority of buyers can be so influenced, the general results may still be much as Edgeworth described.

As an illustration take again with certain alterations the same problem with which the present study begins. Let the conditions now be as follows: (1) The cost of any quantity produced and sold by either of two competitors *A* and *B* is again as shown in Table III. (2) The total demand for the commodity still conforms with the schedule in Table II. (3) Either competitor by lowering his price 0·01 below his rival's can take away from him an amount of business equal to *one-sixth* the total amount demanded, but no more. (4) Of the remaining quantity demanded at any given price, one-half is demanded only of *A*, likewise an equal amount of *B*. For simplicity in calculation it is assumed that devoted customers in each case are not influenced by any price offered by the rival seller no matter how much lower it may be. (5) Neither competitor practises any sort of price discrimination.

When the market opens, suppose *A* sells at price 1·00. By quoting a price 0·01 lower *B* cannot take away all *A*'s business, but he can take away a considerable part of it. It is to his immediate advantage to do so. *A* then retaliates with a price of 0·98. Prices continue to fall with results as shown in Table VIII, each competitor in turn taking all marginal business away

[1] The assumption is commonly embodied in a *continuous* demand curve for the offerings of each individual seller. Such demand is more truly represented in most cases by a *discontinuous* curve broken into parts at certain price levels. For further criticism see *American Economic Review*, Vol. XXIV (1934), Supplement No. 1, pp. 30–32; A. J. Nichol, "The Influence of Marginal Buyers on Monopolistic Competition," *Quarterly Journal of Economics*, November 1934. Cf. also Marshall, *Principles of Economics*, eighth edition, p. 105 n.

TABLE VIII

Step.	*A*'s Price.	*B*'s Price.	*A*'s Sales to		*B*'s Sales to	
			Established Customers.	Marginal Buyers.	Established Customers.	Marginal Buyers.
1	1·00	—	30,000	12,000	—	—
2	1·00	0·99	30,000	0	30,500	12,200
3	0·98	0·99	31,000	12,400	30,500	0
4	0·98	0·97	31,000	0	31,500	12,600
23	0·78	0·79	41,000	16,400	40,500	0
24	0·78	0·77	41,000	0	41,500	16,600
25	0·76	0·77	42,000	16,800	41,500	0
26	0·76	0·75	42,000	0	42,500	17,000
27	0·74	0·75	43,000	17,200	42,500	0

from his rival. This advantage, however, gradually becomes much less pronounced in comparison with the possibility of raising one's price and dealing only with established customers. The turning-point is reached upon the completion of step 27 in Table VIII. As shown in Table IX, it is more profitable for *B* at this point to lift his price to 0·98 rather than cut it again to 0·73. In previous steps continued reductions in price have been more profitable. When *B* lifts his price to 0·98, *A* raises his also to 0·97. Another cycle is thus begun, and prices continue

TABLE IX

Results of Two Possible Price Quotations by B *following Step* 27, *Table VIII.*

Price.	Sales to			Gross Receipts.	Total Cost.	Net Profit.
	Established Customers.	Marginal Buyers.	Both Combined.			
0·98	31,000	0	31,000	30,380	19,104·17	11,275·83
0·73	43,500	17,400	60,900	44,457	33,543·38	10,913·62

to fluctuate between the limits of 0·98 and 0·74. Although marginal buyers in this case constitute only one-sixth of the total, the range of price oscillation is almost as great as in the original problem, *i.e.* 0·24 as compared with 0·28.

The main virtues of Edgeworth's analysis, as the present writer sees them, are as follows :—

I. Edgeworth implicitly assumed that when a few are selling to many, only the sellers name prices. Buyers decide whether to buy or not to buy—and if they buy, from whom and how much. Buyers have an indirect influence on prices but no direct voice. This general condition conforms with reality, as everyone knows, though economists have given it little attention.

II. Each duopolist in Edgeworth's market is at liberty to choose his own price. He is not forced to conform with the general action of the rest of the market as under unlimited competition. His price is not determined by competitive bidding among buyers as in an auction sale, or in Cournot's false theory.

III. Edgeworth broke away from the artificial assumption of an absolute one-price market. Looking beyond his work, taking into consideration certain additional elements of competition, we may still expect to find duopoly prices usually uniform; but the assumption that the prices of two competitors must always be equal is contrary to reality and common sense. This assumption is also a handicap in theoretical analysis, particularly that of intermediate pricing processes and alternative possibilities.

IV. Edgeworth's assumption that all buyers are marginal in their choices between competing products cannot be applied to many real situations, but it emphasises the fact that such buyers exist and the importance of their influence.

V. Edgeworth's theory is significant as a study in disequilibrium. That disequilibrium is perpetual need not be admitted, but disequilibrium is certainly recurrent. Edgeworth's analysis brings to light features of disequilibrium and reasons for disequilibrium not recognised elsewhere.

In certain particulars this article is a defence of Edgeworth, but total acceptance of his theory is by no means advocated. It is subject to the following faults :—

I. The general results do not conform with reality. Duopolists are not observed to engage in perpetual price wars. Duopoly prices are no more chaotic than other prices. It is no wonder that some economists have turned from Edgeworth back to Cournot. Despite the unreality of the process Cournot described, Cournot's general conclusions have the semblance of reality.

II. Edgeworth created the general impression that nothing definite could be known about competition among the few. Strangely enough, this impression discouraged detailed study of his own work. Economists unable to accept Edgeworth's conclusions have struck out in quite different directions, and have not been encouraged to utilise the results of his own pioneering.

III. According to Edgeworth competitors consider profits

only of the immediate present, and not over a period of time. The latter goal is much more sensible.

IV. In actual business buyers do not immediately transfer their patronage from one seller to another because of a difference in price. It takes time for the difference in price to become known; it takes time for buyers to change their buying habits. Thus, although a price difference continued for a considerable length of time may bring about a decided shift in patronage, the immediate advantage gained by one seller in cutting his price is not nearly so great as in Edgeworth's simplified market.

V. An Edgeworthian duopolist does not realise that by cutting his own price he prompts his rival to cut also. As a result, both are worse off than in the beginning. More far-sighted competition has been analysed by Professor Chamberlin.

VI. Edgeworth totally ignored the effect of unstable prices on the original demand situation. In conformity with his approach it has been tacitly assumed in the body of this article that general and individual demand schedules remain unaffected by constant variation in price. As a matter of fact, most buyers, observing the price of an article to fluctuate, postpone part of their purchases when the price rises, and wait for it to fall. Thus price oscillation distorts demand, and the distortion of demand in turn tends to eliminate price oscillation. If Edgeworth's sellers, however, are totally lacking in foresight, so also are his buyers.

On the whole Edgeworth's theory is a brilliant mixture of truth and falsity, but those who ignore or deny him are likely to fall into errors themselves.

A. J. NICHOL

Duke and Yale Universities.

[3]

LEADING BRITISH STATISTICIANS OF THE NINETEENTH CENTURY

Paul J. FitzPatrick
Catholic University of America

This paper explores statistical contributions of eleven outstanding British statisticians of the nineteenth, century. They are Playfair, Porter, Babbage, Farr, Guy, Newmarch, Jevons, Rawson, Galton, Giffen, and Edgeworth. This treatment represents one aspect of British statistical thought not previously developed.

INTRODUCTION

This paper aims to present leading British statisticians whose main statistical contributions were made in the nineteenth century. So far, very little history has been written about British statistical thought. The eleven individuals who are considered here stand out among the British statisticians of that century as having made the best contributions to the field of statistics by means of original statistical ideas and techniques and by their direction of outstanding statistical organizations. Four different kinds of statistical work are distinguished, namely, (1) techniques of presentation; (2) bodies of material compiled; (3) substantial investigations employing statistical techniques; and (4) contributions to statistical theory. On the occasion of the search for statistical contributions of leading American statisticians of the nineteenth century, statistical activities of eleven British statisticians came to light. It was considered desirable to develop this aspect of the history of statistics so that American students of statistics might become familiar with their work.

These British statisticians are William Playfair, the founder of graphic methods of statistics; George R. Porter, head of the statistical department of the Board of Trade who directed so well the development of this newly-created organization; Charles Babbage, the founder both of Section F—Statistics—in the British Association for the Advancement of Science in 1833 and of the Statistical Society of London in 1834, as well as the inventor of calculating machines; Dr. William Farr, the founder of British vital statistics and well known statistician of the Annual Reports of the Office of the Registrar General; Dr. William A. Guy, another leading authority in the field of British vital statistics, editor of the *Journal of the Statistical Society of London,* and honored by the establishment of the famous Guy medal; William Newmarch, leading authority on monetary and banking statistics, editor of the *Journal of the Statistical Society of London,* and one of the few British statisticians of his time to perceive the need for utilizing a greater measure of mathematics in describing and analyzing economic and social problems; W. Stanley Jevons, more famous as an economist and logician, who made a number of important statistical contributions in the form of the ratio chart, the geometric mean, and measures for analyzing secular trend, seasonal variation and cyclical fluctuations; Sir Rawson W. Rawson, an authority on international statistics, editor of the *Journal of the Statistical Society of London,* and first president of the International Institute of Statistics (1885–98); Sir Francis Galton, an eminent scientist, who developed the idea of correlation and other statistical measures, including the quartile deviation, the median, and the index of correlation; Sir Robert Giffen, well-known head of the statistical department of the Board of Trade, and editor of the *Journal of the Statistical Society of London;* and Francis Ysidro Edgeworth, the philosopher of statistics, probably the outstanding statistician in the nineteenth century because of his work in probability, correlation and index numbers, and the distinguished editor of the *Economic Journal.*

1. WILLIAM PLAYFAIR (1759–1823)

William Playfair, economist, journalist, inventor, and statistician, is regarded as the founder of graphic methods in statistics. He wrote several works containing excellent charts between 1786 and 1821 [49, p. 190; 50, p. 101; 56], but his contemporaries paid little or no attention to these volumes. Playfair had earned much ill-will because of previous caustic and unfriendly writings, and no English economist or statistician took any notice of his charts until 1879 when the famous English economist and statistician W. Stanley Jevons remarked at the June 17, 1879 meeting of the Statistical Society of London that "Englishmen lost sight of the fact that William Playfair, who had never been heard of in this generation, produced statistical atlases and statistical curves" [32, Vol. 42, p. 657].

Indeed, we find many statistical tables in English economic and statistical works and journals in the first half of the nineteenth century, but very few charts. Funkhouser's investigation reveals that graphs first appeared in the *Journal of the Statistical Society of London* in 1841. The first fifty volumes of this *Journal* (1837–1887), contain about fourteen charts. As far as the United States is concerned, little or no evidence of the use of graphs appears before 1843, when George Tucker's work, *Progress of the United States in Population and Wealth in Fifty Years* appeared with three charts, two being line charts and one a bar chart. Much the same condition prevailed in western Europe, notwithstanding the favorable reception of Playfair's works in France. Moreover, some continental scholars, such as Jacques Peuchet (1805) and P. A. Dafau (1840) in France, and Carl Knies in Germany, were strongly opposed to the use of graphs.

Playfair's first volume (1786) containing charts bears the title *The Commercial and Political Atlas.* Its long sub-title reads "representing by means of stained copper-plate charts, the exports, imports and general trade of England . . . with observations. . . . To which are added, charts of the revenue and debts of Ireland." This volume contains forty-four charts, all but one being time series, the other a bar graph. Funkhouser describes them in these words:

> They are well executed copper-plate engravings colored by hand in three and four colors. Twenty of these represents the trade of England with other countries from the year 1700. The line of imports is stained yellow, that of exports, red; the space between is colored blue when the balance is favorable to England and pink when the balance is unfavorable [16].

The work was again published in 1787 and in 1801. In the introduction to the third edition of this work (1801), pages ix–xii, Playfair explains the use of his "lineal arithmetic" as follows:

> The advantage proposed, by this method, is not that of giving a more accurate statement than by figures, but it is to give a more simple and permanent idea of the gradual progress and comparative amounts, at different periods, by presenting to the eye a figure, the proportions of which correspond with the amount of the sums intended to be expressed.
>
> Suppose the money received by a man in trade were all in guineas, and that every evening he made a single pile of all the guineas received during the day, each pile would represent a day, and its height would be proportioned to the receipts of that day; so that by this plain operation, *time, proportion*, and *amount*, would be all physically combined.
>
> Lineal arithmetic then, it may be averred, is nothing more than those piles of guineas represented on paper, and on a small scale, in which an inch (suppose) represents the thickness of five millions of guineas . . . as much information *may be obtained in five minutes as would require whole days to imprint on the memory* . . . by a table of figures.[1]

A French edition had appeared in 1789, published by H. Jansen of Paris, bearing the title *Tableaux d'arithmétique linèaire du commerce, des finances, et de la dette nationale de l'Angleterre*. This work also carries a long sub-title. This translation was very well received in France. In 1801, Playfair published in London his volume, *The Statistical Breviary*, with the long sub-title: *shewing, on a principle entirely new, the resources of every state and kingdom in Europe; illustrated with stained copper-plate charts, representing the physical powers of each distinct nation with ease and perspicuity*. This volume contained four plates, three being circle charts of different sizes, proportional to the nature of the data presented. They employ the colors, green, pale red, red, and yellow. A French edition appeared in 1802.[2]

Funkhouser, who has made a detailed study of Playfair's works, points out that Playfair:

> published his many excellent examples of the line graph, circle graph, bar graph and pie diagram and accompanied them with pointed expositions of the advantages of the new method for the discovery and analysis of economic trends [16].

Playfair obtained his ideas about charts from several sources.[3] Funkhouser and Walker quote this statement by him:

> At a very early period of my life, my brother, who, in a most exemplary manner, maintained and educated the family his father left, made me keep a register of a thermometer, expressing the variations by lines on a divided scale. He taught me to know that whatever can be expressed in numbers may be represented by lines [17].

Later on, Playfair worked for James Watt, the inventor of the steam engine, who had developed a gauge on his engine for registering the steam pressure.

[1] Italics are Playfair's.

[2] In 1796 another work appeared with the title *A Real Statement of the Finances and Resources of Great Britain; illustrated by two copper-plate charts*. In 1798 Playfair published *Lineal Arithmetic*, bearing the long sub-title: *applied to show the progress of the Commerce and Revenue of England during the present century, which is represented and illustrated by thrity-three copper-plate charts*. In 1805 and again in 1807 he published *An Inquiry into the Permanent Causes of the Decline and Fall of Powerful and Wealthy Nations, illustrated by four engraved charts. Designed to shew how the prosperity of the British Empire may be prolonged*. In 1805 Playfair translated a small pamphlet entitled *A Statistical Account of the United States of America*, written by D. F. Donnant, a Frenchman, and published it as a supplement to *The Statistical Breviary*. In this pamphlet, Playfair refers to Thomas Jefferson's "Statistical Account of Virginia." (The correct title is: *Notes on the State of Virginia* (1787), London: John Stockdale.) In 1821 he wrote *A Letter on our Agricultural Distresses, Their Causes and Remedies, accompanied with tables and copper-plate charts, shewing and comparing the prices of wheat, bread, and labour, from 1565 to 1821*. Addressed to the Lords and Commons. It contained bar charts.

[3] As this paper goes to press, an article "A Note on the History of the Graphical Presentation of Data" by Erica Royston comes to my attention. It was published in *Biometrika*, 43 (1956).

Moreover, Playfair, having been a draftsman, was familiar with the Cartesian system of plotting lines.

As Funkhouser and Walker point out:

> from the standpoint of the history of statistics his graphs are astonishing in that they were made at a time when large collections of reliable quantitative data were not yet available, when the passion for weighing, measuring, counting, and tabulating was not yet consonant with the spirit of the age, and when the development of statistical method still waited upon the collection of large bodies of mass data [17].

Playfair, the fourth son of the Rev. James Playfair, born at Benvie near Dundee, in Scotland, received little formal education. His older brother, John Playfair (1748–1819), well-known mathematician and geologist, was at one time professor of mathematics and philosophy at the University of Edinburgh. This brother, elected a Fellow of the Royal Society in 1807, was one of the original members of the Royal Society of Edinburgh. Their father died when William was thirteen years old, and John undertook to care for the family. William was sent to serve as an apprentice to the millwright Andrew Meikle of Prestonkirk, the inventor of the threshing machine. John Rennie, later to become famous as engineer of the Waterloo bridge, was a fellow-apprentice. In 1780, at the age of twenty-one, Playfair served as a draftsman for the firm of Boulton and Watt at Birmingham. Watt was the James Watt, famous as the inventor of the steam engine. Possessing an inventive talent, Playfair secured a number of patents in the field of mechanics. He left his Birmingham employment to open a shop in London in order to sell various items which he had invented and made, but he was unsuccessful in this venture. In 1787 Playfair went to Paris, where he became interested in the promotion of the Scioto (Ohio) land company. About 1792 he attacked the 1789 French Constitution in his writings, and for several years he became involved in French politics. He thought it best to leave France and about 1793 he returned to London, after visiting Frankfort. He opened a so-called security bank to handle small loans, but this venture was also unsuccessful [1; 10, Vol. 15, pp. 1300–1; 42, Vol. 3, pp. 116–7].

About 1795 he engaged in various writings, one attacking the French Revolution, and another advocating an issue of forged assignats. About 1795 he established a "critical and satirical newspaper (called) the *Tomahawk*," which he edited and owned. In 1808 he founded a weekly paper, *Anticipation*, which published about twenty-five issues during its short life. Later he went to Paris again, and edited "*Galignani's Messenger* newspaper for a short time." He published in 1806 his annotated edition of Adam Smith's *Wealth of Nations* with some uncomplimentary remarks, which earned him the ill-will of the influential *Edinburgh Review* and of others. Playfair was a prolific writer. It is estimated that he wrote over a hundred items, mostly articles. *The Gentleman's Magazine*, an English periodical, listed forty of his writings in its June 1823 issue.

2. GEORGE R. PORTER (1792–1852)

George Richardson Porter, economist, executive and statistician, is well known for his contribution to British statistics by directing so well the development of the newly-created statistical department of the Board of Trade. Porter was a pioneer in England in advocating the use of statistics to place economics on a sound scientific basis. His famous work, *The Progress of the Nation*, contains numerous statistical tables.

Porter's chief task as a civil servant was to digest and arrange for the Board of Trade the mass of information appearing in Parliamentary reports and papers, and this position furnished him an excellent opportunity to show his statistical talent. Sir Jervoise Athelstane Baines, C.S.I., President of the Royal Statistical Society (1909–1910), reports:

> The Statistical Branch . . . was started by Porter, by whom the incoherent mass of periodical tables (official government returns) then prepared was for the first time reduced to orderly and comprehensive returns, accompanied by lucid explanations of the meaning and limitations of the figures. Moreover, he took advantage of the wide scope afforded by his commission to collect returns from other sources, adding them to his review, and giving it a comparative character by including the figures for a series of years [5].

Baines also reveals that "this Board was the only government department in which official statistics were dealt as a special subject, and to this day, it stands out as the premier representative of the scientific interpretation of publications" [5].

Porter played a strong part in the formation of the Statistical Society of London. When this Society was formed in 1834, Porter was one of its active founders, and he served as a member of its first council. He was a member of the Publication Committee of the *Journal* of the Society when it was first published in May 1838 under the editorship of Rawson W. Rawson, and he was also a contributor to this periodical. Porter served, moreover, as treasurer of the Society from 1841 until his death in 1852 [51, pp. 15–16, 57, 298]. He was regarded as one of its "most esteemed members." After his death, the council of the Society ordered his contributions to its *Journal* to be bound in a separate volume "partly as a permanent tribute to his memory, and partly for convenience of those who may wish to peruse his valuable papers in a collected form" [47]. Furthermore, Porter was one of the active members of the British Association for the Advancement of Science from the time of its founding, and contributed several papers to Section F—Statistics. F. W. Hirst, editor of the *London Economist*, regarded Porter as "a thoroughly painstaking statistician."

Porter is best known as the author of *The Progress of the Nation in its Various Social and Commercial Relations from the Beginning of the Nineteenth Century to the Present-Day*, published in three small volumes, London, 1836–43. A revised one-volume edition appeared in 1847 and 1851. This work "was a statistical and descriptive study of the social, economic, commercial and fiscal changes which took place in the United Kingdom during the first half of the nineteenth century." In 1912, it was republished with additional material under the direction of F. W. Hirst. Professor Hewins, Director of the London School of Economics and Political Science, termed this work as "an invaluable record of the first half of the nineteenth century. It is remarkable for the accuracy and variety of its information, and for the skill with which the results of statistical inquiry are presented." A review in the *Journal of the Statistical Society of London* called it "a compendious and valuable library of British Statistics."

Porter was a pioneer in the use of index numbers, as Westergaard reveals:

> He treated the prices of 1833–7 in the same way as Shuckburgh Evelyn, but his material was much more complete. For each month in these five years he gives the average of index-numbers for fifty articles comprising the "principal kinds of goods that enter into foreign commerce." It is his aim in this way to find "the mean variation in the aggregate of prices from month to month" [57, p. 203].

Porter contributed Section Fifteen, entitled "Statistics," to Sir John F. W. Herschel's *Manual of Scientific Inquiry* (1849), which was prepared for the use of Her Majesty's Navy. His twenty-page treatment of statistics deals with the taking of a census and suggests subjects such as population, manufactures, agriculture, mining, education, domestic and foreign trade, etc. He did not include any discussion of statistical methods. Incidentally, the fourth edition of Porter's contribution was slightly corrected by William Newmarch in 1871.

Porter was born in London, the son of a London merchant, and was educated at the Merchant Taylors' School. His father intended him to manage the family's sugar-broker business, but Porter failed to make a success of it. He prepared a paper on Life Assurance for Charles Knight's *Companion to the Almanac* in 1831 which attracted attention. He married Sarah Ricardo, a well-known writer on educational subjects and a sister of the famous economist David Ricardo [10, Vol. 16, p. 178; 13, Vol. 4, p. 946; 42, Vol. 3, p. 170]. In 1832 Porter was appointed to the Board of Trade by Lord Auckland upon the recommendation of Charles Knight, after the latter had refused the position. He served as head of the newly-established statistical department for many years.[4] In 1840 he was made senior member of the railway department of the Board of Trade, and in 1841 he was appointed joint secretary of the Board. Porter proved to be an able official [57, p. 137]. He was a Fellow of the Royal Society and a member of a number of learned societies.

Porter probably influenced Professor George Tucker of the University of Virginia to take a deep interest in statistics. When Tucker spent the summer of 1839 in England, he lodged part of the time with Porter. Tucker mentioned that he enjoyed meeting Thomas Tooke, the author of the well-known work, *The History of Prices*, and he also met Professor George Long, the editor of the *Penny Cyclopaedia*. Tucker later published his famous American statistical work, *Progress of the United States in Population and Wealth in Fifty Years*, (1843) which originally appeared in installments in Hunt's *Merchant's Magazine* from July 1842 to December 1943 (Vols. 7, 8, and 9). Walter Willcox of Cornell University considered this work as "the most important American book on statistics to appear in the first half of the nineteenth century." He added that Tucker "displayed remarkable insight in utilizing scanty census material" [15, p. 690].

In 1845, Porter collaborated with Professor George Young and Professor George Tucker in publishing a volume *America and the West Indies*. Besides his other writings, he contributed several papers for Lardner's *Cabinet Cyclopaedia*, including "A Treatise on the Origin, Progressive Improvement, and Present State of the Silk Manufacture," and "A Treatise on the Origin, Progressive

[4] As this article goes to press, a book, *The Board of Trade and the Free-Trade Movement, 1830–42*, New York: Oxford University Press, 1958, by Lucy Brown, comes to my attention.

Improvement and Present State of the Manufacture of Porcelain and Glass" [49, p. 191–2; 50, p. 102].

3. CHARLES BABBAGE (1792–1871)

Charles Babbage, economist, inventor, mathematician, scientific mechanician, and statistician, played a very prominent part in the founding in 1833 of Section F—Statistics—in the British Association for the Advancement of Science of which he was the first president. He played a similar part in the founding of the Statistical Society of London in 1834. Dr. William Farr, in his presidential address before the Statistical Society of London on November 21, 1871, made the statement that Babbage "was, in reality, more than any other man its founder" [32, Vol. 34, p. 411]. Babbage was also one of the founders of the British Association for the Advancement of Science in 1831, an organization that was formed in part as a result of his attack on the Royal Society in a work *Reflections on the Decline of Science in England* (1830).

In establishing Section F, Babbage was assisted by the famous economist, Rev. Thomas R. Malthus, Rev. Richard Jones, Professor of Political Economy, King's College, London, and Adolphe Quetelet, eminent astronomer, mathematician and statistician, director of the Royal Observatory at Brussels who was at that time in England attending the meeting. Babbage reports: "The Section was formed for the purpose of promoting statistical inquiries which were of considerable importance. They had been assisted by a distinguished foreigner, Quetelet, possessing a budget of most valuable information." Although the British Association for the Advancement of Science insisted that Section F should adhere "to facts, relating to communities of men, which are capable of being expressed by numbers, and which promise when sufficiently multiplied to indicate general laws," Babbage was urged by Quetelet to form a statistical society in London. A meeting of the Committee of the Section F—Statistics—was held on February 21, 1834, at Babbage's home. Those present were Charles Babbage (President), William Empson, an economist, Rev. Richard Jones, Rev. Thomas R. Malthus, William Ogilby, Lieut.-Col. Sykes, G. W. Wook, M.P., and John Drinkwater (Secretary). Edward Strutt, M.P. and W. W. Whitmore, M.P. were also present. On a motion made by Malthus, seconded by Jones, it was unanimously voted to establish a statistical society in London. At a public meeting, March 15, 1834, held at the rooms of the Horticultural Society, with the Marquis of Lansdowne, a descendent of Sir William Petty, the well-known author of *Political Arithmetick*, presiding, Babbage moved: "That a Society be established in the name of the Statistical Society of London, the object of which shall be the collection and classification of all facts illustrative of the conditions and prospects of Society, especially as it exists in the British Dominions." Rev. Richard Jones seconded the motion, which was unanimously carried. Quetelet was chosen the first foreign member of the society. It was then moved, seconded and unanimously voted that "Charles Babbage, Esq., M.P., Rev. Richard Jones, M.A., Henry Hallam, Esq., and John Elliot Drinkwater, Esq., M.P., be appointed a Provisional Committee to prepare Regulations for the conduct of the Society." Their report with some changes was later accepted by the Society [51, pp. 4–11; 22–28; 57, p. 174; 33, p. 15].

About 1812 Babbage conceived the idea of inventing a calculating machine, the forerunner of our current calculating machines, and this model was completed around 1822. He described the design of this machine and its workings in a brief paper before the Astronomical Society in June 1822 where it was favorably received. The Society awarded him its first gold medal on June 13, 1823. Babbage then enlisted the support of the Royal Society in the construction of a larger-scale calculating machine. He also contacted Mr. Robinson, Chancellor of the Exchequer, for a government grant, and he was awarded the sum of 1500 pounds. Later on, Babbage received additional grants. In 1828, upon his return from France where he had gone to improve his health, he attempted to secure additional government funds, but he was unsuccessful. Babbage later decided to construct a calculating machine on an entirely different principle. However, only a smaller machine was built and exhibited at the 1862 International Exhibition. One of his machines is now in the South Kensington Museum. Thus Babbage spent much time and money between 1822 and 1843 developing and perfecting his calculating machines [4].

Babbage wrote several statistical papers: "Sur les constantes de la nature," (1853–55), "Notice statistique sur les Phares," (1853–55), and "On the Antecedents of International Statistical Congresses," (1860–61), all three appearing in the *Congres International de Statistique.* One paper appeared in the *Journal of the Statistical Society of London* (Vol. 19, 1856) bearing the title "Analysis of the Statistics of the Clearing House during the year, 1839." This pioneering study of seasonal variations contained nineteen tables and several charts "too large for engraving." Another paper, "An Examination of Some Questions Connected with Games of Chance," was read March 21, 1820, and appeared in Volume 9 (1823), of *Transactions of the Royal Society of Edinburgh.*

Babbage was born near Teignmouth in Devonshire and received his early education at private schools at Alphington and Enfield. His father was a member of the banking firm of Praed, Mackworth and Babbage. In 1811 Babbage enrolled at Trinity College, Cambridge, and graduated in 1814. He received the M.A. degree from this institution in 1817. In 1816 he was elected a Fellow of the Royal Society. He was one of the founders of the Analytical Society in 1812 and of the Astronomical Society in 1820, holding several offices in the latter. From 1828 to 1839 he held the Lucasian Chair of Mathematics at Trinity College, Cambridge [10, Vol. 1, pp. 776–8; 12, Vol. 2, p. 374; 42, Vol. 1, pp. 75–7].

He wrote on a variety of subjects, including infant mortality, geology, life insurance, light-houses, mathematics, taxation, and others. His chief work, *On the Economy of Machinery and Manufactures* (1832; third edition, 1833, fourth edition, 1835), is an excellent description of the subdivision of labor and economic function of machines. It contains a wide range of practical illustrations of the factory system. This work was translated into four foreign languages and republished in the United States. Babbage is the author of altogether some eighty writings, many being brief papers or sketches or pamphlets. The titles are listed in the appendix of his book *Passages from the Life of a Philosopher*, his autobiography. His *Table of the Logarithms of the Natural Numbers from 1–108,000* (1827) was well regarded and reprinted in several foreign countries. Other works are *A Comparative View of Various Institutions for the Assurance of Lives* (1826), *Thoughts on the Principles of Taxation* (1848; second edition, 1851, third edition, 1853), and *The Exposition of 1851* (1851) [49, pp. 15–16; 50, p. 5].

4. DR. WILLIAM FARR (1807–1883)

Dr. William Farr, physician and founder of British vital statistics, is widely known as the statistician of the *Annual Reports* of the British Office of the Registrar General. He joined this newly-established organization in 1838 as Compiler of Abstracts in the statistical department. Later he was made superintendent of the department. He gave up medical practice and remained with this organization as Deputy Registrar-General until his retirement in 1879. Farr first served under T. H. Lister, who held office until 1842 when he was succeeded by Major George Graham. It should be remembered that the registration of all deaths and causes of death was first started in 1837. Farr foresaw the urgent need of placing English public health on a scientific basis, and was a pioneer in the use of statistical data and techniques to achieve this objective. He played a great part in developing the nomenclature of causes of death. Farr succeeded so well that one noted authority, Sir Arthur Newsholme, claims:

> Farr is rightly regarded as the founder of the English national system of vital statistics. For over forty years he supervised the actual compilation of English vital statistics, introduced methods of tabulation which have stood the test of time and a classification of causes of death which has been the basis of all subsequent methods. On the basis of national statistics he compiled life tables still used in actuarial calculations [12, Vol. 6, p. 133].

Another statistician, Simeon North, President of the American Statistical Association (1910), points out:

> The world acknowledges with undying gratitude the inspired genius with which Dr. William Farr, of England, organized this work of registration. . . . Under his hands, the great problems to which vital statistics are the key and clew, were converted into scientific truths, and the general principles established which determine the relationship of density of population and hygienic conditions, to disease and death. Dr. Farr was the pioneer in the protection of the people against a thousand insidious sources of infection. He first showed, by statistical method, the relation of cause and effect. He organized the British "Annual Reports of the Registrar General of Births, Deaths, and Marriages,"—a splendid and unrivalled series of demographic statistics . . . [41, pp. 30–1].

The first census in England was taken in 1801. The census of 1851, organized under Dr. Farr, is said to have been the first fairly complete one. In the 1851 and 1861 censuses he was an assistant commissioner, in the 1871 census, commissioner [40, pp. 25–26; 22, pp. 65–70].

As superintendent of the statistical department of the Office of the Registrar General, Farr was responsible for more than forty volumes of reports on births, marriages, and deaths. After Farr's death, Sir Robert Giffen, in his presidential address before the Statistical Society of London, spoke highly of Farr by indicating:

> At least two remarkable monuments of his later labours, the special report to the Registrar General on the mortality of the 1861–1871 decade, which was completed only seven or eight years ago, and his paper on the mode of estimating the value of stocks having a deferred dividend. What he has left is a noble monument of industry and ingenuity, full of example to all of us who have devoted time and strength to statistics [51, pp. 115–116].

Farr compiled three English Life tables (1843, 1853, and 1864), the third being the most elaborate. They are based on English censuses of 1841 and 1851 and records of deaths, 1838–54 [57, pp. 137, 144, 147, 161, 219].

Farr was a very active member of the Statistical Society of London, and read many papers relating to vital statistics before this Society which were published in the Society's *Journal*. He was a liberal donor to its library. He served on the council from 1840–1882 with the exception of 1847, and he held the office of treasurer from 1855 to 1867, and that of president from 1871 to 1875 [51, pp. 60–61, 95–96]. He proposed and seconded no less than 216 persons as members of the Society. In 1864 he was president of Section F—Economic Science and Statistics—of the British Association for the Advancement of Science. He was also president of the Public Health Section of the Social Science Association in 1866. Moreover, being an official delegate of the British Government, he took an active part and manifested a deep interest in the work of the nine International Statistical Congresses which were held in Brussels (1853), Paris (1855), Vienna (1857), London (1860), Berlin (1863), Florence (1867), The Hague (1869), St. Petersburg (1872), and Budapest (1876). He and Dr. D'Espine played a prominent part at the First International Statistical Congress in 1853 in attempting to bring about the adoption of an international list of the causes of death. Their recommendations were adopted at the Second International Statistical Congress in 1855 [40, pp. 173, 177; 14].

Farr was born at Kenley in Shropshire, and, as his parents were in humble circumstances, was adopted at an early age by Mr. Joseph Pryce, squire of Dorrington, near Shrewsbury. Both Mr. Pryce and the Reverend J. J. Beynon directed his early education. Farr assisted Mr. Pryce in his various affairs. From 1826–28 he studied medicine under Dr. J. Webster, a promising young physician, and assisted Mr. T. Sutton, a surgeon at the Shrewsbury Infirmary. Mr. Pryce at his death in 1828 left Farr a legacy of 500 pounds for his future education, and Dr. Webster at his death in 1837 left Farr a similar amount of money along with his library. In May 1829 Farr went to Paris where he enrolled at the University of Paris to study medicine for two years, and it was while he was in that city that he first became interested in medical statistics [10, Vol. 6, pp. 1090–1; 11, Vol. 10, p. 187; 13, Vol. 6, pp. 993–4]. One of his teachers was the famous French physician, P. Ch. A. Louis, who is generally regarded as the father of medical statistics. In 1831 he returned to London to study at University College, and in March 1832 he became a licentiate (L.A.S.) of the Apothecaries' Society. In the same year he started to practice medicine. He then edited the *Medical Annual*, wrote for medical journals, and in 1837 with the assistance of his close friend, Dr. R. Dundas Thompson, he edited the *British Annals of*

Medicine. He wrote an article on "Vital Statistics" for McCulloch's *Statistical Account of the British Empire,* Vol. 2 (1837) [42, Vol, 2, pp. 33–35].

Farr was a prolific writer who contributed not only to the *Journal of the Statistical Society of London* and the *Congres International de Statistique,* but also to the *Lancet,* the *Reports* of the British Association for the Advancement of Science and the Social Science Association [49, p. 76; 50, p. 42]. Many of his important views may be found in a memorial volume entitled *Vital Statistics* (1885), edited by Noel A. Humphreys for the Sanitary Institute of Great Britain [27].

Farr was honored in many ways. The Royal Society elected him a Fellow in 1855. The University of New York gave him the honorary degree of M.D. in 1847, Oxford University bestowed upon him the honorary D.C.L. in 1857, the Royal Medical and Chirurgical Society elected him an Honorary Fellow in 1857, and the King and Queen's College of Physicians in Dublin also elected him an Honorary Fellow in 1867.

5. DR. WILLIAM A. GUY (1810–1885)

Dr. William Augustus Guy, editor, physician and statistician, while well known for his writings in public health, is better known for his many activities on behalf of the Statistical Society of London. Guy, like Farr, was strongly of the opinion that statistics was seriously needed for the study of medical problems. At King's College Hospital, he collected data on out-patients which resulted in three papers relating to the "Influence of Employments Upon Health," read before the Statistical Society of London and published in its *Journal* [57, p. 157]. Some other medico-statistical papers read before the Society and published in its *Journal* were: "On the Health of Nightmen, Scavengers and Dustmen," "Temperature and Its Relation to Mortality," "Mortality of London Hospitals, and Deaths in the Prisons and Public Institutions of the Metropolis," and "Annual Fluctuation in the Number of Deaths from Various Diseases." Guy's contribution to statistics rests primarily on the compilation of bodies of material relating to public health, and on his informative papers dealing with the history of statistics.

Guy was a very active member of the Statistical Society of London, serving for many years as its honorary secretary, 1843–1869, editor of its *Journal,* 1851–1856, and as its president, 1873–75. He was also for many years treasurer of its informal group known as the Statistical Dining Club. Incidentally there are two references to this club. One account reports:

> Outside the work of the Society as such, but still closely connected with it, is the Statistical Dining Club. The only detailed reference to it in the Minutes of the Council is to be found under date 11 January 1839, where it is entered that Mr. Porter reported that a statistical Club had been formed "and had appointed to dine together on the days of the Ordinary Monthly Meetings; that the terms were an annual subscription of one guinea, and 10 s. each on dining with the Club." The Club is limited to forty members and "clubability" is an indispensable prerequisite for election; at each gathering the lecturer of the evening is received as a guest and treated hospitably. It has few rules, no minutes, no records, and only one officer, the Treasurer. The Club is a select body [51, p. 69].

The second account reveals, at the time of its one hundredth anniversary, that:

> At a meeting of the Council of the Statistical Society on January 11, 1839, Mr. George R. Porter reported that a Statistical Club has been formed and "had appointed to dine together on the days of the Ordinary Monthly meetings." That Club has now completed the first hundred years of its life, and the members, in order to mark the occasion, decided that a special Centenary dinner should be held and that Mr. Macrosty should compile a record of the Club for circulation among the members. That account has now been printed, with "recollections" by prominent members, and though no records exist for the first fifty years, it has been found possible to recover the names of 163 past and present members. The membership is limited to forty and there were in February three vacancies.
>
> The Centenary Dinner was held at the Trocadero after the Ordinary Meeting on February 21st, 1939, under the Chairmanship of the President of the Society, Professor A. L. Bowley. Fifty-one persons took part, namely twenty eight members, six Club guests, and seventeen private guests [54].

This club is still going strong under the same rules. It is reported that at one time it had one of the best cellars in the city, but this was destroyed by the bombing of London.

Guy contributed many papers which were read before the Society and published in its *Journal.* One statement records "that in twenty years, 1844–63, Dr. Guy read 15 papers" [57, pp. 60–2, 96, 103]. Noting his death in December 1885, another statement records:

> The Council minuted: "Dr. Guy was a constant and liberal donor to the Library and the numerous papers which he read before the Society, exceeding in number and variety of subjects those of any other Fellow were of exceptional value. He further testified to his constant interest in the prosperity of the Society by the large number of Fellows whom he introduced to it, and finally by bequeathing to it a legacy of £250 and a reversionary interest of considerable value" [51, p. 152].

Some of Guy's papers relating to statistics, which were read before the Society and published in its *Journal,* were: "On the Relative Value of Averages Derived from Different Numbers of Observations," (Vol. 13, 1850), "On the Original and Acquired Meaning of the term 'Statistics,' and on the Proper Functions of a Statistical Society," (Vol. 28, 1865), "John Howard as Statist," (Vol. 36, 1873), "John Howard's True Place in History," (Vol. 38, 1875), and "On Tabular Analysis" (Vol. 42, 1879) [51, pp. 150–1, 153, 156–7]. In the *Jubilee Volume* of the Society (1885), he has a paper, "Statistical Development, with Special Reference to Statistics as a Science." The 1861 issue of *Congres Internationale de Statistique* contains his "Statistical Methods and Signs" [33, pp. 72–86, 363-4; 49, pp. 105–6; 50, pp. 53–4].

Guy was held in high esteem as a statistician. Sir Rawson W. Rawson, K.C.M.G., C.B., President of the Society (1884–86), called attention to "his industry, and high capacity, his professional knowledge, and statistical insight." Sir Arthur Newsholme, K.C.B., M.D., F.R.C.P., an outstanding authority in the field of vital statistics, regarded Guy as "one of the ablest early English statisticians [40, p. 314].

Because of Guy's many activities on behalf of the Society, the Royal Statistical Society voted in 1891 to establish in his honor, the "Guy Medal." One account reveals:

> At the Council Meeting on 21 May, 1891, a motion was put forward by Sir R. W. Rawson and T. H. (afterwards Sir Thomas) Elliott that in memory of Dr. Guy a gold medal should be awarded "at the discretion of the Council in recognition of the original statistical work placed at the disposal of the Society." This was approved at the Annual Meeting in June. . . . The definition was further expanded by the Council. "The Guy Medal of the Royal Statistical Society—founded in honour of the distinguished statistician whose name it bears—is intended to encourage the cultivation of statistics, in their strictly scientific aspects, as well as to promote the application of members to the solution of the important problems in all the relation of life to which the numerical method can be applied, with a view, as far as possible, to determine by its methods the laws which regulate them." Then the scheme was expanded: a Gold Medal for "work of high character founded upon original research performed specially for the Society"; a Silver Medal for "work founded on existing materials" [51, pp. 160–2].

As to the Guy Gold Medal, two persons were awarded this honor in the nineteenth century, The Rt. Hon. Charles Booth, F.R.S., in 1892 and Sir Robert Giffen, F.R.S., in 1894. From 1900 to 1930 inclusive, six additional persons won this honor, namely, Sir Jervoise Athelstane Baines, C.S.I., in 1900, Professor Francis Y. Edgeworth, F.B.A., in 1907, Major P. G. Craigie, C.B., in 1908; Professor George Udny Yule in 1911, Dr. T. H. C. Stevenson, C.B.E., in 1920, and Sir Alfred W. Flux, C.B. in 1930. As to the Guy Silver Medal, five persons won it during the nineteenth century, and twenty persons between 1900 and 1930 [51, pp. 301–2].

Guy was born in Chichester, "where his male ancestors for three generations had been medical men." He studied at both Christ's Hospital and Guy's Hospital. In 1831 he was awarded the Fothergillian medal of the Medical Society of London for the best paper on asthma. He enrolled at Pembroke College, Cambridge, receiving the M.B. degree in 1837. His college career in England had been interrupted by two years at Heidelberg and Paris, where he studied under leading medical men. In 1838 Guy was appointed to the chair of forensic medicine at King's College, and in 1842 he was made physician to King's College Hospital, having the care of outpatients. From 1846 to 1858 he served as dean of the medical faculty, and in 1869 he was also appointed professor of hygiene. In 1844 he was admitted a Fellow of the Royal College of Physicians, and he served as censor in 1855, 1856 and 1866, and as examiner in 1861–63. At the Royal College he was also Croonian (1861), Lumleian (1868) and Harveian (1875) lecturer. In 1862 he was examiner in forensic medicine at the University of London. He was Swiney prizeman in 1869. Because of his intense interest in vital statistics, he retired from medical practice. He served on a number of commissions [10, Vol. 8, pp. 835–6; 24].

Dr. Guy was an outstanding physician and was "often consulted in medico-legal cases." He wrote several medical works, as *Principles of Forensic Medicine* (1884), which was frequently reedited, and *The Factors of the Unsound Mind* (1881). Another work was *Public Health; A Popular Introduction to Sanitary Science*, part I (1870) and part II (1874).

6. WILLIAM NEWMARCH (1820–1882)

William Newmarch, banker, economist, editor and statistician, an authority on monetary and banking statistics, editor of the *Journal of the Statistical Society of London*, was one of the few British statisticians of his time to perceive the need of utilizing mathematics in describing and analyzing economic and social problems.

Newmarch's contributions to Tooke's *History of Prices* is regarded as a masterly statistical review of the economic history of Great Britain, and this work contains many elaborate statistical tables. He was an early user of index numbers. He was honorary secretary of the Society from 1854 to 1862, its president for two years, 1869–71, succeeding the Rt. Hon. W. E. Gladstone, M.P., and served as editor of its *Journal* for five years, 1855–61, making a number of important changes in this periodical for which he was praised. The Society's publication also records that "the Council expressed 'their approbation' of Mr. Newmarch's 'valuable services' and their knowledge of 'the practical and scientific character of the *Journal* under his editorship.' It is for others to say how far his successors have lived up to his standard" [51, p. 88].

Newmarch, in his presidential address, "Progress and Present Conditions of Statistical Inquiry," before the Statistical Society of London in 1869, reveals greater insight and foresight than most of his contemporaries when he said, among other things:

> Let me now state what appears to me to be the fields of statistical research which in this country most require early attention.

Then he goes on to enumerate eighteen fields, the last one being:

> 18. Investigations of the mathematics and logic of Statistical Evidence; that is to say, the true construction and use of Averages, the deductions of probabilities, the exclusion of superflous integers, and the discovery of the laws of such social phenomena as can only be exhibited by a numerical notation.

Later on in this address, he emphasizes:

> The last subject (division eighteen) in the list, relates to the mathematics and logic of Statistics, and therefore, as many will think, to the most fundamental enquiry with which we can be occupied. . . . It is certain that by means of averages, and variations of increase and decrease, presented by large masses of figures representing social phenomena which occur within longer or shorter intervals of time and within defined limits, it is possible to arrive at conclusions which so far resemble the law of several cases that they justify the enunciation of probabilities and predictions [32, Vol. 32, pp. 365–6, 373].

Newmarch enjoyed two distinctions as president of the Statistical Society of London. First, until he became president of the Society in 1869, all previous presidents had been either high government officials or members of the royalty. Secondly, he instituted the custom "of a regular series of Presidential Addresses." The inaugural addresses are given at the commencement of each presidential term. Previously they had been made at the close of the term—a practice established in 1851 by the Rt. Hon. Earl of Harrowly, K.G., D.C.L., at the end of the second term of office. As the *Annals* records: "Since that time each succeeding President . . . has enriched the records with an address, and in their mass their addresses form a contribution to the history and development of statistics which is unrivalled elsewhere."

Newmarch was an outstanding member of the Statistical Society of London. He was regarded as "one of its most eminent members." One publication of the Society records: He "had for more than thirty years been identified with its work, having contributed many papers on the leading economical questions of the day, and taken a prominent and guiding part in its discussion" [51, p. 115]. Robert Giffen, K.C.B., F.R.S., a distinguished economist and statistician, claims that Newmarch "was remarkable not merely as a statistician but as a man of business and as an economist" [51, p. 115].

Newmarch was an early user of index numbers. Westergaard reports that:

> In 1859 W. Newmarch published index-numbers for nineteen articles with the New Year, 1851, as a starting point, and in the following two years he treated a similar material, extending his investigations to twenty-two articles, with the years 1845–50 as a basis [57, p. 204].

Newmarch published several articles for the *Journal of the Statistical Society of London,* after having read them before the Society. Some are: "Progress and Present Condition of Statistical Inquiry" Vol. 32, p. 359; "Electoral Statistics of Counties and Boroughs in England and Wales from the Reform Act of 1832 to the Present Times" Vol. 20, p. 169; "Electoral Statistics of England and Wales, 1856–58," Vol. 22, p. 101; "Attempts to Ascertain the Magnitude and Fluctuations of the Amount of Bills of Exchange in Circulation at one time in Great Britain, England, Scotland, Lancashire, and Cheshire, respectively, and of Bills drawn on Foreign Countries during each Year, 1828–47," Vol. 14, p. 143. An article "On the Statistical Society of London" appeared in the 1860–61 issue of the *Congres International de Statistique.*

Newmarch collaborated with Thomas Tooke in completing the two concluding volumes, 5 and 6, of the well-known work, the *History of Prices and the State of the Circulation, From 1793 to 1857* (London, 1857), the six volumes covering the period from 1793 to 1856. Newmarch's two concluding volumes, covering the years from 1836 to 1856, are not only a masterful statistical review containing many elaborate statistical tables but also a careful monetary and banking analysis. He entertained great hopes of bringing the *History of Prices* up to date, but pressure of many duties prevented it. These two volumes attracted much attention and were translated into German and used in several German universities [42, Vol. 3, pp. 17–8]. When Mr. Tooke passed away, Newmarch played a leading part in securing funds to establish the "Tooke Professorship of Economic Science and Statistics" at King's College [48, Vol. 34, pp. xvii–xix].

In 1863 he inaugurated an annual section, "Commercial History of the Year," in the London *Economist* which continued up to 1882. During his connection with the *Economist,* he served under the editorship of Wilson, Bagehot and Palgrave.

Newmarch was an authority on monetary and banking problems and appeared several times before a number of Parliamentary committees. He also appeared in 1857 before the Select Committee of the House of Commons investigating the Bank Act, being a leading critic of the famous Peel's Bank Act passed in 1844 [23]. After 1846 he was a frequent contributor to the *Morning Chronicle* [48, Vol. 34, pp. xvii–xix]. Some of his articles dealing with the supply of gold attracted much attention and were later published in 1853 with additions as a book entitled *The New Supplies of Gold*. Part of this work had been read as a paper before the Statistical Society of London in 1851. Besides his contributions to the *Morning Chronicle*, he wrote for the *Economist*, *Fortnightly Review*, *Pall Mall Gazette*, the *Statist*, and the *Times*. Some of his writings were anonymous [33, pp. 367–8; 49, p. 176; 50, p. 93].

Newmarch was born at Thirsk, Yorkshire, and educated in the schools at York. He held several positions as a clerk in his hometown, first under a stamp distributor and then with the Yorkshire Fire and Life Office. Newmarch moved to Wakefield in 1843 to serve as one of the cashiers in the banking house of Leathem, Tew, and Co., and remained with this firm until 1846 when he joined the managerial staff of the Agra Bank of London. This change furnished him the opportunity to become acquainted with many leading persons, some being Thomas Tooke, Alderman Thompson, M.P., and Lord Wolverton [39]. In 1851 he resigned to become actuary and secretary of the Globe Insurance Company and distinguished himself by carrying out several important financial transactions. In 1862 he resigned to be appointed manager of the banking house of Glyn, Mills and Company and he remained with this firm nineteen years until his retirement in 1881 when he was striken with paralysis. He was also a director of several business enterprises [10, Vol. 14, pp. 352–4; 12, Vol. 11, pp. 368–9]. He was elected a Fellow of the Royal Society in 1861. He was, moreover, for many years secretary of the Political Economy Club, and also an active member of both the Adam Smith and the Cobden Clubs. Besides serving one time as secretary, Newmarch was in 1861 also president of Section F of the British Association for the Advancement of Science [9 (1861), pp. 201–203]. Incidentally, Arthur Bowley in his presidential address before Section F (1906) states that "from 1835 to 1855 Section F of the British Association was devoted to 'Statistics,' and it is only from 1856 onwards that it has received the curious name, 'Economic Science and Statistics' " [32, Vol. 69, p. 540].

His colleagues' high esteem of Newmarch is partly reflected by three memorials: After his death the Statistical Society of London "subscribed twenty guineas to the Newmarch Memorial Fund" [51, p. 115]. Mr. H. D. Pochin, a member of the Council of the Society placed at its disposal 100 pounds for a Newmarch Memorial Essay [33, p. 35]. Finally, 1420 pounds and 14 shillings were subscribed toward "the foundation of the Newmarch Professorship of Economic Science and Statistics at the University College, London."

7. W. STANLEY JEVONS (1835–1882)

William Stanley Jevons, economist, logician and statistician, is well known for his influential writings in the fields of logic and economics. He should be equally well known for his important statistical contributions. Jevons was a pioneer in statistical methods in several ways: First, in emphasizing the superior value of the geometric mean over the arithmetic mean; second, in strongly recommending the use of the chart, now known as the ratio chart, as a graphic means of showing per cent of change; third, in calling attention to the several problems involved in the proper construction of an index number; and finally, in improvising statistical means of measuring time series in the form of secular trend, seasonal variation and cyclical fluctuations.

Jevons' early interest in statistics dates at least from October 1860, when at the age of twenty five years "he began to form diagrams to exhibit some statistics" he had been collecting in the British Museum Library for the purpose of developing a *Statistical Atlas*. Later in a letter dated April 7, 1861, he wrote to his brother, Herbert:

> I am very busy at present with an apparently dry and laborious piece of work, namely, compiling quantities of statistics concerning Great Britain, which are to be exhibited in the form of curves, and if possible, published as a *Statistical Atlas*. . . . Almost the whole of the statistics go back to 1780 or 1800, a large part extend to 1700 or 1720, and some—for instance, the price of corn—as far back as 1400. The quantity of statistics which I shall exhibit in about thirty plates will, I think, rather astonish people.

He then goes on to enumerate the various items dealing with population, foreign and domestic commerce, money and banking, agriculture, government debt, etc, which he intends to cover. Then in this same letter, he says:

> Most of the statistics, of course, are generally known, but have never been so fully combined or exhibited *graphically*. . . . The mode of exhibiting numbers of curves and lines has, of course, been practiced more or less any time on this side of the Deluge. At the end of the last century, indeed, I find that a book of *Charts of Trade* [correct title of Playfair's work was the *Commercial and Political Atlas*, 1786] was published, exactly resembling mine in principle; but in statistics, the method, never much used, has fallen almost entirely into disuse. It ought, I consider, to be almost as much used as *maps* are used in geography [30, p. 157–8].

In a letter dated December 3, 1861, to his brother Tom, Jevons remarks: "My statistical matters proceed slowly, and the mere drawing of diagrams takes up an incredible deal of time."

Jevons wrote in his journal on December 8, 1861:

> About October 1860, having then recently commenced reading at the Museum Library, and met some statistics, I began to form some diagram to exhibit them. . . . After doing two or three diagrams the results appeared so interesting that I contemplated forming a series for my own information. Then it occurred to me that publication might be possible, and I finally undertook to form a statistical atlas of say thirty plates, exhibiting all the chief materials of *historical statistics*. For the last year this atlas has been my chief employment. . . . Towards the end of last October I had some twenty-eight diagrams more or less finished in the first copy, and thought it time to arrange for publication [30, p. 161].

However, Jevons was unsuccessful in his efforts with several publishing houses to have the atlas published. They were of the opinion that the work would involve too great an expense in view of the limited market, he records in his journal on December 8, 1861. He also records how Mr. Newmarch "looked at my diagrams without *interest*, and almost without a word, so that I soon left him" [30, p. 162]. It appears that the academic and the business worlds were not ready to appreciate these statistical tools and the knowledge they could impart about the immediate future.

In his letter of December 28, 1862, Jevons wrote his brother Tom:

> I am at present going on with my old work of diagrams. I am now thinking of a small atlas with plates about 6 by 8 inches, from 1844–62, comprising monthly quotations

> of prices, exports, imports, etc., all fully reduced, analyzed, etc., so as to make quite a small gem of work. . . . It is somewhat the same idea with which I just began nearly two years ago but I have learnt so much by experience that my first diagrams were quite laughable besides the little gems I now produce. . . . The atlas would contain perhaps twelve plates [30, p. 173].

However, this atlas met the same unfortunate fate.

In September 1862 Jevons sent two papers to be read at the annual meeting of Section F of the British Association for the Advancement of Science. One paper entitled "On the Study of Periodic Commercial Fluctuations" was read and approved, while the second paper, "Notice of a General Mathematical Theory of Political Economy," was merely read [9, Vol. 32, pp. 157–9]. This little-noticed second paper was to be further developed later and published as a book, *The Theory of Political Economy* (1871). This mathematical description of economic principles was to earn Jevons a world-wide reputation as an economist. He states in the preface of the second edition (1879) that: "I do not write for mathematicians, nor as a mathematician, but as an economist wishing to convince other economists that their science can only be satisfactorily treated on an explicitly mathematical basis." This work thus reveals Jevons to be a pioneer in the field of mathematical economics, and, as will be seen, he was a trailblazer also in the field of econometrics.

In the former paper, "On the Study of Periodic Commercial Fluctuations," Jevons studied the nature of seasonal variations by computing monthly as well as quarterly averages. He found that "it is interesting to observe that the monthly and quarterly variations are of precisely the same character." He employed four diagrams revealing "Average Rate of Discount, 1845–61 and 1825–61," "Total Number of Bankruptcies, 1806–60," "Average Price of Consols, 1845–60," and "Gazette Average Price of Wheat, 1846–61." This investigation enabled Jevons to discover the nature of secular trend movement of prices [29, pp. 2–11].

Analyzing this study, Keynes points out that Jevons:

> was not the first to plot economic statistics in diagrams; some of his diagrams bear, indeed, a close resemblance to Playfair's with whose work he seems to have been acquainted. But Jevons compiled and arranged economic statistics for a new purpose and pondered them in a new way. . . .
>
> Jevons was the first theoretical economist to survey his material with the prying eyes and fertile, controlled imagination of the natural scientist. He would spend hours arranging his charts, plotting them, sifting them, tinting them nearly with delicate pale colours like the slides of the anatomist, and all the time pouring over them and brooding over them to discover their secret. It is remarkable, looking back, how few followers and imitators he had in the black arts of inductive economics in the fifty years after 1862 [35, pp. 523–4; 53].

Next year he brought out his pamphlet of seventy-three pages, *A Serious Fall in the Value of Gold Ascertained, and Its Social Effects Set Forth With Two Diagrams* [28], a very important statistical treatment. For one thing, Jevons, in this pioneering study explains on page 7 the value of using the geometric mean as an average in place of the arithmetic mean to combine wholesale monthly prices near the middle of the month, the prices being those of 39 chief commodities for the years 1845 to 1862 [57, pp. 203–4]. He proposed the use of the geometric mean by calculating the arithmetic mean of the logarithms instead of using the original numbers. Secondly, he demonstrates the use of diagrams with logarithmic vertical scale for observing "proportional variation of prices" with the horizontal scale showing arithmetic progression. This diagram, the forerunner of our current ratio chart, appears to be a variant of Playfair's charting technique. Thirdly, he offers an excellent demonstration of the problems involved in constructing index numbers by examining various aspects such as the question of weighting, the choice of an average, the number and kinds of commodities to include, etc. Seventy-nine minor items were also employed as a check on his results. He even applied the theory of probability to his work. Thus Jevons is regarded by some as "the father of index numbers."

Keynes again appraises Jevons:

> For unceasing fertility and originality of mind applied, with a sure touch and unfailing control of the material, to a mass of statistics, involving immense labours for an unaided individual ploughing his way through with no precedents and labour-saving devices to relieve his task, this pamphlet stands unrivalled in the history of our subject. The numerous diagrams and charts which accompany are also of high interest in the history of statistical description [35, 525–6; 53].

It is, indeed, unfortunate that after Jevons' pioneering efforts the theory and use of index numbers were to mark slow progress until 1887 when Professor Francis Y. Edgeworth commenced his excellent studies in this area [9, (1887), pp. 247–301; (1888), pp. 181–232; (1889), pp. 133–64; (1890), pp. 485–8].

The last page of Jevons' pamphlet contains an advertisement reporting that he had "in preparation" *The Merchant's Atlas and Handbook of Commercial Fluctuationo.* This original effort indicates that Jevons was again a pioneer in planning to sell business men information about the current status of business conditions. No reason, however, can be found for the failure to publish this *Merchant's Atlas.* It is quite likely that the poor sales for his pamphlet, *A Serious Fall in the Value of Gold,* may be the answer. It sold only 74 copies.

In 1865 he brought out another statistical paper "On the Variation of Prices, and the Value of the Currency Since 1872" which he read before the Statistical Society of London in May 1865 and published in its *Journal* in June 1865 (Vol. 28). This paper represented a further development of the theory of index numbers, and contained data going back to the eighteenth century. He continued to use the geometric mean and the ratio chart. In 1865 his famous book, *The Coal Question,* appeared, which attracted considerable attention. In Chapter 9, entitled "Of the Natural Law of Social Growth," he pointed out that many economic and social phenomena experience a law of geometric growth, some at a greater rate than others. He goes on to apply this idea to the growth of Great Britain. Jevons advanced the thesis that future prosperity of Great Britain would increase the demand for coal in the form of geometric progression leading to a possible exhaustion of coal. This book resulted in the appointment of a royal commission to examine the available coal reserves. Thus Jevons can be considered as a pioneer in the field of secular trend measurement. In 1866, he brought out another statistical paper, "On the Frequent Autumnal Pressure in the Money Market, and the Action of the Bank of England," which was read before the Society in April 1866, and published in its *Journal* in June 1866 (Vol. 29).

Jevons was a student of business cycles, then known as commercial crises, pointing out that there is a strong relation between the solar period and the price of corn. His first paper, "The Solar Period and the Price of Corn," was read in 1875 before Section F—Economic Science and Statistics—of the British Association for the Advancement of Science. Corrections were made in subsequent papers, entitled "Commercial Crises and Sun Spots," which were published in two articles in *Nature:* Part I appeared in the November 14, 1878 issue and Part II in that of April 24, 1879. Another paper, "The Periodicity of Commercial Crises and its Physical Explanation," was read in August 19, 1878 before Section F of the British Association for the Advancement of Science and published in Volume 7 of the *Journal of the Statistical and Social Inquiry Society of Ireland.* Wesley C. Mitchell, in his famous book *Business Cycles* (1927), pays tribute to Jevons by stating: "It was left for W. Stanley Jevons to give the first powerful impetus to statistical work in economic theory."

Jevons was a very active member of the statistical Society of London and "made numerous donations to its Library." He served as its honorary secretary from 1877 to 1880 [51, p. 115], and read several papers before the Society which were published in its *Journal.* Some are: "On the Variation of Prices, and the Value of the Currency since 1782" (Vol. 28, 1865), "On the Frequent Autumnal Pressure in the Money Market, and the Action of the Bank of England" (Vol. 29, 1866), "Condition of the Metallic Currency of the United Kingdom, with Reference to the Question of International Coinage" (Vol. 31, 1868), and "Statistical Use of the Arithomometer" (Vol. 41, 1878). The latter article referred to the use of a French calculating machine. The *Annals* reports that "no other economist so distinguished was so closely connected with the Society." In 1870 he served as president of Section F of the British Association for the Advancement of Science.

While living in Manchester Jevons was also an active member of the Manchester Statistical Society. He served as its vice president in 1868–69, and as its president, 1869–71 [2]. He read several papers before this Society, for example, "The Work of the Manchester Society in connection with the Question of the Day" (1869–70), and "The Progress of the Mathematical Theory of Political Economy, with an Explanation of the Principles of the Theory" (1874–75). Furthermore, he wrote a paper, "The Periodicity of Commercial Crises and its Physical Explanation," which was published in the *Journal of the Statistical and Social Inquiry Society of Ireland* (Vol. 7, 1876–1879). This paper examined the nature of the relationship between commercial crises and sun spots.[5]

Jevons, born the ninth of eleven children, at Liverpool, was the son of an iron merchant who was a writer on economic and legal matters. He received his early education at the hands of a private tutor, and at the Mechanics Institute High School. But he remained only a short time at this institution and then

---

[5] Jevons was the author of a number of other works [49, pp. 134–5; 50, p. 66]. In economics, *Primer of Political Economy* (1878) which was translated into French and German, *Money and the Mechanism of Exchange* (1875), *The State in Relation to Labour* (1882), and *Methods of Social Reform* (1883). In the field of logic, *Elementary Lessons in Logic* (1870), *Primer of Logic* (1876), and *Pure Logic and Other Minor Works* (1890), *Studies in Deductive Logci,* (1880). Another work was *The Principles of Science: A Treatise on Logic and Scientific Method,* 2 volumes (1874), and one volume (1877). He was a contributor to Australian newspapers in earlier years. Later he contributed to the *Spectator, London Quarterly Review, Contemporary Review, National Review, Times, Macmillan Magazine.*

enrolled at Beckwith's private school. In 1850, at the age of fifteen, he attended the University College School at London, and in 1851 he enrolled at the University College, where he studied mathematics, chemistry, biology, and metallurgy. By the midsummer of 1851 he had won five prizes—three being first prizes and two second prizes. Because of financial circumstances (his father having become a bankrupt in January 1848), Jevons was forced to leave college when halfway through his studies. This business failure of Jevons and Sons probably resulted from the depression of 1847. Late in 1853 at the age of eighteen he left England to accept the position of assayer in the newly-established Royal Mint at Sydney, Australia. Gold had recently been discovered in Australia. En route he stopped off at Paris where he spent two months at the Paris Mint studying assaying. He arrived at Sydney in October 1854 [48, Vol. 35, pp. i–xii]. At first he was interested in meteorology, but his interest later shifted to Adam Smith's *Wealth of Nations* and John Stuart Mill's *Logic.* His residence of about five years in Australia is said to have given him much opportunity to reflect on various problems and subjects, a development which is well indicated in his writings after his return to England. Early in 1859 he resigned his position and returned to London by way of South America and the United States, where he visited a number of cities. In October 1859 he enrolled at the University College to study mathematics, political economy and logic, receiving the A.B. degree in 1860, and the Ricardo scholarship and the M.A. degree in June 1863. He won the gold medal in philosophy and political economy [31; 12, Vol. 8, pp. 389–91]. In 1863 at the age of twenty eight he became a tutor at Owens College, a young institution in Manchester, where in 1866 he was appointed professor of logic and mental and moral philosophy and in 1867 also Cobden Lecturer in Political Economy [10, Vol. 10, pp. 811–5; 11, (1957), Vol. 13, pp. 30–1]. In 1864 he joined the Statistical Society of London and remained an active member for the remainder of his life. While living in Manchester he became an active member of the Manchester Statistical Society. In 1868 Jevons was appointed an Examiner in Political Economy at the University of London. In 1874 and 1875 he served as an Examiner in the Moral Science Tripos at the University of Cambridge. In 1876 he was Examiner in Logic and Moral Philosophy at the University of London. In 1872 he was elected a Fellow of the Royal Society, the first economist so honored since Sir William Petty, famous author of *Political Arithmetick.* In 1876 he resigned his teaching position at Owens College in order to accept the chair of Political Economy at the University College at London. Because of ill health, because of his dislike for lecturing, and because of his intense desire to devote all his time to his writing projects, he resigned from teaching in 1880. In 1875 he received the honorary degree of LL.D. from the University of Edinburgh [42, Vol. 2, pp. 474–9; 38, p. 1202].

8. SIR RAWSON W. RAWSON, C.B., K.C.M.G., (1812–1899)

Sir Rawson William Rawson, administrator, editor and statistician, an authority on international statistics, is remembered as the first editor of the *Journal of the Statistical Society of London* (1838–40), and is well known as the first president of the International Institute of Statistics during its formative years (1885–98).

Rawson became a member of the Statistical Society of London in March 1835, was elected to the council in 1836, served as honorary secretary from 1836 to 1842, and as editor of its *Journal* beginning with the first issue of May 1838 [45]. This scholarly periodical continued as a monthly until April 1839 when it became a quarterly. It has been published continuously since that date and is probably the most outstanding statistical journal in the world. As editor, Rawson was assisted by "a Publication Committee (Mr. Porter, Dr. Lister, Mr. Heywood, Mr. Romilly, and Mr. Boileau)" [51, p. 57]. In 1840 Rawson was succeeded by Joseph Fletcher as editor. The *Annals* reports that during the first decade of the Society, "Mr. R. W. Rawson contributed 6 of the papers." It also mentioned "13 contributions on as many separate subjects by R. W. Rawson" [51, pp. 60–2]. His articles were of a critical nature because it was "the custom to comment on parliamentary papers and other state documents." *Proceedings of the Statistical Society, 1834–1837*, a volume published by the Society, contains papers prepared and read during the years before the publication of its *Journal*. In this volume Rawson has four papers, one being "On the Collection of Statistics."

"On his return from a distinguished colonial career," he again took an active part in the Statistical Society of London [51, p. 155]. In 1876 he was reelected to the council and remained a member of it until his death. Five times he was elected vice president during the period from 1876 to 1884, and he served as president in 1884–86. In 1885 the official title of the Society was changed to the Royal Statistical Society. In his address at the Golden Jubilee meeting of the Society, he mentioned that "my public career in the colonies afterwards separated me from active participation in the work of the Society for the third of a century." This Golden Jubilee, postponed one year on account of the death of the Duke of Albany, was held in London, June 22, 23 and 24, 1885. In planning this Golden Jubilee, the Society had set up a Committee "to consider in what manner the Jubilee of the Statistical Society may be utilized for the advancement of Statistical Science and the extension of the Statistical Society." The objectives of the Jubilee became: "1. To review the work of the Statistical Society during the past fifty years. 2. To consider what has been achieved by the International Statistical Congresses, or by other means, in the direction of the uniformity of statistics, and by what means that object may be further promoted. 3. To consider the possibility of establishing an International Statistical Association" [51, pp. 139–40].

The Golden Jubilee meeting was an outstanding one with distinguished guests in attendance from many countries. General Francis A. Walker, President of the American Statistical Association, was the sole representative from the United States. An excellent set of statistical papers, read by distinguished economists and statisticians, such as Edgeworth, Levasseur, Galton, Guy, Marshall, Mouat, Giffen, Korosi, von Neumann-Spallart, and others, are published in the Society's *Golden Jubilee* volume. Sir Rawson, presiding over these sessions, delivered the opening address [33, pp. 2–12]. He was elected the first president of the International Institute of Statistics, founded at this meeting, which held its first meeting in Rome in 1887 [57, pp. 246, 260].

Rawson was regarded as "the Nestor of British statisticians." He suggested in one of his papers "the use of varying price of an *average ton* of exports or imports as a sort of an index number for measuring the change in the value of money" [46]. Rawson was chairman of the Library Committee of the Society, and he left the statistical portion of his library to the Society. One obituary records that "the Society has been deprived of both its senior Fellow and of one who has done more than perhaps anyone else toward placing it in its present satisfactory condition" [45].[6]

Rawson, the eldest son of Sir William Rawson, K.B., was born in London and educated at Eton. In 1830 he was appointed private secretary to Mr. Poulett Thompson, vice president of the Board of Trade, and served in the same capacity to Mr. Alexander Baring who succeeded Mr. Thompson in 1834. He again served in the same capacity to William Gladstone in 1841 who was then vice president. In 1842 he was appointed civil secretary to the Governor General of Canada, and in 1844 treasurer to Mauritius. In 1854 he became colonial secretary at Cape of Good Hope, during which period he was honored with the C.B. In 1864 he was appointed governor of the Bahamas, and in 1869 he succeeded to the governorship of Windward Islands. In 1875 he retired from public service, and in the same year he was honored with K.C.M.G. [59, Vol. 1, pp. 588–9].

9. SIR FRANCIS GALTON (1822–1911)

Sir Francis Galton, eugenist, explorer, psychologist and statistician, the father of correlation analysis, created a number of statistical tools. As early as 1869, Galton, in his work *Hereditary Genius*, began to develop statistical techniques, stating on page 20. "The method I shall employ . . . is . . . theoretical law of 'deviation from an average'," which he acknowledges has been used by the famous Belgian statistician Quetelet. Galton claims that he is the "first to treat the subject in a statistical manner." In the preface of this work, Galton says:

> The theory of hereditary genius, though usually scouted, has been advocated by a few writers in the past as well as in modern times. But I may claim to be the first to treat the subject in a statistical manner, to arrive at numerical results, and to introduce the "law of deviation from an average" into discussion on heredity.

As to the idea of correlation, Galton describes the incident which gave rise to its development as follows:

> As these lines are being written, the circumstances under which I first clearly grasped the important generalisation that the laws of Heredity were solely concerned with deviations expressed in statistical units, are vividly recalled to my memory. It was in the grounds of Naworth Castle, where an invitation had been given to ramble freely. A temporary shower drove me to seek refuge in a reddish recess in the rock by the side of the pathway. There the idea flashed across me, and I forgot everything else for a moment in my great delight [18, p. 300].

---

[6] Besides contributing many papers to its *Journal*, Rawson also was the author of a number of other works, including Reports on Mauritius Census of 1851, *Immigration of Coolies and Valuation of the Rupee in Mauritius, 1845–64, Statistical Description of the Bahamas, and an Account of the Hurricane of 1866 in those Islands, Reports on Barbados Census of 1871 and Rainfall of Barbados 1873–74, British and Foreign Colonies (1884), International Vital Statistics (1885), Synopsis of the Tariffs and Trade of the British Empire, 1884–85, Our Commercial Barometer (1890–91), Ocean Highways or Approaches to the United Kingdom (1894)* [49, pp. 200–1; 50, p. 107].

The date of this famous idea is 1888. Galton also relates another incident, which pertains to the regression line:

> I had given much time and thought to Tables of Correlations, to display the frequency of cases in which the various deviations say in stature, of an adult person, measured along the top, are associated with the various deviations of stature in his mid-parent, measured along the side. I had long used the convenient word "mid-parent" to express the average of the two parents, after the stature or other character of the mother had been changed into its male equivalent. But I could not see my way to express the results of the complete table in a single formula. At length, one morning, while waiting at a roadside station near Ramsgate for a train, and poring over the diagram in my notebook, it struck me that the lines of equal frequency ran in concentric ellipses. The cases were too few for certainty, but my eye, being accustomed to such things, satisfied me that I was approaching the solution. More careful drawing strongly corroborated the first impression [18, 302].

Galton first used the term "correlation" on December 20, 1888, when his paper, "Co-relations and Their Measurement" was read before the Royal Society. It was not until the publication of his *Natural Inheritance* in 1889 that the terms "correlation" and "regression" became known [57, pp. 226–7, 268, 270–2].

Thus 1869 marked the beginning of Galton's many contributions to the theory of statistics. He devised the ogive curve (1875), the symbol of the coefficient of correlation, *r*, (which first meant reversion, but later changed to regression), (1877), the quartile deviation (1879), the median (1883)—although Fechner had the same idea independently—the percentile system (1885), the index of correlation (1888), and the use of the normal curve for grading children. Galton was responsible for the introduction of graphical methods in mapping the weather, and he was the originator of the use of statistical methods in the field of biology. Galton's statistical contributions are so well described by two well-known authorities, Karl Pearson and Helen M. Walker, that readers are urged to consult them [43, 55].

Galton joined the Statistical Society of London in 1860, "but his association with the Society was not close" [51, pp. 179, 225]. He served on the council from 1869 to 1879, and was vice president in 1875. He read three papers before the Society.

Galton, born in Duddeston, in Warwickshire, was the youngest of seven children. His father, a member of the Society of Friends, was a banker, and his mother was related to a number of prominent persons. His two grandfathers were both Fellows of the Royal Society, and his cousin was the famous Charles Robert Darwin (1809–1882). After being educated at several private schools, Galton attended King Edward VI's grammar school, then studied at the Birmingham Hospital, and completed his medical education at King's College. His parents wished him to be a physician, but he later changed his mind about medicine and enrolled in 1840 at Trinity College, Cambridge, graduating in 1843. His father passed away in 1844, leaving him a considerable financial inheritance, and so he was able to spend much time in foreign travel for the next few years. In 1850 he, along with Dr. Charles J. Andersson, explored certain unknown areas in Africa. An account of his experiences resulted in a book, *The Narrative of an Explorer in Tropical South Africa* (1853), which went through several editions. This exploration earned him in that year the gold medal of the Royal Geographical Society and in 1854 the silver medal of the French Geographical Society [19]. In 1855 Galton wrote another work, the *Art of Travel*, which also went through several editions. In 1856 he was elected a Fellow of the Royal Society. During the years 1860–63 he was the editor of an annual volume, *Vacation Tourists and Notes of Travels*. Galton now became interested in meteorology and in 1863 published his work *Meteorographica*. This was followed by other writings in meteorology so that he became a member of the meteorological committee and its successor, the meteorological council, as well as being connected with the Kew Observatory. He was thus associated with the meteorological committee for about forty years, ever since its beginning [10, Supp. Vol. 2, pp. 70–3; 11, Vol. 11 (1910) pp. 427–8; 12, Vol. 6, pp. 553–4]. The publication of the *Origin of Species* by Charles Darwin in 1859 encouraged Galton to make a study of heredity which resulted in several works, *Hereditary Genius* (1869), which went through several editions, *English Men of Science* (1874), *Inquiries Into Human Faculty and Its Development* (1883), and *Natural Inheritance* (1889). At the 1884 International Health Exhibition in London he set up the first Anthropometric Laboratory, which measured over 9,000 persons. At the close of this exhibition, the laboratory was established at the Science Museum, South Kensington. This later became the foundation of the well-known biometric laboratory at the University College, London [38, pp. 1167–72; 44]. Because of the possible anthropological significance, Galton now turned his talents to the study of fingerprints, and several works appeared, namely, *Finger Prints* (1892), *Blurred Finger Prints* (1893), and *Finger Print Directories* (1895). This system is now employed all over the world.

Galton was a most prolific writer [49, p. 89; 50, p. 47]. His *Memories* in 1908 lists 182 writings. Pearson has listed over 220 papers and fifteen books. He was, moreover, a member of many scientific and learned societies at home and abroad. He was the recipient of honorary degrees from Oxford, which conferred the D.C.L. on him in 1894, and from Cambridge, which honored him with the D. Sc. in 1895. The Royal Society bestowed upon him three medals: The Royal Gold Medal in 1886, the Darwin Medal in 1902, and the Copley Medal in 1910. In 1908 the Linnaean Society gave him a medal in honor of the Darwin-Wallace Celebration. In 1901 the Anthropological Institute awarded him the Huxley Medal. He was knighted in 1909 [58, pp. 562–3; 59, pp. 265–6].

Galton was general secretary of the British Association for the Advancement of Science from 1863 to 1868, and twice he declined the presidency. Four times he was president of its Sections; twice of its Geographical Section in 1862 and 1872, and twice of its Anthropological Section in 1877 and 1885. He was president of the Anthropological Institute from 1885 to 1888. Galton served for several years on the Council of both the Royal Geographical Society and Statistical Society of London, and was vice president of the latter in 1875. He was also Chairman, Committee of Management, Kew Observatory of the Royal Society 1889–1900. In his will he left a sum of 45,000 pounds for the establishment of a Chair of Eugenics to be occupied by his close friend, Karl Pearson.

10. SIR ROBERT GIFFEN (1837–1910)

Sir Robert Giffen, economist, economic journalist, editor and statistician, is well known as the head of the statistical department of the Board of Trade, as the editor of the *Journal of the Royal Statistical Society* (1876–1891), and as a prolific writer on economic statistics. In 1867 Giffen became a member of the Statistical Society of London, and he first served on the council in 1871. He was elected its honorary secretary for 1873–74 and 1876–82, and he was editor of its *Journal* from 1876 to 1891. He was vice president of this Society, 1880–81, and its president for two years 1882–84 [51, pp. 227–8]. He read eleven papers before the Society and three before Section F of the British Association for the Advancement of Science. He was twice president of Section F in 1887 and 1901. He assisted in the founding of the International Statistical Institute in London in 1885. He was an outstanding member of the Political Economy Club from 1877 to 1910. He was also one of the founders of the *Statist*, to which he contributed a number of articles, and of the British Economic Association in 1890, now known as the Royal Economic Society, in which he held office as vice president at one time. He contributed articles, known as *City Notes*, "received from R.G.," to the *Economic Journal* from its first volume in 1891 up to his death in 1910. The Royal Statistical Society honored him with its Guy Gold Medal in 1894.

As a statistician Giffen was highly regarded. He was chief statistical adviser to the British Government, for which he prepared various reports, and he was frequently called upon to present his views before royal commissions and committees. One obituary notice observed that he "was the most popular, if not the ablest, statistician of modern times. . . . He was singularly painstaking and careful in weighing statistical data, and his power of imagination was of immense use in suggesting to him the key to many an economic problem" [20, p. 529]. Another notice contains this quotation:

> I think that one of the features of Sir Robert Giffen's work which impressed me most was its extraordinary rapidity and certainty, whether he was piercing to the heart of a complicated mass of statistics and extracting their real significance, or whether he was composing the luminous and original memoranda, which he tossed off at lightning speed with little apparent effort. He has an almost unique power of carrying his statistics in his head; they were always at his command, and he was never overwhelmed by them. In the most complicated mazes of figures he never lost his grip on the realities for which the figures stood, and he never seemed to lose his bearings or his fine sense of proportion. . . .
>
> With an acute perception of the things that were not measured or unmeasurable, he first surrounded the official statistics with an atmosphere of caution, and then cleared away the mist by the use of bold estimates. For these estimates he had an arithmetical sense almost amounting to genius, a feeling for the probable error of the factors used, and a courageous rejection of measurement where the inaccuracy was too great. He had an intuitive feeling for the relative importance of numbers. He used to express his conclusion as to the adequacy of the data by saying he could, or could not, "give a figure." He appears to have had little or no knowledge of the modern mathematical theory of statistics, but arithmetical sense was so strong that he was able to proceed safely and with knowledge through calculations whose validity could only be established mathematically [21, pp. 319–21].

This obituary closes with the last sentence reading: "Giffen deserves to be honored with the Masters of Statistical Science."

One writer states:

> Giffen, a prolific writer on economic, financial, and statistical subjects, possessed a luminous and penetrating mind, great store of information, an intimate acquaintance with business matters and methods, and shrewd judgment. His instructive handling of statistics and his keen eye for pitfalls contributed greatly to raise the reputation and encourage the study of statistics in this country, though he did not develop its technique by the higher mathematical treatment [10, Supp. Vol. 2, pp. 104–5].

Another writer declares: "Giffen's numerous statistical studies are models of clear exposition and of legitimate statistical inference. He paid little attention to the mathematical analysis of statistical data and was acutely aware of the limitations commonly inherent in quantitative material" [12, Vol. 6, pp. 656–7].

Some of his papers are regarded as classics. One is his presidential address before the Statistical Society of London in 1883, entitled "The Progress of the Working Classes in the Last Half Century," which was followed in 1886 with "Further Notes on Progress of Working Classes During Last Half Century." Another is "Recent Accumulations of Capital in the United Kingdom," (1878) followed by "Accumulations of Capital in the United Kingdom, 1875–85," (1890). Still another is "The Use of Import and Export Statistics," (1882). His book, *The Growth of Capital* (1889), is one of the early estimates of national wealth. His papers and books comprise a remarkable record for a top official who wrote most of them outside his regular departmental duties. They reveal his wide acquaintance with many problems and his "unusual power of accurate generalization from voluminous and complex evidence." Richmond Mayo-Smith, a distinguished American statistician, who termed Giffen as "the greatest living statistician in England," was critical at times of Giffen's handling of some statistics, although at other times he praised Giffen's statistical writings [37].

During his twenty-one years with the board he was mainly responsible for the noteworthy improvements in official economic statistics, and he rendered much valuable assistance to royal commissions and committees. He directed the first national census of wages in 1886.[7]

Giffen was born in the small Lanarkshire town of Strathaven, and received his early education in the village school. His father was a small merchant and an elder of the Presbyterian Church. At the age of thirteen, Giffen moved to Glasgow, where he spent several years (1850–1855) as a clerk in a solicitor's office. He attended part of the time classes at the University of Glasgow, but did not graduate. In later years (1844) this University honored him with the degree of doctor of laws. In 1860 he became a reporter and sub-editor of the *Stirling Journal*. In 1862 he moved to London where he worked for the *Globe*

[7] He was the author of many books, some being *American Railways as an Investment* (1872); *Stock Exchange Securities; An Essay on the General Causes of Fluctuations in Their Price* (1877); *Essays in Finance, First Series* (1880; fifth edition 1890); *Essays in Finance, Second Series* (1886; third edition 1890); *The Growth of Capital* (1889); *The Case Against Bimetallism* (1892; second edition in the same year); and *Economic Enquiries and Studies*, two volumes (1904) which contains miscellaneous writings and addresses. He left a manuscript which was published in 1913 as a book, *Statistics*, edited by Henry Higgs with the assistance of G. Udny Yule. This volume contains nothing on statistical methods [49, p. 99; 50, p. 49].

as sub-editor and served until 1866. He then joined the *Fortnightly Review* under John Morley (later Viscount Morley), and in 1868 he became associated with the *London Economist* under the famous Walter Bagehot, as an assistant editor for the years 1868–76. During part of this period of 1873 to 1876, he contributed articles to the *Times* and the *Spectator*, and also served as city editor of the *Daily News* [11, Vol. 12 (1910), p. 4]. He joined the Board of Trade in 1876 as chief of its statistical department. In 1882 he was made assistant secretary of the board, and was also placed in charge of the commercial department. This had previously been entrusted to the foreign office, but was now made a part of the statistical department. In 1892, a third department, labour, was merged with the statistical department and Giffen was then appointed Controller-General of the Commercial, Labour and Statistical Department [57, p. 184]. Giffen was responsible for the considerable improvement of official economic statistics. In 1897, at the age of sixty, he retired from this position. He was honored in 1895 with the rank of K.C.B., after being made a C.B. in 1891 [58, p. 582].

11. FRANCIS YSIDRO EDGEWORTH (1845–1926)

Francis Ysidro Edgeworth, originally named Ysidro Francis Edgeworth, economist, editor, and statistician, is highly regarded by many as the philosopher of statistics. Some claim he is the oustanding statistician of the nineteenth century. His writings, scattered in many English and foreign periodicals, cover a wide variety of subjects, including probability, law of error, law of change, correlation, index numbers, types of averages, method of least squares, banking, prices, rates of births, deaths and marriages [57, p. 261; 8].

The decade of the 1880's marks Edgeworth's initial and strong interest in the theory of statistics. At that time six papers on the theory of probability appeared (1883–84), the first one bearing the title of "The Law of Error" and appearing in the *Philosophical Magazine* (1883). This paper was the foundation of a later paper of the same title appearing in the *Cambridge Philosophical Transactions* (1905). At the beginning of this same period in 1880, Edgeworth was appointed Lecturer in Logic at King's College. In 1885, at the Golden Jubilee of the Royal Statistical Society, he delivered a remarkable paper, "Methods of Statistics," employing ideas of leading thinkers such as Laplace, Lexis, and Venn, wherein he advanced the scientific basis for the theory of statistics [33, pp. 181–217; 57, pp. 230–1]. This epoch-making paper served to bring the calculus of probability into practical use and demonstrated that "in the apparatus for eliminating chance the most important piece of mechanism is the *law of error* or *probability* curve" [51, p. 179–80]. During this decade Edgeworth was greatly influenced by three works: Lexis' *Zur Theorie der Massener-scheinungen*, Todhunter's *History of Probability* and Venn's *Logic of Chance*. In the 1880's Edgeworth was a lonely pioneer in the somewhat unknown world of statistical theory, and it was not until around 1895 that Bowley, Pearson and Yule became his statistical companions [51, p. 180]. From 1887–90, Edgeworth was busily engaged in the study of index numbers, holding also office as secretary of the committee of Section F of the British Association for the Advancement of Science. In this scholarly work he not only examined carefully such aspects as the relative value of averages, the appropriate weights to employ, the application of the law of error, etc., but he also showed considerable interest in the several economic angles of this problem [9, 1888–1891 volumes]. In 1890 he was appointed Tooke professor of economic science and statistics at King's College, a chair distinguished for its outstanding professors, some being Reverend J. E. Thorold Rogers, Reverend William Cunningham, E. J. Urwick, and Friedrich A. von Hayek. In 1891 he resigned this chair to succeed Thorold Rogers as Drummond Professor of Political Economy at Oxford University, and served until he retired as Emeritus Professor in 1922 [10, Vol. 1922–30, pp. 284–5]. In 1892 his first paper on correlation bearing the title, "On Correlated Averages," appeared in the *Philosophical Magazine*. As to his statistical writings, Bowley points out that:

> The numerous statistical studies published between 1893 and 1926 are to a very large extent the working out of ideas expressed or latent in the papers already named, with numerous applications to a great variety of problems and with critical and explanatory references to the work of other writers. Throughout the two score papers listed for these years run the thread of the importance of sound fundamental ideas on probability in all mathematical statistics as opposed to purely empirical work [52, p. 622; 7, p. 118].

Edgeworth, regarded as "one of its most admired and trusted leaders," joined the Royal Statistical Society in 1883, served on its council, with short intervals, from 1886 to 1912, and was its president in 1912–14. The *Annals* records:

> His work for the Society lay mainly, either through papers or through contributions to Miscellanea, in the application of mathematics to the study of social and other problems. No subject was too great or too small for the use of his analysis—the theory of banking, the flow of wasps through a cycle of operations, variations in the rates of births, marriages, and deaths, chance in examinations, the rationale of exchange, psychical research were only a part of the material to which he vigorously applied his tools. . . . He was the greatest academic figure in the inner circles of the Society in the last fifty years and the most charming of friends to all those who were honoured by his acquaintance [51, pp. 237–9].

Since Bowley has so well classified and described Edgeworth's statistical writings, the reader is referred to this valuable memorial work. In the introduction Bowley states:

> In the arrangement of subjects I have endeavoured to follow the logical sequence that was always present to his mind. . . . First comes "Probability" and "Credibility," in which the philosophic basis of the whole is laid. Secondly, "The Law of Error" and the "The Method of Translation," in which the implications of the postulate of plural causation are worked out in the light of the theory of pure probability. Thirdly "Applications to Special Problems," where, cases being taken to which the theory is definitely applicable, the use of the method in measuring variations, and in distinguishing the accidental (or random) from results of direct causation ("the elimination of chance") is illustrated in many practical statistical problems. Edgeworth held very definitely the opinion that it was not sufficient to measure the variation of a statistical result simply by the statement of a standard deviation, but that it was necessary to connect this standard deviation with a law of error, to assign the probability that it (or a multiple of it) would be exceeded, and to relate this probability to credibility by the inverse method, The modulus in this use always performs this complete function. Fourthly, a short section on "The Best Mean" is mainly devoted to an explanation of Edgeworth's championship of the median, which depends on an understanding of parts of the previous sections. There follows an account of his

early contributions to the theory of correlation, so that it may be determined how far a claim for priority in its development is valid, and finally a note on his concept,on of the relations between the theories and methods of probability and of political economy [6, pp. 4–5].

Edgeworth was an active member of the British Association for the Advancement of Science, holding office as president of Section F in 1889. He was elected a Fellow of the British Academy in 1903. He was a very active member of the Royal Economic Society, serving a term as vice president. He distinguished himself, moreover, by serving first as editor, then as chairman of the editorial board, and finally as joint editor with John Maynard Keynes, of the *Economic Journal* since its first issue in March 1891. He served up to the day before his death, February 13, 1926. Under his inspiring influence, this scholarly journal achieved international prominence.

Edgeworth, born at Edgeworthstown, County Longford, Ireland, was the youngest of five sons. He was educated at home under tutors until the age of seventeen, and in 1862 attended Trinity College, Dublin, but apparently did not graduate. In 1867 he went to Oxford, and in 1868 to Balliol College, where he was awarded first class honors in Literis Humanioribus, the great school of Philosophy, the following year, although he did not receive the A.B. degree until 1873 [58 (1926), pp. 875–6]. In 1877 he obtained the M.A. degree and in the same year he was admitted to the bar, but he never practiced. He preferred to spend his time writing and lecturing [12, Vol. 5, pp. 397–8]. In 1877 he published a paper-covered volume of 92 pages, *New and Old Methods of Ethics,* being a commentary on Henry Sidgwick's *Methods of Ethics* (1874). In 1881 he published a slender volume of about 150 pages, *Mathematical Psychics: An Essay on the Application of Mathematics to the Moral Sciences.* In 1883 he wrote his first paper for the *Journal of the Statistical Society of London* (now the Royal Statistical Society), bearing the title "The Method of Ascertaining a Change in the Value of Gold." In 1884, his paper "The Philosophy of Chance" appeared in *Mind,* this being a critique of Venn's *Logic of Chance* (1883). In 1887 he published his third and last work, *Metretike, or the Method of Measuring Probability and Utility.* These three works are the only books Edgeworth produced in his life. He was apparently more inclined to write numerous articles and many book reviews, as well as to edit the *Economic Journal,* the official quarterly of the Royal Economic Society. These activities took the greater part of his time during the last thirty-five years of his life [34, p. 234; 36, p. 151]. His principal writings in economics were selected, edited and revised by Edgeworth, and published in three volumes, *Papers Relating to Political Economy,* by the Royal Economic Society in 1925. They contain thirty-four papers and seventy-five reviews. His contributions to statistical theory, embracing seventy-four papers and nine reviews are collected and arranged by Bowley in 139-page volume entitled *F. Y. Edgeworth's Contributions to Mathematical Statistics,* which the Royal Statistical Society published in 1928.

CONCLUSIONS

Many interesting features stand out in the lives and accomplishments of the men whose work has been reviewed in the preceding pages. Of the eleven leading British statisticians, six, Babbage, Edgeworth, Farr, Galton, Guy and Jevons, were college graduates, while five, Giffen, Newmarch, Playfair, Porter, and Rawson, were not. Only Edgeworth had any legal training. Two, Farr and Guy, were physicians, intensely interested in vital statistics, for one thing, to find some means of reducing the death rate. Only four, Babbage, Edgeworth, Galton, and Jevons, had post-graduate training. Not one taught a course in statistics. Only one, Farr, was connected with the national census, namely that of 1851, 1861 and 1871. Eight, Babbage, Farr, Galton, Giffen, Guy, Jevons, Newmarch, and Porter, were Fellows of the Royal Society, while three, Edgeworth, Playfair and Guy, were not. Four, Giffen, Guy, Newmarch and Rawson, were editors of the *Journal of the Statistical Society of London*, now the *Journal of the Royal Statistical Society*. Six, Edgeworth, Farr, Giffen, Guy, Newmarch and Rawson, were presidents of the Statistical Society of London, known since 1885 as the Royal Statistical Society, while five, Giffen, Guy, Jevons, Newmarch and Rawson, served as honorary secretaries. Three, Galton, Giffen and Rawson, were knighted by their government. Giffen won the Guy Gold Medal of the Royal Statistical Society, while none received the Guy Silver Medal. Rawson was for many years president of the International Institute of Statistics, founded in 1885. Finally six, Babbage, Edgeworth, Farr, Giffen, Jevons and Newmarch, were at one time president of Section F—Statistics—of the British Association for the Advancement of Science.

Three outstanding contributors to the theory of statistics were Edgeworth, Galton and Jevons; Edgeworth in the areas of probability, correlation and index numbers, Galton in the field of correlation, and Jevons in the fields of averages, index numbers, ratio chart, seasonal variation, secular trend, and crises, now known as business cycles. Edgeworth distinguished himself as editor of the *Economic Journal*. Newmarch made a significant contribution when he suggested the use of variations from the average, now known as dispersion, and particularly in his 1869 presidential address when he stated that statistics should be placed more on a mathematical basis. He thus seems to have possessed more statistical insight and foresight than most of his contemporaries. Babbage will be remembered as the founder of two important statistical organizations, Section F—Statistics—of the British Association for the Advancement of Science in 1833, and the Statistical Society of London in 1834—warmly aided by his friend Quetelet, the famous Belgian statistician. Playfair will be remembered as the founder of graphic methods in statistics, and Farr for his outstanding work in developing British vital statistics; Porter and Giffen for establishing and developing the well-known statistical department of the Board of Trade.

Finally, it appears that, even in the nineteenth century, British statisticians were making newer and more significant contributions to the theory of statistics than American statisticians, probably because of the fact that British statisticians in general had a better mathematical training.

REFERENCES

[1] *Annual Biography and Obituary*, Vol. 8, London: Longman, Hurst, Rees, Orme, and Brown, 1824.

[2] Ashton, T. S., "The Work of Stanley Jevons and Others," *The Manchester Statistical Society, 1833–1933*. London: P. S. King and Son, Ltd., 1934.

[3] Babbage, Charles, *Passages From the Life of a Philosopher*, London: Longman, Green, Longman, Roberts and Green, 1864.

[4] Babbage, Henry Prevost, *Babbage's Calculating Engines*, London: E. and F. N. Spon, 1889.

[5] Baines, Sir Jervoise Athelstane, C. S. I., "The History and Development of Statistics in Great Britain and Ireland," *The History of Statistics*, John Koren, editor, NewYork: The Macmillan Company, 1918.

[6] Bowley, A. L., *F. Y. Edgeworth's Contributions to Mathematical Statistics*, London: Royal Statistical Society, 1928.

[7] Bowley, Arthur L., "Francis Ysidro Edgeworth," *Econometrica*, 2 (1934), 113-24.

[8] Bowley, A. L., "Miscellaneous Notes; F. Y. Edgeworth," *Journal of the American Statistical Association*, 21 (1926) 224.

[9] British Association of the Advancement of Science, *Reports of*, London: various volumes.

[10] *Dictionary of National Biography*, London: Oxford University Press, various volumes.

[11] *Encyclopaedia Britannica*, Cambridge: Cambridge University Press, 1910, various volumes.

[12] *Encyclopaedia of the Social Sciences*, New York: The Macmillan Company, various volumes.

[13] *English Cyclopaedia, Division III, Biography*, London: Bradbury and Evans, various volumes.

[14] "Dr. William Farr, C.B., D.C.L., etc.," *Journal of the Statistical Society of London*, 46 (1882), 350-1.

[15] Fitzpatrick, Paul I., "Leading American Statisticians of the Nineteenth Century—II," *Journal of the American Statistical Association*, 53 (1959).

[16] Funkhouser, H. Gray, "Historical Development of the Graphical Representation of Statistical Data," *Osiris*, 3 (1937), 280-90. Also contains several photographs of Playfair's charts.

[17] Funkhouser, H. G. and Walker, Helen M., "Playfair and His Charts," *Economic History*, 3 (1935), 103-9. Also contains several photographs of Playfair's charts.

[18] Galton, Francis, *Memories of My Life*. London: Methuen and Co., 1908.

[19] "Obituary—Sir Francis Galton, D.C.L., D.Sc., F.R.S.," *Journal of the Royal Statistical Society*, 74 (1911), 314–20.

[20] "Obituary—Sir Robert Giffen, K.C.B., F.E.S., LL.D.," *Journal of the Royal Statistical Society*, 73 (1910), 529–33.

[21] "Sir Robert Giffen," *Economic Journal*, 20 (1910), 318-21.

[22] Greenwood, Major, *Medical Statistics from Graunt to Farr*, Cambridge: Cambridge University Press, 65, 69–71, 1948.

[23] Gregory, T. E., *Select Statutes, Documents and Reports Relating to British Banking, 1832–1928*, Vol. 2, Oxford: Oxford University Press, 1929.

[24] "Dr. William A. Guy, F.P.C.P., F.R.S.," *Journal of the Statistical Society of London*, 48 (1885), 650–1.

[25] Hayek, F. A., "The London School of Economics, 1895–1945," *Economica*, 13 (1946), 6–8.

[26] Hotelling, Harold, "British Statistics and Statisticians Today," *Journal of The American Statistical Association*, 25 (1930), 186–90.

[27] Humphreys, Noel A., *Vital Statistics*, London: Edward Stanford, 1885.

[28] Jevons, W. Stanley, *A Serious Fall in the Value of Gold Ascertained, and Its Social Effects Set Forth in Two Diagrams*, London: Edward Stanford, 1863.

[29] Jevons, W. Stanley, *Investigations in Currency and Finance*, H. S. Foxwell, ed., London: Macmillan and Co., 1884.

[30] Jevons, H. A., *Letters and Journal of W. Stanley Jevons*, London: Macmillan and Co., 1886.

[31] "Professor William Stanley Jevons, F.R.S.," *Journal of the Statistical Society of London*, 45 (1882), 484–7.

[32] *Journal of the Statistical Society of London*, various volumes.

[33] *Jubilee Volume*, Statistical Society of London, London: Edward Stanford, 1885.
[34] Keynes, John Maynard, *Essays in Biography*, London: Rupert Hart-Davis, 1951.
[35] Keynes, J. M., "William Stanley Jevons, 1835–1882," *Journal of the Royal Statistical Society*, 99 (1936), 523–4.
[36] Keynes, J. M., "Francis Ysidro Edgeworth," *Economic Journal*, 36 (1926), 151.
[37] Mayo Smith, Richmond, book review of Giffens' *Essay on Finance* (Second Series), *Political Science Quarterly* (1886), 337–8.
[38] Newman, James R., *The World of Mathematics*, Vol. 2, New York: Simon and Schuster, 1956.
[39] "The Death of Mr. William Newmarch, F.R.S.," *Journal of the Statistical Society of London*, 45 (1882), 115–21.
[40] Newsholme, Sir Arthur, *The Elements of Vital Statistics*, rev. ed., London: Allen and Unwin, 1923.
[41] North, S. N. D., "Seventy-Five Years of Progress in Statistics," *The History of Statistics*, John Koren, Ed. New York: The Macmillan Company, 1918.
[42] Palgrave's *Dictionary of Political Economy*, London: Macmillan and Co., 1926, various volumes.
[43] Pearson, Karl, *Life, Letters and Labours of Francis Galton*, Vol. 3A, Cambridge: Cambridge University Press, 1924 and 1930.
[44] Pearson, Karl, *Francis Galton, 1822–1922—A Centenary Appraisal*, Cambridge: Cambridge University Press, 1922.
[45] "Sir Rawson W. Rawson," *Journal of the Royal Statistical Society*. 62 (1899), 677–9.
[46] "Sir Rawson Rawson, K.C.M.G.," *Economic Journal*, 9 (1899), 665–6.
[47] "Report of the Council," *Journal of the Statistical Society of London*, 16 (1853), 97–8.
[48] Royal Society of London, *Proceedings of*, London: various volumes.
[49] Royal Statistical Society, *Catalogue of the Library of the Royal Statistical Society*, London: The Royal Statistical Society, 1908.
[50] Royal Statistical Society, *Catalogue of the Library of the Royal Statistical Society*, London: The Royal Statistical Society, 1921.
[51] Royal Statistical Society, *Annals of the Royal Statistical Society, 1834–1934*, London: The Royal Statistical Society, 1934.
[52] Spiegel, Henry W., "Bowley on Edgeworth," *The Development of Economic Thought*, New York: Wiley, 1952.
[53] Spiegel, Henry W., "Keynes on Jevons," *The Development of Economic Thought*, New York: Wiley, 1952.
[54] "The Statistical Dinner Club, 1839–1939," *Journal of the Royal Statistical Society*, 102 (1939), 292–4.
[55] Walker, Helen M., *Studies in the History of Statistical Method*, Baltimore: Williams and Wilkins, 1931.
[56] Wenzlick, Roy, *William Playfair and His Charts*, privately printed, 1950.
[57] Westergaard, Harald, *Contributions to the History of Statistics*, London: P. S. King and Son, Ltd., 1932.
[58] *Who's Who (1904)*, London: Adam and Charles Black, Ltd., various volumes.
[59] *Who Was Who (1897–1916)*, Vol. I, London: Adam and Charles Black.

[4]

PROFESSOR FLEEMING JENKIN, 1833–1885 PIONEER IN ENGINEERING AND POLITICAL ECONOMY

By A. D. BROWNLIE *and* M. F. LLOYD PRICHARD

I

HENRY CHARLES FLEEMING JENKIN (Fleeming pronounced Flemming) was one of the intellectual giants of the Victorian period who made important contributions in several fields. Trained as an engineer, he wrote on engineering subjects and was appointed to the Chair in Engineering at University College, London, at the age of thirty-three. He was also a competent electrical engineer and he wrote distinguished articles on electrical engineering. He was, moreover, an inventor. His best-known invention was his system of *telpherage*. His literary and scientific papers were numerous, and these were published in 1887 in two volumes, prefaced by a memoir by Robert Louis Stevenson. In the second volume appeared Fleeming Jenkin's pioneering work as an economic theorist and a study of this indicates that he anticipated Alfred Marshall on several points. Before examining his interesting papers on economics, a brief review of his life and career will demonstrate the range of this remarkable figure.

Fleeming Jenkin was born in Kent on 25 March 1833. His father was a commander in the British Navy and his mother achieved some success as a novelist. He went first to Dr. Burnett's school in Jedburgh and later to the Edinburgh Academy. In 1846 his parents were forced by reduced economic circumstances to live on the Continent. He continued his schooling there, learnt French, and showed a taste for mathematics. The Revolution of 1848 drove the family from France to Italy. Here, again, they were in the midst of a rising at Genoa, but they stayed in that city and Fleeming Jenkin attended the university as the first Protestant student.

Robert Louis Stevenson says in his memoir that the young man was fortunate in his choice of university. 'The physical laboratory was the best mounted in Italy. Bancalari, the professor of Natural Philosophy, was famous in his day; by what seems an odd coincidence, he went deeply into electro-magnetism and it was principally in that subject that Signor Flaminio, questioned in Latin and answering in Italian, passed his Master of Arts degree with first-class honours.' He completed his degree in 1850 and started his engineering career in a locomotive shop in Genoa under Philip Taylor of Marseilles. In 1851, however, his family returned to England and to Manchester, where he became an apprentice in Fairbairn's works. He made many friends in and around Manchester (he was a frequent visitor at Mrs. Gaskell's house) and, in spite of continuing poverty and Manchester weather, he was happy.

His first employment after finishing his apprenticeship was to help with a survey for the Lukmanier railway in Switzerland. He returned to England in 1855 and was engaged as a draughtsman in Penn's marine engineering works at Greenwich. Shortly afterwards he transferred to the service of Messrs. Liddell & Gordon, a civil engineering firm engaged on railway work. This firm was associated with Newall in the manufacture of wire rope and had begun to take an interest in marine telegraphy. From 1857 Fleeming Jenkin gained experience in the employment of Messrs. Newall at Birkenhead. The firm was engaged in the manufacture of the first Atlantic cable, and he was given charge of their engineering and electrical work. He superintended machine construction in the factory, designed picking-up and paying-out machinery, fitted up steamships for electric cables, and supervised electric testing. In 1859 he made the acquaintance of Professor William Thomson and a profitable working relationship began. Thomson wrote:

> In the first week of our acquaintance, the electric telegraph and particularly submarine cables and the methods, machines and instruments for laying, testing and using them, naturally formed the chief subject of our conversations and discussions; it was in fact the practical object of Jenkin's visit to me in Glasgow; but not much of the week had passed before I found him remarkably interested in science generally and full of intelligent eagerness on many particular questions of dynamics and physics. When he returned to Birkenhead, a correspondence commenced between us which continued without intermission to the last days of his life.

Fleeming Jenkin and Thomson were engaged together on many enterprises. The former worked with Thomson on important experiments on the resistance and insulation of electrical cables, and in 1861 he was the bearer of Thomson's proposal for the Committee on Electrical Standards named by the British Association. Thomson encouraged his collaborator to write, and from this period begins Jenkin's contribution to scientific journals. The eighth edition of the *Encyclopaedia Britannica* carried Jenkin's measurements for the resistance of gutta-percha given as the only absolute measurements of the kind made at that date. As Secretary to the Committee on Electrical Standards, Jenkin wrote their reports, published in 1869. In 1862 he produced, for the Philosophical Transactions, *Experimental Researches on the Transmission of Electrical Signals through Submarine Cables.*

In 1859 Fleeming Jenkin was elected A.I.C.E. and in the same year he was examined before the Royal Commission on the Submarine Telegraph. At the Exhibition of 1862 he was made Juror for Physical Apparatus and named Reporter for Electrical Apparatus. In 1866 he was appointed Professor at University College, London, and he gave the Cantor Lectures on the Construction, Laying and Testing of Submarine Cables. In 1868 he was appointed to the Chair of Engineering at Edinburgh University, and Stevenson says that now 'pecuniary embarrassments passed for ever out of his life'. He was elected M.I.C.E. and he gave evidence before the Select Committee on Scientific Instruction.

It was in Edinburgh that Fleeming Jenkin began his seminal work in economics. In March 1868 he contributed an article to the *North British Review* entitled 'Trade unions: how far legitimate?' This was a review of the reports of the Commissioners appointed to inquire into the organization and rules of trade unions and other associations. Two years later he contributed to *Recess Studies* (edited by Sir Alexander Grant) an article on 'The graphic representation of the laws of supply and demand and their application to labour', and he followed this with a contribution to *The Proceedings of the Royal Society of Edinburgh* (session 1871–2) entitled 'On the principles which regulate the incidence of taxes'.[1]

Until 1873 Jenkin was also engaged in the laying of submarine telegraph cables. He helped with the manufacture of part of the first Atlantic cable (as we have noted) and also with the Red Sea cable, the Singapore–Batavia cable, and important Mediterranean cables, including the first Malta–Alexandria cable. He accompanied various expeditions helping to lay cables, and from 1868 he entered into an agreement with Thomson to act as joint engineers to submarine cable companies. He was also adviser to the government on submarine cables while these were being transferred to the Post Office and he was responsible for testing cables acquired. The story of his journeys may be read in the letters quoted in Stevenson's memoir, and the reader will be entertained by the sketches made by Jenkin of Latimer Clark and other shipmates.

In 1873 Jenkin wrote *Magnetism and Electricity* for Longman's Science Series. Many editions followed, and the book was translated into Italian and German. For the ninth edition of the *Encyclopaedia Britannica* he

[1] These articles, plus two unpublished manuscripts, viz. 'The time-labour system: or how to avoid the evils caused by strikes' (1879–1881) and 'Is one man's gain another man's loss?' (1884), were included in *Papers Literary, Scientific, &c.*', by Fleeming Jenkin, F.R.S., LL.D., with a memoir by R. L. Stevenson, edited by Sidney Colvin and J. A. Ewing, 1887, containing also a note on the contributions by Fleeming Jenkin to electrical and engineering science by Sir William Thomson, 2 volumes. The London School of Economics reprinted *The Graphic Representation of the Laws of Supply and Demand and other Essays on Political Economy* in 1931.

wrote an article on Bridges, afterwards published as a separate treatise in 1876. A paper 'On the application of graphic methods to the determination of the efficiency of machinery', read before the Royal Society of Edinburgh and published in the *Transactions*, 1876–8, earned for him the Keith gold medal. Thomson stated that the paper 'was a continuation of the subject treated in Relaux's Mechanism and . . . supplied the elements required to constitute from Relaux's kinematic system a full machine receiving energy and doing work'. In 1879 Jenkin was elected Vice-President of the Royal Society of Edinburgh.

In the 1870's also, Jenkin made a substantial contribution in connexion with sanitary reform. His interest developed as a result of correspondence in *The Times* on the health and sewage of towns in which he took part. In 1877, lecturing to the Philosophical Institution of Edinburgh, he proposed the establishment of a Sanitary Protection Association on the same lines as the Steam Boiler Protection Association proposed by Sir William Fairbairn. The Edinburgh Sanitary Protection Association was formed in consequence, and other societies followed in London and elsewhere, to some of which Jenkin was made consulting engineer. In 1878 Jenkin published *Healthy Houses*, the substance of lectures delivered in Edinburgh, and from 1880 to 1885 further publications on the same subject were written by him.

The last years of Jenkin's life were spent in working out a system of electrical transport called by him telpherage. This was suggested to him by Professors Ayrton's and Perry's description of the electric railway block system. In a paper read before the Society of Arts in 1884, Jenkin said that telpherage was intended to 'designate all modes of transport effected automatically with the aid of electricity'. Stevenson tells us that the invention was costly to Jenkin because it 'consumed his time, overtaxed his strength and overheated his imagination'. Be that as it may, the hopes which he cherished for its success heightened the close of his life, and Stevenson concludes: 'However Fleeming chafed among material and business difficulties, the rainbow vision never faded . . . he may be said to have died upon a pleasure.' On 12 June 1885, after a trifling operation on his foot, Jenkin's life ended. A telpher line was opened at Glynde, Sussex, in October 1885 (with Professor Perry as engineer for the Telpherage Company) and two other lines were erected in Weston.

The notice of Fleeming Jenkin in the *Dictionary of National Biography* comments: 'In practical engineering, thoroughness and soundness marked all Jenkin's work. His determinative work in electricity is of the highest value, while his varied originality as an inventor is testified by his 35 British patents and by his scientific papers.' His work as an economist has not received much notice[1] but, as will be shown, this, too, was noteworthy.

II

In Palgrave's *Dictionary* Edgeworth wrote that Jenkin had '... contributed to political economy some very original papers of the highest theoretical importance and of considerable practical interest'.[2] Much later Schumpeter claimed Jenkin to be '. . . an economist of major importance, whose main papers . . . form an obvious stepping stone between J. S. Mill and Marshall'.[3] With such credentials from high authority it is surprising that, as far as we are aware, no complete account and assessment of Jenkin's contributions to economics has appeared. We hope that the present article will go some way towards filling this gap.

Being a mathematician it was natural for Jenkin to think that economic relations could be '. . . stated as accurately, and defined in the same manner, as any mathematical laws affecting quantities of any description' (p. 76).[4] His applications of the mathematical method to economics are all related to the partial equilibrium analysis of individual markets which has since become Marshall's trade-mark. Jenkin first analyses 'what determines the price of a given commodity at a given time in a given market . . .' (p. 76) by means of the following model (pp. 17–18, n. 1):

$$(1)\ D = f(A+1/x),$$

$$(2)\ S = F(B+x),$$

$$(3)\ D = S,$$

where D is the quantity of a particular commodity demanded, S the quantity supplied, x the variable price, and A and B unknown variable quantities. From equations (1) to (3) the equilibrium price is given by $f(A+1/x) = F(B+x)$.

Although Jenkin did not rigorously examine the form of these demand and supply functions [equations (1) and (2)] he stressed that they are subjectively based. 'In a given market, on a given day, the elements of the demand and supply curves already exist in the minds of purchasers and sellers' (p. 88). And: 'Enough has now been said to show how much the value of all things depends on simple mental phenomena, and not on laws having mere quantity of materials for their subject' (p. 93).

[1] But see the account of him in Palgrave's *Dictionary of Political Economy*. Marget, Schumpeter, and Whittaker are three writers who have paid attention in recent years to this neglected economist.

[2] Op. cit., vol. ii, p. 473.

[3] *History of Economic Analysis*, p. 837, n. 10.

[4] The references in brackets after quotations are to vol. ii of Jenkin's collected papers; see p. 206, n. 1.

With respect to demand: 'The value which buyers and sellers set on any article depends on different motives. The demand in the buyer's minds corresponds to the utility which, in their opinion, attaches to the article' (p. 98). Since equation (1) represents an inverse relation between demand and price some notion of diminishing marginal utility would seem to be implied. With respect to market supply, as the total available quantity is fixed, the basis of equation (2) cannot be found in the conditions of production. In making the statement '. . . price of all . . . limited commodities depends on a conflict between the desire for the commodity and the reluctance to sell it' (p. 21), Jenkin appears to have been thinking of the possibility of producers' consumption, particularly as wheat is one of the main examples used (pp. 77–84). But this basis for the form of equation (2) cannot apply to manufacturers because they 'rarely desire the article they make for itself, but make it only with the object of selling it' (p. 88). Short-run supply should, in this case, be constant regardless of price. Jenkin, however, invokes expectations to support a direct relation between supply and price. 'There are always a few holders who would only sell if the price were much higher than the market price,—these are the people who expect price to rise; there are some who are just willing to sell at the market price, but who will not sell a penny below; and there are others, weak holders, who expect prices to fall, and these would really, if pushed to extremity, sell below the market price' (p. 109).

Equation (3) is an equilibrium condition reached by the operation of market forces. 'If x were to rise by what we may term an accident for a day or two above the value determined by the equation [i.e. $f(A+1/x) = F(B+x)$] . . . the quantity supplied would be in excess of that required, competition would therefore at once lower the price to its true value as determined by the equation' (p. 17, n. 1). In other places Jenkin fully discusses the various market reactions of buyers and sellers that maintain price at the equilibrium level where supply equals demand (e.g. pp. 78 and 123). This discussion is very similar to that currently used in textbooks.

In representing the analysis graphically, Jenkin follows the mathematical convention of locating the dependent variable on the vertical axis; the reverse, of course, of the convention initiated by Marshall. In Fig. 1 D is the demand curve, S the supply curve, and Ox the equilibrium price. Although Jenkin does not consider stability conditions, the demand and supply curves are so drawn that the equilibrium price given by the intersection of the two curves is stable. Shifts in these curves would be caused by: changes in the total fixed supply; changes in men's minds, including their expectations; and changes in buyers' income—'The funds available for purchase at any price are limited, and this, which may be called the purchase fund, limits the possible demand' (p. 79). Jenkin uses a series of graphs (pp. 80–83) to examine the effect on equilibrium of various plausible shifts in the curves; for example, the effect of an increase in income is shown by a shift of the demand curve to D_1.

The foregoing analysis relates to a very short period. 'In the long run, the price of the manufactured article is chiefly determined by the cost of its production, and the quantity manufactured is chiefly determined by the demand at that price' (p. 89). Thus, buyers' 'opinion of the utility of the article does not ultimately affect the price' (p. 99). It

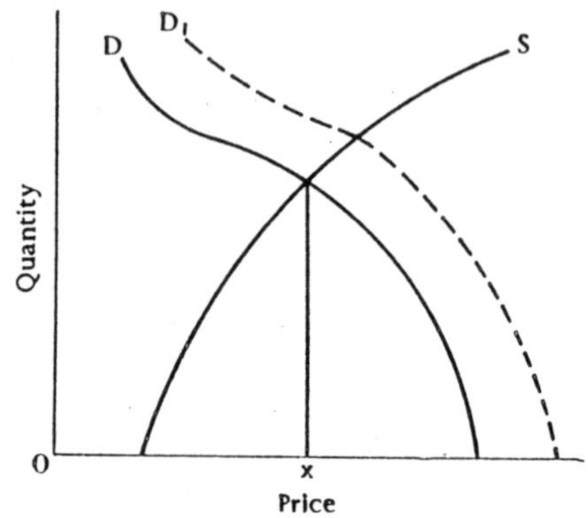

FIG. 1

is producers' reactions that equate price and cost because, if there is insufficient demand 'at cost price (including what they think a fair profit), they will cease to produce, or produce only as much as the demand at that price requires. While, if the demand equals or exceeds the supply at a higher price than cost price as above defined, makers will be tempted to produce more' (pp. 88–89), and 'new makers will produce, and by their competition soon reduce cost to that which represents an ordinary profit on outlay' (p. 24). Jenkin drew long-run demand and supply curves similar in shape to those in the above diagram, with particularly steep supply curves. The form of the supply function is now based on production conditions, decreasing returns being the typical case: '. . . the cost of production will gradually increase with the quantity produced, owing to the limitation of labour, of capital and of raw material' (p. 91) and: 'The cost of production varies with the quantity to be produced, because as more is wanted a higher price is generally required to tempt more capital and labour into the given walk [industry]' (p. 92). This account of cost conditions would appear to contradict Jenkin's statement that value is unrelated to utility. It is, however, recognized that 'Only in the case in which the supply curve is a vertical line at one price [i.e. constant costs] is it strictly true that the cost of production determines price without reference to demand; but for all those cases in which the cost of production varies little with the quantity produced, the statement is approximately true' (p. 92).

It should now be clear that Jenkin anticipated, in print at least, Marshall's synthesis of the ideas of Jevons and others about demand with those of Ricardo and Mill about cost of production and supply. There is, for example, little in Marshall's celebrated scissors analogy that is not represented in Jenkin's diagrams. Jenkin, moreover, was the first Englishman to discuss demand functions and he introduced the diagrammatic method into English economic literature. Although diagrams had been used earlier by such continental writers as Cournot, Dupuit, and von Mangoldt, his use of them was more thoroughgoing and basic to the analysis. Furthermore, Jenkin was evidently unaware of Dupuit's work (see p. 110) and so was probably unacquainted also with other continental writers. His value theory was thus possibly a rediscovery.

Jenkin developed his analytical apparatus for two main purposes: to examine the relation between trade unions and wage determination and to elucidate the effects of commodity taxation. He wrote at a time when there was considerable public criticism of the activities of trade unions. They were charged, *inter alia*, with: injuring the quality of products by reducing competition among workmen; discouraging piecework and overtime; opposing the use of machinery; and using force and criminal tactics. Jenkin suggested that the 'one argument in favour of permitting combinations of workmen to bargain with their employers is that these combinations do enable men to make a more advantageous bargain with the capitalist' (p. 7). To support this view he explored wage theory, starting with a consideration of the then current wages-fund doctrine. Mill had stated the doctrine thus: 'Wages depend . . . on the proportion between the number of the labouring population and the capital or other funds devoted to the purchase of labour' (p. 8). Jenkin recognised this to be a mere truism. 'Very clear and very true. When you know the number of recipients and the sum to be paid them, divide the number of shillings by the number of men, and you obtain the mean wages. . . . Diminish the number of men, diminish your divisor, says Mill, and your quotient will be larger' (p. 8). Jenkin also disagreed with the argument that changes in the wages fund depended only upon the profits of capital since it 'may increase by obtaining a larger share of the gross receipts from the sale of produce, though profits may be less; it may be swelled by the increased savings of the community made in the face of a diminished average rate of interest; it may rise by an increase in the gross receipts received by the maker from the consumer' (pp. 13–14). Thus: 'A manufacturer will generally work his mill or factory to the utmost so long as he does obtain a profit; he does not voluntarily set aside a certain sum for wages, diminishing and increasing that sum according to profits, but he employs as many men as he can, and pays them what he must' (p. 10). Jenkin's disagreement with Mill's hypothesis that saving varies directly with interest is based on the idea that '. . . if men can get 10 p.c. for their money they will consider they have made sufficient provision for their family by investing 10,000 l.; if they can get only 5 p.c. they feel compelled to provide 20,000 l. before retiring from business' (p. 11). Criticism of the wage-fund theory by Jenkin (1868), Longe (1867), Thornton (1867), and Leslie (1868) led Mill to make his famous recantation in 1869.

Jenkin thought that, in the short run, wages, like the price of all other limited commodities, depended upon market supplies and demand, with the important reservation that they may be affected by bargaining between employer and employee (pp. 19–26). He also applied his long-run analysis: 'The cost of production of his labour may be defined as the cost of maintaining the labourer from his birth to his death; . . . labourers do not produce and keep a family until their wages equal the cost of maintenance, including such enjoyment of comfort as in their opinion make life tolerable. . . . The labourer if dissatisfied with his comforts, does not cumber himself with a wife and family—he even emigrates, or, in the last resort goes on the parish, and dies' (pp. 99–100). '. . . If we begin by raising the standard of comfort which our labourer desires, we shall both limit the population and raise wages. The limitation of population is the intermediate machinery by which the desired end is to be effected, but the motive power must be sought in individual self-interest or discontent' (p. 102). 'The trade union, therefore, has a permanent action in raising wages, because it enables men to accumulate a common fund, with which they can sustain their resolution not to work unless they obtain such pay as will give increased comfort' (p. 104). But, while 'It is the seller of labour who determines the price, . . . it is the buyer who determines the number of transactions' (p. 105); thus unemployment could result from pressure to increase wages.

After recognizing that higher wages may alter the distribution of income Jenkin wrote: 'Looking at the relative position of the rich and poor, we do not think that the permission to combine should be withheld because it tends to diminish the present inequality of condition. Great inequality is necessary and desirable (. . . observation seems to show that trade will extend faster with large profits and small wages than with small profits and large wages) but it is at present great enough to admit of some reduction' (pp. 31–32). In any case, the total abolition of trade unions was 'out of the question as impolitic, undeserved, and impossible . . .'; consequently, '. . . in the interest of society and in protection of the rights of the minority . . . we must insist that the great power granted to the bodies of workmen shall be administered under stringent regulations' (p. 67). Jenkin proceeds to examine alleged abuses and makes many practical proposals (pp. 35–75) about which Edgeworth stated: 'much weight attaches to his advice as to the rights and limitations of combination'.[1]

A further improvement of the labour market suggested by Jenkin was the introduction of a time-labour system of engagement to replace the personal system. 'Each engagement ought not to be a contract with a man to keep him individually for a whole year or other period, but should provide on the one hand that the master shall employ one competent hand for the given time at the given rate, and on the other hand that the workman shall not leave without providing a competent substitute who will work until the end of the given time at the given rate' (p. 134). He did not, however, entertain much hope for its acceptance: 'Neither party would, by adopting the time-labour system, gain the smallest advantage over the other; a fact which may, for some time, prevent it from finding an advocate' (p. 138).

The theory of wages, particularly in regard to the influence of trade unions, was greatly improved by Jenkin. Schumpeter, indeed, claims that he must 'be added to the list of the builders of modern wage theory'[2] and goes so far as to suggest that his making explicit and actually drawing a labour demand curve 'implies an embryonic marginal productivity theory'.[3]

The second use Jenkin found for his analytical apparatus was to investigate the incidence of commodity taxes. First: 'The graphic method may . . . be employed to indicate the advantage gained by each party in trade, and to show how it may be estimated in money' (p. 108). In Fig. 2 *DN* and *SR* are demand and supply curves.

'Looking at the demand curve, the ordinate x_A from the axis OY to A represents the value set on some of the goods by some buyers, but these buyers have got the goods for the sum represented by the ordinate $x = OM''$; the difference between these two ordinates $x_A - x$ is the difference in price between what was given and what might have been given for a certain small quantity Δy of goods. $\Delta y(x_A - x)$ is, therefore, the benefit reaped by buyers from the purchase of the quantity Δy; and integrating the benefits derived from the sale of each successive quantity, we find the area $M''PN$ represents the whole gain to buyers by the purchase of

[1] Palgrave, vol. ii, p. 473. [2] *History of Economic Analysis*, p. 942. [3] Op. cit., p. 664.

the quantity OQ of goods. Similarly, it is easy to show that the area $M''PR$ represents the gain to sellers by the same transaction; these areas represent the gain in money, each product $\Delta y(x_A - x)$ being the product of a quantity by the gain in money per unit of quantity. Thus the whole benefit to the two leading communities is represented by the sum of the two above named areas, and the partition of the benefit between the two communities is perfectly definite' (p. 109). Since the curves 'for given

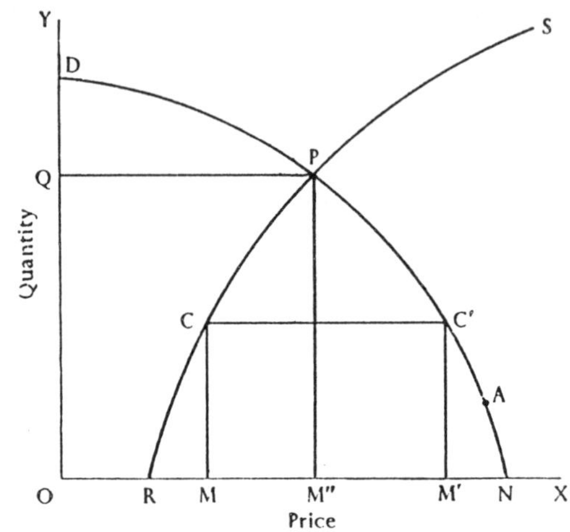

Fig. 2

goods might be determined experimentally by observing from year to year variations of quantities bought or quantities supplied at various prices' (pp. 107–8) it might be possible to give 'a numerical estimate in money of the value of any given trade . . .' (p. 110). Jenkin then demonstrates that the relative values of the two surpluses depend upon the steepness of the demand and supply curves.

He next considers 'the incidence of a tax on trade, levied as a fixed sum per unit of goods. . . .. The effect of such a tax is to produce a constant difference between the price paid by the buyer and the price received by the seller. The market prices are determined in the diagram . . . by the points between which a line parallel to OX, and equal in length to the tax, can be fitted between the two curves' (pp. 112–13). Thus if 'CC' be the amount of the tax per unit of goods, then OM is the market price to the supplier, OM' the market price to the buyer, and the difference MM' is equal to the tax' (p. 113). From this construction Jenkin calculates the relative losses of producers' and consumers' surplus and points out both that each party's loss is greater than the tax paid and that these losses increase with the rate of tax.

Jenkin had rediscovered (see p. 110) not only the theory of consumers' surplus that Dupuit had propounded but also the approximation Dupuit used to apply it. He was, furthermore, the first both to publish an account of producers' surplus and to develop and apply to problems of taxation the full surplus analysis.

Economists have always found the temptation to comment on the welfare implications of free markets difficult to resist. Jenkin was no exception. He tended to take a favourable view of market mechanisms: 'Whatever school of religion or philosophy we belong to, we cannot deny that each man, acting rationally for his own advantage, will conduce to the good of all; and if the motive be not the highest, it is one which at least can always be counted on' (p. 105). And: 'In a rapidly advancing community those who make improvements may become rapidly rich relatively to those who make none, but they nevertheless benefit the stationary class. Their own benefit is wholly derived from their own products and from the productions of those who, like themselves, make improvements' (pp. 147–8). He did, however, have some reservations about the labour market: 'They [labourers] think it monstrous that one of two parties to a bargain should be told to shut his eyes and open his hands and take the wages fixed by Political Economy, which allegorical personage looks very like an employer on pay day' (p. 26).

Although we may claim for Jenkin objective priority on a number of aspects of economic analysis, his work appears to have had little influence on the development of economic thought. Whittaker[1] suggests that this may be because he was not a professional economist and because the two writers he is most likely to have influenced, Jevons and Marshall, treated him shabbily, to say the least.

Contact between Jevons and Jenkin is disclosed by H. Stanley Jevons who wrote, in the preface to the fourth edition of *The Theory of Political Economy*,[2] that in one of his father's manuscript notes there is mention of correspondence with Jenkin about mathematical economics. It appears, moreover, that the publication of Jevons' *Theory* might have been delayed if it were not for the appearance of Jenkin's essays. Jevons, in commenting on 'The graphic representation of the laws of supply and demand', says: 'The essay is ingenious and instructive, and probably correct at almost all points; but I may add that from about the year 1863 I regularly employed intersecting curves to illustrate the determination of the market price in my lectures at Owens College.'[3] There is evidence that a 'book of careful lecture notes taken down by a member of his class . . . do, indeed, include a sketch of a demand curve'.[4] But,

[1] *A History of Economic Ideas*, pp. 452–3. [2] p. lvii. [3] Ibid., p. 333.
[4] J. M. Keynes, 'William Stanley Jevons', *Journal of the Royal Statistical Society*, 1936, p. 539.

clearly, either Jevons was exaggerating or this particular student of his did not have a very strong appetite for graphs.

If Jevons's reference to Jenkin was uncharitable, Marshall's was inadequate. The only acknowledgement is inappropriately located in Book V and appears at the end of a long footnote. This concerns consumers' surplus and reads: 'The graphic method has been applied, in a manner somewhat similar to that adopted in the present chapter, by Dupuit in 1844; and independently by Fleeming Jenkin (*Edinburgh Philosophical Transactions*) in 1871.'[1] Although as early as 1872 Marshall was acquainted with Jenkin's work[2] he denied any relation between his own analysis and that of Jenkin in a letter to Seligman dated 6 April 1896: '. . . my obligations are solely to Cournot; not to Fleeming Jenkin or Dupuit. I had given the main substance of my doctrines in lectures a year or two before he read his paper at Edinburgh. . . .'[3] Keynes substantiates this in his memoir of Marshall. 'The evidence as to the order of his studies is as follows: In 1867 he began with the development of diagrammatic methods. . . . By 1871 his progress along these lines was considerably advanced. He was expounding the new ideas to pupils and the foundations of his diagrammatic economics had been truly laid.'[4]

If the above testimony is accepted, then the influence of Jenkin on the development of economic doctrine may be regarded as slight. His personal achievement, however, is remarkable. He was not a trained economist, appears to have read little other than J. S. Mill, and his main economic papers were spread over a period of only four years. Yet the clarity and originality of his economic theorizing were of the highest order.

University of Auckland

[1] *Principles of Economics* (8th ed.), p. 476.
[2] See Marshall's review of Jevons' *Theory* in *Academy*, 1 Apr. 1872.
[3] J. Dorfman, 'The Seligman correspondence III', *Political Science Quarterly*, 1941, p. 407.
[4] 'Alfred Marshall 1842–1924', *Economic Journal*, 1924, p. 330.

[5]

A CORRECTION: ON THE GENEOLOGY OF THE SO-CALLED EDGEWORTH-BOWLEY DIAGRAM

VINCENT J. TARASCIO*
University of North Carolina at Chapel Hill

Presumably, when a tag bearing an individual's name is attached to a concept or conceptual device, it is done to designate priority of discovery. In that case, the box diagram so extensively used in the literature and generally attributed either to Edgeworth or to Edgeworth and Bowley is mislabelled. To my knowledge, the box diagram does not appear anywhere as such in Edgeworth's writings, and Bowley was not the first to use the box device.[1] The purpose of this note is to show where and when the diagram really originated.

It is curious that, with very few exceptions, when the box device is attributed to Edgeworth or Edgeworth-Bowley, no sources are cited at all. So far as Edgeworth is concerned, in the few instances where a source is cited, it is *Mathematical Psychics* (1881), but usually without page reference.[2] Baumol alone, among the authors I have consulted, gives a page reference.[3] Neither on that page nor anywhere else in *Mathematical Psychics* nor in the three volumes of Edgeworth's *Papers Relating to Political Economy* is a box diagram to be found.

It might be argued that the idea of a box construction is *suggested* in *Mathematical Psychics* in either of two diagrams (pp. 28 and 114). Can Edgeworth's graphs be converted to a box apparatus by simple geometric manipulation? The answer is no—a geometric manipulation of Edgeworth's diagram on page 28 of *Mathematical Psychics* results in a box diagram which is nonsensical in terms of the conventional box diagram.[4]

*The author is indebted to Professor William Jaffé, who first suggested the subject of this paper, for his helpful comments.

1. I say "as such" because it can be argued that Edgeworth's contract curve diagram [3, p. 28] implies a box diagram. Simply because it can be depicted as a box diagram does not mean that Edgeworth so depicted it.

2. Scitovsky [12, p. 70] speculates that "the idea [of the box diagram] probably originated with F. Y. Edgeworth (in his *Mathematical Psychics*) ...." Peter Newman [7, p. 80] points out that in Edgeworth's *Mathematical Psychics*, "the contract curve first made its appearance, together with indifference curves," and then goes on to suggest, on the basis of this, that the box diagram is attributed to Edgeworth.

3. To use his words: "This device [the box diagram], as well as the concept of the contract curve, described below, was invented by Edgeworth. See F. Y. Edgeworth, *Mathematical Psychics*, pp. 17 ff." [1, p. 326n.].

4. It turns out that the indifference curve for one trader is parallel to the indifference curve of the other trader. It might be argued that Edgeworth had a "box" in this sense: the ordinate of Figure 1 (p. 28) is amount of labor (time) *given up* by Friday; the abcissa is the remuneration received by Friday. Then Y is *received* by Crusoe, and X is given up. Hence quantities are conserved in the diagram; this mode inherently limits the quadrant to tenable points. This property is used to prove that the contract curve shrinks as the number of traders rises. But a "box" in this sense has nothing in common with the conventional box used today; it merely possesses some similar properties. In any event, Edgeworth never depicted a box in either sense.

In the case of the diagram contained in Edgeworth's Appendix on "Jevons' Formulae of Exchange," (p. 114) such a process leads to results that are inconsistent with the theory underlying the analysis.[5] Also, although Edgeworth uses the term "indifference *curves*" (in plural form in this Appendix), the term is meant to apply to the indifference curve of each of two individuals: nowhere in *Mathematical Psychics* does one find an indifference mapping consisting of more than one curve per individual. Furthermore, his indifference curves are curves of *indifferent exchanges* or "indifferent trades."

The first person to use explicitly a *system* of indifference curves for *each* person was Irving Fisher in 1892 [5, p. 68].[6] Later Pareto, in an article published in *Encyklopädie der mathematischen Wissenshaften* in 1903 [8], developed a system of indifference curves for each individual which at the same time explicitly avoided cardinal measures of utility. Edgeworth's review of Pareto's article makes a crucial point:

> Among Pareto's original contributions to the subject we may notice his study on the quantitative data with which the mathematical economist has to deal. As we understand Professor Pareto, these data do not comprise measurements of utility: psychical quantities, unlike physical, cannot be expressed as a sum of so many units. The exercise of *choice*, the preference of the economic man for one combination of goods to another, results in a *system* [my italics] of *indifference-curves* which are comparable with the isobars or isotherms of physical science in that each successive curve denotes a greater intensity of the attribute under consideration, but differ in that the economic, unlike the physical, curves cannot be each labelled with a number [4, III, p. 44].

In this citation, Edgeworth recognizes not only the idea of ordinal utility generally attributed to Pareto, but also the significance of Pareto's use of a system of indifference curves (i.e., indifference "maps"). Such a system is a necessary prerequisite for constructing a box diagram. Therefore it is not surprising that in 1906 the box diagram appears in several places in Pareto's *Manuale*, and for the first time in its familiar form in the economic literature.[7]

5. Again, the result is parallel indifference curves. If, on the other hand, one begins with individual diagrams and then superimposes them by reversing the origins and the axes, the result is tangent indifference curves along a contract curve, but the direction of the contract curve is from the northwest to the southeast and the indifference curves are not concave to/from the origins.

6. Although Fisher began with the assumption of measurable utility (as did Edgeworth), in his definition of indifference curves he was forced to discard that assumption as well as the existence of utility when he encountered difficulties arising from interdependent goods. See [11, p. 1065].

7. Cf. Pareto [9, pp. 187, 333, 338].

Eighteen years after the publication of Pareto's *Manuale*, the year following Pareto's death, Arthur Bowley published his *Mathematical Groundwork*. The first Chapter contains an elaborate version of the box diagram [2, p. 5], which presumably is the basis for attributing the diagram to him.[8] The situation with Bowley is somewhat different from that of Edgeworth, since in the latter's *Mathematical Psychics*, which predated Pareto's work, there was the question of priority and originality. In the case of Bowley, the matter of priority is of no concern in view of Pareto's earlier apparatus. The question that remains is whether Bowley was in any sense an independent, though belated, discoverer.

It is, indeed, unlikely that Bowley devised his box diagram without inspiration from earlier writers. In the Preface of his book he mentions Pareto and Edgeworth (as well as Cournot, Jevons, Marshall, Pigou and Johnson), adding that "since I cannot be sure that I have not in some cases misrepresented these writers, I have not given many detailed references and must content myself with this general acknowledgment of indebtedness" [2, pp. v-vi]. In any event Bowley did not claim any originality. The fact that he was familiar with Pareto's *Manuale* (or the French edition) is quite clear.[9]

Actually, as in the case with most concepts, the derivation of the box diagram had its roots in several innovations, all of which contributed to its development. It might be worthwhile to summarize these in order to give credit where credit is due.

(A) Jevons, *Theory of Political Economy* (1871), pp. 98-100.

(1) $\dfrac{\phi_2 x}{\psi_2 (b - y)} = \dfrac{y}{x}$, the *offer curve* of y,

where ϕ_2 and ψ_2 are the marginal utilities of goods X and Y, respectively.

(2) $\dfrac{\phi_l (a - x)}{\psi_l y} = \dfrac{dy}{dx}$, *equilibrium condition (individual),*

(3) $\dfrac{\phi_l (a - x)}{\psi_l y} = \dfrac{y}{x} = \dfrac{\phi_2 x}{\psi_2 (b - y)}$, *equilibrium in exchange,*

where ϕ_l, ϕ_2, ψ_l, ψ_2 are the marginal utilities of individuals 1 and 2 for goods X and Y.

8. Scitiovsky [12, p. 70] believes that the box diagram was first used by Bowley. Newman argues that the box diagram is attributed to Bowley as well as Edgeworth because the former "included a much more explicit treatment of the 'box' construction..." [7, p. 80].

9. Cf. [2, pp. 1-3, 5-18].

(B) Edgeworth, *Mathematical Psychics* (1881).

(4) $(\zeta - x)\left(\frac{dP}{dx}\right) + (\eta - y)\left(\frac{dP}{dy}\right) = 0$, the *indifference curve equation* (p. 21), where P is the total utility of one individual and x and y quantities of commodities X and Y.

Taking Jevons' (3) and using his own notation:

(5) $\frac{dP}{dx}\frac{d\Pi}{dy} - \frac{dP}{dy}\frac{d\Pi}{dx} = 0$, the *contract curve* (p. 21),

where P and Π are the respective total utilities of two individuals for quantities of x and y.

Taking Jevons' (1):

(6) $\frac{\phi_1(a - x)}{\psi_1(y)} = \frac{y}{x}$, the *demand curve* of x (p. 113).

(C) Fisher, *Mathematical Investigations in the Theory of Value and Prices* (1892).
System of indifference curves for one individual (p. 68).

(D) Pareto:

(a) "Anwendungen der Mathematik auf Nationalökonomie," (1903).

(7) $f(x_a, x_b) = z$, *system of indifference curves*,
where z is a parameter and x_a and x_b are quantities of commodities A and B.

(8) $F_a dx_a + F_b dx_b = 0$,
differential equation of an indifference curve (Edgeworth's (4)), where F_a and F_b are the partial derivatives of (7).

(b) *Manuale* (1906).
The *box diagram* (pp. 187, 333, 338) and a statement of the mathematical conditions of the Appendix.

(E) Bowley, *Mathematical Groundwork* (1924).
Diagram (p. 5) contains Offer Curves (Jevons), Indifference Curves (Edgeworth), Indifference Mapping (Fisher-Pareto), Contract Curve (Edgeworth), Box Construction (Pareto).

My purpose has not been to denigrate the contributions of Edgeworth or to dispute a claim that Bowley *himself* never made. It seems paradoxical that, of the names usually associated with the box apparatus, the person who has undisputed claim to priority and originality is never mentioned. I have not taken the time to trace the origin of this oversight, since it is not really important that the source of the error be established. What is more important is the fact that the oversight has persisted for so many years. For those who are fond of using terms to designate the *geneology* of a concept, Samuelson's "Jevons-Edgeworth-Bowley-Lerner" designation [10, p. 233] should be modified to "Jevons-Edgeworth-Fisher-Pareto-Bowley-Lerner," which is rather tedious. Why not simply Pareto Box Diagram?

REFERENCES

1. W. J. Baumol, *Economic Theory and Operations Analysis*. Englewood Cliffs 1965.
2. A. L. Bowley, *The Mathematical Groundwork of Economics* (1st ed., 1924). New York 1965.
3. F. Y. Edgeworth, *Mathematical Psychics*. London 1881.
4. ———, *Papers Relating to Political Economy*, 3 Vols., London 1925.
5. I. Fisher, *Mathematical Investigations in the Theory of Value and Prices*. New Haven 1892.
6. W. S. Jevons, *The Theory of Political Economy* (1st ed., 1871). London 1888.
7. P. Newman, *The Theory of Exchange*. Englewood Cliffs 1965.
8. V. Pareto, "Anwendungen der Mathematik auf Nationalökonomie," in *Encyklopädie der mathematischen Wissenschaften*, I, Heft 7, 1903.
9. ———, *Manuale d'economie politica*, Milano, Societá editrice librariá, 1906. French translation and revision: *Manuel d'économie politique*, Paris 1909.
10. P. A. Samuelson, *Foundations of Economics Analysis*. Cambridge 1955.
11. J. A. Schumpeter, *History of Economic Analysis*. New York 1954.
12. T. Scitiovsky, *Welfare and Competition*. Chicago 1951.

[6]

EDGEWORTH'S THEORY OF RECONTRACT[1]

I. *The Current Interpretation of Competitive Recontract.*
II. *Edgeworth's Early Views on the Formation of Prices.*
III. *The Transitional Phase of Edgeworth's Thought.*
IV. *Edgeworth's Recontract Model.*
V. *Conclusions.*

In recent years there has been a great deal of interest in Edgeworth's brilliant and suggestive analysis of the formation of prices, and papers on exchange continue to be published in which it is asserted that their inspiration is drawn from him. An accurate interpretation of his work is therefore desirable, but the current one is erroneous. In an effort to provide a better understanding of his thought, the present study examines Edgeworth's early writings, shows that initially his exposition of the recontract process was incomplete, and then demonstrates that he developed a recontract model that differs from the kind attributed to him.

I. The Current Interpretation of Competitive Recontract

The current interpretation of Edgeworth's theory of competitive recontract has its origin in an article of Kaldor's. He said that " Edgeworth's assumption " is that " buyers and sellers . . . make only *provisional* contracts . . ." (Kaldor (1934), p. 126). Edgeworth made this assumption, Kaldor stated, in order to ensure that trade takes place exclusively at the solution price determined by the intersection of the market demand and supply curves that are associated with the initial distribution of assets (*ibid.*, p. 127). In Kaldor's view, Edgeworth's and Walras's models " . . . come to much the same thing; they should both be considered as attempts to formulate the conditions under which buyers and sellers are able to find out the true ' equilibrium price ' *before* they undertake any exchange activity. . . . Edgeworth . . . thought that this state of affairs followed from the ' principle of re-contract ' and is thus a property of ' perfect competition ' " (*ibid.*). Kaldor concluded:

> " While Edgeworth's analysis may be slightly obscure and Walras's assumption slightly ridiculous, the main idea stands clear: . . . in so far as there is any initial ' higgling and bargaining ' this should be done by playing with ' chips ' and not with ' hard cash ' (by making only ' provisional ' and not ' final ' or ' irrevocable ' contracts). The formation of prices must *precede* the process of exchange and not be the result of it " (*ibid.*).

[1] This study has benefited greatly from the comments and criticisms of William Jaffé, from the observations of Sir Roy Harrod, and from the constructive suggestions of the referee.

Kaldor's interpretation has now become generally held.[1] Indeed, the view that Walras's and Edgeworth's theories are essentially the same has become so firmly entrenched that the term " Walras–Edgeworth *tâtonnement* " now appears in the literature.[2]

II. Edgeworth's Early Views on the Formation of Price

The development and general acceptance of the current view of Edgeworth's recontract model has been made possible by the character of his early work. His literary style was elusive, and his early thought on price formation was incomplete. These features of his work invite the reader to supply his own interpretation of its meaning and implications.[3] Furthermore, the indefiniteness of Edgeworth's early thought allowed him to entertain simultaneously two different notions of the equilibrating mechanism of a competitive market. Their differences were not clear to Edgeworth, so his writings shifted from one to the other, blending them, and treating them as equivalent analyses, with the result that it is possible for a reader to take elements of each, supplement them with modern refinements, and emerge with the contemporary interpretation of the theory of recontract. On the one hand, Edgeworth subscribed to a Walrasian point of view, which was an abstract mathematical and logical conception of an ideal perfectly competitive market model. On the other hand, he wanted to develop an analysis of the historical dynamic processes whereby actual markets move towards equilibrium, for which purpose he developed his theory of recontract. Walras's thought had similar characteristics. His *tâtonnement* theory of market equilibrium was in fact a mathematical paradigm, and indeed he was aware of this at the time that he constructed it (Walras (1900), p. VIII; Jaffé (1951), p. 37), yet he fell into the habit of describing his theory as an account of what really happens (Walker (1970), pp. 693–4). Although Walras never eliminated this confusion, and remained tied to his *tâtonnement* model, it will be seen that Edgeworth's recontract analysis grew into a dynamic theory and completely displaced his Walrasian strain of thought.

When Edgeworth presented the Walrasian view of ideal price formation he was concerned with the determination of market price on a single day in pure exchange markets. In these markets there is a given number of traders who hold fixed aggregate stocks of assets that have already been

[1] See, for example, Schumpeter (1954), p. 984; Negishi (1961), p. 122; Newman (1965), chapters 3–5; Walker (1970), p. 693. Kaldor's interpretation also appears throughout the literature on the analysis of coalitions and the competitive core. See Debreu and Scarf (1963), p. 165 Rader (1964), p. 175; Aumann (1964), p. 390; Vind (1964), p. 165.

[2] See, for example, Guarnieri (1971), p. 202.

[3] As Stigler has observed, Edgeworth characteristically did not " tarry long at one point . . . often, alas, he was content to pass on immediately to a new problem. . . ." (Stigler (1941), p. 108). "One must," Stigler remarked, " accordingly interpret and supplement Edgeworth's writings, otherwise they are frequently incomprehensible " (*ibid.*, p. 109). See also Stigler (1957), pp. 6–7.

produced, and who engage in a simple redistribution of the assets through exchange. Edgeworth said that in this situation the competitive equilibrium price and volume of transactions are determined by the point of intersection of the supply and demand curves (Edgeworth (1881), p. 31). This proposition, he wrote, is " generally accepted " (*ibid.*, p. 30); it follows from the assertion that competition is perfect; and any necessary explanation has already been provided by writers such as Marshall, Walras, and Auspitz and Lieben (*ibid.*, pp. 30, 31; Edgeworth (1925), vol. 2, p. 297).[1] Writing in the Walrasian vein, Edgeworth neglected the recontract process, and stated that there are neither provisional nor irrevocable disequilibrium contracts in a competitive market: " You might suppose each dealer to write down his *demand*, how much of an article he would take at each price, without attempting to conceal his requirements; and these data having been furnished to a sort of market-machine, the *price* to be passionlessly evaluated " (Edgeworth (1881), p. 30). Edgeworth's market machine is the same as Walras's *calculateur* (Walras (1874); Walras (1883), p. 16; Walker (1972), p. 346), and, like Walras, Edgeworth was describing a market that operates as though the traders, instead of bargaining about the terms of their agreements, freely report their excess demand functions to an omniscient price setter. The price setter, an *intellectus angelicus*,[2] then calculates and publishes the initial solution price, the only price that is quoted and the only price at which trade is allowed to occur. Similarly, when Edgeworth formally set out the properties of a perfectly competitive market he introduced the equality of desired market demand and supply as a *postulate*, as an assumed condition of a market model, not as a derivative consequence of recontract (Edgeworth (1881), p. 42; and see Edgeworth (1925), vol. 2, pp. 291–7). Repeatedly he stated that trade in a competitive market takes place subject to Jevons's law of indifference (Jevons (1957), pp. 91–2), the law that " all portions of a commodity shall be exchanged at the same rate " (Edgeworth (1925), vol. 2, p. 295; and see also Edgeworth (1881), pp. 31, 39, 113, 115, 190; Edgeworth (1925), vol. 2, pp. 306–7; Jaffé (1965), Letter 856), which is precisely the condition that is fulfilled in a Walrasian *tâtonnement* model.

The second conception of price formation found in Edgeworth's early work, the recontracting procedure, had within it the possibility of becoming a theory with behavioural content, but prior to 1900 Edgeworth had not formulated the specific details of the competitive recontract process, nor had he even thought out all the broad lines of its general character. This view is supported by evidence provided by *Mathematical Psychics* and other relatively early writings of Edgeworth's, and by the contrast between those

[1] In fact Walras and Marshall differ in their theories of competitive exchange (Walker (1969)) and Walras was in disagreement with Auspitz and Lieben on fundamental aspects of the determination of market prices (Jaffé (1965), Letters 913, 970, 978, 1200 enclosure).

[2] See Jaffé (1967), p. 2, where this term is aptly used to describe the characteristics that the Walrasian market machine would have to possess, and see also Uzawa (1960), p. 184 and *passim.*

sources and the position he took in articles and comments written after 1900.

In his early discussion of recontract, Edgeworth stated that he was going to analyse what happens to the number of possible equilibrium asset distributions when the number of traders is progressively increased (Edgeworth (1881), pp. 35–43). He explained that the possible equilibrium asset distributions lie on the contract locus. Each time that new traders enter the market there is a new contract locus, and new sets of contracts are formed until an equilibrium is once again achieved. The range of possible equilibrium distributions diminishes as the number of traders is increased, and when the number becomes indefinitely large the contract locus shrinks to a point, the multi-dimensional co-ordinates of which are the competitive equilibrium stocks of the assets held by the traders (*ibid.*, p. 39). What is this distribution and the associated equilibrium price? Edgeworth was unclear on this matter.

A first reason for his lack of clarity is that Edgeworth makes two different assumptions about what happens when the number of traders is increased. In one exposition Edgeworth implied that when additional traders are introduced into the market, thus initiating a new market day, the traders who participated in the market on previous days are assumed once again to hold their pre-trade stocks of the assets; and therefore when the competitive market day begins, the supply and demand functions are those for which the pre-trade asset distribution is a parametric condition (*ibid.*, pp. 31, 42; Edgeworth (1925), vol. 2, p. 312). In Edgeworth's other account (Edgeworth (1881), pp. 34–41), at the beginning of each new day the participants on the previous day are assumed to hold the old equilibrium stocks that they acquired when they moved to the previous contract locus. Consequently, at the start of the market day that begins with indefinitely many traders there is the pair of supply and demand functions associated primarily with the asset distribution that evolves as a result of the sequence of actual exchanges which occur when one after another equilibrium is upset as the market becomes progressively more competitive. This pair leads to an equilibrium price and distribution that are not, in general, the same as those to which the market is led by the pre-trade endowment pair.

A second source of Edgeworth's obscurity is that he did not explain how the recontract process operates as an equilibrating mechanism within each new alternative market day with given parameters, that is, when each new constant number of traders is in the market, with their particular individual stocks of the assets, and their particular preference functions. He said that traders form and re-form agreements, but he did not explain important aspects of the recontract procedure. He made statements about the consequences of recontracting, but he did not show how they occur. In two places Edgeworth referred to producers " . . . selling products among a set of consumers . . ." (*ibid.*, p. 31; and see p. 146), which implies that the theory of recontract can apply to normal-value analysis, but his early work does not explicitly mention whether recontracting deals with normal price or market price. This means that important parametric conditions of the recontract model were not specified, and therefore the model itself remained incompletely defined.

Third, the examples used in *Mathematical Psychics* have different implications. In one type of example the inherent nature of the commodities traded is such as to restore the original endowments at the beginning of each new contract time. This type leads to the view that Edgeworth had in mind a non-*tâtonnement* market that reaches equilibrium after a succession of days, but in which the initial conditions are the same at the beginning of each day, so that the equilibrium price is the same as if there were no disequilibrium transactions. For instance, Edgeworth wrote that " . . . a landlord *on expiry of lease* recontracts, it may be, with a new tenant" (*ibid.*, p. 17; emphasis added). Here Edgeworth stated that disequilibrium contracts are not provisional, that they last until the end of the contract period, but that they are not renewed on the same terms, which is entirely different from saying that they are annulled. The land is privately owned, and it endures forever, so the landlord regains control of his stock of land at the end of the contract period. Edgeworth did not, however, indicate the possible implications of his brief statement, or provide any information about the character of recontracting in his subsequent extended discussion of the renting of land (*ibid.*, pp. 138–46). A complete explanation would point out that if contracts are not made on equilibrium terms the conditions of the new contracts would be closer to the equilibrium conditions, and would describe the rules and processes by which the equilibrating mechanism operates. Edgeworth also mentioned or dealt with labour markets (*ibid.*, pp. 17, 28–9, 31, 146; Edgeworth (1925), vol. 2, pp. 318–19), perhaps on the supposition that the capacity of a worker to undertake labour is the same at the beginning of each new day, and with the realisation that the worker can have no accumulated stock of past labour to bring to the market.

By contrast, in *Mathematical Psychics* Edgeworth also referred to the " . . . use of capital from among sets of capitalists . . ." (Edgeworth (1881), p. 31; and see p. 146), international traders (*ibid.*, p. 146), and, as has been seen, producers and consumers (*ibid.*, pp. 31, 146). There is, he said, a " substantial unity of the theory of *contract* (*whatever* the *articles*) " (*ibid.*, p. 139).[1] The assertion that recontracting can be assumed to occur in a market for *any* type of commodity would require a model that is free from special assumptions regarding the type of commodity exchanged, but no such alternative recontract process appears in Edgeworth's early work.

[1] Emphasis added to *whatever*. In one place ((1881), p. 28) Edgeworth uses *articles of contract* to mean the alternative possible terms of different contracts regarding two given commodities, but on the next page, and elsewhere, he uses the term to mean *the commodities traded* (*ibid.*, pp. 17, 19, 29, 49, 139).

III. The Transitional Phase of Edgeworth's Thought

During the ten years after 1881 Edgeworth's views of price formation underwent a process of evolution, in the course of which he came to distinguish between his own ideas and the Walrasian variety of theory. As part of clarifying this distinction he developed an analysis of normal value, and constructed a non-*tâtonnement* theory of recontract in bilateral monopoly.

It was observed above that in 1881 Edgeworth thought that Walras had accurately stated how supply and demand are equalised, but eight years later Edgeworth made the judgment that the theory of *tâtonnement* is " after all, not a very good idea " (Edgeworth (1889), p. 435; and see Edgeworth (1925), p. 281).[1] Subsequently he enlarged upon this view, arguing that Walras's theory of *tâtonnement* is defective, that it is not a dynamic theory of the movement of the economic system, and that the theory of recontract offers a different and a better explanation of the matter (Edgeworth (1891), pp. 12 ff.). Edgeworth explained that Walras had described an hypothetical equilibrating process, one by which economic equilibrium is reached in his model. But the *tâtonnement* process is not the way that the real economic system actually follows (Edgeworth (1889), p. 435; Edgeworth (1891), p. 20; Edgeworth (1925), vol. 2, p. 311). In fact, " Walras's laboured description of prices set up or ' cried ' in the market is calculated to divert attention from a sort of higgling which may be regarded as more fundamental than his conception, the process of *recontract* . . ." (Edgeworth (1925), vol. 2, p. 311).

Two years later Edgeworth unequivocally applied his theory of recontract to the analysis of a market in which there are flows of production and consumption, and in which there are firms and consumers (Edgeworth (1891), p. 15). Of course, Walras had also constructed a model of flows of production and consumption, but, like his exchange market, it was a *tâtonnement* model. By contrast, in Edgeworth's analysis the industry moves to equilibrium through a non-*tâtonnement* process in which the terms of successive irrevocable disequilibrium transactions are varied through competition between the sellers. Equilibrium is reached when " the increased costs resulting from the increased production just counter-balance the profit that can be drawn " from attracting another buyer (*ibid.*).

In his theory of bilateral exchange Edgeworth also treated recontract as a non-*tâtonnement* process. This view first emerged in *Mathematical Psychics*. " Why, indeed," he wrote, "should an isolated couple exchange every portion of their respective commodities at the same rate of exchange? " (Edgeworth (1881), p. 109; and see *ibid.*, pp. 28–9; Jaffé (1965), Letter 856). Then in 1891 Edgeworth presented his complete model of bilateral

[1] On this point see Stigler (1941), p. 245; Walras (1954), translator's note to Lesson 11, p. 515; and Walker (1970), pp. 692–3.

exchange ((1925), vol. 2, pp. 315–7).[1] The contracts made by the traders at different prices within a given market day are irrevocably fulfilled, and the initial endowments are not renewed at the beginning of each new contracting period, so the point that represents the asset distribution in the commodity space traces a path of segmented line sections from the initial endowment point to the point of equilibrium. Each successive segment is an opportunity line with a slope equal to the new price agreed upon in the new contract (*ibid.*, vol. 2, p. 316). Ordinarily the traders reached the contract curve, and the slope of the last segment along which they move to reach that curve is the equilibrium price. The equilibrium price and asset distribution therefore depend upon the particular sequence of trading prices and the associated sequence of transactions.[2]

IV. Edgeworth's Recontract Model

During the ten years after 1891 Edgeworth finished working out the main characteristics and the appropriate setting of the competitive recontract model, introducing disequilibrium transactions into the model, and beginning the integration of exchange and production theory.

In 1902 Edgeworth wrote that

> " two kinds of higgling may be distinguished as appropriate respectively to short and long periods. *First,* we may suppose the intending buyers and sellers to remain in communication without actually making exchanges, each trying to get at the dispositions of the others, and estimating his chances of making a better bargain than one that has been provisionally contemplated. By this preliminary tentative process a system of bargains complying with the condition of equilibrium is, as it were, rehearsed before it is actually performed " (Edgeworth 1925, vol. 1, p. 40).

This is the *tâtonnement* process that is currently thought to be Edgeworth's recontract model, but Edgeworth said it is not. He offered an alternative hypothesis: " Or, *second,* one may suppose a performance to take place before such rehearsal is completed " (*ibid.*). By this he meant that, on his second supposition, irrevocable disequilibrium transactions occur.[3] He went on to describe explicitly the principal features of the competitive recontract model that he had finally developed, and the resulting determination of what may be called Edgeworthian normal value:

[1] His article does not in fact deal with the kind of normal-value recontract model that his editorial note of 1925 (Edgeworth (1925), pp. 313–4) described it as analysing.

[2] Compare Newman ((1965), p. 68). Edgeworth's theory of barter has been correctly described and generalised by Uzawa (1962) and by Negishi ((1962), pp. 660–3).

[3] It is perfectly reasonable to assume in a competitive market model that trade occurs at disequilibrium prices. This has been shown by Marshall (1920), pp. 334–5; Walker (1969); and by those who have developed modern competitive non-*tâtonnement* models. See, for example, Negishi (1961); Hahn and Negishi (1962); Hahn (1962); Negishi (1962); Hahn (1963); Negishi (1964); Morishima (1964); Quirk and Saposnik (1968), pp. 191–93; Arrow and Hahn (1971), pp. 324–46.

" On the first day in our example a set of hirings are made which prove not to be in accordance with the dispositions of the parties. These contracts terminating with the day, the parties encounter each other the following day,[1] with dispositions the same as on the first day, —like combatants *armis animisque refecti*,—in all respects as they were at the beginning of the first encounter, except that they have obtained by experience the knowledge that the system of bargains entered into on the first occasion does not fit the real dispositions of the parties. The second plan of higgling . . . is more appropriate to ' normal ' value.

[1] They *recontract*, in the phraseology of *Mathematical Psychics* (ibid., vol. 1, p. 40, and p. 40, n. 3)."

It can be seen from Edgeworth's footnote that he had come to want the competitive recontracting process dealt with in *Mathematical Psychics* to be interpreted as a non-*tâtonnement* process. Unlike Walras's equilibrating procedure, which takes place within a single " day," Edgeworth's occurs over a sequence of days. Until equilibrium is reached, each day ends in disequilibrium after transactions have occurred at disequilibrium prices, revealing to the traders the magnitude and sign of the excess demand. From day to day, as the traders' knowledge of the state of the market increases, they progressively modify their behaviour, changing the price in such a way that the market converges to equilibrium: they " meet again and again . . . and . . . resume bargains until a system of contracts, not likely to be varied by re-contract, has been set up " (*ibid.*, vol. 2, p. 331; see also *ibid.*, vol. 2, pp. 333–4).[2]

Once he had attained a clear view of recontracting, Edgeworth's examples, and the context in which he presented them, also became unambiguous. Thus the labourers and the employers in the example (*ibid.*, vol. 1, pp. 35–6, 39, 40) to which he refers in the above quotation start each morning with the same supply-of-labour and demand-for-labour functions respectively, and enter into wage contracts. Each set of contracts is binding for the work day on which it is made, but if the market supply and demand quantities are not equal, then the terms of the next day's contracts are changed. Eventually, the equilibrium contract terms are found. The participants subsequently renew those terms at the beginning of each new market day, until some parametric change occurs.

The other theme that Edgeworth began to sketch out, the integration of exchange and production theory, was an early statement of stock-flow analysis, and it was a further step towards a theory of real dynamic systems.

[2] By 1902 Edgeworth had adopted Marshall's view of the likelihood that current wage bargains are affected by past contracts, and his view that labour markets as a result have unique characteristics (Marshall (1920), pp. 335–56). Edgeworth observed that the terms of any particular contract may affect the traders' preference functions. In labour markets, previous contracts may affect the workers' habits and efficiency (Edgeworth (1925), vol. 1, p. 41; *ibid.*, vol. 2, p. 319), and may also affect the magnitude of the stocks of assets held by workers and employers at the beginning of each new recontracting period. The terms of past contracts can therefore cause the market demand and supply functions to shift.

Edgeworth came to regard recontracting within a given market day and from day to day as important and interesting for the reason that it leads towards the establishment of the equilibrium values of the variables that are determined by underlying normal forces (*ibid.*, vol. 1, p. 40; *ibid.*, vol. 2, p. 333), and he became insistent that the recontract model should be used for the analysis of normal price. He referred to Marshall's use of the contract curve in the treatment of market price in a barter situation: " I am about to adapt a similar construction to a somewhat different purpose, contemplating not market value but normal value " (*ibid.*, vol. 2, p. 331). Marshall's treatment of barter " . . . has in view a market in a special sense distinguished from normal, whereas the process which I analyse has much in common with the determination of normal equilibrium " (*ibid.*, vol. 2, p. 313). Edgeworth wrote that in the analysis of value

> " . . . Zawadski makes an assumption about the data which we regard as important. For the purpose of the abstract theory—which ' affords an approximate image of the real phenomenon '—we should think of ' dealers who often meet having each at his disposal . . . about the same quantity of goods.' . . . Again, ' the economic tendencies imaged by the abstract theory are the more decided . . . the more the phenomena are regular, continually repeated under analogous conditions.' . . . And again, with special reference to *production*: ' Only transactions frequently repeated under analogous circumstances can present a certain character of regularity, so it is only to these that our theory is in general applicable. . . .' " (Edgeworth (1925), vol. 2, pp. 452–53).

Edgeworth then referred (*ibid.*, vol. 2, p. 453, n.) to his recontract model as a " cognate conception " with Zawadski's, and supported this position by quoting the passage about non-*tâtonnement* recontracting that he had written in 1902.

It can now be seen that many of the assumptions of Edgeworth's theory of competitive recontract are designed to perform the same type of function as the assumptions made by Marshall in his analysis of short-run normal value. In Edgeworth's competitive recontract model there is a set of points " . . . like initial conditions continually renewed " (*ibid.*, vol. 2, p. 331) that are required to maintain the constancy of the position of the market supply and demand curves at the beginning of each new day. These conditions are similar in nature to those that are required in a Marshallian normal short-run market to maintain the position of the market supply and demand curves during the equilibrating process that takes place after some shock has displaced the price. In Marshall's model, as in Edgeworth's, the set of demanders and their preference functions are assumed to be constant. Both models assume that the demanders' purchasing power is constant, as well as the other parameters of the market demand function. Similarly, both models require that there be a fixed number of sellers, and that the preferences of the sellers are constant. Marshall's short-run normal analysis of output markets assumes constancy of the conditions that determine the form and position of the supply curve of each input, and that constancy is also a tacit assumption which lies behind the individual supply curves in an Edgeworthian output market. Marshall's normal short-run labour market model, just as Edgeworth's treatment of labour markets, assumes that the number of workers in the industry, their work—income preferences, their efficiency, and their wealth are all constant.

Disequilibrium transactions occur in the models of both writers. In Edgeworth's model " . . . agreements are renewed or varied many times. A ' final settlement ' is not reached until the market has hit upon a set of agreements which cannot be varied with advantage to all the re-contracting parties " (*ibid.*, vol. 2, p. 314). This is similar to what happens in a Marshallian normal market, although Marshall described the equilibrating mechanism in terms of changes in the rate of production, the volume of transactions, and the price, rather than in the terminology of " recontract " and " settlements."

V. Conclusions

Edgeworth's early work on price formation dealt with a variety of incompletely explained situations. At no point, however, did he describe recontracting in the way that is now thought to characterise his work. After 1881 Edgeworth's ideas on exchange underwent a process of evolution, and by 1902 he had developed a recontract model which differs from the one currently ascribed to him in two major respects. First, its purpose is the analysis of a type of normal price, not market price. Second, it is concerned with markets that are characterised by irrevocable disequilibrium prices and transactions, and that may be in a state of disequilibrium for an extended period of time. The formation of equilibrium prices in his model does not precede the actual exchange of commodities. On the contrary, exchange at disequilibrium prices is an essential part of the equilibrating process.

If the current interpretation of Edgeworth's model were correct, we would indeed have to conclude that it is a " fanciful " (Newman (1965), p. 69) scheme. Doubtless that is why Edgeworth rejected the *tâtonnement* approach. His alternative was an advance over the Walrasian conception, an early step in a new direction towards a line of investigation that is still being slowly worked out—a dynamic non-*tâtonnement* theory of exchange, production, and consumption.

Donald A. Walker

Indiana University of Pennsylvania.

Date of receipt of final typescript: May 1972.

References

Arrow, Kenneth and Hahn, Frank H., *General Competitive Analysis*. San Francisco and Edinburgh: Holden-Day and Oliver and Boyd, 1971.

Aumann, Robert J., " Markets with a Continuum of Traders," *Econometrica* 32, nos. 1–2 (January–April 1964), pp. 39–50.

Debreu, Gerard, and Scarf, Herbert, " A Limit Theorem on the Core of an Economy," *International Economic Review* 4, no. 3 (September 1963), pp. 235–46.

Edgeworth, Francis Y., *Mathematical Psychics*. London: C. Kegan Paul & Co., 1881.

——, " The Mathematical Theory of Political Economy," *Nature* 40 (September 5, 1889), pp. 434–6.

——, " La théorie mathématique de l'offre et de la demande et le coût de production," *Revue d'économie politique* 5, no. 1 (January 1891), pp. 10–28.

——, *Papers Relating to Political Economy*, 3 vols. London: Royal Economic Society, 1925.

Guarnieri, Raymond L., " 1970—Q5," *Journal of Political Economy* 79, no. 1 (January/February 1971), p. 202.

Hahn, Frank H., " On the Stability of a Pure Exchange Equilibrium," *International Economic Review* 3, no. 2 (May 1962), pp. 206–13.

——, " On the Disequilibrium Behaviour of a Multi-Sectoral Growth Model," Economic Journal 73, no. 291 (September 1963), pp. 442–57.

Hahn, Frank H., and Negishi, Takashi, " A Theorem on Non-*Tâtonnement* Stability," *Econometrica* 30 (July 1962), pp. 463–9.

Henderson, James M., and Quandt, Richard E., *Microeconomic Theory*, 1st ed. New York: McGraw-Hill, 1958.

Jaffé, William (ed.), *Correspondence of Léon Walras and Related Papers*, 3 vols. Amsterdam: North-Holland, 1965.

——, " Walras' Theory of *Tâtonnement:* A Critique of Recent Interpretations," *Journal of Political Economy* 75, no. 1 (February 1967), pp. 1–19.

Jevons, William S., *The Theory of Political Economy*, 5th ed. New York: Kelley and Millman, 1957.

Kaldor, Nicholas, " A Classificatory Note on the Determinateness of Equilibrium," *Review of Economic Studies* 1 (February 1934), pp. 122–36.

Marshall, Alfred, *Principles of Economics*. New York: Macmillan, 1920.

Morishima, Michio, *Equilibrium, Stability, and Growth: A Multi-Sectoral Analysis*. London: Oxford University Press, 1964.

Negishi, Takashi, " On the Formation of Prices," *International Economic Review* 2, no. 1 (January 1961), pp. 122–6.

——, " The Stability of a Competitive Economy: A Survey Article," *Econometrica* 30, no. 4 (October 1962), pp. 635–69.

——, " The Stability of Exchange and Adaptive Expectations," *International Economic Review* 5, no. 1 (January 1964), pp. 104–11.

Newman, Peter, *The Theory of Exchange*. Englewood Cliffs, N.J.: Prentice-Hall, 1965.

Quirk, James, and Saposnik, Rubin, *Introduction to General Equilibrium Theory and Welfare Economics*. New York: McGraw-Hill, 1968.

Rader, John T., " Edgeworth Exchange and General Economic Equilibrium," *Yale Economic Essays* 4 (Spring 1964), pp. 133–80.

Schumpeter, Joseph A., *History of Economic Analysis*. New York: Oxford University Press, 1954.

Stigler, George J., *Production and Distribution Theories*. New York: Macmillan, 1941.

——, " Perfect Competition, Historically Contemplated," *Journal of Political Economy* 65 (February 1957), pp. 1–17.

Uzawa, Hirofumi, " On the Stability of Edgeworth's Barter Process," *International Economic Review* 3, no 2 (May 1962), pp. 218–32.

——, " Walras' Tâtonnement In the Theory of Exchange," *Review of Economic Studies* 27 (June 1960), pp. 182–94.

Vind, Karl, " Edgeworth-Allocations in An Exchange Economy with Many Traders," *International Economic Review* 5, no. 2 (May 1964), pp. 165–77.

Walker, Donald A., " Marshall's Theory of Competitive Exchange," *Canadian Journal of Economics* 2 (November 1969), pp. 590–8.

——, " Léon Walras in the Light of his Correspondence and Related Papers," *Journal of Political Economy* 78 (July/August 1970), pp. 685–701.

——, " Competitive *Tâtonnement* Exchange Markets," *Kyklos* 25, fasc. 2 (June 1972), pp. 345–63.

Walras, Léon, " Principe d'une théorie mathématique de l'échange," *Séances et travaux de l'Académie des Sciences morales et politiques*. The *Collection* 101, New Series 33rd year (January (1874), part I, pp. 97–116. Republished in Walras 1883, pp. 7–25.

——, *Théorie mathématique de la richesse sociale*. Lausanne: Corbaz, 1883.

——, *Eléments d'économie politique pure*. Lausanne: F. Rouge, 1900.

——, *Elements of Pure Economics*, translated by William Jaffé. Homewood: Irwin 1954.

[7]

Edgeworth's Contract Curve: Part 1. A propaedeutic essay in clarification

William Jaffé

This propaedeutic essay is intended primarily to lay the groundwork for a sequel[1] in which two historical antecedents of Edgeworth's Contract Curve will be explored. With this limited purpose in mind, I shall here confine myself to the purely formal aspects of Edgeworth's analysis of isolated bilateral barter in two commodities,[2] without reference either to his own elaborations and applications of the theory or to subsequent accretions and developments introduced by others in recent literature. At the same time, I propose to pry out certain latent implications contained in Edgeworth's own formulation of his theory, stressing principally those implications which help reveal conceptual links between Edgeworth's Contract Curve and its historical antecedents.

It may come as a surprise, to those who rely exclusively on secondary sources for information on past analytic achievements, to learn that nowhere in Edgeworth's published writings is there anything resembling what is so frequently referred to as an "Edgeworth box diagram." To my knowledge, the earliest adumbration of a true box diagram is found on page 288 (Fig. 16) of the fifth instalment of Vilfredo Pareto's article, "Considerazioni sui principii fondamentali dell'economia pura," which appeared in October 1893, twelve years after the publication of Edgeworth's *Mathematical Psychics*.[3] Technically speaking, Edgeworth's

WILLIAM JAFFÉ *is Professor of Economics at York University and a frequent contributor to this journal.*

1. Part 2 of this article, subtitled "Two Figures in Its Protohistory: Aristotle and Gossen," will appear in the Winter issue of this journal.

2. Though the case is often designated as one of "bilateral monopoly," this term will be avoided in the present context because of its ambiguity which has been pointed out in Schneider 1932, pp. 78–82, and 1952, pp. 259–83; and in Hicks 1935, p. 16.

3. The Paretian origin of the "box diagram" has been noted in several places, e.g., in Schneider 1952, p. 261 of Hutchison's translation; in Shackle 1967, pp. 71–80, where Edgeworth's "lines of indifference" and Pareto's "indifference curves" are carefully distinguished; in Dobb 1969, p. 13; and in Tarascio 1972. Singh 1963, pp. 45–56, without referring to a box diagram, calls attention to the differences between Edgeworth's "indifference curves" employed in his theory of barter and the Fisher-Pareto type of "indifference curves" designed to portray a *consumer's* scale of preferences.

Contract Curve diagram could only be converted into a box diagram of specific dimensions if the initial endowments, which Edgeworth deliberately chose to leave implicit,[4] were explicitly specified.

The unqualified identification of Edgeworth's construction with Pareto's box diagram is so persistent and widespread in the literature that a simplified recapitulation[5] of Edgeworth's original argument seems opportune, not only as a frame of reference for probing earlier manifestations of the key concepts involved, but also in the interest of historical verity. Let us turn, therefore, to Edgeworth's pristine diagram, as it appeared in the *Mathematical Psychics* of 1881,[6] shorn however of lines of no immediate concern for present purposes[7] and lettered here less esoterically, as in Fig. 1, where CC′ is the Contract Curve.

4. That Edgeworth's omission of the initial endowments from the arguments of his utility functions was deliberate is evident from his statement on p. 21 of the *Mathematical Psychics* that there is a correspondence between his differential equation of the Contract Curve,

$$\text{“}\frac{dP}{dx}\frac{d\Pi}{dy}=\frac{dP}{dy}\frac{d\Pi}{dx}\text{,”}$$

in which the utility function of one of the barterers is defined as $P=F(x,y)$ and that of the other barterer as $\Pi=\Phi(x,y)$, and "Professor Jevons's equation

$$\frac{\phi_1(a-x)}{\psi_1(y)}=\frac{\phi_2(x)}{\psi_2(b-y)}\text{.”}$$

Edgeworth was more explicit in an article published in Italian ten years later, where a footnote reads: "Faciliterà forse la formazione di concetti precisi se si pone U (e, *mutatis mutandis,* pure V) uguale a $\Phi_1(a-x)+\Psi_1(y)$, espressione in cui Φ_1 e Ψ_1 sono gli integrali di ϕ_1 e di ψ_1 che Jevons ha reso conosciutissimi (*Theory*, chapt. IV). Senonchè, non occorre punto, nè limitare in tale modo la forma di U, nè esprimere la provvista originale (a) esplicitamente" (Edgeworth 1891, p. 235, n. 2). Or in English: "It may assist in the formation of correct conceptions if we put U (and, mutatis mutandis, V) equal to $\Phi_1(a-x)+\Psi_1(y)$, an expression in which Φ_1 and Ψ_1 are integrals of ϕ_1 and ψ_1, the well-known symbols of Jevons's *Theory* (chap. 4). It is not necessary to limit ourselves to this form of U [for which Edgeworth substituted the general form $F(x,y)$] *or to specify the original endowment* (a) *explicitly*" (my translation; italics inserted). Cf. Edgeworth 1925, 2:315, n. 1, for his weaker English version. See below, note 17.

5. The need for simplification in the restatement arises from Edgeworth's "peculiarities of style." For one thing, as J. M. Keynes has observed, Edgeworth was often clumsy and awkward "in his handling of the mathematical instrument" (Keynes 1963, p. 224). For another, recourse to the original is likely to be disconcerting, not only because of Edgeworth's "obscurity of connection, his inconclusiveness of aim, his restlessness of direction," but also because, again in Keynes' words, "Quotations from the Greek tread on the heels of the differential calculus, and the philistine reader can scarcely tell whether it is a line of Homer or a mathematical abstraction which is in course of integration" (ibid., p. 225).

6. Edgeworth 1881, 1932, p. 28, Fig. 1. Cf. Edgeworth 1891, p. 236, Fig. 1; Edgeworth 1925, 2:316, Fig. 1; and Marshall 1961, 1:844, n. XII *bis*.

7. The lines omitted from Fig. 1 relate to Edgeworth's second law, which he

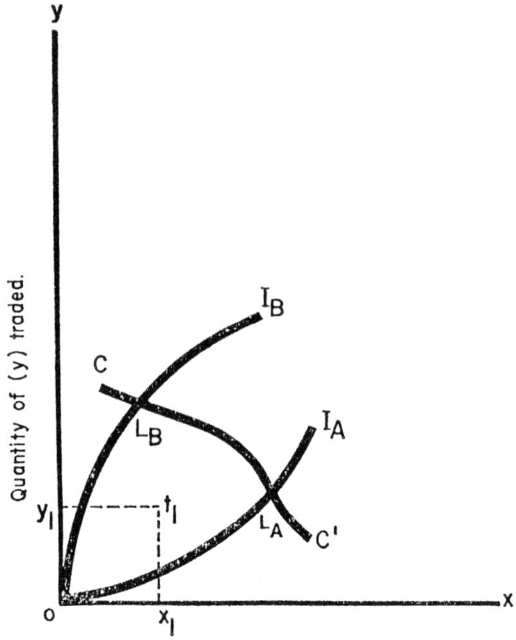

Fig. 1

This device was designed to illustrate the range of possible final contracts between isolated barterers, say Mr. A and Mr. B, trading commodity (X) for commodity (Y). Along the Ox axis is measured the quantity of (X) *traded* and along the Oy axis the quantity of (Y) *traded* by the two barterers. Or as Shackle put it,[8] in an exchange between two barterers, "what one gives up and the other receives is measured on one axis, and what the other gives up and the first receives is measured on the other." Thus, to paraphrase Edgeworth,[9] any point, for instance t_1, denotes the exchange of, or contract for the exchange of, the number of units of (X) represented by the abscissa Ox_1 against the number of units of (Y) expressed by the ordinate Oy_1. Then x_1t_1/Ox_1 (i.e., the slope of a ray from the origin to t_1) may be defined as the price per unit of (X) in terms of (Y).

In order more fully to appreciate the significance of Edgeworth's

designated as (β): "Contract under *perfect* competition is perfectly determinate." Edgeworth 1881, 1932, p. 20. For the limited purposes of this article I am confining my attention to Edgeworth's first law (α): "Contract without competition is indeterminate." Ibid.

8. Shackle 1967, p. 72. Cf. Shackle 1972, pp. 97–101.

9. Edgeworth 1925, 2:316.

lines, here designated as OI_A, OI_B, and CC′, it may be useful, especially in view of their current unfamiliarity, to represent them together with the additional lines $y_1I'_A$, $y_2I''_A$, $x_1I'_B$ and $x_2I''_B$ in a four-quadrant diagram, where Edgeworth's Contract Curve reappears in the N.E. quadrant, derived from curves in the N.W. and S.E. quadrants.[10]

In the construction of this diagram, it is assumed that both commodities (X) and (Y) are infinitely divisible. Each of the curves in the N.W. and S.E. quadrants represents a schedule of equi-satisfactory alternative "contracts for exchange" such that the barterer concerned is indifferent between any two of them. The nature of such schedules is seen in the following three examples referring respectively to Mr. A's curves I_A, I'_A, and I''_A in the N.W. quadrant of Fig. 2. By Schedule 1, bartering, for example, 30 units of (X) for 14 units of (Y) procures for A precisely the same satisfaction as bartering 34 units of (X) for 20 units of (Y), or indeed as engaging in no barter at all, this last-mentioned alternative being alternative (1) in Schedule 1.

MR. A's SCHEDULE 1
(Coordinates of selected points of Curve I_A in Fig. 2)

Alternative	*Quid* (−) Units of commodity (X) given up in exchange	*Pro Quo* (+) Units of commodity (Y) received in exchange
(1)	0	0
(2)	−10	+2
(3)	−20	+6
(4)	−30	+14
(5)	−34	+20

In a second case (Schedule 2), bartering, for example, 20 units of (X) for 17 units of (Y) procures for A precisely the same satisfaction as bartering 26 units of (X) for 22 units of (Y), or indeed as receiving

10. I have arbitrarily assumed, as Edgeworth did, that one party (Mr. A) only barters (X) for (Y), while the other party (Mr. B) only barters (Y) for (X), without inquiring into the constraints which determine their trading propensities. It is possible to take the constraints into account by deriving Edgeworth's "lines of indifference" from the conventional Fisher-Pareto type of indifference maps to which Edgeworth's construction is *analytically* related, but such a procedure would entail the precise specification of initial endowments which Edgeworth decided to leave implicit (see above, note 4). *Historically* a derivation of this sort would be anachronistic. Edgeworth's Contract Curve apparatus first appeared on the scene in 1881, antedating Irving Fisher's indifference curves (Fisher 1892, 1925, p. 68, Fig. 18) by eleven years and Pareto's indifference map (Pareto 1906, chap. 4, §§43–70) by twenty-five years. Even if we include the still earlier "Kurven konstanter Befriedigung" of Rudolf Auspitz and

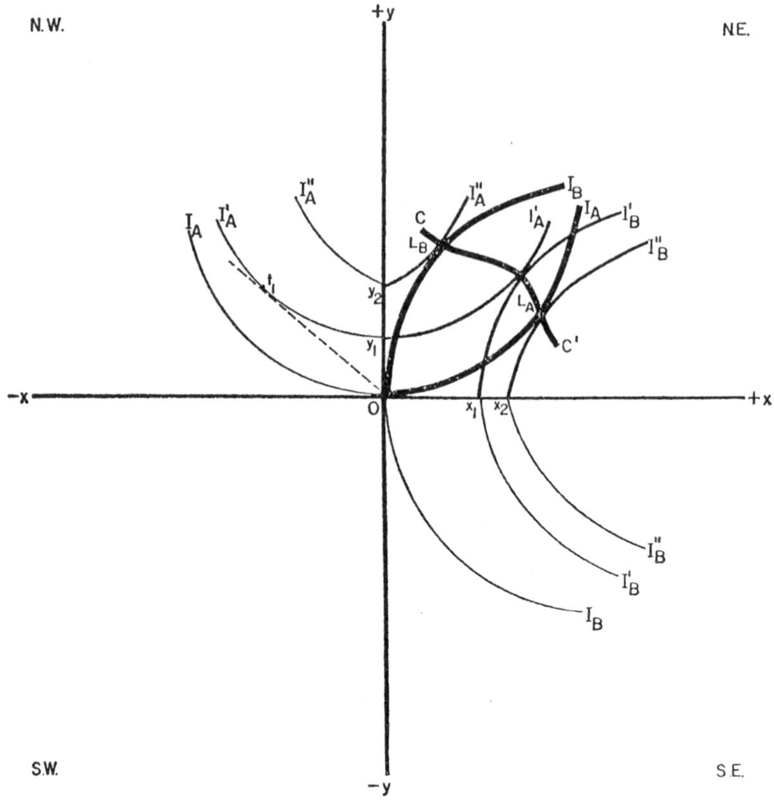

Fig. 2

11 units of (Y) gratuitously, this last-mentioned alternative being alternative (1) in Schedule 2.

In a third case (Schedule 3), bartering, for example, 6 units of (X) for 23 units of (Y) procures for A precisely the same satisfaction as bartering 16 units of (X) for 36 units of (Y), or indeed as receiving 20 units of (Y) gratuitously.

Richard Lieben (Auspitz and Lieben 1889, 1914, app. II, §3), whom Irving Fisher acknowledged as a source of inspiration (Fisher 1892, 1925, pp. v, 65 n., and 69), Edgeworth's invention preceded theirs by eight years. It is, however, possible to remain within the framework of Edgeworth's conception of his isolated barter example without having recourse to anachronistic derivations and still ensure that Mr. A is disposed to trade (X) for (Y) and Mr. B is disposed to trade (Y) for (X) rather than the other way around, simply by postulating that at the point (0,0) in the N.E. quadrant of Fig. 2 the slope of the price ray from the origin be greater than the slope of Mr. A's boundary curve I_A and smaller than the slope of Mr. B's boundary curve I_B at the same point. More meaning than this Edgeworth's construction need not be asked to bear.

MR. A's SCHEDULE 2
(Coordinates of selected points of Curve I'_A in Fig. 2)

Alternative	*Quid* (−) Units of commodity (X) given up in exchange	*Pro Quo* (+) Units of commodity (Y) received in exchange
(1)	0	+11
(2)	−10	+12
(3)	−20	+17
(4)	−26	+22
(5)	−30	+28

It is clear that in passing from Schedule 1 to Schedule 2 and from Schedule 2 to Schedule 3, provided Mr. A always prefers more of commodity (Y) to less in exchange for a given quantity of (X), his satisfaction must increase, for at any alternative in Schedule 1 he is no better or worse off than if he had not traded at all, while at any alternative in Schedule 2 it is as if he had received a free gift of 11 units of (Y); and in Schedule 3 he is still better off, since any alternative is equivalent to his receiving 20 units of (Y) gratuitously.

MR. A's SCHEDULE 3
(Coordinates of selected points of Curve I''_A in Fig. 2)

Alternative	*Quid* (−) Units of commodity (X) given up in exchange	*Pro Quo* (+) Units of commodity (Y) received in exchange
(1)	0	+20
(2)	−6	+23
(3)	−10	+26
(4)	−14	+32
(5)	−16	+36

Barterer B, of course, has his own set of schedules referring respectively to his curves I_B, I'_B, and I''_B in the S.E. quadrant of Fig. 2. These schedules and their corresponding curves are established on the same principle as Mr. A's, but are as different from Mr. A's as his propensities to trade are different. These propensities are assumed to be such as to permit the drawing of as dense a family of curves of equal satisfaction as we please within each of the quadrants considered. Whether in Mr. A's N.W. quadrant or in Mr. B's S.E. quadrant, the further any curve is from the origin, the more satisfactory to the barterer concerned is the set of equi-satisfactory alternatives indicated on that curve. In the N.W. quadrant the negative abscissa and the positive ordinate of any point measure respectively the amount of (X) Mr. A gives up and the amount of (Y) he receives in the exchange indicated by the point, while at any point in the S.E. quadrant it is the negative ordinate and the positive abscissa which measure respectively the amount of (Y) Mr. B gives up and the amount of (X) he receives in the exchange indicated by that point.

Following Edgeworth, I have assumed that his barterers are strictly speaking "catallactic molecules," i.e., pure traders whose only concern is to maximize their respective trading advantages without regard to any ulterior motive, whether it be consumption, provision for gifts, or anything else. That is why I have avoided using the term "utility," which, as we know from the example set by Gossen, is too apt to be identified with the satisfaction derived in the course of consumption.

It would have been out of character for one so thoroughly steeped as Edgeworth was in the Benthamite utilitarian tradition to be troubled by such inhibitions. Without treating either of his "catallactic molecules" as consumers, Edgeworth nevertheless ascribed "utility" functions to each of the barterers: to one of them, say Mr. A, the "utility" function $P = F(x,y)$ and to the other, say Mr. B, the "utility" function $\Pi = \Phi(x,y)$. Then considering $P - F(x,y) = 0$ and $\Pi - \Phi(x,y) = 0$ as surfaces, he set himself the problem of finding a point "such that, in whatever direction we take an infinitely small step [in the course of bartering], P and Π do not increase together, but that, while one increases, the other decreases." He then gave as a necessary property of the required point,

$$\frac{\partial P}{\partial x}\frac{\partial \Pi}{\partial y} - \frac{\partial P}{\partial y}\frac{\partial \Pi}{\partial x} = 0, \qquad (1)$$

and called the locus of such points the *Contract Curve*.

Geometrically, the same Contract Curve can be derived simply by turning Mr. A's "curves of indifference" in the N.W. quadrant over rightwards on the Oy axis as on a hinge, and Mr. B's "curves of indifference in the S.E. axis upwards and over on the Ox axis until we obtain superimposed mirror images of these curves in the N.E. quadrant, where the axes have the same significance as those of Fig. 1 above. If we had drawn a dense mass of these curves in the N.W. and S.E. quadrants and turned all of them over in the manner just described onto the N.E. quadrant, given certain properties of the curves, this procedure would reveal a continuum of points of tangency between Mr. A's curves and Mr. B's curves where they have like positive slopes. It is precisely the locus of such points of tangency which constitutes Edgeworth's Contract Curve.

In fact, Edgeworth's "lines of indifference" were endowed with just those properties which make the tracing of his Contract Curve possible. They appear, in the first place, as continuous functions of two variables, twice differentiable: each line in the N.W. quadrant with the equation

$$P = F(x,y) = \text{constant};$$

and each line in the S.E. quadrant with the equation

$$\Pi = \Phi(x,y) = \text{constant}.$$

The constants are parameters that increase from curve to curve northward in the N.W. quadrant and eastward in the S.E. quadrant. Secondly, every "line of indifference," whether in the N.W. quadrant or in the S.E. quadrant, is downward sloping, because, saturation with either commodity having been excluded by assumption, neither barterer could remain on the same "curve of constant satisfaction" unless an increase in what he gives up (a minus quantity) is associated with an increase in what he receives (a plus quantity). Finally, these curves are, in each case, as Edgeworth states it, "convex to the sacrifice axis and concave to the acquisition axis."[11] This last property is equivalent to the assumption of an increasing marginal rate of substitution of (X) for (Y) in the N.W. quadrant and of (Y) for (X) in the S.E. quadrant, an assumption which may be justified on grounds of marginal utility analysis, but which, if such grounds are rejected, can only be justified as convenient and generally plausible.[12] Of course, the standard attribution of "rationality" to the barterers precludes any two "lines of indifference" from crossing each other in either the N.W. or S.E. quadrants. When these curves are turned over onto the N.E. quadrant, they form two superimposed sets (or families) of continuous, non-intersecting curves, both sets upward sloping, but one set (Mr. A's) convex to the Oy axis and the other set (Mr. B's) convex to the Ox axis. The way is now open for members of Mr. A's and Mr. B's families of curves to "meet and touch" at the required points of tangency.

The whole purpose of the Edgeworthian contrivance was to define the range of indeterminacy of "final settlements" in an isolated two-party barter of two commodities, one for the other. The indeterminacy is, however, limited to a segment of the Contract Curve precisely demarcated in theory, the limits being L_A and L_B in Figs. 1 and 2. It is true that the Contract Curve extends in the southeast direction beyond

11. Quoted in Singh 1963, p. 45, without citation of exact source.

12. Cf. Edgeworth 1881, 1932, pp. 35–36. Edgeworth's analytical justification of the convexity property of his "lines of indifference" is hedged and inconclusive.

L_A and in the northwest direction beyond L_B in the sense that beyond these limits there continue to be points of contact between A's and B's "lines of indifference." It should be noted, however, that at points of tangency to the southeast of L_A, Mr. A would find his "lines of indifference" all inferior in satisfaction to his boundary line I_A, while at points of tangency to the northwest of L_B, Mr. B would, on his side, find his "lines of indifference" all inferior in satisfaction to his boundary line I_B. Hence only "final settlements" in the range between L_A and L_B are admissible in voluntary exchange. Within these limits it is to Mr. A's advantage to reach a "final settlement" as near to L_B as possible, just as it is to Mr. B's advantage to reach a "final settlement as near to L_A as possible, though in the atmosphere of bluff and concealment that generally pervades the bargaining process, neither barterer ever really knows where the other barterer's true limit lies. The attainment of the highest possible advantage by one barterer at the expense of the other barterer's gains from trade depends upon the relative nimbleness of the two parties in the practice of "dissimulation and objectionable arts of higgling," or simply upon luck and chance.

Though Edgeworth did mention in passing "an interior indifference curve, as may be said,"[13] in one place, and only in one place, in the *Mathematical Psychics,* and though his differential equation of the Contract Curve implies the existence of "interior indifference curves," in his diagrams he never actually drew any curves like I'_A, I''_A or I'_B, I''_B in the N.E. quadrant of Fig. 2 above, where the first two are "interior" to I_A and the second two "interior" to I_B. When such curves are drawn, their intercepts on their respective "axes of acquisition" acquire a theoretical significance apparently unsuspected by Edgeworth.

Consider the intercept of the I'_A curve on the Oy axis at the point y_1. As we have already observed, the ordinate Oy_1 of this point is tantamount to a free gift of Oy_1 units of (Y) since the abscissa of y_1 in the N.W. quadrant is zero. Any other point on the I'_A curve in that quadrant, say t_1 (it need not be the optimum point shown in Fig. 2), represents by its abscissa the quantity of (X) traded by Mr. A for a quantity of (Y) measured by the ordinate of that point. Though there is no question of a free gift implied in such a trade, the gain from the trade is subjectively equivalent to a gift of Oy_1 units of (Y), since both t_1 and y_1 are on the same curve of equal satisfaction. Similarly, the gain from trade at any point on the I''_A curve east of the Oy axis is measurable by the quantity Oy_2 of (Y). In the same manner, Mr. B's gain from any trade specified by the coordinates of a point on the I'_B curve

13. Edgeworth 1881, 1932, p. 36.

in the S.E. quadrant is measurable by Ox_1 units of (X); just as Mr. B's gain from any trade specified by a point on the I''_B curve is measurable by Ox_2 units of (X).

Seen in this light, the Edgeworth Contract Curve diagram reveals hidden implications that were surely not intended by its author. Once the diagram is filled in with "interior indifference curves" and the economic significance of the intercepts of these curves on their respective axes of acquisition is taken into account, the third dimensions P and Π of Edgeworth's "utility" surfaces are shown to be unnecessary. Thus the whole nebulous concept of "utility" is revealed as superfluous for the analysis of a trader's behavior. Nothing more is needed than a trader's scale of preferences depicted by the (increasing) distances from the origin to the intercepts of the successive "interior indifference curves" on his "axis of acquisition."[14] While these distances on the "axis of acquisition" represent cardinal measures of gains from trade in terms of the acquired commodity, they cannot be considered as cardinal measures of the trader's gains in the subjective sense unless it is assumed that the measure of a trader's satisfaction is a strictly linear function of his objective gains from trade subject only to the choice of an arbitrary unit of measurement of satisfaction, the origin having already been given by the assumed zero gain at the point where his boundary curve meets the axis of acquisition. If, however, the assumption that objective measures of gains from trade are translatable via a linear transformation into subjective measures is discarded "on the principle of Occam's razor," as Hicks would say, then Edgeworth's Contract Curve theory is reduced to a theory of the strictly ordinal variety. Now the gains from trade in terms of the acquired commodity can serve as a consistent Paretian monotonically increasing index of satisfaction from trading. Moreover, since each trader's gains are measured only in terms of his own acquired commodity, which is different from the commodity ac-

14. Mr. A's *objective* gains from trade could have been represented just as well by vertical distances between I_A and "interior curves" anywhere in the N.W. quadrant at any assigned value of $-x$ less than zero, but the *subjective* gains would still be the same as those afforded by the corresponding free gifts measured along the Oy axis where $-x$ equals zero. Similarly Mr. B's *objective* gains from trade could have been represented by horizontal distances between I_B and "interior curves" anywhere in the S.E. quadrant at any assigned value of $-y$ less than zero, but again the *subjective* gains would be the same as those afforded by the corresponding free gifts, in this case measured along the Ox axis where $-y$ equals zero. This geometric portrayal of gains from trade on the axes is, in certain respects, formally analogous to (but in substance different from) the Hicks-Henderson representation of Marshall's consumer's surplus in all-or-none bargains. Hicks 1941, pp. 108–10, and 1946, pp. 38–41; Henderson 1941, pp. 117–19. A still earlier formally analogous construction is found in Pareto 1906, pp. 173–74, Fig. 9, chap. 3 §75.

quired by his counterpart, and since there can be no exogenously predetermined fixed ratio of exchange between the two commodities traded, interpersonal comparisons of gains from trade, even when objectively considered in their cardinally measurable aspects, are precluded. It is one of the paradoxes of history that Edgeworth, so doughty a champion of cardinal measurement of utility and of interpersonal comparisons, invented a means that could serve so well to make it possible to dispense with his own cherished hedonistic preconceptions, which later economists have stigmatized as irrelevant and unfortunate.

There is more to Edgeworth's Contract Curve theory than definition, which is all that has been discussed so far. However defined, whether in a cardinal sense or an ordinal sense, the Contract Curve apparatus remains a device designed to analyze a particular process of exchange which renders the "final settlement" indeterminate. Indeed, as Erich Schneider has shown,[15] the indeterminacy of outcome even in the case of isolated two-party barter in two commodities is not inevitable, but depends upon the "modes of behavior" of the two barterers. In the *Mathematical Psychics* of 1881, Edgeworth said very little about this apart from the following hint, found on page 109 of the *Mathematical Psychics*: "Why, indeed, should an isolated couple exchange every portion of their respective commodities at the same rate of exchange? What meaning can be attached to such a law [i.e., to Jevons's Law of Indifference] in their case? The dealing of an isolated couple would be regulated not by the theory of exchange . . . [i.e., by the law of supply and demand], but by the theory of simple contract. . . ." Edgeworth repeated the same idea privately on November 8, 1888, in a letter to Léon Walras: ". . . Jevons's formula applies *only* to a perfect market, not to exchanges between individuals" (Edgeworth's underlining).[16] It was however, not until 1891, in his article entitled "Osservazioni sulla teoria matematica dell'economia politica con riguardo speciale ai Principi di economia di Alfredo Marshall"[17] that Edgeworth actually speci-

15. Schneider 1952, pp. 363–66. See below, note 21.

16. Jaffé 1965, 2:274, Letter 856.

17. Edgeworth 1891, 1925. Edgeworth's English summary of his Italian article published thirty-four years earlier furnishes an interesting example of his tergiversations, "his inconclusiveness of aim, his restlessness of direction" (see above, note 5). In 1891 Edgeworth had described the utility function of barterer A entirely in accord with the idea of leaving initial endowments unexpressed, as follows: "Sia *U* la utilità, o il vantaggio, di A, in quanto dipende da un lato dal numero di noci che egli guadagna e dall'altro dal numero di mele che egli perde." Edgeworth 1891, p. 235. Here *U* had been presented simply as a function of the quantity of nuts acquired and the quantity of apples given up by Mr. A in exchange. But in 1925 he paraphrased the above sentence in English so as to read: "Let *U* be the utility, or satisfaction, of A so far as it depends on the one hand

fied in detail the particular dynamic adjustment process required for his Contract Curve theory. In fact, he had found the description of the process he needed ready-made in the first edition of Alfred Marshall's *Principles of Economics,* which had appeared in 1890. There, in his "Note on Barter," Marshall developed his famous apples-and-nuts example without mathematics or diagrammatics.[18] In the aforementioned Italian article, which was a comment on Marshall's "Note," Edgeworth illustrated Marshall's process analysis by means of a diagram[19] which was then reproduced in Mathematical Note XII *bis* of the second edition (1891) of Marshall's *Principles.*[20]

The behavioral pattern subsumed by both Edgeworth and Marshall includes, besides "final settlements," anterior settlements, which, like the "final settlements," are not provisional agreements subject to revision, but binding agreements that are irrevocably fulfilled. "Recontract," which has its place in Edgeworth's competitive model, is, as Edgeworth

on the number of nuts that he gains, and on the other *the number of apples that he retains, that is the number initially in the basket less by the number that he has parted with.*" Edgeworth 1925, 2:315; italics inserted. The first argument of the function U is the same as before because Edgeworth always pictured his barterer A as having no nuts to begin with, but the second argument is now no longer the quantity of apples given up, but rather the balance of apples remaining to barterer A after trading a certain quantity of his original stock of apples for nuts. The Italian version is consistent with his "lines of indifference" as he first conceived them in the *Mathematical Psychics*; the English version is not. The latter renders any geometrical construction founded upon it indistinguishable from the Fisher-Pareto type of indifference curves depicting a consumer's preferences. Though the change from 1891 to 1925 is analytically trivial, the unambiguously catallactic character of the original formulation is lost. Professor Donald A. Walker (1973) narrates with remarkable clarity and meticulous scholarship the successive changes which Edgeworth made, as time went on, in his theory of recontract, and incidentally sheds light on the modifications and emendations to which Edgeworth subjected his theory of isolated barter.

18. Marshall 1961, 1:791–92 and 2:790, note *a,* referring to 1:791.

19. Edgeworth's diagram was used in his Italian article (1891) in connection with an argument which falls outside the scope of this study. Edgeworth insisted that the indeterminacy or uncertainty of outcome in isolated two-party barter was due to the absence of competition and not, as Marshall had contended, to the variability of the marginal utilities of both commodities as the quantities traded varied. Cf. Marshall 1961, 2:791–98, "Editorial Appendix to Appendix F."

20. Marshall 1961, 1:844–45. Marshall, however, was not quite accurate in Mathematical Note XII *bis* where he reported that Edgeworth "takes U to represent the total utility to A of apples and nuts when he has given up x apples and received y nuts. . . ." This repeats what Marshall had read into Edgeworth in his review of the *Mathematical Psychics* when it first came out in 1881: "He [Edgeworth] supposes that if X. exchanges an amount x of his commodity for an amount y which Y. has to dispose of, the total gratification which X. will get from what is left of his commodity after subtracting x from it, together with that which he will get from an amount y of the other commodity, may be represented by $P = F(x,y)$." Marshall, 1881, p. 457. Cf. Edgeworth 1881, 1932, p. 20, and see above, note 17.

perceived, ruled out in strictly isolated two-party barter where neither barterer has the option of recommencing negotiations at his initial starting point or of looking elsewhere for a better bargain.

Suppose, under these circumstances, that at the outset one of the barterers, say Mr. A, manages, either by guile or by chance, to persuade

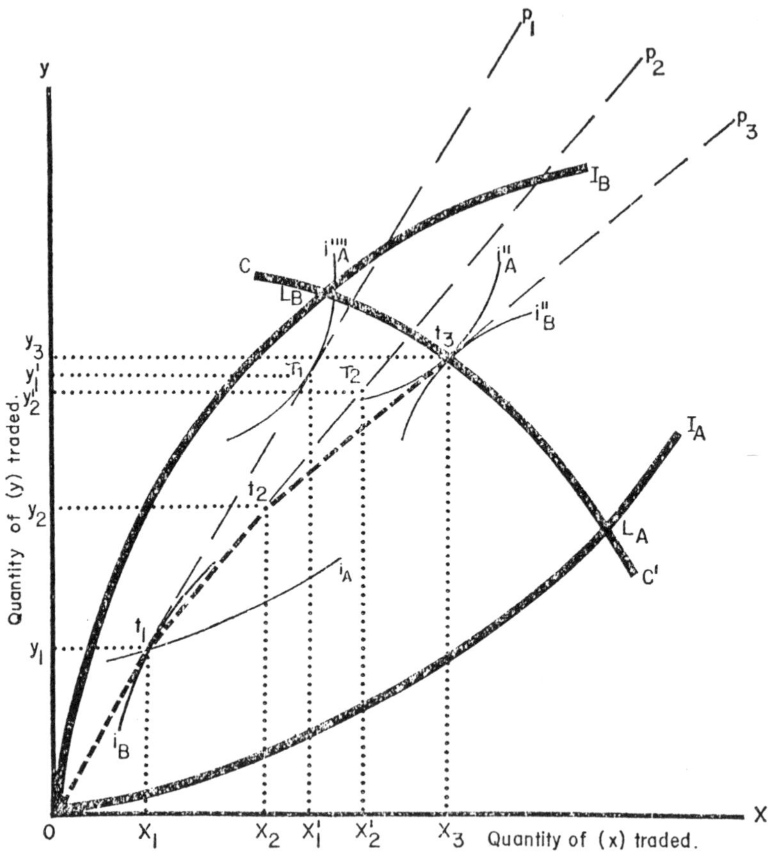

Fig. 3. Note that A's "lines of indifference," convex to the Ox axis, in the order of increasing advantage to A, are: I_A, A's boundary line; i_A, through t_1; i'_A (not drawn, through t_2); i''_A, tangent to t_2p_3 at t_3; i'''_A (not drawn, tangent to t_1p_2 at τ_2); and i''''_A, tangent to Op_1 at τ_1.

B's "lines of indifference," convex to the Oy axis, in the order of increasing advantage to B, are: I_B, B's boundary line; i_B, tangent to Op_1 at t_1; i'_B (not drawn, tangent to t_1p_2 at t_2); and i''_B, tangent to t_2p_3 at t_3.

his counterpart, Mr. B, to trade Oy_1 of (Y) for Ox_1 of (X), as these quantities are measured on the axes in Fig. 3. In the same Fig. 3 the implicit ratio of exchange governing this initial transaction is given by the slope of the ray Op_1 passing through the point t_1. It is evident that at this ratio, Mr. A would have been eager to acquire Oy'_1 of (Y) at a sacrifice of Ox'_1 of (X), since τ_1 rather than t_1 denotes his optimum position; but the furthest B could possibly go without sinking to a "line of indifference" inferior to i_B, was to give up precisely Oy_1 of (Y) for Ox_1 of (X). Upon the completion of the transaction, A and B will be at t_1 where A's "line of indifference" i_A intersects the ray Op_1 and B's line i_B is tangent to the ray. Now Mr. A, always seeking to reach a superior "line of indifference," will find it to his advantage to be a little less rapacious and offer (or consent, if B, who is no less interested than A in improving his position, takes the initiative) to engage in further exchanges at an implicit ratio more favorable to B. Let the next trade be y_1y_2 of (Y) in exchange for x_1x_2 of (X). The new implicit ratio governing their second transaction is given by the slope of the ray t_1p_2. At this stage, as would be plain if A's line of indifference i'''_A tangent to t_1p_2 at τ_2 had been drawn in Fig. 3, A would have been eager to acquire $y_1y'_2$ of (Y) at a sacrifice of $x_1x'_2$ of (X), but B, whose "line of indifference" i'_B (not drawn) is tangent to t_1p_2 at t_2 could not go further than that along t_1p_2 without worsening his position. Now that both barterers find themselves at t_2 where A's "line of indifference" i'_A (not drawn) intersects the price ray t_1p_2, the stage is set for at least one more trade, provided that the next pair of quantities changing hands is such as to imply a ratio of exchange still more favorable to B than the previous one given by the slope of the ray t_1p_2. Accordingly, let the new quantities exchanged be x_2x_3 of (X) and y_2y_3 of (Y). The implicit ratio will then be given by the slope of the ray t_2p_3. If at that ratio, given their point of departure t_2, both barterers find it simultaneously to their greatest advantage to be at t_3 and "neither seek nor covet more," than the point at which the whole series of piecemeal transactions culminates will be on the Contract Curve, and after that no concession made by either party will be acceptable to the other.[21]

21. For an elegant analytical generalization of Edgeworth's theory of barter, see Uzawa 1962, pp. 223 ff., and Negishi 1962, pp. 660–63. More recently, however, Maurice Bouchard (1971, pp. 93–102), taking an uncompromisingly rigoristic stand, has severely condemned Edgeworth's Contract Curve theory principally on two grounds: first, that it violates the canons of pure science; and second, that the assumed behavior of the barterers in Edgeworth's model is incompatible with "freedom in trading" ("liberté des échanges"). According to Bouchard, a proper "scientific" theory of barter would be one in which the system of postulated relations is sufficient, and no more than sufficient, to determine the

The last piecemeal transaction constitutes the "final settlement," and the broken line $Ot_1t_2t_3$ traces one of an indefinite number of possible paths leading toward a point on the Contract Curve, each path depending upon the relative bargaining acumen which the barterers exhibit in the course of their successive barters. Since the economist knows no laws that would define the path in a unique way under the assumed transaction rules, the particular culmination of a path in a "final settlement" necessarily remains indeterminate between the limits L_A and L_B of the Contract Curve.

These are the bare formal features of Edgeworth's Contract Curve, which, in the guise of the now familiar "box diagram," has become one of the most fascinating contrivances in the modern economist's arsenal. But it is more than a technical contrivance, more than a mere tool, for its initial conception betrays its origins in age-old ruminations on the human predicament, as will be seen in Part 2 of this article, which is to follow.

ACKNOWLEDGMENTS

I wish first of all to express my gratitude to Professor Georgescu-Roegen for taking exception to my propaedeutic interpretation of Edgeworth's Contract Curve theory as I presented it in an early draft of this article read as a paper before the economics seminar of Vanderbilt University. He was right, but I did not fully appreciate the significance of his criticism until my colleague, Professor Marcel Boyer, showed me the way out of the difficulty and painstakingly guided me through a complete revision of that part of the paper. I am deeply indebted to him, as I am to Professors Louis Lefeber, John Buttrick, and Michael Copeland for helpful comments and suggestions. A penultimate version of this article was submitted as a paper to a conference held in Chicago, May 30–31, 1973, under the auspices of the History of Economics

values of its variables; and, indeed, he demonstrates that if there were no intermediate disequilibrium transactions (which he denounces as an empirico-inductive intrusion, alien to pure theory) and if no actual trading took place until both barterers simultaneously attained their relative maxima of utility, the solution of the isolated barter problem, arrived at *uno actu*, would be determinate, though not in all cases unique, allowance being made for the possibility of multiple equilibria. Moreover, only under these conditions would "freedom in trading" be realized, for Bouchard defines "liberté des échanges" in terms of the absence of constraints in an individual's exercise of choice of quantities traded. In Edgeworth's process analysis, as Bouchard sees it, this freedom of choice is not available to both parties at a point on the adjustment path where one party is constrained by the other to trade in smaller quantities than he prefers and where the other party is conceived to resign himself submissively to terms of trade imposed by the superior guile ("fourberie") of the first party.

Society, on which occasion I reaped the benefit of critical observations offered by Professor Samuel Hollander of the University of Toronto. I need hardly add that none of these good Samaritans should be held responsible for what remaining shortcomings the reader may detect. I owe thanks also to the Canada Council for a research grant in support of work on a project of which this article is a by-product.

REFERENCES

Auspitz, R. (with R. Lieben). *Untersuchungen über die Theorie des Preises.* Leipzig, 1889. French translation by Louis Suret, *Recherches sur la théorie du prix,* 2 vols. Paris, 1914.

Bouchard, M. *L'homo economicus: Essai sur l'échange et les prix.* Montréal, 1971.

Dobb, M. *Welfare Economics and the Economics of Socialism.* Cambridge, 1969.

Edgeworth, F. Y. *Mathematical Psychics.* London, 1881. Series of Reprints of Scarce Tracts, no. 10. London, 1932.

———. "Osservazioni sulla teoria matematica dell'economia politica, con riguardo speciale ai Principi di economia di Alfred Marshall." *Giornale degli economisti,* Ser. 2, 2 (March 1891):233–45. Edgeworth published an abbreviated version of this article in English in his *Papers* . . . (1925), 2:313–19, under the title "On the Determinateness of Economic Equilibrium."

———. *Papers Relating to Political Economy.* 3 vols. London, 1925.

Fisher, I. "Mathematical Investigations in the Theory of Value and Prices." *Transactions of the American Academy,* vol. 9 (July 1892). Reprinted, New Haven, 1925.

Henderson, A. "Consumer's Surplus and the Compensating Variation." *Review of Economic Studies* 8, no. 2 (Feb. 1941):117–21.

Hicks, J. R. "Annual Survey of Economic Theory: The Theory of Monopoly." *Econometrica* 3, no. 1 (Jan. 1935):1–20.

———. "The Rehabilitation of Consumer's Surplus." *Review of Economic Studies* 8, no. 2 (Feb. 1941):108–16.

———. *Value and Capital.* 2d ed. Oxford, 1946.

Jaffé, W., ed. *Correspondence of Léon Walras and Related Papers.* 3 vols. Amsterdam, 1965.

Keynes, J. M. *Essays in Biography.* New ed. New York, 1963.

Marshall, A. Review of *Mathematical Psychics* by F. Y. Edgeworth, *The Academy* 19, no. 476 (18 June 1881):457.

———. *Principles of Economics.* 9th (variorum) ed., with annotations by C. W. Guillebaud. London, 1961.

Negishi, T. "The Stability of a Competitive Economy: A Survey Article." *Econometrica* 30, no. 4 (Oct. 1962): 635–69.

Pareto, V. *Manuale di economia politica con una introduzione alla scienza sociale.* Piccola Biblioteca Scientifica no. 13. Milan, 1906. English rendition by A. S. Schwier, *Manual of Political Economy.* Edited by A. S. Schwier and A. N. Page. New York, 1971.

Schneider, E. *Reine Theorie monopolisticher Wirtschaftsformen.* Tübingen, 1932.

———. *Pricing and Equilibrium.* Translated by T. W. Hutchison from the first edition of E. Schneider's *Einführung in die Wirtschaftstheorie:* II. Teil. *Wirtschaftspläne und wirtschaftliches Gleichgewicht in der Verkehrswirtschaft* (1952). London, 1952.

Shackle, G. L. S. *The Years of High Theory: Invention and Tradition in Economic Thought, 1926–1939.* Cambridge, 1967.

———. *Epistemics and Economics: A Critique of Economic Doctrines.* Cambridge, 1972.

Singh, H. K. M. *Demand Theory and Economic Calculation in a Mixed Economy.* London, 1963.

Tarascio, V. J. "A Correction: On the Genealogy of the So-Called Edgeworth-Bowley Diagram." *Western Economic Journal* 10, no. 2 (June 1972):193–97.

Uzawa, H. "On the Stability of Edgeworth's Barter Process." *International Economic Review* 3, no. 1 (May 1962):218–32.

Walker, D. A. "Edgeworth's Theory of Recontract." *Economic Journal* 83, no. 329 (March 1973):138–49.

[8]

Edgeworth's Contract Curve: Part 2. Two figures in its protohistory: Aristotle and Gossen

William Jaffé

Part 1 of the present article,[1] which appeared in the last number of this journal, was designed as an analytical prelude to the historical study which now follows. Though Francis Ysidro Edgeworth (1845–1926) was the first to give the Contract Curve its name and the first to sketch its characteristic geometric and analytical properties, which subsequent writers refined and refashioned, nevertheless the underlying rationale of indeterminacy of outcome within a bounded range in isolated bilateral barter in two commodities has a hoary history. Indeed it is protohistory insofar as it antedates any evidence of continuity or of a clear line of acknowledged filiation between earlier intimations and Edgeworth's initial formulation of the theory in his *Mathematical Psychics* of 1881.

We know that Turgot[2] more than a hundred years before Edgeworth, and Carl Menger[3] a full decade before Edgeworth, had both fore-

1. Jaffé 1974.

2. Turgot 1844, pp. 84–91. Turgot did not have a straightforward theory of indeterminacy in the case of isolated two-party barter in two commodities, though he came tantalizingly close to it. Unfortunately he lost his way in a "labyrinthe de calculs" (ibid., p. 89) of his own making. He started out well enough, defining for each of the two traders the furthest limit to which he would consent to go in his offer rather than not trade at all, but Turgot failed to notice that his particular arithmetic example precluded trading altogether. According to Turgot's hypothetical figures, the maximum each trader would be willing to offer of his own commodity for a given quantity of the other's commodity was below the minimum the other trader would be willing to accept rather than forgo trading. Turgot thought that the solution lay in "splitting the difference" (or, as he put it, in the "valeur estimative *moyenne* entre celle que les deux contractants attachent à chaque objet"). This might have made some sense, though it would still have been far from a correct analytical solution, if the two limits in Turgot's arithmetical example, instead of being each trader's "valeur estimative" (i.e., the outside value each trader attaches to his own commodity in terms of the other's commodity), were each trader's initial trial bid based on his estimate of the other trader's minimum acceptable "price." It is noteworthy, however, that Turgot was probably the first to use an isolated barter theory, such as it was, as a steppingstone to a theory of price formation in the case of multiparty competition. See below, note 10.

3. Menger 1871, pp. 175–77, where § 1 of chap. 5 is headed, "Die Preisbildung

shadowed, however imperfectly, Edgeworth's theory of isolated exchange.[4] It has not been noticed, however, as far as I am aware, that over two millennia before the appearance of the *Mathematical Psychics*, Aristotle had divined certain aspects of Edgeworth's Contract Curve theory—as now appears in the light of S. Todd Lowry's interpretation of Aristotle's analysis of exchange.[5] Nor has it been sufficiently noticed that Gossen,[6] in a labyrinthine demonstration of his own invention, had come closest to anticipating Edgeworth's analysis in technical detail, or indeed that he had treated the problem at all. De Quincey[7] and John Stuart Mill,[8] also, had touched upon isolated exchange, but their analy-

beim isolirten Tausche," corresponding to pp 194–97 of the Dingwall and Hoselitz translation. Wicksell in 1924 (1958, p. 108), while observing that Menger had considered "pricing in the case of the *isolated* exchange of two goods" as "a determinate problem only within more or less wide limits," did not seize the opportunity to refer to Edgeworth's later treatment of the problem. Chipman (1965, pp. 43–44), on the other hand, after exposing the defects of Menger's analysis, pointed out that it remained for Edgeworth eventually to clarify the problem.

4. Groenewegen 1970, p. 189, nn. 55 and 56. Turgot's and Carl Menger's theories of isolated exchange had previously been alluded to in Kauder 1953, pp. 645–47, in the course of a discussion that offered no occasion to mention Edgeworth. Notwithstanding Groenewegen's impression that "Turgot was the only eighteenth-century economist with a theory of isolated exchange" (op. cit., p. 196, n. 77), there was another in that century, Condillac (1798, pp. 26–28), who discussed isolated exchange very much as Turgot had done, though with less theoretical firmness.

5. Lowry 1969. Lowry expressly refrained in this article from any "attempt . . . to examine systematically the evidences of Aristotelian analysis in modern economic theory" (p. 46, n. 9). This explains why he did not name Edgeworth in the course of his ingenious interpretation of Aristotle's passages on isolated barter. See below, note 20.

6. Gossen 1854, 1927, pp. 80–85. Cf. Walras 1954, Translator's Note [7] to Lesson 16, pp. 523–24.

7. De Quincey 1844, pp. 24–28. The passage is found quoted in J. S. Mill 1848, 1965, Book III, chap. 2, § 1, pp. 462–63 (2d vol.). Edgeworth (1925*a*) rejected De Quincey's own interpretation of his "famous parable of the musical snuff-box" and denied that it is illustrative in general of the outcome "of a bargain between two isolated individuals."

8. Chipman (1965, p. 44) cites both Mill's *Principles* (1848, 1965, Book III, chap. 2, § 1, pp. 462–64 of 2nd vol.) and Mill's *Fortnightly Review* article, "Thornton on Labour and Its Claims, I" (1869, 1967, pp. 633–46) as evidence of Mill's concern with "the indeterminacy of bilateral monopoly." Actually, it was only in the *Fortnightly Review* article—and then not in Part I, except for a passing allusion on p. 643, but in Part II, pp. 657–58, in the course of a discussion of collective bargaining between "tacit combinations of employers and trade unions" —that Mill had anything to say about indeterminacy. Edgeworth himself referred to Mill's "review of Thornton on *Labour*" in a footnote on p. 52 of the *Mathematical Psychics*, but only in relation to utilitarian justice. Moreover, in Edgeworth's view (1881, 1932, p. 44, n. 1), unless there is "*complete solidification* of the whole operative-interest and the whole employer-interest," the contract that ensues from collective bargaining is qualified, more or less, by competition, so

tical remarks had little or nothing in common with Edgeworth's formulation. Edgeworth's Contract Curve is thus revealed as an example, among countless others in the history of science, of "what oft was thought, but ne'er so well expressed."

This is not to say that so prodigiously learned a scholar as Edgeworth was unacquainted with the writings of his celebrated forerunners or that he was unaware of antecedent commentaries on isolated exchange. In the *Mathematical Psychics* he alluded to "solitary couples, such as those which political economists delight to place in lonely islands",[9] but nowhere did he acknowledge that his Contract theory owed anything to these political economists. The only earlier works which Edgeworth recognized as *analytically* related to his Contract Curve were Jean Gustave Courcelle-Seneuil's rather little known *Traité théorique et pratique d'économie politique*[10] and W. Stanley Jevons's much better known

---

that whatever indeterminacies subsist are not the same as those of strictly isolated bilateral barter (cf. Jaffé 1974, p. 343, n. 2). The passages in Mill to which Chipman refers, as also Book III, chap. 1, § 5, pp. 460–61 of the *Principles* to which Chipman does not refer, deal with other indeterminacies of price than those engendered by "bilateral monopoly," e.g., indeterminacies arising from such imperfections of market organization as discontinuities of aggregate demand and supply functions, noncompeting groups, monopolistic discriminatory pricing practices, etc.

9. Edgeworth 1881, 1932, p. 115. Edgeworth probably had in mind Courcelle-Seneuil's woodcutter and hunter who "vivent seuls dans une île" (1867, 1:219). When these two lonely woodsmen meet and engage in barter, Courcelle-Seneuil, following Turgot's example to the letter (see above, note 2), calls them "deux contractants," which may have suggested the term "Contract Curve" to Edgeworth.

10. Edgeworth cited Courcelle-Seneuil (1867) three times in his *Mathematical Physics* (pp. 30, 44, and 109), and in one place (p. 30) quotes Courcelle-Seneuil's passage: "à mesure que le nombre des concurrents augmente, les conditions d'échange deviennent plus nécessaires, plus impersonnelles en quelque sorte" (Courcelle-Seneuil 1867, 1:229). This evidently suggests a line of filiation between Edgeworth's theory of the emergence of determinate outcomes as the number of competing traders in a market increases and Courcelle-Seneuil's earlier adumbration of the theory. But Courcelle-Seneuil himself was undoubtedly inspired by Turgot's "Valeurs et monnaies" (c. 1769, 1844), which he praised unreservedly in another place in the volume as "l'étude la plus profonde qui ait été faite sur l'échange" (1867, 1: 482). Indeed Courcelle-Seneuil's §§ 2 and 3 of chap. 2 in Book II of the *Traité* (1:219–32) closely followed the order of Turgot's analytical discussion of trading between "deux sauvages" who chance to meet "dans une île déserte" (Turgot, c. 1769, 1844, 1:84). Courcelle-Seneuil, however, managed to steer clear of Turgot's analytical confusion (see above, note 2) by evading the issue, for instead of considering a set of alternative feasible transactions at a moment of time, he traced the course of successive isolated barter transactions, allowing the circumstances and dispositions of the barterers to change from transaction to transaction. Moreover, he expatiated as Turgot had not done upon the conditions which would give one of the isolated barterers a bargaining advantage over the other. From the modern standpoint the most remarkable of his additions to Turgot's discussion was his footnote comment (1867, 1:223, n. 1) on the real cost of higgling in time lost—long before it became common practice for economists to advert to transaction costs at all.

Theory of Political Economy.[11]

In this article, I propose to consider two unwitting harbingers of the advent of the Contract Curve, Aristotle and Gossen, not only because they appear to have been almost completely overlooked as precursors of Edgeworth but also because, like Edgeworth, they resorted to geometric images in elucidating their theories.

Aristotle

Plato and Aristotle, following in the footsteps of Socrates, included within the scope of philosophy an inquiry into the meaning of good and evil in human affairs and were thus led to turn their attention, on occasion, to the specific problem of justice in trading. They both held professional traders and moneymakers in disdain, Aristotle more uncompromisingly than Plato,[12] but they fully recognized the social and economic need for trading as such. The question nevertheless remained, how to distinguish between trading that was compatible with virtue and trading that was morally degrading.

Already in the seventh and sixth centuries B.C., when Greece was in the throes of transition from the old order of sequestered rustic simplicity to the new order of febrile commercial expansion, Solon, the great Athenian lawgiver, had declaimed against "hearkening to the call of wealth" and censured those "who knew not how to check their greed."[13] To curb the avarice of sellers in the marketplace, Plato in the fourth century B.C. proposed in his *Laws* that "whoever sells anything in the market is never to assign two prices to the wares he sells, but only one; if he do not obtain this, his proper course would be to remove his wares, and he is not to lower or to raise the price on this day nor is there to be any praising of or taking an oath about the article that is for sale."[14] In the same spirit, Edgeworth proclaimed his repugnance to the "dissimulation and the objectionable arts of higgling" which he denounced as "an accessory evil of indeterminate contract."[15] Aristotle, a younger contemporary and pupil of Plato, placed the whole

11. For the manner in which Edgeworth related Jevons's theory to his own, see Jaffé 1974, p. 344, n. 4.

12. Soudek 1952, p. 57.

13. Laistner 1923, p. 1. From Solon's *Fragments,* 4.

14. Ibid., p. 126. From Plato's *Laws,* Book XI, 917.

15. Edgeworth 1881, 1932, pp. 29–30. Alfred Marshall, on the other hand, described the same incidents of two-party dealing with dispassionate neutrality: "the terms of the contract depend to a great extent upon the advantageous position with regard to bargaining, and the skill in bargaining, of the several parties concerned" (Marshall 1881). Cf. Marshall 1961, 1:333, V. II. § 2.

problem of justice and injustice in exchange on a philosophical footing. And he looked for an answer in an analysis of barter.

Aristotle's theory of exchange in Book V of the *Nicomachean Ethics* is by no means easy to decipher. One of the difficulties, especially for the modern reader who is impatient with anything but *wertfrei* theorizing, is that Aristotle's analysis of exchange is imbedded in his discussion of reciprocal justice.[16] Even after making allowance for that, the analysis remains obscure and it is impossible to say how much of the obscurity of the extant passages dealing with exchange may be charged to Aristotle and how much to corruptions of the text perpetrated by countless generations of copyists. As they stand now, these passages have frequently tempted latter-day economists to impose upon them interpretations that are more a reflection of the commentator's convictions and preconceptions than of Aristotle's intended meaning.

What, indeed can one make of such a passage as this from Book V of the *Ethics*?

"Now acts of mutual giving in due proportion may be represented by the diameters of a parallelogram, at the four angles of which the parties and their wares are so placed that the side connecting the parties be opposite to that connecting the wares and each party be connected by one side with his own ware, as in the accompanying diagram" (Fig. 1).[17]

Fig. 1

16. For a discussion of Aristotle's three categories of "particular justice," see Spengler 1955, pp. 381–85. Aristotle's "reciprocal justice," i.e., justice in exchange, was later transmuted by medieval theologians into "commutative justice," which was quite a different thing. Cf. Finley 1970, pp. 10–12, esp. n. 37.

17. Quoted in Theocharis 1961, p. 4, from *The Nicomachean Ethics of Aristotle*, translated by D. P. Chase, Book V, 5, 1133a. The same passage in the

It hardly helps when one reads on:

"For example, let A be a builder, B a shoemaker, C a house, and D a shoe. It is required that the builder shall receive from the shoemaker a portion of [his product], and give him a portion of [his own]. . . . As therefore a builder is to a shoemaker, so must such and such a number of shoes be to a house . . .; for without this reciprocal proportion, there can be no exchange and no association; and it cannot be secured unless the commodities in question be equal in a sense."[18]

A little further on, after a brief digression on the *raison d'être* of exchange and the role of money, Aristotle continued his geometrical argument as follows:

"Retaliation or reciprocity will take place, when the terms have been so equated that, as a husbandman is to a cobbler, so is the cobbler's ware to the husbandman's. But we must bring the terms to a figure of proportion not after the exchange has taken place [otherwise one of the two extremes will have both excesses], but when both parties still retain their own wares. Then they will be equal and capable of association, because it is possible to establish the proper equality between them. Thus let A be a husbandman, C food, B a cobbler and D his wares, which are to be equated. . . . But if this kind of reciprocity were impossible, there would be no association."[19]

---

more commonly quoted translation by W. D. Ross reads simply, "Now proportionate return is secured by cross-conjunction" (Spengler 1955, p. 384; Gordon 1964; p. 121; cf. Soudek 1952, p. 59), which is certainly closer to the Greek text, but less elucidating than Chase's free elaboration of the "original" version. It appears that in the "original" text, the geometrical argument was not accompanied by a box diagram or any other diagram. All that is known is that Nicole Oresme (c. 1326–1382 A.D.) "illustrated his commentary with such a figure" (Lowry 1969, pp. 57–58).

18. Rackham 1926, pp. 283–85; *Nicomachean Ethics V*, v. 10. I prefer Rackhams' translation of this passage to the usually quoted Ross translation (see below, note 19), mainly because Rackham comes closer to removing the ambiguity of the Greek *to ergon*, which he translates as "product of labor" while Ross translates it as "work." Since *ergon*, like "work" in English, is used in several senses, it seems preferable to translate it as I have done in square brackets, in a manner that plainly fits the context and leaves no room for equivocation, lest the passage be taken to lend further support to the view (quite erroneous, in my opinion) that Aristotle held anything like a classical labor-cost theory of value. Cf. Soudek 1952, p. 65; and Gordon 1964, pp. 120–23.

19. Quoted in Monroe 1930, p. 28, from a translation by J. E. Welldon, with an insertion in square brackets giving H. Rackham's version (similar to Ross's version) of the crucial phrase (Rackham, 1926, p. 285, *Nicomachean Ethics V*, v. 12; V, 5, 1133a–b). The justification for citing alternative versions lies in the doubtful reliability of the extant texts and the obscurity of the passages here quoted that are open to more than one interpretation (Rackham 1926, pp. xxii–xxv and p. 283, note c). I have not collated the various English translations available with extant Greek texts; what little knowledge of classical Greek I may once have had is now too faded for that. In venturing (rashly, perhaps) to piece together

When these perplexing passages are viewed in the light of S. Todd Lowry's remarkably penetrating interpretation,[20] they are seen as expressions of an ethical solution of the selfsame problem of isolated two-party barter which Edgeworth considered analytically. Even Aristotle's puzzling "parallelogram," though belonging to another age, is then revealed to bear a fleeting family resemblance to Edgeworth's Contract Curve, like the resemblance of a collateral ancestor to a remote descendant. As might well be expected, this has not escaped the attention of so profound a student of the history of economics as Professor J. J. Spengler, who clearly perceived not only the relation, but also the nature of the relation, between Aristotle's prescriptive design and Edgeworth's geometrical metaphor.[21]

---

different translations, I have been guided by one of Alexander Fraser Tytler's principles of translation which I have attempted to apply to the choice and emendation of translations by others: "Where the sense of an author is doubtful, and where more than one meaning can be given to the same passage or expression (which, by the way, is always a defect in composition), the translator is called upon to exercise his judgment, and to select that meaning which is most consonant to the main train of thought in the whole passage, or to the author's usual mode of thinking, and of expressing himself. To imitate the obscurity or ambiguity of the original, is a fault; and it is still a greater, to give more than one meaning . . ." (Tytler 1791, 1907, pp. 17–18). From the standpoint of Tytler's principle, a commendable translation of the passages under consideration—for a purpose, however, other than mine—is that of C. I. Litzinger, quoted by Hollander (1965, pp. 617–18) from vol. 1 in the Library of Living Catholic Thought series, which contains St. Thomas Aquinas' *Commentary on the Nichomachean Ethics* together with parallel citations from Aristotle translated into English not directly from the Greek but from a medieval Latin version generally attributed to William of Moerbeke of the thirteenth century (Litzinger 1964, p. xii).

20. Lowry 1969. The wisdom of Lowry's self-denying ordinance (see above note 5) is best appreciated when one sees how other learned commentators, who did not refrain from attempts "to examine systematically the evidences of Aristotelian analysis in modern economic theory," succumbed to the temptation to enroll Aristotle of the fourth century B.C. in their favorite camp of latter-day economists. Josef Soudek (1952, pp. 65–68) and Samuel Hollander (1965, pp. 616–23) recount the vicissitudes of those interpretations of Aristotle which portray him as a glory-shedding ancestor either of a cost-of-production theory of value à la Adam Smith or of a (marginal) utility theory of value à la Menger, or indeed of a "dualistic" theory à la Marshall (Gordon 1964, p. 128). Professor Hollander properly questions the relevancy of such interpretations, for in his view, as in mine, "Aristotle did not give an analytical explanation of the determination of price. His doctrine was an ethical 'prescription' " (1965, p. 623).

21. Spengler 1955, p. 286, n. 59. The last paragraph of that note is eminently worth quoting: "Aristotle does not concern himself with how prices are formed in the market, at most implying that parties to a transaction bargain with each other before settling upon terms and completing the transaction. He supposed, of course, that 'all or most men choose what is advantageous' (*Nic. Eth.* 1162b. 35ff.). Had Aristotle had the concept of a contract locus at his disposal, he would probably have said that justice in exchange was to be found in the middle region of the locus, provided that this was compatible with receipt by the exchangers of rewards which correctly reflected the difference between their respective skills."

In Aristotle's age, as Lowry pointed out, technology of production was far from having reached the point of furnishing the market with uniform standardized products, so that "the individual bargain was more likely to characterize trade than general market price."[22] Moreover, in view of the further fact that in Aristotle's day full knowledge of market opportunities was very difficult to come by, "the actual, specific price [was] left to be determined either by bargaining between two parties or by the courts."[23] If this is true, then it is fair to assume, as Lowry did, that what Aristotle had in mind in his theorizing on value was the question of justice in the outcome of higgling and bargaining between a buyer and seller over a uniquely differentiated article, which is the same thing, once the veil of money is drawn aside,[24] as the question of justice in the outcome of isolated barter. To quote Lowry, "This made the problem of justice in distribution [of surpluses generated by trade] something akin to modern analysis when applied to exchange between two parties."[25]

It is, therefore, nothing short of anachronistic to conjecture, as Schumpeter did in his effort to make sense of the above-cited passages from Aristotle, that "Aristotle may have taken normal competitive

---

The proviso at the close of Spengler's last sentence is susceptible of being misunderstood unless carefully qualified. Spengler's word "skill," which, like *technē* in Greek, has a variety of usages, must be taken in this context to mean a trade, a craft, a profession, or a calling, and not expertness or proficiency in the performance of a given task. In evaluating "skills" in this sense for the purpose of defining the principle of equality between the ratio of exchange of two products (or services) and the ratio of the producers of the two products (or services) exchanged, Aristotle had in mind, at least as I read him, a ranking of "skills" on the basis of his conception of moral excellence or merit and not according to economic criteria. See below note 31.

22. Lowry 1969, p. 65.

23. Ibid., p. 66. Soudek too noted that Aristotle was "preoccupied with isolated exchange and not with the exchange of goods by many sellers and buyers competing with each other" (1952, p. 46, quoted with approval by Gordon 1964, p. 123), but it was Lowry who called attention to the reasons for this preoccupation.

24. Though Aristotle recognized that money performs the function of a "store of value" as well as the functions of a "medium of exchange" and a "unit of account" (Soudek 1952, pp. 68–72), he envisaged the "store of value" function strictly in terms of an extension of its "medium of exchange" function, whereby not only is the necessity of the "double coincidence of barter" obviated, but the exchange of goods for goods is divided into two transactions effected at different times—for the convenience of the household. If the sale of goods for money had any other object, like the accumulation of wealth in the form of money for its own sake, that would entail an "unnatural" use of money which Aristotle condemned both on moral grounds and as an absurdity exemplified by the Midas fable. In final analysis, all transactions where money is used properly (in Aristotle's sense) thus resolve themselves into barter.

25. Lowry 1969, p. 46.

prices as standards of commutative justice."[26] And it is still more anachronistic to impose upon Aristotle paradigms of a much, much later date, as both Schumpeter and Theocharis did when they ascribed to Aristotle a labor theory of just price.[27]

Lowry's interpretation, on the other hand, is founded not only on the particular conditions of price formation in Aristotle's own time but also on the conceptual framework of Aristotle's whole philosophical system. Lowry's approach displays an historical integrity which is rare among commentators upon past economic analysis. When Aristotle's cryptic pronouncements on value are considered in this spirit, they fall into place within the Aristotelian system of philosophy, acquire coherent meaning, and, in addition, take on a distinctly Edgeworthian flavor.

For example, Aristotle's statement, "We must bring the terms to a figure of proportion not after the exchange but when both parties still retain their own wares," immediately suggests the limiting positions in propensity to trade taken by each of Edgeworth's two barterers prior to effecting any exchanges. These are the same positions depicted in Edgeworth's Contract Curve diagram by the initial boundary "lines of indifference" OI_A and OI_B shown in Figs. 1, 2, and 3 of Part 1 of this article.[28] It is only with reference to these positions that the gains from trade to be divided between the two barterers can be measured. Furthermore, Aristotle's caveat—"otherwise one of the two extremes will have both excesses"—suggests the essential character of either of the limits of the Contract Curve, L_A or L_B,[29] where all of the advantages of barter are hogged by one party.

Such complete hogging is all the more likely in the case envisaged by Aristotle where one of the commodities traded (a house) is by its nature an indivisible unit, so that anything like the Edgeworth-Marshall

26. Schumpeter 1954, p. 61. In the nature of things, ideas as hoary as those of ancient Greece can only come down to us at best as mummies, at worst as skeletons. And these remains of minds long dead are never fully within the reach of our comprehension. "They had lived so long ago, their time was so unlike the present, their hopes and motives were so widely removed from ours, that between them and the living there seemed to stretch a gulf too wide for even a spirit to pass" (Thomas Hardy, *The Mayor of Casterbridge*, chap. 9). Only a poet could appreciate the dimensions of this gulf. The prosaic *savant*, on the other hand, with his delusions of grandeur shaped by high technical achievements of recent days fondly imagines he has bridged the gulf, only to fall into it—still crying Eureka! Not so M. I. Finley who has taken a truer measure of the difficulty (see Finley 1970).

27. Ibid., p. 60, n. 1; and Theocharis 1961, p. 4.

28. See Jaffé 1974, pp. 345, 347, 355.

29. Ibid.

dynamic adjustment process[30] is excluded. It may well turn out, especially in a transaction accomplished necessarily in a single step, that the variable quantity of the other commodity (shoes) is such as to leave the disadvantaged party in a situation similar to that indicated by L_A or L_B on the Contract Curve. There "one of the two extremes will have both excesses," i.e., he will have all the gains from trade that would otherwise have been shared by the two barterers in one proportion or another. If the sum total of gains from trade accrued to one barterer to the exclusion of the other, such a division would strike Aristotle as eminently unjust.

Where, then, in the bounded range between these limits of unjust trading does "reciprocal justice" lie? It lies, according to the Aristotelian philosophy of merit and just due, at a point where the gains from trade are so divided between the two barterers that they are proportional, not to the labor embodied in the articles traded, not to the quality of the labor performed, not even to the respective marginal utilities of the two articles to each of the barterers, but to the relative merits of the barterers and their corresponding status in society.[31] It is precisely this proportionality that Aristotle's geometric argument was designed to elucidate. If the same principle entailing the injection of ethical considerations into the analysis were applied to Edgeworth's Contract Curve, it would remove the indeterminacy and define a unique point on the curve. The point would be nearer L_B if Mr. A were the barterer of superior merit, or nearer L_A if Mr. B were the barterer of superior merit, or halfway between if the barterers were of equal merit. Of course, the process of arriving at such a unique division of the gains from trade would be different, no longer by chaffering and intermediate transactions, but by the imposition from the outside of an ethical judgment formulated without regard to the private maximization motives of the individual barterers.

Despite these differences, if the above is a true representation of

30. Ibid., pp. 353–57.

31. Aristotle's allusion to want or need (*chreia*) as the raison d'être of exchange (*Nicomachean Ethics* V, 5, 1133a, 25; cf. Soudek 1952, p. 60) should not, as I see it, be taken to imply that he regarded the influence of want or need on the evaluation of goods to be exchanged as unidirectional. It seems to me more in accord with Aristotle's *Weltanschauung* to suppose that he considered it to be at least as true that the relative merit of a producer in terms of virtue confers upon his product a corresponding place in the scale of desirability as that the relative need for a product confers upon its producer a corresponding place in the hierarchy of "skills" (see above, note 21). After all, Aristotle did not need to be reminded that "values which can be measured in terms of money [i.e., market criteria] are not the only ones that ought to count" (Robinson 1962, p. 147).

Aristotle's theory of exchange, he must be accounted a clearly identifiable figure in the protohistory of the Edgeworth Contract Curve.

Gossen

Over two millennia elapsed before another geometrically formulated theory of isolated two-party barter appeared in the literature. It is found on pp. 80–85 of Hermann Heinrich Gossen's *Entwicklung der Gesetze des menschlichen Verkehrs und der daraus fliessenden Regeln für menschliches Handeln,* first published in 1854. There, virtually hidden within the convolute folds of Gossen's highly original marginal utility theory, is his analysis of barter,[32] which though bizarre in geometric aspect was in fact very much closer to Edgeworth's than that of any other previous author.

In Gossen, as in Aristotle, thought is enveloped in obscurity, a different kind of obscurity, but no less perplexing.[33] Otherwise, how can it be explained that only one commentator has, to my knowledge, ever alluded to Gossen's anticipatory approximation of Edgeworth's Contract Curve theory?[34] Stranger still is the fact that Edgeworth, whose detailed description of Gossen's technical economics filled six columns in *Palgrave's Dictionary of Political Economy,* never once mentioned Gossen's minute analysis of indeterminacy in isolated barter.[35]

32. Gossen's *Entwicklung* is not divided into parts or chapters and has neither table of contents nor index. Occasionally a long dash across the page marks off the division between topics, as is the case on page 80, where Gossen, after having established the laws of maximization of utility for a self-sufficient solitary individual producing all his own goods, passed to his analysis of maximization of utility (or enjoyments) via exchange. For an ample summary of the contents of the *Entwicklung,* see W. Stark 1943, pp. 149–208. Stark, however, neglects the technical side of Gossen's theory, concentrating instead upon its philosophical aspects. On the other hand, Pantaleoni (1889, 1898, pp. 28–32 of the English translation) furnishes an interesting technical restatement of Gossen's theory of maximization of utility, but stops short of Gossen's theory of barter exchange except insofar as he discusses a Gossen-like theory of isolated barter without particular reference to Gossen (pp. 137–46 of the English translation). For a fuller technical summary of the *Entwicklung,* see Edgeworth 1925*b*.

33. Part of the difficulty lies in Gossen's peculiar language, which even native German scholars find difficut and repelling. As Stark (1943, p. 150, n. 1) tells us, "Gossen wrote in the unattractive style of the Prussian bureaucracy to which he belonged, and his mode of expression is by no means improved by his rather clumsy endeavor to clothe his ideas in high-sounding pathetic sentences. . . . His work cannot be translated literally."

34. Walras 1954, pp. 523–24, Translators Note [7] to lesson 16.

35. Edgeworth 1925*b*. The only comment Edgeworth made on Gossen's exposition of the theory of exchange was that it "bears comparison with the constructions of the mathematical economists who have succeeded him" (p. 233).

It is difficult to understand why this is so. After all, it does not require a Champollion to decipher Gossen's geometric hieroglyphics. Nothing more is needed than patience plus an ability to pierce the haze of Gossen's confused and faulty exposition,[36] due in all probability to the haste with which Gossen put his book together when serious illness afflicted him and he felt near death's door.

One explanation for the persistent neglect may be the judgment pronounced by von Hayek in his "Vorwort" to the 1927 reproduction of the *Entwicklung*. There he called Gossen's pages 80 to 85 "ganz verfehlt," a complete mistake, despite a perfectly correct point of departure.[37] So shocked was von Hayek by Gossen's acquiescence in interpersonal comparisons of utility that he did not stop to investigate to what extent the assumption of interpersonal comparisons impaired the validity of Gossen's theory.

Gossen began his analysis of two-party exchange with disarming simplicity. He wanted to demonstrate the general principle of gains from trade arising from the reciprocal exchange of two different commodities between two persons. His two persons were Mr. 1, owning initially a certain quantity of commodity (X) but no (Y), and Mr. 2, owning a certain quantity of commodity (Y) but no (X). To simplify, Gossen assumed, to start with, that Mr. 1 and Mr. 2 have identically the same (linear) marginal utility curves for each of the two commodities: *cb* for commodity (X) and *c′b′* for commodity (Y) as shown in Fig. 2.[38]

He further posited that Mr. 1 possesses *ad* units of commodity (X), $ad = 2ab$; and Mr. 2 possesses *a′d′* units of commodity (Y), $a'd' = 2a'b'$. As is clear from the graphs of Fig. 2, Mr. 1 has no use for *bd* units of his stock of (X), and Mr. 2 has no use for *b′d′* units of his stock of (Y). Gossen, then, had the two individuals simply swap their respective superabundant supplies without regard to the ratio of exchange implied. Lo and behold! from this simple act both parties benefit wondrously. Whereas before the swapping, Mr. 1's total utility from his possessions amounted to no more than is represented by the area of the

36. Though the tenor of Gossen's geometrical argument on p. 84, lines 14–39, is unmistakable, such is the confusion of lettered references to points on his graphs that the reader is left dazed and never quite sure whether or where Gossen may have made a slip in detail. In reproducing in Fig. 3 the graphs of Gossen's Fig. 20 (p. 83), I have simplified the lettering which in the original was made up of nearly all the letters in the Greek and Roman alphabets. This has entailed calling his trader A and trader B, Mr. 1 and Mr. 2 respectively.

37. Gossen 1927, p. xix.

38. Ibid., p. 82, Fig. 19. For simplicity, Gossen chose to represent his marginal utility curves as linear functions, though he conceded that they might take any form, provided it is monotonically decreasing throughout (ibid., pp. 8–9).

$$\mathrm{MU}_x = \frac{du}{dx}, \quad u = f(x)$$

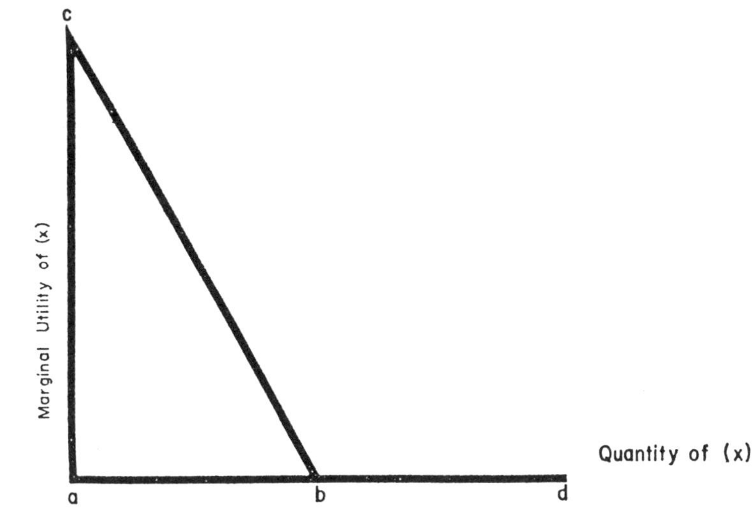

$$\mathrm{MU}_y = \frac{du}{dy}, \quad u = f(y)$$

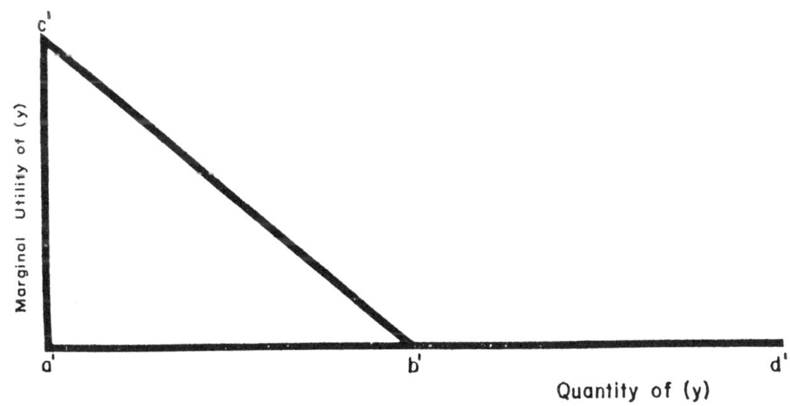

Fig. 2

triangle *acd*, and Mr. 2's total utility from his possessions amounted to no more than is represented by the area of the triangle *a′c′b′*, after the swapping each of the parties has both commodities to the point of satiety, Mr. 1 enjoying *acb* + *a′c′b′* of utility, and Mr. 2 enjoying *a′c′b′* + *acb*. As the example was set up, both parties were destined to reach the equilibrium of perfect bliss, after which neither party had any reason to contemplate further exchanges.

This would certainly have been sufficient to prove that a voluntary interchange of commodities can make each of the two parties better off. Gossen, however, was not content with that. He wanted to show in what measure such an interchange of commodities can increase "die Summe des Werthes,"[39] i.e., the sum of utilities enjoyed by both parties taken together. Consequently, he compared the sum of utilities of the two parties before the swapping,

$$acb + a'c'b',$$

with the sum after the swapping,

$$(acb + a'c'b') + (a'c'b' + acb) = 2(acb + a'c'b'),$$

the latter sum double the former!

Obviously, such a result cannot be demonstrated without presuppos-

39. Ibid., p. 82. In this context, Gossen used the term "Werth" not in the sense of value in exchange, but in the sense of subjective satisfaction or utility, as is clear from many passages, for instance the passage which reads "Die Aussenwelt hat für uns Werth, und es folgt daraus, dass der Werth der Aussenwelt für uns genau in demselben Masse steigt und sinkt, wie die Hülfe, die sie uns gewährt zur Erreichung unseres Lebenszwecks, *dass die Grösse ihres Werthes demnach genau gemessen wird durch die Grösse des Lebensgenusses, den sie uns verschafft*" (p. 24; Gossen's emphasis). Money did not enter the picture in the analysis of barter. When later on in the book, Gossen did take money into account, he did not assume that its marginal utility was constant. He suggested that, *faute de mieux*, the utility of a unit of the commodity used as money might serve as a standard for measuring the utility of other things, albeit such a standard would be no less variable than the utility of a unit of any other commodity. The relevant passage reads ". . . von der Grösse verschiedener Genüsse können wir uns daher nur dadurch einen Begriff machen, dass wir sie gegen einander vergleichen, wie wir dieses ja auch bei Bestimmung der Grösse von anderen Gegenständen thun müssen. Von der Grösse verschiedener Räume erhalten wir nur dadurch einen Begriff, dass wir einen bestimmten Raum zum Mass-stab nehmen, von der Schwere verschiedener Körper nur dadurch, dass wir einen von bestimmter Schwere als Gewicht benutzen u.s.w. So müssen wir denn auch hier einen Genuss als Mass-stab feststellen, und hierzu erhalten wir Gelegenheit, dass bei der Rechnung ein Genuss unbestimmt bleibt. Welchen Genuss man hierzu wählt, ist an und für sich gleichgültig. Vielleicht dürfte es für die Folge einige Bequemlichkeiten gewähren, als Einheit denjenigen zu benutzen, den uns der Gegenstand verursacht, dessen wir uns zu Geld bedienen" (p. 123). In Stigler's excellent translations, this passage reads: "We can conceive of the magnitudes of various pleasures only by comparing them with one another, as, indeed, we must also do in measuring other objects. We can measure the magnitudes of various areas only by taking a particular area as the unit of measurement, or the weights of different bodies only by taking a particular weight as the unit. Similarly, we must fix on one pleasure as our unit, and hence an indefiniteness remains in the measurement of a pleasure. It is a matter of indifference which pleasure we choose as the unit. Perhaps the consequences will be most convenient if we choose the pleasure from the commodity which we use as money" (Stigler 1965, p. 84).

ing the respective utilities of the two parties to be addible. However strenuously one may object to interpersonal comparisons of utility, it must be admitted that Gossen's final summing of utilities was a work of supererogation, which was neither necessary nor fatal to his analytical proof of the principle of gains from trade.

Gossen clearly perceived that up to this point he had dealt with a very much oversimplified case. He then passed to a more complex case, where Mr. 1's and Mr. 2's marginal utility functions for each of the two commodities were no longer the same. He now needed four marginal utility curves, as in Fig. 3.[40] There Mr. 1's and Mr. 2's marginal utility curves for (X) are respectively *cb* (graph i) and G′F′ (graph iv), quite different from each other; and so are their marginal utility curves for (Y), GF (graph ii) being Mr. 1's curve and *c′b′* (graph iii) Mr. 2's. As in the oversimplified case, Gossen assumed Mr. 1's initial endowment to consist in *ad* (graph i) units of (X), but no (Y); and Mr. 2's initial endowment to consist in *a′d′* (graph iii) units of (Y), but no (X), the superfluities *bd* and *b′d′*, however, standing in no specified relation to other given quantities.

Gossen began his analysis of the complex case as in the oversimplified case by letting Mr. 1 and Mr. 2 simply swap their respective superabundant supplies, *bd* of (X) for *b′d′* of (Y), regardless of the implicit ratio of the exchange. Mr. 1 thus acquires DB (graph ii) = *b′d′* (graph iii) units of (Y) in exchange for *bd* (graph i) of (X), losing thereby no utility whatsoever, but gaining DGEB (graph ii) in utility; and Mr. 2 acquires D′B′ (graph iv) = *bd* (graph i) units of (X) in exchange for *b′d′* (graph iii) of (Y), also losing no utility thereby, but gaining D′G′E′B′ (graph iv). In the complex case, however, the utility curves and the initial endowments of each of the traders are such that while both traders benefit appreciably from the swapping of their respective superfluities, neither achieves bliss, so that each has reason to contemplate further exchanges.[41]

In his analysis of the true trading that must now be undertaken, Gossen's trick of leapfrogging from graph over graph to graph became so disconcertingly intricate that he himself occasionally tripped over his own feet. The difficulty lay in the fact that upon the completion of carefree swapping, trading entails a sacrifice of utility as well as a gain. Gossen managed to take this into account fairly neatly, despite the

40. Gossen 1854, 1927, p. 83, Fig. 20. See above, note 36.

41. Cf. Turgot 1844, 1:84–85. So striking are the occasional resemblances between Turgot's model and Gossen's model that one is inevitably left with the impression that Gossen was directly inspired by Turgot, though he never mentioned Turgot's name.

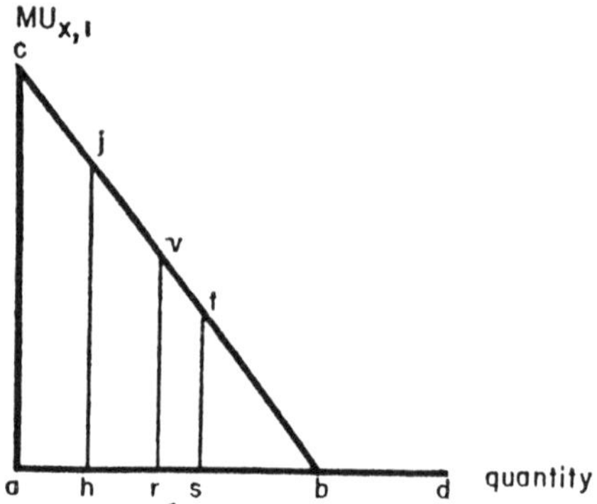

Mr. 1's marginal utility curve for commodity (X).

graph i

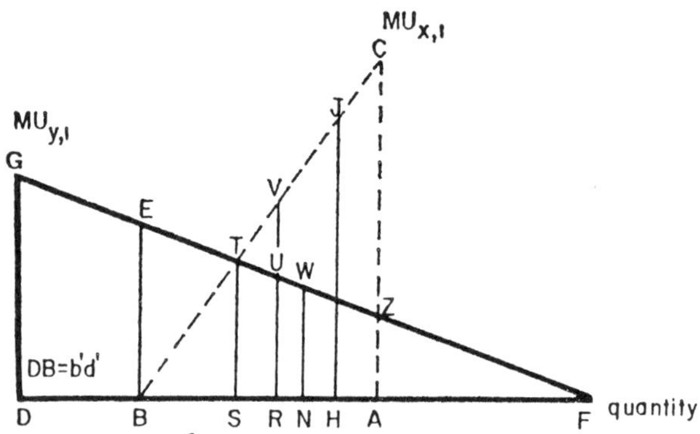

Mr. 1's marginal utility curve for commodity (Y), with reversed $MU_{1,x}$ curve BC superimposed.

graph ii

Fig. 3

unwieldiness of his geometrical apparatus, by assuming the true trading to open at a one-to-one ratio of exchange between (X) and (Y). This permitted him to superimpose Mr. 1's marginal utility curve of (X), viz., *cb* (graph i), after reversing it as seen in the dashed line BC (graph ii), on Mr. 1's marginal utility curve GF of (Y). The superimposed curve was placed in such a way that the point *b* of graph i coincided with the already determined point B of graph ii. Similarly, under the same assumption of a unit-for-unit ratio of exchange, Gossen superimposed Mr. 2's marginal utility curve of (Y), viz, *c′b′* (graph iii), after reversing it as seen in the dashed line B′C′ (graph iv), on Mr. 2′s marginal

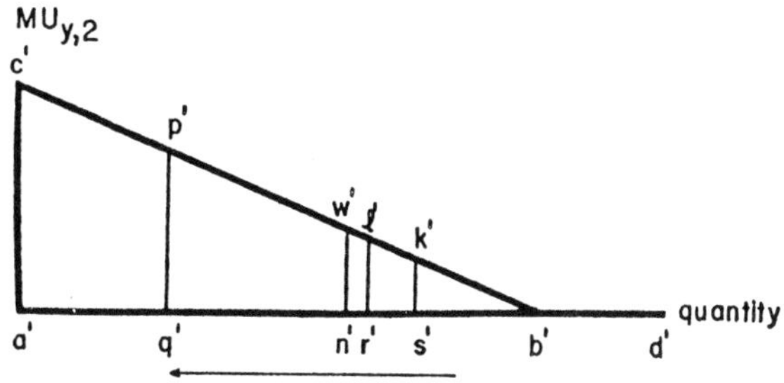

Mr. 2's marginal utility curve for commodity (Y).

graph iii

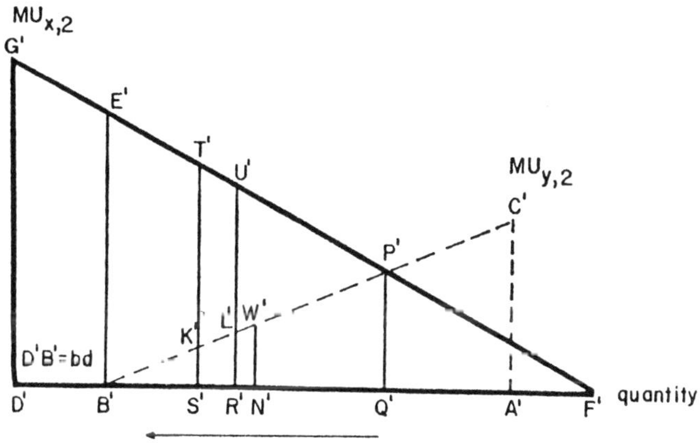

Mr. 2's marginal utility curve for commodity (X), with reversed $MU_{y,2}$ curve B' C' superimposed.

graph iv

utility curve G′F′ of (X), with the reversed curve so placed that the point *b′* of graph iii coincided with the already determined point B′ of graph iv. Hence, moving rightwards from B in graph ii, or from point B′ in graph iv, either a quantity of (X) or a quantity of (Y) can be measured along the same horizontal axes as the analysis may dictate. For instance, in graph ii, when the analysis calls for a consideration of the diminishing utility of (Y) to Mr. 1 as he acquires more and more of (Y) in exchange for (X), the segment EF of the falling curve GF becomes relevant and the quantities of (Y) acquired in trade are measured along the segment of the horizontal axis BF. When, however, account needs to be taken of the increasing marginal utility of (X) as

Mr. 1 cedes more and more of it in exchange for (Y), then the rising dashed line BC is relevant and the segment BA of BF, along which quantities of (Y) acquired were just measured, now serves for measuring the quantities of (X) ceded.

Given this construction, it is clear that Mr. 1 will strive to obtain as much as possible of the area of *net* gain from trade BET (graph ii), while Mr. 2, on his side, strives to obtain as much as possible of his area of *net* gain, B′E′P′ (graph iv). At the opening ratio of exchange, one of (X) for one of (Y), Mr. 2 would be eager to exchange B′Q′ (graph iv) of (Y) for an equal number of units of (X), in order to reap the maximum subjective gain realizable, B′E′P′ (graph iv); but Mr. 1 will not be willing to yield more than BS (graph ii) = B′S′ (graph iv) of (X) for an equal number of units of (Y). If Mr. 1 went beyond that, i.e., to the right of the point S in graph ii, his net gain in utility, BET (graph ii), would be reduced by a vertical segment of the area of loss in utility TCZ (graph ii) commensurate with the increase in amount traded. Hence at the one-to-one ratio of exchange, trading cannot go beyond the interchange of B′S′ units of (X) and (Y) as measured on the horizontal axis of graph iv. Then Mr. 1's net subjective gain from trade will be BET (graph ii), and Mr. 2's will be B′E′T′K′ (graph iv).

At this opening stage of Gossen's sequential analysis, the close similarity between Gossen and Edgeworth leaps to the eye. Gossen arrived at the first negotiated exchange of BS (graph ii) units of (X) for B′S′ (graph iv) units of (Y) by exactly the same route as Edgeworth arrived at his first negotiated exchange of Ox_1 units of (X) for Oy_1 units of (Y) as shown in Fig. 3 of Part 1.[42] In this same Fig. 3 of Part 1, at the implicit price given by the slope of the ray Op_1, one of Edgeworth's barterers, Mr. A, would have liked to trade Ox'_1 of his (X) to bring him to τ_1, just as Gossen's barterer Mr. 2 would have liked to trade B′Q′ of his (Y) to bring him to P′ at the one-to-one ratio of exchange. In both cases these barterers were prevented from getting to their (relative) optimum positions by the intransigence of their respective counterparts, who could not go beyond trading BS of (X) in Gossen's example, or Oy_1 of (Y) in Edgeworth's example, without suffering a diminution in their subjective gains from trade.

After so auspicious a beginning, Gossen seemed well on the way toward a geometrical portrayal of isolated barter which, but for the difference in the geometrical devices employed, would wholly anticipate the design of Edgeworth's sequential analysis culminating in a Contract Curve.[43] Gossen, like Edgeworth, perceived that trading would not

42. See Jaffé 1974, p. 355.
43. Ibid., pp. 345–52.

necessarily come to a standstill at the close of the first round when all the trading that both parties could engage in at the given (explicit or implicit) ratio of exchange was consummated. As in Edgeworth, so in Gossen, one of the two parties was left in midcourse and therefore entirely disposed to make a concession in the terms of trade that would induce the other party to resume trading. Edgeworth's geometrical apparatus enabled him to show the change in the terms of trade quite elegantly by breaking off the first implicit price ray Op_1 at t_1 (Fig. 3 of Part 1) and tacking on a new price ray t_1p_2 less steeply sloped. Not so Gossen's apparatus; and yet Gossen succeeded in devising a method of depicting the changed ratio of exchange despite the forbidding awkwardness of his graphs. After assuming a new exchange rate of more than 1 of (Y) for 1 of (X)—let us say 1½ of (Y) for 1 of (X)—Gossen measured the additional amount of (Y) Mr. 1 consents to acquire at the new ratio along the horizontal axis in graph ii by the segment SN which is 1½ times the length of the segment SR measuring the amount of (X) given up in exchange. Similarly, Gossen measured the additional amount of (Y) Mr. 2 gives up at the new ratio (limited, according to the example, by the amount Mr. 1 consents to receive) along the horizontal axis in graph iv by the segment S′N′ = SN (graph ii), 1½ times the length of the segment S′R′ = SR (graph ii) measuring the amount of (X) Mr. 2 receives in exchange. It is only from this point on, as we can see with the benefit of hindsight informed by Edgeworth's later achievement, that Gossen went astray and the parallelism with Edgeworth's sequential analysis breaks down, though anticipatory contact with Edgeworth's scheme is not completely lost.

In his analysis of the first round of true trading when the exchange ratio was one-to-one, Gossen demonstrated graphically that Mr. 1 attains the (relative) maximum subjective gain from trade BET (graph ii) when he exchanges BS of (X) for an equal number of units of (Y), but in his analysis of the second round Gossen's geometrical apparatus was too primitive to permit him to follow through with a like demonstration. After the completion of the first round, what then determines the additional amount of (X) Mr. 1 is willing to exchange for (Y) at the more attractive ratio of exchange? How did Gossen arrive at SR of (X) for SN of (Y)? Why not larger or smaller amounts? Surely Mr. 1 would want to maximize his net subjective gain at the second round as he did at the first. But Gossen lost this from sight and, in fact, could not have shown such a maximum on the graphs he was using. The only justification he offered for the determination of Mr. 1's trade of SR of (X) for SN of (Y) in the second round was that SNWT $\geqq$ SRVT. Gossen apparently thought it sufficient that the subjective sacrifice SRVT incurred in giving up SR of (X) should not be less than the subjective gain SNWT accruing to Mr. 1 in acquiring SN of (Y) in exchange.

Gossen, now on a false scent, went on to the mistaken conclusion that the process of compensating Mr. 1 for the increasing sacrifice of utility on further resumptions of trading could be carried to the point H (graph ii) where the area of the triangle BJH equals the area of the triangle DGF. This Gossen described as the limit to which Mr. 1 might conceivably be persuaded to go, for at that limit Mr. 1 would be no better (or worse) off than if he had not engaged in any trading at all. The point H obviously corresponds to L_B on Edgeworth's Contract Curve (Fig. 3 of Part 1), but Gossen arrived at it the wrong way. That Gossen's way was incongruous is evident when seen in the light of Edgeworth's sequential analysis. It is as if Edgeworth's broken line $Ot_1t_2t_3$ (Fig. 3 of Part 1) with a decreasing positive slope could end up at L_B. In Edgeworth's example, it will be recalled, Mr. A, like Mr. 2 in Gossen's example, consistently held the upper hand in the bargaining process, but in neither example did the more canny barterer enter upon the scene as a perfectly discriminating monopolist. In Gossen's example, only if there had been no superfluities like *db* (graph i) and *d′b′* (graph ii) to swap and only if from the outset of trading Mr. 2 (or Mr. A in Edgeworth's example) had been assumed to act as a perfectly discriminating monopolist making his counterpart pay through the nose for every unit from the very first traded, could the entire sequence of transactions have left Mr. 1 (or Mr. B in Edgeworth's example) no better off after the trading than he was before.

Were it not for this error and had Gossen constructed a more tractable geometrical apparatus, he might well have produced an exact equivalent of Edgeworth's Contract Curve. His analysis of the first round of true trading took precisely that promising direction. As it was, the Contract Curve or anything resembling it eluded him, but Gossen must be given credit for defining two limiting positions, "Grenzen" as he called them, which in fact play the same role in his theory as L_B and L_A in Edgeworth's Contract Curve theory. Gossen's second limiting position, corresponding to Edgeworth's L_A, is defined in Gossen when the bargaining advantage or acumen is all on Mr. 1's side and Mr. 2 is driven to effect all his exchanges so as to leave him no better off than if he had done no trading at all. Gossen went still further in anticipation of Edgeworth when he concluded "dass die Werthsvermehrung beim Tausch eine sehr verschiedene ist, je nachdem derselbe zu Stande kommt."[44]

44. Or in English, ". . . that the increase in utility from exchange will be one thing or quite another thing, depending upon how the trading is carried out" (my translation). Cf. Turgot 1844, 1: 85–87.

From this it is evident not only that Gossen recognized, at least by implication, a range of indeterminacy not unlike the range between L_B and L_A on Edgeworth's Contract Curve, but more importantly that he understood the final division of the subjective gains from trade between two isolated barterers to be dependent upon the path taken in the barter process.

It should be noted that up to this point Gossen's analysis was in no way contingent upon or tinged with any assumptions of interpersonal comparisons of utility. It was only after this point, when Gossen proceeded to formulate an ideal solution of the problem of the division of subjective gains from trade between the two isolated barterers, that the assumption of interpersonal commensurability of utilities was called into play.[45]

We have seen above how Aristotle tried to solve this problem. Turgot's and Menger's solutions, which fall outside the scope of this article, rested on the principle of King Solomon's judgment: divide the gains of trade in two, with half going to one of the barterers and half to the other.[46] Suffice it to say that Gossen's solution, which is described in analytical terms in Translator's Note [7] to Lesson 16 of Léon Walras's *Elements of Pure Economics*,[47] consisted in such a division as would maximize the sum of subjective gains of both parties taken together. This was a far cry from Edgeworth's solution, which was indeterminate precisely because it consisted in the simultaneous attainment of any one of an indefinite number of pairs of relative maxima by the two parties considered separately rather than the realization of an absolute maximum of utility for the two parties together. As Walras was the first to point out,[48] Gossen's solution not only entails the assumption of interpersonal comparisons of utility but also implies that the trading, if it is to result in

45. Cf. Edgeworth 1881, 1932, p. 53, n. 1, and pp. 102–04.

46. Of course, neither Turgot nor Menger supposed the equal division to be determined by fiat or decree. Turgot (1844, 1:86–87) considered it rather as the equilibrium outcome of bargaining arrived at *uno actu*, without intervening effective transactions. Menger thought the equal division theoretically plausible, since, as he expressed it, "there is no reason for assuming that one or the other of the two bargainers will have an overwhelming economic talent, or that other circumstances will operate more in favor of one than the other. Under the assumption of economically equally capable individuals and equality of other circumstances, I venture to state, as a general rule, that the efforts of the two bargainers to obtain the maximum possible gain will be mutually paralyzing, and that the price will therefore be equally far from the two extremes between which it can be established" (Menger 1871, 1950, p. 196 of the Dingwall and Hoselitz translation, corresponding to pp. 177–78 of the original).

47. Walras 1954, pp. 523–24.

48. Ibid., pp. 204–5, § 162. This section first appeared in the second edition of Léon Walras's *Eléments d'économie politique pure,* 1889, as § 160.

an overall maximum sum of utilities, would require the intervention of an authority and could no longer be voluntary.

The hand of destiny has dealt cruelly with Gossen's pioneer innovations in economic analysis. Gossen's discoveries were from the start condemned to belated recognition years after subsequent economists, unaware of the *Entwicklung*, made the same discoveries, which they developed more attractively and with greater technical proficiency. First it was the revelation of Gossen's marginal utility theory that earned him the reputation of a neglected anticipator of Menger, Jevons, and Walras, and now it is the rescue of his barter theory from almost complete oblivion[49] that shows him as an anticipator of Edgeworth as well. Paradoxically enough, the unhappy fate of the *Entwicklung* was due, in part at least, to its author's ruling passion to discover prescriptive rules which he thought divinely ordained for the guidance of mankind in pursuit of its greatest happiness. In the course of this eccentric endeavor, he hit upon analytical ideas of the highest importance. Surely justice requires that Gossen be accorded his well-deserved place, alongside Aristotle, among the figures that played a praiseworthy role in the protohistory of Edgeworth's Contract Curve.

ACKNOWLEDGMENTS

See Jaffé 1974, pp. 357–58.

REFERENCES

Chipman, J. S. "The Nature and Meaning of Equilibrium in Economic Theory," *Functionalism in the Social Sciences*, Monograph No. 5 of the American Academy of Political and Social Science (Feb. 1965), pp. 35–64.

Condillac, E. B. de. *Le Commerce et le gouvernement*. Vol. 4 of the *Oeuvres complètes de Condillac*. Paris, 1798.

Courcelle-Seneuil, J. G. *Traité théorique et pratique d'économie politique*, 2 vols., 2d edition. Paris, 1867.

De Quincey, Thomas. *The Logic of Political Economy*. Edinburgh, 1844.

Edgeworth, F. Y. *Mathematical Psychics*. London, 1881. Series of Reprints of Scarce Tracts, no. 10. London, 1932.

———. "Thomas De Quincey," 1925*a*. In *Palgrave's Dictionary* 1925, 1:568–70.

———. "Herman Heinrich Gossen," 1925*b*. In *Palgrave's Dictionary* 1925, 2:231–33.

49. Schumpeter (1954, p. 911) barely hints, without saying more about it, that Gossen, among others, had a barter theory postulating the "conditions under which ranges of possible exchange ratios must be substituted for uniquely determined ones."

Finley, M. I. "Aristotle and Economic Analysis." *Past and Present* 18, no. 47 (May 1970):3–26.

Gordon, B. J. "Aristotle and the Development of Value Theory." *Quarterly Journal of Economics* 78, no.1 (Feb. 1964):115–28.

Gossen, H. H. *Entwicklung der Gesetze des menschlichen Verkehrs und der daraus fliessenden Regeln für menschliches Handeln.* Brunswick, 1854. Republished with a Foreword by F. A. von Hayek. Berlin, 1927.

Groenewegen, P. D. "A Reappraisal of Turgot's Theory of Value, Exchange, and Price Determination." *History of Political Economy* 2, no. 1 (Spring 1970):177–96.

Hollander, S. "On the Interpretation of the Just Price." *Kyklos* 18, no. 4 (1965):615–34.

Jaffé, W. "Edgeworth's Contract Curve: Part 1. A Propaedeutic Essay in Clarification." *History of Political Economy* 6, no. 3 (Fall 1974), pp. 343–59.

Kauder, E. "Genesis of Marginal Utility Theory." *Economic Journal* 63, no. 251 (Sept. 1953):638–50.

Laistner, M. L. W. *Greek Economics.* London and Toronto, 1923.

Litzinger, C. I., translator. *St. Thomas Aquinas, Commentary on the Nichomachean Ethics.* Chicago, 1964. Vol. 1.

Lowry, S. T. "Aristotle's Mathematical Analysis of Exchange." *History of Political Economy* 1, no. 1 (Spring 1969):44–66.

Marshall, A. Review of F. Y. Edgeworth's *Mathematical Psychics. The Academy,* 19, no. 476 (18 June 1881):457.

———. *Principles of Economics,* 9th (variorum) ed., with annotations by C. W. Guillebaud. London, 1961.

Menger, C. *Grundsätze der Volkswirtschaftslehre.* Vienna, 1871. Translated by James Dingwall and Bert F. Hoselitz, *Principles of Economics.* Glencoe, Ill., 1950.

Mill, J. S. *Principles of Political Economy.* 1st ed. London, 1848. Variorum ed., vols. 2 and 3 of *Collected Works of John Stuart Mill.* Toronto and London, 1965.

———. "Thornton on Labour and Its Claims." *Fortnightly Review,* Part I (May 1869); Part II (June 1869), n.s. 5:505–18 and 680–700. Republished in vol. 5 of *Collected Works of John Stuart Mill,* the second of two volumes of *Essays on Economics and Society,* pp. 633–68. Toronto and London, 1967.

Monroe, A. E., ed. *Early Economic Thought.* Cambridge, Mass., 1930.

Palgrave's Dictionary of Political Economy, 3 vols. London, 1925.

Pantaleoni, M. *Principii di economia pura.* Florence, 1889. Translated by T. Boston Bruce, *Pure Economics.* London and New York, 1898.

Rackham, H., translator. *Aristotle, the Nicomachean Ethics.* Loeb Classical Library. London, 1926.

Robinson, J. *Economic Philosophy.* London, 1962.

Schumpeter, J. A. *History of Economic Analysis.* New York, 1954.

Soudek, J. "Aristotle's Theory of Exchange: An Inquiry into the Origin of Economic Analysis." *Proceedings of the American Philosophical Society* 96, no. 1 (1952):45–75.

Spengler, J. J. "Aristotle on Economic Imputation and Related Matters." *Southern Economic Journal* 21, no. 4 (April 1955):371–89.

Stark, W. *The Ideal Foundations of Economic Thought: Three Essays on the Philosophy of Economics*. London, 1943.

Stigler, G. *Essays in the History of Economics*. Chicago, 1965.

Theocharis, R. D. *Early Developments in Mathematical Economics*. London, 1961.

Turgot, A. R. J. "Valeurs et monnaies," (circa 1769). In *Oeuvres de Turgot*. Edited by E. Daire. 2 vols. Paris, Guillaumin, 1844, 1:75–93.

Tytler, A. F. *Essay on the Principles of Translation*. London and New York, 1907.

Walras, L. *Elements of Pure Economics*. Translated by William Jaffé. London, 1954.

Wicksell, K. "The New Edition of Menger's *Grundsätze*." First published in Swedish, *Ekonomisk Tidskrift*, 1924, pp. 1–10. English translation in Knut Wicksell, *Selected Papers on Economic Theory*, edited by Erik Lindahl. London, 1958, pp. 193–203.

[9]

EDGEWORTH'S PROPOSITIONS ON ALTRUISM

I

I FIND it a little surprising that recent contributors[1] to the theory of altruistic behaviour have paid scant attention to some fundamental contributions by Edgeworth.[2] Consequently, this paper attempts to set out these propositions and to put minor glosses upon them. It will be convenient to refer to them, though Edgeworth himself did not, as the *shrinking and non-twisting theorems*.

II

The following are among the relevant passages from *Mathematical Psychics*:

> "between the frozen pole of egoism and the tropical expanse of utilitarianism [there is]... the position of one for whom in a calm moment his neighbour's utility compared with his own neither counts for nothing, nor 'counts for one', but counts for a fraction. We must modify the utilitarian integral by multiplying each pleasure, except the pleasures of the agent himself, by a fraction—a factor doubtless diminishing with what may be called the social distance between the individual agent and those of whose pleasures he takes account." (Appendix IV, "On Mixed Modes of Utilitarianism.")

> "between the two extremes of Pure Egoistic and Pure Universalistic there may be an indefinite number of impure methods; wherein the happiness of others as compared by the agent (in a calm moment) with his own, neither counts for nothing, nor [misprinted as 'not'] yet 'counts for one', but *counts for a fraction*." (P. 16.)

We know that Edgeworth thought highly of Sidgwick's *Methods of Ethics* and these passages stand squarely in the tradition of what might be termed *positive utilitarianism*; they assert that people do, indeed, attach weights to the utilities of others. But Edgeworth also asserted, with John Stuart Mill, a *normative utilitarianism* such that each would count for one. Thus:

> "The whole creation groans and yearns, desiderating a principle of arbitration, and end of strife." (P. 51.)

> "the utilitarian settlement may be selected, in the absence of any other principle of selection, in virtue of its moral peculiarities: its satisfying the Sympathy (such as it is) of each with all, the sense of justice and utilitarian equity." (Pp. 53–4.)

The fascinating aspect of Edgeworth's treatment is that these high themes were integrated into contract and exchange theory *at its inception*:

[1] See, for example, H. Frisch, "Die Contraktkurve bei Interdependenzen im Konsum," *Kyklos*, Vol. XXIV (1971), pp. 644–59; L. D. Schall, "Interdependent Utilities and Pareto Optimality," *Quarterly Journal of Economics*, 1972, pp. 19–24; R. H. Scott, "Avarice, Altruism and Second Party Preferences," *Quarterly Journal of Economics*, 1972, pp. 1–18.

[2] F. Y. Edgeworth, *Mathematical Psychics* (1881, L.S.E. Reprint 1934).

"we might suppose that the object which X (whose own utility is P), tends—in a calm, effective moment— to maximise, is not P, but $P+\lambda\Pi$; where λ is a *coefficient of effective sympathy* [Edgeworth's italics]. And similarly Y—not of course while rushing to self-gratification, but in those regnant moments which characterise an ethical 'method'—may propose to himself as end $\Pi+\mu P$. What, then, will be the contract curve of these modified contractors? *The old contract curve between narrower limits* [Edgeworth's italics] . . . As the coefficients of sympathy increase, utilitarianism becomes more *pure*, the *contract curve narrows down to the utilitarian point*." (P. 53, n. 1.)

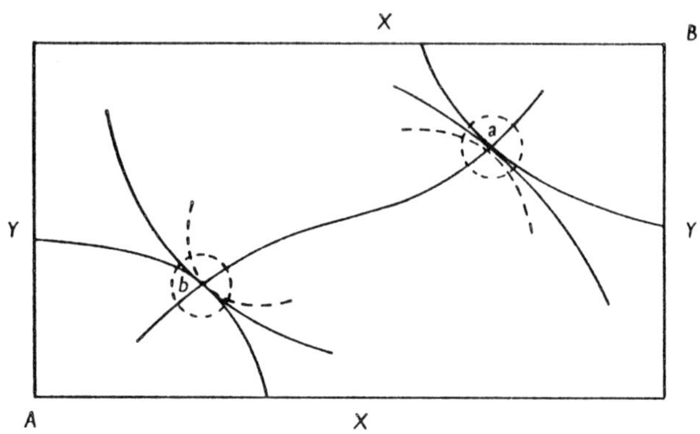

FIG. 1

Consider as Edgeworth does, the indifference curves as two sets of concentric circles (in which case the contract curve is a straight line):

"The contract curve is easily seen to be the line joining the centres. Supposing that the distance between the centres is less than the less of the radii, part of the contract curve is *impure*. If the index, as Mr. Marshall might call it, be placed anywhere in this portion it will run up to a centre. But between the centres the contract curve is *pure*; the index placed anywhere in this portion is immovable..." (P. 25.)

Edgeworth proceeds to a more general algebraic statement:

"it appears that the pure and impure parts of the contract curve are demarcated by the points where $DP/D\Pi$ changes sign, that is (in general) where either $DP/d\sigma$ or $D\Pi/d\sigma$ ($d\sigma$ being an increment of the length of the contract curve) either vanishes or becomes infinite. Accordingly the maximum and minimum of P and Π present demarcating points." (Pp. 25–6.)

Two propositions may be separated out:

(1) The locus of the contract curve is unaffected by the presence of λ and μ (the non-twisting theorem).

(2) The contract curve, or range of core outcomes, shrinks as λ and μ increase (the shrinking theorem).

(2*a*) The curve shrinks to a single point, the *utilitarian point*, when $\lambda = \mu = 1$.

They are illustrated in the accompanying Edgeworth Box diagram, Fig. 1. (Edgeworth did not himself make this construction.)[1] It is convenient to change Edgeworth's notation. Hence the two individuals are A and B and the two goods X and Y. The continuous indifference curves are of the ordinary "selfish" type while the dotted curves assume specific values of λ and μ between zero and unity. Given these weights the points a and b represent maximum utility for A and B respectively. The range of the contract curve between a and b is *pure* and the remainder *impure*.[2]

III

Is the non-twisting theorem true? It is intuitively clear that non-twisting has something to do with the assumption that weights are attached to the *utilities* of others, not to specific goods in their bundles. That is to say, there is nothing paternalistic in Edgeworth's benevolence. One is indifferent as to whether the other's enjoyment (utility given) is worthy or unworthy. But it turns out that this assumption is a sufficient though not a necessary condition.

In the two-person case goods are allocated either to one person or the other so that $dx_B/dx_A = -1$. Then the general condition for Pareto-optimality with interdependent utility is

$$\frac{\partial u_A/\partial x_A - \partial u_A/\partial x_B}{\partial u_A/\partial y_A - \partial u_A/\partial y_B} = \frac{\partial u_B/\partial x_B - \partial u_B/\partial x_A}{\partial u_B/\partial y_B - \partial u_B/\partial y_A} \quad . \quad . \quad . \quad (1)$$

In Edgeworth's case

$$\partial u_A/\partial x_B = \lambda\, \partial u_B/\partial x_B$$

and

$$\partial u_B/\partial x_A - \mu\, \partial u_A/\partial x_A$$

where λ and μ are the altruistic weights.

Substituting these, (1) reduces to the familiar condition

$$\frac{\partial u_A/\partial x_A}{\partial u_A/\partial y_A} = \frac{\partial u_B/\partial x_B}{\partial u_B/\partial y_B} \quad . \quad . \quad . \quad . \quad . \quad (2)$$

Thus Edgeworth's statement of his non-twisting theorem is correct. But does it generalise?

Returning to equation (1) write

$$\partial u_A/\partial x_A - \partial u_A/\partial x_B, \quad \text{etc.}$$

as

$$S_{Ax}\, \partial u_A/\partial x_A, \quad \text{etc.}$$

[1] I have benefited from correspondence with William Jaffé on this and, indeed, on what he calls "the mysteries of Edgeworth's idosyncratic modes of mathematical expression".

[2] Frisch (*op. cit.*) similarly distinguishes between the "Kooperations-Kurve" and the "Konflict-kurve".

Then (1) reduces to (2) if

$$S_{Ax}/S_{Ay} = S_{Bx}/S_{By},$$

a condition which may be defined as proportionate *sympathy*.[1] When this condition does not hold the selfish and altruistic loci will differ; the contract curve will have twisted.[2]

IV

Edgeworth's propositions (2) and (2 *a*) will now be considered together. The first point to notice is that the weights λ and μ are not adjusted to take account of relative incomes but, rather, each actor has sufficient sympathy to perceive the other's increasing marginal utility as his bundle of goods decreases.

Presumably B's marginal utility becomes very high indeed with small bundles so that A's point of maximum utility (a) will definitely move to the south-west as λ increases. Under these assumptions the *pure contract curve* will definitely shrink as both λ and μ increase.

Proposition (2 *a*) says that *a* and *b* will coincide when $\lambda = \mu = 1$. It is easy to show that this is correct. More interestingly they will coincide whenever $\lambda\mu = 1$. That is there will be a perfect *consensus* not only when A and B behave utilitarianly but whenever the one's weak altruism is offset by the strong altruism of the other.

To show this consider, as did Edgeworth, an index (σ) of the contract curve ($0 \leqslant \sigma \leqslant 1$) from A's origin. Let the two individuals experience direct (hedonistic) utilities but also some concern for one another, as follows:

$$\left.\begin{aligned} V_A &= u_A(\sigma) + \lambda u_B(1-\sigma) \\ V_B &= u_B(1-\sigma) + \mu u_A(\sigma) \end{aligned}\right\} \quad . \quad . \quad . \quad . \quad . \quad (3)$$

Now let σ^* be a point of complete agreement or consensus. Then

$$du_A/d\sigma^* - \lambda\, du_B/d\sigma^* = -du_B/d\sigma^* + \mu\, du_B/d\sigma^* = 0 \quad . \quad (4)$$

From which[3]

$$\lambda\mu = 1 \quad . \quad . \quad . \quad . \quad . \quad . \quad (5)$$

The same result may be achieved rather more simply by considering the matrix of weights:

[1] For a similar treatment in a different context see A. K. Sen, "Labour Allocation in a Cooperative Enterprise," *Review of Economic Studies*, Vol. XXXIII (4), Oct. 1966, pp. 361–71.

[2] In which case Pareto-optimal redistribution can no longer be restricted to general purchasing power but may require redistribution in kind.

[3] See J. de V. Graaff's formula (15) in his appendix to chapter IV of *Theoretical Welfare Economics* (Cambridge, 1957) for the slope of the utility possibility curve. The careful reader will notice, by the way, that the formula is slightly misprinted. With perfect consensus there will be no downward sloping portion of the utility possibility curve. If one inserts Edgeworth's notation into de Graaff's formula one obtains, for consensus, $(1-\lambda\mu)\,(\partial u/\partial x) = 0$. That is, either $\lambda\mu = 1$ or "satiation".

	To → *A*	To → *B*
By ↓ *A*	1	λ
By ↓ *B*	μ	1

A and *B* may be said to use identical social weights whenever one row is simply a multiple of the other.[1] As we have constrained the diagonal weights to unity the condition $\lambda\mu = 1$ follows immediately.

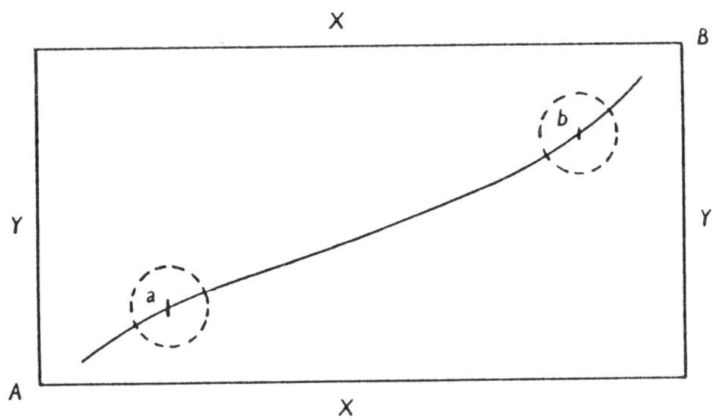

Fig. 2

Edgeworth's proposition (2*a*) may therefore be generalised in a simple way.

(2*a*′) For any consensus (σ^*) there exists a set of supporting weights λ^*, μ^* where $\lambda^*\mu^* = 1$. The special utilitarian consensus ($\hat{\sigma}$) is supported by $\lambda = \mu = 1$. The dual to this theorem is that for any set of supporting weights $\lambda^*\ \mu^*$, where $\lambda^*\mu^* = 1$ there exists a consensus (σ^*).

Such consensus points would be reached only by a remarkable fluke. But as long as $\lambda, \mu \neq 0$ there will be a consensus *range* (the pure contract curve). Redistribution from points outside the range will make *both* parties better off, i.e. there will be scope for so-called "Pareto-optimal" redistribution. But there will be no guarantee, of course, that actual weights will be such as to support any prescribed consensus range.

VI

In the last section it was suggested that Edgeworth's proposition (2*a*) may be taken as a special case of a *consensus theorem*. Edgeworth did not go on to consider what would happen should *A* and *B* be "excessively" altruistic ($\lambda\mu > 1$). Point *a* would then lie to the south-west of point *b*. Apparently each

[1] The two social welfare functions are then essentially identical. I am grateful to Stan Katz and Maurice McManus for discussion on this and the more general *n* person case.

would reach an optimal bundle before the total was exhausted. Hence the economic problem has disappeared. I am tempted to call this the *vanishing theorem.*[1] But the situation should not be confused with satiety proper as it remains the case that each would truly like more goods were it not for the fact that he would thereby deprive the other. It would be open to them to cleave the knot by accepting some arbitrary rule to allocate whatever is "left-over".[2]

In terms of the diagram the range *a–b* is still the pure contract curve (points on it are better than points off it) and allocations to the south-west of *a* or north-east of *b* will not be sustained. However, the situation is the reverse of the usual one in that each would prefer the *other* to have more.

VII

Summary and Conclusions

I have suggested that two theorems, the "non-twisting" and "shrinking" theorems, are to be found in Edgeworth's analysis of altruism and are correct on his assumptions. Additionally his remarks about the "utilitarian point" may be generalised into a "consensus" theorem and into a "vanishing" theorem when altruism is excessive.

David Collard

University of Bristol.

Date of receipt of final typescript: October 1974.

[1] It is *as though* both parties were sated. Thus David Hume in a brilliant passage: "[the poets] easily perceived, if every man had a tender regard to another, or if nature supplied abundantly all our needs and desires, that the jealousy of interest, which justice supposes, could no longer have place. . . *encrease to a sufficient degree the benevolence of men, or the bounty of nature, and you render justice useless*" (*Treatise* (my italics)).

[2] Another possibility, as a referee has pointed out, is that the parties revise their expectations about scarcity. Each would perceive that dx_i/dx_j was zero, not -1, and points like "*a*" would be adjusted upwards until the resource constraint again became tight.

[10]

J. R. Statist. Soc. A (1978),
141, *Part* 3, *pp.* 287–322

Francis Ysidro Edgeworth, Statistician

By Stephen M. Stigler

University of Wisconsin

[Read before the Royal Statistical Society, at a meeting organized by the Research Section on Wednesday, March 15th, 1978, Professor J. F. C. Kingman in the Chair.]

Summary

Edgeworth's major early work in statistics is reviewed in the context of the history of statistics in the nineteenth century. Edgeworth's intellectual development before 1890 is discussed, and his style of writing and its effect upon the spread of his ideas is considered. Special attention is given to Edgeworth's methodology for the comparison of means and his early efforts to test goodness of fit, and an 1885 anticipation of an analysis of variance for two-way classifications is discussed at length.

Keywords: HISTORY; JEVONS, W. S.; GALTON, F.; PEARSON, K.; SIGNIFICANCE TESTS; ANALYSIS OF VARIANCE; COMPONENTS OF VARIANCE; GOODNESS OF FIT; CORRELATION

1. Introduction

The history of probability and statistics, as usually told, emphasizes one compact and coherent line of mathematical development: from Fermat and Pascal to Bernoulli and De Moivre to Gauss and Laplace to Galton and Pearson; from combinatorial probability to limit theorems to least squares to correlation. But if the story gains a certain elegance from its inclusion of nearly every great name in the history of mathematics, its simplicity is not achieved without cost. By stressing mathematical development, it tends to neglect the interplay between statistical concepts and the scientific and practical problems that spawned them. The result is a history that at first glance is coherent, yet yields many paradoxes and anomalies upon closer investigation. If the mathematics of statistics holds the key to the development of statistical concepts, then how, for example, are we to view the continued use of significance tests since four centuries before Fermat's birth? (Stigler, 1977). Or, to come to a more recent time, how can we account for the century lag between the development of the techniques of mathematical statistics in astronomy and their adoption in the social sciences? In this paper we shall focus upon this latter question through the work of one remarkable man, Francis Ysidro Edgeworth.

F. Y. Edgeworth (1845–1926) produced a life's work inextricably bound up with the quantification of economic science, both with the development of mathematical economics and with the incorporation of probability and statistics into the analysis of social and economic data. His role in this was a central one, and his influence upon theoretical statistics was great, yet Edgeworth has remained one of the least known major figures in the history of our field. Before turning to Edgeworth's life, his work, and the nature of his roles in the histories of social science and statistics, we shall briefly survey the situation as it was before 1880.

At the death of Laplace in 1827, statistical theory had developed to a remarkably high level. By mid-century, knowledge of the techniques of mathematical probability and statistics was widespread, as treatises of Laplace, Lacroix, Poisson, Cournot and encyclopedia articles by De Morgan made them easily accessible to any with an interest and a background in calculus. But while the application of these techniques, particularly the method of least squares, was routine in astronomy and geodesy, the spread to other fields was slow.

An important case in point, and a figure we shall meet later in this paper, was W. Stanley Jevons. Jevons was taught probability and least squares by Augustus De Morgan at University College London, and he was both a bold innovator in mathematical economics and an enthusiastic proponent of the use and usefulness of mathematics in the social sciences. Jevons was also a great statistician, in the sense the term was used in the 1860's. While he was not the originator of index numbers and graphical displays, at least Jevons realized their potential and pursued them with a perspicacity far beyond his predecessors', and he displayed such keen good sense in the analysis of large quantities of data that we can still today describe him as a statistician without apology or serious qualification. If there was any nineteenth-century empirical social scientist who could have been expected to develop the techniques of the theory of errors into tools for the quantification of uncertainty in social sciences it was W. Stanley Jevons. But he did not.

Like many others, from Condorcet to Quetelet, Jevons may have believed in and even preached the use of probability in social research. Yet Jevons's use of probability in his own empirical investigations, like that of Quetelet, did not extend to an attempt to quantify the uncertainty of his estimates, to the assessment of the statistical significance of differences or the likely variability in sample averages. Jevons's greatest statistical investigations were his pamphlet of 1863, *A Serious Fall in the Value of Gold Ascertained, and its Social Effects Set Forth*, and a paper in this *Journal* (Jevons, 1868). Both were model statistical investigations, the first for its telling use of index numbers to assess the effects of the gold discoveries in California and Australia upon the value of gold, the second for its intelligent handling of extraordinarily difficult sampling problems in the estimation of the quantity and condition of circulating gold coinage. Both are notable also for the lack of the use of probability in assessing the uncertainty of the estimates found, a lack which, with only one partial and minor exception, extended to the rest of Jevons's empirical investigations.

Nor did Jevons overcome the conceptual barriers to the extension of statistical methods to social science in his major methodological treatise, *The Principles of Science* (1874). Jevons intended this to be a significant statement on logic and scientific method, but although it is a learned work containing much common sense, it is curiously sterile, lacking the boldness that characterized much of Jevons's other work. It dealt almost exclusively with physical science, and among other things sought to show scientific logic could be reduced in the end to a principle Jevons called "the substitution of similars". (C. S. Peirce (1890) wrote sarcastically that the substance of Jevons's idea was in its name: "Cicero had a wart on his nose; so Burke would be expected to have something like it.") Jevons discussed, even emphasized, probability and the theory of errors, but he made no effort to extend these methods beyond their original applications.†

Jevons's lack of use and development of probability-based statistical methods in his empirical work was typical of even the best efforts before the 1880's. The change in this situation over the next half century was slow, and no single individual was responsible for what has become the major methodological advance in the past century. In this paper we shall emphasize the work of Francis Edgeworth, however, both because of its importance and because of its relative neglect in histories of this subject.

In the next section we shall discuss Edgeworth's life, with emphasis upon his intellectual development before 1890. Section 3 discusses Edgeworth's writing style, and its inhibiting effect upon the spread of his ideas. Section 4 reviews his work in statistics generally, with a heavy emphasis upon the work published before 1893. Section 5 contains a long and detailed

† Jevons's *Principles of Science* did make one contribution to statistics that is worth noting; it helped give us "correlation". The book does not present the concept of correlation (it would be easier to find a denial of the usefulness of statistical correlation in the book than an affirmation); rather it seems to have been Galton's source for the word. The word was in common use at that time, for example by Darwin in the *Origin of the Species* (1859) and by W. R. Groves in *The Correlation of Physical Forces* (1865), but while two correlated ideas would be "inseparable even in mental conception", the asymmetric sense that "one . . . cannot take place without involving the other" (Groves, 1865, p. 183) was emphasized. Jevons, however, wrote: "Things are correlated (*con, relata*) when they are so related or bound to each other that *where one is the other is, and where one is not the other is not*" (Jevons, 1874, p. 354). In his personal copy of Jevons's book, Francis Galton marked this passage and wrote in the margin: "Nice wd. never so with the common meaning (Grove's). Thus where motion is there heat may *not* be, but when motion is not then heat will [not] be." (Galton's 1888 spelling of "co-relation" was apparently to distinguish his usage from Grove's.)

discussion of Edgeworth's 1885 anticipation of an analysis of variance for two-way classifications. Finally, in Section 6 we attempt an assessment of Edgeworth's place in the history of statistics in the nineteenth century.

2. Francis Ysidro Edgeworth

Daniel Bernoulli was born February 8th, 1700, at Groningen in Holland, into an enormously creative and celebrated family, and over a long and varied career made fundamental contributions to mathematical economics (particularly to the mathematical study of utility) and to mathematical statistics (including the study of maximum likelihood estimators). Francis Ysidro Edgeworth was born February 8th, 1845, in Edgeworthstown, Ireland, but otherwise the foregoing statements apply as well to Edgeworth as to Bernoulli. In fact, the details of Edgeworth's early intellectual development are so sparse and paradoxical that the astrological conjunction of his and Daniel Bernoulli's birth dates may be as illuminating an explanation for his subsequent career as any.

Many of Edgeworth's forebears had excelled in literary fields. The widely known and respected novelist Maria Edgeworth was his aunt, the poet Thomas Lovell Beddoes was his first cousin, and his grandfather Richard Lovell Edgeworth was a pioneer in education. Edgeworth's father had studied philosophy and written poetry, and his mother, a Spanish refugee, appears to have shared her husband's literary interests. With such a family background it seems only natural that Edgeworth's attention and interests should be drawn to literary and philosophical fields, and indeed they were. In 1862 Edgeworth entered Trinity College, Dublin, and for several years concentrated on the Classics with marked success. He took first prizes in Greek Prose and Verse Composition, and was considered by his tutors the very ablest man in his class. A fellow student and later Professor of Latin, R. Y. Tyrrell, wrote: "He obtained all the highest honours and prizes.... In Trinity College, there are two verdicts pronounced on every student of eminence; one that of the Lecturers and Examiners, the other that of the élite of the students. The latter verdict was pronounced in favour of Mr. Edgeworth with an enthusiasm to which I can remember no parallel."

In 1867 Edgeworth entered Oxford University. He graduated in 1869 as a member of Balliol College, having taken a First Class at the Final Examination in Literae Humaniores. It would appear, however, that while Edgeworth was respected and well thought of at Oxford, no one of his tutors considered him the class genius he had been at Dublin. The recurrence of restrained praise in the testimonials he later solicited from them, of phrases such as "diligent and successful" and "thoroughly competent to undertake the instruction of young men", may help explain the subsequent direction his career took. Edgeworth, perhaps convinced that he could not attain the top rank of classical scholarship that had seemed his destination when he left Dublin, now undertook the study of commercial law. There is little information available about Edgeworth's life from 1870 until he was called to the bar in 1877, but well before 1877 he must have realized that a career as a barrister could not satisfy either his intellectual curiosity or his ambition for recognition as a scholar.

One indication that Edgeworth's pursuit of the law was not wholehearted is the fact that in late 1875 he applied for the vacant Professorship of Greek at Bedford College, of the University of London. College records show that his application was unsuccessful (he was but one of three candidates), although later, in what may have been his first academic appointment, he served temporarily as teacher of Greek at Bedford College from November 1877 through June 1878. He received £29 10s. for his services. But more telling evidence of his changing interests is available in the direction his wide-ranging reading and study took after leaving Oxford. There is no indication in existing records that Edgeworth's early training in mathematics, including that at Oxford, went beyond elementary algebra. Sir William Rowan Hamilton had visited Maria Edgeworth at Edgeworthstown when Edgeworth was a baby and had been a great friend of his father, but the main points of interest they had held in common had been poetry and philosophy, not mathematics. It may then have come as a surprise to all (except Daniel Bernoulli's spirit) that after leaving Oxford and while studying law, Edgeworth undertook a programme of self-study in mathematics that was the equal of any university programme of that time.

The depth of Edgeworth's newly acquired mathematical talents is apparent in his earliest publications. His first substantial effort, *New and Old Methods of Ethics*, was published in 1877 shortly after he was called to the bar, and it already showed a confident and creative mastery of the calculus of variations, not to mention some knowledge of mathematical physics, and a thorough familiarity with the mathematical psychophysics of Fechner, Delbœuf, Helmholtz and Wundt. By the early 1880's it is clear his competence had expanded to the full spectrum of the mathematical sciences: Fourier's theory of heat, Poisson's mechanics, Cournot, Gossen, Jevons and Walras on mathematical economics, Airy, Thomson and Tait, Clerk Maxwell on physics and, above all else, Laplace on the theory of probability.

Edgeworth had already read widely in literature and philosophy while at Oxford, and his efforts to return to academic scholarship from the law were initially in this direction. His short monograph of 1877, *Methods of Ethics*, was an attempt to apply mathematics to ethics, using the calculus of variations to derive conditions of maximum pleasure in a mathematical utilitarianism he called the "calculus of hedonics". It was probably about the time of its publication that Edgeworth obtained a post lecturing on Logic, Mental and Moral Science, and Metaphysics to pupils reading for the open Competitive Examination for admission to the Civil Service of India. The post was at a private institution in London, and its head, a Mr Walter Wren, later wrote that "a very high standard of knowledge was needed in both teacher and taught—especially in the teacher. Mr. Edgeworth's punctuality, zeal, and earnestness with his classes, matched well his extensive learning." Edgeworth remained with Wren's institution for two years; in 1880 he moved to King's College, London, as Lecturer on Logic.

It was while he was lecturing to Evening Classes in Logic at King's College (and on Political Economy to the Ladies' Department at Kensington) that he published the work that first brought him wide recognition. *Mathematical Psychics: An Essay on the Application of Mathematics to the Moral Sciences* was published in early 1881, and was a bold attempt to extend his earlier mathematical treatment of ethics to economics, in particular to incorporate utility theory with an analysis of economic contract and competition. The favourable notices the work received included reviews by the foremost economists of the day. Alfred Marshall, in the second of only two book reviews he ever published, wrote that "this book shows clear signs of genius, and is a promise of great things to come". Marshall wished the author had worked his theory through more fully before publication (advice Marshall himself followed to excess), "but, taking it at what it claims to be, 'a tentative study', we can only admire its brilliancy, force, and originality". W. Stanley Jevons, whose *Theory of Political Economy* had been the subject of Marshall's only other review, was also generally favourable in a review in *Mind*. But while Jevons found the book a "very remarkable one" and saw in it "unquestionable power and originality", he also found the author's style puzzling and the book hard reading. "The book is one of the most difficult to read which we ever came across, certainly the most difficult of those purporting to treat of economic science."

This latter review led to early correspondence between Edgeworth and Francis Galton. Not long after the Jevons review appeared, Galton wrote to Edgeworth:

42 Rutland Gate SW
Oct. 28/81

Dear Sir:

Permit me to express the very great interest with which I have been reading your powerful work of Math. Psychics, and especially those parts of it that claim the right of Mathematics to deal even with the loosest quantitative data. I write more especially, because I was led to a knowledge of your book by an article by Prof. Jevons in "Mind", in which he happens to speak of its being an unnecessarily difficult book to read. With that verdict I am totally at issue. It strikes me that you have handled topics very difficult in themselves, with great lucidity and vivacity; and I do sincerely hope that you will not suffer yourself to be discouraged by that verdict and still less by those of such reviewers as the writer of the Saturday Review article which you quote. It is always the case with the best work, that it is misrepresented, and disparaged at first, for it takes a curiously long time for new ideas to become current, and the older men who ought to be capable of taking them in freely, will not do so through prejudice. It is a grand attempt that you are making, and by successive efforts more will assuredly be won. I trust you will continue to work at various branches of this wide subject.

* * *

Believe me faithfully yours
Francis Galton

Edgeworth's contacts with Galton continued over the years. Indeed, although Edgeworth had read Laplace and Venn on probability before 1881, it seems reasonable to surmise that conversations with Galton helped intensify Edgeworth's interest in statistics in the early 1880's, just as Edgeworth's work had had an important reciprocal influence upon both Galton and Venn by the late 1880's. However, Galton's interest was focused on problems in psychology, heredity and anthropometry, while Edgeworth's goal was the application of probability to the moral or social sciences. Edgeworth drew examples and analogies from Galton's fields, and he read, used and extended Galton's work, but his very different focus precluded the type of close working relationship Pearson would later develop with Galton.

From 1887 through 1889 Edgeworth served as secretary to two Committees of the Economic section of the British Association. His work on index numbers done for one of these committees, and his many contributions to this *Journal* over this period, helped build his reputation to the point where he received the Professorship of Political Economy at King's College, London, in 1888, became Tooke Professor at King's in 1890 and finally, in early 1891, was appointed Drummond Professor of Political Economy at All Souls College, Oxford.

During this period Edgeworth's work on topics in probability and statistics continued at a furious pace. From 1883 through 1893 he published nearly forty notes and articles in these fields, one small book (*Metretike*), and many reviews (including a review of Galton's *Natural Inheritance* for *Nature*). Indeed, a letter from John Venn to Francis Galton dated February 23rd, 1890, testifies to the fact that Edgeworth was the leading theoretical statistician at the time. Venn suggested that a popular treatise on the theory of statistics was needed, particularly as the "Theory of Statistics" had been formally introduced into the schedule of the Moral Sciences Tripos at Cambridge, in the Department of Scientific Logic. He seems to have had a collaborative effort in mind, and added, "If it were desirable to go into the mathematical foundation of the various rules, no one would do it better than Edgeworth". Galton's respect for Edgeworth was such that in February 1891 he tried to convince Edgeworth to accept a Professorship at the Royal Institution in London, but as Edgeworth's Oxford appointment had just come through the effort came to nought.

Edgeworth held his chair at Oxford until he resigned in 1922, at the age of 77. His years at Oxford were in large part devoted to economics, both to extensive writing on economic theory and to the *Economic Journal*, of which he was Editor from the first issue in March 1891 until his death, February 13th, 1926. But while he did most of his deepest and most influential work in economics in this period, the diminution of his efforts in probability and statistics was scarcely noticeable. From 1894 on he published nearly sixty articles in these fields, including twenty-seven concerned principally with the generalized law of error and the Edgeworth Series. During 1912–14, Edgeworth served as President of the Royal Statistical Society, and according to the *Annals* of this Society, he was the only President in the Society's first century to have the title "Professor"!

3. EDGEWORTH'S STYLE

All investigators of Edgeworth's work must at some point come to grips with his unique style of writing. Modern commentators will frequently use the word "obscure" to describe it, but I think this word, with its implications of vagueness, ambiguity and imprecision, is at best misleading, even though an experienced and conscientious reader of Edgeworth's work can well understand the frustration that gives rise to it. One of the better assessments, although it too is slightly more harsh than necessary, was given by Jevons in his 1881 review of *Mathematical Psychics*.

> "There can be no doubt that in the style of his composition Mr. Edgeworth does not do justice to his matter. His style, if not obscure, is *implicit*, so that the reader is left to puzzle out every important sentence like an enigma. It is probable that most of the propositions are worth puzzling out, and that they would be puzzled out if some great engineering work depended upon their comprehension. But social science has not yet taken such a rank that students feel bound to master any new truths propounded; and it is a misfortune, therefore, that a book, which at all events purports to contain a new science, should be such hard reading."

Edgeworth's work requires effort for its full understanding, but unlike the work of so many, the effort is rewarded, and with practice his "charming amalgam of poetry and pedantry, science and art, wit and learning" (Keynes, 1933) can become addictive. At first such devices as the liberal use in his very earliest writing of untranslated phrases or even sentences in Greek or Latin are distracting, but as they become rarer in his later work we come to enjoy them, as we might some other eccentricity in an old friend. Even more than that we come to look for his seemingly endless analogies and metaphors; presented with wry humour and often singularly instructive.

For example, in several papers in the 1880's Edgeworth likened the normal curve to the outline of a gendarme's hat, a phrase he credited to "a lively French statistician" (Edgeworth, 1888c). Edgeworth, however, turned this similarity in shape to the purpose of instruction, contrasting it with a whole wardrobe of hats. Aggregates of marks on examinations fluctuate according to "the normal law above figured as the 'gens d'armes' hat' whatever the mode in which the individual item oscillates: for instance, if . . . the uncertain wavering with regard to each particular question were represented by a college cap on edge"; a skew density is "a sort of hat blown on one side" (Edgeworth, 1888c). If a given gendarme's hat does not agree in scale with the data "it may be necessary to crumple up or spread out the observed hat", and rather than rescale the data based upon the extremes (which he likened to the "rim" of the "hat", "which is the least steady part, in fact consisting of a sort of lace or ribbon which flutters about irregularly"), it is better to use two points "nearer the centre of the hat, say about the positions in which ventilating holes are sometimes inserted in hats". Also, statistical analyses may be performed "with the aid of the gens d'arme's hat—from which, as from a conjuror's, so much may be extracted" (Edgeworth, 1890).

To Edgeworth, chance could take many forms: "The swarm of probabilities flying hither and thither, does not settle down on any particular point" (Edgeworth, 1887c, p. 42). "The Calculus of Probabilities is an instrument which requires the living hand to direct it" (Edgeworth, 1887c, p. 18). "What real and permanent tendencies there are lie hid beneath the shifting superfices of chance, as it were a desert in which the inexperienced traveller mistakes the temporary agglomerations of drifting sand for the real configuration of the ground" (Edgeworth, 1898). And who but Edgeworth would describe the conditions under which the central limit theorem would hold for non-identically distributed summands in political terms: "The constituents of the normally fluctuating average must form a republic, but not necessarily a perfect democracy" (Edgeworth, 1909).

Occasionally a new word or a new use for an old word may catch the eye. His use of the term "probabiloid" for the ellipsoidally contoured multivariate normal density is concise and suggestive (Edgeworth, 1887b). Similarly, the word "monocephalous" (literally, having one head) which Edgeworth used for a unimodal density that is no more than mildly asymmetrical could perhaps be resurrected for modern use (Edgeworth, 1888a).

Edgeworth's mathematical style may be the greatest source of difficulty for most readers. One problem is that the organization of the work was often orderly to the point of being tedious. In what may be the only apparent influence of his training in the law, he had a habit of classifying subjects according to a series of dichotomies, in a logical tree that either could then be explored totally, or one could more restrictively follow only one line in a manner he once likened to "the devolution of real property according to English law" (Edgeworth, 1885d). In one extreme case (Edgeworth, 1885a), an eight-way classification produced up to 256 cases to be covered!

More serious difficulties were, however, due to the actual presentation of his mathematics, which was often sparse of detail. In this, and in the level of rigour, he seems to have followed Laplace and others of the early years of the nineteenth century. Questions of regularity conditions are seldom mentioned explicitly, although he was only rarely led to erroneous conclusions, and those comments he did make sometime show a grasp of subtle points of mathematical detail that was unusual for the time. For example, in proving the asymptotic normality of the sample median by a convergence of densities argument, Edgeworth wrote: "The probability of the error z is therefore proportioned to $1-2p^2z^2/n$; or (by a step* frequent in this region of mathematics, and which success and the authority of Laplace sanction) $e^{-\frac{2p^2z^2}{n}}$" (Edgeworth, 1886c). The asterisked footnote read, "I desiderate a more rigid proof of this step; such as I have attempted to give for the general case of the law of error", and gave reference to a characteristic function proof. The problem that bothered him was not whether or not $(1+xn^{-1})^n \to e^x$ as n increases, but a more basic one: did convergence of densities entail convergence of distributions? That Edgeworth could not resolve this difficulty in 1886 is not surprising; that he seems to have noticed it, is.

On many occasions, as in the previous quotation, Edgeworth cited "authority" to support an argument. This may have the appearance of an uncritical acceptance of all that has gone before, an obsequious deference to great names. The contrary was true. While Edgeworth was polite, he subjected his sources to critical evaluation, and would accept the authority of their word only when no better test existed, and only where the authority was proved in other ways. To Edgeworth, the practices and statements of great scientists and philosophers were like experimental data, to be incorporated with appropriate weights into an informal weighted mean. "The Doctrine of Errors supplies the *rationale* of the common-sense practice of deferring to authority .... All that authority can do is—what, according to Horace, all that philosophy can do—to get rid of a large portion of error" (Edgeworth, 1888b).

Edgeworth's implicit style can indeed be "hard reading" as Jevons said, and we shall encounter many examples in later sections. But it can also be eloquent and inspiring, as when he argued in *Mathematical Psychics* for the use of mathematical reasoning in social science: "He that will not verify his conclusions as far as possible by mathematics, as it were bringing the ingots of common sense to be assayed and coined at the mint of sovereign science, will hardly realize the full value of what he holds, will want a measure of what it will be worth in however slightly altered circumstances, a means of conveying and making it current" (Edgeworth, 1881, p. 3). Despite the problems he presents, Edgeworth must be counted one of the most subtle and interesting writers to grace our field.

4. EDGEWORTH'S WORK IN STATISTICS

After the appearance of *Mathematical Psychics* in mid-1881, Edgeworth published little before October 1883. What did appear (a few reviews and an outline of an article on rent) gave no indication of a shift in the direction of Edgeworth's thought, but internal evidence in later work suggests he had devoted considerable time and energy in this period to a wide and deep study of the literatures of probability and the method of least squares. It is evident from citations in the *Mathematical Psychics* that Edgeworth had some knowledge of probability before 1881; he had read Laplace's *Essai philosophique des probabilités*, John Venn's *Logic of Chance*, and was familiar with some aspects of the works of Galton and Quetelet. By 1885, however, his knowledge of this literature had broadened to the point where it was unequalled in England, and even rivalled that of the indefatigable Czech bibliographer Emanuel Czuber in all but superficiality.

Probability had played only a minor role in the *Psychics*, and Statistics had played none at all, but in late 1883 Edgeworth began publication of a sequence of articles devoted exclusively to these topics. Viewed separately and out of the context of his work, they are puzzling, eccentric pieces. The title of those published in the *Philosophical Magazine* and *Mind* from October 1883 through 1884 appear to describe their contents, but they give no indication of a common link: "The law of error", "The method of least squares", "The physical basis of probability", "The philosophy of chance", "On the reduction of observations" and "A priori probabilities".

At first glance these works present themselves as essays on standard topics in the theory of errors and the foundations of probability. embellished with Edgeworth's own unique style of writing and its attendant difficulties. The discussions show great perspicuity, but no dramatically novel approach. A reader familiar with Laplace will find much that is known to him in these articles; indeed Edgeworth's copious footnotes make it easy to trace the antecedent of many of the ideas in the literature of the previous century. In many cases Edgeworth has extended, developed, enlarged upon and even corrected the analysis of his predecessors, and in all cases he has given critical comments and interpretations of the ideas that differ in subtle ways from earlier accounts.

These early works do contain a number of surprises for a modern reader. For example, in the very first of them we find a derivation of an early version of the Edgeworth series for symmetric densities by a type of argument that has only recently recurred in the theory of diffusion processes (Edgeworth, 1883a). Letting u_{xs} be the density (evaluated at x) of the sum of s independent random variables, each with density $f(x)$ (assumed symmetric about zero), he first derived the recursive relationship $u_{x,s+1} = \int f(z)\, u_{x+z,s}\, dz$. Then, approximating $u_{x,s+1} = u_{xs} + (u_{x,s+1} - u_{x,s})$ by $u_{xs} + du_{xs}/ds$, and expanding

$$u_{x+z,s} \cong u_{xs} + z\frac{du_{xs}}{dx} + \frac{z^2}{2}\frac{d^2 u_{xs}}{dx^2},$$

he was led (since $\int f(z)\, dz = 1$ and $\int z f(z)\, dz = 0$) to the heat equation

$$\frac{du}{ds} = \frac{c^2}{4}\frac{d^2 u}{dx^2}$$

(where $c^2 = 2\int z^2 f(z)\, dz$) as having solutions which would provide asymptotic approximations to the solutions to the recursive equation. Then a series solution to the heat equation which Poisson had given in his *Traité de Mécanique* led to a series approximation to u_{xs}, the leading (and usually asymptotically dominating) term of which was the normal distribution. Crofton (1885) published a similar argument about this time, as a proof of the central limit theorem. Edgeworth was later (Edgeworth, 1905) to refer generously to this as Crofton's Method.

Another example of a surprise is what may be the earliest appearance in any form of the Student's t distribution. Edgeworth called it the "subexponential" distribution, and derived it as the posterior distribution of the mean μ of a normal distribution, given uniform prior distributions for μ and $h = \sigma^{-1}$ (Edgeworth, 1883b; Welch, 1958; Pearson, 1967). But to dwell too long on such tidbits is to risk missing the fundamental point of novelty, the grandly ambitious design that lay behind these sometimes random notes.

Edgeworth's plan, as is clear both from the context of his work and from a closer study of these pieces themselves, was to do at last what had been talked about and assumed possible for over a century, but had never been accomplished: adapt the statistical methods of the theory of errors to the quantification of uncertainty in the social, particularly economic, sciences. The type of question Edgeworth sought to treat, and the difficulties he saw in their treatment, were described in an 1884 review of a posthumously published collection of Jevons's papers, *Investigations in Currency and Finance.* Edgeworth commented upon the beautiful diagrams of time series in the book, which he thought would assist the reader

> "to estimate the probability that the differences in the averages for different weeks and months are not accidental. The question which has been just indicated, one of the most delicate in statistics—namely, under what circumstances does a difference in figures correspond to a difference of fact—comes up often in these pages. Thus Mr. Jevons, comparing the amount of bills created in the different quarters of the year, speaks of a variation to the extent of about six per cent as 'no great difference'. On the other hand, he regards it as noteworthy that, 'out of 79,794 bankruptcies which were gazetted from the beginning of 1806 to the end of 1860, 28,391 occurred in the second month of the quarter, 26,427 in the third month, and only 24,976 in the first month'. No doubt a similar disparity between 'heads' and 'tails' in the result of so many throws of a coin would prove a cause, a want of symmetry in the coin. But our knowledge of the behaviour of tossed coins rests at bottom upon observation and experiments such as those which Mr. Jevons once performed. That what is true of games of chance is true of bankruptcies is not to be assumed without examination" (Edgeworth, 1884).

Edgeworth was to provide this examination.

Edgeworth's key work on this topic, and what was among his most influential works in statistics, was contained in a series of four papers read in the year 1885. The first of these, "Observations and statistics; An essay on the theory of errors of observation and the first principles of statistics", was read on May 25th, 1885, to the Cambridge Philosophical Society; it concentrated on statistical theory, and summarized and extended his work of the previous two years. The second, "Methods of statistics", was read less than a month later, on June 23rd, to the international gathering to celebrate the Jubilee of this Statistical Society; it was concerned with methodology and presented, through an extensive series of examples taken from all manner of fields, an exposition of the application and interpretation of significance tests for the comparison of means. The third and fourth, "On methods of ascertaining variation in the rate of births, deaths, and marriages" and "Progressive means", were read at meetings of the British Association in September and October. The third presented a remarkable analysis for two-way classifications which anticipated many ideas of the analysis of variance, and it will be discussed in detail in the next section. The fourth article, "Progressive means", was a brief discussion of the use of linear least squares for detrending time series, including the estimation of the coefficients' variability to permit significance tests for trend or comparisons of different series.

The range of these four articles is such that a detailed examination of all will not be possible here. Nonetheless a brief discussion of some aspects of the first two, probably the most widely read of all of Edgeworth's statistical works, will be required to provide perspective for the next section.

For Edgeworth, the distinction between *observations* and *statistics* was an important one:

> "Observations and statistics agree in being quantities grouped about a Mean: they differ in that the Mean of observations is real, of statistics is fictitious. The mean of observations is a cause, as it were the source from which diverging errors emanate. The mean of statistics is a description, a representative quantity put for a whole group, the

best representative of the group, that quantity which, if we must in practice put one quantity for many, minimizes the error unavoidably attending such practice. Thus measurements by the reduction of which we ascertain a real time, number, distance are observations. Returns of prices, exports and imports, legitimate and illegitimate marriages or births and so forth, the averages of which constitute the premises of practical reasoning, are statistics. In short, observations are different copies of one original; statistics are different originals affording one 'generic portrait'. Different measurements of the same man are observations; but measurements of different men, grouped round *l'homme moyen*, are *primâ facie* at least statistics" (Edgeworth, 1885a).

Edgeworth's aim was to apply the tools developed in the previous century for *observations* in astronomy and geodesy, where a more or less objectively defined goal made it possible to quantify and perhaps remove nonmeasurement error and meaningful to talk of the remaining variation as random error, to social and economic *statistics* where the goal was defined in terms of the measurements themselves and the size and character of the variation depended upon the classifications and subdivisions employed. To do this he would first disassemble these tools to determine most carefully what lay beneath them: what conditions, what assumptions, what interpretations lay behind their successful use?

"Observations and statistics" focused on one theoretical aspect of this problem, the choice of a best estimate of a mean. While the problem was presented as one of estimation, the underlying motivation, the implicit use to which the mean would be put, was the comparison of different sets of statistics. Edgeworth examined the philosophical interpretations of probability as applied to inference. He gave careful consideration to the objective frequentist or sampling theory view (he called it "ordinary induction", "assumed inversion", or the "indirect method"), but in the end he adopted the inverse probability or Bayesian view, after giving cogent refutations to criticisms of this view by Cournot, Boole and Venn. He gave qualified endorsement to the use of uniform prior distributions, but only when based on experience: "We have a rough general experience that one value of the measurable occurs as often as another at any rate between the limits with which we are practically concerned" (Edgeworth, 1885a). Like Laplace, Edgeworth's embrace of inverse probability was neither metaphysical (his priors were grounded on experience) nor dogmatic. Like Laplace, Edgeworth was inconsistent in his application of inverse probability, reverting to sampling distributions when comparing means by significance tests.

In the selection of a best mean, Edgeworth preferred choosing that value that minimized the posterior expected loss, with a general loss function. He extensively discussed the relationship between the population distribution (the "facility-curve") and the best mean, his examples including the family of stable laws and others where averaging was detrimental, and densities where the median was to be preferred. He focused special attention upon the normal distribution (the "law of error" or "probability-curve"), which he parametrized as

$$y = (C^2\pi)^{-\frac{1}{2}} \exp[-x^2/C^2],$$

and he called C the *modulus* of the curve. He defended $2\Sigma(x_i - \bar{x})^2/n$ as an estimate of C^2 on the grounds that it maximized the posterior density, while $2\Sigma(x_i - \bar{x})^2/(n-1)$ "does not appear to correspond to the maximum of anything in particular" (Edgeworth, 1885a). In employing the normal distribution for the comparison of means, Edgeworth emphasized that he was appealing to the asymptotic normal approximation to the sampling distributions of means, not to an assumption that the populations were themselves normal. "What is required for the elimination of chance is not that the raw material of our observations should fulfill the law of error; but that they should be constant to any law" (Edgeworth, 1885b).

The basic significance test employed in the "Methods of statistics" was extremely simple. Given two "means" (which could be medians or other estimates), first estimate their "fluctuations", a term Edgeworth invented to mean the modulus-squared or, in modern terminology, twice the variance. If one "mean" was a sample mean, $\bar{x}$, he recommended $2\Sigma(x_i-\bar{x})^2/n^2$ as an estimate of its fluctuation; if one were the median he would use $(2ny^2)^{-1}$, where y was the value of the population density (if known) at the median. Then, if C_1^2 and C_2^2 represent estimates of the fluctuations of the two "means", $\surd(C_1^2+C_2^2)$ estimated the modulus of the difference of the "means" (in modern terminology, $\surd 2$ times the estimated standard deviation), and the test was performed by comparing the difference of the "means" with this modulus. If the "means" differed by more than twice this modulus, it was judged "exceedingly improbable" that the difference was accidental, and some other cause was indicated. This was a rather exacting test (corresponding to a two-sided test at level 0·005), and Edgeworth would take smaller differences (say 1·5 times the modulus) as worthy of notice, although he admitted the evidence was then weaker.

The main portion of "Methods of statistics" was given over to examples (often worked in several alternative ways) showing how this simple test, borrowed from the calculus of observations, could be used to assess the significance of statistical data on anthropometry, rates of births, deaths and marriages, economic statistics, and such exotica as the flow to and from a wasps' nest, the attendance at club dinners and the metre of Virgil's poetry. Edgeworth had encountered the work of Wilhelm Lexis in mid-1885 (Edgeworth, 1885a), and in "Methods of statistics" he explained and criticized Lexis's methods for dealing with population statistics. One of the examples he gave was the data on bankruptcies that Jevons had presented, and that Edgeworth had commented on in his 1884 review of Jevons's collected papers. (Jevons's offhand assessment of significance was found by Edgeworth to be "abundantly justified".)

Not all of Edgeworth's comparisons showed significant differences, and one of the more amusing examples concerned a wasps' nest. Edgeworth found the traffic rates at 8 a.m. and at noon on September 4th, 1884, of a nest in Edgeworthstown, Ireland. Edgeworth's motivation for considering these data, which he gathered himself, was to show by analogy how import and export statistics might be handled. The rate at noon was slightly less than that at 8 a.m., and he commented: "If in an insect republic there existed theorizers about trade as well as an industrial class, I could imagine some Protectionist drone expressing his views about 12 o'clock that 4th day of September, and pointing triumphantly to the decline in trade of 2½ per cent. as indicated by the latest returns." Edgeworth found the difference, half the modulus, to be "insignificant".

Edgeworth's 1885 articles, particularly "Observations and statistics" and "Methods of statistics", were widely noticed, both in England and on the continent, and until the end of the century when texts such as Bowley's *Elements of Statistics* began to appear, they served as basic references for the theory and application of statistical techniques to social and economic data.

After 1885 Edgeworth directed his attention more specifically to statistical applications to economic problems and to related statistical theory. In "The mathematical theory of banking" (read 1886, published 1888) and a companion paper (Edgeworth, 1886c), he made a pioneer study in inventory theory, showing how records of past demands on the reserves of a bank could be used to estimate the odds that a given level of reserves will in the future prove insufficient. Among other things, the analysis was notable in that it recognized the existence of serial correlation in a series of returns of Bank of England notes, suggested that their behaviour might be similar to that of a moving average of independent random terms, and gave rough indications as to how this might be taken into account in estimating the variability of means of such series.

The major focus of Edgeworth's work in the years 1886–89 was problems related to index numbers. Edgeworth's interest in index numbers dated at least from 1883 when a short note of his, "On the method of ascertaining a change in the value of gold", appeared in this *Journal* (Edgeworth, 1883c). It seems likely that he had first taken up the subject after reading Jevons's work, as this early note was primarily concerned with criticism of Jevons's arguments in favour of a geometric mean. It also is plausible that concern with index numbers contributed to his decision to focus the 1885 "Observations and statistics" on estimation and the problem "What is the best mean?" If Jevons was primarily responsible for showing the potential power of index numbers in economic investigations, however, it was Edgeworth who first thoroughly investigated their properties from the standpoint of statistical theory. Jevons had made one (and only one) computation of a probable error (Jevons, 1865); Edgeworth investigated the distribution of price changes, the "best means" which follow from assumed distributions, and the performance of those means under failure of assumptions.

The economic implications of Edgeworth's work were published at length with the Reports of the British Association (and reprinted in Volume 1 of his collected papers; Edgeworth, 1925). The theoretical investigations, however, appeared in several papers in the *Philosophical Magazine*, with little or no reference to the index number problems which helped to motivate them. The papers were wide ranging, and included Edgeworth's earliest work on asymmetrical laws of error (with an almost Pearsonian differential equation approximation to a difference equation satisfied by binomial probabilities; Edgeworth, 1886b) and several thoughtful discussions of the rejection of outliers (see Stigler, 1973b).

One of the more striking of Edgeworth's works of this period was an article on testing goodness of fit. In "The empirical proof of the law of error", published in 1887, he described how empirical distributions, such as those of bank reserves or price changes could be examined to see if they supported the hypothesis of normality. He proposed first testing symmetry, then determining whether or not the normal distribution provided the best fit among a limited class of symmetric curves. The test of symmetry he favoured was to compare the sample mean and sample median. If they differed by more than twice the estimated modulus, this would indicate asymmetry. In estimating the required modulus, he made an error in treating the mean and median as uncorrelated, despite the fact that Laplace had presented their joint asymptotic distribution correctly in work Edgeworth was familiar with and cited frequently (see Stigler, 1973a).

As a test of goodness of fit Edgeworth recommended breaking the range of the data into two classes (the points of division depending upon the particular alternative of interest), and testing normality by comparing the observed frequency counts with those expected under a hypothesis of normality. The test, based on a normal approximation to a binomial distribution, is formally equivalent to a χ^2 test for this simple situation, although later correspondence with Karl Pearson (see Pearson, 1965) indicates Edgeworth did not know how to extend the test to counts of more than two classes. In one of two applications he gave, to measurements of the heights of 683,068 Italian recruits, he found "the odds against the Probability-curve [the normal density] being exact are enormous". He speculated that a mixture of normal curves with different means would give a better approximation, but he calculated that compared with a selection of other "simple" symmetric curves (a triangular density, a parabolic density and the double exponential density) supposed *a priori* approximately equally likely, then "the odds in favour of the Probability-curve are stupendous". Edgeworth's test was more limited in scope than Pearson's later χ^2, but his interpretation of the results lacked the dogmatic literalism sometimes given χ^2 tests, even by Pearson.

Edgeworth's investigations of the usefulness of various "means" as index numbers stressed the manner in which the choice depended upon the distribution of prices and the economic purpose to which the index would be put. He allowed that "if there were required a uniform treatment to be administered, like Dr. Sangrado's hot water cure, this general method would undoubtedly be the Arithmetic Mean" (Edgeworth, 1888d). But he emphasized that for many purposes the asymmetric distributions met in practice would be better handled by the mode, the geometric mean or the median. In most of this work he laid particular stress upon the median, because of its insensitivity to discordant measurements. He called special attention to the weighted median, which Laplace had derived as a solution to a least absolute deviations estimation problem (see Stigler, 1973a, b) and he proposed algorithms for extending this "method of situation" (as Laplace called it) to more complicated regression models. After

1889 Edgeworth turned his attention to other areas, although he commented frequently in book reviews on others' works on index numbers.

From 1890 on, with the notable exception of the "generalized law of error", Edgeworth's work in statistics consisted of brief flurries of activity, either on topics not closely related to his earlier work or on brief extensions or applications of earlier work. In 1892 and 1893 he wrote a series of articles on correlation, starting with "Correlated averages" (Edgeworth, 1892a). These were directly inspired by Galton's work, and sought both to develop a mathematical apparatus for handling multivariate normal distributions and the related conditional distributions which arise in multiple regression, and to show how these distributions might be best fitted to data. The treatment was incomplete and not totally successful, but these works had a great influence upon Karl Pearson's first work on correlation, upon the direction of his investigations and the tools he used in successfully dealing with these questions. Pearson acknowledged this influence in his original work, although in his later recollections (Pearson, 1920) he sought to downplay Edgeworth's role, and he was, I think, overly defensive and insufficiently generous. The most prominent modern reminder of Edgeworth's role in the early history of correlation is the phrase "coefficient of correlation", which he introduced. In May and June of 1892, Edgeworth delivered six Newmarch Lectures at University College, London, "On the uses and methods of statistics". The lectures summarized his theoretical work to that point, including his work on multiple correlations and tests of fit, and were delivered nearly five months before Karl Pearson's first public discussion of any of these topics.

In 1908–9 Edgeworth published a multipart investigation of the precision of estimates. The work is notable for its study of the asymptotic behaviour of maximum likelihood estimators, both from the point of view of inverse probability and from that of frequency theory. Edgeworth's anticipation in this series of some of Fisher's later work, including his proof of the asymptotic efficiency of maximum likelihood estimators, has been pointed out on several occasions, and has been recently discussed in detail by John Pratt (1976).

After 1896, Edgeworth's major statistical preoccupation was the "law of error". As we have already noted, his interest in symmetric generalizations to the normal distribution dates from 1883, and in asymmetric curves from 1886. This early work contains the seeds of what was to become known as the Edgeworth series. Another approach Edgeworth later took toward generalizing the normal distribution was to consider the distributions of families of transformed normal random variables. This line of work which dates from an 1892 article, "The law of error and correlated averages" (Edgeworth, 1892b), was later named the "method of translation". While the ideas behind Edgeworth's generalization of the law of error predate (and helped inspire) Karl Pearson's first work on general frequency curves, the major development of these themes came later, and was in fact a competitive (and not very successful) response to Pearson's family of curves. A reasoned appreciation of the role of this work in the development of statistics would require extensive discussion of Karl Pearson's and continental work on this topic, and we shall not pursue the topic here. Bowley (1928) has provided an extensive (if impenetrable) discussion of Edgeworth's voluminous work on this topic.

5. Edgeworth and Two-way Classifications

5.1. *Edgeworth in* 1885

That Ronald A. Fisher was primarily responsible for originating that body of techniques we call the analysis of variance has not been seriously questioned. From 1922 on, Fisher's development and exploitation of a methodology for testing complicated multiple hypotheses, his calculus of sums of squares and the associated models and significance tests, have had an immense influence upon statistical thought and practice. As it is with all scientific innovations, however, we can identify many anticipations and precursors to the analysis of variance, early works that are of interest not only as they help us judge the novelty and real advances of Fisher's work, by presenting us with a view of the intellectual background to his efforts, but also in their own right, as incomplete, not totally successful, early gropings toward the solutions of important problems. Of all these anticipations, Edgeworth's may be the most remarkable.

Prior to 1885 a number of works related to this area had appeared, of which the best known were by Dormoy (1874, 1878, pp. 37–47) and Lexis (1876, 1879). These writers had described measures of dispersion for series of relative frequencies, ratios of a measure of variability under homogeneous binomial assumptions (Lexis called this the "combinatorial" case) to an estimate of probable error not based on this assumption (the "physical" case). The measures were essentially descriptive, no attempt has made in this early work to assess statistical significance, and their applicability was restricted to only certain types of relative frequency data. In 1885, however, Edgeworth published a paper on the analysis of two-way tables that went considerably further.

Edgeworth's paper, "On methods of ascertaining variations in the rate of births, deaths, and marriages", was read on September 12th, 1885, at the meeting of the British Association for the Advancement of Science at Aberdeen. This meeting is already famous in the history of statistics as that where Francis Galton presented his address "Regression towards mediocrity in heredity stature", developing regression (and introducing the term) in the context of the bivariate normal distribution. It is far less well known that two days after Galton gave the world "regression", Edgeworth showed how to perform an analysis of variance for a two-way classification. His paper is remarkable both for its insight and difficulty, and is well worth examining in detail.

Edgeworth's paper, published in this *Journal* in December 1885, took as its problem a particular case of the determination of a modulus C or a fluctuation C^2. Recall that in Edgeworth's terminology the modulus is $\sqrt{2}$ times the standard deviation, so C^2 is just twice the variance, and that when faced with a simple set of independent measurements $X_1, \ldots, X_n$ Edgeworth preferred, on both theoretical and practical grounds, to estimate C^2 by $2\Sigma(X_i - \bar{X})^2/n$. (He used the same term "fluctuation" indifferently for both C^2 and its sample estimate, a practice that did not confuse Edgeworth but could mislead a reader.) The particular case Edgeworth considered was that where the data were cross-classified and one wished to assess the statistical significance of differences between table entries. He began by briefly reviewing some of the methods and concepts he had presented in his "Methods of statistics" paper, including the role of the modulus in statistical comparisons, and the fact that while there is a strong tendency for data to be homoscedastic ("Paradoxically as it sounds, fluctuation is one of the least flux things in the world"), estimates of the fluctuation based on small samples are quite unreliable ("The 'probable error' of a value based on sixteen observations is as much as an *eighth part* of the real thing observed. A *quarter* [of $2\sigma^2$] would not be a very improbable error"). The problem he proposed to treat was the disentangling of "entangled moduli".

Edgeworth had introduced this problem, without solution, in his "Methods of statistics", by noting as an example that if one wished to use the registrar-general's records of marriages to determine if one class had a higher propensity to marry than another (to "test a theory that any particular class was more addicted to marriage, had a higher "Matrimoniality' . . . than some other class"), then there may be some difficulty in determining the modulus of the class's marriage rate. The registrar-general's records would be classified by place and year, and the fluctuation of a randomly selected return could be thought of as $C_t^2 + C_p^2 + C^2$, where C_t^2 was a "time-fluctuation", C_p^2 a "place-fluctuation" and C^2 a fluctuation independent of year and place. Then, if one's data on social classes were from a single county, $C_t^2 + C^2$ would be the relevant fluctuation for making comparisons, while if it was from a single year, $C_p^2 + C^2$ would be the relevant quantity. In either case, if one wished to use the records of the registrar-general to enlarge the data base beyond that available for social classes separately (thus improving the accuracy of the estimate of fluctuation used for comparisons), then it would be necessary to extract separate estimates of C^2, C_t^2 and C_p^2 from the registrar-general's two-way classification. In his "Methods of statistics" Edgeworth had done little more than formulate the problem in terms of this variance components model, promising a solution later. In the B.A.A.S. paper he fulfilled this promise.

5.2. *Virgilian Hexameter*

Edgeworth began his discussion of "Entangled moduli" with an example, which he termed a "lemma", from what to those unfamiliar with Edgeworth must have seemed an exotic source, Virgil's *Aeneid.* Table 1 gives Edgeworth's data, with corrections for some of his approximate calculations of fluctuations indicated in an additional row and column.

What Edgeworth had done, classical scholar that he was, was to take the first 75 lines of Book XI of the *Aeneid,* and classify each of the first four feet in a line as a dactyl or not.† Thus of lines 1–5, three have dactyls in their first foot, and of lines 51–55, only one has a dactyl in its fourth foot. He had treated similar data in a more limited way in "Methods of statistics" where he had noted that "The gusts of passion to which the rhythm is accommodated cannot be treated as perfectly fortuitous. Nevertheless it appears that the causes at work are sufficiently numerous and independent to fulfil the conditions required for the elimination of chance." In the earlier paper Edgeworth had shown that Lexis's urn models and "thesis of pure sortition" were inappropriate for these data, that "If we could imagine dactyls and spondees to be mixed up in the poet's brain in the proportion of 16 to 24, and shaken out at random, the modulus in the number of dactyls would [exceed that actually found, contrary to Lexis's unconstrained model]". In the B.A.A.S. paper he sought to show an appropriate way of analysing these data.

Edgeworth used almost no mathematical notation in describing his analysis, probably in the belief that his intended audience, the members of the B.A.A.S. and the readers of this *Journal,* would not have felt at home in a sea of symbols. He may have been correct at that time, but 93 years later the *Journal's* readers may find notation useful in appreciating what Edgeworth was doing. Accordingly we shall discuss this and a later example in the now conventional notation for a two-way classification, taking X_{ij}, $i = 1, \dots, I$, $j = 1, \dots, J$ as the number occurring in the ith row and the jth column, a measurement of the ith level of treatment j. In the Virgil example X_{ij} is the number of dactyls in the ith foot of the jth group of five lines, $I = 4$, $J = 15$, treatment A is associated with feet and treatment B with lines.

Edgeworth sought "to elicit the entangled from the explicit fluctuations of dactyl-frequency". We shall see that by "entangled" he referred to row, column and residual, while "explicit" meant total variation. For each row and column he gave the sum, mean and fluctuation separately. Thus for lines 51–55 he found the sum to be 6, the mean 1·5, the fluctuation 3. Edgeworth's calculations of fluctuation were approximate (he gave an example of a calculation, so there is not doubt what was intended), but it will be essential for our discussion to have the correct values; these have been added in final rows and columns.

Several entries in Edgeworth's table require further explanation, those at the intersections of the fluctuations column (and row) with those for sums and means. In each case there are two entries; the uppermost is the sum (or, respectively, mean) of the corresponding list (column or row) of fluctuations. The lower entry, in parentheses, is the fluctuation of the corresponding list of sums (or, respectively, means). Thus at the intersection of the row "means" and the column "fluctuations, FYE" we find 2·5 and (0·6), indicating that Edgeworth found 2·5 for the mean of the four row fluctuations and 0·6 for the fluctuation of the 15 column means. Had he carried out his calculations with greater precision he would have found 2·64 and 0·67, respectively; these are given in the adjacent column.

Edgeworth focused attention upon these double entries. Regarding those at the intersection of the "means" row and "fluctuations" column, 2·5 and (0·6), he wrote:

> "The relation of the last two figures is instructive. They ought to be equal, if the fluctuation of the four rows was not only equal, but *identical* in this sense: that,

† A dactyl is a metrical foot consisting of one long syllable followed by two short syllables. Lines in Virgilian hexameter consisted of six feet, all either dactyls or spondees (two long syllables), of which the last foot was always a spondee, and the next-to-last usually a dactyl.

TABLE 1

Edgeworth's counts of dactyls in the first four feet of lines 1–75 of Book XI of Virgil's Aeneid
(*Figures in parentheses are fluctuations*)

	Lines																	*Fluctuations*	
Foot	1–5	6–10	11–15	16–20	21–25	26–30	31–35	36–40	41–45	46–50	51–55	56–60	61–65	66–70	71–75	*Sums*	*Means*	*FYE*	*Corrected*
First	3	3	5	5	4	4	2	2	2	1	2	4	3	2	4	46	3·07	2·8	2·79
Second	1	4	0	3	3	3	5	2	2	4	3	1	2	3	2	38	2·53	3·2	3·16
Third	1	2	4	2	5	2	1	2	2	2	0	2	2	0	1	28	1·87	3·1	3·16
Fourth	2	2	1	0	3	1	2	0	2	1	1	2	1	1	0	19	1·27	1	1·46
Sums	7	11	10	10	15	10	10	6	8	8	6	9	8	6	7	131	8·73	10 (10)	10·57 (10·79)
Means	1·75	2·75	2·5	2·5	3·75	2·5	2·5	1·5	2	2	1·5	2·25	2	1·5	1·75	33	2·18	2·5 (0·6)	2·64 (0·67)
Fluctuations																			
FYE	1·5	2·5	9	7	3	3	5	2	0	3	3	2·5	1	3	2·5	48 (208)	3·2 (0·9)	—	—
Corrected	1·38	1·38	8·50	6·50	1·38	2·50	4·50	1·50	0·00	3·00	2·50	2·38	1·00	2·50	4·38	43·38 (207·38)	2·89 (0·92)	—	—

whenever one went up or down, the others did so also to the same extent; if in short the four waves might be regarded as sections of the same great wave. This result would be unaffected, though we supposed the mean height of the four waves to be different; as [if] it were an identical fluctuation executed in four canals of different level. Again, if the fluctuations were all independent, the fluctuation of the means should be a quarter of the mean fluctuation. Lastly, the fluctuation of the means ought to be less than a quarter of the mean fluctuation, if the primitive waves were *compensatory* in this sense: that wherever there was a trough in one, there was apt to be a crest in the other; as if a dactyl in the first foot was frequently followed by a spondee in the second.

"Now as a matter of fact the fluctuation of the means, 0·6, is just a quarter of the mean fluctuation 2·5. The second hypothesis therefore is the true one."

These passages are succinct and, despite a possible first impression, precise. Their meaning becomes clear if we determine exactly what Edgeworth's "mean fluctuation of the four first rows" (2·5) and "fluctuation of the row of means" (0·6) are. In our modern notation with $X_{i.}$ and $X_{.j}$ for the ith row and jth column means, and $X_{..} = (\Sigma\Sigma X_{ij})/IJ$, we find that

$$FL_R = \text{fluctuation of the row of means}$$
$$= 2\sum_{j=1}^{J}(X_{.j}-X_{..})^2/J,$$

and

$$\overline{FL}(R) = \text{mean fluctuation of the rows}$$
$$= \left[\sum_{i=1}^{I}\left(2\sum_{j=1}^{J}(X_{ij}-X_{i.})^2\right)\Big/J\right]\Big/I.$$

Now let $SSA = J\Sigma(X_{i.}-X_{..})^2$ and $SSB = I\Sigma(X_{.j}-X_{..})^2$ be the row and column sums of squares, and $SSE = \Sigma\Sigma(X_{ij}-X_{i.}-X_{.j}+X_{..})^2 = \Sigma\Sigma(X_{ij}-X_{i.})^2 - I\Sigma(X_{.j}-X_{..})^2$, the residual sum of squares. We can then see that $FL_R = 2SSB/IJ$, $\overline{FL}(R) = 2(SSE+SSB)/IJ$, and

$$\overline{FL}(R) - FL_R = 2SSE/IJ.$$

Thus the two figures Edgeworth compared are multiples of sums of squares, their difference is a multiple of the residual sum of squares, and their ratio,

$$\overline{FL}(R)/FL_R = 1 + SSE/SSB = 1 + (I-1)/F_c,$$

where F_c is the usual F-statistic for testing column effect in a two-way classification. Thus a modern statistician would recognize that Edgeworth's examination of the relationship between the "figures" $\overline{FL}(R)$ and FL_R is equivalent to a comparison of the column and error sums of squares.

His first case, that they be equal, will hold only if $SSE = 0$, that is only if $F_c = \infty$ and an additive effects model fits the data perfectly: $X_{ij} = \mu + \alpha_i + \beta_j$. (Approximate equality would have to be understood to mean SSE was small relative to SSB, F_c was large.) This is what Edgeworth meant when he spoke of the fluctuation of the rows as *identical*, as his analogies to waves and canals makes clear. His second case, that $FL_R = \overline{FL}(R)/4$, will hold only if $\overline{FL}(R)/FL_R = 4$, that is, only if $F_c = 1$. Here, in line with the wave and canal analogies, we should take his condition that "the fluctuations were all independent" to mean that there is no column effect, $\beta_j \equiv 0$ all j. His third case, $FL_R < \overline{FL}(R)/4$, is equivalent to $F_c < 1$, and he noted that this would be expected if the counts within lines (within columns) are negatively dependent.

To summarize, Edgeworth described three extreme cases which we now see are equivalent to $F_c = \infty$, $F_c = 1$ and $F_c < 1$, and he associated them, respectively, with a perfect fit to an additive model, no column effect, and a negative dependence within columns. He found

$FL_R/\overline{FL}(R) = 0{\cdot}6/2{\cdot}5 = 0{\cdot}24$, which would correspond to $F_c = 0{\cdot}95$ (the corrected values would give $F_c = 1{\cdot}02$), and concluded the second hypothesis, no column effect, was supported; Virgil's metre was homogeneous from line to line. His procedure is formally equivalent to the correct analysis of variance test; although he lacked a distribution theory for his test, his understanding of the situation extended to a case seldom (if ever) mentioned in texts today, the fact that within column negative correlation could produce values of F_c less than one!

Edgeworth then went on to investigate row (or foot) effect in a similar manner. He found $\overline{FL}(C)/J = 3{\cdot}2/15\ (\cong 0{\cdot}2)$ to be much less than $FL_C = 0{\cdot}9$; the corresponding value of $F_R = (J-1)(\overline{FL}(C)/FL_C) - 1)^{-1}$ is 5·48; the corrected value woud be $F_R = 6{\cdot}54$. He considered this significant, writing: "We are driven then to the supposition that the transverse, or columnar, fluctuations are not independent"; that is, the within lcolumn variability (which we would associate with a *row* effect) was not as one would expect under the hypothesis of independence, if there were no row (or foot) effect. Edgeworth entertained two possible explanations for this lack of "independence".

The first possible explanation he gave for the large F_R was that there might be a positive correlation within columns (within groups of five lines). He went so far as to concoct a model that would produce just the value observed, where feet 1–3 were always identical, feet 4–6 were always identical, but there was independence between lines and between halves of lines. He dismissed this possibility as "evidently contrary to fact", although he provided no analysis to back up this impression. He did, however, cite an investigation he had presented in "Methods of statistics" as inconsistent with the existence of a line-to-line correlation within groups of five lines. He had shown there that the fluctuation of a mean of five lines was just about a fifth (actually 23 per cent) of that of a single line. His tests for positive correlation may not have been conclusive when viewed from the perspective of a century later, but the fact that in the pre-correlation environment of 1885 he thought to make them at all is remarkable.

Edgeworth's second possible explanation was the one he accepted. "There remains the hypothesis that the rows are at a different level. And this is proved to be true." His conclusion, which is in agreement with that reached by an F test, was supported by several significance tests. First, he noted that the difference between the means for the first and fourth feet ($3{\cdot}06 - 1{\cdot}27 = 1{\cdot}8$) was about four times the estimated modulus (about 0·5; his text contains several misprints here but he clearly intended to calculate $(2{\cdot}8/15 + 1{\cdot}0/15)^{\frac{1}{2}}$). He made no allowance for the fact that multiple comparisons had been made, but noted that the other differences were "slighter, but still real". As further support he performed sign tests: "this conclusion may be verified by one of the humbler methods of statistics. Out of fifteen trials, so to speak, the first foot is only *five* times less than the second. The preponderance of the first over the third and fourth is even more marked."

Edgeworth's analysis of Virgilian hexameter did not end here. He went on to show how the "entangled" moduli could be extracted, and verified his conclusions with a sampling experiment (sampling at random from his data table) and further data. He also used these further data to give a more careful consideration to possible within line correlation, finding a slight, but not significant, negative correlation or "compensation" indicated by a comparison of the fluctuations of individual feet with that of the first and second together. But his understanding of the methods he was using will be clearer if we move to his discussion of a second example.

5.3. *Death Rates and the Additive Effects Model*

Taking leave of the *Aeneid*, Edgeworth wrote: "It is time to proceed from the parade ground to the campaign, and to employ the arts which have been acquired in the field of Virgilian statistics to attack the more difficult and important problem." His intention was to apply what he was to call the "method of extrication" to a table of death rates, but before proceeding he paused to explain more fully the model he had in mind, using a metaphor.

Throughout Section 5.2 we tacitly assumed that the now standard additive effects model,

$X_{ij} = \mu + \alpha_i + \beta_j + \varepsilon_{ij}$, where α_i and β_j are row and column effects and ε_{ij} are random, is what Edgeworth had had in mind. Any doubts that this is true are demolished by the following passage, which gives as clear and elegant a statement of this model as can be found in any work to date.

"The site of a city," Edgeworth hypothesized, "consists of several terraces, produced it may be by the gentler geological agencies. The terraces lie parallel to each other, east and west. They are intersected perpendicularly by ridges which have been produced by igneous displacement. We might suppose the volcanic agency to travel at a uniform rate west to east, producing each year a ridge of the same breadth. It is not known prior to observation whether the displacement of one year resembles (in any, or all, the terraces) the displacements in the proximate years. Nor is it known whether the displacement in one terrace is apt to be identical with that in the neighbouring terraces. Upon the ground thus intersected and escarped are built miscellaneous houses. The height of each housetop above the level of the sea is ascertainable barometrically or otherwise. The mean height above the sea of the housetops for each acre is registered. It is required from these data to elicit the fluctuation of the height of houses above the ground."

In one short paragraph Edgeworth tells the reader more without mathematical symbols than many recent texts convey in pages of algebra. The rows and columns of a two-way table are given physical meaning, and the fluctuation sought is clearly described, regardless of whether or not the effects are conceived of as fixed or random. With this image planted in the reader's mind, he moved immediately to an example.

Edgeworth introduced his data as a strip of death rates for all ages, extracted from the registrar-general's Report for 1883, and announced that he had treated it in the same manner as he had the Virgilian hexameter data; see Table 2. Here the "means" are presented to one more significant digit than Edgeworth gave them, and a misprinted 186 (for 166) for Hertfordshire in 1881 is corrected.

The problem Edgeworth considered important here was the estimation of the fluctuation of death rates after year and county variation had been disentangled. When he had been interested in examining row and column effects, he had proceeded in a manner formally equivalent to the calculation of an F statistic, and his table provides all the information one needs for an analysis of variance table. We might then expect him to estimate the error fluctuation by $\overline{FL}(R) - FL_R$ or $\overline{FL}(C) - FL_C$, which would agree in giving $2SSE/IJ$, except for the approximate nature of Edgeworth's calculations. (We would not expect him to find $2SSE/(I-1)(J-1)$, since he saw no virtue in unbiased estimation.) But he did not quite do this, and the way he did proceed sheds light on both the depth and limitations of his understanding. His analysis was cryptic, and was misinterpreted by Bowley (1928) in the only commentary about it I know of. He wrote:

"Let C^2 be the fluctuation which it is required to determine; put $C^2 + C_t^2$ for the fluctuation of a row. The mean value of $C^2 + C_t^2$ is [190, misprinted 189]. The fluctuation of the fringe row [row of 8 'means'] is $C^2/6 + \alpha C_t^2$; where α is a coefficient depending on the degree of *identity* prevailing between the fluctuations of the different rows. If we trace the curves formed by the rows, there will appear in them a considerable sameness. However, α must fall short of unity. The value of the fringe fluctuation is 146. Eliminating C_t^2 from the two equations which have been stated, we have

$$C^2 = (\alpha 190 - 146)/(\alpha - (1/6)).$$

It is clear C^2 increases with α. Therefore as α cannot exceed 1, we have for a superior limit of C^2, 44/(5/6) or 53.

"Proceeding similarly with the vertical rows and the vertical fringe, we have

$$C^2 + C_p^2 = 88. \quad C^2/8 + \beta C_p^2 = 46.$$

TABLE 2

Death rates from the Registrar-General's report for 1883, as given by Edgeworth (with minor corrections)
(figures in parentheses are fluctuations)

	Year										Fluctuations	
	1876	1877	1878	1879	1880	1881	1882	1883	*Sums*	*Means*	*FYE*	*Corrected*
Berks	175	172	187	186	181	153	169	166	1,389	173·6	224	224·0
Herts	174	165	185	184	176	166	163	188	1,401	175·1	176	169·2
Bucks	182	171	186	195	179	162	177	183	1,435	179·4	172	171·5
Oxford	179	182	194	183	180	169	167	166	1,420	177·5	162	161·5
Bedford	196	174	203	195	198	171	181	184	1,502	187·8	246	246·9
Cambridge	173	177	190	191	187	165	171	181	1,435	179·4	158	158·0
Sums	1,079	1,041	1,145	1,134	1,101	986	1,028	1,068	8,582	1,073	1,138	1,131·00
Means	179·8	173·5	190·8	189·0	183·5	164·3	171·3	178·0	1,630	178·8	190 (146)	188·50 (141·44)
Fluctuation FYE	124	55	77	50	107	68	73	152	—	88 (46)	—	—
Corrected	123·6	55·2	76·9	48·7	105·8	67·8	73·1	152·5	—	88·97 (40·91)	—	—

"Whence $C^2 = (\beta 88 - 46)/(\beta - (1/8))$. And as β cannot be greater than unity, we have for a superior limit of C^2, $42/(7/8)$ or 48."

This is all Edgeworth said; he gave no more explicit definitions. Even if we accepted C_t^2, C_p^2 and C^2 to be as defined in "Methods of statistics", that is as a "time-fluctuation", a "place-fluctuation" and fluctuation independent of year and place, and as we shall see the matter is not quite so simple, there would remain the question of the meanings of the mysterious α and β. A footnote indicating that *identity* is used in the same sense as in the analysis of Virgilian hexameter apparently does not clear matters up, and were the author not Edgeworth we might suspect an argument *ad hoc* and abandon the question. But let us follow Jevons's admonition that Edgeworth's style is implicit, not obscure, and attempt a more reasoned, if speculative, explanation.

Earlier, Edgeworth had used *identical* to indicate a situation in which the additive effects model $X_{ij} = \mu + \alpha_i + \beta_j$ fit the data perfectly. In the passage just quoted, he clearly meant the coefficient α to be a measure of agreement with this model. This would seem to suggest that we consider the more general two-way classification model with interaction, and see if we can account for Edgeworth's unsubscripted α in terms of it. Let us consider, then, the model $X_{ij} = \mu + \alpha_i + \beta_j + \gamma_{ij} + \varepsilon_{ij}$, with $\Sigma_i \alpha_i = \Sigma_j \beta_j = \Sigma_i \gamma_{ij} = \Sigma_j \gamma_{ij} = 0$, and ε_{ij}'s independent, $E\varepsilon_{ij} = 0$, and $\mathrm{var}(\varepsilon_{ij}) = \sigma^2$. Edgeworth had set $\overline{FL}(R) = C^2 + C_t^2$ and $FL_R = C^2/6 + \alpha C_t^2$, and we may recall that $\overline{FL}(R) = 2(SSE + SSB)/IJ$ and $FL_R = 2SSB/IJ$. Now Edgeworth eschewed unbiased estimators of fluctuations but nonetheless we get a useful view of what $\overline{FL}(R)$ and FL_R *are* estimating if we look at their expected values. Letting $\sigma_B^2 = (J-1)^{-1} \Sigma \beta_j^2$ and $\theta^2 = (IJ)^{-1} \Sigma\Sigma \gamma_{ij}^2$, standard results for expected mean squares give

$$E(FL_R) = ((J-1)/J)(2\sigma^2/I + 2\sigma_B^2), \quad E(\overline{FL}(R)) = ((J-1)/J)(2\sigma^2 + 2\sigma_B^2 + 2\theta^2 J/(J-1)).$$

If we then follow Edgeworth's apparent intention and consider FL_R as an estimate of $2\sigma^2/I + 2\sigma_B^2$ and $\overline{FL}(R)$ as an estimate of $2\sigma^2 + 2\sigma_B^2 + 2\theta^2 J/(J-1)$ (for had he wished unbiased estimators, he would have multiplied by $J/(J-1)$), we are then led by his statements to the identifications $C^2 = 2\sigma^2$, $C_t^2 = 2(\sigma_B^2 + \theta^2 J/(J-1))$, and finally, since $\alpha C_t^2 = 2\sigma_B^2$,

$$\alpha = \sigma_B^2/(\sigma_B^2 + \theta^2 J/(J-1)).$$

Thus Edgeworth's coefficient α is just a measure of interaction, equal to one if there is no interaction ($\theta^2 = 0$), otherwise $\alpha < 1$! Since there is no replication, Edgeworth cannot estimate this coefficient, and goes to the worst case, $\alpha = 1$, for an estimate of an upper bound for $C^2 = 2\sigma^2$. Similarly, $\beta = \sigma_A^2/\{\sigma_A^2 + \theta^2 I/(I-1)\}$, where $\sigma_A^2 = (I-1)^{-1} \Sigma_{i=1}^{I} \alpha_i^2$.

This admittedly speculative reconstruction suggests that Edgeworth had remarkable insight into yet one more aspect of his model—the behaviour of his estimates in the event the model fails to hold and interaction is present. Lacking further details it is impossible to be sure exactly what calculations he had done, and exactly how he interpreted the result. While we may be fairly certain that further calculation of the type we have given lay behind his statements, one aspect of them suggests that his algebraic formulation did not go very far, and that a strong intuition played a role. In our modern notation, the two upper bounds given are just $2SSE/J(I-1)$ and $2SSE/I(J-1)$. Edgeworth evidently did not realize that

$$\overline{FL}(R) - FL_R = \overline{FL}(C) - FL_C = 2SSE/IJ$$

is a mathematical identity, and the approximate nature of his calculations helped to mask the fact that his two upper bounds were essentially the same. This suggests that he had not subjected the model to a detailed algebraic treatment. If he had he might have noticed this identity or perhaps derived a maximum likelihood estimate of the fluctuation he sought. This suspicion is confirmed by a later, similar example in this same article, where $I = J = 7$ and the bounds should agree, and yet due to the roughness of his calculations Edgeworth found the widely differing values 77 and 56!

After presenting this method of estimating C^2, Edgeworth sought confirmation through the use of three alternative ways of determining C^2. These were, first, the method of *collation*, second, a direct method based on additional data for several districts with populations 10,000–15,000 for 1861, and third, the calculation of Lexis's "combinatorial" modulus, based upon a binomial model for deaths. (Edgeworth considered Lexis's method, which purported to give a lower bound for C^2, as capable of confirming but not contradicting his other calculations, writing that "we ought to be disposed towards [Lexis's] *à priori* calculation, as the literary man in 'Punch' to his critic, 'I don't care twopence for your opinion, but if you say something favourable I shall be pleased' ".)

The first of these methods, *collation*, was the more interesting, and amounted to another, more direct, groping toward an estimate based on the residual sum of squares. Taking two columns of his table, for 1876 ($j = 1$) and 1881 ($j = 6$) he calculated the residual sum of squares from the additive effects model for this reduced table, divided by the number of rows,

$$I^{-1}\sum_{i=1}^{I}(X_{i6}-X_{i1}-(X_{.6}-X_{.1}))^2.$$

He then repeats this calculation comparing column 6 with each of five others and averaged the results. He also performed a similar operation with pairs of rows, to get yet another value for C^2. His article ended by showing how his results could be used to evaluate the significance of differences in death rates for different occupations.

Edgeworth's work on two-way classifications contained surprising insights for the time. He presented a method of calculation from which an analysis of variance table could today be easily extracted, he gave a way of separately measuring row and column effects that is equivalent to the appropriate F statistics, he considered subtle types of correlation as alternative models to account for large or small values of the F statistics, he gave estimates of error variation based on the error or residual sum of squares, and he showed an appreciation of the effect of interaction upon these estimates. He did not give a full algebraic development of the model, and he did not present a distribution theory for his novel measures. But in nearly every case that an interesting effect was noticed, or an important estimate presented, he did make attempts to assess the significance of the effect or reliability of the estimate, usually by pairwise comparisons or calculations of a "modulus".

This work of Edgeworth's had little direct impact upon subsequent investigators. He himself referred to the article often, but he did not publish further examples of those calculations (although he mentioned having done them). His implicit style and the amount of tedious arithmetic involved certainly helped dissuade others from understanding or adopting his methods, but the primary reason for the lack of impact seems to be that Edgeworth's development of the methods and his exploration of their potential were insufficient to overcome the inherent resistance to their use in social science. The commonly heard assent to the usefulness of probability in the social sciences was little more than lip service; as we have earlier noted (and shall elaborate upon in Section 6), a broad basis of empirical confirmation of this usefulness at a very rudimentary level would be needed before the more refined methods would achieve acceptance. Edgeworth's other work, the "Methods of statistics" and his work on banking and index numbers in particular, began to develop this basis. But adoption of his analyses of qualitative classifications would not be possible until the simpler methods of comparison had proved their worth through much more extensive experience than Edgeworth was to provide; acceptance of the techniques would have to await Fisher's rediscovery and more elegant and complete development of these techniques.

6. CONCLUSION

Edgeworth's influence, his impact upon his contemporaries and the development of statistics, was like his writing: subtle and profound. The subtlety of his work and the difficult and diffuse manner in which he presented it have prevented both Edgeworth's contemporaries and posterity from pointing with assurance at his most significant accomplishments.

Edgeworth was never elected to the Royal Society, and a letter concerned with that failure highlights the problems faced in evaluating his work. Galton was greatly impressed with Edgeworth's work and sought on at least three occasions, with the assistance of John Venn and others, to gain election to the Royal Society for Edgeworth. On November 27th, 1889, Galton wrote to Venn: "I am anxious to put up F. Y. Edgeworth's name for the Roy. Soc. I have long had a very high opinion of his work." Another try was made in 1894, and another in 1896. On this latter occasion Weldon agreed to join in supporting Edgeworth, writing to Galton on January 5th, 1896 that "I shall, of course, be glad to sign Edgeworth's certificate; but I hope he will not prevent Pearson's election. It seems to me that both men should already be fellows!" Pearson was elected that year, but Edgeworth was not. On April 26th, 1896, Venn wrote to Galton, apparently in response to the news of the election,

> "I am sorry to hear what you say about Edgeworth, but I think your remarks exactly hit the point. I have a very high opinion of the aggregate of his contributions to the Theory of Statistics, and have felt the help of his work in a number of directions; but it is difficult to point to any single essay of his which, like K. Pearson's, is decisive at once in the way of power and originality. I feel strongly that Edgeworth ought to be on the R.S., and I can't but think that if I had a vote it would go for him, but the more I think about it the more difficult I feel it to say anything quite *definite* which ought to decide others in his favour."

Venn's difficulty in articulating Edgeworth's contributions has been shared by many later commentators, and Edgeworth is best known to today's statisticians as a shadowy eminence, an economist who expanded frequency distributions in series and may have anticipated Fisher on maximum likelihood, but who was nonetheless totally overshadowed by Karl Pearson. And yet, after a close examination of Edgeworth's work and its context, I would argue that he should rank with Galton and Karl Pearson as among the most profoundly influential figures in our field in the century between Laplace and Fisher.

Edgeworth's influence was great both in the application and the theory of statistics. He played a key role in the past two centuries' progress toward the application of probability and statistics to the quantification of uncertainty in social and economic science. It may be hard to believe that workers before Edgeworth did not use the theory of errors to assess the significance of differences between means calculated from social data, but there is more than ample testimony to this fact in early volumes of this *Journal*, and in other statistical journals and books of the mid-nineteenth century. Quetelet, Galton and Lexis all used probability in their work, but it played a primarily descriptive role. They and many others fit normal and binomial distributions to social data, and they used these fits to draw qualitative conclusions about the homogeneity of these data. But they did not take the conceptual step Edgeworth took that was required to apply probability to the choice and comparison of means of social data.

Cournot, Quetelet and Jevons wrote excellent, even brilliant books on the use of probability in scientific inference. All three argued that social science needed probability, that no other mathematical tool could make social science a science. Yet even these far-sighted geniuses could not bring themselves to action on this pronouncement. All three discussed the variability of means and gave methods of estimating this variability, yet all three only used astronomical, geodetic or meteorological data as examples of the usefulness of this technique.

The successful application of probability to social data required two conceptually difficult and perhaps even contradictory steps. First, agreement had to be made to group as homogeneous a large mass of data, to forget individual labels and treat groups of births, prices, marriages or bankruptcies as alike and subject to the same causes. Second, agreement had to be made to separate the data into fine enough subclassifications so that the grouping done would provide meaningful conclusions, leading to testable hypotheses and results that could be checked under other sets of conditions. Both steps were easily made with astronomical data, where, for example, observations of a given comet were naturally grouped together and future sightings permitted verifiability of conclusions. But with social data these concepts were slow to develop.

By the 1880's the first step had been largely accomplished, in the works of Quetelet, Galton and Jevons. A passage Jevons wrote in 1869, defending himself against charges that he was wrong in grouping prices of different commodities together in his analysis of the variation in the value of gold, may be taken as an announcement of this:

> "Not a few able writers . . . are accustomed to throw doubt upon all such conclusions, by remarking that until we have allowed for all the particular causes which may have elevated or depressed the price of each commodity we cannot be sure that gold is affected. Were a complete explanation of each fluctuation thus necessary, not only would inquiry into this subject be hopeless, but the whole of the statistical and social sciences, so far as they depend upon numerical facts, would have to be abandoned" (Jevons, 1869).

The second step took longer. Galton's regression and Lexis's measures of dispersion may be taken as advances in this direction, as early quantitative techniques for discovering if a collection of data previously considered homogeneous could be properly and profitably divided into subclasses. But the early use of these techniques was descriptive and qualitative, notwithstanding their probabilistic origin. It remained for Edgeworth and later workers to develop these methods, to produce tests of significance and of appropriateness of assumptions, and to develop a mathematical methodology for "disentangling moduli" and evaluating deviations in complex situations, allowing the statistical significance of differences to be judged.

Edgeworth's success in this was only partial. He invented and preconized a methodology to handle the problems he faced, but he did not create a sudden revolution in the analysis of economic data. Rather the general acceptance of the methods he espoused was almost glacially slow. The full adoption of the quantitative machinery of mathematical statistics to the analysis of social and economic data would require an extensive and extended empirical base, a variety of examples and applications that could not be gathered in a short time, and Edgeworth lacked the evangelical zeal that Karl Pearson was later to bring to the building of a similar empirical base for biometry. But Edgeworth did make a beginning.

Edgeworth lectured widely, and his work was widely recognized outside of England and often cited. He had repeated, almost heated, exchanges in print in the 1890's with von Bortkiewicz which, while not successful in converting von Bortkiewicz to Edgeworth's non-Lexian approach, had an influence upon the direction of von Bortkiewicz's development of Lexis's dispersion theory (Edgeworth, 1896a, b; von Bortkiewicz, 1895, 1896). Edgeworth visited the United States in 1902, perhaps the first European mathematical statistician to do so, and gave several lectures. His interaction with Irving Fisher on this and other occasions must have played a role in influencing Fisher's approach to economic data and his work with index numbers (Fisher, 1956, pp. 92–94).

In England, Edgeworth's impact upon the application of statistics to economic data was felt both generally, as through Bowley's work on wage statistics and his text *Elements of Statistics* (1901), and more specifically through the adoption and spread of the statistically motivated index numbers that followed his British Association Committee report.

Edgeworth's impact upon the theory of statistics has also not received due recognition. His development of a mathematical approach to the theory of estimation, his investigations (well before Karl Pearson) of general families of symmetric and asymmetric probability distributions, his attempts in 1892 at a mathematical analysis of multiple correlation surfaces, his statistical tests of fit in 1887 (including one equivalent to χ^2 in a simple case), his advocacy and extension of the asymptotic methods of Laplace, and his defence, development and application of inverse probability as an approach to inference: all of these had, I would argue, an immediate, long-lasting and profound effect upon the development of our field. Works such as Edgeworth's analysis of two-way classifications and his proof of the efficiency of maximum likelihood estimators may not have been appreciated at the time, but they were so intimately connected with other work of his that was appreciated that it would be incorrect to speak of rediscoveries 25–50 years later as truly independent of Edgeworth, even where the rediscoverer (R. A. Fisher) may not have read the particular works in question. Edgeworth's influence on the modern theory of statistics was perhaps most deeply felt through his direct effect upon the direction and approach of Karl Pearson's mathematical work in statistical theory. A full and balanced discussion of the intellectual relationships between these statistical pioneers and their contemporaries in England, on the continent and in America must, however, be deferred to another place.

In most historical accounts of the development of statistics, Edgeworth has remained in the background. In this respect his position is similar to that of an ancestor of his, the Abbé Edgeworth, in another revolution, the French. The Abbé Edgeworth (his grandfather's cousin) had been on the scaffold at the beheading of Louis XVI, as father confessor (C. S. Edgeworth, 1815; Woodgate, 1945). Francis Edgeworth also oversaw the final break with the past in what has been called the modern revolution in statistics, but unlike the Abbé, Francis Edgeworth played a vital role in producing that revolution.

In March of 1925 Edgeworth forwarded to his closest relatives a set of his three-volume *Papers Relating to Political Economy* which had been published that year by the Royal Economic Society. In a separate letter he wrote: "I trust that the Statistical Society, following the handsome precedent set by the Economic Society, will in due time republish the numerous papers which I have contributed to the Journal during a period of forty years." Perhaps, with over half a century's perspective on the work of this remarkable man, "due time" has come.

ACKNOWLEDGEMENTS

The research was completed while I was a Fellow of the John Simon Guggenheim Memorial Foundation. I would also like to acknowledge the assistance I have received from many librarians and archivists at Bedford College, London, University College London, Nuffield College, Oxford, All Souls College, Oxford, the Galton Laboratories, and the University of Durham, and from Professor David Butler of Nuffield College. I am grateful to William Kruskal, Frederick Mosteller, John Pratt and George Stigler for their comments on an early draft.

BIBLIOGRAPHICAL NOTE

All accounts of Edgeworth's life begin with Keynes's excellent essay (Keynes, 1933), and most end there. Other valuable sources include Bonar (1926), Price (1926), Bowley (1934) and Kendall (1967). Another recent account is Hildreth (1968). The present article has drawn upon letters and papers in the possession of Professor David E. Butler of Nuffield College, in the Nuffield College Library, in the Galton Archive at University College London, and at the Galton Laboratories. In 1928 the Royal Statistical Society published a synopsis of Edgeworth's work in statistics by Arthur L. Bowley (Bowley, 1928). This volume (recently reprinted) can be a useful guide to parts of Edgeworth's work, and should be consulted by any serious student of Edgeworth, but it should not be taken as an adequate substitute for reading Edgeworth's original papers. It contains inaccuracies and omissions, and additions to or changes in Edgeworth's analyses are neither always announced nor always warranted. The union of Bowley's bibliography and Edgeworth (1925) includes most of Edgeworth's articles. In addition, Edgeworth published nearly 200 book reviews in the *Economic Journal*, *The Academy*, *Journal of the Royal Statistical Society*, *Nature*, *Mind* and the *Journal of Education*, over 130 articles in Palgrave's *Dictionary of Political Economy*, and three short biographies in the *Dictionary of National Biography* (Thomas Baker, Richard Balam, Thomas Baxter).

Apparently no bibliography has ever been published of these minor pieces that approaches completeness. Edgeworth's work in economics has been commented on frequently, although G. J. Stigler (1941, Chapter 5) has not been superseded. G. J. Stigler (1965) also discusses Edgeworth's work in several essays.

References

BONAR, J. (1926). Memories of F. Y. Edgeworth. *Economic Journal*, **36**, 647–653.

BORTKIEWICZ, L. VON (1895). Kritische Betrachtungen zur theoretischen Statistik, II. *Jahrbücher für Nationalökonomie und Statistik* (Third Series), **10**, 321–360.

—— (1896). Kritische Betrachtungen zur theoretischen Statistik, III. *Jahrbücher für Nationalökonomie und Statistik*. (Third Series), **11**, 671–705.

BOWLEY, A. L. (1901). *Elements of Statistics*. London: P. S. King.

—— (1928). *F. Y. Edgeworth's Contributions to Mathematical Statistics*. London: Royal Statistical Society. (Reprinted 1972 by Augustus M. Kelley, Clifton, N.J.)

—— (1934). Francis Ysidro Edgeworth. *Econometrica*, **2**, 113–124.

CROFTON, M. W. (1885). Probability. *Encyclopaedia Britannica* (9th ed.).

DORMOY, E. (1874). Théorie mathématique des assurances sur la vie. *Journal des Actuaires Français*, **3**, 283–299, 432–461. (Reprinted in Dormoy (1878), pp. 1–47.)

—— (1878). *Théorie mathématique des assurances sur la vie*, Tome 1. Paris: Gauthier-Villars.

EDGEWORTH, C. SNEYD (1815). *Memoirs of the Abbé Edgeworth; containing his narrative of the last hours of Louis XVI*. London: Rowland Hunter.

EDGEWORTH, F. Y. (1877). *New and Old Methods of Ethics, or "Physical Ethics" and "Methods of Ethics."* London: James Parker.

—— (1881). *Mathematical Psychics: An Essay on the Application of Mathematics to the Moral Sciences*. London: C. Kegan Paul. (Reprinted 1967 by Augustus M. Kelley, New York.)

—— (1883a). The law of error. *Philosophical Magazine* (Fifth Series), **16**, 300–309.

—— (1883b). The method of least squares. *Philosophical Magazine* (Fifth Series), **16**, 360–375.

—— (1883c). On the method of ascertaining a change in the value of gold. *J. Roy. Statist. Soc.*, **46**, 714–718.

—— (1884). Review of *Investigations in Currency and Finance*, by W. S. Jevons. *Academy*, July 19th, 1884, 38–39.

—— (1885a). Observations and statistics. An essay on the theory of errors of observation and the first principles of statistics. *Transactions of the Cambridge Philosophical Society*, **14**, 138–169. (Abstract in *Proc. Camb. Phil. Soc.*, **5**, 310–312; corrigendum in *Proc. Camb. Phil. Soc.*, **6**, 101–102.)

—— (1885b). Methods of statistics. *Jubilee Volume of the Statistical Society*, 181–217.

—— (1885c). On methods of ascertaining variations in the rate of births, deaths and marriages. *J. Roy. Statist. Soc.*, **48**, 628–649. (Abstract in *Report* of the B.A.A.S. for 1885, 1165–1166.)

—— (1885d). Calculus of probabilities applied to psychical research, I. *Proc. Soc. Psych. Res.*, **3**, 190–208.

—— (1886a). Progressive means. *J. Roy. Statist. Soc.*, **49**, 469–475.

—— (1886b). The law of error and the elimination of chance. *Philosophical Magazine* (Fifth Series), **21**, 308–324.

—— (1886c). Problems in probabilities. *Philosophical Magazine* (Fifth Series), **22**, 371–384.

—— (1887a). The empirical proof of the law of error. *Philosophical Magazine* (Fifth Series), **24**, 330–342.

—— (1887b). On observations relating to several quantities. *Hermathena*, **6**, 279–285.

—— (1887c). *Metretike: or the Method of Measuring Probability and Utility*. London: Temple.

—— (1888a). The mathematical theory of banking. *J. Roy. Statist. Soc.*, **51**, 113–127. (Abstract in *Report* of the B.A.A.S. for 1886, 776–778.)

—— (1888b). The value of authority tested by experiment. *Mind*, **13**, 146–148.

—— (1888c). The statistics of examinations. *J. Roy. Statist. Soc.*, **51**, 599–635. (Abstract in *Report* of the B.A.A.S. for 1888, 763.)

—— (1888d). Some new methods of measuring variation in general price. *J. Roy. Statist. Soc.*, **51**, 346–368.

—— (1889). Review of *Natural Inheritance*, by F. Galton. *Nature*, **39**, 603–604.

—— (1890). The element of chance in competitive examinations. *J. Roy. Statist. Soc.*, **53**, 460–475, 644–663. (Abstract in *Report* of the B.A.A.S. for 1890, 920.)

—— (1892a). Correlated averages. *Philosophical Magazine* (Fifth Series), **34**, 190–204.

—— (1892b). The law of error and correlated averages. *Philosophical Magazine* (Fifth Series), **34**, 429–438, 518–526.

—— (1896a). Bemerkungen über die Kritik meiner "Methoden der Statistik" von Dr. v. Bortkewitsch. *Jahrbücher für Nationalökonomie und Statistik* (Third Series), **11**, 274–277.

—— (1896b). Eine Erwiderung. *Jahrbücher für Nationalökonomie und Statistik* (Third Series), **12**, 838–845.

—— (1898). Miscellaneous applications of the calculus of probabilities, contd. *J. Roy. Statist. Soc.*, **61**, 119–131.

—— (1905). The law of error. *Trans. Camb. Phil. Soc.*, **20**, 36–65, 113–141.

EDGEWORTH, F. Y. (1908–1909). On the probable errors of frequency-constants. *J. Roy. Statist. Soc.*, **71**, 381–397, 499–512, 651–678; **72**, 81–90.
—— (1909). On the application of the calculus of probabilities to statistics. *Bull. de l'Inst. Intern. de Stat.*, **18**, 505–537.
—— (1925). *Papers Relating to Political Economy* (3 vol.). London: Royal Economic Society.
FISHER, IRVING N. (1956). *My Father, Irving Fisher.* New York: Comet Press.
GROVE, W. R. (1865). *The Correlation of Physical Forces* (4th ed.). As reprinted in *The Correlation and Conservation of Forces* (E. L. Youmans, ed.). New York: D. Appleton & Co.
HILDRETH, C. (1968). Francis Ysidro Edgeworth. In *International Encyclopaedia of the Social Sciences* (David L. Sills, ed.). Macmillan and Free Press.
JEVONS, W. STANLEY (1865). The variation of prices and the value of the currency since 1782. *J. Roy. Statist. Soc.*, **28**, 294–320. (Reprinted in Jevons, 1884.)
—— (1868). On the condition of the metallic currency of the united kingdom, with reference to the question of international coinage. *J. Roy Statist. Soc.*, **31**, 426–464.
—— (1869). The depreciation of gold. *J. Roy. Statist. Soc.*, **32**, 445–449. (Reprinted in Jevons, 1884.)
—— (1874). *The Principles of Science: A Treatise on Logic and Scientific Method.* London: Macmillan. (Second edition (1877) reprinted in 1958 by Dover Publications, New York.)
—— (1881). Review of *Mathematical Psychics*, by F. Y. Edgeworth. *Mind*, **6**, 581–583.
—— (1884). *Investigations in Currency and Finance.* London: Macmillan. (Reprinted in 1964 by Augustus M. Kelley, Clifton, N.J. A second, differently paged edition published in London in 1909.)
KENDALL, M. G. (1968). Francis Ysidro Edgeworth, 1845–1926. *Biometrika*, **55**, 269–275. (Reprinted in Pearson and Kendall, 1970.)
KENDALL, M. G. and PLACKETT, R. L. (1977). *Studies in the History of Statistics and Probability*, Vol. 2. London: Griffin.
KEYNES, JOHN MAYNARD (1933). F. Y. Edgeworth. In *Essays in Biography*. New York: Harcourt, Brace & Co. (Frequently reprinted; originally published in the *Economic Journal* (1926), **36**, 140–153.)
LEXIS, W. (1876). Das Geschlechtsverhältnis der Geborenen und die Wahrscheinlichkeitsrechnung. *Jahrbücher für Nationalökonomie und Statistik*, **27**, 209–245.
—— (1879). Ueber die Theorie der Stabilität statistischer Reihen. *Jahrbücher für Nationalökonomie und Statistik*, **32**, 60–98.
MARSHALL, ALFRED (1881). Review of *Mathematical Psychics*, by F. Y. Edgeworth. *Academy*, June 18th, 1881, 457.
PEARSON, E. S. (1965). Some incidents in the early history of biometry and statistics 1890–94. *Biometrika*, **52**, 3–18. (Reprinted in Pearson and Kendall, 1970.)
—— (1967). Some reflexions on continuity in the development of mathematical statistics, 1885–1920. *Biometrika*, **54**, 341–355. (Reprinted in Pearson and Kendall, 1970.)
PEARSON, E. S. and KENDALL, M. G. (eds) (1970). *Studies in the History of Statistics and Probability*. London: Charles Griffin.
PEARSON, KARL (1920). Notes on the history of correlation. *Biometrika*, **13**, 25–45. (Reprinted in Pearson and Kendall 1970.)
PEIRCE, CHARLES S. (1890). Review of *Pure Logic, and Other Minor Works* by W. Stanley Jevons. *The Nation*, **51**, No. 1305, p. 16.
PRATT, JOHN W. (1976). F. Y. Edgeworth and R. A. Fisher on the efficiency of maximum likelihood estimation. *Annals of Statistics*, **4**, 501–514.
PRICE, L. L. (1926). Francis Ysidro Edgeworth. *J. Roy. Statist. Soc.*, **89**, 371–377.
STIGLER, GEORGE J. (1941). *Production and Distribution Theories: The Formative Period.* New York: Macmillan. (Reprinted 1968 by Agathon Press.)
—— (1965). *Essays in the History of Economics.* Chicago: University of Chicago Press.
STIGLER, S. M. (1973a). Laplace, Fisher, and the discovery of the concept of sufficiency. *Biometrika*, **60**, 439–445. (Reprinted in Kendall and Plackett, 1977.)
—— (1973b). Simon Newcomb, Percy Daniell, and the history of robust estimation 1885–1920. *J. Amer. Statist. Assoc.*, **68**, 872–879. (Reprinted in Kendall and Plackett, 1977.)
—— (1977). Eight centuries of sampling inspection: the trial of the Pyx. *J. Amer. Statist. Assoc.*, **72**, 493–500.
WELCH, B. L. (1958). "Student" and small sample theory. *J. Amer. Statist. Assoc.*, **53**, 777–788.
WOODGATE, M. V. (1945). *The Abbé Edgeworth (1745–1807).* Dublin: Browne and Nolan.

[11]

History of Political Economy 12:2

Some recent interpretations of *Mathematical Psychics*

John Creedy, University of Durham, England

> I trust that I shall not suffer like the plaintiff in the old state of the English law who lost his case because in describing an article which had been stolen from him he spoke of a "ham" where he should have used the words "part of a ham."
>
> —*F. Y. Edgeworth*[1]

I. *Introduction*

The above quotation comes from Edgeworth's introduction to the reprint of part of his paper "The Determinateness of Equilibrium."[2] It is therefore rather ironic that the conventional interpretation of *Mathematical Psychics* has recently been questioned by a number of writers. For example Walker (1973, p. 139) asserts that "the indefiniteness of Edgeworth's early thought allowed him to entertain simultaneously two different notions of the equilibrating mechanism of a competitive market" and that "at no point . . . did he describe recontracting in the way that is now thought to characterise his work" (p. 147). Furthermore Tarascio (1972, p. 193) has argued that the diagram used by Edgeworth (1881, p. 28) "has nothing in common with the conventional Box used today." He goes so far as to suggest (p. 193) that "a geometrical manipulation of Edgeworth's diagram . . . results in a box diagram which is nonsensical in terms of the conventional box diagram." Tarascio's suggestion has been followed in papers by Jaffé (1974) and Weatherby (1976).[3] The acceptance of these assertions would mean that Edgeworth would have to be regarded as rather confused and inconsistent, merely suggesting a few 'lines of inquiry,'

1. *Papers* (1925), 2:314. For further discussion of Edgeworth's contribution to the theory of exchange and competition, see Creedy 1978.

2. He continued, "At any rate before condemnation is passed, reference should be made to the writer's essay on *Mathematical Psychics*." Unfortunately this plea has not always been heard sympathetically. Edgeworth was at one time a barrister-at-law!

3. The first two papers are very similar, though Jaffé (p. 343 n.3) mentions Tarascio only in a footnote.

rather than as a highly original theorist who developed some of the most basic results of modern microeconomics.[4]

The purpose of this article is, then, to examine these interpretations of what Stigler (p. 246) has called "probably the most elusively written book of importance in the history of economics." Section II below considers the arguments of Walker, while Section III considers those of Jaffé et al. First, it is perhaps useful to very briefly summarise the conventional interpretation of Edgeworth's contribution.

The models of exchange available before *Mathematical Psychics* were explicit in their assumption that all individuals took prices as 'given' (that is, parametric). Individuals were assumed to be unable to affect the rate of exchange at which their own transactions were conducted.[5] The equilibrium rate of exchange which would eliminate all excess demand and supply was then obtained as the solution to a set of simultaneous equations (using a given initial distribution of resources and preferences)—and no genuine 'competition' between individual buyers or sellers was necessary. Walras used his well-known *tâtonnement* process, and Jevons openly stated that he was unable to say anything about the process by which an equilibrium might actually be achieved.

Edgeworth then presented his *recontracting* model whereby buyers and sellers freely communicate with each other within the context of what is now called a cooperative game. The making and breaking of *provisional* contracts provides a free flow of information within the market; and if the number of competitors is sufficiently large the solution of such a game exactly corresponds to the Walrasian equilibrium. Again, the order in which the provisional contracts are made cannot be determined, although this does not affect the final solution. A major contribution of Edgeworth's model was that it explicitly introduced the role of *numbers* into the analysis of competition, showing that where there are few competitors the solution is indeterminate and depends on "the objectionable arts of higgling." It is now well known that these more subtle parts of *Mathematical Psychics* were long neglected until the important paper by Shubik (1959), which revealed the precise relationship between game theory and Edgeworth's model.

4. See Samuelson, p. 1277 n.19, and Schumpeter, p. 831, for panegyrics. Walker (p. 139 n.1) does not actually mention the main results, but suggests that the later game-theory interpretations are wrong. Very clear expositions of recent results can be found in Hildebrand and Kirman 1976 and Bacharach 1976.

5. Menger, in the *Grundsätze*, paid much more attention to factors like quality differences, imperfect information, etc., which would prevent equalisation of the rate of exchange. Edgeworth does not refer to Menger in 1881.

II. *The Interpretations of Walker*

It is this conventional view of Edgeworth that Walker challenges. First, it is argued that Edgeworth was inconsistent in his view that the uniformity of prices was the *result* of his model, rather than an initial assumption. Secondly, Walker argues that Edgeworth was inconsistent in his assumption that contracts are provisional.

Uniformity of prices

Walker first claims that the current interpretation of Edgeworth "has been made possible" because "his literary style was elusive, and his early thought on price formation was incomplete" (Walker, p. 139).[6] Walker suggests (p. 140) that Edgeworth simultaneously held two views about competition, and "writing in the Walrasian vein . . . neglected recontract." As evidence of this assertion Walker then quotes Edgeworth 1881, p. 30, as saying, "you might suppose each dealer to write down his *demand*, . . . these data having been furnished to a sort of market-machine, the *price* to be passionlessly evaluated." It is perfectly clear, however, that Edgeworth was simply contrasting this kind of *deus ex machina* with his own approach, involving as it did the "objectionable arts of higgling" (1881, p. 30). Indeed, just before the part quoted by Walker he says explicitly, "with this procedure . . . (that is, barter) . . . is contrasted the smooth machinery of the open market." He says quite clearly that the model involving recontract is an improvement over Walras' model, especially in showing how the result of his procedure is equivalent to one in which all agents are 'price takers' only in the special case of perfect competition.[7] Thus, "the advantage of this general method is that it is applicable to the particular case of imperfect competition; where the conceptions of *demand and supply at a price* are no longer appropriate."

Walker (p. 140) then states that "when Edgeworth formally set out the properties of a perfectly competitive market, he introduced the equality of desired market demand and supply as a *postulate*, as an as-

6. There is, of course, no doubt that his style was elusive and his mathematics clumsy, but Walker (p. 139 n.2) also repeats the suggestion made by Stigler that Edgeworth did not, "tarry long at one point." But Edgeworth often had his papers privately reprinted with additional sections, and regularly quoted from his own work. As Bowley notes (1928, p. 3), "Each time a problem was attacked afresh there were references to the results of former work, just as an Act of Parliament is to be interpreted by reference." Presumably to suggest a lack of clarity, Walker (p. 142 n.1) notes that Edgeworth used the words *articles of contract* in two different senses, but he fails to point out that Edgeworth consistently used italics for the meaning given in 1881, p. 28.

7. The quotation reproduced in Walker (p. 143) from Edgeworth 1925, 2:311, and meant to show a change in Edgeworth's thought, is simply a repetition of the same point made in 1881.

sumed condition of a market model, not as a derivative consequence of recontract." To refute this suggestion it is only necessary to quote Edgeworth 1925, 2:311: "The proposition that there is only one price in a perfect market may be regarded as *deducible* from the more axiomatic principle of recontract (*Mathematical Psychics*, p. 40 and context)."[8] The importance of this result is that in large markets the recontracting process—where individuals obtain information through free communication—leads to the same unique rate of exchange as in a system where prices are parametric and individuals make choices without reference to others (though the equilibrium price has to be set by an omniscient *intellectus angelicus*).[9]

The nature of recontract

A further part of Walker's argument concerns the meaning of recontract. He suggests that Edgeworth assumed that exchange takes place at the formation of each coalition or contract.[10] In support of this he quotes Edgeworth as saying, "a landlord, on expiry of lease recontracts, it may be, with a new tenant" (Walker, p. 142: Edgeworth 1881, p. 17). It is, however, surprising that he does not quote the preceding part of the paragraph: "It is . . . *Pax* or *pact* between contractors during contract, *war*, when some of the contractors *without the consent of others recontract*. Thus an auctioneer having been in contract with the last bidder (to sell at such a price *if* no higher bid) *recontracts* with higher bidder." While the statement about landlords is not very clear, there is no doubt about this earlier part. The phrases "*if* no higher bid" and "*without the consent of others*" can only mean that no actual exchange takes place. Thus the process of recontract involves no wealth changes until the *final settlement* (defined in 1881, p. 19) is reached. Edgeworth (1881, p. 19) also adds, "any individual is free to *recontract* with another independently of, *without the consent being required of*, any third party." There would be no need to add the condition about consent if actual exchange were assumed to take

8. This was a note added in 1925, which refers to his original presentation. Also, in 1925, 2:453, Edgeworth repeated, "The existence of a uniform rate-of-exchange . . . is perhaps not so much axiomatic as deducible from the process of competition in a perfect market."

9. See also Edgeworth 1881, p. 31 n.1. He explicitly stated that his model qualified the results of Walras and Jevons: "It must be carefully remembered that Prof. Jevons' formulae of exchange apply not to isolated individuals . . . but . . . to individuals clothed with the properties of a market." There are no grounds for Walker's statement, "what is the associated equilibrium price? Edgeworth was unclear on this matter" (Walker, p. 141). See Section III, "The indifference map," below. Walker's comments at the bottom of page 141 are also not substantiated.

10. Walker says (p. 142), "they last until the end of the contract period, and he continues to talk about market days. This is considered further below.

place. Later (1881, p. 35) he adds, "it will generally be in the interest of the X of one couple and the Y of the other to rush together, leaving their partners in the lurch." Again this clearly shows that the coalition was only a provisional and conditional contract.[11] Furthermore it is difficult to see how a close reading of pp. 35–49 of Edgeworth 1881 could suggest that he had not fully worked through his recontract process.[12]

It is also worth noting that Edgeworth 1881 nowhere talks about 'market days,' whereas Walker confuses the discussion by the introduction of such 'days.' As Weintraub (p. 16) has pointed out, "the core . . . seems to embody a process dynamic . . . *there is not, however, any notion of time involved in this process*."

Walker (p. 133) then attempts to show that in his later work Edgeworth used a "competitive recontract model, introducing disequilibrium transactions into the model." On the basis of his earlier argument that Edgeworth in 1881 was inconsistent and incomplete, Walker is then able to discount all later references by Edgeworth to his earlier work.[13] Walker's argument mainly rests, however, on a quotation selected from Edgeworth 1925, 1:40, which mentions two cases; one where "intending buyers and sellers . . . remain in communication without actually making exchanges," and the second where "hirings are made" (Edgeworth here is explicitly considering a labour market without unions), but "the parties encounter each other the following day, with dispositions the same as on the first day,—like combatants *armis animisque refecti?*" Walker argues (p. 145) that the second case is a non-*tâtonnement* process which Edgeworth used, "once he had a clear view of recontracting."

It is, however, perfectly clear that these two cases are *formally equivalent*. Furthermore Walker fails to note the very important sentence which states that "two kinds of higgling may be distinguished as appropriate respectively to short and long periods" (*Papers*, 1:40). The

11. Again in Edgeworth 1925, 2:313: "The dispositions and circumstances of the parties are assumed to remain throughout constant. But it is supposed that agreements are renewed or varied many times." Stigler (p. 247 n.25) also refers to "recontract, the institution which allows tentative contracts to be broken without penalty."

12. On first stating the main results Edgeworth (1881, p. 20) says, "*Conclusions* rather, the mathematical demonstration of which is not fully exhibited." Later (p. 35) when considering replication, he says, "for the sake of illustration (not of the argument)"; and more significantly, on page 38: "If this reasoning does not seem satisfactory, it would be possible to give a more formal proof; bringing out the important result that the common tangent to both indifference curves at the point $\zeta\eta$ is the vector from the origin." These comments seem to indicate that his statements were much more than 'conjectures,' the term used by later game theorists.

13. For example, Walker (p. 145) says: "It can be seen . . . that he had come to want the competitive recontracting process . . . to be interpreted as a non-*tâtonnement* process." In Edgeworth 1925, 1:36, a new footnote is added to the paper on distribution, which repeats the argument of 1881.

reference to short and long periods is crucial here, and of course was written after the introduction of these concepts by Marshall. It is also the first time that Edgeworth uses the parable of market days to explain the process. It can therefore be argued that far from changing his views about recontract, Edgeworth was simply trying to show that his model may be of more than academic interest; that it could be applied to certain kinds of contracts—in this case labour contracts on a 'daily' or 'short term' hire[14]—where the 'exchange' does not really involve a *permanent* redistribution of wealth (the labourer has the same amount of labour to offer the next day and has gained information from his earlier contract).

III. *The Interpretation of Jaffé et al.*

The Box Diagram

Tarascio, Jaffé, and Weatherby all point out that Pareto first published the Edgeworth Box Diagram in its familiar form,[15] but this can surely be no surprise. Indeed, Blaug (p. 311) merely states, "Instead of the now conventional box diagram introduced by Pareto . . . Edgeworth turns the axis around." Pareto's debt to Edgeworth has, however, long been recognised. Thus Pantaleoni (p. 548) notes, "Pareto . . . elaborated a system of general economic equilibrium . . . with materials only partially his own, . . . he would not have been what he has been without the author of *Mathematical Psychics* and the author of *Mathematical Investigations into the Theory of Value and Prices*."[16]

The suggestion, noted above, that Edgeworth's diagram bears no relation to the conventional Box Diagram is, however, more serious. The argument rests on the proposition that Edgeworth did not specify the initial endowments. Jaffé (p. 344) thus says, "Edgeworth's contract curve diagram could only be converted into a box diagram of specific dimensions if the initial endowments, which Edgeworth deliberately chose to leave implicit, were explicitly specified."

Although Edgeworth did not write the length of each axis in the dia-

14. Similarly, this may be applied to the case where goods are perishable within the day, but are 'cropped' daily in regular amounts. In his paper on distribution Edgeworth often talked of hiring a daily mountain guide. Again in 1925, 3:453, he mentions situations "continuously repeated under analogous conditions."

15. Rather than Bowley (1924), who anyway acknowledged Pareto and claimed no originality. Weatherby (1976) actually suggests that the box was attributed to Edgeworth because of Marshall's discussion in his appendix on barter (Marshall, 1:844), and the controversy, first reported at length in 2:790–98!

16. Pantaleoni, a great friend and correspondent of Pareto, also noted (p. 585): "In economics this work, I submit, consisted in bringing to a great perfection a machine which was to a very large extent already built up." See also Shackle 1967.

gram (1881, p. 28)—for reasons discussed below—he was nevertheless quite explicit about the initial endowments in the text. Thus (1881, p. 20) he states, "let x and y be the portions interchanged, as in Prof. Jevons' example. Then the utility of one party, say X, may be written $\Phi_1(a-x) + \Psi_1(y)$; and the utility of the other party, say Y, $\Phi_2(x) + \Psi_2(b-y)$; where Φ and Ψ are the integrals of Prof. Jevons' symbols ϕ and ψ.[17]

The person X therefore begins with an amount a of his own good (which Edgeworth also denotes by the letter X, for obvious reasons). Similarly person Y has an amount b, of good Y only. This is the initial situation which Edgeworth took from Jevons' consideration of exchange, and which was used consistently throughout *Mathematical Psychics*.

Edgeworth then defined utility P of individual X as $P = F(x,y)$,[18] and although the initial endowments are implicit in the function F, the reason for this presentation is fully discussed in his Appendix V (1881, p. 105). He showed that mathematically there is no point in writing, say, $P = P(a-x, y)$. Edgeworth preferred to write $P = F(x, y)$ because he was primarily interested in deriving a theory of *exchange*, and it makes more sense to have the amounts exchanged as the arguments of the function. The later more pedagogic uses of the Box Diagram are usually concerned with *allocation* between individuals. Edgeworth (1881, p. 105) also defines the demand curve of person X for good Y (in terms of the offer of x of good X). He transforms to polar coordinates $P = p(\rho \cos\theta, \rho \sin\theta)$, where θ is the rate of exchange, and defines the demand curve as $dP/d\rho = 0$. Jaffé (p. 344 n. 4) seems to have missed this point when he quotes Edgeworth as saying, "it is not necessary . . . to specify this initial endowment [a] explicitly." Edgeworth was simply making a mathematical point about the equilibrium condition.

Similar considerations apply equally to the diagram, and once it had been constructed there was no need to write down the length of each axis since Edgeworth was primarily interested in discussing the choice by individuals of quantities *exchanged*. The emphasis on exchange, rather than allocation, also explains why Edgeworth's diagram is rotated by 90° when compared with the conventional textbook figure; with amounts *exchanged* measured along each axis it would be idiosyncratic to place the origin anywhere other than in the southwest corner.[19]

17. On the next page he compares the definition of the contract curve with Jevons' ratio of marginal utilities. All this is clearly understood in Marshall's review; see Whitaker, p. 266.

18. The comma has been added here and below. Edgeworth actually wrote $P = F(xy)$. See also Whitaker, p. 266 n.8.

19. Stigler (p. 105) refers to 'asymmetrical axes,' but the asymmetry only applies to

The indifference map

A further rather surprising argument is that Edgeworth did not actually use a 'system' of indifference curves. Tarascio (p. 194) says, "Nowhere in *Mathematical Psychics* does one find an indifference mapping consisting of more than one curve per individual," and "the first person to use explicitly *a system* of indifference curves for *each* person was Irving Fisher in 1892."[20] Jaffé (p. 358) also states that Edgeworth mentioned "in passing 'an interior indifference curve'. . . in one place, and only in one place, in the *Mathematical Psychics*."[21]

Edgeworth of course did not *draw* a family of indifference curves; indeed he very rarely used diagrams and was much more concerned to emphasise that the results are obtained by the 'mathematical method.' It is, however, clear that the definition of the contract curve implies a 'system' of indifference curves. Thus a point on the contract curve is defined as where "their *lines of indifference* are coincident" (1881, p. 22). Furthermore, "these settlements are represented by an *indefinite number* of points" (p. 29). In Edgeworth's discussion of the introduction of additional traders (1881, pp. 35–38), the 'system' of indifference curves is explicit, both in the mathematics and in the discussion. On page 38 he says, "the common tangent to both indifference curves at the point $\zeta\eta$ is the vector from the origin." But Edgeworth obviously felt that it would be otiose to actually draw these additional curves. This contention of Tarascio and Jaffé is even more surprising considering the statement (1881, p. 40), "let the indifference curves consist of families of concentric circles." Edgeworth's discussion in Appendix V is also relevant; for example, the problem of deriving the offer curve is, he says (p. 113) to "find the locus of the points where lines from the origin *touch* curves of indifference." Similarly, "for all points *above* Q where a *curve of indifference* of B touches the *demand-curve* of A" (p. 116).[22]

the formulation $P = F(x,y)$, not to the diagram. There is no asymmetry from the point of view of *exchange*.

20. Edgeworth's characteristically 'modest' review (1925, 3:39) is of interest here. After discussing Fisher's use of indifference curves he notes: "These conceptions, received by Dr. Fisher from his predecessors, have been greatly improved by him." Fisher's independent 'discovery' is, however, now recognised. Edgeworth was surprised and interested by Fisher's discussion of the integrability problem: "Soaring . . . beyond the furthest heights of his predecessors, . . . he attains . . . a conclusion which seems to us of unexpected value" (1925, 3:40). Pareto also discussed the same problem, of course. Indeed Pantaleoni (p. 584) notes that Pareto's first publication was in the theory of elasticity in solid bodies and "researches concerning the integration of the differential equations determining their equilibrium."

21. Jaffé (p. 351) also suggests, "when such curves are drawn, their intercepts on their respective 'axes of acquisition' acquire a theoretical significance apparently unsuspected by Edgeworth."

22. Also on page 113 Edgeworth refers to "the differential equation of our '*curves of*

IV. *Conclusions*

It is therefore argued, in contradiction to the authors discussed above, that Edgeworth's recontract model was clearly worked out in 1881, that he consistently used the same concept of recontract, and that the current interpretation used in the literature on cooperative games is substantially correct. In 1928 Bowley produced a remarkable survey of Edgeworth's contributions to mathematical statistics. His statement (1928, p. 3) may also be applied to Edgeworth's work on exchange and competition: "The impression obtained is that his work is singularly consistent; the germs of the last analysis are to be found in his earliest papers."

I am very grateful to Professor D. P. O'Brien for encouragement and helpful comments on an earlier draft of this article.

REFERENCES

M. Bacharach. *Economics and the Theory of Games*. New York, 1976.
M. Blaug. *Economic Theory in Retrospect*. London, 1968.
A. L. Bowley. *Mathematical Groundwork in Economics*. Oxford, 1924.
———. *Edgeworth's Contributions to Mathematical Statistics*. London, 1928.
J. Creedy. "Edgeworth's Contribution to the Theory of Exchange." *Scottish Journal of Political Economy*, 1979.
F. Y. Edgeworth. *Mathematical Psychics: An Essay on the Application of Mathematics to the Moral Sciences*. London, 1881.
———. *Papers Relating to Political Economy*, 3 vols. London, 1925.
W. Hildebrand and A. Kirman. *General Equilibrium Analysis*. Amsterdam, 1976.
W. Jaffé. "Edgeworth's Contract Curve: A Propaedeutic Essay in Clarification." *History of Political Economy* 6 (1974).
A. Marshall. *Principles of Economics*. Ninth variorum edition. Edited by C. W. Guillebaud. London, 1961.
M. Pantaleoni. "Pareto: An Obituary." *Economic Journal* 33 (1923).
P. A. Samuelson. "Complementarity: An Essay on the Fortieth Anniversary of the Hicks-Allen Revolution in Demand Theory." *Journal of Economic Literature* 12 (1974).
G. L. S. Shackle. *The Years of High Theory*. Cambridge, 1967.
J. A. Schumpeter. *History of Economic Analysis*. London, 1954.
M. Shubik. "Edgeworth Market Games." In R. Luce and A. W. Tucker, eds., *Contributions to the Theory of Games*, IV, *Annals of Mathematical Studies* 40 (1959). Princeton.
G. J. Stigler. *Essays in the History of Economics*. Chicago, 1964.
V. J. Tarascio. "A Correction: On the Genealogy of the So-Called Edgeworth-Bowley Diagram." *Western Economic Journal* 10 (1972): 193–97.

---

indifference,' " and again on the same page, "if . . . the *curves of indifference* consist of a series of circles." Further, on page 114 is found, "the equation of *any* indifference curve"; and again, p. 116, "B's *curves of indifference*."

D. A. Walker. "Edgeworth's Theory of Recontract." *Economic Journal* 83 (1973).
J. L. Weatherby. "Why Was It Called an Edgeworth-Bowley Box? A Possible Explanation." *Economic Inquiry* 14 (1976).
E. R. Weintraub. "The Microfoundations of Macroeconomics: A Critical Survey." *Journal of Economic Literature* 14 (1977).
J. K. Whitaker. *The Early Economic Writings of Alfred Marshall*, vol. 2. London, 1975.

[12]

History of Political Economy 12:2

Some recent interpretations of *Mathematical Psychics*: a reply

Vincent J. Tarascio, University of North Carolina at Chapel Hill

Professor Creedy's note on some recent interpretations of Edgeworth involves several different articles and authors. I shall confine myself to those points he raises in connection with my paper on the genealogy of the so-called Edgeworth-Bowley diagram.[1] Since my paper was published in another journal and is therefore not immediately accessible to the readers of this journal, I shall outline the contents of that paper before responding to his arguments.

In my original paper I attempted to trace the origin of the so-called Edgeworth-Bowley diagram. I argued (p. 195): "as is the case with most concepts, the derivation of the box diagram had its roots in several innovations, all of which contributed to its development." I then went on to summarize these innovations in order to give credit where credit is due. Below is my original summary (pp. 195–96):

(A) Jevons, *Theory of Political Economy* (1871), pp. 98–100.

(1) $\dfrac{\phi_2 x}{\psi_2(b - y)} = \dfrac{y}{x}$, the *offer curve* of y,

where ϕ_2 and ψ_2 are the marginal utilities of goods X and Y, respectively.

(2) $\dfrac{\phi_1(a - x)}{\psi_1 y} = \dfrac{dy}{dx}$, *equilibrium condition (individual)*,

(3) $\dfrac{\phi_1(a - x)}{\psi_1 y} = \dfrac{y}{x} = \dfrac{\phi_2 x}{\psi - (b - y)}$, *equilibrium in exchange*,

where $\phi_1, \phi_2, \psi_1, \psi_2$ are the marginal utilities of individuals 1 and 2 for goods X and Y.

(B) Edgeworth, *Mathematical Psychics* (1881).

(4) $(\zeta - x)\left(\dfrac{dP}{dx}\right) + (\eta - y)\left(\dfrac{dP}{dy}\right) = 0$, the *indifference curve equation* (p. 21), where P is the total utility of one individual and x and y quantities of commodities X and Y.

1. Vincent J. Tarascio, "A Correction: On the Genealogy of the So-Called Edgeworth-Bowley Diagram," *Western Economic Journal* 10 (June 1972); 193–97.

Taking Jevons' (3) and using his own notation:

(5) $\frac{dP}{dx}\frac{d\Pi}{dy} - \frac{dP}{dy}\frac{d\Pi}{dx} = 0$, the *contract curve* (p.21),

where P and Π are the respective total utilities of two individuals for quantities of x and y.

Taking Jevons' (1):

(6) $\frac{\phi_1(a - x)}{\psi_1(y)} = \frac{y}{x}$, the *demand curve* of x (p. 113).

(C) Fisher, *Mathematical Investigations in the Theory of Value and Prices* (1892).
System of indifference curves for one individual (p. 68).

(D) Pareto:

(a) "Anwendungen der Mathematik auf Nationalökonomie" (1903).

(7) $f(x_a, x_b) = z$, *system of indifference curves*, where z is a parameter and x_a and x_b are quantities of commodities A and B.

(8) $F_a dx_a + F_b dx_b = 0$.
differential equation of an indifference curve (Edgeworth's (4)), where F_a and F_b are the partial derivatives of (7).

(b) *Manuale* (1906).
The *box diagram* (pp. 187, 333, 338) and a statement of the mathematical conditions of the Appendix.

(E) Bowley, *Mathematical Groundwork* (1924).
Diagram (p. 5) contains Offer Curves (Jevons), Indifference Curves (Edgeworth), Indifference Mapping (Fisher-Pareto), Contract Curve (Edgeworth), Box Construction (Pareto).

I concluded by saying that my purpose was not to denigrate the contributions of Edgeworth nor to dispute a claim that Bowley himself never made, but if terms are to be used to designate the genealogy of a concept, Samuelson's Jevons-Edgeworth-Bowley-Lerner designation should be modified to Jevons-Edgeworth-Fisher-Pareto-Bowley-Lerner. Because of the tediousness of such a label I suggested simply Pareto Box Diagram.

The above review has been necessary in order to put Creedy's arguments in their proper context, since an uninformed reader might conclude that I wished to deny Edgeworth his proper place in the development of the box diagram.

Now let us turn to Creedy's paper. The two issues he raises which are of concern to me are (1) the relationship of Edgeworth's diagram to the conventional box diagram and (2) the indifference map.

Regarding the issue of the box diagram, I wrote (p. 193) as follows:

> It might be argued that the idea of a box construction is *suggested* in *Mathematical Psychics* in either of two diagrams (pp. 28 and 114). Can Edgeworth's graphs be converted to a box apparatus by simple geometric manipulation? The answer is no—a geometric manipulation of Edgeworth's diagram on page 28 of *Mathematical Psychics* results in a box diagram which is nonsensical in terms of the conventional box diagram.

In note 4 on p. 193, I explain why:

> It turns out that the indifference curve for one trader is parallel to the indifference curve of the other trader. It might be argued that Edgeworth had a "box" in this sense: the ordinate of Figure 1 (p. 28) is amount of labor (time) *given up* by Friday; the abcissa is the remuneration received by Friday. Then *Y* is *received* by Crusoe, and *X* is given up. Hence quantities are conserved in the diagram; this mode inherently limits the quadrant to tenable points. This property is used to prove that the contract curve shrinks as the number of traders rises. But a "box" in this sense has nothing in common with the conventional box used today; it merely possesses some similar properties. In any event, Edgeworth never depicted a box in either sense.

With respect to the diagram on page 114 of Edgeworth's *Mathematical Psychics*, I said (p. 194) "such a process leads to results that are inconsistent with the theory underlying the analysis." In note 5 on p. 194 I explained why:

> Again, the result is parallel indifference curves. If, on the other hand, one begins with individual diagrams and then superimposes them by reversing the origins and the axes, the result is tangent indifference curves along a contract curve, but the direction of the contract curve is from the northwest to the southeast and the indifference curves are not concave to/from the origins.

Creedy does not address himself to this issue, directly. Instead he raises the distinction between exchange and allocation. The issue is simply this: The *contracted* term "Edgeworth-Bowley" is a misnomer, because today it is used to refer to an apparatus which first appeared in Pareto's writings and which continues to be used in the same manner as first presented by Pareto without modification in applicability and meaning. Why call an apple an orange?

Finally, I turn to the issue of indifference curves. In my paper (p. 194) I stated:

> Also, although Edgeworth uses the term "indifference *curves*" (in plural form in this Appendix), the term is meant to apply to the indifference curve of each of two individuals: nowhere in *Mathematical Psychics* does one find an indifference mapping consisting of more than one curve per individual. Furthermore, his indifference curves are curves of *indifferent exchanges* or "indifferent trades."
>
> The first person to use explicitly a *system* of indifference curves for *each* person was Irving Fisher in 1892. . . . Later Pareto, in an article published in *Encyklopädie der mathematischen Wissenschaften* in 1903 . . . , developed a system of indifference curves for each individual which at the same time explicitly avoided cardinal measures of utility.

Creedy's response is that, "Edgeworth of course did not *draw* a family of indifference curves; indeed he very rarely used diagrams and was much more concerned to emphasise that the results are obtained by 'mathematical method.' " Yet he is unable to offer any mathematical expressions, from the works of this mathematical economist, which indicate a system of indifference curves for each individual. Of course, we can look for and find in Edgeworth a prose statement or two which might *suggest* the possibility of systems of indifference curves as Creedy has done, but such speculations are superfluous (and misleading) in the case of Edgeworth, whose demonstrations were mathematical. Certainly the mathematical demonstration should be given precedence over mere fragments of scattered prose in this case: if Edgeworth intended to use systems of indifference curves he would have included them in his mathematical exposition, as did Pareto in equation (7) above.[2]

2. In any event the examples which Creedy gives to support his position that Edgeworth has in mind systems of indifference curves are incorrect, because his examples refer to cases of one indifference curve per trading partner or the indifference curve of one trader who shares characteristics similar to another trader. All of Creedy's examples fall into either category. His references to Edgeworth (*Psychics*, pp. 22 and 29) fall into the first category and his reference to pp. 38, 40, 113, and 116 fall into the second category. Since Creedy believes that his strongest case lies in the latter, I shall discuss this category.

On p. 40 of *Psychics* Edgeworth is referring to indifference curves of similar but not equal individuals showing X's characteristics and Y's characteristics, or the Xs and Ys as he refers to them. Here again reference is with respect to the single indifference curve of *each* of these four individuals, which agrees exactly with the diagram on p. 41, and not with Creedy's interpretation. On p. 113 Edgeworth gives an equation of the "curves of indifference," but it turns out that the expression is in fact an equilibrium

It seems that Creedy has missed the important issues in my paper. His speculations regarding what might have been or what could have been add little, if anything, to the literature which he challenges.

---

condition for the individual; see Jevons' equation (2) above in the text. Edgeworth then goes on to discuss two individuals A and B. Later on, on p. 116, Edgeworth refers to "B's curves of indifference," which suggests he had a system in mind. But in his n.1 he explains, "If, however, the competition between the Bs is *not perfect*, it may happen that they cannot force each other up to T, the intersection of the demand curves. . . ." Hence although the diagram referred to involves A and B, it is clear that Edgeworth is talking about two Bs and the statement above refers to the indifference curve of one person combined with that of another person, so they are taken together as a system, and not the system for one person. This is a subtle and confusing point.

[13]

JOURNAL OF ECONOMIC THEORY 24, 1–39 (1981)

Rawls, Edgeworth, Shapley, Nash: Theories of Distributive Justice Re-examined

MENAHEM E. YAARI*,†

Department of Economics, Hebrew University, Jerusalem, Israel

Received October 4, 1979; revised January 23, 1980

I. INTRODUCTION

While preparing for a seminar on "Economics Justice," I was rather perplexed to find the existing theory of distributive justice in what looked like a state of considerable disarray. Here was an enormous body of writing, dating back almost as far as writing itself, that was as amorphous as putty and almost as yielding when you tried to sink your teeth in it. One could hardly find two writers agreeing on what a third writer had said, to say nothing of the existence of an agreed body of assertions—no matter how small or sketetal—that everyone could adopt as a common point of reference. And it was on this kind of ground that economists were merrily running along, producing such things as "Benthamite" or "Rawlsian" taxation schemes.

Having mentioned John Rawls, I should hasten to say that, in my opinion, one of the most valuable contributions of Rawls' book [19] is indeed its attempt to answer the foregoing criticism. For Rawls had undertaken to state precisely what questions a theory of distributive justice is meant to answer and to lay down a general methodology that would make the answers to these questions deducible from certain ethical premises. Rawls then

* This paper is an outgrowth of a seminar that took place at the Hebrew University of Jerusalem in 1977/1978. I had the pleasure of sharing the responsibility for that seminar with Avishai Margalit, and it is here that I wish to record my debt to him, incurred through many conversations both in and out of the classroom. Thanks are due also to Maya Bar-Hillel, to Gideon Schwartz, and to Amartya Sen for their comments.

† In this paper, I have made an attempt to provide a coherent account of the issues that make up the theory of distributive justice, to the best of my understanding. The paper is an economist's way of reading the theory of distributive justice and it focuses on issues which economists tend to raise when discussing problems of distribution. Yet, I should like to emphasize that the paper is intended also for non-economists, and this fact has had an obvious influence upon the style of presentation. To a large extent, this is an essay in the history of thought, so the reader should be alerted not to look for the types of results which usually appear in papers being published in this *Journal.*

0022-0531/81/010001-39$02.00/0

proceeded to use this methodology to construct his own theory, called "justice as fairness," and to compare it with other theories of distributive justice, most notably with utilitarianism. Rawls makes a very determined effort to define utilitarianism (as a theory of distributive justice) in terms of the framework that he himself had laid down, so that the differences between the two theories might come into focus. But here I find that Rawls meets with but limited success, and his discussion of utilitarianism, in many instances, is vague and imprecise. Witness the many comments that have appeared since 1971 on the relationship between Rawls and utilitarianism (Arrow [2], Barry [5, Chap. 10], Gordon [9], Harsanyi [12], Lyons [15], Sen [22], among others) no two of which seem to agree on what the issues are, let alone on how they might be resolved. Seeing that this was the case, and with a seminar soon to get underway, I had no choice but to sit down and undertake the exercise of writing precisely what it was, to the best of my understanding, that utilitarianism as a theory of distributive justice did say, and then to do the same with what I understand to be Rawls' position, so as to be able to carry out a rigorous comparison between the two. I started by taking advice from Rawls himself, who says [19, p. 22] that "in order to bring out the underlying differences in the simplest way... the kind of utilitarianism I shall describe is the strict classical doctrine which receives perhaps its clearest and most accessible formulation in Sidgwick." Now, I did not find Sidgwick [24] all that clear, and at certain points I had the feeling that he was being deliberately vague. So, I decided to call in F. Y. Edgeworth as a kind of reinforcement. Edgeworth's [7] articulate and methodical account of utilitarian distribution theory is more orthodox and audacious than Sidgwick's and yet, at the same time, Edgeworth clearly sees himself as building upon the foundations that Sidgwick had laid. Therefore, any contrast that one might draw between Rawls and Sidgwick would no doubt be accentuated and brought more sharply into focus with Edgeworth in the picture.

My version of the confrontation between Sidgwick and Edgeworth on the one hand and Rawls on the other ended very differently from the confrontation that Rawls himself had set up in his book. Using a standard minimax theorem, I was able to argue that, under very general assumptions, the Sidgwick–Edgeworth theory and the Rawlsian theory are equivalent. So, if one still wants to hold the view that Rawls and classical utilitarianism are fundamentally different from each other, then one would have to show either that I have misstated the Sidgwick–Edgeworth position or that I have misstated Rawls' position, or else that the general assumptions under which the two positions are equivalent are fundamentally controversial and that the difference between the two theories rests on the failure of these assumptions.

The Sidgwick–Edgeworth brand of utilitarianism has long been passé, mainly because the pseycho-physical foundations of utility have been debunked and exposed as useless pseychologism. This immediately brings up a very important question: Can a theory of distributive justice that is founded upon utilitarian principles be consistent with modern utility theory? One would have thought that finding the answer to this question would by now be a matter of looking up the appropriate page in some standard text on social philosophy, social choice, or welfare economics. And a very promising source to look up is Chapter 9 of Sen's fine book [21]. But neither this source nor any other source that I have been able to consult gives a definitive answer to the question posed above. The feeling one gets is that, with so many "impossibility theorems" floating around, the answer is probably that a theory of distributive justice which would be both utilitarian and utility–theoretic is impossible. My own position on this question is less pessimistic, and I derive my mild sense of optimism from a framework suggested by Shapley [25] which appears to me to provide a powerful tool for constructing utilitarian theories of social interaction. (To make my position clear, I should emphasize that the reference here is to the general methodology of Shapley's paper, and not to the specific conept—the so-called Shapley value—which he uses as a solution for situations of social choice with conflicting interests.)

It makes no sense to try and carry out a direct comparison between Rawls [19] and Shapley [25] because the two theories rest on different foundations. However, it does make sense to try and see what happens when Shapley's methodology is applied to Rawls' ethics. Such an experiment, one might hope, would lead to a theory of distributive justice that would be true to Rawls' principles and yet be free of conflict with modern utility theory. Intrigued to see what would emerge, I performed the experiment, only to find myself re-discovering Nash's [17] theory of bargaining.

These tales and others will be told in the sequel.

II. Framework

I propose to study distributive justice within the general framework of social choice theory. (See, for example, Sen [21].) To capture the essentials of a simple but non-trivial distribution problem, let me start with two building blocks: First, a non-empty set X and, second, a list of n real-valued functions $u_1, u_2, \ldots, u_n$, defined on X. The set X is the universe of discourse and its elements are entities among which society could conceivably be called upon to exercise a choice. For the sake of concreteness, I shall refer to the elements of X as *distribution schemes*, with the interpretation of this term depending on the specific context of any given discussion. Thus, the elements of X could be given such divergent interpretations as alternative constitutions, alternative institutional structures, alternative tax structures, alternative ways of dividing up the net national product, alternative ways of cutting a cake at a birthday party, and so forth. The set X of all conceivable distribution schemes will be referred to as the *choice space.* As for the functions $u_1, u_2, \ldots, u_n$, they will be referred to as the *utilities* of the individuals who make up the society under consideration. In other words, "society" consists of n individuals who are identified by the utilities $u_1, u_2, \ldots, u_n$ all of which are functions assigning real numbers to elements of the choice space X. Utilities are assumed to convey information about the individuals' preferences. The formula

$$u_i(x) > u_i(y)$$

has the obvious interpretation that individual i prefers the scheme x over the scheme y, in the sense that i would rather see x chosen than y. But utilities can also be assumed to convey information about the *intensity* of preferences. For example, the formula

$$u_i(x) - u_i(y) > u_i(w) - u_i(z)$$

could be taken to mean that individual i's preference for x over y is stronger than his preference for w over z. Statements of this form will not appear explicitly in the present essay. However, much of the discussion will be based, implicitly, on the assumption that such intensity statements are meaningful. Now, the most demanding interpretation of the utilities $u_1, u_2, \ldots, u_n$ is one where they are assumed also to convey information about interpersonal comparisons. For example, one could think of the formula

$$u_i(x) > u_j(y)$$

as comparing individual i's position when the scheme x is chosen with individual j's position when the scheme y is chosen, and asserting the former to be more favorable than the latter. The assumption that such interpersonal comparison statements are meaningful is very strong and hardly warranted. Nevertheless, some authors do assume these interpersonal comparisons to be meaningful and therefore, in stating these authors' positions, it will for a while be necessary to make the same assumption here as well. This issue will be examined in detail in Sections VII and X.

The choice space X consists of all conceivable distribution schemes that might arise as options in any hypothetical social choice situation. Now, every *specific* social choice situation is, however, characterized by a *subset* of X, consisting of those options that happen to be feasible in that choice situation, taking into account such things as resource limitations, institutional rigidities, etc. This gives rise to the notion of the *set of feasible distribution schemes* (or the *feasible set*, for short) for which the symbol F will be used.

Given the feasible set F, one can go ahead and define a set U in the following manner:

$$U = \{(a_1, \ldots, a_n) | u_1(x) = a_1, u_2(x) = a_2, \ldots, u_n(x) = a_n \text{ for some } x \in F\}.$$

U is called the set of *feasible utility profiles* (or the *utility-possibilities set*). If one defines a vector-valued function $\mathbf{u}$ by writing $\mathbf{u}(x) = (u_1(x), \ldots, u_n(x))$ for all $x \in X$, then U is given simply by the statement

$$U = \mathbf{u}(F),$$

U being the image of F under $\mathbf{u}$. Each choice that society can feasibly make is translated into a "profile" (an n-tuple) of utility numbers and the collection of these utility profiles is the set U.

It is now possible to state a fundamental assumption, which I shall take to be an axiom in much of the present analysis (the removal of this assumption will be discussed in Section IX).

PRINCIPLE OF NON-POLARIZATION. *The set U, of feasible utility profiles, is convex.*

The first thing to be noted is that this principle would always be fulfilled if society were allowed to make randomized choices (such as to announce an option under which the toss of a coin would determine which of the two schemes, x or y, will be selected) and if all individuals have von Neumann–Morgenstern utilities. In the absence of randomized choices, the Principle of Non-polarization could still be shown to hold in many specific settings as, for example, in a setting where the object is to split a bundle of perfectly divisible and freely disposable goods among n individuals having concave utilities. In any case, it should be clear that the Principle of Non-polarization can only be defended in a serious way if one is willing to accept the point of view that utilities convey information not only on preferences but also on the *intensity* of preferences. And even with this much granted, it is still easy to construct theories of social interaction that would violate the Principle. (A good example would be a theory of distribution in an economy where production is subject to increasing returns to scale.) My own impression is that such fundamental departures from the Principle of Non-polarization lead, invariably, to social theories that are Marxian in spirit (as is indeed the case when production is subject to increasing returns to scale). For it is basically a Marxist tenet which holds that society is always faced with polarized alternatives—favoring one group or another—with no way for an intermediate compromise. However, for the systems that I shall attempt to discuss in the forthcoming pages, the adoption of the Principle of Non-polarization is certainly consistent, even though the principle may not actually be written down in so many words. (Rawls [19] mentions convexity only in one place—p. 68—while discussing the idea of efficiency. He does not seem to attach much importance to the notion of convexity but, as far as I can see, his analysis is entirely in keeping with this notion. It is clear, for example, in the discussion of the Original Position [19, pp. 130–136] that in Rawls' view, the concept of justice is *prior* to the concept of an institutional structure. Thus, in a very fundamental sense, if society ever finds itself constrained by an institutional structure that violates non-polarization, then it is possible that the structure is itself unjust. This is precisely where a Marxian would rise to object. For him, giving justice a priority over institutional structure would be out of the question.)

The framework for the analysis is now complete in the sense that we have before us a well-defined social choice problem, namely, the problem of how to select a distribution scheme from the set F of feasible schemes, given the utilities $u_1,..., u_n$. What I propose to do in the sequel is to examine how, under the Principle of Non-polarization, certain systems of social thought—notably some variants of utilitarianism and Rawls' justice as fairness—would treat this problem and how these treatments are related to one another.

But before I can turn to this task, I find it necessary to enter a brief disclaimer concerning the priority of liberty. I disagree with Rawls' contention that utilitarianism is incapable of granting an absolute priority to liberty. However, this issue is not directly related to the topics that will be discussed in this essay. Therefore, it seems desirable to sidestep this issue altogether by agreeing that the problem shall be limited to the case where the choice which society is called upon to make is solely in matters unrelated to liberty. More precisely, let us assume, for the purposes of the present discussion, that the set F of feasible distribution schemes has the following property. If x and y are elements of F, then x and y lead to identical distributions of liberty among individuals. On the liberty scale, then, all feasible distribution schemes are equal.

III. The Utilitarian Program

The first thing that a utilitarian—*any* utilitarian—would do when faced with the problem of how society should select from the feasible set F is to construct a measuring rod, in the following manner. For any n-tuple of nonnegative weights, $\boldsymbol{\lambda} = (\lambda_1,..., \lambda_n)$ having the property that $\lambda_1 + \lambda_2 + \cdots + \lambda_n = 1$, and for any distribution scheme x (feasible or not) the utilitarian would define $W(x, \boldsymbol{\lambda})$ by writing

$$W(x, \boldsymbol{\lambda}) = \lambda_1 u_1(x) + \lambda_2 u_2(x) + \cdots + \lambda_n u_n(x)$$

so that $W(x, \boldsymbol{\lambda})$ is the weighted average, using the set of weights $\boldsymbol{\lambda}$, of the individuals' utilities at x. Let S be the set describing all the ways of assigning weights to individuals:

$$S = \left\{ \boldsymbol{\lambda} = (\lambda_1, \ldots, \lambda_n) \;\middle|\; \begin{array}{l} \lambda_1, \lambda_2, \ldots, \lambda_n \text{ are non-negative real} \\ \text{numbers and } \lambda_1 + \lambda_2 + \cdots + \lambda_n = 1 \end{array} \right\}.$$

(S is usually referred to as the *unit simplex* of dimension $n - 1$.) Then, W is a real-valued function defined on the Cartesian product $X \times S$. This function will be called *the utilitarian form*.

Now, why should this function, W, be the first thing that a utilitarian (and as we shall see, not only a utilitarian) would consider? The answer is given by the **Pareto Principle**, which may be stated as follows:

THE PARETO PRINCIPLE. *Let x be a feasible distribution scheme ($x \in F$). If there exists a feasible scheme y ($y \in F$) satisfying $u_i(y) > u_i(x)$ for $i = 1, \ldots, n$, then the scheme x is irrelevant for social choice.*

Under this principle, only so-called *Pareto-efficient* distribution schemes are relevant for social choice, provided of course that such Pareto-efficient schemes exist in sufficient abundance. (A feasible scheme $x \in F$ is said to be Pareto-efficient—in the weak sense—if there does *not* exist a feasible scheme $y \in F$ with $u_i(y) > u_i(x)$ for $i = 1, \ldots, n$.)

The connection between the Pareto Principle and the utilitarian form W emerges as soon as one writes down the following well-known proposition:

PROPOSITION. *Under the principle of non-polarization, a feasible scheme x ($x \in F$) is Pareto-efficient if and only if there exists a system of weight $\boldsymbol{\lambda}$ ($\boldsymbol{\lambda} \in S$) such that $W(x, \boldsymbol{\lambda}) \geqslant W(y, \boldsymbol{\lambda})$ for all feasible schemes y ($y \in F$).*

In other words, a feasible scheme x is Pareto-efficient if and only if it *maximizes* the utilitarian form W, for some choice of weights $\boldsymbol{\lambda}$. The Pareto Principle may therefore be re-phrased as follows. If Pareto-efficient schemes can be assumed to exist then, under non-polarization, the problem of selecting a scheme x from the feasible set F is equivalent (up to a matter of indifference for all individuals) to the problem of choosing a set of weights $\boldsymbol{\lambda}$ in S and then looking only at those schemes x for which $W(x, \boldsymbol{\lambda})$ is a maximum on F. This makes the utilitarian form W relevant not only in utilitarian theories, but in any theory which adopts the Pareto Principle.

The Pareto Principle enjoys wide acceptance, by utilitarians and by non-utilitarians alike (see, e.g., Rawls [19, p. 17]). The main reason for accepting this principle in a theory of distributive justice is that a failure to do so would lead to the untenable position that justice may have to be enforced, against the will of *all* individuals. It is one thing to say that justice may require enforcement upon *some* individuals, perhaps even as many as all except one. But if all individuals hold, unanimously, that a distribution scheme, say x, is strictly preferable to some other scheme, say y, then it is very hard to accept that justice should demand, nevertheless, that y be chosen over x. This point has been brought forth very effectively by Nozick's [18, pp. 160–164] famous "Wilt Chamberlain" example. (Nozick himself draws a very different moral from this example, namely, that "no end-state principle or distributional patterned principle of justice can be continuously realized without continuous interference with people's lives" [18, p. 163]. I confess that I am puzzled by this conclusion taking the place of what appears to me to be the obvious conclusion, namely, that one of the principles of distributive justice had better be the Pareto Principle. Nozick's own explanation [18, p. 164, footnote] does little to relieve my sense of puzzlement, because his new example—unilateral transfers or bequests—is still based on taking an initial situation which is not Pareto-efficient.) Now, strong and persuasive as the case for the Pareto Principle might be, there is of course no guarantee against another principle, perhaps equally as persuasive, coming up later in the discussion and turning out to be incompatible with the Pareto Principle. In the face of such a conflict of principles, some people would choose to abandon one principle, others would abandon another, and still others would abandon the analysis altogether. (See McClelland and Rohrbaugh [16] for an attempt to study the extent to which people who are forced to make judgements in the face of conflicting principles tend in fact to abandon the Pareto Principle.) In the present essay, no postulates will arise that are in conflict with the Pareto Principle, so adopting it here seems to be in order.

Convinced of the reasonableness of the Pareto Principle, the utilitarian is now ready to lay down a general procedure for social choice. I shall refer to this procedure as "the utilitarian program":

THE UTILITARIAN PROGRAM. *First, use ethical judgments to determine what the right set of weights, say* λ^*, *should be, for the given feasible set* F. *Then select the distribution scheme* x^* *in such a way that* $W(x, \lambda^*)$ *shall be a maximum, over all* x *in* F, *at* $x = x^*$.

At this stage, I neglect the problem of ties and how they should be broken.

IV. ON MAXIMIZING THE SUM-OF-UTILITIES: A CRITICAL REMARK

As you read the literature on social choice (and on distributive justice as a branch of social choice theory) you find a tendency among authors to identify utilitarianism with the proposition that society should always select the alternative that maximizes the sum of the individuals' utilities. I confess that I find the cavalier manner in which this pronouncement is usually made rather infuriating. Even as careful a writer as Sen [22, 23] is, in my opinion, not careful enough on this point.

Equating utilitarianism with the maximization of the sum-of-utilities is equating it with the proposition that the "correct" set of weights, $\boldsymbol{\lambda}^*$, to be used in the utilitarian form W is the same for *all* feasible sets F. This point of view sees the utilitarian as solving social choice problems by looking always for a Pareto-efficient scheme at which the rates of transfer of utility among individuals are in accordance with some universal constants $\boldsymbol{\lambda}^*$. Even the most naive utilitarians cannot be characterized as having argued in this way.

In one (trivial) sense, the assertion that utilitarianism coincides with the maximization of the sum-of-utilities is always true, by definition. Consider the utilitarian program, described in the last paragraph of Section III and suppose that, in one way or another, a set of weights $\boldsymbol{\lambda}^* = (\lambda_1^*, ..., \lambda_n^*)$ has already been determined. Let the functions $v_1, v_2, ..., v_n$ be defined by $v_1(x) = \lambda_1^* u_1(x)$, $v_2(x) = \lambda_2^* u_2(x), ..., v_n(x) = \lambda_n^* u_n(x)$ for all $x \in X$, where $u_1, ..., u_n$ are the individuals, utilities, given originally. Then, by this definition, the utilitarian program would always have x^* chosen to maximize the sum $v_1(x) + v_2(x) + \cdots + v_n(x)$. Clearly, on this interpretation, to equate utilitarianism with maximization of the sum-of-utilities is to confuse *ex-ante* with *ex-post*, because the utilities whose sum is being maximized are themselves an outcome of the analysis.

But what other interpretation can there be for the sum-of-utilities maxim? Arguing in a somewhat simple-minded fashion, one can say that the very act of writing the symbol "+" in an expression like $u_1(x) + u_2(x) + \cdots + u_n(x)$ means that the utilities $u_1, u_2, ..., u_n$ have been jointly calibrated and converted into a *common* unit, so that the u_i's whose sum is being taken are, in fact, the v_i's of the previous paragraph. There is no way to calibrate the utilities $u_1, ..., u_n$ and convert them to a common unit, except by using conversion factors which, even if equal in magnitude, are not equal in unit of measurement. Thus, by forcing the addition of utilities to be well-defined, one automatically introduces the assumption that utilities have been re-defined so as to incorporate the appropriate conversion rates. This looks almost like a *proof* that the (trivial) *ex-post* interpretation of the sum-of-utilities maxim is the only one possible. Almost, but not quite. After all, there do exist structures that are amenable to extensive-additive measurement. Let us, for a moment, take a look at the conditions that would have to be satisfied in order for the utilities of different individuals, jointly, to be a structure admitting extensive-additive measurement. There are four such conditions (here, I follow Krantz, Luce, Suppes, and Tversky [13, pp. 71–75]):

(i) There exists a non-empty set, E, of unambiguously defined entities having the attributes of pleasure and pain. Elements of E will be referred to as *experiences*.

(ii) There exists a binary relation $\gtrsim$ on E which is reflexive, transitive, and connected. (That is, $\gtrsim$ is a complete weak order of E.) If e and e' are experiences, then the statement $e \gtrsim e'$ has the interpretation that e is at least as pleasurable or at most as painful as e'.

(iii) There exists a binary operation $*$ on E, called *concatenation* (or *joining together*) so that any two experiences (not necessarily of the same individual) may be concatenated, and the result is once again an experience. This binary operation satisfies such algebraic laws as associativity and cancellation.

(iv) The relation $\gtrsim$ and the operation $*$ fit together nicely in two different ways. First, if e, e', f, f', are experiences such that $e \gtrsim f$ and $e' \gtrsim f'$, then $e * e' \gtrsim f * f'$. Second, experiences are Archimedean, in the sense that if ε is any experience such that $\varepsilon * \varepsilon \neq \varepsilon$ then, by concatenating ε with itself sufficiently many times, one gets a new experience lying outside any preassigned $\gtrsim$-interval of the form $\{e \in E \mid e_1 \gtrsim e \gtrsim e_2\}$.

Anyone equating utilitarianism with the sum-of-utilities maxim (in a non-trivial *ex-ante* sense) is actually equating utilitarianism with the adoption of these four conditions, (i) through (iv), as postulates.

Technical remark. Some readers will object here and say that in order to derive the sum-of-utilities maxim it is enough to have a social preference order, defined on utility profiles, which is symmetric and additively separable. But this would be wrong, because utility profiles are not invariant to changes of individuals' utility indicators.

As far as I know, the only utilitarian who could conceivably be stretched to the point of adopting these four postulates is Edgeworth, who thought that the notion of a "just-perceptible increment" could be used to construct a universal unit for measuring pleasures and pains (see Section VI). But as we shall see, even Edgeworth's theory of social choice has more to it than a mere maximization of the sum-of-utilities.

Now, what about the argument that derives the sum-of-utilities maxim from considerations of choice under uncertainty? The argument goes something like this (see Harsanyi [11]): Suppose you had to select a distribution scheme x from the feasible set F before knowing what individual characteristics you were going to have. In particular, suppose you believed that your utility could be one of the functions $u_1, u_2, \ldots, u_n$ and that it would be just as likely to be one or the other. Then, if your choice behavior satisfies certain axioms, you would select x^* to maximize the expected utility

$$\frac{1}{n}u_1(x)+\frac{1}{n}u_2(x)+\cdots+\frac{1}{n}u_n(x)$$

over all x in F, which is the same thing as maximizing the sum $u_1(x)+u_2(x)+\cdots+u_n(x)$. This reasoning is valid for all participating individuals, and therefore, by unanimity, social choice should seek to maximize the sum-of-utilities after all. How about that? Well, to begin with, I should hasten to set the record straight by noting that this is not what Harsanyi proves. Indeed, Harsanyi [11, Theorem 5] is very precise in stating that the rule which he seeks to establish using these probabilistic considerations is one where social choice is governed by the maximization of a *weighted* sum-of-utilities, with weights that are not necessarily equal and have nothing to do with the probabilities of the underlying decision-making situation. As for the point itself, one must remember only that probabilities, like relative frequencies, are pure numbers (unit-less magnitudes). Therefore, if $p_1, p_2, \ldots, p_n$ are probabilities, then the expected utility $p_1u_1(x)+p_2u_2(x)+\cdots+p_nu_n(x)$ is well-defined only after the functions $u_1, u_2, \ldots, u_n$ are jointly calibrated and converted to a common unit. We are right back where we started.

A final comment may be in order, for readers who might wonder how summing utilities can meet with so much wrath when, all along, *weights* were being added together, in expressions like $\lambda_1+\lambda_2+\cdots+\lambda_n=1$. Are not λ_i and λ_j measured in different units? Is writing $\lambda_i+\lambda_j$ not like summing apples and oranges? The answer should be apparent upon a moment's reflection: In the maximization of the utilitarian form, $W(x, \boldsymbol{\lambda})$, only the *relative* magnitudes of the weights (i.e., ratios of the form λ_i/λ_j) play a role. Therefore, each weight may be divided by the sum of all weights, without changing anything.

V. Modern Utilitarianism: Shapley's Proposal

Anyone proposing a theory of social interaction which is consistent with the Principle of Non-polarization and with the Pareto Principle can be thought of as carrying out what I have termed "the utilitarian program." Yet it seems that for a theory of social interaction to be called *utilitarian*, it must also, in one way or another, incorporate the idea of *utility trade-offs* among individuals. When somebody proposes a social change that would benefit me but harm you, it becomes the utilitarian's task to offer a way of weighing my benefit against your loss. For the modern utilitarian, this task is very difficult indeed, because he must somehow subsist on what is left after modern utility theory and Arrow's impossibility theorem have each taken their shares. A general and ingenious proposal for meeting this modern utilitarian challenge has been made in a contribution due to Shapley [25]. Shapley's proposal has already been applied in several directions, and the results so far have been encouraging. (See, for example, Aumann and Kurz [4] who use Shapley's procedure to study the effect of the political structure on taxation.)

What Shapley says is this. Consider the weights $\boldsymbol{\lambda} = (\lambda_1, \ldots, \lambda_n)$ appearing in the utilitarian form $W(x, \boldsymbol{\lambda})$. These weights play the role of conversion rates that transform individual utilities into some universal unit. In particular, these weights act also as *rates of transformation* or *rates of exchange* between individual utilities. For example, if society has chosen the weights $\boldsymbol{\lambda} = (\lambda_1, \ldots, \lambda_n)$ then, by so doing, society has in fact decreed that one unit of individual i's utility is exchangeable for λ_j/λ_i units of individual j's utility. In other words, every choice of weights $\boldsymbol{\lambda} = (\lambda_1, \ldots, \lambda_n)$ defines a system of transferable utility between individuals (provided none of the λ_i vanishes) where the ratio λ_j/λ_i defines the rate at which utility side-payments between individuals i and j are to be made. But once utility is transferable, so says Shapley, we can bring to bear a very powerful theory, namely, the theory of games with transferable utility. So, for every choice of weights, $\boldsymbol{\lambda} = (\lambda_1, \ldots, \lambda_n)$, we are told to construct a game, say $G(\boldsymbol{\lambda})$, which would describe our social choice problem in terms of what individuals can achieve under each distribution scheme, on the assumption that the total utility obtained by any group of individuals can be divided up in any manner among its members, using the rates of transfer $\lambda_1, \ldots, \lambda_n$. There are usually several ways to construct the game $G(\boldsymbol{\lambda})$, with different sets of rules for how the game is to be played. This fact accounts for the generality of Shapley's proposal. Now, once the game $G(\boldsymbol{\lambda})$ is constructed, one can appeal to some solution concept, for games with transferable utility, to tell us how society should divide up the total utility which it can obtain under the rules of the game. (The solution concept recommended by Shapley is the so-called "modified Shapley value" but this is not essential to his proposal.) Let us say, then, that some solution concept has been selected and that, under this solution concept, the distribution of total utility among individuals in the game $G(\boldsymbol{\lambda})$ is given by $\boldsymbol{\mu}(\boldsymbol{\lambda}) = (\mu_1(\boldsymbol{\lambda}), \ldots, \mu_n(\boldsymbol{\lambda}))$. That is, for each set of weights $\boldsymbol{\lambda}$, the game $G(\boldsymbol{\lambda})$ is constructed and then resolved into an n-tuple of numbers, $(\mu_1(\boldsymbol{\lambda}), \ldots, \mu_n(\boldsymbol{\lambda}))$, describing the utility payoffs that individuals get in the game $G(\boldsymbol{\lambda})$, under the adopted solution concept. In general, the utility profile $(\mu_1(\boldsymbol{\lambda}), \ldots, \mu_n(\boldsymbol{\lambda}))$ *will not be feasible* in the original distribution problem. That is, there will not in general exist a feasible distribution scheme x $(x \in F)$ having the property that $u_1(x) = \mu_1(\boldsymbol{\lambda})$, $u_2(x) = \mu_2(\boldsymbol{\lambda}), \ldots, u_n(x) = \mu_n(\boldsymbol{\lambda})$. If this is the case—the utility profile $(\mu_1(\boldsymbol{\lambda}), \ldots, \mu_n(\boldsymbol{\lambda}))$ not being feasible—then the system of weights $\boldsymbol{\lambda}$ has *failed to justify itself* in the sense that these rates of utility transfers, $\boldsymbol{\lambda} = (\lambda_1,..., \lambda_n)$, do not correctly reflect the realities of the underlying choice situation. Therefore, a new set of rates for utility transfer must be examined and the process must be repeated until a set of weights, say $\boldsymbol{\lambda}^* = (\lambda_1^*,..., \lambda_n^*)$, is found having the property that the utility profile $(\mu_1(\boldsymbol{\lambda}^*),..., \mu_n(\boldsymbol{\lambda}^*))$ is feasible in the original distribution problem. Only a set of weights $\boldsymbol{\lambda}^*$ having this property can be a candidate for use in the utilitarian form $W(x, \boldsymbol{\lambda})$.

For the sake of brevity, let me say that a set of weights $\boldsymbol{\lambda} = (\lambda_1,..., \lambda_n)$, in the unit simplex S, is *self-justifying* if there exists a feasible distribution scheme x $(x \in F)$ such that $u_1(x) = \mu_1(\boldsymbol{\lambda})$, $u_2(x) = \mu_2(\boldsymbol{\lambda}),..., u_n(x) = \mu_n(\boldsymbol{\lambda})$, where $(\mu_1(\boldsymbol{\lambda}),..., \mu_n(\boldsymbol{\lambda}))$ is the distribution of utilities in the solution of the game $G(\boldsymbol{\lambda})$. Shapley's contribution consists of two separate items. First, he proves that, for a large class of games $G(\boldsymbol{\lambda})$ and using any solution concept satisfying certain general requirements (continuity and the Pareto Principle), *there always exists in S a set of weights $\boldsymbol{\lambda}^*$ which is self-justifying.* Second, Shapley offers a heuristic argument (based on "counting equations and unknowns") to show that, in most cases, there exists in *S one and only one* set of weights $\boldsymbol{\lambda}^*$ that is self-justifying. (Here, the meaning of "in most cases" is vague, but it can be made precise.) Now, if it happens in any specific model (as, for example, in Aumann and Kurz [4]) that self-justifying weights are in fact unique, then the argument for using precisely these weights in the utilitarian form W is very hard to resist. For suppose that society decides to select some Pareto-efficient distribution scheme, say x^*, from the set of feasible schemes F. Under non-polarization, there will exist a set of weights $\boldsymbol{\lambda}^* = (\lambda_1^*,..., \lambda_n^*)$ corresponding to x^*. Thus, by selecting the scheme x^*, society is in fact asserting that it is correct to pretend that utility is transferable between individuals at the rates $\lambda_1^*,..., \lambda_n^*$. But if pretending that utility is transferable at the rates $\lambda_1^*,..., \lambda_n^*$ does not lead back to a distribution scheme where these are, in fact, the local rates of transfer (i.e., back to x^* itself) then the pretending was clearly incorrect. Thus, Shapley's proposal may be summarized as follows: *Never select a distribution scheme whose implicit rates of utility transfer would lead you to want to move away from that scheme.* This sounds like a rather minimal consistency requirement, but in many cases it suffices to determine a unique selection.

But how would ethical principles, without which there cannot be a theory of justice, fit in Shapley's framework? The answer, quite clearly, is that such principles would have to go in through the specification of the games $G(\boldsymbol{\lambda})$ and through the choice of a solution concept for these games. For example, it is possible to construct the games $G(\boldsymbol{\lambda})$ in such a way as to incorporate the principle that each person's utility payoff should reflect the share of total wealth that this person brings into the game at the outset (something like "to each according to his wealth"). And there is a specific way to do this, whereupon Shapley's procedure leads directly to the distributive mechanism known in economics as the competitive equilibrium. In principle, one can design the games $G(\boldsymbol{\lambda})$ to reflect any ethical or distributional postulate and then use Shapley's procedure to derive the corresponding distributive mechanism. In Section X, I shall attempt to do just that, using Rawls' Difference Principle as the underlying ethical postulate.

VI. Classical Utilitarianism

My task in this section is to try and translate the classical utilitarian doctrine into the language of finding an appropriate set of weights, $\boldsymbol{\lambda} = (\lambda_1, \ldots, \lambda_n)$, for the utilitarian form $W(x, \boldsymbol{\lambda})$, and picking a distribution scheme x^* that maximizes $W(x, \boldsymbol{\lambda})$ among all feasible schemes x ($x \in F$). Since classical utilitarians did not all speak in one voice, my translation is bound to contain an element of interpretation and I shall try, needless to say, to convince the reader that my interpretation is indeed correct. But, perhaps more importantly, I shall argue that my interpretation of classical utilitarianism is no different from Rawls' interpretation of the same doctrine. Why this should be important will be seen later, when I discuss the alleged contrast between classical utilitarianism and Rawls' own theory. But first, let me try to formulate as rigorous a statement as I can of classical utilitarianism. In this attempt, I shall rely for the most part on the writings of Sidgwick [24] and Edgeworth [7]. Sidgwick's account of this doctrine is, perhaps, the most balanced and deliberate (sometimes to the point of being noncommittal) while Edgeworth's is probably the most spirited and enthusiastic.

In Section IV, the problem of selecting a set of weights, $\boldsymbol{\lambda} = (\lambda_1, \ldots, \lambda_n)$, for the utilitarian form $W(x, \boldsymbol{\lambda})$ was discussed in terms of the theory of measurement: Can individual utilities be converted into a common unit and, if so, how? For classical utilitarians, this problem was no different from the problem of converting, say, the lengths or weights of individual physical objects into a common unit. Happiness, or pleasure, was thought of as a psycho-physical quantity given to objective measurement that makes it commensurable between individuals (Edgeworth [7, p. 59]). Furthermore, it was proposed that the Weber–Fechner notion of a just-perceptible stimulus could very well be used to construct a universal unit of utility that would enjoy the same degree of efficacy as do the gram or the centimeter in physical science. Thus, Edgeworth says [7, p. 60]: "Just perceivable increments of pleasure, of all pleasures for all persons, are equateable." (See also Edgeworth's discussion of "hedonimetry" [7, pp. 98–102] where he argues that there is no reason for the margin of error in hedonimetric measurements to exceed the margin of error in physical measurements. Sidgwick's position on this [24, 3rd ed., pp. 146–147] is similar to Edgeworth's, albeit more hesitant.)

For classical utilitarians, then, the individual utilities $u_1, u_2, ..., u_n$ may be taken, at the outset, as measured in terms of a common unit. End of story? Not quite. The weights $\boldsymbol{\lambda} = (\lambda_1, ..., \lambda_n)$ still have a major role to play, but they are not interpreted as rates of conversion in a system of measurement. Rather, the interpretation of these weights is that λ_i stands for the *proportion of individuals of type i in the population.* In classical utilitarianism, the structure as well as the size of the population was very much an object for social choice, especially after Malthus and his followers had spoken of what would happen if population were not made an object for conscious social policy. Both Sidgwick and Edgeworth are quite clear on this. Sidgwick says [24, 3rd ed., p. 412]: "But a further question arises when we consider that we can to some extent influence the number of future human (or sentient) beings. We have to ask how, on Utilitarian principles, this influence is to be exercised." And Edgeworth [7, p. 56] opens the section on Utilitarian Calculus as follows: "*Problem.* To find (α) the distribution of means and (β) of labour, the (γ) quality and (δ) number of population, so that there may be the greatest possible happiness." Edgeworth speaks explicitly of two different ways for influencing population structure, namely, migration and something called evolution. Migration is clear enough, as is its position among the prominent issues of social policy. As for "evolution," what Edgeworth had in mind was a process affecting population structure and lying somewhere between outright population control and a "Darwinian" theory in which the distribution of happiness is viewed as affecting, possibly, the rates of reproduction and survival.

To make a long story short, we are now given a list of utilities $u_1, ..., u_n$, each representing a *type* of individual or a social class (or a "section" as Edgeworth calls it) and the problem of social choice is to select a distribution scheme x and a set of population parameters $k_1, ..., k_n$ so as to maximize the quantity

$$k_1 u_1(x) + k_2 u_2(x) + \cdots + k_n u_n(x),$$

among all $(x, k_1, k_2, ..., k_n)$ lying in some feasibility set. Here, k_i is the number of individuals of type i, or the size of the ith social class. If one lets the size of the total population be denoted N (that is, $N = k_1 + k_2 + \cdots + k_n$) and if one defines the proportions $\lambda_1, ..., \lambda_n$ by writing $\lambda_i = k_i/N$, then the social choice problem becomes one of finding a distribution scheme x, a system of weights $\boldsymbol{\lambda}$, and a population size N so as to maximize—under suitable constraints—the expression $NW(x, \boldsymbol{\lambda})$, where $W(x, \boldsymbol{\lambda})$ is now interpreted as the (weighted) *average happiness* which would result if the policy x

were adopted and if $\boldsymbol{\lambda} = (\lambda_1, ..., \lambda_n)$ were the proportions of the various types of people in the population.

All this is taken right out of Sidgwick [24, 3rd ed., p. 413] who says "the point up to which, on Utilitarian Principles, population ought to be encouraged to increase, is not that at which average happiness is the greatest possible, but that at which the product formed by multiplying the number of persons living into the amount of average happiness [i.e., the product formed by multiplying N into $W(x, \boldsymbol{\lambda})$] reaches its maximum." Edgeworth, for his part, refers explicitly [8, p. 19] to this passage in Sidgwick, calling it "the nearest approach to an absolutely new idea of first-rate importance in morals."

The maximization of something like $NW(x, \boldsymbol{\lambda})$ seems to provide a reasonable formulation for Hutcheson's celebrated maxim: "that action is best which procures the greatest happiness for the greatest numbers." $W(x, \boldsymbol{\lambda})$ is "happiness" while N is "numbers" so maximizing their product is an attractive explication of Hutcheson's maxim. It may therefore appear curious that Edgeworth should have been so contemptuous of it. He says [7, p. 117]: "is this [maxim] more intelligible than 'greatest illumination with the greatest number of lamps'?" If one takes the view, as Edgeworth did, that man is a pleasure machine, then by definition, the greater the numbers, the greater the aggregate of pleasures. So, what sense is there in speaking of the greatest pleasure for the greatest numbers? The resolution of this apparent difficulty emerges as soon as the maximization of $NW(x, \boldsymbol{\lambda})$ is spelled out more carefully. For this maximization takes place under *two* separate sets of constraints. One set of contraints is physiological, describing what Sidgwick and Edgeworth call "the capacity for happiness" of the various types of individuals. Specifically, if k_i is the number of individuals of type i and if u_i is the utility level enjoyed by a person of type i, then, in maximizing the sum $k_1 u_1 + k_2 u_2 + \cdots + k_n u_n$, the utility profile $(u_1, ..., u_n)$ must be taken from some specific set, U, which describes the different capacities for happiness of the different types of individuals. For example, if there are only two types of individuals, type 1 and type 2, and if individuals of type 1 have precisely twice the capacity for happiness as do individuals of type 2, then the set U will consist of all pairs (u_1, u_2) of nonnegative real numbers satisfying $u_1 + 2u_2 \leqslant K$, where K is some constant that may be normalized so as to have $K = 1$. In general, the set U describes the psycho-physically determined rates of transformation between the happiness of different types of individuals and it has nothing whatsoever to do with the feasibility or lack of feasibility of one social action or another. (Recall that, in previous sections of this essay, the set U was the image, in utilities-space, of the set F of socially feasible distribution schemes.) By Fechner's law of diminishing ability to perceive incremental stimuli of constant magnitude, U is some convex subset of Euclidean n-space, so that, in this theory, the Principle of

Non-polarization follows from the laws of pseycho-physiology. At any rate, the maximization of $k_1 u_1 + k_2 u_2 + \cdots + k_n u_n$ over all $(u_1, u_2, \ldots, u_n)$ lying in U is meaningless, since "numbers"—that is, the k_i's— can be made as large as we please, thereby making the maximand arbitrarily large. This is the meaning of Edgeworth's mocking paraphrase—"greatest illumination with the greatest number of lamps."

The maximization problem becomes meaningful when a second family of constraints is recognized, having to do with the availability of resources. If resources were unlimited, then the quantity $NW(x, \boldsymbol{\lambda})$ would have no maximum in the sense that infinitely many people would be able to enjoy infinite happiness. So, the problem of social choice arises only when resources are limited. Sidgwick and Edgeworth themselves did not use the term "resources" but preferred a term that is more general and much more vague, namely, "the means of happiness." Edgeworth discusses this vagueness explicitly [7, p. 69], indicating how difficult it would be to tell how much happiness could be produced from a given amount of means (= resources). It is clear, however, that at any given moment, there exists a *technology* that describes the various ways for converting means of happiness into happiness, and it is through this technology that the limited availability of resources acts as a constraint on social choice. It is quite easy to write all this down very formally, but this seems to me rather an idle exercise. Instead, I shall try to bring out the essentials of the problem in a simpler setting, where total happiness itself acts as the limiting factor. In other words, I shall assume that society must act under the constraint that total welfare (= total happiness = Sidgwick's "quantum of happiness" = Edgeworth's "lot of happiness") cannot exceed some number, say $\bar{W}$. Here, the reader will no doubt wonder: If $NW(x, \boldsymbol{\lambda})$ cannot exceed $\bar{W}$ then, obviously, one should set $NW(x, \boldsymbol{\lambda}) = \bar{W}$, so what on earth is left to be maximized? The "physiological" requirement that the utility profile must lie in the set U is of no help because, as has already been mentioned, the number N can always be adjusted to have $NW(x, \boldsymbol{\lambda}) = \bar{W}$. Indeed, for *any* "physiologically" feasible pair $(x, \boldsymbol{\lambda})$ one can go ahead and calculate $W(x, \boldsymbol{\lambda})$ and then set N to satisfy $NW(x, \boldsymbol{\lambda}) = \bar{W}$, so that any pair $(x, \boldsymbol{\lambda})$ is as good as any other. It appears as though we keep coming back to Edgeworth's "greatest illumination with the greatest number of lamps" except that now we set the number of lamps in accordance with some fixed total amount of available illumination. But a careful writing down of who-maximizes-what-with-respect-to-which-variables shows that this is not so. Suppose that the weights $\boldsymbol{\lambda} = (\lambda_1, \ldots, \lambda_n)$ have already been determined somehow. Then, there is no question but that the classical utilitarian would select x^* to maximize $W(x, \lambda)$ among all feasible x—i.e., among all "physiologically" feasible utility profiles—and then let total population be determined from the equation $N = \bar{W}/W(x^*, \boldsymbol{\lambda})$. (The set F of feasible distribution schemes plays no role in this discussion but I am retaining it nevertheless, along with phrases like "picking x^* to maximize $W(x, \boldsymbol{\lambda})$ among all feasible x," for the purpose of keeping consistent terminology throughout the essay. It may be worthwhile to point out that, also in the other sections of this essay, it is not the set F as such which determines the structure of a distribution problem, but rather the set U of feasible utility profiles. Here, this same set, U, is given the "physiological" interpretation described above.) Furthermore, society—being fully rational—*knows* that after it decides on the population proportions $\boldsymbol{\lambda}$, it will in fact follow the procedure of selecting x^* to maximize $W(x, \boldsymbol{\lambda})$. Therefore, in deciding which proportions $\boldsymbol{\lambda}$ to pick, society takes this knowledge into account. Now, $W(x^*, \boldsymbol{\lambda})$ will be the average happiness enjoyed by a representative individual, and this average is at a maximum, given the proportions $\boldsymbol{\lambda}$. Let us write

$$x^* = \xi(\boldsymbol{\lambda})$$

to mean that x^* is that choice of x, among all x in F, for which $W(x, \boldsymbol{\lambda})$ is at a maximum. It is assumed that this choice is unique or, more precisely, that other principles will have to be relied upon in case of a tie that needs to be broken. Now, when it comes to picking the proportions $\boldsymbol{\lambda}$ themselves, the object should be to let the greatest possible numbers enjoy the level of happiness $W(\xi(\lambda), \boldsymbol{\lambda})$, this being the maximum happiness enjoyed by a representative individual, under the proportions $\boldsymbol{\lambda}$. In other words, the population proportions should be picked so as to *maximize* N, subject to the constraint that $NW(\xi(\boldsymbol{\lambda}), \boldsymbol{\lambda})$ cannot exceed the total amount of happiness, $\bar{W}$. In symbols, one gets—

$$\max_{\boldsymbol{\lambda} \in S} N \qquad \text{subject to} \quad NW(\xi(\boldsymbol{\lambda}), \boldsymbol{\lambda}) = \bar{W},$$

or, substituting for $\xi(\boldsymbol{\lambda})$—

$$\max_{\boldsymbol{\lambda} \in S} N \qquad \text{subject to} \quad N[\max_{x \in F} W(x, \boldsymbol{\lambda})] = \bar{W},$$

which I now take to be the explication of Hutcheson's maxim. The maximum inside brackets stands for "the greatest happiness" and the maximum of N on the left stands for "the greatest numbers." Each maximization takes place with respect to a different decision variable: The former takes place with respect to the choice of a distribution scheme (or utility profile) and the latter with respect to the choice of a population structure. Edgeworth [7, pp. 61–75] recognizes these two levels of social choice quite explicitly and he offers optimal rules for both of them. His solution for the optimal population structure [7, pp. 70–71] is given by a kind of "bang-bang" policy which, no doubt, sounds rather weird: All persons whose capacity for happiness is greater than some critical value should be encouraged to reproduce at the maximum possible rate, while all persons whose capacity for happiness lies below that critical value should not be allowed to reproduce at all. Edgeworth himself is concerned that this conclusion might "appear outlandish" [7, p. 71] so he hastens to qualify it in various ways, some of them not unamusing. In Section VIII, I shall argue that Edgeworth's fear to appear outlandish was without foundation. For Edgeworth's population policy— so I shall argue—is in fact an early forerunner of Rawls' Difference Principle. The outlandish aspect is not in the principle itself but rather in its application to the problem of population planning. Indeed, if Rawls had tied his Difference Principle to population planning (something like "only those in the least-favored position should be allowed to reproduce") would this not appear equally outlandish?

To recapitulate, what I have been trying to do in these last few pages is to convince the reader that classical utilitarianism, as a framework for social decision making, can be summarized as follows. Find a distribution scheme x^* and a system of weights λ^* so that the pair (x^*, λ^*) shall provide a solution for the problem

$$\max_{\lambda \in S} N \qquad \text{subject to } N[\max_{x \in F} W(x, \lambda)] = \bar{W},$$

where the sets S and F are as defined above. A moment's reflection makes it clear that this optimization problem can be reformulated in a way that avoids explicit reference to N and $\bar{W}$. This leads to another statement of classical utilitarianism, equivalent to the previous one, namely:

CHOICE UNDER CLASSICAL UTILITARIANISM. *Find a distribution scheme x^* and a system of weights λ^* so that the pair (x^*, λ^*) shall provide a solution for the problem*

$$\min_{\lambda \in S} \max_{x \in F} W(x, \lambda).$$

Except for tie-breaking, we have here a complete proposal for how to carry out the utilitarian program (see Section III) telling us which weights, λ^*, to use in the utilitarian form, whose maximization then leads to the choice of a distribution scheme, x^*. The specific interpretation which classical utilitarians had given the weights λ^*—the proportions of the various types of individuals in the population—is completely independent of the formal principle itself, and it is possible to adopt the principle without adopting the interpretation. Thinking of the weights λ^* as population parameters is a consequence of the classical utilitarians' commitment to a pseycho-physiological calculus of pleasures and pains. For anyone not committed to such a calculus, the need to interpret $\boldsymbol{\lambda}^*$ in this way disappears.

But, interpretations aside, it is very important to note how the weights $\boldsymbol{\lambda}^*$ are to be determined, according to classical utilitarianism. The guiding principle is clearly one of economy, calling for the weights to be selected in such a way as to stretch a given amount of total social welfare as far as possible. Suppose that, upon working out the classical utilitarians' proposal, we were to find that $\lambda_i^* > \lambda_j^*$, for some i and j: Individual i is assigned greater weight than individual j. Is this because i is more deserving than j? Or, perhaps, because i's needs are greater than j's? Or is there a legal case showing that i is entitled to more than j? Or has i's utility been stated in the wrong units, relative to j's? It is none of these. Individual i is assigned greater weight than individual j merely because such an assignment allows a given quantity of happiness to be stretched farther than would an alternative assignment. Persons are distinguished from one another only according to considerations of efficiency. Ethics, like economics, is seen as derived from a general mechanical principle—say Hamilton's Principle of Least Action—which says that rules of human conduct and behavior, like equations of motion, have their roots in a universal tendency toward efficiency. At this point, how can I resist reproducing that much-cited passage from Edgeworth [7, p. 21]: " 'Mécanique Sociale' may one day take her place along with 'Mécanique Celeste,' throned each upon the double sided height of one maximum principle." This celebrated passage reinforces my belief that the formulation of classical utilitarianism given above is indeed correct. For if one takes the utilitarian form W as the social analogue of the Hamiltonian form and the weights $\boldsymbol{\lambda}$ as the social analogue of Hamilton's "auxiliary variables" (which always enter linearly) one finds that the analogue of Hamilton's Principle comes out to be precisely that $W(x, \boldsymbol{\lambda})$ shall be a maximum with respect to x and a minimum with respect to $\boldsymbol{\lambda}$.

The impersonal, mechanistic aspect of classical utilitarianism is indeed striking. This is also the conclusion reached by Rawls [19] who examines classical utilitarianism at some length. (In Rawls' discussion, a great deal of emphasis is given to the notion of an impartial sympathetic spectator as being central in classical utilitarianism. This construction—the impartial spectator—had been invented by early utilitarians for the purpose of handling the problem of how individual desires and wants are to be assessed and compared. However, apparently due to the advant of Fechnerian psychophysics, this construction was no longer deemed necessary, so it was simply dropped. This is evidenced by the fact that neither in Sidgwick's account of utilitarianism nor in Edgeworth's can an appeal be found to the notion of an impartial spectator. In any event, the impartial spectator was merely a vehicle designed to lead to certain principles and it is these principles, not the vehicle, which define classical utilitarianism.)

Perhaps a good way to summarize Rawls' view of classical utilitarianism is by quoting a few passages from his book [19]. When discussing classical utilitarianism, Rawls says

> Social justice is the principle of rational prudence applied to an aggregative conception of the welfare of the group. (p. 27)
>
> On this conception of society, separate individuals are thought of as many different lines along which rights and duties are to be assigned and scarce means of satisfaction allocated in accordance with rules so as to give the greatest fulfillment of wants. (p. 27)
>
> [In classical utilitarianism, we think of society] as the efficient administration of social resources to maximize the satisfaction of the system of desires constructed by the impartial spectator from the many individual systems of desires accepted as given. (p. 33)

Rawls criticizes classical utilitarianism repeatedly for what he calls "the conflation of all desires into one system of desires" which he sees as "failing to take seriously the distinction between persons" [19, e.g., pp. 187–188]. Now, as Arrow [2] has pointed out, any attempt to design a coherent system of social values that would take account of the desires of all individuals is bound to contain an element of "conflation" of these desires. Nevertheless, I think that Rawls is correct to point out the failure of classical utilitarianism in coming to grips in a serious way with the phenomenon of human diversity. Human beings differ from one another in the same way that engines differ from one another, in the efficiency with which they generate energy from fuel (Edgeworth [7, p. 2]). And just as there is nothing fundamental about an engine having some specific efficiency rating, so there is nothing fundamental about a person having some specific individual characteristic. In both cases, differences among individuals matter only insofar as they can be made to work in the service of some higher principle that tells you how to allocate your scarce resources among their various potential uses. No wonder, therefore, that Rawls [19, pp. 179–180] should regard this point of view as being in conflict with Kant's imperative, that men shall treat one another not as means but as ends in themselves.

VII. Rawls' Difference Principle

Having thus rejected classical utilitarianism, Rawls sets out to propose a system of ethics that would not only "take seriously the distinction between persons" but would in fact take the distinction between persons as primary and fundamental. ("If we assume that . . . the plurality of distinct persons with separate systems of ends is an essential feature of human societies, we should not expect the principles of social choice to be utilitarian" [19, p. 29].) Moreover, Rawls' position leads hims to reject *all* forms of utilitarianism, and not just the classical variety. ("The merit of the classical view is that it clearly recognizes what is at stake, namely the relative priority of the principles of justice and of the rights derived from these principles" [19, p. 33]. This is why Rawls chooses to discuss utilitarianism mainly in its classical version. But he makes it clear that his critique is meant to apply, perhaps in varying degrees, to all forms of utilitarianism.) Rawls rejects utilitarianism because he views the very principle of weighing one person's utility againt another's, even when it is proposed that relative weights be derived from ethical considerations, as unacceptable [19, e.g., pp. 33, 180]. For the utilitarian, whether he be classical or preclassical or modern, the concept of a *solution* for a social choice problem emerges from considerations of *trade-offs* between utilities of different persons. Thus, what Rawls sets out to do is to change the very notion of what constitutes a solution for a given problem of social choice.

Now, the *data* of any given social choice problem cannot be affected by whatever debate there might be as to what constitutes a solution of the problem. For the types of problems discussed in this essay, the data consist of a choice space, denoted X, whose elements are distribution schemes, a subset F of X that tells which distribution schemes are feasible, and, finally, a list of individuals' utility functions, $u_1, u_2, \ldots, u_n$. Rawls' new solution concept must therefore be definable in terms of these entities. And since Rawls views "the plurality of distinct persons with separate systems of ends" as essential, it is natural that he should start by examining the utilities $u_1, u_2, \ldots, u_n$. A sufficient condition for there to be *no* plurality of distinct persons with separate systems of ends is that all the utilities $u_1, \ldots, u_n$ coincide on X, i.e., that for all $x \in X$ and for all pairs of individuals, i and j, the condition $u_i(x) = u_j(x)$ should hold. This means that a *necessary* condition for the existence of the plurality upon which Rawls intends to build is that there should exist a distribution scheme x and a pair of individuals, i and j, such that $u_i(x) \neq u_j(x)$. In most contexts, this condition cannot be regarded as *sufficient*, and from the inequality $u_i(x) \neq u_j(x)$ one cannot usually infer that individuals i and j are "different" in any essential way. It is therefore a shortcoming of Rawls' system that he does regard this inequality, $u_i(x) \neq u_j(x)$, as sufficient for conveying certain information on the difference between i and j. Specifically, Rawls assumes that the utilities $u_1, \ldots, u_n$ are given in a manner that permits the inequality $u_i(x) > u_j(x)$ to be read as individual i being better off than individual j, if x is the chosen distribution scheme. (If I understand it, Rawls' discussion of "primary social goods" is meant to provide a rationale for this supposition.) This issue has been discussed extensively in the literature (e.g., Arrow [3], d'Aspremont and Gevers [6], Sen [23], and references therein). Right now, my intention is not so much to criticize Rawls' assumptions, but rather to examine his theory on its own grounds. I shall therefore accept the premise that the utilities $u_1, \ldots, u_n$ can be used to rank the relative well-being of different individuals. In Section X, I shall return to this matter and attempt to present a version of Rawls' theory where this premise is absent.

The possibility of performing an ordinal comparison between the relative well-being of different individuals means that one can speak of a widening or a narrowing of the *gap* between two individuals. Let x and y be two distribution schemes, and let u_i and u_j be the utilities of two arbitrarily chosen members of society. If it happens that the following conditions hold

$$u_i(x) > u_i(y) > u_j(y) > u_j(x), \qquad (*)$$

then one can surely say that the gap between i and j is *narrower* under y than under x. (Notice that the inequalities in (*) are written so that i is better off than j both under x and under y, but the gap is smaller under y than under x.) Suppose for a moment that society consists of these two individuals, i and j, alone and that the inequalities (*) hold. Should society pick x over y, or should it pick y over x? A utilitarian might possibly say that the answer to this question depends on the degree to which the choice between x and y affects the two individuals. If j is only slightly better off under y than under x while i is substantially better off under x than under y, then picking x over y may be justified, even though such a choice results in a wider social gap. Indeed, the utilitarian would be able to make a pretty strong case for this answer, based on continuity considerations. Such an argument might go something like this: Suppose that the inequalities (*) hold in a whole sequence of situations. Suppose also that, as we proceed along this sequence, individual j changes in such a way that the inequality $u_j(y) > u_j(x)$ tends to equality. Then, in the limit, we have $u_j(y) = u_j(x)$ and, by a strong version of the Pareto Principle, society should pick x over y. Therefore, by continuity, if the difference $u_j(y) - u_j(x)$ is sufficiently small, but positive, society should still pick x over y. When all is said and done, Rawls' system rests precisely on denying that calculations of this kind may be justified. Accordingly, he enunciates the following value judgement:

LEAST DIFFERENCE PRINCIPLE. *If society consists of individuals i and j alone, and if (*) holds, then society should never pick x over y.*

This is as weak a version as I can find for Rawls' own Difference Principle. The word "least" in Least Difference Principle can be read in two different ways, both of them appropriate. If we read "least" as modifying "difference," we get the notion that smaller differences (gaps) are better; and if we read "least" as modifying "principle," we get the notion that this is, so to speak, the least of all difference principles. (The Least Difference Principle is quite similar to Hammond's [10] Equity Axiom, but it is weaker.)

Rawls' discussion indicates that he is, in fact, prepared to make a value judgement that seems to be much stronger. Suppose that society consists of $N+1$ individuals, of whom N are just like individual i (i.e., their utilities coincide with u_i) and the last one being poor Mr. j. The integer N may be as large as we please. Suppose the inequalities (*) hold. We now have a situation where a great many individuals would benefit if x were to be chosen and only one individual—Mr. j—would benefit if y were to be chosen. Rawls' interpretation of the Kantian imperative (see Rawls [19, pp. 179–180]) leads to the value judgement that no matter how large N is, if (*) holds then society should not pick x over y. For Rawls, the denial of this judgement would constitute the instance of a person (Mr. j in this case) being treated as means and not as an end in itself. (It is not made clear, in Rawls' book, why picking x treats j as means while picking y cannot be regarded as treating i—or all those having i's utility—as means. See Harsanyi [12].)

It is easy to produce hypothetical examples where this extremely uncompromising value judgement leads to ludicrous implications (Harsanyi [12]). However, if one is willing to accept that social choice is to obey certain structural requirements (see, e.g., Arrow [3]) then it turns out that the denial of this uncompromising value judgement has consequences that are no less extreme and equally easy to expose as ludicrous. In particular, under certain widely acceptable structural requirements, the denial of the above value judgement automatically affirms the extreme opposite judgement, namely, that even if society consists of only one individual having utility u_i and N individuals having utility u_j (reversing the situation of the previous example) and if the inequalities (*) still hold, then x should always be picked over y, no matter how large the number N.

The "structural requirements" referred to in the foregoing paragraph have been discussed extensively in the literature (Arrow [3], d'Aspremont and Gevers [6], Hammond [10], and Strasnick [26]) and there seems to be little point in dwelling upon them here once more. I shall therefore be content with the following brief and somewhat informal summary.

Let a process of social choice be called *nicely behaved* if the following five conditions are satisfied.

(1) Social choice from a finite set of feasible alternatives is always possible.

(2) Let F and F' be two feasible sets, describing two social choice situations. Assume that $F' \subset F$. If any of the schemes chosen under F are still feasible under F', then these schemes, and only they, are chosen under F'. (In particular, if under F society happens to select a unique scheme, x^*, and if $x^* \in F'$, then x^* must also be the unique selection under F'.)

(3) Consider a society with n individuals having utilities $u_1, \ldots, u_n$ and let x and y be two distribution schemes. Now let the individuals' utilities be

changed to $v_1,..., v_n$ in such a way that, for all i and j, $v_i(x) \geqslant v_j(y)$ if and only if $u_i(x) \geqslant u_j(y)$. (In other words, the information concerning the well-being of individuals, when only the schemes x and y are considered, does not change, even though utilities have been changed.) Then, x is chosen over y *before* the change from $u_1,..., u_n$ to $v_1,..., v_n$ if and only if x is chosen over y *after* the change.

(*Note*: In the literature, conditions (2) and (3) have both come to be known as *independence of irrelevant alternatives*, which has been causing a great deal of confusion.)

(4) Let the situation be as in (3) above, but now assume that the list of utilities $v_1,..., v_n$ is merely a re-arrangement (permutation) of the original list $u_1,..., u_n$. If x is chosen over y *before* the change, then x is chosen over y *after* the change.

(5) Consider a society where the individuals' utilities are given by $u_1,..., u_n$ and let x and y be two distribution schemes. If $u_n(x) = u_n(y)$—individual n being indifferent between x and y—then social choice between x and y must coincide with the choice between x and y in a society with $n - 1$ individuals having utilities $u_1,..., u_{n-1}$.

Conditions (1) and (2) are designed to guarantee that social choice is always guided by a criterion of picking that feasible alternative which is highest in some social rank-ordering. (See Arrow [1, Theorem 3].) Condition (3) makes the social ranking of x against y dependent on information concerning x and y alone. Condition (4) guarantees equal treatment of equals, by making the information as to who has which utility irrelevant. Condition (5) requires that individuals who are indifferent between x and y not be allowed to affect the choice that society would make when forced to select between x and y.

The following proposition is a consequence of a theorem due to Hammond [10] and Strasnick [26].

PROPOSITION. *Consider a society with n individuals having utilities $u_1,..., u_n$ defined over the choice space X. Let the set of feasible distribution schemes be denoted F, $F \subset X$, and let x^* be a scheme chosen from F. If social choice is nicely behaved, then, under the Pareto Principle and the Least Difference Principle, the scheme x^* must be one of the (possibly many) schemes for which the quantity*

$$\min[u_1(x), u_2(x),..., u_n(x)]$$

is a maximum, for $x \in F$.

This is the so-called Maximin Rule, and the proposition can be viewed as a formalization of the process by which Rawls attempts to derive this rule from basic ethical and structural principles. Rawls argues at length that individuals gathered in an original position to select a mechanism of social choice, behind a veil of ignorance, would all agree that the mechanism to be selected should comply with the Pareto Principle and with the (Least) Difference Principle. Presumably, the parties in the original position would also agree that social choice should be nicely behaved, although this aspect is not discussed in Rawls' book. Therefore, it follows that the parties in the original position would agree, unanimously, that social choice be governed by the Maximin Rule.

VIII. On the Equivalence of Rawls and Classical Utilitarianism

Consider a society with n individuals, having utilities $u_1,\ldots, u_n$. These utilities, it will be recalled, are real functions defined on some choice space, X. As before, let F be the feasible set, i.e., that subset of X from which society must actually choose, and let U be the set of feasible utility profiles, $U = \{(u_1(x),\ldots, u_n(x)) \mid x \in F\}$. The Principle of Non-polarization asserts that U is a convex set. Recall also that the *utilitarian form*, W, has been defined by writing

$$W(x, \boldsymbol{\lambda}) = \lambda_1 u_1(x) + \lambda_2 u_2(x) + \cdots + \lambda_n u_n(x)$$

for all x in X and for all $\boldsymbol{\lambda} = (\lambda_1,\ldots, \lambda_n)$ in the unit simplex, S.

For the sake of brevity, I shall say that a distribution scheme x^* in F *is a maxmin* if the quantity

$$\min[u_1(x), u_2(x),\ldots, u_n(x)]$$

has a maximum on F at $x = x^*$.

The following is a kind of duality theorem which is very close in form to the Kuhn–Tucker Theorem of non-linear programming (see, for example, Uzawa [27]). It is also obviously related to the minimax theorem for two-person zero-sum games.

Theorem. *Let the Principle of Non-polarization be satisfied. Then, a distribution scheme x^* in F is a maxmin if, and only if, there exists a system of weights $\boldsymbol{\lambda}^* = (\lambda_1^*,\ldots, \lambda_n^*)$ in S such that the inequalities*

$$W(x, \boldsymbol{\lambda}^*) \leqslant W(x^*, \boldsymbol{\lambda}^*) \leqslant W(x^*, \boldsymbol{\lambda}) \tag{1}$$

hold for all $x \in F$ and for all $\boldsymbol{\lambda} \in S$.

When the inequalities (1) are satisfied, it is common to say that the pair

(x^*, λ^*) is a *saddlepoint* of the utilitarian form $W(x, \lambda)$, for $x \in F$ and $\lambda \in S$. Using this terminology, what the theorem says is that, under non-polarization, x^* is a maxmin if and only if x^*, together with some system of weights λ^*, is a saddlepoint of the utilitarian form, W.

The proof of the foregoing theorem relies on the separation theorem for convex sets, and it is virtually the same as the proof of the minimax theorem for two-person zero-sum games. So, there is no point in reproducing the proof here.

Somewhere on page 12 of Edgeworth's book one would have expected to find a sentence that would read roughly as follows: "Just as mechanical action is governed by the law that the Hamiltonian Form shall be at a saddlepoint, so social action is governed by the law that the Utilitarian Form shall be at a saddlepoint." Edgeworth clearly had something like this in mind, so if he had actually said it, my task of showing that (under non-polarization) Rawls' theory is equivalent to Edgeworth's would now be complete. But Edgeworth did not quite say it, so completing my task is going to require some writing.

One thing ought to be clear: If the pair (x^*, λ^*) is a saddlepoint of W, that is, if the inequalities

$$W(x, \lambda^*) \leqslant W(x^*, \lambda^*) \leqslant W(x^*, \lambda)$$

hold for all $x \in F$ and $\lambda \in S$, then the pair (x^*, λ^*) is a solution of the problem

$$\min_{\lambda \in S} \max_{x \in F} W(x, \lambda).$$

Therefore, the foregoing theorem tells us right away that a distribution scheme, say x^*, selected from the feasible set F by Rawls' Difference Principle must, under non-polarization, satisfy the classical utilitarians' rule for social choice (see Section VI). In other words, under non-polarization, if a Rawlsian were to recommend some social action, based on Rawls' Difference Principle, then a classical utilitarian would always concur.

Now, what about the converse? Would a Rawlsian always be inclined to concur in a recommendation made by a classical utilitarian? The answer is yes, *provided* one takes into account the classical utilitarians' rule for breaking ties. Consider a problem of social choice for which a solution, according to Rawls' Maxmin Rule, exists (so the question posed above is meaningful). By the theorem, this Rawlsian solution would have to be *one* of the solutions that a classical utilitarian would recommend. In particular, if the social choice rule of classical utilitarianism leads to a unique solution, then this solution must coincide with the Rawlsian solution, i.e., the Rawlsian would concur with the utilitarian. However, if the choice rule of classical utilitarianism leads to *several* solutions, locked in a tie, then all we know is that one of these would be Rawlsian, but not necessarily all. Thus, it appears as though, in case of a tie, a classical utilitarian might end up making a recommendation in which a Rawlsian would not concur.

EXAMPLE. Take a two-person case, and let the set U of feasible utility profiles consist of all pairs (u_1, u_2) of non-negative utility numbers satisfying $u_1 + u_2 \leqslant 1$. In this case, classical utilitarianism leads to the result that *all* the Pareto-efficient utility profiles—i.e., all feasible pairs (u_1, u_2) satisfying $u_1 + u_2 = 1$—are locked in a tie. Among these, the only configuration satisfying Rawls' Maxmin Rule is the one for which $u_1 = u_2 = \frac{1}{2}$.

But classical utilitarians were fully aware that, in cases where the principle of greatest happiness results in a tie, a further principle is needed to decide the issue. Here is the appropriate passage from Sidgwick [24, 3rd ed., pp. 413–414] on this point:

> It is evident that there may be different ways of distributing the same quantum of happiness among the same number of persons; in order, therefore, that the Utilitarian criterion of right conduct may be as complete as possible, we ought to know which of these ways is to be preferred ... Now the Utilitarian formula seems to supply no answer to this question: at least we have to supplement the principle of seeking the greatest happiness on the whole by some principle of Just or Right distribution of this happiness. The principle which most Utilitarians have either tacitly or expressly adopted is that of pure equality.

Thus, classical utilitarianism amounts to the use of two principles, arranged in a hierarchy: The principle of greatest happiness should be applied first. If this principle is not sufficient, in the sense that it leads to several solutions locked in a tie, then the principle of greatest equality should apply, to break the tie. (In the simple example given above, the principle of greatest happiness led to all non-negative pairs (u_1, u_2) satisfying $u_1 + u_2 = 1$ as being equally good. Therefore, by the principle of greatest equality, the tie-breaking pair is given by $u_1 = u_2 = \frac{1}{2}$, which coincides with the solution according to the Maxmin Rule.) A moment's reflection reveals that, in the presence of the theorem stated above, this hierarchy of principles always leads, under non-polarization, to a selection that conforms with Rawls' Maxmin Rule.

IX. ON DROPPING NON-POLARIZATION

The equivalence of Rawls' theory of distribution and that of classical utilitarianism rests heavily on the assumption of non-polarization. This assumption is justified when it is believed either that society can make randomized choices or else that goods are smoothly transferable among individuals, that social policies are capable of gradual implementation, and that individuals are subject to some form of diminishing marginal utility. Conceivably, under some circumstances, these beliefs may be unwarranted. When this is the case, i.e., when it is not reasonable to suppose that the set U of feasible utility profiles is convex, the difference between Rawls' and classical utilitarianism springs up and becomes pronounced. Without nonpolarization, classical utilitarianism tends to push social choice towards extremes, whereas Rawls' Difference Principle tends to work in favor of moderation, to the extent that moderation is feasible. A simple example may serve to illustrate this contrast.

Suppose that society consists of two individuals, having utilities u_1 and u_2, and assume that the set U of feasible utility profiles is as depicted in Fig. 1. In this situation, Rawls' Maxmin Rule would select the utility profile B. On the other hand, classical utilitarianism, guided by the rule $\min_\lambda \max_x W(x, \lambda)$, would select the profiles A and C indifferently, without being able to decide between them. (Applying to the principle of greatest equality, as a tie-breaker, is clearly of no use in a comparison between A and C.)

Another case where non-polarization does not hold is one where the number of options open to society is finite. In practice, of course, society never faces a choice among infinitely many alternatives, and the question of finitely versus infinitely many alternatives is one of selecting a *model*. If the situation is such that the finite-options model is more appropriate, then non-polarization fails so that Rawls' Maxmin and classical utilitarianism diverge. Moreover, it can be shown that Rawls' theory is, in this case, more powerful than classical utilitarianism. By "more powerful" I mean that Rawls' theory results in an unambiguous choice more often than does classical utilitarianism. Once again, a simple example, with two individuals having utilities u_1 and u_2, may serve to illustrate the point. Suppose that society faces a choice between two isolated policies leading, respectively, to the

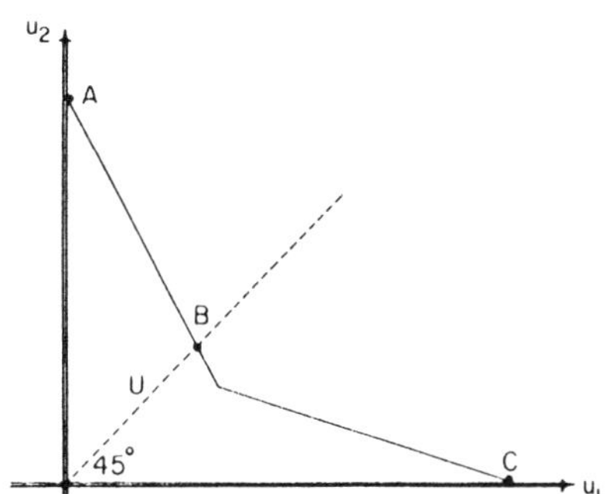

FIGURE 1

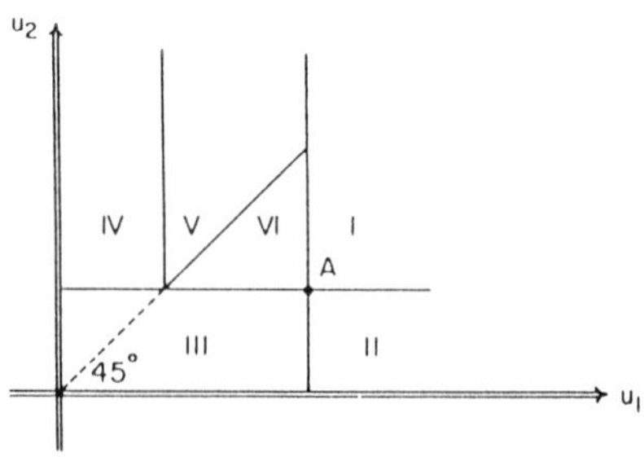

FIGURE 2

utility profiles A and B. In Fig. 2, the utility profile A has been marked and then, using the point A, the non-negative quadrant has been divided into six regions marked by Roman numerals, I through VI. If the utility profile B falls in one of the regions marked I, II, III, or VI, then both Rawls' Maxmin and classical utilitarianism are capable of deciding the issue and, in fact, the choices made by the two theories are the same (in this simple two-alternative case). However, if B happens to fall either inside IV or inside V, then classical utilitarianism is not capable of deciding between A and B, while Rawls' Maxmin is. Specifically, Rawls' Maxmin will pick A over B if B lies in IV and will pick B over A if B lies in V. The only case where neither theory is capable of deciding the issue is the one where B happens to fall right on the vertical line separating IV and V. (If B happens to fall on the horizontal line passing through A, then both Rawls' and classical utilitarianism require the *strong* version of the Pareto Principle in order to decide between A and B.) In this sense, it may be said that Rawls' Maxmin is more powerful than classical utilitarianism. Now, when the number of isolated alternatives is greater than 2, the situation becomes much more complicated. However, it is still true that in all configurations where classical utilitarianism leads to a unique choice so does Rawls' Maxmin, but not conversely.

X. RAWLS' DIFFERENCE PRINCIPLE WITHOUT INTERPERSONAL COMPARISONS

Before proceeding, let me reinstate the Principle of Non-polarization, which will be assumed to hold throughout the remainder of this essay: The set U of feasible utility profiles is convex.

As has been pointed out in Section VII above, the theory of distribution proposed by Rawls [19] rests on the stipulation that assertions of the form $u_i(x) > u_j(y)$ are meaningful. (Here, as always, $u_1, \ldots, u_n$ are the utilities of the individuals who make up the society under consideration.) Specifically, the inequality $u_i(x) > u_j(y)$ is shorthand for the statement "individual i is better off under the distribution scheme x than individual j under the distribution scheme y." Now, this element of Rawls' theory is regarded by most people as a significant shortcoming because the meaningfulness of an inequality of the form $u_i(x) > u_j(y)$ implies that u_i and u_j—and therefore all the utilities $u_1,..., u_n$—are measured in the same units. Not only is your utility assumed to be the same entity as my utility, the units used to measure the two utilities are assumed to be the same. These common units can be used to construct a procedure for "objective" measurement of well-being, and this is a conclusion to which utility theory (whether in ordinalist or in cardinalist form) simply cannot lend any support.

In this section, I propose to reformulate Rawls' Difference Principle in a manner that does not involve the supposition that utilities are interpersonally comparable. The tenets of utility theory—albeit in its cardinalist version—will be adhered to fully. To achieve this minor feat, I shall appeal to the conceptual framework, due to Shapley [25], that has been outlined in Section V.

The basic idea is quite simple, and it can be summarized in a few sentences. With every Pareto-efficient distribution scheme, one can associate a system of *implicit* conversion rates that transform individual utilities into some common unit of measurement. This common unit of measurement can be used to perform interpersonal comparisons even though the individuals' utilities themselves are not comparable. In Shapley's [25] terminology, one could say this: Let us pretend for a moment that utilities *are* transferable among individuals and that the rates of transfer are given by the weights $\boldsymbol{\lambda} = (\lambda_1,..., \lambda_n)$. That is, we pretend that when person i gives up a unit of his utility, u_i, to be transferred to person j, the gain to person j is λ_i/λ_j units of his own utility, u_j. (Here, all the weights λ_i, for $i = 1,..., n$, are assumed to be positive.) In this kind of never-never land (to use Shapley's phrase) Rawls' Difference Principle would call for a distribution of utility levels $u_1,..., u_n$ that would maximize the least of the quantities $\lambda_1 u_1, \lambda_2 u_2,..., \lambda_n u_n$. But now, seeing that utility is *not* in fact transferable, what we ought to do, according to Shapley, is to keep changing the weights $\boldsymbol{\lambda} = (\lambda_1,..., \lambda_n)$ until we hit upon a particular system of weights, say $\boldsymbol{\lambda}^* = (\lambda_1^*,..., \lambda_n^*)$, having the property that the distribution $(u_1^*,..., u_n^*)$ of utility levels that maximizes the least of the numbers $\lambda_1^* u_1^*,..., \lambda_n^* u_n^*$ (in the transferable utility game defined by $\boldsymbol{\lambda}^*$) can be achieved *without* utility transfers actually being necessary.

To get started, I shall assume, in keeping with Rawls' contractarian framework, that no distribution scheme can be put into effect unless *all* individuals agree. Every individual has the power to veto a proposed distribution scheme, thereby forcing society to stay at the status quo. Staying at the status quo (or, if one prefers, at the "state of nature") is always a feasible option, which will be denoted x_0. In the absence of interpersonal comparability, one may assume that the individuals' utilities have been normalized so as to satisfy $u_1(x_0) = u_2(x_0) = \cdots = u_n(x_0) = 0$. Under this normalization, a distribution scheme x is relevant for social choice only if the utility levels $u_1(x), \ldots, u_n(x)$ are all non-negative. Therefore, I will assume henceforth that the set F of feasible distribution schemes has the property that $x \in F$ implies $u_i(x) \geqslant 0$ for $i = 1, \ldots, n$. Furthermore, I shall assume that there exists at least one social contract where all individuals are actually better off than they would be if society were to stay at the status quo. In symbols, this assumption asserts that there exists a feasible distribution scheme $\hat{x}$ ($\hat{x} \in F$) such that $u_i(\hat{x}) > 0$ for $i = 1, \ldots, n$. Obviously, if this assumption fails, then the Rawlsian notion of maximizing the well-being of the least advantaged individual degenerates into a triviality, because in this case staying at the status quo is always a solution.

Consider the problem of choosing a distribution scheme from a feasible set F, and let x^* belong to F. If $\boldsymbol{\lambda} = (\lambda_1, \ldots, \lambda_n)$ is an n-tuple of non-negative weights satisfying $\lambda_1 + \lambda_2 + \cdots + \lambda_n = 1$ and if the utilitarian form $W(x, \boldsymbol{\lambda})$ is a maximum on F when $x = x^*$, then I shall say that $\boldsymbol{\lambda}$ is a system of weights *corresponding* to the scheme x^*. Let $\boldsymbol{\lambda} = (\lambda_1, \ldots, \lambda_n)$ be a system of weights corresponding to some (Pareto-efficient) distribution scheme x^*, and let x be any distribution scheme. Clearly, the magnitudes $\lambda_1 u_1(x), \ldots, \lambda_n u_n(x)$ are all measured in the same unit. Moreover, if $\boldsymbol{\mu} = (\mu_1, \ldots, \mu_n)$ is a system of weights corresponding to some other scheme, say y^*, then the magnitudes $\mu_1 u_1(x), \ldots, \mu_n u_n(x)$ are still measured in the same unit as were the earlier magnitudes, $\lambda_1 u_1(x), \ldots, \lambda_n u_n(x)$. Therefore, as far as units of measurement are concerned, it is meaningful to compare a quantity of the form $\lambda_i u_i(x)$ with another quantity of the form $\mu_j u_j(y)$, where x and y are any distribution schemes. From a purely formal point of view, the inequality

$$\lambda_i u_i(x^*) > \mu_j u_j(y^*)$$

is a meaningful assertion. The question, however, is: Under the assumption that $(\lambda_1, \ldots, \lambda_n)$ and $(\mu_1, \ldots, \mu_n)$ are systems of weights corresponding, respectively, to x^* and y^*, can this inequality be taken to mean that individual i is better off under x^* than individual j under y^*? In order to answer this question, one must start by examining the case of *intra*personal comparisons, where we take $i = j$. That is, if $\boldsymbol{\lambda} = (\lambda_1, \ldots, \lambda_n)$ and $\boldsymbol{\mu} = (\mu_1, \ldots, \mu_n)$ are systems of weights corresponding, respectively, to x^* and y^*, and if i is some integer satisfying $1 \leqslant i \leqslant n$, can one infer from the inequality

$$\lambda_i u_i(x^*) > \mu_i u_i(y^*)$$

that individual i *prefers* x^* over y^*? Is there any necessary connection between the statement $\lambda_i u_i(x^*) > \mu_i u_i(y^*)$ and the statement $u_i(x^*) > u_i(y^*)$? In the special case of a society that consists of two individuals, the answer to this question is simple and straightforward: If $n = 2$, then the inequality

$$(\lambda_i u_i(x^*) - \mu_i u_i(y^*))(u_i(x^*) - u_i(y^*)) \geqslant 0$$

is true for $i = 1, 2$, with equality holding if and only if either $u_i(x^*) = u_i(y^*)$ or $\lambda_i = \mu_i = 0$. In other words, when $n = 2$, the two differences—$\lambda_i u_i(x^*) - \mu_i u_i(y^*)$ and $u_i(x^*) - u_i(y^*)$—cannot have opposite signs, so it is impossible to have $\lambda_i u_i(x^*) > \mu_i u_i(y^*)$ with the ith individual's preference between x^* and y^* running the other way. (This assertion is implied by the more general assertion that will be stated and proved a few lines below.)

If there are more than two individuals, then the quantities $\lambda_i u_i(x^*) - \mu_i u_i(y^*)$ and $u_i(x^*) - u_i(y^*)$ may have opposite signs, but this has to do with the relationships among individuals other than i himself. If one controls for these relationships, then the desired result emerges again. One way to control for the relationships among individuals other than i is to suppose that $(\lambda_j/\lambda_k) = (\mu_j/\mu_k)$ for all $j \neq i$ and $k \neq i$. What this means is that in the transition from x^* to y^*, rates of conversion between utilities of individuals other than the ith individual are unaffected. Another way, which also leads to the desired result, is to suppose that $(u_j(x^*)/u_k(x^*)) = (u_j(y^*)/u_k(y^*))$ for all $j, k \neq i$, which means that relative welfare positions of individuals other than i do not change in the transition from x^* to y^*. Here, I shall be content to spell out only the first of these two alternatives. The following assertion is true: Let i be an integer satisfying $1 \leqslant i \leqslant n$ and let $\boldsymbol{\lambda} = (\lambda_1, \ldots, \lambda_n)$ and $\boldsymbol{\mu} = (\mu_1, \ldots, \mu_n)$ be systems of weights corresponding, respectively, to x^* and y^*. If the equation

$$\left(\lambda_j \middle/ \sum_{k \neq i} \lambda_k\right) = \left(\mu_j \middle/ \sum_{k \neq i} \mu_k\right) \tag{2}$$

holds true for all $j \neq i$, or if one of the denominators in Eq. (2) vanishes, then the inequality

$$(\lambda_i u_i(x^*) - \mu_i u_i(y^*))(u_i(x^*) - u_i(y^*)) \geqslant 0. \tag{3}$$

holds, with equality if, and only if, either $u_i(x^*) = u_i(y^*)$ or $\lambda_i = \mu_i = 0$. Note that, in the case $n = 2$, the assumption on the relative weights, (2), is always satisfied (trivially) so the previous assertion is entailed in this one.

Proof of the assertion. From the fact that $\boldsymbol{\lambda}$ corresponds to x^* and $\boldsymbol{\mu}$ corresponds to y^*, it follows that two inequalities may be written:

$$\sum_{j=1}^{n} \lambda_j u_j(x^*) \geqslant \sum_{j=1}^{n} \lambda_j u_j(y^*), \tag{4}$$

$$\sum_{j=1}^{n} \mu_j u_j(x^*) \leqslant \sum_{j=1}^{n} \mu_j u_j(y^*). \tag{5}$$

If $\lambda_i = 1$, then (3) follows from (4) and if $\mu_i = 1$, then (3) follows from (5). This takes care of the case where one of the denominators in (2) vanishes. Now assume that $\lambda_i < 1$ and $\mu_i < 1$ and divide (4) and (5), respectively, by $1 - \lambda_i$ and $1 - \mu_i$. This will lead to

$$\sum_{j=1}^{n} \left(\frac{\lambda_j}{1-\lambda_i} - \frac{\mu_i}{1-\mu_i}\right)(u_j(x^*) - u_j(y^*)) \geqslant 0. \tag{6}$$

By (2), all the terms appearing in (6) vanish, except for the ith term. Thus, one gets

$$\left(\frac{\lambda_i}{1-\lambda_i} - \frac{\mu_i}{1-\mu_i}\right)(u_i(x^*) - u_i(y^*)) \geqslant 0, \tag{7}$$

which holds if, and only if

$$(\lambda_i - \mu_i)(u_i(x^*) - u_i(y^*)) \geqslant 0. \tag{8}$$

And since all the quantities appearing in (8) are non-negative—recall that $u_i(x) \geqslant 0$ for all $x \in F$—the desired result, (3), follows readily. ∎

We see, then, that under a certain *ceteris paribus* assumption, the inequality $\lambda_i u_i(x^*) > \mu_i u_i(y^*)$ does indeed admit an interpretation showing a preference for x^* over y^* by individual i. Now, what about the inequality $\lambda_i u_i(x^*) > \mu_j u_j(y^*)$, where $i \neq j$? Here, the only question that one can ask is the following. Suppose, for the sake of argument, that u_i and u_j have somehow been pre-calibrated, for some $i \neq j$, in such a way that the inequality $u_i(x^*) > u_j(y^*)$ is meaningful. *In this case*, will it also be true that $\lambda_i u_i(x^*) > \mu_j u_j(y^*)$? Clearly, if the inequality $u_i(x^*) > u_j(y^*)$ is meaningful, then u_i and u_j must be measured in the same unit which means, in turn, that the rate at which u_i can be converted into any universal unit must coincide with the rate at which u_j can be converted into that unit. Therefore, $\lambda_i = \mu_j$ and the inequality $\lambda_i u_i(x^*) \geqslant \mu_j u_j(y^*)$ must hold, with a strict inequality in all but the extreme case, when $\lambda_i = \mu_j = 0$.

These considerations lead me to conclude that it is not unreasonable to try and reformulate Rawls' Difference Principle on the basis of comparisons of the type $\lambda_i u_i(x^*) > \mu_j u_j(y^*)$, where $(\lambda_1, \ldots, \lambda_n)$ and $(\mu_1, \ldots, \mu_n)$ are systems of weights that correspond, respectively, to x^* and y^*. This can be done formally, using Shapley's procedure, which has two stages. The first stage consists of specifying a rule for distribution in the case of transferable utility. The second stage consists of allowing the rates of transfer of utility to vary until the distribution problem is such that its solution can be achieved *without* utility transfers actually taking place. These two stages will now be taken up in order and described more fully.

In the first stage, a hypothetical set of feasible utility profiles, to be denoted $U(\boldsymbol{\lambda}, K)$, is defined by writing $(v_1,\ldots, v_n) \in U(\boldsymbol{\lambda}, K)$ if and only if $v_1,\ldots, v_n$ are non-negative real numbers satisfying $\lambda_1 v_1 + \lambda_2 v_2 + \cdots + \lambda_n v_n \leqslant K$. Here, $\boldsymbol{\lambda} = (\lambda_1,\ldots, \lambda_n)$ is any system of weights such that $\lambda_i > 0$ for $i = 1,\ldots, n$ and $\lambda_1 + \cdots + \lambda_n = 1$, and K is some non-negative real number. The weights $\lambda_1,\ldots, \lambda_n$ must all be strictly positive because $\lambda_i = 0$ for some i would mean that utility transfers to and from the ith individual are not possible. The constant K represents the maximum amount of welfare that can be achieved by society as a whole in this hypothetical situation, and it is postulated that "welfare" is an entity which can be divided up among individuals in any way, with the weights $\lambda_1,\ldots, \lambda_n$ acting as the rates of conversion of individual utilities into units of this common entity, called "welfare." Now let $(v_1,\ldots, v_n)$ be a feasible utility profile, $(v_1,\ldots, v_n) \in U(\boldsymbol{\lambda}, K)$. Under this profile, person i's well-being, measured in common units of welfare, is given by the quantity $\lambda_i v_i$. Therefore, in this hypothetical setting, Rawls' Difference Principle would dictate that $(v_1,\ldots, v_n)$ be selected from the set $U(\boldsymbol{\lambda}, K)$ so as to maximize the *least* of the quantities $\lambda_1 v_1,\ldots, \lambda_n v_n$. If $(v_1^*,\ldots, v_n^*)$ is a utility profile in $U(\boldsymbol{\lambda}, K)$ at which this maximum is attained, then I shall say, for the sake of brevity, that $(v_1^*,\ldots, v_n^*)$ is a *λ-maxmin utility profile*, for total welfare level K.

In the second stage of the argument, transferable utility is no longer postulated, which means that the set of feasible utility profiles is no longer of the special form, $U(\boldsymbol{\lambda}, K)$, of the previous paragraph. Instead, we are back with our old set U, which is obtained by taking the image of the set F of feasible distribution schemes in the space of utility profiles, $U = \{(u_1(x),\ldots, u_n(x)) \mid x \in F\}$. To handle this situation, Shapley tells us to keep searching through different systems of weights, $\boldsymbol{\lambda}$, locating in each case a $\boldsymbol{\lambda}$-maxmin utility profile for some appropriate welfare level K. The search is over as soon as one finds a system of weights, say $\boldsymbol{\lambda}^*$, having the following two properties: First, there must exist a feasible distribution scheme x^* ($x^* \in F$) such that the n-tuple $(u_1(x^*),\ldots, u_n(x^*))$ is a $\boldsymbol{\lambda}$-maxmin utility profile, with the constant K to be determined by the next requirement. This means that at $\boldsymbol{\lambda}^*$, the transferable utility maxmin is attainable without any transfers actually taking place. Second, the system of weights $\boldsymbol{\lambda}^*$ must correspond to the distribution scheme x^* so that, at x^*, utility is in fact *locally* transferable at the rates implied by $\boldsymbol{\lambda}^*$. (More precisely, $W(x, \boldsymbol{\lambda}^*)$ must be a maximum on F at $x = x^*$, which means that if person i's utility is reduced from $u_i(x^*)$ to $u_i(x^*) - \varepsilon$, then the maximum F-feasible utility gain that person j can get from this is no greater than $\varepsilon(\lambda_i^*/\lambda_j^*)$.) This second requirement determines the value of the constant K appearing in the first requirement. Specifically, $K = \sum \lambda_i^* u_i(x^*) = W(x^*, \boldsymbol{\lambda}^*)$.

All this may now be summarized by a formal definition that will lead to a statement of the ethical principle which has been the object of the present discussion.

DEFINITION. Let F, $F \subset X$, be the set of feasible distribution schemes and let $u_1,..., u_n$ be utilities defined on X. A distribution scheme $x^* \in F$ will be referred to as a *Rawls–Shapley scheme* if there exists a system of weights $\boldsymbol{\lambda}^* = (\lambda_1^*,..., \lambda_n^*)$, with $\lambda_i^* > 0$ for $i = 1,..., n$ and $\lambda_1^* + \cdots + \lambda_n^* = 1$, such that the following two conditions hold:

(i) $\boldsymbol{\lambda}^*$ is a system of weights corresponding to x^*. That is,

$$W(x^*, \boldsymbol{\lambda}^*) \geqslant W(x, \boldsymbol{\lambda}^*) \qquad \text{for all} \quad x \in F;$$

(ii) the n-tuple $(u_1(x^*),..., u_n(x^*))$ is a $\boldsymbol{\lambda}^*$-maxmin utility profile for total welfare level $W(x^*, \boldsymbol{\lambda}^*)$. In other words, the quantity

$$\min[\lambda_1^* v_1, \lambda_2^* v_2,..., \lambda_n^* v_n]$$

is at a maximum on the set $U(\boldsymbol{\lambda}^*, W(x^*, \boldsymbol{\lambda}^*))$ when $v_1 = u_1(x^*)$, $v_2 = u_2(x^*),..., v_n = u_n(x^*)$.

To spare the reader the need to flip pages back and forth, let me repeat the definition of the set $U(\boldsymbol{\lambda}, K)$:

$$U(\boldsymbol{\lambda}, K) = \left\{ (v_1,..., v_n) \;\middle|\; \begin{array}{l} v_1,..., v_n \text{ non-negative real} \\ \text{numbers with } \lambda_1 v_1 + \cdots + \lambda_n v_n \leqslant K \end{array} \right\}.$$

It is now possible to state:

DIFFERENCE PRINCIPLE WITHOUT INTERPERSONAL COMPARISONS. *Society should always select a Rawls–Shapley Distribution scheme.*

An analysis of this new principle would require that three questions be considered. First, under what conditions do Rawls–Shapley distribution schemes exist? Second, if Rawls–Shapley schemes exist, are they typically unique? (If they are not, then a tie-breaking rule may be needed.) Third, what is the axiomatic basis for a principle of social choice demanding that Rawls–Shapley schemes shall always be selected? The following theorem serves to answer all three questions at once.

THEOREM. *Let F ($F \subset X$) be the set of feasible distribution schemes and* *let the Principle of Non-polarization be satisfied. Assume also that there exists in F a distribution scheme $\hat{x}$ with $u_i(\hat{x}) > 0$ for $i = 1, \ldots, n$. A distribution scheme x^*, $x^* \in F$, is a Rawls–Shapley scheme if, and only if, the product*

$$u_1(x) \cdot u_2(x) \cdots u_n(x)$$

is a maximum on F when $x = x^*$.

In other words, x^* is a Rawls–Shapley scheme if, and only if, x^* is the solution on F of Nash's |17| bargaining problem. (Recall that utilities have all been so normalized that $u_i(x_0) = 0$ for $i = 1, \ldots, n$, where x_0 is the so-called status quo.)

Sketch of the proof. One proceeds by showing, first of all, that x^* is a Rawls–Shapley scheme if, and only if, there exists a system of weights $\boldsymbol{\lambda}^* = (\lambda_1^*, \ldots, \lambda_n^*)$ with $\lambda_i^* > 0$ for $i = 1, \ldots, n$ and $\lambda_1^* + \cdots + \lambda_n^* = 1$, such that the following two conditions hold:

(a) $W(x^*, \boldsymbol{\lambda}^*) \geqslant W(x, \boldsymbol{\lambda}^*)$ for all $x \in F$;

(b) $\lambda_1^* u_1(x^*) = \lambda_2^* u_2(x^*) = \cdots = \lambda_n^* u_n(x^*)$.

Showing this is quite straightforward. Now, shifting the discussion into the space of utility profiles, it is possible to write down the problem of finding a Rawls–Shapley scheme as follows: Let U be a subset of the non-negative orthant in Euclidean n-space, and assume that U is convex and that it possesses a point whose components are strictly positive. Find a point $\mathbf{u}^* = (u_1^*, \ldots, u_n^*)$ for which there exists a system of weights $\boldsymbol{\lambda}^* = (\lambda_1^*, \ldots, \lambda_n^*)$ with $\lambda_i^* > 0$ for $i = 1, \ldots, n$ and $\lambda_1^* + \cdots + \lambda_n^* = 1$, such that

(a′) $\sum_{i=1}^{n} \lambda_i^* u_i^* \geqslant \sum_{i=1}^{n} \lambda_i^* u_i$ for all $(u_1, \ldots, u_n) \in U$;

(b′) $\lambda_1^* u_1^* = \lambda_2^* u_2^* = \cdots = \lambda_n^* u_n$.

What remains now is to verify that we have here a procedure for associating a point $\mathbf{u}^*$ with a given convex set U in such a way that all the axioms of Nash's |17| solution of the bargaining problem are satisfied. (See, e.g., Roth |20| for a statement of these axioms in the case of a bargaining problem involving n persons.) This verification completes the proof of the theorem, in view of the fact that, under the hypotheses of the theorem, if a solution to Nash's problem exists, then it is unique.

Here, then, are the answers to the three questions posed above. First, under the premises of the theorem, a sufficient condition for the existence of the Rawls–Shapley scheme is the compactness of the set U of feasible utility profiles (and boundedness of U is in fact a necessary condition). Second, under the premises of the theorem, if a Rawls–Shapley scheme exists then it is unique, up to a matter of indifference for all individuals. Third, the axiomatic basis for selecting a Rawls–Shapley scheme is given by Nash's four well-known postulates, namely, Pareto-efficiency, symmetry, invariance under linear transformations of utilities, and invariance under deletion of non-optimal alternatives.

There is an air of anti-climax about the foregoing theorem: All this work to release Rawls from the clutches of interpersonal comparisons, culminating in a return to a conceptual framework introduced by Nash in 1950. This is particularly disappointing in view of the fact that Nash's bargaining theory is known to have a serious deficiency—when interpreted as a theory of distributive justice—namely, that it leads to distributions that tend to assign greater rewards to persons having utilities that are closer to linearity, and this can be regarded as a bias in favor of the rich and against the poor. (See, for example, Luce and Raiffa [14, pp. 129–130].)

However, it is possible also to turn the matter around and state the moral of the foregoing theorem in a more positive way: We find John Nash's view of how bargaining determines a social contract receiving renewed support from unexpected quarters, namely, from John Rawls' ethics (combined with Lloyd Shapley's method for dealing with interpersonal comparisons). It is possible that a change in the definition of "the status quo" would permit this positive conclusion to stand, while at the same time eliminating the problem of the bias in favor of the rich. But this would be a topic for a separate study.

References

1. K. J. Arrow, Rational choice function and orderings, *Economica, New Series*, **26** (1959).
2. K. J. Arrow, Some ordinalist-utilitarian notes on Rawls' theory of justice, *J. Philos.* **70**, No. 9 (1973).
3. K. J. Arrow, Extended sympathy and the possibility of social choice, *Amer. Econ. Rev.* **67**, No. 1 (1977)
4. R. J. Aumann and M. Kurz, Power and taxes, *Econometrica* **45**, No. 5 (1977).
5. B. Barry, "The Liberal Theory of Justice," Oxford Univ. Press (Clarendon), London/New York, 1973.
6. C. d'Aspremont and L. Gevers, Equity and the informational basis of collective choice, *Rev. Econ. Studies* **44**, No. 2 (1977).
7. F. Y. Edgeworth, "Mathematical Physics," Kegan Paul, London, 1881. (Reprinted 1967 by Augustus M. Kelley, New York.)
8. F. Y. Edgeworth, "Papers Relating to Political Economy," Vol. III, Macmillan & Co., London, 1925.
9. S. Gordon, John Rawls' Difference Principle, utilitarianism, and the optimum degree of inequality, *J. Philos.* **70**, No. 9 (1973).
10. P. J. Hammond, Equity, Arrow's conditions, and Rawls' Difference Principle, *Econometrica* **44**, No. 4 (1976).
11. J. C. Harsanyi, Cardinal welfare, individualistic ethics and interpersonal comparisons of utility, *J. Political Econ.* **63** (1955).

12. J. C. HARSANYI, Can the Maximin Principle serve as a basis for morality? A critique of John Rawls' theory, *Amer. Political Sci. Rev.* **69** (1975).
13. D. H. KRANTZ, R. D. LUCE, P. SUPPES, AND A. TVERSKY, "Foundations of Measurement," Vol. 1, Academic Press, New York, 1971.
14. R. D. LUCE AND H. RAIFFA, "Games and Decisions," Wiley, New York, 1958.
15. D. LYONS, Rawls versus utilitarianism, *J. Philos.* **69**, No. 18 (1972).
16. G. MCCLELLAND AND J. ROHRBAUGH, "Who Accepts the Pareto Axiom? The Role of Utility and Equity in Arbitration Decisions," Research Report No. 202, Institute of Behavioral Science, University of Colorado, 1978.
17. J. F. NASH, The Bargaining problem, *Econometrica* **18** (1950).
18. R. NOZICK, "Anarchy, State and Utopia," Basic Books, New York, 1974.
19. J. RAWLS, "A Theory of Justice," Belknap Press, Cambridge, Mass., 1971.
20. A. E. ROTH, The Nash solution and the utility of Bargaining, *Econometrica* **46**, (1978).
21. A. K. SEN, "Collective Choice and Social Welfare," Holden–Day, San Francisco, 1970.
22. A. K. SEN, Rawls versus Bentham: An axiomatic examination of the pure distribution problem, *Theory & Decision* **4** (1974). (Reprinted *in* "Reading Rawls" (N. Daniels, Ed.), Basic Books, New York, 1974).
23. A. K. SEN, On Weights and measures: Informational constraints in social welfare analysis, *Econometrica* **45**, No. 7 (1977).
24. H. SIDGWICK, "The Methods of Ethics," Macmillan & Co., London, 1874.
25. L. S. SHAPLEY, Utility comparison and the theory of games, *in* "La Décision," Colloques Internationaux du CNRS, CNRS, Paris, 1969.
26. S. STRASNICK, Social Choice and the derivation of Rawls' Difference Principle, *J. Philos.* **73**, No. 4 (1976).
27. H. UZAWA, The Kuhn–Tucker theorem in concave programming, *in* "Studies in Linear and Non-Linear Programming" (K. J. Arrow, L. Hurwicz, and H. Uzawa, Eds.), Stanford Univ. Press, Stanford, Calif., 1958.

[14]

Eastern Economic Journal, Vol. VIII, No. 1, January 1982

Difficulties with the Element of Time and the 'Principles' of Economics or Some Lies My Teachers Told Me

LAWRENCE A. BOLAND*

"The Hatter was the first to break the silence. 'What day of the month is it?' he said, turning to Alice: he had taken his watch out of his pocket, and was looking at it uneasily, shaking it every now and then, holding it to his ear . . .
'Two days wrong!' sighed the Hatter. 'I told you butter wouldn't suit the works!' he added, looking angrily at the March Hare.
'It was the *best* butter,' the March Hare replied."

Lewis Carroll

As a child of the 50's and 60's I never learned to read originals—we were taught to be in a big hurry. Consequently I accepted the many second-hand reports which alleged that the contributions of Robinson, Sraffa, Keynes, Chamberlin, Triffin, et al, represented major or revolutionary advances in economic science. If the truth were told, economic theory is no better off—maybe it is even worse off.

With respect to Marshall's *Principles* the only apparent accomplishment of more modern writings is a monumental obfuscation of the problem that Marshall's method of analysis was created to solve. A clear understanding of the methodological problem that concerned Marshall is absolutely essential for a clear understanding of the Marshallian version of neoclassical economics. Unfortunately, due to our technically oriented training we have lost the ability to appreciate Marshall's approach to the central problem of economic analysis which is based on the methodological role of the element of Time. Laying a new foundation for the appreciation of "the element of Time" and its role in Marshall's neoclassical economics is the aim of this paper.[1]

Unlike neo-Walrasian equilibrium models which take time for granted, Marshall's economics allows time to play a central role. Simply stated, the recognition of the element of time is Marshall's solution to the problem of explanation which all economists face. That problem can only be appreciated in relation to a specific explanatory principle or behavioural hypothesis. Such a relationship was introduced in the preface to Marshall's first edition where he refers to the *Principle of Continuity*. But he does not explain either the role of continuity in the problem of explanation or the problem itself. The problem, it turns out, results primarily from a second explanatory principle, the *Principle of Substitution* which he introduces later (in Book V). I will argue here that Marshall saw an essen-

*Simon Fraser University, Burnaby, BC, Canada V5A 1S6

[1]For a discussion of the problem of time in neo-Walrasian and Austrian models, see [Boland, 1978].

tial role for time in economic explanations for the simple reason that he wished to apply only these two principles to all economic problems.

The Explanatory Principles

Surprisingly, there are only two explanatory principles stated by Marshall—the Principle of Substitution and the Principle of Continuity. These two explanatory principles are distinguished from "laws" (or tendencies) which also play a role in his explanations. The former are assumptions (we assume because we do not know) but Marshall considers the latter to be beyond doubt.

The Principle of Substitution is easily the more familiar of the two. It says, *everyone is an optimizer* (i.e., a maximizer or minimizer) *given his or her situation* (including his or her endowment). But *by itself* it is not sufficient explanation; the Principle of Substitution presumes the truth of the Principle of Continuity. Since Marshall wished to apply the Principle of Substitution to everything, he needs to show that the Principle of Continuity applies to everything. In simple terms, the Principle of Continuity says everything is a relative matter of degree. Consequently, for Marshall there are no class differences, only matters of degree. He takes the same attitude towards the differences between "city men" and "ordinary people," between altruistic motives and selfish motives, between short-run and long-run, between cause and effect, between Rent and Interest, between man and his appliances, between productive and nonproductive labour, between capital and non-capital, and even between needs and non-essentials. In all cases whether the degree in question is more or less is relative to how the distinction is being used *in an explanation.* For example, "what is a short-period for one problem, is a long-period for another" (p. vii).[2]

[2]All page references enclosed in parentheses are from [Marshall, 1964].

I claim that it is because Marshall appreciates the methodological problem of the applicability of the Principle of Substitution, i.e., of what we now call the neoclassical maximization hypothesis, that he postpones its introduction until Book V. The first four Books are devoted to convincing the readers that the assumption of maximization is applicable by demonstrating the universal applicability of the Principle of Continuity—or specifically what modern theorists might call the connectedness of choice options. There must be available a continuous range of possible options over which there is free choice (i.e., substitutability cannot be completely limited), and the choice must not be an extreme (or special) case—otherwise the question would be begged as to what determines the constraining extreme limit. What Marshall stresses (e.g., in his Preface) is that the applicability of the Principle of Continuity (and consequently the applicability of the Principle of Substitution) depends heavily on "the element of Time."

The Element of Time

Substitution Without Time

By ignoring the element of time, our teachers (and their textbooks) would have us believe that the Principle of Substitution is the only hypothetical aspect of the 'Principles'. Samuelson saw that even the notion of a stable equilibrium can be reduced to the Principle of Substitution [e.g., Samuelson 1965, p. 5], i.e., to the matter of constrained maximization. Time, if considered at all, is deemed relevant only for the proofs of the stability of equilibria. Most of us have been trained not to see any difficulty with the element of time—for fear of being accused of incompetence.

Marshall's view was quite the contrary: the element of time is central. For instance, to presume that *at* any point in time a firm has chosen the best labour and capital mix presumes that the time elapsed since the relevant givens were established (viz, the technology, the prices, the market conditions, etc.), and that there was sufficient time for the firm to vary those things over which it has control (viz, the labour hired and the capital purchased) prior to the decision or substitution. Even when its price has gone up the firm cannot respond immediately; nor can it stop production and its employment of labour merely because the price has fallen (cf. p. 298). Contrary to modern textbooks, in Marshall's economics very short-run market pressures are more "the noise" than they are "the signal" *when viewed from the perspective of the businessman's decision process.*[3]

Time and Explanation

Time is an essential element in Marshall's method of explanation. Marshall tells us quite a lot about explanation in economics. He stresses the need to recognize the role of fixed "conditions," but he also stresses that the "fixity" is not independent of the defining "time periods"—remember, according to the Principle of Continuity everything is a matter of degree.

Because Marshall's use of the term "conditions" can lead to confusion, it is relevant to examine his theory of explanation more specifically by distinguishing between dependent, independent and exogenous variables, and between fixed and exogenous conditions. These distinctions crucially involve the element of time.

The relationship between dependent and independent variables is supposed to be analogous to the relationship between causes and effects. But, Marshall cautions us that all such distinctions are relative. For instance, in the very short period the market price is the dependent variable and, given the demand, the quantity supplied is the independent variable. However, in the usual (expected) short-run, the market price is the independent variable and, given technology (i.e., the production function), the quantity supplied is the dependent variable.

In the Preface to the *Principles* Marshall recognizes the usual type of interdependence as being an instance of the Principle of Continuity. He specifically credits Cournot with teaching us to face the difficulty of "mutual determination." Marshall calls this type of interdependence a mathematical conception of continuity although he refers this conception only to the relationship between causes and effects.[4] Today we might say that in Marshall's short period price and quantity are both endogenous variables and are *simultaneously determined* by the exogenously given technology and demand. Thus, the distinction between independent and dependent variables is only a matter of verbal convenience since both are endogenous (see further [Boland 1975; 1978]).

What Marshall calls "conditions" are variables which are "exogenously fixed" during the period of time under consideration. It is their fixity which Marshall relies on in his explanation of behaviour (where the fixed variables are the constraints in a maximization process). The exogenous reason why they are fixed is the logical basis for their use in his explanation. Note, however, that exogenous variables need not be fixed, their fixity only makes things more convenient.

The problem of explanation—in Marshall's view—is one of carefully defining the fixity of the "conditions" by defining the relevant period of time for the operation of the explanatory Principle of Substitution. Of course, what is a relevant period of time depends conversely on what are the relevant exogenous

[3]See (p. 314); the businessman must always make a judgement as to whether day to day changes in the market will be long lasting enough to justify investment and hiring decisions.

[4]His reference to Cournot has often misled modern commentators to think that the mathematical conception is all that Marshall was saying—rather than the more important methodological issue of relative degrees.

conditions for the application of the Principle of Substitution. For example, in Marshall's short-period—"a few months" (p. 314)—virtually everything but the level of output and the amount of labour employed is by definition fixed; but in his long period—"several years" (p. 315)—everything but technology and social conditions is endogenous.

The difficulty with Marshall's approach to explanation when there are many variables is that it is difficult to distinguish between the endogenous conditions which are exogenously fixed for the period of time considered but change as more time elapses (which permits more and more variables to be chosen, e.g., fixed capital) and the truly exogenous conditions that can never be made to submit to the Principle of Substitution (e.g., weather, social conditions, states of knowledge, etc.). In Marshall's economics the truly exogenous variables are the only "causes" in the strict sense. As Marshall views this, if one is to provide a long-run explanation, "time must be allowed for causes to produce their effects" (p. 30). Of course, this ". . . is a source of great difficulty in economics . . ." because ". . . the causes themselves may have changed" (p. 30). Note however, that the changeability of "causes," i.e. of exogenous variables, is *not* the problem of explanation, but rather, it is the more narrow methodological problem of *verifying or refuting* one's explanation.[5]

I will argue that even when changes in the exogenous givens are assumed away, the fundamental problem for all explanations involving time still exists. The logic of explanation (for example, of all the co-determined endogenous variables) requires that we recognize at least one exogenous variable; and given maximization with exogenous tastes and exogenous constraints, changes in endogenous variables are explained as being caused by changes in at least one of the exogenous variables. But this means that an explanation of long-run dynamic behavior requires an exogenous variable which is impervious to the amount of real time elapsed in the long-run (otherwise, the explanation might be circular). The explanatory element of time is then to provide a time-independent exogenous variable—i.e., one which does not change over the defined long-run.

Marshall's Strategy

It would be misleading to suggest that Marshall's problem of explanation is merely a matter of defining long-run equilibrium, for it is also a matter of how the long-run equilibrium is reached. Again, in Marshall's view (p. 304), the explanatory problem is that there are too many exogenous variables in the short-run during which most decisions are made. His strategy is intended to reduce the number of exogenous variables by increasing the number of variables to which the Principle of Substitution can be applied at later stages.[6] Marshall thus considers the problem of explanation to be solvable since he recognizes that there is a different degree of changeability for each variable (another application of the Principle of Continuity). In short, Marshall's strategy is to distinguish between short-run and long-run explanations. Any complete explanation must specifically *assume* which variables can be changed most quickly—i.e., variables must be ordered according to their changeability. Different orderings may yield a different path to the long-run equilibrium. Unless the assumption is very specific it may be impossible to distinguish between a long-run moving equilibrium and a short-run movement toward a new long-run equilibrium.

[5]One must be careful to distinguish between the logical validity of an explanation and its truth status; see [Boland, 1978, pp. 246–9; 1979, Section 1].

[6]The variables to be treated later, then, are "independent" variables.

Marshall's view of explanation recognizes yet another aspect of the element of Time. If the state of affairs at any point in time is to be *explained* as a consequence of someone's optimizing choice, it must *have been* possible to alter one's choices—and this possibility is both a matter of the time available and the continuity of options. Needless to say, it also presumes the ability to know what is the best *option.* Learning what is the best option takes time (p. 284). This question of learning, I would argue, is *the* explanatory problem involving the element of time. Of course, for Marshall, the inductive scientist, time is all that is necessary for the accumulation of the needed knowledge. Unlike the classical school Marshall sees no need to assume "perfect knowledge" because he explicitly wishes to recognize the period of time under consideration—a period he would consider sufficiently long to obtain any "necessary knowledge" [for more on inductivism in economics, see Boland 1982, chapters 1 and 4].

Although Marshall gives a prominent role to the distinction between long and short periods, it is not sufficient to solve his problem of explanation—which, as has been said, is a problem concerning the methodological choice of exogenous variables that are impervious to time. Yet, most commentators seem to think that Marshall's "statical method"—namely the contents of Book V—constitutes his solution to the problem of explanation. This is a mistake.

The first point to be made is that Marshall's "statical" or partial equilibrium method of analysis yields incomplete explanations. The "statical" method is relevant only for decisions "on the margin" or in the neighborhood of an equilibrium position. By itself this method examines the necessary but not the sufficient conditions for equilibrium. The second point to be made is that Marshall does offer a more complete explanation which is based on the contents of Book IV. By itself, Book V deals only with the "noise" in order at best to explain it away. A source of an explanation of an economy's true dynamics and its application of the Principle of Continuity to the element of Time is to be found in Book IV. These two points will be discussed in turn.

The Insufficiency of Book V

I do not think Marshall ever claims that Book V alone represents a complete explanation of an economy's behavior. Yet, judging by modern textbooks, one could easily think that Book V is "the principles of economics." What we call microeconomic analysis today can all be found in Book V. Nevertheless, implicitly Book V provides only the necessary conditions for any equilibrium. That is, on the *assumption* that an economy is in long-run equilibrium at a point in time, certain necessary relationships must hold whenever that assumption is true. It is a "statical" method because it may be relevant only for that one equilibrium position at one point in time. In effect, Book V examines the local stability properties of the *assumed* long-run equilibrium that are the logical consequences of definitions of equilibrium and the long period. But it will be argued below that the stability properties are heavily dependent on the empirical assertions of Book IV.

To be specific, before Book V can be considered relevant for anything, i.e., play a role in economic analysis, a key question must be asked: why should there ever be a long-run equilibrium? Marshall approaches this question in two ways. The most familiar is in Book V in which he defines an ordering of the changeability of the variables with respect to three periods of time—"the very short period," "the short period" and "the long period." The quickest variable in Marshall's world is the market determined price. In fact, his definition of a market is not the textbook one of a *place* where buyers and sellers meet to haggle over the price. Marshall makes the existence of a market depend on whether the price clears *quickly* enough for all producers to face the *same price* regardless of their location. For Marshall then there is no market for any good whose price is either not uniform[7] or not quickly established. In effect, this axiom about market prices makes all firms price-takers since it takes longer to establish their (short-run) decisions than the price itself.

Marshall's definition of the market means that the market price (as opposed to the short-run or long-run equilibrium price) is the only *real time* observable price. This theory of market prices assumes that the supply quantity is fixed—virtually everything is fixed but the price. The remainder of the discussion in Book V is an examination of what happens to the market price over time when more and more of the fixed givens are allowed to change. For example, Marshall begins by allowing the firms to make substitutions in their quantity supplied in response to the current level of the market price (relative to costs). This "short-run" *process* of substitution requires some time—"a few months or a year" (p. 314).

Marshall says that he wishes to argue that demand determines the market price in one extreme—the very short-run—and technology determines the market price in the other extreme—the long-run equilibrium. Implicitly the real world is somewhere in between.[8] Again, the meaning of "determines" is only a matter of necessary relationships of the defined equilibria. If the economy is at a long-run equilibrium, it must also be at a short-run equilibrium, since if it were not there would be short-run incentives to change the givens which are the constraints in the determination of the market price. Similarly, the short-run equilibrium presumes that the market is in equilibrium. In other words, every long-run equilibrium must also be a short-run equilibrium and every short-run equilibrium must be a market-run equilibrium. This "nesting" of the forms of equilibrium is the essence of Marshall's "statical method."

Although it is now very easy to list the necessary conditions for the existence of a long-run equilibrium, the key question still concerns the sufficient conditions for the existence of a long-run equilibrium, which must be consistent with both a short-run equilibrium and a market equilibrium. The question of consistency has been a major source of controversy over the last 50 years. The logical problem is that the absence of excess profits in conjunction with profit maximization in the long period implies that the production function is locally linear-homogeneous (constant returns to scale); but this implication is inconsistent with a downward sloping demand curve, the ultimate constraint thought to be necessary to limit the size of the producer.

Marshall's only line of defense is his other approach, which is based on the Principle of Continuity. Given the continuous operation of the Principle of Substitution, it is quite possible for the price to be above or below the long-run equilibrium price. When it is above there are positive excess profits and when it is below there are losses and, logically, there must be a (long-run equilibrium) point in between where excess profits are zero. The apparent inconsistency is due only to the discussion of the hypothetical and heuristic "stationary state"—which is a very special type of long-run equilibrium that is supposed to hold for a specified period of time. The only inconsistency is between the previously mentioned nesting of equilibria and the stationary state. Specifically, the inconsistency is that the stability of each of the various equilibria that hold at the long-run equilibrium depends

[7]Marshall allows for different prices as the result of transportation costs (p. 271).

[8]That is, the very short-run is not realistic (p. 304), and the logical consequences of a long-run equilibrium is a stationary state (p. 315, footnote 1); but, a stationary state is alleged to be "a fiction" (p. 305).

on the one hand necessarily on the consideration of *different* periods or lengths of time for each whereas, on the other hand, in the stationary state they are all supposed to refer to the *same* period of time.

Leaving the stationary state aside, there is no reason why the stability of the various forms of equilibrium have to refer to the same set of "conditions" or variables or, equivalently, to the same period of time. Hence, the stability relations (e.g., the necessary slopes of curves) for one form of equilibrium will not be statically consistent with those relations necessary for the stability of another form. If one ignores the element of time it is only too easy to "see" an inconsistency where otherwise there is none.

The Methodology of Book V vs. a Complete Explanation

Once one recognizes the necessary element of time it might appear that there is no logical problem with Book V. But to the contrary, there still remains the matter of explaining *why* there should ever be a long-run equilibrium,[9] and this is a question which must be dealt with in an appropriate frame of reference. Like all explanations there must be something exogenous in Marshall's view of the economy—and it must be something whose exogeneity extends to a longer period of time than the "long period" under consideration. Marshall deals with this issue first in Book IV.

Particularly relevant to Marshall's explanation of an economy is what is now called his "life-cycle" hypothesis of the firm. In its most specific form it is an empirical assertion about the history of an individual firm with a life span of three generations [cf. Hague 1958; Loasby 1978]. In its more general form it says that at the beginning of its life the firm benefits from learning so that its ability to produce increases with its size. Implicitly Marshall is only concerned with growing firms—their size is irreversable, hence time and size go together. At the end of its life every firm suffers from diminishing returns. In either case, the life-cycle trajectory is the needed long-run exogenous variable.

By itself, this hypothesis about the beginning and the end of the life of a firm does not seem very relevant. The addition of the Principle of Continuity, however, renders the desired result. This principle allows us to conclude that since returns change from increasing to decreasing, at some point in between there must have been "constant" returns. This point is a possible long-run equilibrium. Given the life-cycle hypothesis and continuity, every firm must pass through this point. Once it is reached the "statical method" can be used; but it remains merely a "snap-shot," relevant only for that one point (in the history of the firm).

There is absolutely no reason why all the firms in an economy should simultaneously reach the point of constant returns—that is, reach the "turning point," as Marshall calls it. It might be interesting for someone to explore such a fantasy world, but nowhere does Marshall seem to be suggesting that such a state of affairs is *necessary*. Book V nevertheless explores the nature of this turning point: Book V ". . . is not descriptive, nor does it deal constructively with real problems" (p. 269). However, Marshall does say Book V ". . . sets out the *theoretical backbone* of our knowledge of the causes which govern value" (pp. 269–70, emphasis added). However, this statement is qualified. He says ". . . it aims not so much at the attainment of knowledge . . ." but rather ". . . at the power to obtain and *arrange* knowledge with regard to two opposing sets of forces . . ." (p. 270, emphasis added).

Marshall's use of the words "theoretical"

[9] Book V discusses only the *logical* possibility of a long-run equilibrium.

and "arrange" is slightly different than usual modern usage. His usage is related to Friedman's *as if* approach to explanation. There is no claim that the method of analysis—of arranging the facts of business—is a true explanation. There is only the claim that the nature of the inevitable turning point can be understood to be the result *if* the world were in a state of equilibrium at a moment in time—or more properly, in a state where forces are balanced.

Like most economists' adventures in methodology, Marshall wishes to be all things to all people; thus his is not a pure example of the Instrumentalism we associate with Friedman. Rather, the Introduction to Book V gives a classic example of what we now call Conventionalist methodology. We are offered a way of looking at things. What is offered is not claimed to be true; it can be judged only to the extent that it is better or worse than some other competing view. Book V is filled with conventions with no claim to their truth status (e.g.,the representative firm, the stationary state, the market, the long-period, etc.). Only in those cases where we know that he thinks a particular convention is a fiction do we have examples of the "as if" methodology [cf. Boland 1979, pp. 512–3].

The methodology discussions of the *Principles* are not very interesting today but his theory of the firm should be. The point at issue is that Book IV is a foundation for a complete theory of the firm: the firm is always to be found somewhere on its life-cycle trajectory. Where it is is determined completely by the time elapsed, (cf. 258), but the value of that position can only be determined as a relative value, relative to its past and its future. There are simply too many contingencies to be able to determine the absolute value. But remember, the Principle of Continuity is only concerned with relative values.

Book V does offer a way of seeing the absolute value as a consequence of external forces, i.e., of competitive market pressures. But there is no reason why the actual, real-time, values would ever be "long period normal" prices. The existence of long period normal prices is merely, one might suggest, a beautiful fiction which lends itself to simple mathematical analysis having no bearing on "real problems" (cf. p. 269).

Inadequacies of Marshall's Method vs. Problems Created By His Followers

Over the last fifty years there have been two major problems in the application of Marshall's principles; both of them involve the element of time. The first concerns the meaning of increasing returns and the nature of the long-run equilibrium. The second concerns the artificial distinction between "historical" and "logical" time.

Problems with the Firm's Long-run Equilibrium

Marshall's Victorian style lends itself easily to distortion. What he meant by certain words in one place may not have the same meaning in another. For example, the term "increasing returns" is used in two different senses; both result from his implict assumption that the firm is always growing; hence size and time go together. In Book V he uses the term to describe the observation that average productivity rises over time for any given input levels (p. 377). This use is at variance with modern usage. Earlier, in Book IV, he employs the term in the limited modern sense to mean an increase in output which is proportionally greater than the increase in the size of the firm (p. 266). A similar confusion derives from his use of the term "margin" when discussing his "representative firm." By definition, the representative firm is at the "turning point" on the life-cycle trajectory. At that point average and marginal cost both equal price; thus it is possible to use the average and marginal magnitudes interchangably. But another use of the term "marginal" emerges when he refers to the representative firm's contribution to its industry's output.

These confusions are merely irritants. The major problem is ignoring the element of time inherent in the "statical method" when applied to long-run equilibria (as noted above). Although the difficulty is primarily logical it results from conjoining four statements whose individual truth status depends on different periods of time. They are the following:

(i) prices are determined before the firm makes its supply choice; hence prices are given.
(ii) the Principle of Continuity applied to all inputs (all inputs are variable) means that the production function of the firm is locally linear-homogeneous and that the level of output is always equal to the sum of the marginal productivities each multiplied by the respective input.
(iii) the Principle of Substitution (i.e., profit maximization) applied to all variable inputs means that the marginal productivity of each input multiplied by the product's price will always equal the price of that input.
(iv) the firm is at the "turning point," i.e., its excess profits are zero.

There is no difficulty with the conjunction of these four statements if they only refer to a single point in time [Boland 1978, pp. 242–3]. Moreover, even over the short-run given (i) any two of the remaining statements imply the other one. So long as the theory of the firm is confined to the "short period" there need not be any logical problems. The problems that are alleged to exist arise only when the theory (i.e., the Principle of Substitution) is applied in the long run period to the short-run *constraints*.

Applications of the Principle of Substitution involve some form of maximization (or minimization) facing fixed constraints. In the short-run, all the variables which cannot (by definition) be varied constitute the short-run constraints (e.g., the short-run may presume capital is fixed but labour is variable). In the long-run everything except the production function is supposed to be variable (by definition); but this raises a major methodological problem. Anything which is variable must logically be the object of the Principle of Substitution. This means that the variables that served as fixed constraints in the short-run become endogenous variables in the long-run. But, this also means that there are no constraints in the long-run and this leaves the Principle of Substitution inoperable in the long-run. In the long period, then, the conjunction of the assumptions of a price-taker, (i), of the changeability of all variables in the production function, (ii), and of profit maximization with regard to all changeable variables, (iii), seems to deny any limit to the size of the individual firms—as if size has nothing to do with time (this interpretation of Marshall's theory of the firm, by its focusing only on the internal logic of maximization, is quite contrary to the views expressed in Book IV).

The methodological problem of explaining the size of the firm (as a consequence of maximization) seems to have troubled many of Marshall's followers although it did not seem to trouble him since his Principle of Continuity discourages extreme viewpoints, such as long-run equilibria. The problem only arises when one attempts to apply the Principle of Substitution to the size of the firm in the long-run. Today this problem is avoided (i.e., hidden under the rug) by saying that one should only explain the size of the industry. But this tactic merely raises other questions such as, what prevents any one firm from taking over the industry as a monopoly?

Although there is considerable discussion of industries in the *Principles,* Marshall's explanatory Principle of Substitution is applied only to the (short-run) decisions of the individual firm. The industry is merely an epiphenomenon—the logical consequence of what individual firms do. This is a standard neoclassical viewpoint. However, this viewpoint has always posed certain puzzles concerning the interaction of demand and supply in the market. The difficulty is that both the market and the industry are defined for a specific good but the market is related to the individual firm only through the going price. The price by itself says nothing about quantities except that aggregate quantity demanded must equal industry supply. But, if individual firms must determine the quantity supplied independently of each other, the aggregate quantity supplied is only an epiphenomenon. In terms of Marshall's individualistic methodology, this approach to the relationship between firm and industry appears rather mysterious.

In order to overcome the mystery, Marshall offers the infamous heuristic fiction, the representative firm. Unfortunately, whenever one tries to use the representative firm, instead of Book IV, to explain the size of the firm as another consequence of an application of the Principle of Substitution, another methodological problem is created. Recall that the representative firm is defined (p. 285) as a firm at the "turning point" and it is also a firm on the margin of the industry (older firms will be making less than normal profits). As a profit maximizer at the turning point (where profits are just normal), the representative firm must face constant returns to scale (at least "locally," see Baumol 1977). On the other hand, as a representative of the industry, it must be constrained by the negatively sloped demand curve. This latter constraint means that we have a fifth statement which must be conjoined with the other four: namely (v) the representative firm's marginal revenue must be less than the price. The problem is that either (v) and (i) are mutually contradictory or one of the other statements must be denied. With respect to any one firm it is not possible for all five statements to be true simultaneously. For example, while profit maximization implies the equality of marginal cost and marginal revenue, zero excess profits implies an equality between average cost and average revenue (the price). Thus, when marginal revenue is less than the price, the firm must be operating where there are increasing returns (since marginal cost must be less than average cost) which is contrary to statement (ii). Note that a firm can still be a price-taker even when its average revenue is falling.

I would speculate that all of the controversies surrounding the long-run theory of the individual firm are merely about which of the five statements should be dropped. Moreover, most of the controversies have ignored the element of time. There is no doubt that *if* one ignores the element of time (which differs according to the statement one is considering) and, instead, views the above statements as holding at a single (static) point of time, then logically some of the statements are mutually inconsistent. As argued by Sraffa and Robinson, something must give. A realistic interpretation is that the idea of a price-taker (i), must go, but Marshall's statical method of dealing with his problem of explanation—distinguishing between very short periods and the short-run—blocks that avenue. Allowing that prices may not be market determined would lead to a conclusion that is contrary to Marshall's objective. If prices were *not* determined in a market, then demand could only play a role in the determination of the size of the *industry*—i.e., given the life-cycle, demand determines the number of firms in an industry—*in the long-run.* Prices are left to be determined by technical and social considerations within and between firms (e.g., without "spoiling the market").

Such conclusions seem to be ideologically unacceptable or mathematically inconvenient for economic theorists—hence they simply have stopped talking about Marshallian economics since what he promised (a role for demand and utility maximization in the determination of prices) seems doomed. What is being suggested here is that things may not be as desperate as everyone seems to fear. Perhaps all that is required is a proper examination of the element of time.

The Distinction between Logical and Historical Time

Contrary to Marshall's view it is claimed by post-Keynesians one must carefully distinguish between "historical" and "logical" time [e.g., Robinson 1974]. Historical time is the usual calendar or clock time within which decision processes are irreversable. In logical time decisions are reversible. For example, the life-cycle hypothesis is in historical time since it is assumed that the firm always gets older; it cannot get younger. One might say that this is because with the passage of time the firm is learning but it cannot "unlearn." The stability analysis of equilibrium theory is in logical time since the analysis is always conducted in terms of questions such as, what *if* the price were higher or lower than the equilibrium price? Logical time is concerned with conceivably possible alternative worlds (regardless of actual events) at any given point in time, whereas historical time may be concerned with the (necessarily) singular event occurring at that time.

The distinction between historical and logical time corresponds respectively to Books IV and V. But, the intellectual separation of these concepts (and Books) into mutually exclusive classes is a direct contradiction of Marshall's Principle of Continuity. Marshall does not claim that these concepts or books should be separated. To the contrary, Books IV and V go together. Reality for Marshall is on the continuum *between* the two extreme concepts, i.e., reality involves both Books in full measure. Any explanation of the behaviour of an enterprise must be both grounded in history (i.e., irreversible past decisions) and explanatorily complete (i.e., it must at least imply a stable determination of the values of the variables to which the Principle of Substitution has been applied.)

Some Closing Remarks

Most of modern economic analysis concerns only the mathematics of Book V. The reason, I think, is simply that Book V is the only part of Marshall's *Principles* that is compatible with the methodological doctrine that dominates economic theory today—Conventionalism: the methodology that restricts research to questions of logical validity instead of empirical truth [see further, Boland 1982, chapters 7 and 8]. Economists today do not wish to discuss the "truth" of economic theories but only examine their logical validity. The reason why logical validity rather than empirical truth is the preferred object is because with the help of mathematical analysis the former can be established more quickly. Even though Marshall stressed the importance of gradual, slow change, those economists in a hurry will find the logic or mathematics of static equilibria more interesting. Logical analysis can be very quick but real change takes real time and thus may not be disposed to easy analysis.

One is reminded of the story of the inebriated gentleman who one evening lost his only quarter far from the nearest streetlight; but he spent all his time looking under the streetlight—because the light was better! I think the profession has devoted enough time searching under the light of *Foundations;* it is time to go back to where the quarter was lost—Book IV of the *Principles.* I am not suggesting that *the* solution to the difficulties with the element of time is to be found in Book IV, but only that in Book IV at least the emphasis is on a realistic approach—an approach which still awaits development and constructive criticism. If teachers wish to be truthful with their students they will tell them where the quarter is.

References

Baumol, W. J. (1977) *Economic Theory and Operations Analysis,* 4th Edition (Englewood Cliffs: Prentice-Hall).

Boland, L. A. (1975) "Uninformative Economic Models," *Atlantic Economic Journal,* vol. 3, pp. 27–32.

Boland, L. A. (1978) "Time in Economics vs. Economics in Time: The 'Hayek Problem,'" *Canadian Journal of Economics,* vol. 11, pp. 240–62.

Boland, L. A. (1979) "A Critique of Freidman's Critics," *Journal of Economic Literature,* vol. 17, pp. 503–22.

Boland, L. A. (1981) "On the Futility of Criticizing the Neoclassical Maximization Hypothesis," *American Economic Review,* Vol. 71, pp. 1031–1036 (Dec.)

Boland, L. A. (1982) *The Foundations of Economic Method,* forthcoming (London: Allen & Unwin).

Hague, D. C. (1958) "Alfred Marshall and the Competitive Firm," *Economic Journal,* vol. 68, pp. 673–90.

Loasby, B. J. (1978) "Whatever Happened to Marshall's Theory of Value?," *Scottish Journal of Political Economy,* vol. 25, pp. 1–12.

Marshall, A. (1964) *Principles of Economics,* 8th Edition (London: Macmillan).

Robbins, L. (1930) "On a Certain Ambiguity in the Conception of Stationary Equilibrium," *Economic Journal,* vol. 40, pp. 194–214.

Robinson, J. (1974) "History versus Equilibrium," Thames Papers in Political Economy.

Samuelson, P. A. (1965) *Foundations of Economic Analysis* (New York: Atheneum).

[15]

Eastern Economic Journal, Vol.VIII, No. 1, January 1982

Biological Theory and Technological Entrepreneurship in Marshall's Writings*

LAURENCE MOSS*

In 1939, Joseph A. Schumpeter explained that the evolution of capitalism "is studded with violent bursts and catastrophes." Schumpeter's entrepreneur disturbed existing business and social structures with the destructive force of a tornado. "We must recognize," Schumpeter continued, "that evolution is lopsided, discontinuous, disharmonious by nature—that the disharmony is inherent in the very *modus operandi* of the factors of progress."[1] It is instructive to begin with Schumpeter's views on economic development because Alfred Marshall's views are exactly the opposite.

In the introduction to his last published work, *Industry and Trade* (1923), Marshall explained that the maxim, "Nature does not willingly make a jump . . . is specially applicable to economic development."[2] Similarly the motto, "Natura non facit saltum," appeared on the title page of Marshall's *Principles of Economics,* and remained there in full view through each of the eight successive editions that appeared between 1890 and 1920. In the introduction to his *Principles,* Marshall attributed the special character of his book to an awareness of "continuity" in both the natural and social world.[3] At one place in his *Principles,* Marshall referred to chapter 14 of Charles Darwin's *On the Origin of the Species* in which Darwin, the illustrious proponent of the natural selection mechanism of evolution, insisted that "natural selection acts *solely* by accumulating slight successive, favorable variations, it can produce no great or sudden modification; it can act only by very short and slow steps. Hence, the canon of 'Natura non facit saltum'. . . ."[4] Like Darwin, Marshall accepted this canon, thereby pledging his allegiance to the naturalist tradition inaugurated by Charles Lyell in the early part of the nineteenth century in his *Principles of Geology* (1830–32). According to that tradition, processes currently at work in the natural world were the same processes at work millions of years ago, and these processes alter the shape and positions of the objects of the natural world slowly over time in small incremental steps.[5] If change in economic life occurs in the same way as change in nature,

*I wish to thank the following individuals for valuable criticisms of an earlier version of this paper: A.W. Coats, Ronald Coase, Frank Genovese, H.S. Gordon, Gerard Koot, Richard Romano, Robert Ronstadt, Donald A. Walker. Any errors that remain are my own.

*Babson College, Wellesly, MA 02157

[1] Joseph A. Schumpeter, *Business Cycles: A Theoretical, Historical and Statistical Analysis of the Capitalist Process* (New York: McGraw-Hill, 1939, p. 102.

[2] Alfred Marshall, *Industry and Trade* (London: Macmillan, 1923), p. 6.

[3] See Alfred Marshall, *Principles of Economics: An Introductory Volume,* 8th ed. (London: Macmillan 1920), ed. C. W. Guillebaud. 2:35.

[4] Charles Darwin, *On the Origin of Species,* Ernst Mayr, ed. (New York: Atheneum, 1967), p. 471.

[5] Lyell, himself, did not advance a "progressive" or evolutionary view of the natural world. Species, like land movements, came and went keeping the natural world in a "steady state." See discussion in Michael Ruse, *The Darwinian Revolution: Science Real Tooth and Claw* (Chicago, 1979), pp. 40–74.

there would seem to be no room for Schumpeter's entrepreneur. Like rivers changing course and mountains rising up, economic development occurs in small incremental steps.

But what if it can be shown that the natural world also evolves in big steps, say, cataclysmic jumps, and radical discontinuities? A great many biologists came to this point of view after rediscovering the pioneering work of Gregor J. Mendel after 1900.[6] Would Marshall have changed his views about economic development? There is evidence to indicate that Marshall was somewhat alarmed by the Mendelian revolution because he understood it to mean that in the area of inheritance and development of new species, nature did move in jumps. By the seventh edition of his *Principles,* Marshall took notice of the Mendelian revolution in biology by stating that whatever the outcome of the debate in biology about explaining evolution in terms of large individual variations, that was simply of no interest to economists because economics deals with aggregates of individuals—average behavior rather than with deviations around the average—and for these problems, gradual continuous change over time was the rule and not the exception. This represents a curious turn of events in the development of Marshall's methodological position. Writing in the *Economic Journal* as early as 1898, Marshall concluded his article on "Mechanical and Biological Analogies in Economics" with the remark that "the Mecca of the economist is economic biology rather than economic dynamics."[7] However, in about a decade the explanatory scheme of biology was to undergo some radical changes that, if copied by economists, would support the Schumpeterian view of economic evolution over Marshall's. Marshall did not react kindly to this change.

I shall organize my discussion in three parts. First, I shall summarize Marshall's view of what constitutes the entrepreneurial function. Marshall's treatment of the technological entrepreneur, in which process innovations are made an ordinary part of everyday business management adds a dynamic element to Marshall's theory of factor substitution. The hypothesis that alterations in relative price encourage innovation, has, since Jacob Schmookler's pioneering work in 1966, turned out to be an empirically significant and reliable guide to policy analysis, thereby adding much empirical support to Marshall's position.[8] In the second part of this paper, I shall attempt to locate precisely those aspects of nineteenth-century biology that Marshall found so congenial to economic analysis. I shall show that the expressions, "survival of the fittest," "natural selection," and "adaptation," all appear in Marshall's writings, but not without undergoing a number of significant qualifications before they are applied to the development of the economy. What was most important to Marshall was the notion of "continuous change"—that economic development, like nature itself, changes in small increments. When twentieth century biologists shifted away from the Lyell-Darwin view of natural processes, Marshall resisted that shift. While Schumpeter, in his theory of economic development and his subsequent use of that theory in his analysis of the behavior of business cycles, flowed with the latest developments in biological research, Marshall held his ground. By the seventh edition of his *Principles,* Marshall appeared to rule out

[6]Loren Eiseley, *Darwin's Century: Evolution and the Men Who Discovered It* (New York, Anchor Books, 1961), pp. 205–232; Hamilton Cravens, *The Triumph of Evolution: American Scientists and the Heredity Environment Controversy 1900–1941* (University of Pennsylvania, 1978), pp. 31–55; Garland E. Allen, "Hugo de Vries and the Reception of the 'Mutation Theory'" *Journal of the History of Biology* 2 (Spring 1969): 55–87. See, however, my remarks in note 55 below.

[7]In Alfred Marshall, *Memorials of Alfred Marshall,* A. C. Pigou, editor (London: Macmillan, 19), p. 318.

[8]See Jacob Schmookler, *Invention and Economic Growth* (Cambridge: Harvard University Press, 1966).

certain modes of investigation purely on methodological grounds regardless of whether or not this meant departing from the precepts of modern biology. The economist had lost his mecca! In the last section of this article I offer a few conjectural remarks about why Marshall found the catastrophean point of view unacceptable to the study of economic development.

I.

The entrepreneurial function consists of moving resources from where they are (relatively) undervalued to where they are (relatively) overvalued across both space *and time*.[9] The presence of time immediately adds a dimension of risk and uncertainty to entrepreneurial function that is not present in, say, currency arbitrage operations where the order to buy undervalued currencies in London and resell them in Zurich can be made in such close temporal proximity that the passing of time is virtually insignificant. Thus, outside of the world of currency arbitrage, entrepreneurial behavior is inherently risky and uncertain and requires a distinctive type of payment that Marshall (following the precedent set by the classical school) termed "profit."[10] Marshall did not use the term "entrepreneurship" but included the function under the general heading "business ability." Business ability included the talent for managing and organizing factors, leadership, forecasting demand, monitoring contracts, and most importantly willingness to experiment with new ideas and take risks.[11] It is common to categorize Marshall along with J. S. Mill and earlier economists as insisting that profit is a return for bearing risk. However, a careful reading of Marshall's oeuvre suggests that in many cases the "risk" that Marshall had in mind was the risk of an innovation failing to operate as planned or failing to increase profits.

Throughout Marshall's *Principles* he repeatedly identified "business ability" with inventiveness, leadership, and *quickness to add* inventions.[12] This idea is not to be found in Marshall's earliest published work, *The Economics of Industry*. Here Marshall followed Adam Smith and attributed new inventions to the workers themselves who are closest to the actual factory processes and suggest to management alternative ways of organizing the factory process.[13] The notion of the "innovative worker" does not appear in his later writings, but the associated idea that innovation is a by-product of the factory process and proceeds in small incremental steps is carried over into all of Marshall's writings. In his *Industry and Trade,* Marshall explained how "the printing press did not rise

[9]Cf. Israel M. Kirzner, *Competition and Entrepreneurship* (Chicago: University of Chicago, 1973). According to Kirzner, entrepreneurs discover disequilibrium phenomena and act to equilibrate particular markets.

[10]Both Kirzner and Schumpeter deny that the entrepreneur *qua* entrepreneur bears any risk (Cf. Kirzner, *Competition* . . . , pp. 30–88; and Schumpeter, *Business Cycles*, pp. 102–109). My claim is simply that the entrepreneur's reputation for successful "alertness" is endangered among the capitalist backers if too many failures occur and that is the risk that the entrepreneur must necessarily assume.

[11]On the manager as a supplier of business ability of what Marshall termed "business power" see Alfred Marshall and Mary Paley Marshall, *The Economics of Industry* (London: Macmillan, 1879), pp. 75, 118 and 143; Marshall, *Principles* I:312–313, 606–607 and 665; II:651, 671–672. On the manager as an organizer of factors see Marshall, *Principles* I:293 and II:659. On the manager as a leader see Marshall, *Principles* I:41 and 297; see also, Marshall, *Industry* . . . , p. 49 and idem., Memorials, pp. 331–337. On the manager as a forecaster see Marshall, *Economics of Industry,* p. 161; idem., *Principles,* 297; and idem., *Industry and trade,* 47 and 164. On the manager's role in monitoring contracts see Marshall, *Principles,* p. 293. On his willingness to experiment and assume risks see all of the above references and also Marshall, *Economics of Industry,* p. 114; idem., *Principles* I:89, 305, 341, 355, 359, 406, 597–98, 665, 293 and II:309; and idem., *Industry and Trade,* 62, and 645.

[12](My italics.) See Marshall, *Industry and Trade,* p. 6.

[13]Marshall, *Economics of Industry,* p. 51. Cf. Adam Smith, *The Wealth of Nations,* Cannon ed. (New York, 1936), p.

to nearly its full power even in a couple of centuries: and the present generation is the first that has seen the whole rise of several great inventions from nothing to dominating positions." The passage immediately concludes with Marshall's maxim that "Nature does not willingly make a jump."[14]

In the *Principles,* Marshall introduced his famous "principle of substitution" as a general description of economizing action on the part of businessmen. According to Marshall, businessmen are constantly searching for the cheaper ways of combining factors of production in order to achieve certain effects. As the scale of production changes, horse power may be replaced by steam power.[15] The implication is that a steam-powered alternative process is known to exist (perhaps in a pilot stage) but managers do not commercialize that invention until it is economically profitable to do so. Thus, innovation is part of the *normal* routine operations of the man possessing ordinary "business ability." Furthermore, the same way individual businessmen substitute one technique for another, the market substitutes one businessman for another! Some firms succeed while others do not, and the less efficient are weeded out by the selection process of the market. Thus, the principle of substitution operates both within firms and between firms![16]

Marshall saw quite readily that invention and innovation are not one and the same thing. Many inventions occur that are not adopted, and those that are adopted take *time* to become diffused. The time that it takes for a profitable invention to become diffused throughout the industry depends critically on both the scale of operation and the relative factor prices expected to prevail over the long view. For Marshall, the entrepreneurial function consisted precisely of discovering the menu of factor combinations available to a firm and choosing the most profitable combination from all those that are available. Marshall's gradualistic conception of technological entrepreneurship has received a great deal of historical support from those who document the actual process of technological change, although this conception has not been particularly identified with Marshall.[17] According to Schumpeter, however, the entrepreneurial function consists of changing the entire menu of factor combinations rather than choosing a technique from a given menu. Schumpeter specifically criticized Marshall on this point and declared that:

> Those [innovating firms] upsetting existing industrial structure and, as it sometimes seems, heading toward monopoly, are in general precisely those which have set up new production functions and which are struggling to conquer their market.[18]

It remains an unsettled question whether changes in technique and organization can be distinguished from changes in the production function itself. Ultimately, what is at stake is whether Marshall's or Schumpeter's conception of the process of innovation is more useful for understanding economic development. We shall say no more about this issue here.

Despite Marshall's reluctance to view the entrepreneurial function in catastrophic terms, there are references to the pressures or stress experienced by businessmen to take "quick advantage of the new inventions."[19] Here we have Marshall's adopting the idea also found in Ricardo's and Marx's writings

[14]Marshall, *Industry and Trade,* p. 6.
[15]Marshall, *Principles,* pp. 339–340.
[16]Ibid., p. 341.

[17]Nathan Rosenberg, "Problems in the Economist's Conceptualization of Technological Innovation," *History of Political Economy* 7 (Winter 1975):456–481. See also, idem., *Perspectives on technology* (Cambridge: Cambridge University Press, 1976).
[18]Schumpeter, *Business Cycles,* I:91.
[19]See Marshall, Economics of Industry, p. 114; and idem., *Principles,* p. 598. See Joseph A. Schumpeter's comments in *History of Economics Analysis* (Oxford: Oxford University, 1953), pp. 893–94.

about the innovator reaping higher-than-normal profits for a period of time before other firms copy the innovator, bring down product prices and/or raise various factor prices.[20] Marshall divided employers into two groups, "those who open out new and improved methods of business and those who follow beaten tracks."[21] The copiers of the innovator's business plan "increase the supply, and lower the price of their wares, until their profits fall to about their old level."[22] Innovators can make, of course, huge financial gains before the innovation becomes widely diffused. Money will be made, Marshall added, even if the innovation is of a rather trifling sort and the businessman of "no more than the normal or average ability of the people who fill such exceptionally difficult posts."[23] And so we have Marshall insisting that, although the innovation process proceeds in small incremental steps, these incremental steps can be immensely profitable.

According to Marshall, "business ability" or entrepreneurship has its own market and receives a normal price. This implies that the amount of business ability available to an economy is a variable and responds to economic incentives. Clearly, if it makes sense to speak of a supply curve of "business ability" then the amount of resources devoted to innovation can be affected by financial incentives.[24] Business ability also depends on the organizational structure of firms. At several places Marshall explained that large, vertically-integrated firms can afford the luxury of experimenting and discovering new knowledge since they can internally appropriate more of the returns to research-and-development than can small firms.[25] It is significant that in his later writings, Schumpeter also identified innovations with large firm size. The extensive statistical literature on the relationship between market structure and innovation effort spurred, in part, by Edwin Mansfield's work, however, tends not to support both Marshall's and Schumpeter's view that larger firms have a greater incentive to invest in research and development or an advantage over small firms when making such investments.[26]

Patents retard the *diffusion* of innovations allowing the patent owner to reap a monopoly return for a longer period of time than would otherwise be possible. This extra return is needed, according to the proponents of the patent system, to help innovators appropriate part of the social returns attributed to their efforts. Without such a return, few would have an incentive to innovate.[27] Those who criticize the patent system do so on grounds that patent monopolies burden consumers to a greater extent than is really needed to encourage innovation. Critics also contend that in the absence of a patent system, diffusion would not be so rapid that it would eliminate the entire monopoly return accruing to the leader. In this interim period many innovators

[20]See David Ricardo, *The Works and Correspondence of David Ricardo* 11 vol. P. Sraffa ed., (Cambridge: Cambridge University Press, 1966), I:386–97.

[21]Marshall, *Principles*, I:597.

[22]Ibid.

[23]Ibid.

[24]Ibid., pp. 312–313.

[25]Marshall, *Principles*, I:284; and idem., *Industry and Trade*, pp. 73–74.

[26]See Edwin Mansfield, *Industries Research and Technological innovation* (New York, Norton, 1968). In his *Economics of Technological Change* (New York, Norton, 1968), Mansfield wrote, "There is little evidence that industrial giants are needed in all or even most industries to promote rapid technological change or rapid utilization of new techniques" (p. 217). For a more recent effort supporting the link between entrepreneurial activity and firm size, see Albert N. Link, "Firm Size and Efficient Entrepreneurial Activity: A Reformulation of the Schumpeter Hypothesis." *Journal of Political Economy* 88 (August 1980), pp. 777–782.

[27]See, for example, Stephen P. Magee, "Information and Multinational Corporation: An Appropriability Theory of Direct Foreign Investment," in J. S. Bhagwati ed., *The New International Economic Order: The North-South Debate* (Cambridge: M.I.T. Press, 1977), pp. 317–340.

could reap more than enough revenue to reward their earlier innovative efforts. A survey of Marshall's scattered remarks about patents suggests that he must be counted among the critics of patenting. Marshall requested that patent revenues *not* be counted in calculations of national wealth and that liberal bankruptcy laws were more than enough to encourage innovation and at all times perferable to patent monopolies.[28]

Much of the same antimonopoly attitude carries over into Marshall's discussion of business secrecy. Marshall explicitly criticized those who try to withhold information from others in the market. Marshall considered a businessman's desire for secrecy and isolation due to his "lack of imagination" something that education would help eliminate from the modern world.[29] Marshall considered trade secrecy immoral because the holder of the secret withholds opportunities from others in the market. Marshall's reform liberal sentiments are no better illustrated than in the following passage:

> There is every reason to hope that the progress of trade morality will continue, aided in the future as it has been in the past, by a dimunition of trade secrecy and by increased publicity in every form; and thus collective and democratic forms of business management may be able to extend themselves safely in many directions in which they have hitherto failed and may far exceed the great services they already render in opening a large career to those who have no advantages of birth.[30]

In *Industry and Trade* Marshall praised the advent of trade associations to help disseminate information among the firms in an industry and break away from old habits of secrecy and the private appropriation of business information.[31] At another place in his work, Marshall explained that, as a practical matter, even if a businessman tries to use a "secret process . . . enough information about them often leaks out to set others soon on a track near to his own."[32]

When suggesting a research program for economics as early as 1886, Marshall wrote that "one of the most important of the unwritten chapters in Economics is that of the time that elapses between economic causes and their effects in consequence of the slowness with which knowledge diffuses itself."[33] It is clear that Marshall favored the rapid diffusion of information in the economy. First, because it disseminated business opportunities to the lowest orders of society helping to alleviate poverty; second, it eliminated monopoly practices and (thereby) increased national wealth; and third, because Marshall considered the conscious withholding of proprietary information an example of morbid behavior and a relic of less civilized times. With the widespread dissemination of knowledge about inventions and related business information, the entrepreneurial function consisted of an alertness as to when a body of business or technical information becomes applicable to a particular business situation. The businessman is viewed as drawing knowledge from a preexisting inventory of information and because of this smooths out the clustering of innovations that Schumpeter and others considered to be characteristic of the innovation process.[34]

[28]See Marshall, *Economics of Industry*, pp. 212, 79, 94 and 180; idem., *Principles* I:60; other references to patents include 280; idem., *Industry and Trade*, p. 244 and 398.

[29]Marshall, *Principles* I:285; and idem., *Industry and Trade*, p. 101, 583.

[30]Marshall, *Principles* I:303–304.

[31]Marshall, *Industry and Trade*, p. 101. Compare idem., *Principles* I:278–90. See also John K. Whitaker, "Some Neglected Aspects of Alfred Marshall's Economic and Social Thought," *History of Political Economy*, 9(1977):161–97.

[32]Marshall, *Industry and Trade*, p. 204.

[33]Marshall, *Economics of Industry*, p. VII.

[34]Cf. Alvin H. Hansen, "Schumpeter's Contribution to Business Cycle Theory" in S. E. Harris, *Schumpeter: Social Scientist* (Cambridge: Harvard University Press, 1951), p. 81.

II.

Marshall's conception of a community of businessmen increasingly united by the communication and exchange of ideas was entirely consistent with what he understood to be the great scientific advances in biology. According to Marshall there is a "fundamental unity of action between the laws of nature in the physical and in the moral world."[35] That unity consists of the "increasing subdivision of functions between [society's] separate parts, on the one hand, and on the other a more intimate connection between them."[36] This is an important and fruitful observation and one that reflects Herbert Spencer's towering influence on Victorian social thought.[37] The example Marshall presents, and the one we shall consider here, is the division of labor. As individuals become more specialized and enjoy expanding wealth, they also become more interdependent. This interdepence can be something supportive of social structure inasmuch as interdependent areas find it expensive to fight wars. On the other hand, interdependence makes cyclical variation more likely. For example, in a highly developed money economy, an attempt on the part of the majority of traders to build up their (average) cash balances will cause excess supplies to build up in commodity markets. Excess commodity supplies may trigger an overall decline in the level of economic activity. In Marshall's words, "each part gets to be less and less self-sufficient, to depend for its well-being more and more on other parts, so that any disorder in any part of a highly-developed organism will affect other parts also."[38] As examples of the "intimate connection," Marshall refers to trade credit, road, rail and telegraph communications.[39a] He does not discuss the *sharing* of a common body of knowledge about inventions and know-how perhaps because this phenomenon takes place mostly within a particular industry rather than among all industries in an economy.

Marshall also adopted Spencer's familiar phrase, "survival of the fittest' and correctly explained that, when applied to individuals, it offered no standard of moral excellence. An individual might survive simply because he is best "fitted to utilize the environment for [his] own purposes." The environment might be an unfortunate one, and the individual's purposes might be purely ignoble. Thus, there was no necessary connection between moral excellence and survival—at least on the level of the individual behavior. And morality (at the level of the individual) was extremely important to Marshall.[39b]

All was qualitatively different, however, when it came to the study of large groups of individuals such as "races" of men. According to Marshall, whose point of view reflects preference for nineteenth century holism, in the "long run those races of men ... survive in which the individual is most willing to sacrifice himself for the benefit of those around him; and which are consequently the best adopted collectively to make use of their environment."[40] There were exceptions to this rule also. Consider Marshall's theory of parasitic races where the success of one race of men

[35] Marshall, *Principles* I:241.

[36] Ibid.

[37] See J. W. Burrow, *Evolution and Society: A Study in Victorian Social Theory* (Cambridge: Cambridge University, 1966), pp. 179–227. Marshall's close friend, W.K. Clifford, was described as the "leading spirit" of the Grote Club. The Grote Club was a small group of Cambridge friends who, as Sir F. Pollack described, were "carried away by a wave of Darwinian enthusiasm .... Natural Selection was to be the master-key of the universe; ... to solve all riddles and reconcile all contradictions. Among other things it was to give us a new system of ethics, combining the exactness of the utilitarian with the political ideals of the transcendentalist," cited in Whitaker, "Some Neglected ...,"p. 194.

[38] Marshall, *Principles* I:241.

[39a] Ibid. On Marshall's morality of Schumpeter, *Ten Great Economists: From Marx to Keynes* (New York: Galaxy, 1965), pp. 91–109.

[39b] Ibid.

[40] Ibid., pp. 241–43.

depends on living off the efforts of another race. The parasitic race "turn the peculiarities of [the other] race to good account for their own purposes without giving any good return." The economic demand for money-dealers in Eastern Europe and Asia allows the Jewish and Armenians to prosper even though neither of these races has the virtues needed for independent greatness. But as a general rule "those races survive and predominate in which the best qualities are most strongly developed."[41]

A race, Marshall argued, steadily improves through the slow gradual development of its culture, practices and other institutions. Each generation *inherits* the customs, attitudes and practices of the previous generation. Naturally each succeeding generation inherits traits that helped in the struggle to survive. Not all of these traits are completely moral or unselfish. Consider the notion that large segments of the population must be sacrificed during "special exigencies." This manner of segmenting the population, as existed under the caste system, was needed in earlier times. But the sacrifice of the urban poor and their children to the production of wealth in a modern industrial society seems entirely unnecessary and in "some respects . . . a case of atavism."[42] By atavism Marshall referred to the anomolous biological phenomena whereby early traits lost in evolution seem to make a startling reappearance in modern generations.[43]

But as a reform-liberal Marshall firmly believed that the existing English race could (and would) be improved by education. The education might also require the encouragement of a more chivalrous attitude among businessmen and an appreciation for promoting the higher values among the working class. Public parks, sanitation reform and publicly supported education would all spark economic and social progress. This type of progress must necessarily be slow and result in some sacrifice of the "immediate efficiency of production," but any economy that consciously "allows the higher faculties of the lower grades of industry to go to waste, is open to grave suspicion."[44] Presumably English society, descended from Teutonic stock, would not permit this waste to occur.

Despite Marshall's favorable references to Darwin and the theory of "natural selection," there is little evidence to suggest that he appreciated the finer details of the *modus operandi* implied by Darwin's vast mechanism of natural selection. According to the theory of natural selection, it is only the slightest and subtlest of individual variations within a species that give their individual owners a slight edge in the inter and intra species struggle for survival.[45] This selection process takes eons to finally produce a new species and the application of this sort of mechanism to the development of human society was anachronistic if not blatantly absurd.[46] Yet Darwin was guilty of this logical lapse as was Marshall himself.[47]

[41]Ibid., p. 244.

[42]Ibid. p. 245. It seems that Marshall set the tone for the application the racially-based instinct theories in economics. This doctrine, articulated by Frank A. Fetter, Robert Hoxie and for a while Irving Fisher, holds that "biological drives are the foundation of individual economic behavior and that these drives differ among races," [See Robert Cherry, "Biology, Sociology and Economics—An Historical Analysis" *Review of Social Economy 38* (October 1980): 141–154].

[43]Himmelfarb, *Darwin*, pp. 312–36. Interestingly, Schumpeter also used the biological concept of "atavism" to explain the persistence of imperialism in modern industrial society. See his *Imperialism* (New York, Meridian, 1955). According to Professor G. Koot, Hobson used this concept during the Boer War (correspondence 6 April 1981).

[44]Ibid., p. 249. cf. Whitaker, "Some Neglected . . . ," pp. 175–85.

[45]Michael Ruse, "Charles Darwin's Theory of Evolution: An Analysis," *History of Biology* 8 (Fall 1975):219–41.

[46]The application of the mechanism of natural selection to species creation was also challenged on exactly these grounds. Ruse writes, ". . . the criticism that (rightly) worried Darwin the most [was Kelvin's claim later supported by F. Jenkin] that physical considerations show that the world is far younger than uniformitarian

In most of the discussions about evolution contained in the *Principles,* Marshall was much more comfortable with Lamarck's idea that species develop by adapting to their environments and then passing the favorable traits they acquire on to their descendants. The process is much speedier than natural selection and at least does not require a statistical process of the slow accumulation of random variations.

In subsequent editions of his *Origin,* Darwin himself reintroduced the Larmarkian theory of the inheritance of acquired characteristics complete with the concept of "genetic momentum", where a variation in the characteristic of a species in one direction increases the likelihood of another variation in the same direction.[48] Apparently, Marshall followed Darwin in emphasizing these mechanisms of evolution. In the first edition of the *Principles,* Marshall offered a note about the proverbial evolutionary giraffe. Marshall wrote:

> The giraffe whose long neck enables it to survive by feeding on the shoots of trees when the grass is dried up, may possibly lengthen its neck yet further by stretching it, and thus further increase its power of surviving; but this effect is not purposely sought ... The longer, within certain limits, the giraffe's neck is, and the more exclusively he feeds on the shoots of trees, the more will his chance of survival depend on the length of his neck; and the greater will be the force which the struggle for survival will exert in tending to accelerate that growth ...[49]

A mathematical appendix translates this evolutionary example into mathematics. In Note XI Marshall defines f(t) to represent the length of the giraffe's neck and time t and notes that by Taylor's theorem

$$f(t+h) = f(t) + hf'(t) + \frac{h^2}{1 \cdot 2} f''(t + \theta h);$$

then if h is large and h^2 very large, then f(t + h) will be much greater than f(t) even though the other terms in the expression are small. According to Marshall this illustrates how "the rate of increase of the neck increases ... with every increase in the neck"—a clear application of the Darwinian notion of "genetic momentum."[50] In the third edition of Marshall's *Principles,* Marshall switched from the giraffe example to one involving the webbed feet of duck, but the notation was unchanged. In particular, the symbol f(t) now interpreted to mean the size of the web between the birds' toes—everything else was left intact. Following this example Marshall explained:

> In sociology as well as biology we are learning to watch the accumulated effects of forces which, though weak at first, get greater strength from the growth of their own effects; and the universal form, of which every such fact is a special embodiment is Taylor's Theorem. . . .[51]

The reason, Marshall wrote, that Taylor's Theorem is amenable to this problem of accumulated effects is because "There is more than a superficial connection between the advance made by the applications of the differential calculus to physics at the end of the eighteenth century and the beginning of the nineteenth, and the rise of the theory of evolution."[52] That more than superficial connection had to do with the analysis of change and motion in small incremental steps!

geology supposes, and certainly far younger than the time span demanded by the theory of evolution through natural selection." (*Darwinian Revolution,* p. 223). cf. also, Bruce Glassburner, "Alfred Marshall on Economic History and Historical Development," *Quarterly Journal of Economics* (November 1955):582.

[47]This is one of the central themes of Gertrude Himmelfarb's controversial treatment of Darwin the "Scientist" who did not understand his theories, see her *Darwin and the Darwinian Revolution* (New York: Norton, 1962): esp. 311–378.

[48]Ruse, *Darwinian Revolution,* pp. 210–11.

[49]Marshall, *Principles* II:834.

[50]Ruse, *Darwinian Revolution,* pp. 210–11.

[51]Marshall, *Principles* I:843–44.

[52]Ibid., p. 844.

By the seventh edition of the *Principles* in 1916 the brilliant work of Mendel was rediscovered by European experimentalists Hugo de Vries, Carl Correns, and Erick von Tschermak-Seysenegg. Rapidly biology moved from the real of naturalist observation and armchair speculation to the modern experimental laboratory.[53] After years of neglect, Mendel's laws were confirmed in repeated experiments on plants and flies. According to the new biologists, biological traits did not blend together or disappear with evolution but appeared from generation to generation in predictable ratios in accordance with certain basic laws.[54] As the Mendelian Hugo de Vries explained, new species appeared only when radical mutations occurred and not by the slow gradual process such as Darwin hypothesized. According to G. E. Allen, "In emphasizing mutations as the large scale, discrete steps by which evolution occurred, de Vries and his followers placed their work in direct opposition to Darwin and neo-Darwinians."[55] Suddenly the natural world did make jumps and apparently quite a few big jumps indeed.

In the seventh edition of the *Principles* Marshall added several lines to his Note XI:

> This conclusion [about the rate of increase of f(t)] will remain valid even if further investigation confirms the suggestion, made by some Mendelians, that gradual changes in the race are originated by large divergences of individuals from the prevailing type. *For economics is a study of mankind, of particular nations, of particular social strata; and it is only indirectly concerned with the lives of men of exceptional genius or exceptional wickedness and violence.*[56]

Unfortunately, it is not clear what Marshall meant by this rather bold and sharp retreat from methodological individualism into holism. Was not the reason economics concerned itself with groups of individuals rather than single agents because change was slow and gradual in both the natural and social worlds? If now nature does in fact move in large jumps as the mutationists claimed, then are we not entitled to attribute to single individuals the power to alter the course of economic development? Might not the social world, like the natural world, admit of something like Schumpeter's entrepreneur? What does it mean to say that economics is only "indirectly concerned with the lives of men of exceptional genius"? After all, is not the exceptional individual precisely the one who alters the average? Is the Mecca of the economist no longer to be found in biology now that biology has moved in the direction of discontinuous change?

III.

We are now in a position to summarize how Marshall's theory of entrepreneurship was related to the biological theories of his day. First, on the issue of technological entrepreneurship Marshall claimed that most innovations proceed in the form of incremental improvements diffused rather quietly in the market. This way of thinking about evolution is consistent with the main teachings of Lyell and Darwin. The process of economic evolution was slow and gradual, not one that required the catastrophic uprooting of the economy. There is much in the recent literature on innovation that supports Marshall's description rather than Schumpeter's. The second reason Marshall had for denying that

[53]Cravens, *Triumph*, p. 39.

[54]Ibid., pp. 33–40.

[55]See G.E. Allen, "Hugo de Vries," p. 72. I wish to point out that there is nothing about Mendel's laws of heredity that requires that evolution proceed in jumps or be discontinuous. Marshall, like many others since, viewed Mendelian genetics as based on mutations because of the intermediaryship of de Vries who was *both* a Mendelian and a mutationist. One can be a Mendelian without necessarily being a mutationist! Apparently, mutationist biology is again in the news, this time in the form of "punctuated equilibria," see "Is Man a Subtle Accident?" *Newsweek* (3 November 1980):95–96.

[56]Marshall, *Principles* I:844 (my italics).

the entrepreneur could affect the economy in the manner Schumpeter described was a methodological one based on Marshall's organic view of nature and his commitment to the methodological rule or, as Darwin called it, "the canon" that nature does not move in large steps. After the Mendelian revolution of the 1900s and biology's return to catastrophic processes of change, in the writings of de Vries, we find Marshall in the seventh edition taking a different tact. Reluctant to follow the post-Mendellian wave of biologists into the world of catastrophic change, Marshall implied that even if particular isolated entrepreneurs were disruptive their average behavior would not be. But why should the aggregate behavior of a group of destabilizers be stabilizing? Why should the aggregate behavior of a group of stabilizers be stabilizing? Marshall did not say.

It may be that Marshall's commitment to unilateral improvement of man and society was in some fundamental way threatened by a mutation theory of evolution. The continuity and the orderliness of change suggested that social progress was uni directional and always moving closer to that ideal. The millenium was approaching with economic life improving as society moved toward a new era in which poverty would be lessened and business chivalry nourished into a highly cultivated art.[57] A mutation theory suggested discontinuity, randomness and, very simply, a process without direction and without end. Marshall could accept none of this and ruled such investigations improper on methodological grounds. Entrepreneur-induced catastrophes were simply not proper Victorian economics!

[57]Talcott Parsons, "Wants and Activities in Marshall," *Quarterly Journal of Economics* 46 (November 1931):128–131.

[16]

J. R. Statist. Soc. A (1983),
146, *Part* 2, *pp.* 158–162

F. Y. Edgeworth's Mathematical Training

By J. CREEDY

University of Durham, UK

SUMMARY

F. Y. Edgeworth made important contributions to mathematical economics and statistics, although he does not seem to have had a formal training in advanced mathematics. This paper examines the question of how, and under what incentive, Edgeworth acquired his mathematics. It is unlikely that this question could be answered with certainty. However, this paper examines a number of connections, the most important being with W. R. Hamilton and W. K. Clifford, which have not previously been mentioned in studies of Edgeworth.

Keywords: EDGEWORTH'S FAMILY BACKGROUND; MATHEMATICAL TRAINING; TRINITY COLLEGE DUBLIN; SAVILE CLUB

1. INTRODUCTION

F. Y. Edgeworth (1845–1926) is widely recognized as a leading figure in the development of mathematical economics and statistics. He seems to have been the first to use the calculus of variations, lagrange multipliers and determinants to make significant progress in economics. Of about 170 published papers, approximately 3/4 were concerned with statistical theory; he was a Guy Medalist (Gold) in 1907 and was President of the Royal Statistical Society 1912–14. His contribution to statistics was examined shortly after Edgeworth's death by Bowley (1928), and more recently by Stigler (1978). In view of his important contributions, it is interesting that Edgeworth does not seem to have had a formal training in advanced mathematics. Thus Samuelson (1974, p. 1279, n. 1) refers to him as a "self-taught barrister". Bowley (1934, p. 114) refers to his "want of systematic training", and Edgeworth once said of his own work that it "could be presented by a professed mathematician more elegantly and scientifically" (1881, p. 24).[1] †

In discussing Edgeworth's mathematics, Kendall (1970, p. 258) suggests that, "It would . . . be of considerable interest if we could discover how and when Edgeworth acquired his mathematics, and under what incentive". It is this question, which has received surprisingly little attention, which is considered here. The paucity of direct information makes it unlikely that it can ever be answered with certainty. However, there are a number of connections which have not previously been indicated in studies of Edgeworth, the most important of them being with W. R. Hamilton and W. K. Clifford. It is first necessary to dismiss the suggestion (made by Eisenhart in discussion of Stigler, 1978, p. 319) that Sir Francis Beaufort (1774–1857) may have been influential. Although Beaufort was a close friend of Edgeworth's grandfather, Richard Lovell Edgeworth, it is unlikely that his mathematics were sufficiently advanced; furthermore, he died when Edgeworth was only 12 years old.[2]

2. TRINITY COLLEGE DUBLIN

The possibility that Edgeworth may have been exposed to serious mathematics at Trinity College Dublin, despite the fact that his main training was in the classics and literature, is worth

† The footnotes appear grouped together at the end of the paper. This deviation from the house-style of the *Journal* makes pagination easier and is consistent with historical studies.

Present address: Professor John Creedy, Department of Economics, The University, 23/26 Old Elvet, Durham DH1 3HY, UK.

 0035–9238/83/146158 $2.00

considering. Unfortunately, no direct records are available, although Bowley suggests that when Edgeworth entered Trinity in 1862, "it may be presumed he studied both mathematics and classics" (1934, p. 113). In this connection it is of interest that a tutor of Edgeworth at Trinity was J. K. Ingram (1823–1907),[3] but although Ingram initially showed promise as a mathematician he later regretted the time spent on mathematics, was strongly averse to its application in economics and had little sympathy with *a priori* reasoning.[4]

Of greater relevance is the fact that Trinity College Dublin had an excellent curriculum in mathematics. This was largely the result of efforts by Rev. Bartholomew Lloyd who was Professor of Mathematics, Natural Philosophy, Greek and Divinity, and later became provost of the college and president of the Royal Irish Academy. Lloyd instituted a revolution in mathematics teaching after 1812, when he introduced French textbooks into the college and had other texts written in order to teach the work of the continental mathematicians. His son Humphrey Lloyd (1800–81) became Vice Provost of Trinity in 1862, the year in which Edgeworth entered. There are several further points worth noting. Humphrey Lloyd's first research, in optics, was directly stimulated by a question from William Rowan Hamilton (discussed further below). He was later involved with much work on terrestrial magnetism. In *Mathematical Psychics* (1881, pp. 13–14), Edgeworth presented a complex analogy involving electro-magnetic fields.

3. FAMILY INFLUENCES

Despite the strong scientific (as well as literary) interests of the large Edgeworth family,[5] there seems to be no clear evidence concerning Edgeworth's mathematical training. However, it is known that although Edgeworth's father Francis Beaufort Edgeworth (1809–46) hated mathematics,[6] he was a close friend of Sir William Rowan Hamilton (1805–65). Hamilton kept in touch with Edgeworth's mother after Francis Beaufort's death, and spent most of his life at the Dunsink Observatory near Dublin. He did original work in the calculus of variations and is famous for his theory of biquaternions.[7] In view of Edgeworth's eulogistic remarks about Lagrange in *Mathematical Psychics* it is worth noting Hamilton's comment on the *Mechanique Analytique*, that it could only be described as "a scientific poem" (see Ball, 1924, p. 408). The beauty of Lagrange's work was that everything was deduced, using the calculus of variations, from a single principle (the principle of least action). When Edgeworth referred to Hamilton in *Mathematical Psychics* (1881, p. 94) he was talking of the use of utilitarianism as the "one central idea". Hamilton's work was characterized by a high degree of abstraction and generality, which made it difficult to read and meant that, like Edgeworth's work, it was some time before its value was fully recognized.

Another family connection concerns the Rev. Thomas Romney Robinson (1792–1882), astronomer and mathematical physicist.[8] He was from 1823 in charge of the Armagh observatory, and his publications include work on electricity, magnetism, heat and mechanics, in addition to astronomy. Robinson's second wife was Lucy Jane Edgeworth (1805–97), an aunt of Edgeworth, and Robinson was a frequent guest at Edgeworthstown.

Robinson also provides an additional family connection, through his daughter, Mary Suzanna Robinson.[9] In 1857 she married Sir George Gabriel Stokes (1819–1903), Lucasian Professor of mathematics at Cambridge from 1849 until his death. Stokes was a close friend of William Thomson (Lord Kelvin). Both Stokes and Kelvin are mentioned in *Mathematical Psychics*, but there seems to be no direct evidence on the extent of any contact between Edgeworth and Stokes. Stokes's successor as Lucasian Professor was Joseph Larmor, who was known to have admired Edgeworth's mathematics (see Price, 1946, p. 41).

4. OTHER CONNECTIONS

It is clear that Edgeworth's family background was sufficient to stimulate scientific and mathematical interest, in addition to classical and literary interests, but a further connection should be mentioned. A clue is provided by the psychologist James Sully, who was friendly with Edgeworth. Sully read the proofs of *New and Old Methods of Ethics* (1877), and Edgeworth was acknowledged by Sully for help with the latter's *Pessimism* (1877). In his autobiography Sully

(1918, p. 164) discusses his association with the Savile Club, and says, "It was the same sociable club which introduced me to W. K. Clifford, the brilliant young mathematician and thinker; to F. Y. Edgeworth . . . as well as to other lovers of ideas.[10] William Kingdon Clifford (1845–79) was not only a brilliant mathematician, but had wide interests in literature and philosophy. He had worked on the mechanics of fluids and gases,[11] and was an effective teacher. For example, Ball (1924, p. 491, n. 1) says that, "His remarkable felicity of illustration and power of seizing analogies made him one of the most brilliant expounders of mathematical principles'. Edgeworth refers directly to Clifford (in 1877, pp. 13, 25, 87) and, while there seems to be no direct evidence, it is quite possible that he knew and was influenced by Clifford.

It is interesting that Edgeworth did not meet Jevons and Marshall until 1879 (see Creedy, 1981, p. 96, n. 8). Clifford was at University College London, where Jevons was appointed in 1875, and he was an active member of the Grote Club, which included Marshall.[12] However, there is no evidence that Edgeworth had any strong interest in economics before 1879 (see Keynes, 1972, p. 148, n. 4) and it seems likely that he was introduced to Jevons by Sully.[13]

It must again be stressed that the mathematicians mentioned above may *possibly* have provided stimulus and help to Edgeworth, but that no direct evidence has been found. There is a further question which may briefly be considered. Did Edgeworth acquire mathematics in order to examine particular philosophical and economic questions, or did he come to see that his knowledge of mathematics could be applied to these subjects? It seems fairly clear that the latter is the case. Edgeworth said that on first seeing Marshall's work he "discerned a new power of mathematical reasoning" (see Pigou, 1925, p. 66), and in *Mathematical Psychics* he referred to a vast range of work on psychology and the natural sciences, in addition to mathematics. Edgeworth's intellectual pursuits and remarkable abilities covered many different fields, and it was not until his middle thirties that he finally concentrated on economics and statistics. These interests came, following his meeting with Jevons, from a realisation that utilitarianism, reinforced by mathematical methods, could be applied to problems of economic exchange and distribution.[14]

FOOTNOTES

* I should like to thank Mrs C. Colvin for information about the Edgeworth family, and a referee for helpful comments on earlier drafts of this paper.

1. See also Edgeworth (1881, p. 96). It is often suggested that Edgeworth's mathematics are difficult to follow; see Baumol and Goldfeld (1968, pp. 189–190), Keynes (1970, p. 256) and Bowley (1934, p. 114). This cannot, however, be used as strong evidence of lack of training; Edgeworth's literary style is also difficult, and some highly trained mathematicians were more obscure than Edgeworth.
2. On Beaufort's friendship with Edgeworth's grandfather see Butler (1972, p. 130, n. 2) and Friendly (1977). In fact Richard Lovell's fourth wife was Beaufort's eldest sister Francis Anne (1769–1865), and Beaufort's second wife was Honora Edgeworth (1791–1857), a daughter of Richard Lovell by his third wife. On the complex family relationships, see Butler and Butler (1927) and Colvin (1971).
3. See Stigler (1978, p. 320).
4. See, for example, Ingram (1878, 1893) for clear statements of his views on methodology.
5. Details of the scientific work and circle of friends of Richard Lovell Edgeworth are given in Schofield (1963). The range of contacts of the Edgeworths is well illustrated in the published letters of Maria Edgeworth; see Colvin (1971, 1979).
6. His Cambridge tutor stated that he was "ignorant of mathematics and determined to remain so", and because of his unwillingness to learn mathematics he did not graduate from Cambridge.
7. He was responsible for this new approach which involved abandoning the commutative laws of algebra and led to further work in matrix theory. P. G. Tait (mentioned several times by Edgeworth in the *Psychics*) was one of Hamilton's supporters; they were in correspondence from 1858; see also Tait (1867). Hamilton's close connection with the Edgeworths is clearly shown in Graves, R. P. (1882–85).

8. The family relationship with Galton should not be forgotten. Galton is mentioned several times in the *Psychics*, but there does not seem to have been much direct contact, and Edgeworth is not mentioned in Forrest (1974). See also Stigler (1978), who quotes an encouraging letter from Galton to Edgeworth after the publication of the *Psychics*.
9. Susanna Robinson (d. 1899) was a daughter by Robinson's first marriage to Eliza Isabelle Rambaut (d. 1837).
10. Edgeworth's membership of the Savile is also mentioned by Bowley (1934, p. 122), Keynes (1972, p. 266) and Price (1946, p. 38). Sully was elected to the Savile in 1875. There are no records of Edgeworth's election, but in 1872 he proposed his brother Antonio E. Edgeworth for membership. One of the seconders was Alfred P. Graves, a friend of Edgeworth from Trinity College (see Graves, A. P., 1931, p. 129). Sully only once mentions Edgeworth by name (1918, p. 164); but see also pp. 167, 177–179, 181).
11. Clifford also worked on the theory of biquaternions. There are many analogies with the motion of fluids in the *Psychics*. For further details of Clifford's work see the introduction of his *Lectures and Essays* (1879).
12. In a lecture of 1877, Clifford took Jevons's work as his point of departure (see *Papers*, 1882, pp. 1–16). See also Keynes (1972, pp. 167, 174, n. 3). Other members of the Savile included Bonamy Price, Fleeming Jenkin, Cliffe-Leslie, Leslie Stephen, T. H. Green and Henry Sidgwick.
13. Sully's friendship with Jevons did not develop until after Sully moved to Hampstead in 1878; see Sully (1918, pp. 180, 223). Edgeworth, Sully and Jevons all lived in Hampstead, so that there is unfortunately very little correspondence. Part of a letter from Jevons to Sully is given in the volume edited by his wife (1886, p. 407), but Sully is mentioned only briefly (as a professor of chemistry!) in the biography included in Black and Konekamp (1972, p. 50).
14. For an examination of Edgeworth's early work in economics, see Creedy (1981).

REFERENCES

Ball, N. W. R. (1924) *A Short Account of the History of Mathematics*. London: Macmillan.

Baumol, W. J. and Goldfeld, S. M. (1968) *Precursors in Mathematical Economics: An Anthology*, London School of Economics Reprints of Scarce Works in Political Economy, No. 19.

Black, R. D. C. and Konekamp, R. (1972) *Papers and Correspondence of William Stanley Jevons, Vol. I, Biography and Personal Journal*. London: Macmillan for the Royal Economic Society.

Bowley, A. L. (1928) *Edgeworth's Contribution to Mathematical Statistics*. London: Royal Statistical Society.

——— (1934) Francis Ysidro Edgeworth. *Econometrica*, **1**, 113–124.

Butler, H. J. and Butler, H. E. (1927) *The Black Book of Edgeworthstown and other Edgeworth Memories 1585–1817*. London: Faber and Gwyer.

Butler, M. S. (1972) *Maria Edgeworth, A Literary Biography*. Oxford: University Press.

Clifford, W. K. (1879) *Lectures and Essays*. 2 vols (L. Stephen and F. Pollock, eds). London: Macmillan.

——— (1882) *Mathematical Papers* (ed. R. Tucker). London: Macmillan.

Colvin, C. (1971) *Maria Edgeworth, Letters from England, 1813–1844*. Oxford: University Press.

——— (1979) *Maria Edgeworth in France and Switzerland*. Oxford: University Press.

Creedy, J. (1981) Francis Ysidro Edgeworth 1845–1926. In *Pioneers of Modern Economics in Britain* (D. P. O'Brien and J. R. Presley, eds). London: Macmillan.

——— (1981) The development of F. Y. Edgeworth's early work. *University of Durham, Department of Economics Working Paper*, No. 34.

Edgeworth, F. Y. (1877) *New and Old Methods of Ethics*. Oxford: James Parker & Co.

(1881) *Mathematical Psychics: An Essay on the Application of Mathematics to the Moral Sciences*. London: Kegan Paul.

Forrest, D. W. (1974) *Francis Galton; The Life and Work of a Victorian Genius*. London: Elek.

Friendly, A. (1977) *Beaufort of the Admiralty, the Life of Sir Francis Beaufort 1774–1857*. London: Hutchinson.

Graves, A. P. (1931) *To Return to all That*. London: Jonathan Cape.

Graves, R. P. (1882–85) *Life of William Rowan Hamilton*. London: Longmans, Green & Co.

Ingram, J. K. (1878) The present position and prospects of Political Economy. Reprinted in *Essays in Eonomic Method* (R. L. Smyth, ed.), London: Duckworth, 1962.

——— (1893) *History of Political Economy*. Edinburgh: A & C Black.

Jevons, H. A. (ed.) (1886) *Letters and Journal of W. Stanley Jevons*. London: Macmillan.

Kendall, M. G. (1970) F. Y. Edgeworth. In *Studies in the History of Statistics and Probability* (E. S. Pearson and M. G. Kendall, eds). London: Griffin.

Keynes, J. M. (1972) *Essays in Biography*, Vol. X of the *Collected Writings of Keynes*. London: Macmillan for the Royal Economic Society.

Pigou, A. C. (ed.) (1925) *Memorials of Alfred Marshall*. London: Macmillan.

Price, L. L. (1946) Memoirs and Notes on British Economists, 1881–1946. (MSS, Brotherton Library, University of Leeds.)

Samuelson, P. A. (1974) Complementarity: an essay on the 40th anniversary of the Hicks–Allen revolution in demand theory, *J. Econ. Literature*, **12**, 1255–1289.

Schofield, R. E. (1963) *The Lunar Society of Birmingham, A Social History of Provincial Science and Industry in Eighteenth-Century England*. Oxford: Clarendon Press.

Stigler, S. M. (1978) Francis Ysidro Edgeworth, Statistician. *J. R. Statist. Soc.* A, **141**, 287–322.

Sully, J. (1877) *Pessimism: A History and a Criticism*.

——— (1918) *My Life and Friends*. London: T. Fisher Unwin.

Tait, P. G. (1867) *Elementary Treatise on Quaternions*. London: Macmillan.

THE ECONOMIC JOURNAL

MARCH 1983

The Economic Journal, **93** (*March* 1983), 1–12
Printed in Great Britain

THE SCOPE AND METHOD OF ECONOMIC SCIENCE*

Phyllis Deane

The title I have chosen to sail under on this occasion is a deliberate echo, modified in one particular only, of the title John Neville Keynes gave to the monograph which was designed to signal the end of the methodological crisis that developed in the 1870s.[1] For there is a parallel, it seems to me, between the crisis of confidence in the central tenets of their discipline that afflicted the intellectual community of economists a century ago and the current disarray on questions of economic method. Then, as now, economists seemed to feel that the glaring lack of consensus on fundamental principles compromised the scientific status of their discipline, and there were strong professional and public pressures to establish a new orthodoxy which could speak authoritatively on economic matters. The interesting question is how far did our predecessors succeed in reconciling their deep methodological differences and how far did they merely stop quarrelling about them?

A hundred years ago it was classical political economy that was under fire from a variety of directions. Nineteenth century social reformers confronting the policy problems of an industrialising society were repelled by what they saw as its doctrinaire adherence to the principles of laissez-faire, its arid detachment from all ethical issues and its narrow focus on a mythical economic man. Conservatives were uncomfortable with the stark conflicts of interest between capital and labour which the socialists were able to infer from Ricardo's theory of income distribution. Academic economists found their authority as teachers undermined, and undergraduates lacked confidence in the discipline of political economy, when its leading theorists differed on matters of principle. But it was not until 1869, when the most prestigious social scientist of his generation, John Stuart Mill, publicly recanted the Ricardian wage-fund doctrine, that the facade of orthodox classical political economy cracked wide open.

The substantive issue in question was whether trade unions could actually influence the level of real wages or whether that was predetermined by the capital funds available for investment. The central economic theory at stake was the cost of production theory of value on which the whole system of classical ideas seemed to rest. Mill's well-known assertion: 'Happily there is nothing in the laws of value which remains for the present or any future writer to clear up;

* Presidential Address to the Royal Economic Society, 21 July 1982.

[1] J. N. Keynes, *The Scope and Method of Political Economy*, 1st edn. 1891, 4th edn. 1930.

the theory of the subject is complete'[1] still stood, unrevised in the 1871 edition of his *Principles* after the ground had evidently been cut from under it. The 'last of the classical economists' J. E. Cairnes, did not have Mill's magisterial authority and his attempts to shore up what he himself described as 'the present vacillating and unsatisfactory condition of the science in respect of fundamental principles',[2] were unconvincing in face of the forceful arguments of those who insisted that if political economy were to qualify for scientific status it needed to acquire a more convincing method of inquiry.

In the methodological debates of the 1870s and 1880s the polar extremes were represented by the historicists on the one hand and the mathematical school on the other. The historical school had already established for themselves a distinguished academic reputation in Germany and spoke from the vantage of a respectable empirical research programme. Their contempt for the characteristic deductive technique of Ricardian theorising gathered conviction when the world trade boom of the 1850s and 1860s ran out of steam and the mid-century moves towards freer international trade lost momentum everywhere but in Britain. Confidence in what critics of classical political economy called 'hypothetical science' depended on the manifest success of its predictions and when the Mid-Victorian Boom turned into the Great Depression the introspectively-based postulates of armchair economics lost much of their credibility. Meanwhile, current views of the Baconian inductive procedures that were supposed to characterise all the natural sciences[3] provided a justification for the empirical bias of the historicists.

At the other methodological extreme the abstract theorists succeeded in capturing the imagination of a rising generation of economists with the aid of an analytical tool based on the calculus. The marginal technique of analysis could be used to reconstruct the weakest link in the classical theoretical system – the cost of production theory of value – without denting the hard core of orthodox classical doctrine. It was a particularly attractive development for economists who had ambitions to mimic the methods of the natural sciences for three sorts of reasons: first because the most progressive natural sciences were obviously benefitting from mathematical tools of analysis; second, because retention of the hard core doctrine of the self-regulating economic system under competitive conditions implied the continuity of classical and neo-classical economics and made it easier to believe in the cumulative advance of economic theory; and thirdly because the independent application of the marginal technique in three separate geographical locations in the early 1870s[4], gave the intellectual community of economists a sense of international consensus which is rare for social scientists.

Arguments about fundamental principles tend to acquire the bitter and divisive qualities of theological disputes and the methodological divisions of the 1870s were no exception. Jevons' angry reaction against the 'noxious influence

[1] J. S. Mill, *Collected Works*, Toronto edition, vol. III, p. 456.
[2] J. E. Cairnes, *The Character and Logical Method of Political Economy*, 1888 ed., p. 21.
[3] It was of course a myth that natural sciences did not use deductive procedures.
[4] W. S. Jevons, *Theory of Political Economy* (1871), Carl Menger, *Grundsätze der Volkwirtschaftslehre* (1871) and Leon Walras, *Eléments d'économie pure politique* (1874–7).

of authority' and the 'monotonous repetition of current questionable doctrines' is well known.[1] The historical economists condemned the hypothetico-deductive method of the classical economists as being hostile to empirical research, irresponsibly speculative and, most wounding of all, ideologically biased. In effect, the classical economists were accused of devising amoral (if not immoral) theories involving implicit presumptions in favour of a laissez-faire stance in economic policy at a time when ethical considerations demanded a programme of legislation to protect the underprivileged sectors of the economy. Then, as now, ideological preconceptions concerning the appropriate agenda for government economic policy were often the key to an economist's choice of sides in the methodological debate.

This was the background against which J. Neville Keynes began his attempt to clarify the scope and method of political economy roughly a century ago. He wrote essentially for undergraduates confused by the tendentious arguments of leading economists quarrelling about the basic nature and validity of economic knowledge. Neville Keynes' main strength as a teacher of political economy was a clear, logical mind and a capacity to detach himself from the partisan passions aroused by the current methodological debates. He had already published a successful undergraduate textbook on formal logic[2] and his *Scope and Method* grew, as so many textbooks do, out of a course of lectures.[3] When he announced to his friend and contemporary, J. S. Nicholson, that he proposed to develop the lectures into a book the latter (as reported by Keynes in his diary) said scornfully that 'anyone could write such a book as that. He says he is sick of disquisitions on method and that what we want is useful *applications* of the right method.'[4]

As it happened, however, the time was ripe for a book of the kind Keynes contemplated. For the marginal techniques of analysis were steadily gaining international acceptance, the economic historians were producing impressive research results of obvious relevance to applied economics[5] and Marshall was already writing what was to be the bible of a new economic orthodoxy, neoclassical economics. Evidently there was more than one progressive research programme on the march and a new generation of economists was persuaded that important advances were taking place in economic knowledge.

In the event, Keynes' *Scope and Method* and Marshall's *Principles of Economics* proceeded side by side, with each author systematically reading and criticising the other's chapter drafts or proofs. They were published within half a year

[1] See for example the preface to the 1879 edition of his *Theory of Political Economy*: 'When at length a true system of Economics comes to be established, it will be seen that that able but wrong-headed man, David Ricardo, shunted the care of Economic Science on to a wrong line, a line, however, on which it was further urged towards confusion by his equally able and wrong-headed admirer John Stuart Mill.'

[2] J. N. Keynes, *Studies and Exercises in Formal Logic*, 1st ed. 1884, 4th ed. 1928.

[3] When Marshall left Oxford in January 1885 to take up his Cambridge Chair Keynes lectured in his place (but on a subject of his own choosing) for the rest of the academic year.

[4] J. N. Keynes *Diaries*, Cambridge University Library Add. MSS. 7834, 2-6 85.

[5] In the early 1880s Arnold Toynbee gave his remarkable Oxford lectures on the industrial revolution (published posthumously in 1884), Cunningham's *Growth of English Industry and Commerce* appeared in 1882, Seebohm's English Village Community in 1883. These were the first of a stream of exciting new works by economic historians. Most significant of all perhaps, an economic historian, Thorold Rogers, was elected to the Drummond Chair of Political Economy at Oxford in 1888.

of each other, Marshall's *Principles* in mid-1890 and Keynes' book in January 1891. The latter was accepted by a majority of reviewers as being the definitive methodological text for the new political economy (in Britain identified with Marshall's *Principles*), and as ending the long and tedious *Methodenstreit.* Edgeworth, for example, who reviewed it twice (in *Nature* and in this JOURNAL) said in *Nature* 'on a subject which it is undesirable to be always re-opening it may be hoped that Mr Keynes' work will prove final.'[1] James Bonar, reviewing it in *The Academy* said, (in a passage which Keynes was proud to transcribe into his diary): 'In a sense it is true that his book simply sums up the views about scope and method which have in the last twenty years been gradually taking shape in the minds of English and American economists under the influence of Jevons, Marshall and Walker.'[2] Nor was it only English-speaking economists who were already adopting deliberately non-controversial views on scope and method. Similar ideas were appearing in the methodological pronouncements of leading continental writers such as Cossa in Italy or Wagner in Germany or Böhm-Bawerk in Austria.[3] Suddenly, it would appear, there was a consensus on the methodology of economics.

At the heart of the consensus was a determination to re-establish the scientific credentials of a discipline which had been publicly discredited by internal dissension on fundamental principles. The scientific validity of the 'new political economy' was accordingly justified along three main lines:

(1) by tracing its continuity with classical political economy, so as to establish the cumulative quality of progress in economic knowledge;

(2) by accepting that the inductive-empirical researches of the historical school and the deductive-analytical researches of the mathematical school had complementary roles to play in furthering economic knowledge; and

(3) by insisting that the basic postulates of the discipline were value free, that they were objectively given by the industrial and organisational conditions of modern society to which the resulting economic analysis was intended to be applied.

The first route involved a blurring of the methodological differences between the old and the new political economy and a systematic interpretation of radical changes in economic theory as being evolutionary rather than revolutionary. It was an interpretation that sat easily in the intellectual environment of the second half of the nineteenth century, buzzing with Darwinian or Spencerian ideas of natural selection, social evolution and unity of the sciences.

The second route involved recognition of different types of economic inquiry and turned away from the narrow-minded intolerance inherent in the *Method-*

[1] Keynes reproduced this passage in his diary for 28th February 1891, Add MSS 7841. The ECONOMIC JOURNAL Review appeared in 1891, pp. 420–3, it was longer and more critical as befitted a professional audience but equally determined to stress the book's 'finality' on the methodological issues 'on which authorities appear to be substantially, if not in phrase, agreed.' (p. 423).

[2] J. Bonar, *The Academy*, March 7, 1891 p. 227.

[3] See e.g. L. Cossa, *Guide to the Study of Political Economy* (1880). Translated by W. S. Jevons from the 2nd Italian edition (1878); Wagner on the Present State of Political Economy, *Quarterly Journal of Economics*, October, 1886; and E. Böhm-Bawerk, 'The Historical vs the deductive method in political economy', in *Annals of the American Academy of Political and Social Science*, October, 1890.

enstreit. Neville Keynes for example distinguished between three kinds of economics, a positive science, a normative or regulative science and an art. 'The object of a positive science is the establishment of *uniformities*, of a normative science the determinants of *ideals*, of an art the formulation of *precepts*.'[1] Adolf Wagner writing from a different tradition envisaged a division of labour between economists. 'Nothing is, in my opinion more harmful for the true advance of a branch of knowledge than that a given tendency in it, which happens to fit the abilities, the turn of mind, the training of individual scholars, which may indeed be fruitful and necessary, is carried so far as to demand for itself an exclusive control and to pretend that in it is the only true science...The result is that a valuable line of thought, first entered on by great leaders, continues to be followed mechanically by a set of commonplace imitator – men it may be, of high technical training and the more arrogant for that...The truth is that there are minds that tend to deductive reasoning, to systematic exposition, to generalising and dogmatising; there are other minds of a more 'historical' bent that turn to induction, to historical and statistical investigation...Each tendency has its strengths and weaknesses, its merits and defects.'[2]

The third route to consensus involved denying that the classical assumption of perfect competition and the associated bias towards laissez-faire policy prescriptions were essential features of the more general, positive, kind of economic theorising that was rising on the shoulders of the old orthodoxy. Thus Neville Keynes defended the traditional postulates on two ostensibly objective grounds: first, in relation to perfect competition, because 'it is best to take the simplest case first'; and second, because 'in modern economic societies laissez-faire has been as a matter of fact the general rule'. But as 'a maxim of conduct' he dismissed laissez-faire as being irrelevant to the pure economics that he equated with positive economic science and relegated it to the art of political economy.[3] Marshall, who seems to have been more sensitive than Keynes to the charges of ideological bias that were often levelled against economists, was prepared to go still further, both in disowning the convenient concept of the economic man and in throwing overboard the utilitarian heritage. The account of his speech seconding the vote of thanks for Goschen's presidential address to the Royal Economic Society reported Marshall's assertion that 'the economists of today dispensed with the economic man altogether' and also that classical political economy was 'wholly independent of the utilitarian doctrine: it was, when rightly understood, common property to all ethical creeds.'[4]

In effect then the academics who embraced the 'new political economy' of the late nineteenth century justified their claims for the scientific status of their discipline by distinguishing an abstract deductive core of 'pure' economics aimed at explaining the logic of economic behaviour in the market place without prejudice from its ethical or political implications. Accusations that political

[1] Keynes *Scope and Method,* 1930 ed. p. 35. The distinction between political economy as an art and political economy as a science goes back to Bentham.

[2] Translated by C. F. Dunbar, 'Wagner on the Present State of Political Economy', *Quarterly Journal of Economics,* October, 1886.

[3] J. N. Keynes, *op. cit,* p. 66–7.

[4] ECONOMIC JOURNAL, September, 1893, p. 388.

economy was speculative or unethical or biased towards the preservation of a particular economic system could be brushed aside from the objective core of economic *science* on the grounds that questions of empirical validity or distributional justice or policy desiderata simply did not arise at the theoretical level. They could be relevant only within the more flexible periphery of applied economics.

Acceptance of the idea that there was a central core of continuously evolving economic theory, insulated from irreconcilable conflicts between ethical or political value systems, represented a victory for the theorists over the anti-theorists, the historicists. For although the leading theorists acknowledged the necessity for increased research in applied economics they left little doubt that progress in economic science (as opposed to political economy) could take place only at the theoretical core where they focused most of their own research efforts.

Walras, for example, had originally set himself a research programme which involved the writing of three volumes of basic economic principles – the first on pure economics, the second on applied economics 'or the theory of Agricultural, Industrial and Commercial Production of Wealth' and the third on social economics 'or the Theory of the Distribution of Wealth via Property and Taxation.'[1] The first book came out in two instalments in 1874 and 1877 and he spent most of the rest of his life improving on it. The research projects which were to have underpinned the second and third books were never developed, though he published two books of essays under these titles. Similarly Marshall, who spoke strongly in favour of applied economics and put a great deal of historical and empirical material into the first edition of his *Principles*, went on steadily shifting the balance towards pure theory in each successive edition of this his major work.[2]

The effect of thus lifting the central body of economic theory out of the arena of ethical and political debate was twofold. It narrowed the scope of the theoretical core of the economists' research programme so that it was largely reducible to a theory of exchange under competitive conditions: and at the same time it took the passion and the point out of the debates on method that had characterised the 1870s and 1880s. It did not eliminate all methodological differences: for example the debate on whether pure economics should become an essentially mathematical science continued. But such arguments were more decorously conducted in correspondence between individual economists or in the pages of the learned journals. They did not shake the foundations of the discipline. Indeed the fact that leading theorists such as Marshall openly downgraded the role of mathematics enabled the largely innumerate rank and file of

[1] Leon Walras, *Elements of Pure Economics* or 'The Theory of Social Wealth', (translated by W. Jaffé 1954) p. 35, quoting from the Preface to the 4th ed. 1900.

[2] There is a significant passage in one of his letters to Neville Keynes, on the question of the reform of the Cambridge Economics Tripos to the effect that: 'Gradually I have been forced to the conclusion that unless the empirical treatment of economics is completely to oust the scientific and analytical – to which you and I are almost the only elderly middle-aged English economists who are perfectly loyal (I don't count Edgeworth because he is so extreme) we must throw over the mischievous and untrue statement that according to the classical economists "it was only on the assumption of free competition that their principles and technology could apply".' *Marshall Papers*, Marshall Library, Cambridge.

professional economists to retain a sense of confidence in their own scientific contribution.

There remained, of course, an 'awkward squad', mainly composed of economic historians, which was not able to accept the terms of the consensus and persisted in raising questions of scope and method which the new school of economic science did not wish to know about. In particular, the economic historians continued to baulk at the idea that abstract economic theory or 'pure economics' as it was commonly labelled, was the sole source of the discipline's scientific progress. Leaving aside the traditional historians such as Archdeacon Cunningham, for whom the study of economic history was a branch of political history, and who had little interest in, or understanding of, either classical or neo-classical political economy,[1] there was emerging a new breed of economic historians, such as Thorold Rogers or William Ashley, for whom the study of economic history was a branch of applied economics. The new economist-historians had their own followings in the academic community of economists and were as capable of assessing the strengths and weaknesses of the new political economy as the innovating theorists themselves. Ashley, for example, in a careful exegesis of Ricardo's labour theory of value, provoked by the first edition of Marshall's *Principles*, effectively demonstrated the distortions involved in the latter's attempt to establish a classical pedigree for the marginal revolution.[2]

Some sixteen years later in his presidential address to Section F of the British Association, Ashley reviewed the international revolution in economic ideas that had taken place over the previous two decades and sharply criticised the over-simplifications and the limitations of the marginal analysis. 'Instead of leading us to the very heart of the problem – the doctrine of marginal value seems to me to remain entirely on the surface: it is not much more than a verbal description of the superficial facts at a particular point of time.'[3] He also pointed out that the consensus was only skin-deep, being limited to a common belief in the value of abstract, general reasoning 'and the common employment of a few specialist terms...So long as the student keeps to a particular set of writings, he may cherish the impression of a triumphant analysis, solving all difficulties for intelligent men in the same way; when he extends his reading, he will find that there are at least three main groups, following respectively the lead of Cambridge, of Vienna and of New York; while among the younger men there are all sorts of ingenious but mutually irreconcilable attempts at eclectic compromise.'[4]

Nevertheless economists who were prepared to narrow the scope of their 'science' to some aspect of the theory of markets operating under perfect

[1] Cunningham was a waspish critic of Marshall but his attacks were rarely on target for he did not understand what the new political economy was all about. See, e.g. W. Cunningham, 'The perversion of economic history', ECONOMIC JOURNAL, 1892, and Marshall's reply in the same volume.

[2] W. J. Ashley, 'The rehabilitation of Ricardo', ECONOMIC JOURNAL, 1891, See for example the last paragraph which after freely acknowledging that 'The *Principles of Economics*...casts into the background almost all that has been written in England since John Stuart Mill; it sums up the economic movement of the last forty years, and furnishes the point of departure for a new and fruitful development', concluded 'The economic historian, we are told, is apt to be confused in theory; I am afraid we must add that the sympathetic theorist runs the risk of being unhistorical.'

[3] W. J. Ashley, 'The present position of political economy , ECONOMIC JOURNAL, December, 1907, pp. 476–7.

[4] *Ibid.* p. 478.

competition, were able to convince themselves that they were engaged in a progressive research programme, for which the neo-classical orthodoxy supplied the necessary paradigm.

Those whose inquiries took them in directions where the theory of money was relevant found (then as now) that they had no such disciplinary consensus from which to begin. Wicksell, for example, in his inaugural lecture at Lund in 1904 said, in terms which would not look out of place nearly 80 years later: 'Within the whole of his [the economist's] science, or what he insists on calling science, no generally recognised result is to be found, as is also the case for theology and for roughly the same reasons; there is no single doctrine taken to be a scientific truth without the diametrically opposed view being similarly upheld by authors of high repute.' And, giving examples of perennial conflict between economists, he went on: '...when it is a matter of finding the cause of general changes in the price of commodities, and especially the influence on those of credit and the institutions regulating credit, some maintain that cheap and easy credit, in other words, a low rate of interest, will tend to increase the amount of means of payment in circulation and the demand for goods and this will tend to increase the general level of prices; while others maintain the contrary, that cheap credit means the same things as cheaper costs of production and so tends to lower the level of prices, not to raise it; and naturally...there is no lack of more moderate opinion between the two extremes, eclectics who say that the influence of credit on prices is sometimes in one direction, sometimes in another and is sometimes nil.'[1]

None of these doubts, however, was allowed to threaten the analytical core of 'pure economics' and for several decades the dominant belief inspiring the intellectual community of economists was that they shared a common nucleus of views in the scope and method of economic *science*. They could go on teaching successive generations of undergraduates from the same, or similar, textbooks of economic theory and could assume that, whatever the intractability of the problems posed in the applied areas of their discipline, they were building on virtually impregnable analytical foundations. There *were* methodological differences between theorists but they could be regarded as differences of degree rather than of substance; and they could be subsumed in the narrower or broader conceptions of the *scope* of the discipline adopted by different theorists.[2]

The reason why the economic historians found it impossible to observe the truce on scope and method was that they started from the belief that economic theory should illuminate the study of history and they were dismayed therefore

[1] K. Wicksell, Inaugural Lecture (1904) reprinted in E. Lindahl, *Ends and Means in Economics* (1958).

[2] For example when Wicksteed, in his 1913 presidential address to Section F of the British Association, restated the essence of the marginal theory of value in Jevonian terms, which were markedly narrower than the Marshallian version, the result was simply that it led him to restrict the scope of political economy (in relation to sociology) more narrowly than mainstream neoclassicals would have done. P. H. Wicksteed, 'The Scope and Method of Political Economy in the light of the 'marginal' Theory of Value and Distribution,' ECONOMIC JOURNAL, March, 1914. See, e.g. p. 785 '...the so-called supply curve is simply a part of the total demand curve'; or p. 784 '...the better we understand the true function of the "market" in its widest sense, the more fully we shall realise that it never has been left to itself, and the more deeply shall we feel that it never must be. *Economics must be the handmaid of sociology*' (my italics).

by the gap that seemed to be widening between theoretical and applied economics. So in 1922 Clapham tried to confront the leading theorists on their own ground with his article on 'empty economic boxes'.[1] The main burden of his argument was that the strategic concepts of economic theory were empty of relevance to the real world; that even Marshall and Pigou could make little practical use of the abstract items of 'mental furniture' on which the contemporary consensus in economic theory rested. 'I think a great deal of harm has been done' he complained 'through omission to make clear that the Laws of Returns have never been attached to specific industries; that we do not, for instance, at this moment *know* under what conditions of returns coal or boots are being produced'.[2]

Pigou wrote a suitably crushing reply in the next issue of this JOURNAL.[3] He began by distinguishing two sorts of knowledge: 'pure' knowledge such as is sought in mathematics and logic; and realistic knowledge concerned with subject-matter presumed to be central, such as is sought by physicists. Within the second sort of knowledge must be further distinguished knowledge that cannot and knowledge that can give us direct help in the practical conduct of affairs. This second distinction seems to be somewhat blurred in Dr Clapham's mind.'[4] The gap was maintained then between pure and applied economics and a further ditch was dug between applied economic research which could not be justified in terms of its applicability to practical policy problems (of which research in economic history was a telling example) and a vaguely-defined but evidently limited area of directly useful knowledge. Pigou concluded by pouring scorn on the idea that economic theory was useless because its concepts could not clearly be related to the real world: 'It is as though Dr Clapham, in choosing between two suits of clothes (he will forgive the horrible suggestion that he might buy such things ready-made) should refuse to inquire which of them will fit him best, because there is another consideration also relevant to his choice, namely the amount of money that they respectively cost.'[5] In short Clapham was firmly put down for being confused and naive and above all for wasting time in quarrelling about methodological issues that he did not properly understand.[6]

Still, Clapham did make it into the ECONOMIC JOURNAL and he did rate a reply from high authority. Other critics of orthodox economic theory found it hard to attract any sort of response. I have found no evidence, for example, that Ashley's lecture on Evolutionary Economics, written in 1923 for the Birkbeck College Centenary, drew any response from the theorists though it argued more

[1] J. H. Clapham, 'Of empty economic boxes', ECONOMIC JOURNAL, September, 1922.
[2] *Ibid.* p. 312.
[3] A. C. Pigou, 'Empty boxes: a reply.' ECONOMIC JOURNAL, December, 1922.
[4] *Ibid.* p. 458.
[5] *Ibid.* p. 464.
[6] Clapham's rejoinder, also in the December 1922 ECONOMIC JOURNAL showed that he was sensitive to the rebuke 'whose point is sharpened by the references to ready-made clothes and "a certain naivete"' but he claimed his right to raise the issue of economic method: 'Mounted on the smoothly running machine which he handles with such incomparable skill Professor Pigou may be a trifle impatient of suggestions that a differently constructed model might have a longer and more useful life; but that is no reason why the suggestions should not be made, even by a much less expert driver.'

systematically than Clapham and in terms that now seem persuasive, for 'new theoretical ways of looking at things.'[1] Ashley's argument was that in so far as economics could lay claim to being a scientific body of knowledge its validity depended on its capacity to adjust its assumptions, concepts and analytical apparatus to changes in the institutional and organisational context of industrial and commercial behaviour: and he listed a number of obvious ways in which the existing corpus of economic theory was plainly out of date. Of these the most important was in its clinging to the assumption that competition was the 'normal' state of affairs in an industrial world where 'it is almost as true to say that our condition is one of various degrees of combination checked by competition as to describe it as one of various degrees of competition checked by combination.'[2] But, persuasive or not, it was easy to ignore such criticisms of established economic science when they were being levelled by those whose researches were confined to the fringe areas such as economic history or the 'art' of political economy.

In Britain, the pure theoretical research tradition continued to dominate through the 1920s and early 1930s while resisting externally-generated winds of change.[3] The demonstration by Piero Sraffa that there were logical inconsistences in the laws of returns[4] had more effect than the applied economists' complaints of unrealism in stimulating the search for new models based on the assumption of imperfect competition; and it was not until Maynard Keynes published his *General Theory* that the central assumption of the self-regulating market economy came under direct fire again. This time it was not too easy to paper over the methodological divisions that re-surfaced. True there was a golden decade or so of superficial harmony when Keynesian macroeconomic theory and neo-classical micro-economic theory inhabited separate compartments of the post-World War II textbooks, and while the growing army of professional economists in the service of national governments and international agencies was given credit for a prolonged post-war boom. When stagflation reared its ugly head, however, bringing with it a nasty mixture of high unemployment and high inflation for which neither Keynesian nor neo-classical theory had a plausible explanation a new crisis of confidence developed. The methodological debates flared up again and economists began to re-consider the terms on which their discipline could lay claim to scientific status. The fact that the philosophers of science have also been re-considering the demarcation

[1] Sir W. Ashley, 'Evolutionary Economics', *Birkbeck Centenary Lectures, 1823–1923* (1924).

[2] *Ibid.* p. 60. Among the other changes in the nineteenth century economic environment which Ashley identified as calling for radical reconstruction of orthodox economic theory were the increasing capital intensity of industrial production (calling for new approaches to the 'study of the relations between Capital and Labour', to the theory of price formation and to the theory of saving and investment) and the dropping of the gold standard (calling for a revision of the Quantity Theory of Money as an explanation of inflation).

[3] In the United States the institutionalists' revolt against the doctrine that abstract theorising was the main source of scientific progress in economic knowledge seems to have had more impact on economists generally than did the economic historians in Britain. No doubt this was largely due to the personal qualities of Wesley Mitchell and to the fact that he concentrated his research efforts on the most pressing economic problem of the early twentieth century – business cycles. But it probably owed a great deal also to the human and financial resources of the National Bureau of Economic Research through which Mitchell was able to mount an impressively fruitful empirical research programme.

[4] P. Sraffa, 'The laws of returns under competitive conditions,' ECONOMIC JOURNAL, December, 1926.

lines between science and non-science, and the nature of scientific progress generally, has added new dimensions to these debates.

This background noise of dissent dividing the leaders of the discipline on fundamental issues does not constitute a comfortable working environment for the would-be *normal* practitioners and there is no lack of external as well as internal pressures to encourage the search for a new consensus. The difference today, however, as compared with a hundred years ago, or even fifty years ago, is that there is now a plethora of 'new theoretical ways of looking at things' and it is not going to be as easy in the 1980s as it was in the 1880s to pretend that there is a hard core of cumulative economic knowledge to which – if it is defined carefully enough – the majority of economists could confidently subscribe. Econometricians are stuffing suitably trimmed empirical data into the new economic boxes almost as fast as the theoretical innovations appear in print, though it is not obvious that the recent explosion of quantitative research in mathematical models has improved the explanatory or predictive power of the economist's 'engine of thought'.

In the end, however, it is the external pressures for consensus that are likely to be most potent. For economics is more vulnerable than most other sciences to the immediate practical demands of social policy. To quote one of the most distinguished of twentieth century econometricians, Ragnar Frisch: '...at the global level the goal of economic theory is to lay bare the way in which different economic factors act and interact on each other in a highly complex system, and to do this in such a way that the results may be used in practice to carry out in the most effective way, specific desiderata in the steering of the economy.'[1] It is here, in its implications for policy prescriptions that dissension amongst economists is most disturbing.

The lesson, it seems to me, that we should draw from the history of economic thought is that economists should resist the pressure to embrace a one-sided or restrictive consensus, There *is* no one kind of economic truth which holds the key to fruitful analysis of *all* economic problems, no pure economic theory that is immune to changes in social values or current policy problems. The scope and method of our discipline needs at all times to be defined in relation to the social problems which give purpose to it and there is room for more than one progressive research programme in operation at the same time. We ought indeed to profit from the divergent approaches of leading theorists, provided that they and their disciples avoid the kind of arrogance of which Wagner complained a century ago and are scrupulously open-minded in the conduct of the necessary debates. In any case, there is now no prospect of fudging the difficult political and ethical issues by drawing a distinction between the science of pure economics and the art of political economy. For it is evident that designing economic models for direct use in the process of policy formulation is a research activity which is as likely to suggest fruitful 'new theoretical ways of looking at things' as is fundamental theoretical research of a primarily abstract nature.

If economics is a science – and it is not as clear as it used to be what *that* is

[1] R. Frisch, Nobel Prize Lecture, 'From Utopian Theory to Practical Applications: The Case of Econometrics.' Reprinted in *American Economic Review*, December, 1981, p. 6.

– it is evidently a science whose powers of prediction and control are limited, largely because the phenomena it seeks to explain are subject to persistent change and often for reasons that may lie outside the traditional boundaries of the discipline. In these circumstances successful explanation, or prediction, must depend on the economist's willingness to renew, discard and adapt theories, concepts and analytical techniques and even to adjust the boundaries of the discipline. What we need is not a new orthodoxy on scope and method but a readiness to listen seriously to our colleagues who take opposing views on fundamental principles and to admit to the natural scientists, or the politicians, or the students, who are crying out for economic truth, that the right answers are unlikely to come from any pure economic dogma.

University of Cambridge

Date of receipt of final typescript: July 1982

[18]

Francis Ysidro Edgeworth

by Sir John Hicks

I am a little embarrassed by the task that has been laid on me, to speak of F.Y. Edgeworth in this series of lectures on Irish economists. I am not at all sure that he can be reckoned to have been an Irish economist. It is true that he was born in Ireland, and brought up in Ireland; but he rarely speaks of Ireland in his works. When one thinks that he is going to do so, he usually turns off to some other subject. There is however a good deal to be said about his Irish background. I shall allow myself to talk about that at some length, before I come to his economics.

But perhaps I ought to make clear, before I come even to that, that I feel myself to have a rather special relation to him. I had no personal contact with him. I think I once saw a figure on the other side of a street, and was told that it was Professor Edgeworth; that is all. I did not start to work at all seriously on economics until after he was dead. But then quite soon afterwards, really quite soon after he was dead, I found myself drawn to him. Much of my own early work on economic theory is a continuation of his. So I got to think of him, almost as if he had been my teacher. It was in his footsteps that I was trying to walk.

Years later I had the honour (I hope you will understand from what I have just said how great an honour I felt it to be) of succeeding him, at two removes, as Drummond Professor of Political Economy in Oxford. That carried with it, for me as it had done for him, a Fellowship at All Souls College. He was Fellow of the College for thirty-five years, from 1891 to his death in 1926; I have followed him, so far, for thirty-one years, since 1952. We have a splendid photograph of him, which hangs in our common room, and which I have had copied; but for the rest I have not found it easy to collect recollections of him.[1] It is quite a long time ago.

[1] I have to make acknowledgements, for help received in the biographical parts of this paper (1) from my colleague, Mr J.S.G. Simmons, formerly librarian of the Codrington Library, All Souls (2) from Mrs Christina Colvin, herself a descendant of Michael Pakenham Edgeworth, Frank Edgeworth's full brother, who is now living in Oxford and has done much work on the Edgeworth family papers, and (3) from Raymond Carr, Warden of St Anthony's College, who is an expert on the nineteenth-century history of Spain.

Sir John Hicks

There are one or two things which our college archivist has been able to collect for me, and one or two which I have got from other sources in Oxford; I shall make use of them later. But in the main I have had to rely on Keynes's well-known memoir, supplemented by the *Black Book of Edgeworthstown,* the history of the Edgeworth family. Keynes knew him well, since for years they were joint editors of the *Economic Journal.* I don't think that Keynes had much sympathy with Edgeworth's approach to economics; he had little understanding of those parts of Edgeworth's work which now seem to be of particular importance. But for Edgeworth as a person he is the source on whom we have most to rely.

Now for the family history, which indeed is an Irish story. One need not go further back than his grandfather, Richard Lovell Edgeworth, a remarkable figure, quite an ornament of the age of Burke and of Grattan, one of the more distinguished periods of Irish history. He had inherited the family estate at Edgeworthstown, County Longford, and lived there a good part of his time. But he made visits to England, finding his way to Lichfield, where he became a member of that notable group of literary people, scientists and inventors, which was a focus of the technological revolution then taking place. He was himself a bit of an inventor; his inventions, though unsuccessful, were quite forward-looking. He organised a semaphore, ancestor of the telegraph; and he tried to make a caterpillar-wheeled vehicle which could climb over walls. But he is best known for his progressive views on education, where he began as a follower of Rousseau, but turned, by experience, into something not less original, but more sensible.

He had a lot of experience, for he married four times, successively, and by each of his wives he had a family, eighteen children in all. So he had quite a school of his own to educate. But they can never have been in his school together; there were too many years between them. Maria Edgeworth, the novelist, came from the first of these families; there is no doubt, you will know, that she belongs to Ireland. (She was said, at the time, to have done for Ireland what Walter Scott was to do for Scotland.) She was thirty years older than her half-brother Frank (Francis Ysidro's father) who came from the fourth family.

But before coming to him, I would like to say a word about another descendant. One of Maria's (full) sisters was the mother of Thomas Lovell Beddoes, that strange but rather appealing figure, who wrote poems that one likes to think as having the same relation to Shelley's as Webster's to Shakespeare's. He died, by his own hand, when Francis Ysidro was two years old; there is something appropriate in the fact that they were both of them grandsons of Richard Lovell.

I turn to the other side of Francis Ysidro's ancestry. His mother was Spanish (that is where the Y for Ysidro comes from); but I suppose we may now say that that need not make him any less Irish. The story of how his parents met is romantic.

The year (this is important) is 1831. Frank Edgeworth was then 22 years of age. As a very much younger son of so large a family, he did not have much money. But he had managed to visit Italy. On returning to London, with the intention of setting out on further travels, he was shown, by mistake, into a room that was full of ladies. 'They proved to be the wife and daughters of General Eroles, a Spanish exile.' (That is what the *Black Book* says.) Being an Irishman, he came back next day, with a bouquet; and three months later he had married Rosa Eroles, then aged sixteen.

Now just who was this 'General Eroles' and why was he exiled? I was intrigued by this story, and wanted to discover more about it. With the aid of my friends in Oxford, I have had some success; though there are puzzles, important puzzles, which remain. I would like to report on our investigations.

There have been others who have wanted to find out about the Eroles family, in the first place, very naturally, the Edgeworths themselves. There is extant a letter, dated December 1831, addressed to Charles Edgeworth, Frank's half-brother, of the third family. It is written by Lord Holland, the nephew of Charles James Fox, at whose table the Whig leaders, then in office (the Reform Bill ministry) were so often entertained. Charles had appealed to him for information about these people with whom his brother had got entangled. What he says is: 'I took great interest in the fortunes of Madame Eroles and her daughters at the time her husband somewhat imprudently engaged in the expedition of his countrymen against Ferdinand's government a year and a half ago. . . I am much mistaken if either her father (or uncle)-in-law was not the Baron d'Eroles who commanded a very considerable corps in Catalonia during the revolutionary war and was constantly in communication with our naval commanders.' That is what he says; but I think it can now be shown that he was, just a bit, mistaken.

The Baron, who 'collaborated with the British', is a well-known historical figure. He was in fact what we should now call a resistance leader; he led the popular resistance against Napoleon's invasion, in Catalonia, in the foothills of the Pyrenees. His first name was

Francis Ysidro Edgeworth

Jaoquin. Now it has been ascertained by my friend the archivist (from the 1886 edition of Burke's Landed Gentry, which contains a note on the Edgeworth family) that the name of Rosa Edgeworth's father was Antonio. So we can separate them out; we have their names.

Lord Holland clearly thought that Jaoquin was Antonio's father (or uncle); but it is known that Jaoquin was born in 1781, so that is not possible. We may take it from him that they were related; it would seem most likely that they were brothers. I shall assume they were brothers.

But now for the puzzle. Jaoquin died in 1825; but before he died he had played a part in the Spanish Civil War of 1823, between so-called 'liberals' and supporters of King Ferdinand's government—which was commonly regarded, in England, as the most disreputable of the 'absolutist' governments which had been established, in many continental countries, during the post-Napoleonic Restoration. In that Civil War, Jaoquin, quite definitely, had been on the absolutist side. But Antonio, as we know from Lord Holland, had taken part in a quite abortive expedition, apparently in 1830, *against* Ferdinand's government. Though that expedition was thought, by Lord Holland, to have been 'imprudent', he evidently sympathised with it; he was prepared to help people who had taken part. So while Joaquin had been pro-Ferdinand, Antonio, it appears, was on the other side.

There is no reason why brothers should not have political differences; but this, surely, is rather extreme. I can only guess at an explanation; but there does not seem to be one possible clue. There was an insurrection in Catalonia in 1827, of people who had been pro-Ferdinand in 1823, but who considered that they had not been properly treated by the party they had supported, when it came out on top. Suppose that Antonio had been involved in that insurrection, went into exile after its failure, and so was available to take part in the expedition of 1830 which started from England. That it meant joining up with people against whom Joaquin had been fighting in 1823 would then be intelligible.

Perhaps, after all, there is a basic consistency. Say that the Eroles were neither leftist nor rightist, even in the terms of that time. What they stood for was Catalan independence, of some sort, from Madrid. That would fit, each time. They were always anti-Madrid, whoever was in power at Madrid. There were some Catalans, already, who took that line. Their stronghold was in the Pyreneean foothills; that was the region where Joaquin, in both of his wars,

Sir John Hicks

had his strength. These people kept up their struggle against Madrid, for many years; later on it was to take the form of support from the Carlist pretender. It was a conservative provincialism which did not have much in common with the Catalan nationalism, based on Barcelona, which has been a force in the present century.

I beg pardon for this digression, which has got quite out of scale. Let us go back to Frank and Rosa. They spent the first years of their married life in Florence, then in London; but afterwards they came back to Edgeworthstown, where Francis Ysidro was born in 1845. His father died the next year, but his mother not until 1864. So he must have been brought up by his mother, his education (so Keynes tells us) being given by tutors, from whom he got the Greek and Latin which in his writings he so often displays. And there are other things in his works which reflect that background, as we shall see.

He had one year, here at Trinity College Dublin, in 1862. He afterwards went to Balliol College, Oxford, graduating with a first in 'Greats' in 1869. So his formal education, throughout, was classical; but the substance of his work is mathematical, not classical. Where did he get his mathematics?

I wonder if he was quite self-taught. Anyone who was so mathematically minded as he was, who enjoyed mathematics as he did, must surely have had something of mathematics in his education. He was much more of a natural mathematician than his great contemporary Marshall, who had been a Senior Wrangler at Cambridge, had taught mathematics, and had even thought of becoming a mathematical physicist. Marshall is always putting mathematics away from him; he did not have the affection for it that Edgeworth had. He would never have wanted to campaign for the applicability of mathematics to economics.

I don't see that Edgeworth could have had opportunity, or encouragement, to study mathematics in Oxford; but I wonder about that year at Dublin. There were, in those days, great mathematicians in Dublin. There was Sir William Rowan Hamilton, whose reputation, great at that time, has become even greater since. There must be few modern students of advanced mathematics, or of mathematical physics, who do not know his name. In 1862 his health was failing; but we know that he had some relations with the Edgeworth family, so one would guess that when the boy went to Trinity, he would have been given an introduction to Hamilton. Hamilton was not only a mathematician; he was also a remarkable linguist. If Edgeworth went and talked with him, something could have happened. There was also George Salmon. I have read Salmon's books; I was lucky to pick up a set of them on one of my early visits to Dublin. I can imagine Edgeworth getting from Salmon something like what I myself, at much the same age, got from G.H. Hardy. Salmon was a beautiful expositor; a pupil of his could well have been in love with curves.

But enough of such conjectures. Though one can only guess how Edgeworth's mathematics started, how his economics started is perfectly clear. It was from Jevons. After Edgeworth had graduated, he went to live in London, nominally reading for the bar, but in fact going on with the philosophy, which he had been doing for 'Greats', and gradually turning from that to statistics and economics. When Edgeworth arrived in London, Jevons was still at Manchester; but his *Theory of political economy* (1871) was a link between the Utilitarianism, to which Edgeworth was already committed, and economics—mathematical economics. From 1876 to 1881 Jevons was professor at University College, London. He then lived in Hampstead, where Edgeworth also was living; we know that they used to go for walks on the Heath together. The preface to Jevons's second edition of his *Theory* (1879), in which he gives references to predecessors and contemporaries, obviously served as a reading-list for Edgeworth's first publication on economics—*Mathematical psychics* (1881).

I shall have much more to say on that book (*MP* I shall call it); but let me first proceed to fill in the main lines of biography. Jevons died, in a bathing accident, in 1882; how far he had had time to read *MP* before he died may be doubted. One must however suppose that it was by Jevons's influence that Edgeworth got his first teaching job in economics, at what was then the only other college of London University, King's. He taught there during the eighties, and during the eighties his reputation mounted, so that we find him, already in 1889, President of Section F (the economics section) of the British Association. Then came the great year of 1891, which set course for the rest of his life. He then went to Oxford as Drummond Professor, and at much the same time became editor of the *Economic Journal*—the first editor of that Journal, only just established. He remained as sole editor until 1911, when he handed over to Keynes. There were some later years when they were joint editors. His work for the *Journal* was a great part of his life.

So from 1891 he was living in Oxford, in rooms in All Souls. (He never married.) He kept his lodgings in Hampstead, and used to come to Ireland in the summer, staying (so Keynes informs us) at the St George Club, Kingstown. In his later years the Edgeworths-

Sir John Hicks

town house came into his possession, as the last surviving direct male descendant of Richard Lovell, but he never lived there. Soon after he died it passed away from the family.

I now turn to his work, and chiefly to that early work *MP*, which seems to me to be the centre of his contribution to economic theory. As will have been seen, he went on writing for forty years after that; but his later writings on economics, though they have their own value, and always their charm, are not often constructive like *MP*. They are mostly of the nature of reviews; even the longest are mainly review-articles. There was no other economist, of his period, who read so much of what was appearing, in many countries and in many languages. One must remember that in those days few writings on economics were translated. The modern economist can draw on the world, even if he knows no language but English; but it was not so then. (It was not so even in my own young days, when one had to read German at least to keep up to date; but it is now many years since I have reviewed a book in German.) So Edgeworth's reviews, and review-articles, which are brought together in the three volumes of his *Papers*, are invaluable to the student of the economics of that period. One can read him on Marshall, on Walras, on Pareto, on Böhm-Bawerk, on Fisher, on Cassel; and since it is the same mind that is reflecting on each of them, he ties them together.

But now for *MP*. The curious title, *Mathematical psychics*, was of course intended as a contrast to mathematical physics, already enjoying the vast reputation which it has retained. He is out to show that similar methods can be applied to human studies also. That nowadays needs no defence; so I need not pay attention to the challenge with which he begins. The substance of what he has to say is in what follows: a chapter on positive economics (economical calculus he calls it) and one on what he calls utilitarian calculus (what we should now call welfare economics). To have made a clear distinction between these two branches was the first, and not the least, of Edgeworth's contributions to economic theory. There is no doubt that he made it; I don't think there is anyone who can be claimed to have made it before.

What he has to say on the positive side is confined, almost entirely (in *MP*) to the theory of exchange—that is to say, if one uses the distinction that comes from Adam Smith, the determination of market prices. He does not go on to production theory, even to the determination of the prices of products; one supposes that he was leaving that to Marshall, with whose early work in that field he was

Francis Ysidro Edgeworth

already acquainted when he wrote *MP*. To a Jevonian the market price question came first. One can take it that it was already accepted that in a free market price was determined by demand and supply; that the equilibrium price was that which would bring demand, at that price, and supply at that price, into equality. But just how, and why, would such an equilibrium price be established?

Jevons had seen that this was a question, but had failed to answer it. Walras also had seen it, but had found himself obliged to introduce a fictitious character (modern writers about Walras call him an 'auctioneer', though he is not what I would call an auctioneer) in order to solve it. He is definitely not one of the parties trading. Edgeworth, very properly, would not accept this obviously 'ad hoc' solution. His market has no auctioneer; but if there is enough competition, it does come to equilibrium. He was thus obliged to define, very carefully, what he meant by 'enough competition'.

He begins with a case in which there is no competition, on either side, and then builds up. Then there are just two parties trading, in two commodities; so one of the parties is seller of A and buyer of B, the other is seller of B and buyer of A. Any particular bargain is the exchange of some quantity of A for some quantity of B; so these quantities can be represented by the simple Cartesian co-ordinates of a point on a diagram. If one assumes (as Edgeworth assumed, and it is clearly the general case into which others can be fitted), that each party has some use for each of the commodities traded) we can take it that the seller of A will not give up any A unless he is offered some B in exchange for it; and it is likely that there are other 'bad' bargains which will be similarly refused. For he would then give up what is worth more to him than what he is offered in exchange for it. So one can mark out a region on the diagram, representing those bargains which are impossibly bad from the point of view of the seller of A; and a corresponding region on the side of the seller of B. Any bargain which falls into either of these regions will be rejected, either by one party or by the other. He will prefer to stay where he was, without trading.

The boundaries of these regions are what Edgeworth called *indifference curves;* it was in this context that he invented that name which has become so famous. If either accepted a bargain which was representable by a point that was *on* his indifference curve, he would be not better off (and no worse off) than if he stayed where he was without trading—in the position that is represented by the origin of the diagram. So the indifference curves pass through the

Sir John Hicks

origin; and it makes sense to suppose them to curve round, as shown in Figure 1.

Figure 1

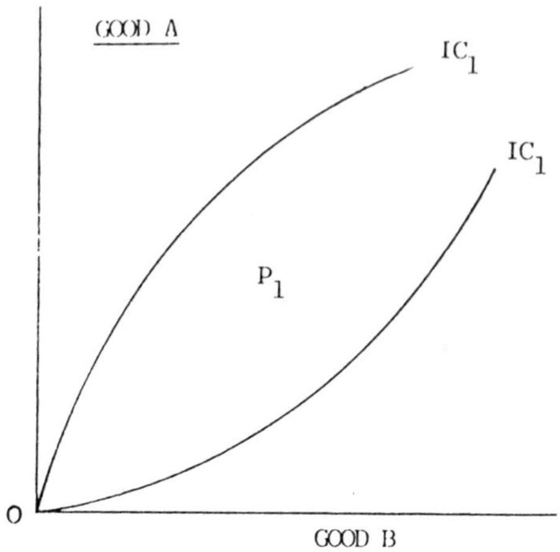

Figure 2

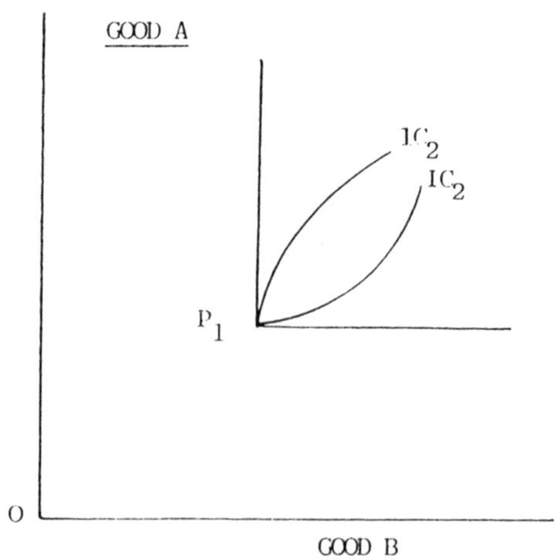

Francis Ysidro Edgeworth

The region between the two boundaries is the region of *practicable bargains*. There is no reason, for anything that has been said so far, why it should not be a wide region. Any point within that region represents a bargain which would give some advantage to each party (over no trading); so if it were to be proposed, and nothing better were on offer, it might be accepted.

But why should nothing better be on offer? Suppose that some bargain, within the practicable region (as shown) were accepted, why should not that be taken as a base for further trading? The possibilities of that can be shown on the diagram. We can take the point P_1, which has been reached in the first bargain, as a new origin, and through that we can draw another pair of indifference curves (Figure 2). Since P_1 was preferred to O, by both parties, any point that is preferred to P_1, by both parties, must also be preferred by both to O; so the practicable region, marked out by the new indifference curves must lie within the old. Suppose that some supplementary bargain, leading to a point within the new practicable region, is accepted. The construction can then be repeated, with a second supplementary bargain, and so on. Each time the practicable region that remains gets smaller; so in the end it must disappear. There is then no opportunity for supplementary trading.

That is as far as one can get, without competition. It is no more than the first step in Edgeworth's theory. It is however already shown, by this process of supplementation, that many of those bargains which appeared at the first round to be practicable, are not practicable as *final* bargains. All those that remain can be shown to lie on a curve, which Edgeworth called the *contract curve*. Once the contract curve has been reached, it is not possible to make an amendment which is to the advantage of both parties. A movement along the curve would be to the advantage of one and to the disadvantage of the other. But there may be a great spread between the two ends of the contract curve. At one end all, or nearly all, the advantage goes to the one of the parties, nearly all to the other at the other end.

Although this construction was no more than a first step, it was already a considerable achievement. It throws a great deal of light on actual, practical, processes of bargaining—more, I think, than is thrown by Games Theory, which (perhaps because of its dependence on abstruse mathematical theorems which were quite outside Edgeworth's reach) has in latter days acquired such prestige. The particular application which Edgeworth had most in mind was to bargaining between a trade union and an employers' association;

Sir John Hicks

and that is a field where it still has its uses. But one now wants to go on to still more important applications, to diplomatic bargaining between states, of which that now proceeding about armaments is a major example. In any of these cases one can see how a bargainer will often refuse a first step towards an agreement, corresponding to P_1 on the diagram I have been using, because he fears that it will set him on course towards a final contract, which, though it 'lies upon the contract curve' will be very unfavourable to him. It is the clash between absolute gain and relative gain which makes bargaining so difficult.

But now for competition. Proceed, at the next step, to introduce a second buyer and second seller, the two pairs being in contact. (All trades are still simple exchanges of good A for good B.) As Edgeworth very rightly shows, this need not by itself make much difference. What it does is to ensure that there can be no final settlement unless the same price is being charged throughout; the rate of exchange at which each pair is trading must be the same. For if it were not so, there would be a tendency to cross over—the less advantaged buyer changing to the seller from whom he could get better terms. But this does not imply that a very one-sided outcome, very favourable to the buyers (or to the sellers) is ruled out. For if separate bargainings had resulted in very similar settlements, then (whatever they were) competition so far would not upset them.

What makes the difference is when one seller can contract with more than one buyer (or vice versa). It is easiest to see this if one takes the case of employment of labour, which was Edgeworth's own example. Say that there are just two (possible) masters and two (possible) servants; I will venture to use those old terms which in this case are not inappropriate. Neither master minds which servant works for him, and neither servant minds which master he works for. Each servant will prefer to work for the master who offers better wages, and each master will prefer to employ the servant who will come for less. So if each master is to keep his servant, each must pay the same wage. But if the wage that was thus established was very low, it might be the case that a master would like to have two servants; but if he got both of them to work for him, the other master would get left out. So one can see him bidding up the wage, in order to keep his one servant for himself. Thus the extremely low wage, which at first sight seemed consistent with a final settlement, is not in fact consistent. The original set of practicable bargains, along the contract curve, is thus reduced in length. Though this does not make as good sense in the case of labour contracts (as Edgeworth noted) there should in principle be a similar closing-in at the other end.

The jump from employing one servant to employing two (as in this simple case) is *relatively* large; so the extent of closing-in, in this illustration, does not look considerable. But when the number of traders, on each side, is increased, the scope for re-arrangements, which will cause some party, on one side or the other, to get left out, becomes larger. It should not take a very large number to make the closing-in essentially complete. A market in which the closing in is complete, so that just one point on the contract curve is left, is what economists, ever since, have regarded as a perfect, or perfectly competitive, market.

I am not suggesting that Edgeworth invented the concept of a perfect market; it was there, in some of the works that he had read, in Cournot and Walras, at least. But by approaching it in the way that he did, he showed that the equilibrium of a perfectly competitive market would be such as could be represented by a point on his contract curve (suitably generalised). That is to say, there is no other set of bargains, which could be substituted for the equilibrium set, and which would not be worse than it is for some party, or parties. There may be other sets of bargains which would pass this test; but the equilibrium set of bargains is one that does pass it.

We are nowadays accustomed to express this proposition by saying that the equilibrium of perfect competition is a Pareto optimum; using that term as a tribute to the use that Pareto made of it. Still, Pareto got it from Edgeworth; there is no doubt of that.

A general proof of this Edgeworth-Pareto theorem, which will satisfy professional mathematicians, is quite difficult; but it is sufficient for most economic purposes just to note that the conditions for the establishment of a perfectly competitive equilibrium, and the conditions for a Pareto optimum, are the same. That Edgeworth clearly saw. So on this track, which has been followed by so many later economists, he did take the first step; and it is a defensible view that it was that first step which chiefly mattered.

That is as far as Edgeworth got, on the positive side, in *MP*; to what he said on the other (welfare) side I shall be coming in a moment. But before I come to that, I should like to say that he seems to me to have missed, at this point, an opportunity. He had given a rather full analysis of simple exchange, of quantities of two commodities (which I called A and B); he might have gone on to consider multiple exchange, in which more than two commodities come into question. He was already acquainted, when he wrote *MP*, with the work of Walras. Walras had gone on to study multiple exchange; but he had done so no more than set out equilibrium conditions. He could not explain the working of his market save by the introduction of his 'auctioneer', the device that Edgeworth rejected. A study of multiple exchange, on Edgeworth lines, would indeed have been more difficult. But if no more than the first steps towards it had been taken, things would have happened.

There can be no simple exchange (such as Edgeworth had been considering) between two parties unless each of them has things the other wants. But suppose that I have things I want to sell, and you have things you want to sell, but I do not want your goods, and you do not want mine.

But then suppose I can find another party, who will take my goods, though all he can offer in exchange is something I do not want. But these goods, which are not wanted by me, are wanted by you. Then I can get what I want, in exchange for what I have to sell, in two steps. (There may of course be more than two steps that are needed.) No final equilibrium, of Edgeworth type, can be achieved unless all such opportunities for indirect trade have been taken.

It will be noticed that it is essential, for such indirect trade to be possible, that there should be people who are willing to take in exchange, for the goods they have to sell, things which they do not themselves want, but are willing to take because they think it to be possible to hand them on to other people. People who take part in this sort of trade may appropriately be described as merchants. I don't think that Edgeworth could have constructed a model of multiple exchange, including indirect exchange, without introducing merchants. He would then have found that these merchants, each of them actual traders, seeking to make a profit, would have taken on most of the functions of Walras' 'auctioneer'.

It seems to me that it would have made a great deal of difference to the development of economic theory, in the years which followed, if Edgeworth had explored the route which I have just been trying to sketch out. For what that route leads to, very soon, is the introduction of *money*. Edgeworth himself never took much interest in monetary theory. Only in quite recent times has the power of an Edgeworthian approach to monetary theory begun to be realised.

So far, then, what Edgeworth had said had been very forward-

Francis Ysidro Edgeworth

looking; he has laid foundations for much of the work that economic theorists have been doing since his time. Of the final section of *MP* (on what he calls 'utilitarian calculus') that cannot be said. To understand it, one must remember that Edgeworth is a Utilitarian, in the strict sense that comes down from Bentham; the 'utility' or 'pleasure' that each individual is seeking to maximise is a quantity, and the aim of policy should be to maximise the sum of those quantities, all added together. Now if individuals are similar, and there is a general rule that marginal utility diminishes with wealth, it follows mathematically that this sum of utilities will be maximised if wealth is divided equally. Edgeworth clearly saw that (he was not the first to have seen it), but it is a conclusion that he was most unwilling to accept:

> Consider Equality, the right of equals to equal advantages and burdens, that large section of distributive justice, that deep principle which continually upheaves the crust of convention.
>
> . . .πολλάων πολίων κατέλυσε κάρηνα
> ἠδ' ἔτι καὶ λύσει. του γὰρ κράτος ἔστι μέγιστον.
>
> All this mighty moral force is deducible from the practicable principle of exact Utilitarianism combined with the simple laws of sentience (*a* and ß).

When one looks up this *a* and ß one finds that they are just the now familiar 'laws' of diminishing marginal utility and increasing marginal disutility).

I have inflicted on you the Homeric quotation, in the original Greek, pronounced as I was taught at school to pronounce it, and I suppose Edgeworth also; but I will venture to translate it, as it is essential to the force of the passage. It comes out, rather literally, as

> Many are the states it has destroyed, and it will go on destroying. For its power is very great.

I am pretty sure that that is what Edgeworth meant.

Now if one wished to avoid that conclusion, while keeping to the strict Utilitarianism so dear to Edgeworth, the only way was to insist on inequality, inequality between persons, in ability to get 'pleasure' or to bear 'pain'. Perhaps what I said in the beginning about his forebears will help to explain why he took this line so strongly. Of course he was helped by the Darwinism, then so fashionable.

Sir John Hicks

> Capacity for pleasure is a property of evolution, an essential attribute of civilisation. The grace of life, the charm of courtesy and courage, which once at least distinguished rank, not unreasonably received the means to enjoy and to transmit. To lower classes was assigned the work of which they seemed most capable; the work of the higher classes being different in kind was not to be equated in severity. If we suppose that capacity for pleasure is an attribute of skill and talent; if we consider that production is an unsymmetrical function of manual and scientific labour; we may see a reason deeper than Economics may afford [*he means, of course, his own positive economics*] for the larger pay, though often more agreeable work, of the aristocracy of skill and talent. The aristocracy of sex is similarly grounded upon the supposed superior capacity of the man for happiness, for the ἐνέργειαι of action and contemplation; upon the sentiment
>
> 'Woman is the lesser man, and her passions unto mine
> Are as moonlight unto sunlight and as water unto wine'.

You will notice the 'supposes' with which these passages are studded; he does not commit himself to this Tennysonian outlook, but still leaves the impression that he is inclined to share it.

I do not know that there is any other economist who has gone so far in the direction of Inegalitarianism as Edgeworth in these passages appears to do. Even Pareto, who (as we have seen) was in many ways a follower of Edgeworth, and who undoubtedly shared Edgeworth's feelings on these matters, felt himself obliged to look for another way out. For him, it was the *strict* utilitarianism of Edgeworth that had caused the trouble. One can keep all that one needs of Jevonian (or Edgeworthian) utilitarianism if it is applied to individual choices only. Utility is just an index of preference, and there is no reason why the index that is used by one chooser, and that used by another, should be capable of being added up. So after Pareto (and after the work that was done by Robbins and others in publicising what had already been done by Pareto) economists need not feel themselves bound to be egalitarian, or anti-egalitarian. These are moral questions, on which not even the welfare economist need feel called on to pronounce.

But to go back to Edgeworth. There is a later work of his, on the *Theory of taxation*, in which he appears to take a very different line from that which he had taken in *MP*. This was written in 1897, sixteen years later. He there comes out, very strongly, in favour of what he calls the principle of 'minimum aggregate sacrifice', as opposed to that of 'equal sacrifice' which been championed by some of his contemporaries. As applied to taxation, his principle clearly tends in the direction of steeper progressiveness than the alternative. For now he has little to say about those differences in 'capacity for pleasure' of which in the earlier work he had made so much. It is evident, from the correspondence of Pareto, that Pareto (who had held firm to his inegalitarianism) thought that Edgeworth had been swayed by the influence of Marshall—that he had sold out to the Cambridge 'Left'.

But Edgeworth did not say that he had changed his mind, so perhaps he thought he had not done so. We must remember the date of the later paper. Progressive taxation was then a novelty. Even the Lloyd George budget of 1909 was still far ahead. No more than a very mild degree of progression was then in question. The total burden of taxation was still very low, in comparison with what it has since become, nearly everywhere. He could well have maintained that for the distribution of that burden, a government could not be expected to pay much attention to the (rather intangible) differences in capacity, of which he had made so much in *MP*. As long as progression remained as moderate, or nearly as moderate, as it was in the nineties, it did not threaten the destruction of which in *MP* he had been afraid.

There is that; but it may well be that there was something else. There is a very large part of Edgeworth's work of which in this paper I have said nothing. I did not feel myself called upon to discuss it, and I fear that I should have been quite incompetent to do so. His work on probability, on the foundations of statistical theory, is voluminous; it has never been brought together. There is a summary of it, by Bowley; but I am not sure, from the small sample I have made of the original writings, that Bowley represents him at all fully. To do justice to his work in this field would require a major effort of research, which I have been quite unable to undertake. It is not at all certain that it would be rewarding, for there is no question that Edgeworth's work in this field (as indeed in much of his economics) is peculiar. The line he worked out is treated with respect by some modern stochasticists; but it has not been generally followed. But that he has so strong an interest in this direction is one of the things that needs to be borne in mind.

There is a paper on 'The application of probability to economics' to be found in his collected papers, but I do not find it to be of much help. It is however to be noticed that (there at least) he endorses the classical *equally likely* principle—'the assumption that any probability-constant of which we know nothing is as likely to have one value as another'—the formulation he quotes himself. We know from other writings of his that he had some doubts about that principle (as others have done); but he was clearly willing, on occasion, to use it himself. I wonder whether it is not in some such way that he would have defended his later view on optimum taxation—against his earlier self, supposed to have risen up as critic. But that is only a guess.

It is indeed not only his work on statistical theory which in this paper I have largely overlooked. He did work on other parts of economics, on monopoly and on international trade, to take leading examples. It is chiefly my own taste which has led me to concentrate on *MP*, that admittedly early book. I do feel, myself, that I would rather lose those later papers than lose *Mathematical psychics*.

[19]

British Review of Economic Issues, Vol. 6, No. 14, Spring 1984, pp.55-82.

ON THE NOTION OF SHORT-RUN AND LONG-RUN: MARSHALL, RICARDO AND EQUILIBRIUM THEORIES[1]

O.F. HAMOUDA
University of Cambridge

INTRODUCTION

The purpose of this paper is to discuss the notions of short-run and long-run relative to historical time and operational time in the context of the works of Marshall and Ricardo, and the equilibrium theorists.[2]

The concepts of short-run and long-run are widely used by economists; sometimes they are taken literally, that is, defined with respect to calendar time (i.e. in terms of days, weeks, years, etc.). At other times, they are conceived in an abstract context in which 'short' and 'long' are flexible and arbitrary, having nothing to do with the duration of time (where a clock is concerned) or historical reference. In the former interpretation short-run and long-run are intimately related. Short-run precedes long-run (in a temporal sense) and both are related to a succession of events in the economic activities of the actual world. In the latter interpretation, it is often the case that short-run and long-run are independent of each other and are usually compatible with description and explanation related to analytical and abstract conceptions.

A failure to distinguish between these two interpretations can be a source of disagreement and controversy between authors and different schools of thought. It can also create confusion in interpreting the work of a single author. To illustrate how short-run and long-run are dealt with in some specific cases, the paper will first consider Marshall's analysis. Marshall has provided definitions which have been accepted but not disputed. Followed then by a discussion on some forms of equilibrium theories (at a glance, it may appear that the issue of short-run and long-run interpretations is irrelevant to these theories but in fact it is one of the major causes which create a sharp division in terms of the methodological approach to market analysis within this economic stream). Finally we will review Ricardo's implicit explanation of these concepts (since the revival of his theory is the object of much discussion).

It will be shown that Marshall, Ricardo and the equilibrium theorists handled the concepts of short-run and long-run differently in their theoretical objectives but that these concepts are subject to interpretation even within their respective theory.

1. SHORT-RUN AND LONG-RUN IN HISTORICAL AND OPERATIONAL TIME

The concepts of short-run and long-run by themselves do not attract economists' attention yet they are part of terminology which is found in almost every economic writing. It is perhaps worthwhile to point out two things: (a) there does not seem to be in economic literature an exhaustive study concerning developments and various interpretations of these terms[3]; (b) in the English economic literature, together with the concepts of short-run and long-run there are other terms such as short-term, long-term, short-period and long-period which are often used synonymously. Without too much intrusion into the meaning of every aspect of these terms, it can be said that although 'short' and 'long' on the one hand, and 'period', 'term', and 'run' on the other hand are used in combination, it must be pointed out that 'short' and 'long' are adjectives, while 'period', 'term', and 'run' as nouns, are the key words. All of these terms (period, term, and run) convey an idea of *time*. However, their significance can be different according to the manner in which they are used: for instance Marshall distinguished 'period' from 'run' but it seems that economists, in general, do not pay any attention to these differences. For the purpose of this paper, these questions of semantics are left aside. It is therefore assumed, unless otherwise indicated, that 'period', 'term' and 'run' are synonymous. Instead the emphasis is placed on the relation of short-run and long-run to historical and operational time.

Since there are a great number of unknowns, heterogenous activities and agents involved in the dynamics of actual production, exchange and distribution, it is extremely difficult to grasp every aspect of these activities at once. In the process of theorizing, transformations are introduced. There are differences between what has or is actually taking place in the economic activity *and* the theoretical expression of that which is happening. It is not denied here that these differences should exist. By definition, theoretical expressions are abstract constructions and are, therefore, different in nature from the world which they are supposed to represent. However, it must be pointed out that in translating the actual happening of the world into theoretical constructs, simplifications are made for convenience but devices and conceptual and technical complications (which often have nothing to do with the actual world) are also introduced.

There are, therefore, on the one hand, developments of events in the economic activity as experienced in the actual world and there is, on the other hand, a supposedly corresponding world conceived for the sake of analysis. It is with respect to these two views of the world that the notion of time is interpreted in this paper. In the former (i.e. the actual world), events are happening in calendar time (or clock time), there is a passage of time and this time is referred to as *Historical Time* (a term often used by Joan Robinson[4] in relation to her description of the dynamics of the actual economic activity). In the latter (i.e. the abstract world), economists are analysing hypothetical situations. Time introduced in relation to the description of hypothetical happenings is referred to as *Operational Time*, a term used by Opie to conceptualize Marshallian Time.

Historical Time is the order in which actual events are succeeding each other. Historical time is said to be uni-directional in the sense that the future becomes the present then the past. Calendar time or clock time is used to locate events and eras with respect to history. A pattern of history is a sequence of states of affairs and events. Events are dated and ordered, once they occur they become history and cannot be changed. In this context, short-run and long-run are portions of calendar time. 'Short' is relative to 'long', and both are temporal measurements.

Operational Time has nothing to do with the nature of world history. "When he (Marshall) distinguished long and short periods he was not using clock-time as a criterion, but 'operational' time, in terms of the economic forces at work... Because assumptions may be made with respect to what is included in the 'factors of production'. In this sense short and long periods may 'shade into one another', but this shading has nothing to do with continuity of time in Nature" [Opie (1921), pp.199-200]. It will be argued that Marshall, in fact, was dealing with both historical time and operational time, and not simply with operational time as Opie seems to maintain. Furthermore, in this paper, Opie's conceptualisation of operational time is extended to every economic analysis which is concerned with hypothetical situations in which hypothetical change is involved. Operational time then, is a hypothetical lapse of time imagined in the mind of economists (independent of calendar time or clock time) when a hypothetical situation (in which economic forces are at work) is analysed. In the context of operational time, short-run and long-run are independent devices used to justify the focus on one specific theoretical issue rather than another; for example, 'market prices' and 'natural prices' are supposed to be, respectively, short-run and long-run phenomena and consequently are treated separately.

It has been argued elsewhere[5] that the interpretation of time in economics is much more complex than the simple explanation of historical time and operational time put forward in this paper. However, it is believed that these two interpretations of time are sufficient for the argument of this paper.

2. MARSHALL

Marshall, perhaps more than any other economist, was aware of the difficulties involved in handling practical matters at an abstract level, and in providing theories which would reflect, as closely as possible, the actual world.[6]

One of his main concerns was the explanation of the price formation which led to the formulation of the general mechanism of Supply and Demand. To arrive at such a construction, he invented a method of approach of his own, that of treating one variable while at the same time assuming the rest *unchanged*. He also invented an economic concept, namely that of *economic period*. He made a clear distinction between the following terminology:

> *Market Period* is a period in which "Supply is taken to mean the stock of the commodity in question which is on hand, or at all events 'in sight'." [Principles, p.378]
>
> *Short-Period*: "a few months or a year. Supply means broadly what can be produced for the price in question with the existing stock of plant, personal and impersonal, in the given time." [Principles, p.378]
>
> *Long-Period*: is "several years. Supply means what can be produced by plant which itself can be remuneratively produced and applied within the given time." [Principles, p.378]
>
> *Secular-Period* is a period in which there is "gradual growth of knowledge, of population and capital, and the changing conditions of demand and supply from one generation to another." [Principles, p.379]

> *Long-Run* is referred to in relation to the concept of the "Normal" or the "Natural" value of a commodity: "it is the average value which economic forces would bring about if the general condition of life were stationary for a run of time long enough to enable them all to work out their full effect". [Principles, p.345]

On the first reading of these definitions (removed from their context), one may conclude that the notion of "Period" related to historical time or calendar time, while "Long-Run" is (since, according to him, there is no such thing as stationarity in the actual world) an abstract concept related to an operational time.

In the context of Marshall's *Principles*, these definitions have been conceived for a specific reason, namely that of constructing a coherent and logical theory of value. Marshall was caught in a dilemma: on the one hand he wanted to construct an accurate and operational theory, but at the same time, he wanted his theory to remain sufficiently open, to reflect the actual world. This has created some confusion about what concerns us here: his treatment of time. His interpretation of the time period constantly oscillates between the idea that it is a device needed for analytical convenience, (where the time referred to is operational time even though it in turn is described in terms of month and year); and references to the actual world. At this level, indeed there is a passage of time in calendar time.

The whole construction of the Demand and Supply schedules and the idea of "Market-Period", "Short-Period", and "Long-Period" Equilibria are purely logical conceptions. For instance, in constructing his Demand schedule, time is discarded altogether (Marshall, p.94). Most of the discussion on the Supply schedule is based on the notion of a "representative firm" which is "a construction of the mind, a device by which to reason quickly and conveniently on the evolution of the market as a whole" [Frisch (1950), p.513]. Concluding the chapter on "Equilibrium of Normal Demand and Supply", in his most important book (V), Marshall says:

> "As a general rule, the shorter the period which we are considering, the greater must be the share of our attention which is given to the influence of demand on value; and the longer the period, the more important will be the influence of cost of production on the value."
> Principles, p.349

Is Marshall, according to this assertion, referring to logical construction or to the actual world? Consider both hypotheses:

If he is dealing with the former then he is assuming an operational time in which "forces are at work". His idea of "Normal" price in the short-period, different from the "Normal" price in the long-period, is tantamount to saying that there are "Long-Run Short-Period" and "Long-Run Long-Period" situations. These situations are *Equilibria* obtained under different conditions. Here, "Long-Run" must be understood as a reference to an arithmetic average value, even though it gives the impression that there is the idea of a tendency to movement. These equilibria are statements about prevailing situations (under different conditions, he gets different prevailing situations). The distinction between "Market-Period", "Short-Period", and "Long-Period" is, at this level, a matter of convention. For example, in a graphical representation, a Supply schedule is drawn vertical, steep and flat, respectively.

If, on the other hand, Marshall is referring to the actual world in which there is a passage of time, then his "Period" notions correspond to historical time. But now, because Demand and Supply are the result of many individuals' and firms' interaction (and these, according to Marshall, are constantly changing) there would never be enough time for economic forces to adjust completely. Therefore the adjustment process itself becomes subject to fluctuations. Along these lines, Marshall could justify that in the actual market economy, there cannot be a "Long-Run" complete adjustment, but constant fluctuation, hence the price formation can only be governed by the interaction of Supply and Demand and not by the cost of production. Referring to the actual market, Marshall says there is no distinction between "Short" and "Long" Period. Along these lines, his entire theoretical conception cannot be constructed. There are actually too many changes going on at the same time. But now, with respect to the actual market, he does not have an operational theory of the market, and therefore cannot say anything definite about market prices.

Marshall is well *aware* of the above two hypotheses and of the limitation of abstract theory. This is perhaps one of the reasons why he says:

> "I never apply curves or mathematics to market values. For I don't think they help much, and market values are, I think, either absolutely abstract or terribly concrete and full of evervarying (though individually vital) side issue."
> [Principles, p.435][7]

It is believed that Marshall has developed his notion of "Period" time to deal primarily with the first hypothesis. Even though he refers to calendar time (months and years), "Period" is an hypothetical lapse of time in which one conceives "as if" forces are at work. But having the second hypothesis in mind (concerned with actual happenings in physical time) has, to a certain extent, prevented him from overrating *theoretical constructions*. It is not at all surprising to find that in the middle of his theoretical analysis of the Demand and Supply (Book V), he asserts that:

> "A man is likely to be a better economist if he trusts his common sense and practical instinct than if he professes to study the theory of value and resolved to find it easy." [Principles, p.368]

It must be pointed out that he is referring to theoretical constructions, particularly with regard to the theory of value *This should by no means be understood as a rejection of theoretical reasoning as a whole, but simply as a warning against too much confidence in technical construction.*

As it can be seen, in the case of Marshall's own work, there is room for interpretation of his notions of "Long-Run" and "Short" and "Long" "Period". These notions have since been widely used in different contexts for different purposes.

3. EQUILIBRIUM THEORIES

The second illustration concerning the interpretation of our terminology is that of a group of theories in which the study of market mechanism is the main concern. Among this group of theories, first, there are those conceived on the basis that the market forces are the result of individual choices, and the outcome of these interactions should be accepted and considered as an equilibrium; second, there are those which contain the idea that, in addition to individual choices and actions, the market contains imperfections which may prevent it from being in equilibrium.

Since the outcome of the market interactions is the result of individual choices, that it must be accepted as a desired situation and this is the simplest way of characterizing the first category of theories is hence, it is regarded as an equilibrium from the actual market process point of view. If one looks at the market process through time, then, according to this belief, the market economy is in a *Moving Equilibrium* situation. There are many variants of this school of thought.

(a) MOVING EQUILIBRIUM THEORIES:

i) There is, first of all, the Neo-Austrian stream.[8] It advocates the belief that the strength of the market economy resides in free choice and free action, which is motivated by wants, tastes and opportunities. These human enterprises are too complex to be reduced to any technical relations. Formalization cannot take into account differences which exist between individual agents and elements of the forces involved. It also cannot take into consideration the actual opportunities which are conveyed in each decision and interaction (this is, they argue, precisely why the market is what it is). All forms of technical formulation of market behaviour are seen as irrelevant. Not only is there no need for deterministic macro-theories, but they should be rejected altogether. Neo-Austrians favour the self-adjusting market mechanism and maintain that if any disturbance arises, then the market forces will quickly correct them, provided there is no interference with its working. *The Neo-Austrian theories are of a pragmatic type, even though they describe and explain market behaviour on the basis of the marginalist framework as developed by K. Menger.* They do not have any special interpretation of short-run and long-run. Since they are constantly referring to the actual world, the interpretation of short-run and long-run is compatible with historical time.

ii) The other variants of moving equilibrium theories are the Intertemporal and Temporal Equilibrium theories, and the Rational Expectation theory. Most of these theories are often very sophisticated in terms of their technical formalization "artillery", but luckily, they are fairly simple in their treatment of time. Intertemporal and Temporal Equilibrium are a family of theories which have been developed by various authors [Hayek (1928), Lindahl (1929), Lundberg (1930), Hicks (1939) and many others]. Unlike the Neo-Austrian theories which are concerned with the actual working of the market mechanism, Intertemporal and Temporal Equilibrium theories are the abstract formulation of what is supposed to be the working of the market mechanism.

The easiest and the simplest of these theories is the Fisherian Intertemporal Equilibrium type. Burmeister's pure role of time[9] is one of the latest illustrations. Time, in his theory, is introduced as an independent variable. Time is conceived as a sub-space in a more general spatial relation (i.e., things are represented with respect to their location), or in other words, it is a fourth dimension in mathematical space. Time in such analysis is an abstract concept which has nothing to do with the passage of time in calendar time. Technically, there is no difference between the formulation of temporal relations and that of spatial relations. Generally, in these Intertemporal Equilibrium theories, there is a constant reference to the notion of a "Point in time", (using symbols such as $t-\infty, \ldots t-1,\ t_0,\ t+1, \ldots t+\infty$), and to "interval of time". These theories are abstract and simply primitive in their economic content.

There was, in the late twenties and thirties, an attempt to integrate another temporal dimension into the Fisherian Intertemporal Equilibrium theory. It consisted of dividing the notion of continuous time into consecutive periods and studying the equilibrium situation, either within a single period (this is Temporal Equilibrium), or with respect to a sequence of periods (this is the Intertemporal Equilibrium or sequential analysis). Periods are not necessarily assumed to be of the same length. This, according to B. Hansson, is perhaps the reason why these analyses were not formulated in difference equations. At the same time, there was also an effort to integrate expectations into the analysis. In both theories, it is assumed that equilibrium prevails during the periods, while changes and adjustments take place in between periods. The length of the "Period" is arbitrary. For instance, in the work of Hicks (1939), it is defined as an abstract "week":

> "The length of our 'week' is fairly arbitrary (that can be made shorter or longer according as we desire more or less exact conclusions) ... it may often be legitimate to spin it out into something like Marshallian 'short-period' - the time during which existing equipment (in a broader or narrow sense) can be taken as given." [Hicks (1965), p.246]

Hicks is very careful in his wording. He does not say that it is *similar* to Marshall's "Short-Period". In fact it is not. In both the Swedish and in Hicks' theory, the "Period" is defined with respect to expectations and not with respect to production capacity:

> "Expectations adjust themselves in a one unit period... the length of the period has been chosen so as to equal the expectational lag." [Hicks (1965), p.63]

For the purpose of this paper, we will ignore the differences which exist between these various theories and concentrate on their general common approach. The dynamic process of Temporal Equilibrium and Intertemporal Equilibrium theories is conceived as a continuous analysis of a sequence of switching temporary equilibria or a sequence of stationary situations. Now, what can be said about the "Period" notion in such an analysis?

Since the notion of a "Period" is related to expectations, then some help can be obtained from the following questions: On what basis are these expectations formed? How long will these expectations remain stationary? How are expectations about the future considered in the analysis?

It must be pointed out that these theories are based on individual behaviour as well as on that of a group of individuals. The latter is the sum of the former. The method consists in taking everything that has happened before the period as given information, available at the beginning of the period. It supposes that prices, plans, decisions, and expectations are quickly formed on the basis of this information and on some *given* future expectations. By "given" expectations, it is meant that every individual and every firm act on the basis that they have a precise idea of what things will be in the future. It is, of course, assumed that prices, plans, and expectations remain unchanged during the period in question and that all decisions are postponed to the beginning of the next period.

It appears as though the analysis is taking the past, present and future into consideration, but what is the nature of the "time" considered?

At an individual level, it is conceivable that such a "period" can refer to a lapse of time in calendar time. At the market level, it raises questions: firstly, if it is a calendar time "Period", then, as described by Neo-Austrians, the market process is continuously changing. There is a continuous flow of partial and conflicting information. Decisions and actions overlap (one can think of the stock exchange environment as an example) hence, there is always some adjustment taking place somewhere. In this case, the period which is conceived to last a period of time collapses to one point in time. Then all of the emphasis placed on the equilibrium analysis becomes a statement about a state of affairs at one point in time. Since the analysis is not really addressing the transitional question, it cannot say very much about the market process. Secondly, if it assumes a hypothetical situation which takes place in hypothetical time in a more orderly process, then it is possible to have an abstract construction as described above. Neither of these authors denies that he is intending to conceive anything more than simple constructions. They believe that at the theoretical level, it is necessary to proceed in such a manner, if one wants to arrive at formulating a theory and then to use it as an "approximation" of the actual process. One question remains: "how approximate are these 'approximations'?". As far as the conceptualization of time is concerned, Temporal and Intertemporal Equilibrium theories are simply logical, and abstract constructions are conceived entirely in Operational time.

The mechanical aspect of the Temporal and Intertemporal Equilibrium theories proliferated again at the end of the sixties and seventies. One successful "outlier" in the renewed interest of this type of analysis seems to be the Rational Expectation theory. When one considers the development of equilibrium theories since the twenties, one easily recognizes that the Rational Expectation Hypothesis theory is neither original in terms of idea, nor new in terms of approach.

The Rational Expectation theory emerged from the Keynesian-Monetarist debate about the effectiveness of policies. It is the most obvious piece of highly theoretical justification for "no need to interfere with the market mechanism".[10] Its theoretical foundation belongs entirely to the above Temporal and Intertemporal Equilibrium theories. Its technical approach is influenced by Friedman's (1968) and Phelps' (1968) work on Phillips curves and by Radner's (1968) information analysis in an equilibrium theory using a stochastic approach. We will put aside the empirical and policy questions for now. Theoretically, the Rational Expectation Hypothesis assumes time to be continuous. The behaviour of an individual at a point in time depends on the information available at a previous point in time and on expectations the individual may make about the following point in time. Expectations are "Rational" in the sense that individuals assume that their expectations are correct and act accordingly. They adjust instantaneously their behaviour according to the information which becomes available. The interval of time between the previous, the present and the following points in time is so short that it can be considered to have shrunk to a single point of time, in which case we have an equilibrium situation. Furthermore, the process is in equilibrium all of the time.

We can sum up what has been said about the second variants of the moving equilibrium theories by saying that *Intertemporal and Temporal Equilibrium theories and Rational Expectation theory are mostly of the equilibrist approach type. They describe and explain the hypothetical situation of a market mechanism process on the basis of rational behaviour of individuals.* Sometimes, however, the notion of "Period" in the Temporal and Intertemporal approach is referred to as "Short-Period", while a sequence of such periods could be interpreted as "Long-Period". [Hicks (1965), p.30]

To make these theories less rigid, and convenient for empirical testing, a random variable is often introduced in the specification of the model. This is the case, for instance, with the Rational Expectation Hypothesis model. The presence of a disturbance element does not really affect the spirit in which they are conceived. The method of approach then becomes stochastic. The Rational Expectation Hypothesis model is specified and tested in such a way as to show that, even in the short-run, fiscal and monetary policies are ineffective. Therefore, the Phillips curve must be refuted and the actual market unemployment must be accepted as the natural rate of unemployment. This result differs from that obtained with Adaptive Expectation Hypothesis models, which are specified and tested in such a way as to show that even though in the short-run, fiscal and monetary policies can have an effect on unemployment, and that in the long-run these effects will vanish. What is the meaning of the short-run and long-run in these contexts? With respect to the model building, these terms are identified with the specifications described above. Hence, in this context, short-run and long-run are conceived in operational time. With regard to policy implications, they are often thought of in terms of calendar time (months and years). 'Short' and 'Long' depend on the kind of policy implemented. For instance, it is much quicker to implement a monetary policy which involves the central bank only, than a fiscal policy which has to be the subject of parliamentary debate.

The next illustration consists of those theories which contain the ideas that there are exogenous or endogenous market imperfections which prevent (either momentarily or continuously) the market from remaining in a state of equilibrium.

(b) DISEQUILIBRIUM WITHIN MOVING EQUILIBRIUM THEORIES:

i) An example of theory built on the basis of exogenous disturbances is Frisch's Eratic Shocks. According to him, the market economy is frequently subject to shocks which disturb its smooth functioning. However, these disturbances are only of a temporary nature. Eventually, if the system does not undergo further shocks, then the economy settles back into its moving equilibrium. Cyclical fluctuations are explained in Frisch's theory in terms of random shocks which in turn can be described in a stochastic process model. With respect to his system of differential equations, "oscillations" and "averages" are conceived in relation to operational time. As far as the application of this theory is concerned, (even though there is a reference to the actual fluctuations in calendar time), it is difficult to say anything precise about their duration or their economic implications because the frequency and the intensity of these shocks are random and exogenous. We could postulate that fluctuations are of short-period duration (the Period being unspecified in its duration) while in the long-run, an idea of an average performance of the economy is considered an equilibrium path.

ii) As a consequence of the observation of periodical crises experienced during the last century and the beginning of this century, there flourished, at one time, theoretical studies of fluctuations. Many theories of the trade (or business) cycle were advocated on the basis of endogenous discrepancies in the working of the market economy. According to the various explanations, fluctuations are the result of: the inadequate effective demand (producing more or less than what is actually required, i.e., people's purchasing power disposed of is more or less sufficient to absorb what is actually provided), [e.g., theories of Under-consumption]; or the discrepancies between the real and the monetary rate of interest (money being a greater or lesser value in relation to its return when invested), [e.g., Wicksell]; or the degree of confidence in the credit facility (expansion and contraction of credit, depending on the amount of optimism and pessimism prevailing), [e.g., Hawtrey]; or the delays between decisions and realisation of investment (*Ex-ante* decisions of investing corresponds to more or less *Ex-post* investment requirement), [e.g., Kalecki]; or the diversion of investment from one sector to another (favouring increased or decreased production of capital goods or consumption goods, according to circumstances of policies), [e.g., Hayek, Robertson]; or inadequate profitability (cost of production being higher or lower in relation to realized receipts), [e.g., Mitchell]; or the class struggle (distribution of a product between the classes involved favours one group more than another), [e.g., Goodwin]; or for any other reason we have not mentioned. Technically, there is no difficulty in proposing any explanation and using it to build a mechanical process describing a cyclical movement. As Burns has pointed out:

> "Any competent logician, especially if he has the command of mathematics, can select a set of simplified conditions and deduce a cyclical path from what he has assumed. (p.2)"

According to statistical analysis, fluctuation movements are usually decomposed into four components (seasonal fluctuation - cyclical fluctuation - the trend - and the random variable). Seasonal fluctuations are usually eliminated from the analysis by smoothing out the data available. It is the cyclical fluctuations which are generally assumed to be the short-period phenomena, while the trend is referred to as a long-run, regular and smooth path.

With regard to cyclical movement, the story is slightly different. Before the thirties, the more noticeable cyclical movements were the Juglar type (i.e., lasting between nine and eleven years). Kondratieff advocated that the trend itself was a long cycle (of fifty to fifty-five years' duration). Kitchin found evidence that there exists a shorter cyclical movement (three to four years) which is contained in the Juglar cycle. There were also other types of cycles, (linked to construction, agriculture, etc.) which were advocated. Apparently, these cycles, which seemed fairly regular before the war, did not occur in the same fashion after the Second World War. For whatever reasons, economic cycles seem to be more frequent and less violent (except in the last decade). Therefore if "Short-Period", "Long-Period", and "Long-Run" are to be defined in calendar time in terms of economic cycles, then one must be prepared: first of all, to find the criteria by which cycles themselves may be defined and, secondly, to revise our definitions according to historical evidence.

Cyclical fluctuation theories are too diverse in terms of their explanation, method of approach, and economic implications. They cannot be lumped together in one category. In general literature, there is little said about short-run and long-run. Often, there is reference to the notion of "Short" and "Long" waves which again depend on the context in which they are used.

The third illustration deals with the classical theory of distribution. Here, the concern is not with distribution as such, but in the manner in which the key concepts such as "tendency", "gravitation" and "natural and market prices" are related to the notions of short-run and long-run. Before attempting to examine these relationships, one can ask what it is that classical economists are trying to achieve. To preserve the clarity of the text, *the focus in the remainder of the following section will be mainly on Ricardo.*

4. RICARDO

Ricardo's objective is "to determine the laws which regulate the distribution" (p.49) of the wealth (which is produced with the use of machinery, capital and labour) among proprietors, owners of the stock of capital and workers. Referring to our concern for the time aspect, we can identify two distinct questions in Ricardo's *Principles:*

(i) What is the explanation of the value of a commodity, wage, profit and rent in relation to the way actual working of the economy proceeds?

(ii) What is the impact of population growth and capital accumulation on the growth of a nation?

Although these two questions are related, the first deals with what is happening NOW, while the second is directed to what will happen LATER. With regard to the first question, Ricardo is interested in observing how production and the market operate, he then tries to explain their functioning in a causal manner, *not* by considering some particular market situation, and then deducing what production and cost of production will be. Even though emphasis is laid on the functioning of the actual economy, there is, however, a logical and abstract conception of its behaviour. There are, therefore, two levels of abstraction: one in which production and the market mechanism are conceived as a set of logical relations in operational time, and the other being what actually takes place in the economy in reference to calendar time.

Given these two levels of abstraction, for convenience, Marshall's analysis is recalled and four different notions of price are assumed.[12] These are:

(i) The "Short-Period" Normal price is the market price as determined by the logical and abstract conception of Supply and Demand schedules.

(ii) The "Long-Period" Normal price is the natural price as determined by the logical conception of cost of production.
(iii) The market price as reflected in the actual market.
(iv) The normal price as reflected in the actual cost of production.

Marshall was dealing, theoretically, with the first two, while constantly referring to the second two. In Ricardo's analysis, the first step (i) does not exist.[13] By analogy, step (ii) is slightly different, while steps (iii) and (iv) are both obvious.

There is not very much Ricardo can say about market prices in step (iii) except that they are determined by supply and demand, and that they are changing through time.

> "It should be recollected that prices always vary in the market, and in the first instance, through the comparative state of demand and supply." (p.139)

However, it is always possible to calculate the cost of production [step (iv)] of any commodity, given the fact that the components used in its production are known. To explain how price and cost of production are related, Ricardo conceived a logical construction [step (ii)] in which the value of a commodity "is divided into two portions only: one constitutes the profits of stock, the other the wages of labour" (p.130), the rent being a surplus generated by those lands which are relatively more fertile than others. Now it is this logical construction [step (ii)] contrasted with the normal prices of step (iv) which are of prime interest and serve as a point of reference to which the market prices [step (iii)] are continuously gravitating. As it can be seen, there is an ongoing overlapping between these levels of abstraction.

One of Ricardo's principal propositions is that:

> "It is the cost of production which must ultimately regulate the price of commodities, and not, as has been often said, the proposition between the supply and demand: the proportion between supply and demand may, indeed for a time, affect the market value of a commodity, ... but this effect will be only of temporary duration." [Principles, p.374]

If one considers this citation on its own (taken, again, out of its context), one may ask numerous questions. What is the meaning of "ultimately regulate"? Is it that the "ultimate" price of a commodity will converge to the value of its cost of production if sufficient time is allowed? Or is it that it will only converge if the economy becomes stationary? Is it really a question of convergence? What is the meaning of "effect will be only temporary"? How long is "temporary"?

To answer these questions, it is crucial to consider how Ricardo developed his arguments. Ricardo has not used the term "convergence"; it is the word "regulate" which appears in many places (e.g. pp.114, 127, 274). In his chapter "On the Influence of Demand and Supply on Prices", he gives two examples in which he explains the meaning of the above citation. Consider a more recent example: the price of Hi-fi stereos in the last twenty years. When the Hi-fi product was first introduced into the market, its price was comparatively high, because the cost of its production was high. As time passed, partly because more is known and cheaper ways of producing are found, and partly because competition stimulates firms to further reduce their costs, over the years the Hi-fi stereo price has been substantially reduced compared to other goods, and despite a huge increase in demand. Hence, according to Ricardo, the price of a commodity will eventually decrease if its production cost has diminished, and vice versa. It is in this sense that Ricardo's "ultimate regulation" must be understood. Also, because production precedes exchange in the market place, it implies that the cost of production is the "Natural" reference for any price formation.

As far as the components of the cost of production are concerned, Ricardo does not say that they are fixed. Capitalists, for instance, "will naturally seek for it (capital) that employment which is most advantageous" (p.111). Furthermore there is a "restless desire on the part of all the employers of stock, to quit a less profitable for a more advantageous business", this "has a strong tendency to equalize the rate of profits" (p.111). Notice that Ricardo does not say there is a unique rate of profit. It is the movement of capital (due to the competition) for a better return which creates tendency forces. Because the system is changing, convergence is never achieved, "this tendency, this gravitation as it were of profits, is happily checked at repeated intervals by the improvements in machinery, ..., as well as by discoveries ..." (p.140). Furthermore, Ricardo says that, a capitalist may sometimes "forego a part of his money profit, in consideration of the security, cleanliness, ease, or any other real or fancied advantage which one employment may pose over another" (p.113), therefore profit maximisation is not always the criterion on which capitalists base their behaviour. It also shows that there is a whole range of rates of profit which depend on risk factors. As capital is moving from a less profitable sector to a more profitable one, it alters the profits and wages relation. As a consequence, there is a transference of both "capital and labour" (p.114). It is the competition and the transference of capital and labour which "prevents the market price of commodities from continuing for any length of time either much above, or much below their natural price" (p.114). On the question of wages, labour "has its natural and its market price" (p.115). Natural price is the price which permits workers "to subsist and to perpetuate their race". The natural price of labour is in turn dependent on the "price of the food". The market price of labour, on the other hand, is the actual price paid for labour. Like a commodity, labour is also subject to "ultimate regulation", and "It is not to be understood that the natural price of labour, estimated even in food and necessaries, is absolutely fixed and constant. It varies at different times in the same country" (p.118). He continues:

> "It appears then that wages are subject to a rise or fall from two causes:
> 1st. The supply and demand of labourers.
> 2nd. The price of the commodities on which wages of labour are expanded." [Principles, p.119]

As it can be seen, Ricardo is not dealing with a stationary state analysis, nor with a purely hypothetical situation. He describes and explains the process of actual price formation. In the course of economic activity, there is a tendency for market prices to move towards their natural values, whilst natural prices themselves change with time due to variations in the components of the cost of production. This may seem a vicious circle on a theoretical level, but it is a cause and effect analysis of the economic market process when calendar time is taken into consideration.

Even though Ricardo's analysis refers to calendar time, it is still nonetheless subject to interpretation with regard to concept of short-run and long-run.

- There is Ricardo's reference to the effect being "only of temporary duration" which can be considered as a short-period fluctuation, but since the market is always fluctuating, it can be said that long-period is a succession of short-period fluctuations. In the long-run, there is an ongoing cause and effect movement due to restless capital movement. This is happening with respect to steps (iii) and (iv).
- There is a logical long-run to be conceived within step (ii). If forces are allowed to exert themselves fully, and provided there is a free mobility of capital and labour, then in the end or in the long-run, market prices will equal their natural value. If there are no changes, then the system will remain stationary.
- There is an actual long-run in relation to actual happenings in the economy. As time passes, there is a tendency for the market price to be regulated by its natural value (as in the Hi-fi example). This corresponds to what is happening in steps (iii) and (iv).
- There is an actual long-run associated with secular movement. As the population grows, because land and resources are limited, there is a possibility of the economy stagnating.

In order to distinguish between whatever interpretations one is dealing with, one must mentally separate:

1 - the logical construction conceived specifically to determine the value of a commodity.

2 - the forces of tendencies due to restless capital movement, which in fact always exists in (the workings of) a capitalist economy.

3 - the actual changes reflected in the market and normal prices as a cause and effect relationship between cost of production and supply and demand, which is described at a conceptual level.

To sum up, we can say that Ricardo's theory uses an open approach to describe and explain: the determination of value; the price formation process; and the inherent forces in those economic activities which are related to capital movement and capital accumulation.

5. SOME CONCLUDING REMARKS

In order to understand why there are different interpretations of short-run and long-run, we have attempted to dissect the reasoning of Abstract Economics, and tried to clarify the various steps involved in conceiving the different levels of abstraction. Conceptually, what is described at a theoretical level never corresponds exactly to the image of what is actually taking place. Hence, all theories are subject to interpretation.

The most important proposition of this paper is the distinction between short-run and long-run with respect to operational and historical time:

- All theories which are developed according to a deterministic approach are, by definition, logical theories, and can only be conceived in operational time (hypothetical time). The distinction between short-run and long-run is not a matter of temporal importance, but a question of the issue treated. Short-run and long-run are two independent concepts associated with different theoretical constructions (e.g. market value and normal value).

- Eclectic theories are generally more open theories. When they are developed with reference to historical time, then short-run and long-run belong together - short-run being a lapse of time of a limited duration, while long-period is a succession of short-periods. No matter what kind of approximation one uses, it is just not possible to translate the process of the actual working of the economy into technical and mechanical relations, yet still incorporate all the human considerations, and preserve an accurate picture of what is actually going on.

It seems, therefore, that we either opt for technical precision and lose a great deal of actual accuracy, or preserve the human and temporal dimensions and face a much more difficult theoretical treatment.

ENDNOTES

1. Some of the ideas in this paper were developed while at Université de Sherbrooke (Quebec), others while visiting Cambridge University. I would like to thank Tom Asimakopulos, Phyllis Dean, Pierre Gregoire, Geoff Harcourt, Prue Kerr, Tony Lawson, Trøels Sorensen and the referees of the *British Review of Economic Issues* for useful comments and suggestions.

2. It must be pointed out that the purpose of the discussion in this paper is not to provide a precise answer or alternative solution to a specific question. It is a methodological exercise in which it shows that simple concepts such as short-run and long-run (which often are taken for granted) are not as obvious as it seems. Their different interpretations have led to fundamentally different methodological approaches in dealing with economic issues. Examples of such views are reflected in debates within different camps: the late Joan Robinson vs. Neo-Ricardians, Hahn vs. Lucas, Neo-Austrians vs. General-Equilibrium, "'Short'-Keynesians" vs. "'long'-Keynesians" and so on.

3. Discussion on some aspect of these concepts is to be found in Opie (1931) and Garegnani (1976).

4. See her *Capital Accumulation* and *Further Essays in Economics.*

5. See my Ph.D. Thesis on "The Treatment of Time in the Theoretical Writings of Sir John Hicks", (McGill, January 1983). Also, my 'Time, Choice and Dynamics in Economics' (forthcoming).

6. For more discussion on Marshall's *Principles*, see Shove (1940), Guillebaud (1940), Beach (1982) and Frisch (1950).

7. *In Memorial of Alfred Marshall*, A.C. Pigou (ed.), 1925, London: Macmillan, p.435, cited by K. Bharadwaj, 1978, p.265.

8. We are referring here to L. Lachmann, I. Kirzner, etc.; see, for example, Dolan (ed.), 1976.

9. See Burmeister, 1980.

10. See Tobin's discussion of continuous market clearing. [Tobin (1980) pp.20-48.]

11. A.F. Burns, 'Hicks on the Real Cycle', *Journal of Political Economy*, 1952, p.2, reprinted in Burns (1954).

12. Prof. Asimakopulos has pointed out that "Demand is involved in long-period normal price as well as in short-period, since Marshall's competitive industries need not be constant cost industries". This is not denied; see discussion on "a graphical representation", p.6. The issue itself, however, does not affect the argument of this paper.

13. For further discussion on this issue, see Garegnani, P., 'The Classical Theory of Wages and the Role of Demand Schedules in the Determination of Relative Prices'.

REFERENCES

Aftalion, A. (1913), *Les crises périodiques de production*, 2 Vols., Paris: M. Rivière.

Asimakopulos, A. (1978), Keynesian Economics, Equilibrium and Time, *Canadian Journal of Economics*, XI, No.4 Supplement, November, pp.3-10.

Asimakopulos, A. (1978), *An Introduction to Economic Theory: Micro-economics*, Oxford University Press.

Beach, E.F. (1982), Marshall's Theory of Industrial Progress, *Eastern Economic Journal*.

Bharadwaj, K. (1978), The Subversion of Classical Analysis: Alfred Marshall's Early Writing on Value, *Cambridge Journal of Economics*, Vol.2, pp.253-271.

Burmeister, E. (1980), *Capital Theory and Dynamics*, Cambridge University Press.

Burns, A.F. (1954), *The Frontier of Economic Knowledge*, Princeton University Press.

Deane, P. (1983), The Scope and Method of Economic Science, *Economic Journal*, Vol.93, March, pp.1-12.

Dobb, M. (1929), A Sceptical View of the Theory of Wages, *Economic Journal*, Vol.39, No.4, December, pp.506-519.

Dolan, E. (ed.) (1976), *The Foundation of Modern Austrian Economics*, Kansas City: Sheed Andrews and Meel.

Frisch, R. (1933), Propagation Problems and Impulse Problems in Dynamic Economics, in *Economic Essays in Honour of Gustav Cassel*, New York: Kelley (1967), pp.171-205.

Frisch, R. (1950), Marshall's Theory of Value, *Quarterly Journal of Economics*, Vol.65, pp.495-524.

Garegnani, P. (1976), On the Change in the Notion of Equilibrium..., in. M. Brown, K. Sato and P. Zarembala, *Essays in Modern Capital Theory*, North-Holland, pp.25-45.

Guillebaud, C.W. (1940), The Evolution of Marshall's Principles of Economics, *Economic Journal*, Vol.LII, pp.330-349.

Hahn, F.H. (1973), *On the Notion of Equilibrium in Economics*, Cambridge University Press.

Hahn, F.H. (1982), *Money and Inflation*, Oxford: Basil Blackwell.

Hansson, B. (1982), *The Stockholm School and the Development of Dynamic Method*, London: Croom Helm.

Harcourt, G.C. (1982a), *The Social Science Imperialists: Selected Essays*, Prue Kerr (ed.), London: Routledge and Kegan Paul.

Harcourt, G.C. (1982b), Post Keynesianism: Quite Wrong and/or Nothing New?, *Thames Papers in Political Economy*, Summer.

Harcourt, G.C. (1982c), Reflections on the Development of Economics as a Discipline, *Paper presented to the History of Thought Conference*, Nottingham, September.

Hayek, F. Von (1928), Das intertemporale Gleichgewichtssystem der Preise und die Bewegungen des Geldwertes, *Weltwirtschaftliches Archiv*, Vol.32.

Hawtrey, R.G. (1927), The Monetary Theory of the Trade Cycle and its Statistical Test, *Quarterly Journal of Economics*, May, pp.471-486.

Hicks, J.R. (1939), *Value and Capital*, Oxford: Clarendon Press.

Hicks, J.R. (1950), *A Contribution to the Theory of the Trade Cycle*, Oxford: Clarendon Press.

Hicks, J.R. (1965), *Capital and Growth*, Oxford: Clarendon Press.

Kaldor, N. (1972), The Irrelevance of Equilibrium Economics, *Economic Journal*.

Kalecki, M. (1971), *Selected Essays on the Dynamics of the Capitalist Economy*, Cambridge University Press.

Keynes, J.M. (1930), *A Treatise on Money*, London: Macmillan.

Keynes, J.M. (1936), *The General Theory of Employment, Interest and Money*, London: Macmillan.

Kondratieff, N .D. (1924), On the Notion of Economic Statistics, Dynamics and Fluctuations, *Sotsialisticheskoe Khoziaistvo*, No.2, pp.349-382.

Kuznets, S.S. (1930), *Secular Movements in Production and Prices*, Boston and New York.

Isard, W. (1942), *A Neglected Cycle: The Transport-Building Cycle*, Harvard University Press, pp.149-158.

Lachmann, L.N. (1956), *Capital and its Structure*, London School of Economics.

Lindahl, E. (1929), Prisbildningsproblemet Fran Kapitalteoretisk synpunk, *Ekonomisk Tidskrift*.

Lucas, R.E. (1972), Expectations and the Neutrality of Money, *Journal of Economic Theory*, Vol.4, April, pp.103-124.

Lucas, R.E. (1977), Understanding Business Cycles, in K. Brunner and Meltzer (eds.), *Stabilization of the Domestic and International Economy*, Carnegie-Rochester Conference Series on Public Policy, Vol.5, Amsterdam.

Lundberg, E. (1930), Om Begreppet ekonomisk jamvikt, *Ekonomisk Tidskrift*.

Machlup, F. (1967), *Essays in Economic Semantics*, New York: Norton.

Marshall, A. (1920), *Principles of Economics*, 8th Edition, London: Macmillan.

Marx, K. (1867) (1885) (1894), *Das Kapital*, Hamburg.

Menger, K. (1950), *Principles of Economics*, Glencoe, Illinois.

Mill, J.S. (1885), *Principles of Political Economy*, New York: D. Appleton and Company.

Mitchell, W.C. (1923), *Business Cycles and Unemployment*, New York: McGraw-Hill.

Opie, R. (1931), Marshall's Time Analysis, *Economic Journal*, Vol.41, No.2, June, pp.199-215.

Phelps, E.S. (1968), Money Wage Dynamics and Labour Market Equilibrium, *Journal of Political Economy*, Vol.76, pp.678-711.

Radner, M. (1968), Competitive Equilibrium Under Uncertainty, *Econometrica*, Vol.36, January, pp.31-58.

Robinson, J. (1965), *The Accumulation of Capital*, 2nd edition, London: Macmillan.

Sargent, T.J. and Wallace, N. (1975), Rational Expectation, the Optimal Monetary Instrument, and the Optimal Money Supply Rule, *Journal of Political Economy*, Vol.83, April, pp.241-257.

Schumpeter, J.A. (1939), *Business Cycles*, New York: McGraw-Hill.

Schackle, G.L.S. (1958), *Time in Economics*, Amsterdam: North Holland.

Schackle, G.L.S. (1965), *A Scheme of Economic Theory*, Cambridge University Press.

Schackle, G.L.S. (1972), *Epistemics and Economics*, Cambridge University Press.

Schackle, G.L.S. (1979), *Imagination and the Nature of Choice*, Edinburgh: The University Press.

Shove, G.F. (1940), The Place of Marshall's Principles in the Development of Economic Theory, *Economic Journal*, Vol.LII, pp.294-329.

Sraffa, P. (1960), *Production of Commodities by Means of Commodities*, Cambridge University Press.

Tobin, J. (1980), *Asset Accumulation and Economic Activity*, Oxford: Basil Blackwell.

Young, A. (1928), Increasing Returns and Economic Progress, *Economic Journal*, Vol.38, No.4, December, pp.527-542.

[20]

History of Political Economy 16:4

CCC 0018–2702/84/$1.50

Edgeworth: utilitarianism and arbitration

John Creedy

I. *Introduction*

It is sometimes suggested that "what was important in marginal utility was the adjective rather than the noun."[1] Following this approach, F. Y. Edgeworth is frequently cited as a prime example of a pioneering neoclassical utilitarian whose analytical contributions can now be used independently of their utilitarian background. For example, Schumpeter (1954, 831) states that "we can leave out the utilitarianism from any of his economic writings without affecting their scientific content." Indeed, Edgeworth himself recognised, following the work of Fisher and Pareto, that ordinal utility is sufficient for some purposes. However, he was always careful to state that where questions involving distribution are concerned, some "principle of justice" is necessary. Despite the many criticisms of utilitarianism, its methods continue to be used and defended by economists.

Following the development of the von Neumann/Morgenstern approach to choice under uncertainty, well-known major re-statements of utilitarianism were made by Harsanyi (1953; 1955) and Vickrey (1960). The maximisation of expected utility, with each individual taking the a priori view that any outcome is *equally likely*, was shown to lead to the use of a social-welfare function which maximises the sum of individual utilities. These approaches, sometimes describes as "contractarian neo-utilitarianism," have been criticised by, for example, Pattanaik (1968).[2] However, a more recent defence has been articulated by Mirrlees (1982), involving preferences with regard to allocations to "alternative selves."

In view of this 'modern' approach, it is of interest to examine the development of Edgeworth's attitude to utilitarianism. This seems to have been neglected in the literature, despite the fact that Rawls (1971, 29) noted that a contractarian approach, "is sometimes suggested by Bentham and Edgeworth, although it is not developed by them in any systematic

Correspondence may be addressed to the author, University of Durham, 23/26 Old Elvet, Durham DH1 3HY, England.

1. Blaug (1978, 322) attributes this remark, without reference, to Hutchison.
2. See also Sen 1970 and Diamond 1967. Vickrey 1961 provides further discussion of his approach.

way."[3] While it is true that Edgeworth did not *formally* develop a mathematical justification for utilitarianism along the lines later taken by Vickrey and Harsanyi, the use of utilitarianism, based on a social-contract view of choice under certainty, can be seen to have been extremely important for Edgeworth.

II. *Edgeworth's Early Work*

Egoism, evolution, and utilitarianism

In considering Edgeworth's attitude to utilitarianism it is necessary to stress the eclectic nature of his early views.[4] The main debates in moral philosophy during the last half of the nineteenth century involved the familiar 'isms' of egoism, evolutionism, idealism, intuititionism, and of course utilitarianism. Edgeworth's brand of utilitarianism in fact embraced the majority of these principles, except for those of the Hegelian Idealists.[5]

His first publication was a short note in *Mind* (1976) on 'Mr. Matthew Arnold and Bishop Butler's doctrine of self love.' Arnold had earlier argued that Butler's term "self-love" should be interpreted to mean, "the pursuit of our temporal good." However, Edgeworth believed Butler to be saying, "duty and interest are perfectly coincident." Thus, at this early stage Edgeworth is seen to be proposing that egoism and utilitarianism could be subsumed under the same principle.[6]

It is also necessary to appreciate the importance to the late Victorians of Darwin's theory of evolution, the growing interest in experimental psychology (especially on the Continent), and the associated growth of sociology. An early attempt to apply psychological work to moral philosophy was made by Alfred Barratt, in *Physical ethics* (1869). Sidgwick's *Meth-*

3. Rawls 1971, 29, described this as, "a deeper and more roundabout justification of utilitarian," although of course he rejected it (see especially 1971, 170) in favour of his "maxi-min" approach. The contractarian approach, with each individual having extreme risk aversion, has in fact been shown to lead to the maxi-min rule; see Atkinson & Stiglitz 1980, 339, 420, and Phelps 1973, 418–23. However, Rawls explicitly rejected this view (see 1971, 172).

4. Edgeworth's remarkable family background undoubtedly influenced his early utilitarianism. His grandfather Richard Lovell Edgeworth and aunt Maria Edgeworth were strong utilitarians. One of R. L. Edgeworth's circle of friends was Joseph Priestley (see Schofield 1963). It was in Priestley's *Essay on government* (1768) that Bentham found the phrase "the greatest happiness of the greatest number." For further references to Edgeworth's background see Creedy 1981 and 1983. The wide range of contacts of the Edgeworths is well illustrated in the published letters of Maria Edgeworth; see Colvin 1971 and 1979.

5. For example, he refers to the, "false friend and dire foe of hedonism . . . the voluptuary and the hegelian" (1877, 70). He refers only once to F. H. Bradley (1877, 9 n. 2), and ignores him in Edgeworth 1881.

6. Edgeworth was fond of quoting from Pope's *Essay on man* (see Creedy, 1981) where it is interesting to find the lines, "Self-love and reason to one end aspire/Pain their aversion, pleasure their desire," and "Even mean self-love becomes, by force divine/The scale to measure others' wants by thine." (Both are from the 'Second Epistle'.)

ods of ethics appeared in 1874 and was reviewed by Barratt in *Mind* (1877). Edgeworth was familiar with a considerable part of the literature on psychological research, and his studies must have been helped by his friendship with the psychologist James Sully.[7] But the publications of Barratt and Sidgwick provided the direct stimulus for Edgeworth's first substantial publication, his *New and old methods of ethics* (1877).

The first part of this book consists of a comparison of the work of Barratt and Sidgwick. Edgeworth takes pains to argue that the main approaches of both can be subsumed under the 'sovereign principle' of utilitarianism. For example, he states: "The egotist, then, may have the power and the motive to cultivate a desire for the general good, not, indeed to the pitch of pure utilitarianism, but to a degree asymptotically approaching it, in the progress of evolution" (1877, 33).

The same theme was repeated in 1882 when Edgeworth reviewed Leslie Stephen's book *The science of ethics* and argued that evolutionism and utilitarianism "become ultimately convergent." Edgeworth often argued that tastes change with evolution and education, and the fact that he was also strongly influenced by the work of Darwin and Galton is clearly shown in his early work.[8]

Optimal distribution

Edgeworth's attempt to provide a synthesis of the various approaches in such a way that they are concerned with the same ultimate ends provided the groundwork for his really original contribution, which formed the second part of *New and old methods of ethics*. Here Edgeworth first applied mathematical techniques to the problem of determining the optimal utilitarian distribution. In view of the considerable respect which Edgeworth had for Sidgwick as an 'authority' it is worth considering the following quotation from Sidgwick which Edgeworth reproduced (1877, 35, n. 1):[9]

7. There are many references to the work of Delbœuf, Fechner, Helmholtz, Weber, and Wundt in Edgeworth 1877 and 1881. On Sully's contact with Edgeworth see Creedy 1983. Sidgwick wrote of Sully that he was, "probably the one Englishman known to German Professors as a writer on physiological psychology" (Sidgwick & Sidgwick 1906, 516).

8. Edgeworth was related to Galton, who married Edgeworth's cousin Louisa Butler in 1853. Galton's mother was Violetta Darwin, daughter of Erasmus Darwin, who was a friend of Edgeworth's grandfather Richard Lovell Edgeworth.

9. The role of 'authority' was very important for Edgeworth, because of the need to make a priori assumptions which are not capable of being tested. His views on authority are similar to those of Austin and Cornewall Lewis, referred to in Edgeworth 1881, 103, 126. As an example of Edgeworth's high regard for Sidgwick as an authority, see his review (1925, 3:147–52) of Sidgwick & Sidgwick 1906. In view of Sidgwick's importance it is necessary to see if the contractarian approach can be found in his work. However, it has not been possible to trace any mention, and the same negative result was reported by Rawls (1971, 29). However, in view of Edgeworth's approach to Butler mentioned above, it is interesting to note the comment by Schneewind (1977, 418) that, "To no major historical figure does Sidgwick have closer affinities than to Bishop Butler."

> That our practical utilitarian reasonings may be rough is no reason for not making them as accurate as the case admits; and we shall be more likely to succeed in this, if we keep before our minds as distinctly as possible the strict type of calculation that we should have to make, if all the relevant consideration could be estimated with mathematical precision [Sidgwick, 1874, Book IV, ch. 1, §2].

This usefully summarises one aspect of much of Edgeworth's work, and indeed that of much modern welfare analysis (see, for example, Atkinson & Stiglitz 1980, 456). The subject of optimal distribution was next examined by Edgeworth in his 1879 paper, the hedonical calculus, when the mathematical treatment of the problem was handled with much more assurance. Edgeworth's synthesis of the various approaches to ethics (other than idealism, of course) can clearly be seen in his attempts to allow for evolutionary changes in the 'quality' of the population, and in particular to incorporate into his work some of the results of Galton on the distribution of 'abilities' in successive generations. Thus Edgeworth's early utilitarianism was not the simple static version sometimes attributed to neoclassical economists. He argued that individuals have a higher capacity for pleasure in higher states of evolution. When suggesting that "higher" pleasures are "most pleasurable," Edgeworth (1879, 395; 1881, 58) referred to the "scientific statement" of this view by his friend Sully.

The importance of the psychological research to the early neoclassical economists has sometimes been neglected. For example Jevons's son had to remind Keynes of the importance of these aspects of W. S. Jevons's work (see Keynes 1972, 153). After mentioning the work of Wundt, Weber, Fechner, and Helmholtz (all referred to by Jevons and Edgeworth), even Schumpeter (1954, 796 n. 1) states, "it has not so far occurred to economists to explore the opportunities this line of research might conceivably offer."[10]

III. *Competition and Arbitration*

It is well known that Jevons's work involved the application of mathematics (of a more elementary nature than those used by Edgeworth) and of psychological research to the analysis of exchange in competitive markets. While it is surprising that Edgeworth did not know of the work of Jevons much earlier, there can be no doubt that he did not see that work until 1879 (see Edgeworth 1881, 34 n. 1; Creedy 1979, 164 n. 4). Two main influences of Edgeworth's contact with Jevons may be identified. First there was the direct stimulus provided by the *Theory of political economy* and the anonymous reviewer of Jevons's book in the *Saturday*

10. For further discussion of this issue and of the technical innovations of Edgeworth (1877 and 1879) see Creedy 1980.

Review.[11] Secondly, it was Jevons who introduced Edgeworth to the work of Marshall. These factors are discussed in turn below.

Jevons and house sales

The crucial development following Edgeworth's contact with Jevons was not simply the realisation that mathematics could be used to examine equilibrium in exchange. Rather it was that in his analysis Jevons explicitly assumed, through his "law of indifference," that all individuals take the equilibrium prices as given. He was concerned with the properties of such an equilibrium and deliberately excluded the role of the number of competitors from his analysis. However, in the section 'Failure of the laws of exchange,' Jevons discussed cases, notably the example of house sales, in which some indeterminacy would result. The reviewer of Jevons in the *Saturday Review* then suggested that indeterminacy would result not, as Jevons had claimed, from the discrete nature of the commodity, but from the lack of competition. This clearly raised the need to examine the role of the number of competitors in the market.[12]

Marshall and wage bargaining

The influence on Edgeworth's mathematical approach of Marshall's *Pure theory of foreign trade and the pure theory of domestic values* (1879) is clear. Edgeworth later said that on first seeing Marshall's work he, "discerned a new power of mathematical reasoning" (see Pigou 1925, 66), and in 1881 he provided the basic analytics, in terms of indifference curves, of Marshall's (reciprocal) demand curves. But the clue to another important influence on Edgeworth's concern with indeterminacy is provided by Edgeworth's reference (1881, 48 n. 1) to Thornton's comparison of the determination of prices in Dutch and English auctions. He gave no bibliographical reference to Thornton, and it seems likely that Edgeworth obtained this reference from a footnote in the Marshalls' joint book, *Economics of industry* (1879). This note states: "If there are very few buyers in a market, it may make a great difference whether goods are sold by Dutch or English auctions. . . . See Thornton *On Labour*, 2nd ed. pp. 56, 7" (1879, 200 n. 1). It is also significant that this footnote was placed in a chapter, 'Influence of trade unions on wages', where the Marshalls suggests that trade unions may secure for workers a large share of the Wages-and-Profits fund. Thus:

11. This is an untitled and anonymous review in the *Saturday Review* 1871. It has been reprinted in Black 1979, 152–57. The question of the authorship of this review is examined in detail in O'Brien et al. 1983.

12. It is interesting to note that the question of the number of traders and indeterminacy was raised directly with Jevons in a letter from R. O. Williams in 1875. He wrote, "I would rather say that the difficulty . . . was in the restricted conditions of the market . . . than in the indivisibility of one of the subjects of exchange." See Black 1978, 4:151.

> If the labourers throughout a country have been in the habit of selling their labour without reserve, they may have received among them a smaller share of the Wages-and-Profit Fund than they would have got if there had been perfectly free competition among employers, or than they would have got if they had been able to offer their labour at a reserve price.
>
> If then the labourers enter into local trade combinations, and refuse to sell their labour except at a reserve price, it is quite possible that they may increase their share of the Wages-and-Profits Fund, and raise wages at the expense of profits [1879, 200].

It is worth pointing out here that Marshall later rejected this first edition, and all subsequent editions of *Economics of industry* simply contain parts of his *Principles*.

These admissions of indeterminacy, arising from the small number of competitors on each side of the market, therefore seem to have stimulated Edgeworth to examine explicitly the role of the number of competitors in the formation of the exchange rate. As is now well known, Edgeworth first examined barter, in which individuals do not take prices as parametric. His analysis, based on his concepts of indifference curves and the contract curve, showed clearly how indeterminacy arises with few competitors. Furthermore he demonstrated that large numbers of competitors produce a determinate rate of exchange which is equivalent to the 'price taking' equilibrium solution of Jevons (and of Walras). The role of combinations of labour, in reducing the number of competitors and increasing the range of indeterminacy in contract, was considered at length by Edgeworth. These major analytical contributions of *Mathematical psychics* are fundamental to modern micro-economics, and are not discussed further here.[13]

IV. *Arbitration and Utilitarianism*

The need for arbitration

The crucial development of Edgeworth's utilitarianism arose from the recognition that, once indeterminacy is shown to exist, there is a need for arbitration. Indeed, Jevons stated clearly that with indeterminacy, "The dispositions and force of character of the parties . . . will influence the decision. These are motives more or less extraneous to a theory of economics, and yet they appear necessary considerations in this problem. It may be that indeterminate bargains of this kind are best arranged by an arbitrator or third party" (1871; reprinted in 1970, 159). Edgeworth's statement of the same point was rather less prosaic: "The whole creation groans

13. For further discussion see, for example, Hildebrand & Kirman 1976; Schotter & Schwodiauer 1980; and Creedy 1979.

and yearns, desiderating a principle of arbitration, an end of strifes" (1881, 51). What is important here is that Edgeworth then used his 'Hedonical Calculus' as a 'principle of arbitration.' The results of his 1879 *Mind* paper therefore acquired a new significance, and the reprinting of this paper as the last part of the *Psychics*, following the 'Economical Calculus,' was perfectly appropriate.[14] The use of the utilitarian principle as a 'principle of arbitration' acquired even more importance when Edgeworth showed that the utilitarian optimum is one of the (infinite number of) efficient exchange positions along the contract curve. Thus, "It is a circumstance of momentous interest that one of the in general indefinitely numerous *settlements* between contractors is the utilitarian arrangement . . . the contract tending to the greatest possible total utility of the contractors" (1881, 53). Edgeworth also argued that other methods of arbitration, such as equal division, would be unstable because they need not necessarily be on the contract curve. There would thus be a potential gain for at least one party by moving to the contract curve. He later suggested that the utilitarian arrangement may be preferable to the competitive equilibrium, although both are on the contract curve (1925, 2:284).

Edgeworth's justification of utilitarianism

Edgeworth recognised that the argument that the utilitarian solution is on the contract curve was not *sufficient* to justify the use of utilitarianism as a principle of arbitration. The contract curve defines a *range* of positions. It was only a necessary condition that the principle of arbitration adopted should place the 'parties' somewhere on the contract curve, since they would otherwise have an incentive to move. His justification for utilitarianism as a principle of justice was as follows:

> Now these positions lie in a *reverse order of desirability* for each party; and it may seem to each that as he cannot have his own way, in the absence of any definite principle of selection, he has about as good a chance of one of the arrangements as another . . . both parties may agree to commute their chance of any of the arrangements for . . . the utilitarian arrangement [1881, 55].

Edgeworth therefore clearly viewed justice in terms of choice under uncertainty, and the assumption of equal a priori probabilities appears *explicitly* in this statement. It recurs many times in his work, and for example was also used by him in his later (Bayesian) analysis of statistical inference. Thus, "there is made an assumption, not statistically verified, concerning the equi-distribution of *a priori* probabilities" (1887, 56).[15]

14. Edgeworth made a number of alternations when the paper was used for the *Psychics* (1881, 56–82); for details see Creedy 1981, 16–22.

15. He also stated (1887, 53) that "the fairest province of Probabilities is held under the suzerainty of the Principle of Utility."

The same justification of utilitarianism was offered by Edgeworth in his analysis of income taxation. He rejected the *quid pro quo* view of taxation, on the argument that public expenditure and taxation decisions do not result from competitive processes. Some principle of justice is required in the framework of a social contract between taxpayers and government. In deciding on the appropriate tax burden

> each party may reflect that, in the long run of various cases . . . of all the principles of distribution which would afford him now a greater, now a smaller proportion of the sum-total ability obtainable . . . the principle that the collective utility should be on each occasion a maximum is most likely to afford the greatest utility in the long run to him individually [1897; in 1925, 102].

The explicit treatment of the question of taxation in contractarian terms involves the *direct* link between the analyses of the appropriate tax burden and of the optimal utilitarian distribution. The use of the criterion of minimum total sacrifice (requiring equal marginal sacrifice) was then of course only a small step to take. This approach marks an important stage in the process of bringing the analysis of taxation within the general framework of 'welfare economics,' involving standard efficiency criteria rather than a special set of 'tax maxims.'

Thus Edgeworth's 'justification' of utilitarianism along 'neo-contractarian' lines was clearly and explicitly articulated and was more important to Edgeworth than is generally recognised. After his analysis of the need of "a world weary of strife" for a principle of arbitration, this approach to the use of utilitarianism became the crucial link between the 'economical' and the 'utilitarian' calculus. Edgeworth's earlier work on optimal distribution acquired a new significance when reprinted in the *Psychics* two years later.

It must also be stressed that Edgeworth referred to his 'neo-contractarian' justification on a number of later occasions (not mentioned by Rawls 1971), and right up to the age of eighty when he prepared his *Papers relating to political economy* for publication. Edgeworth returned to the question of indeterminacy and arbitration in his important paper on the theory of distribution (1904; reprinted in 1925, vol. 1). He again argued in favour of the utilitarian principle, and referred back to relevant passages of *Mathematical psychics* (see 1925, 1:57). In editing his *Papers*, Edgeworth in 1925 added a reference to volume 2 (2:101) where the same argument was made in the reprint of the taxation paper. The same point is referred to again in 1925, 2:322.

Thus Edgeworth's explicit justification, along contractarian terms, for the use of utilitarianism as a principle of distributive justice, his positing of the widespread existence of indeterminacy, his analysis of the special property of the utilitarian arrangement in terms of being on the contract curve of efficient exchanges, his analysis of the role of numbers in competition, and his demonstration that both the price-taking equilibrium and that achieved with recontracting are the same are all distinguishing features of his first contribution to economics, in *Mathematical psychics*. This was quite a spectacular entry into the profession, but a contribution which has taken many years to be appreciated fully.

I am very grateful to Professor Denis O'Brien and two referees of this journal for comments on an earlier draft of this article.

References

Atkinson, A. B., and J. E. Stiglitz 1980. *Lectures on public economics*. London.

Black, R. D. C. 1978. *Papers and correspondence of William Stanley Jevons*, vol. 4, *Correspondence 1873–1878*. London.

——— 1979. *Papers and correspondence of William Stanley Jevons*, vol. 7, *Papers on political economy*. London.

Blaug, M. 1978. *Economic theory in retrospect*, 3d edition. Cambridge.

Colvin, C. 1971. *Maria Edgeworth, letters from England, 1813–1844*. Oxford.

——— 1979. *Maria Edgeworth in France and Switzerland*. Oxford.

Creedy, J. 1979. 'Edgeworth's contribution to the theory of exchange.' *Scottish Journal of Political Economy* 26:163–81.

——— 1980. "The early use of Lagrange multipliers in economics.' *Economic Journal* 90:371–76.

——— 1981. 'Notes on mathematical psychics.' *University of Durham, Department of Economics Working Paper* no. 46.

——— 1983. 'F. Y. Edgeworth's mathematical training." *Journal of the Royal Statistical Society*, Series A:146, 158–62.

Diamond, P. A. 1967. 'Cardinal welfare, individualistic ethics, and interpersonal comparisons of utility: comment.' *Journal of Political Economy*, vol. 75.

Edgeworth, F. Y. 1876. 'Mr. Matthew Arnold on Bishop Butler's doctrine of self love.' *Mind* 1:570–71.

——— 1877. *New and old methods of ethics or 'physical ethics' and 'methods of ethics.'* Oxford.

——— 1879. 'The hedonical calculus.' *Mind* 4:394–408.

——— 1881. *Mathematical psychics: an essay on the application of mathematics to the moral sciences*. London.

——— 1882. 'Mr. Leslie Stephen on utilitarianism.' *Mind* 7:446–447.

——— 1887. *Metretike, or the method of measuring probability and utility*. London.

——— 1925. *Papers relating to political economy*, 3 vols. London.

Harsanyi, J. C. 1953. 'Cardinal utility in welfare economics and in the theory of risk-taking.' *Journal of Political Economy*, vol. 61.

——— 1955. 'Cardinal welfare, individualistic ethics, and interpersonal comparisons of utility.' *Journal of Political Economy* 63:309–21.

Hildebrand, W., and A. Kirman 1976. *General equilibrium analysis*. Amsterdam.

Jevons, W. S. 1970. *Theory of political economy*. Edited with an introduction by R. D. C. Black. London.

Keynes, J. M. 1972. *Essays in biography*, vol. 10 of the *Collected writings of Keynes*. London.

Marshall, A., and M. P. Marshall 1879. *The economics of industry*. London.

Mirrlees, J. A. 1982. 'The economic uses of utilitarianism.' In A. K. Sen and B. Williams, eds., *Utilitarianism and beyond*. Cambridge.

O'Brien, D. P., A. C. Darnell, and J. Peters 1983. 'A statistical technique for the investigation of authorship puzzles.' *University of Durham, Department of Economics Working Paper*, no. 59.

Pattanaik, P. K. 1968. 'Risk, impersonality and the social welfare function.' *Journal of Political Economy*, vol. 76. Reprinted in Phelps 1973, pp. 298–318.

Phelps, E. S., ed. 1973. *Economic justice*. London.

Pigou, A. C., ed. 1925. *Memorials of Alfred Marshall*. London.

Rawls, J. 1971. *A theory of justice*. Oxford.

Review of Jevons's *Theory of political economy* 1871. *Saturday Review*, 11 Nov. 624–25. Reprinted in *Papers and correspondence of W. S. Jevons*, vol. 8, edited by R. D. C. Black (London, 1979).

Schneedwind, J. B. 1977. *Sidgwick's ethics and Victorian moral philosophy*. Oxford.

Schofield, R. E. 1963. *The Lunar Society of Birmingham: a social history of provincial science and industry in eighteenth-century England*. Oxford.

Schotter, A., and G. Schwodiauer 1980. 'Economics and game theory: a survey.' *Journal of Economic Literature* 18:479–527.

Schumpeter, J. S. 1954. *History of economic analysis*. London.

Sidgwick, A., and E. M. Sidgwick. 1906. *Henry Sidgwick: a memoir*. London.

Sen, A. K. 1970. *Collective choice and social welfare*. London.

Vickrey, W. S. 1960. 'Utility, strategy and social decision rules.' *Quarterly Journal of Economics* 74:507–35.

———. 1961. 'Risk, utility and social policy.' *Social Research*. Reprinted in Phelps 1973.

[21]

Cambridge Journal of Economics 1984, **8**, 361–379

Physics and the 'marginalist revolution'

Philip Mirowski*

The mathematician is an inventor, not a discoverer (Wittgenstein, 1978, I, 168).

1. Internal *versus* external histories of science

Interest in the origins of neoclassical theory has a number of motivations. The first is antiquarian: it is concerned with tracing the intellectual antecedents of a given innovation. The second is epistemological: the methods of great discoverers are held to provide an exemplar for currently accepted methods of research. The third is ontological: the occurrence of independent simultaneous discovery is used to suggest the substantiality and reality of the phenomenon identified. William Stanley Jevons, for instance, wrote that, 'The theory in question has in fact been independently discovered three or four times over and must be true' (Jevons, 1972, IV, p. 278). The fourth is practical: it provides a reservoir of metaphors and theoretical suggestions which might serve to prompt novel contemporary lines of inquiry which are obscured or slighted by modern theory. Confusion or doubt over the origins of modern neoclassical economic theory would introduce the possibility of serious historical, epistemological, ontological and practical confusions in its exposition.

At present, the most popular textbook of the history of economic thought attempts to dispose of the issue by absolving itself of any responsibility for discussing origins:

> Therefore, to try to explain the origin of the marginal utility revolution in the 1870s is doomed to failure: it was not a marginal utility revolution; it was not an abrupt change, but only a gradual transformation in which the old ideas were never definitively rejected; and it did not happen in the 1870s (Blaug, 1978, p. 322).

This text denies that there was any unified and self-conscious movement. In its stead, it portrays a haphazard and fragmented agglomeration of economic theorists, whose only common denominators were the twin notions of diminishing marginal utility and utility-determined prices. Since neither notion was particularly novel in the 1870s, it follows from this portrayal that there was no discontinuity in the economic thought of the period, and that economic theory has embodied one continuous discipline from Adam Smith until the present (see Bowley, 1973, ch. 4).

The thesis that innovations in economic theory in the 1870s and 1880s were unexcep-

*Tufts University and University of Massachusetts, Amherst. I should like to acknowledge helpful discussions with Larry Samuelson, Lawrence Boland and Don Katzner on the topic of this paper. None should be implicated in any errors or flights of fancy.

0309–166X/84/040361 + 19 $03.00/0

tional and merely a continuation of the unbroken threads of economic discourse in the preceding half century meets a number of difficulties. The first problem is that not all the major protagonists would have agreed with such an assessment. One cannot read the letters and published works of Stanley Jevons, Léon Walras, Francis Edgeworth, Irving Fisher, Vilfredo Pareto and others without repeatedly encountering assertions that their work represented a fundamental break with the economics of their time. Much of their professional lives was spent promoting the works of this small self-identified côterie. The second impediment to the gradualist view is the fact that the most discontinuous aspect of the 'marginalist revolution' was not the postulate of a utilitarian theory of value, but rather something no historian of economic thought has ever discussed in detail: the successful penetration of mathematical discourse into economic theory. In both their correspondence and in their published work, the early neoclassical economists recognised each other as *mathematical theorists* first and foremost; and when they proselytised for their works, it took the form of defending the 'mathematical method' in the context of economic theory. The third impediment to the gradualist view is the fact that all the major protagonists were concerned to differentiate their handiwork from previous political economy on the explicit ground that it was of a scientific character. While the claim that one's theory is 'scientific' (and therefore deserves respect) echoes throughout the last three centuries of social theory, in the case of Jevons *et al.* this claim assumes a very specific and narrow form, shared by all the principals. An understanding of these three points will lead inexorably to a re-evaluation of the significance of the rise of neoclassical economic theory.

The gradualist view of the genesis of neoclassical theory has generally been prefaced with some methodological remarks on the contrast between 'internalist' and 'externalist' intellectual histories (Blaug, 1978; Black, Coats and Goodwin, 1973). The internalist version, the one presently favoured by neoclassicals, assumes that all ideas are merely reactions to previous developments internal to the discipline under consideration. The job of an intellectual historian is to trace the descent of ideas from scientist to scientist through time, revealing how error was rooted out by the internal criticism of logical deduction and empirical testing, while scientific truths were preserved and nurtured. New insights and concepts are pioneered by key individuals, but the sources of those insights are not an important part of the historian's narrative (Popper, 1965). The historian may use sociological and other external considerations to explain adherence to superseded theories; but adherence to the successful theory is felt to need no other explanation other than its *prima facie* success (Bloor, 1976).

This view is in contrast to externalist intellectual history, which seeks the determinants of successful theories in the political, philosophical and/or social currents of the time. The externalist historian is satisfied to identify the link between an historical interlude and the construction and acceptance of a successful theory, without expending undue effort to trace the intellectual pedigree of its precursors within the science. Undoubtedly, much of the hostility of neoclassical economists to externalist explanations of the 'marginalist revolution' stems from the weak and unconvincing nature of the few attempts: Bukharin (1927) associated it with the rise of a new class of *rentiers* in *fin-de-siècle* Europe, whereas Stark (1944) saw it as a reflection of some general Kantian influences in conjunction with the assertion that the economy of mid-nineteenth century Europe was actually characterised by atomistic competition. It has been observed repeatedly that these portrayals are not historically accurate; nor do they describe correctly the milieu of the major protagonists (Blaug, 1978; Kauder, 1965).

The internalist/externalist dichotomy has itself impeded the understanding of the rise of neoclassical economic theory. It forces the student of history to choose between a tautology and a disdain for theory, which has rendered the history trivial for all present purposes. Further, recent philosophers of science have severely undermined the distinction (Bloor, 1976; Kuhn, 1970). It is particularly necessary for social theorists to be aware of both the social and intellectual parameters of their own practices.

2. An alternative thesis

Our first thesis may be stated simply and directly: there was a readily identifiable discontinuity in economic thought in the 1870s and 1880s which was the genesis of neoclassical theory; and both its timing and intellectual content can be explained by parallel developments in physics in the mid-nineteenth century. The evidence is drawn from (i) the published works of the first neoclassicists; (ii) an example from the physics of the time which reveals the parallels; and (iii), biographical information about the principals.

All the major protagonists of the 'marginalist revolution' explicitly stated in their *published* works the sources of the inspiration for their novel economic theories. Jevons (1970, pp. 144–147) wrote that his equation of exchange does '. . . not differ in general character from those which are really treated in many branches of physical science'. He then proceeds to compare the equality of the ratios of marginal utility of two goods and their inverted trading ratio to the law of the lever, where in equilibrium the point masses at each end are inversely proportional to the ratio of their respective distances from the fulcrum. Note at this stage that Jevons' exposition does not adequately support his statements in the text: since he does not derive the equilibrium of the lever from considerations of potential and kinetic energy, he fails to justify the parallel between the expression for physical equilibrium and his use of differential equations in his own equations of exchange (see further, Section 5).

Far from being an isolated and insignificant metaphor, this invocation of the physical realm is always present in Jevons' writings on price theory. For example, in his defence of the mathematical method before the Manchester Statistical Society, he insists that

> Utility only exists when there is on the one side the person wanting, and on the other the thing wanted. . . Just as the gravitating force of a material body depends not alone on the mass of that body, but upon the masses and relative positions and distances of the surrounding material bodies, so utility is an attraction between a wanting being and what is wanted (Jevons, 1981, VII, p. 80).

When one observes that more than half of Jevons' published work concerns the logic and philosophy of science, one begins to see that the metaphor of physical science was the unifying principle, and not merely a rhetorical flourish. In his major book, *The Principles of Science,* he suggests that the notion of the hierarchy of the sciences justifies '. . . a calculus of moral effects, a kind of physical astronomy investigating the mutual perturbations of individuals' (1905, pp. 759–760). The reduction of social processes to simple utilitarian considerations is compared to the reduction of meteorology to chemistry and thence to physics, implying that there is only one scientific methodology and one mode of explanation—that of physics—in all human experience.

Léon Walras was equally explicit concerning the motivation behind his published work. In his *Elements of Pure Economics* he claims that, 'the pure theory of economics is a science which resembles the physico-mathematical sciences in every respect' (1969,

p. 71). Walras explains in great detail his occupation with 'pure economics' in Lessons One to Four of the *Elements*. In his opinion, a pure science is only concerned with the relationships among things, the 'play of the blind and ineluctable forces of nature' which are independent of all human will. Walras insists that there exists a limited subset of economic phenomena which could be the objects of a pure scientific inquiry: they are the configurations of prices in a regime of 'perfect competition' (for further elaboration see Mirowski, 1981). Such 'pure' relationships justify and indeed, for Walras, *demand* the application of the *same* mathematical techniques as those deployed in mid-nineteenth century physics; other social phenomena tainted by the influence of human will would be relegated to studies employing non-scientific rhetorical techniques.

The proposed unity of technique in physics and economics is fully revealed in Walras's article of 1909, 'Économique et Mécanique' (reprinted in Walras, 1960). In this article he develops the two favourite metaphors of the early neoclassical economists, the rational mechanics of the equilibrium of the lever and the mathematical relations between celestial bodies; he also asserts that the 'physico-mathematical science' of his *Elements* uses *precisely* the identical mathematical formulae. He then proceeds to scold physicists who had expressed scepticism about the application of mathematics to utilitarian social theories on the ground that utility is not a measurable quantum; Walras retorts that the physicists themselves have been vague in their quantification of such basic terms as 'mass' and 'force'. The proposed connections between the terms of the sciences could not have been made more manifest: 'Aussi a-t-on déjà signalé celles des *forces* et des *raretés* comme *vecteurs*, d'une part, et celles des *énergies* et des *utilités* comme *quantités scalaires*, d'autre part' (Walras, 1960, p. 7).

Francis Ysidro Edgeworth was a third partisan of 'mathematical psychics' who was quite explicit about the wellsprings of the neoclassical movement. If only because of his extravagant and florid writing style, he is worth quoting directly:

> The application of mathematics to the world of the soul is countenanced by the hypothesis (agreeable to the general hypothesis that every psychical phenomenon is the concomitant, and in some sense the other side of a physical phenomenon), the particular hypothesis adopted in these pages, that Pleasure is the concomitant of Energy. *Energy* may be regarded as the central idea of Mathematical Psychics; *maximum energy* the object of the principal investigations in that science... 'Mecanique Sociale' may one day take her place along with 'Mecanique Celeste', throned each upon the double-sided height of one maximum principle, the supreme pinnacle of moral as of physical science. As the movements of each particle, constrained or loose, in a material cosmos are continually subordinated to one maximum sub-total of accumulated energy, so the movements of each soul whether selfishly isolated or linked sympathetically, may continually be realising the maximum of pleasure... (Edgeworth, 1881, pp. 9, 12).

Vilfredo Pareto, a fourth confederate of the marginalist cadre, adopted a much more pugnacious but essentially identical position:

> Strange disputes about predestination, about the efficacy of grace, etc, and in our day incoherent ramblings on solidarity show that men have not freed themselves from these daydreams which people have gotten rid of in the physical sciences, but which still burden the social sciences... Thanks to the use of mathematics, this entire theory, as we develop it in the Appendix, rests on no more than a fact of experience, that is, on the determination of the quantities of goods which constitute combinations between which the individual is indifferent. The theory of economic science thus acquires the rigor of rational mechanics... (Pareto, 1971B, pp. 36, 113).

In some ways, Pareto was the most ruthless proponent of the physical metaphor, and because of this, found himself the first of the neoclassicals to have to defend himself from attacks by mathematicians and physicists (Volterra, 1971, pp. 365–396).

Once one recognises these passages for the manifestos that they are, one sees that they are ubiquitous in the writings of early neoclassical economists. They can be found in Fisher (1892), Antonelli (1886), Laundhardt (1885) and Auspitz and Lieben (1889). In fact, the explicit appropriation of this specific physical metaphor is present in every major innovator of the marginalist revolution, with the single exception (discussed later) of the Austrian school of Carl Menger. The adoption of the 'energetics' metaphor and framework of mid-nineteenth century physics is the birthmark of neoclassical economics, the Ariadne's thread which ties the protagonists, and which can lead us to the fundamental meaning of the neoclassical research programme.

3. Physics and economics

Historians of economic thought, and many other economists as well, have long been aware that there are some close familial resemblances between physical concepts and neoclassical economic theory (see Sebba, 1953; Lowe, 1951; Knight, 1956; Weisskopf, 1979; Samuelson, 1972; Thoben, 1982). The reason why these observations have passed without notice is that the extent and significance of the linkage has not been chronicled from the viewpoint of physics. For example, it has become a cliché to refer to neoclassical economics as being 'Newtonian', perhaps bolstered by some offhand assertions that both are atomistic, both have resort to the language of frictions and equilibrium, and, depending upon the disposition of the commentator, perhaps inclusion of a pejorative comment that both are 'mechanistic'. Indeed, if those observations exhausted the sum total of the analogy, then it would merit no further serious consideration. However, recourse to the history of mathematics and physics shows that the characterisation of neoclassical economics as 'Newtonian' is both inept and misleading.

Historians of science are increasingly sceptical of the conventional wisdom that the history of physics consists of two discrete periods: one, stretching from the sequence Galileo–Descartes–Newton to roughly 1895, called Classical Physics; and the second, a twentieth century phenomenon based on quantum mechanics and relativity. To quote a recent textbook:

> The term 'Newtonian' as applied to 18th and 19th century physics implicitly conflates Newton's natural philosophy and the physics of this later period, and is hence a misleading description. The developments in theoretical mechanics in the 18th century show a significant departure from the mechanical and mathematical assumptions of Newton's natural philosophy; and the physics of imponderable 'fluids', active substances and the anomalous forms of matter current in the 18th century contrasts with Newton's theory of nature... Despite the dominance of the program of mechanical explanation ... the term 'Newtonian' is misleading when applied to physics in the 19th century. The conceptual innovations of 19th century physics—energy conservation, the theory of the physical field, the theory of light as vibrations of an electromagnetic ether, and the concept of entropy—cannot be meaningfully be described as 'Newtonian' (Harman, 1982, pp. 10–11).

In point of fact, the word 'physics' was not generally used in English until the middle of the nineteenth century to refer to the united study of mechanics, light, heat, etc., both because of its Aristotelian connections (Cannon, 1978, p. 113, *et seq.*) and because there was no consensus on a unified theory of these phenomena until the rise of energetics in the middle of the century. Problems with Newtonian concepts in the nineteenth century with respect to light, heat and electricity led to the proliferation of types of postulated matter and their associated separate attractions and repulsions, which in turn led to contradictions inherent in the idea of more than one Newtonian force (Agassi, 1971; Harman, 1982). Energetics as a unifying principle was created by Helmholtz's famous 1847 paper 'On the Conservation of Force' (Kahl, 1971), drawing upon earlier study of the conceptualisation of *vis viva* (or 'living force') and the interconvertability of heat and mechanical work. This innovation induced substantial revision of many previous physical doctrines, and created the discipline of physics as the unified study of phenomena linked by energetic principles.

This watershed in physics altered not only the subject matter but the techniques of research and methodological prescriptions as well. It was linked to the mathematical supersession by French analytical methods and Leibniz's notation for the calculus of the English use of the Newtonian calculus of fluxions and the English fondness for geometrical argument (Bos, 1980). It was accompanied by changes in the acceptable standards of theory formation: these included an increasing refusal to specify the underlying nature of phenomena described mathematically; fewer concessions made to intuitive plausibility; increasing imperatives to measure quantitatively without being precise as to what it was that was being measured; and a predisposition to accept the 'usefulness' of a model as a form of proof (Heidelberger, in Jahnke and Otte, 1981; Harman, 1982).

Crucial in this revolution in thought concerning physical processes was the transformation of vague 'forces' into a Protean, unique, and yet ontologically undefined 'energy', which could only be discussed cogently through the intermediary of its mathematical eidolon. In this guise, energy did not characterise Newtonian particles, but rather processes. It shifted the description of motion itself away from vectors such as momentum and towards scalars encompassing the new 'energy'. Its divergence from Newtonian concepts became apparent when the conservation law was enunciated, because the conservation law provided the only means by which to identify an energetic system as in some sense the 'same' as it underwent various changes and transformations (Theobald, 1966; Meyerson, 1962).

Some familiarity with the history of physics, even one as sketchy as that provided above, is necessary for an understanding of the fact that neoclassical economics was not prompted by a Newtonian analogy. Classical economists made reference to the Newtonian analogy in non-essential contexts (see Blaug, 1980, pp. 57–58); but they could not reconcile the inverse square law, the calculus of fluxions and other Newtonian techniques with their overall conception of social processes. The rise of energetics in physical theory induced the invention of neoclassical economic theory, by providing the metaphor, the mathematical techniques, and the new attitudes toward theory construction. Neoclassical economic theory was appropriated wholesale from mid-nineteenth century physics; utility was redefined so as to be identical with energy.

An example may make this clearer for the modern reader.

Consider a point-mass displaced a distance $q(=AB)$ in a two-dimensional plane, as in Fig. 1, by a force vector $\mathbf{F}$. The force vector can be decomposed into its perpendicular components, $\mathbf{F}=\mathbf{i}F_x+\mathbf{j}F_y$ (where $\mathbf{i}$, $\mathbf{j}$ are the unit vectors along the appropriate axes). Similarly, the vector of displacement can also be decomposed into its components, $d\mathbf{q}=\mathbf{i}dx+\mathbf{j}dy$. The work done (i.e. the product of the force and distance moved along the path of its action) in the instance of this displacement is defined as the summation of the forces times the displacements, or:

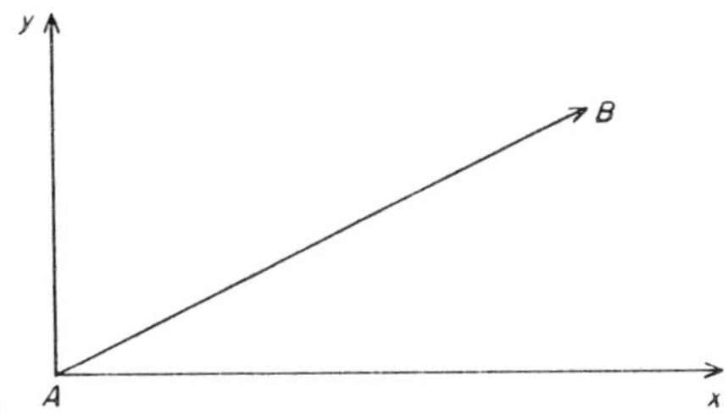

Fig. 1

$$T=\int_A^B (F_x dx + F_y dy) = \tfrac{1}{2}m|\mathbf{v}|_B^2 - \tfrac{1}{2}m|\mathbf{v}|_A^2.$$

Energetics redefined the change in mv^2 (i.e., the *vis viva* of the particle) to be the change in kinetic energy. The vector characterisation could then be translated into a single-valued scalar function, T. In the eighteenth century, there had been much controversy over whether the *vis viva* was conserved; this issue was clarified in energetics in the following manner. Suppose that the above expression in the parentheses were an exact differential; in other words, there existed a function U such that:

$$F_x = -\partial U/\partial x;\ F_y = -\partial U/\partial y;\ U = U(x,y).$$

This uniquely identified scalar function U was interpreted as the unobserved potential energy of the particle. Then it is the *total* energy of the particle, $T+U$, which is conserved through any motion of the particle. The postulate that total energy is conserved was significant, because it allows a rigorous specification of the 'principle of least action'. This principle, in its various forms, dated back to Maupertuis in the eighteenth century, who noted that the actual paths of motion traversed in many mechanical phenomena could be described mathematically as evincing the minimum of the particle's 'action'. William Hamilton in the 1830s pioneered 'the central conception of all modern theory in physics' (Schrödinger, quoted in Crowe, 1967, p. 17) by defining the action integral over time of the path of a particle as:

$$\int_{t_1,A}^{t_2,B} (T-U)\, dt.$$

The Hamiltonian principle of 'least action' asserts that the actual path of the particle from A to B will be the one which makes the action integral stationary. The path may be calculated by finding the constrained extrema, employing techniques of Lagrangean constrained maximisation/minimisation or, in more complicated cases, using directly the calculus of variations. In a conservative system, where $T+U=$ a constant, action is a function of position only, which implies that all motion is fully reversible, and exhibits no hysteresis (Kline, 1972, ch. 30).

To summarise: in the 1820s theoretical treatises in mechanics began to stress the work integral and its mathematical relationship to *vis viva* (Harman, 1982, p. 36). In the 1830s, Hamilton linked this framework to the mathematics of constrained extrema (Hankins, 1980). Starting in the 1840s, the interconvertability of mechanical energy and other energetic phenomena was postulated; by the 1860s, the mathematics of unobservable potentials and constrained extrema were extended to all physical phenomena.

Walras insisted that his *rareté* equations resembled those of the physical sciences in every respect. We may see now that he was very nearly correct. Simply redefine the variables of the earlier equations: let **F** be the vector of prices of a set of traded goods, and let q be the vector of the quantities of those goods purchased. The integral $\int \mathbf{F}.\mathrm{dq} = T$ is then defined as the total expenditure on these goods. If the expression to be integrated is an exact differential, then it is possible to define a scalar function of the goods x and y of the form $U = U(x,y)$, which can then be interpreted as the 'utilities' of those goods. In exact parallel to the original concept of potential energy, these utilities are unobservable, and can only be inferred from theoretical linkage to other observable variables. Relative prices are equal to the ratios of the marginal utilities of the goods by construction: the 'potential field' of utility is defined as the locus of the set of constrained extrema, although the early marginalists reversed this logic in their expositions of the principle. Instead of treating utility as a derived phenomenon, they postulated the utility field as the fundamental exogenous data to which market transactions adjusted. The mathematics, however, are the same in both instances.

There *is* one major difference, however, between the mathematics of energetics and its transplanted version in neoclassical economics. The conservation principle in energetics does not translate directly into neoclassical theory: the sum of income and utility is not conserved, and is meaningless in the context of economic theory. Does this mean that neoclassical economics has managed to dispense with the artifice of a conservation principle? This may appear to be the case, because neither the progenitors of neoclassicism nor any of its modern adherents have ever seriously discussed this aspect of the physical metaphor (see Mirowski, 1984C). Yet to cast any problem in a constrained maximisation framework, the analyst *must* assume some sort of conservation principle. In physics, it is widely understood that the conservation principle is the means by which the system being considered retains its analytical identity.

In other words, the adoption of the energetics metaphor in economics has imposed an analytical regimen, the rigours of which have hitherto gone unnoticed. Neoclassical theorists, from the 1870s onwards, have surreptitiously assumed some form of conservation principle in their economic models. In the period of our present concern, the principle took two forms: (a) the income or endowment to be traded is given exogenously and, further, is assumed to be fully spent or traded; thus, for practical purposes, T is conserved; and/or (b) the transactors' estimation of the utility of the various goods is a datum not altered by the sequence of purchase, nor any other aspect of the trading or consuming process (or, as Marshall sheepishly admitted, desire was equated with satisfaction *by assumption*); so in effect the utility field U is conserved (see Mirowski, 1984C). In this case, the analogy between physics and economics would be as if physical theory had managed to preserve what has proved to be an anachronistic element: as if Hamilton had somehow managed to preserve the conservation of *vis viva* (kinetic energy) within the new mathematics of energetic extrema.

Once the parallels between mid-nineteenth century physics and neoclassical economic theory are outlined, and it is acknowledged that the progenitors themselves openly admitted them in their published writings, most would accept the thesis that the 'marginalist revolution' should be renamed the 'marginalist annexation'. Should doubts linger, however, the thesis should be clinched by an examination of the biographical particulars of the protagonists.

The most obvious and straightforward case is that of the most respected of neoclassical progenitors, Léon Walras. In his first effort to mathematicise his father's concept of *rareté,* Walras attempted to implement a Newtonian model of market relations, postulating that 'the price of things is in inverse ratio to the quantity offered and in direct ratio to the quantity demanded' (Walras, 1965, I, pp. 216–217). Dissatisfied with this model, Walras tinkered with various formulations, but none involved the constrained maximisation of utility until the late autumn of 1872. At that time, a professor of mechanics at the Academy of Lausanne, Antoine Paul Piccard, wrote a memo to Walras sketching the mathematics of the optimisation of an unobserved '*quantité de besoin*' (Walras, 1965, I, pp. 308–311) along the lines outlined above. Although Walras trained originally as an engineer at the École des Mines, he did not possess a deep understanding of the new energetics: this can be opbserved in his reactions to the letters of Charles Émile Picard (Walras, 1965, III, pp. 417–420) correcting his errors of interpretation and mathematical representation. While these letters did prompt him to write 'Économique et Mécanique', they did not prompt him to revise his *Elements* significantly. This suggests that Walras did not comprehend the real thrust of these letters, which question the appropriateness of various aspects of the physical metaphor. It was left for his successors Antonelli and Pareto to explore some of the *social* implications of the mathematics of energetics.

It is significant that all the earliest members of the Lausanne school were trained as engineers. Giovanni Antonelli was an Italian civil engineer whose monograph *On the Mathematical Theory of Political Economy* explicitly discusses utility theory in the manner described above (pp. 366–368) (Antonelli, 1886). He is now considered a pioneer in the problem of integrability, which here we interpret as an acknowledgement and extrapolation of the implications of conservation principles. The significance of this problem did not receive widespread attention until well into the twentieth century (Samuelson, 1950). Vilfredo Pareto was also trained as an engineer, and this expertise enabled him to explore the implications of the path-independence of the realisation of utility, a direct extrapolation of the path-independence of equilibrium energy states in rational mechanics and thermodynamics (Pareto, 1971A). This work was consigned to oblivion partly because Pareto and Antonelli gave up economic theory in later life, and partly because no one outside a very limited circle of engineers who had a working knowledge of the new economic theory could read it. The English-speaking world had to wait until the 1930s when an influx of physicists—and engineers—manqués into economics led to the revival of their work.

The biographical evidence in the case of Jevons is not as direct, but is substantial. Prompted by his father to become an engineer, Jevons studied chemistry and mathematics in London. He attended some of Michael Faraday's renowned public lectures at the Royal Institution, at which Faraday claimed that magnetic forces did not obey the Newtonian force rule (Jevons, 1972, I, p. 82). This is significant because in the land of Newton in the 1850s Faraday was one of the very few partisans of field theories and energetics: indeed, Jevons' letters make clear his enormous respect for Faraday. We also have evidence that Jevons was familiar with the writings of Thomson and Joule on the interconvertability of heat and mechanical work, writings which led to the enunciation of the theory of the conservation of energy (Jevons, 1972, II, p. 66). Later in his life Jevons remained conversant with the field of energetics, and even wrote to James Clerk Maxwell arguing a point of controversy in Fourier's theory of heat (Jevons, 1972, IV, pp. 207–208).

If there was a difference between Jevons and Walras, it was this: Walras did not evince any deep understanding of mid-nineteenth century physics, and applied the mathematical techniques and the metaphor in a mechanical and unimaginative manner, leaving it for others to draw out the logical and connotative implications of the physical metaphor. Jevons, on the other hand, was even less of a mathematician than Walras, but did dedicate his life's work to drawing out the meaning of the metaphor of energetics for the sphere of the economy. This point is not readily apparent, because Jevons' work is rarely considered as a whole. His major achievements were the *Theory of Political Economy*, *The Coal Question,* his work on sunspots and the business cycle, and *The Principles of Science*. The connection between the four can best be summarised in Jevons' own words, from his paper 'The Solar Influence on Commerce' (Jevons, 1972, VII, p. 97): 'Long ago George Stevenson acutely anticipated the results of subsequent scientific inquiry when he said that coal was sunshine bottled up; now it is among the mere commonplaces of science that all motions and energies of life . . . are directly or indirectly derived from the sun.' The maximisation of utility, the prediction that England was rapidly exhausting energy stocks in the form of coal, and the lifelong theme that economic crises must be caused by energy fluctuations exogenous to the social operation of the economy, are all direct extrapolations from the energetic movement of the mid-nineteenth century (Mirowski, 1984A). The last point gains credibility when one notes that Jevons recorded in his journal that Faraday explicitly discussed the periodicity of sunspots in his lectures of 1853 (Jevons, 1972, I, p. 82). As for the *Principles of Science,* it can be read as a plea for the unity of methodology in all sciences, in the face of the serious upheavals and discontinuities which erupted both in subject matter and in research methods in mid-nineteenth century physics. The fact that his own conception of scientific endeavor was highly coloured by the rise of energetics can be observed in the *Principle's* definition of science: 'Science is the detection of identity, and classification is the placing together, either in thought or in the proximity of space, those objects between which identity has been detected' (Jevons, 1905, pp. 673–674).

4. The Austrians were not neoclassicals

Those familiar with conventional histories of neoclassical economic theory must, by this point, be impatient to object: what about Menger and the Austrians? Do they fit the thesis which links the rise of neoclassical theory to the rise of energetics in physics?

Although it has become conventional wisdom to cite the triumvirate of the marginal revolution as Jevons, Walras and Menger, these three actors themselves did not accept this regimentation. Jevons did not mention Menger once in all his writings: a curious reticence in one so determined in later life to uncover all predecessors and fellow revolutionaries. Walras did correspond with Menger, but only to discover to his amazement that Menger did not recognise his contribution on account of its mathematical nature. This was sufficient for Walras to deny Menger's role in the revolution, writing in a letter to Bortkiewicz in 1887 that Menger's and Bohm-Bawerk's efforts to describe the theory of 'Grenznuten' in 'ordinary language' was unsuccessful, and even painful (Walras, 1965, II, p. 232). Walras viewed Menger's 1871 *Principles* as merely an attempt at *translation* of marginalist ideas into ordinary language, and a failed one at that: there was nothing novel or original there; he thus denied Menger any status as an equal. (Interestingly enough, this opinion seems to be shared by many modern neoclassical economists. In this regard, see Samuelson, 1952, p. 61.) Menger did not conform to

Walras's main criteria for a neoclassical theorist: he was not mathematical, he did not adhere to the norms of physical science, and therefore he was not 'scientific'.

In contrast, historians of economic thought are persistently perplexed by Menger's recalcitrance at being elevated to membership in the triumvirate. Howey, the most careful of these writers, notes:

> ... although Menger talked about the Austrian school, no one would gather from his words in any of his publications after 1871 down to his death that the Austrian School had the slightest connection with the Marginal Utility School. He either did not admit the connection, or wished to minimise it, or took it for granted. Menger never publicly admitted any kinship with Walras or with Jevons (Howey, 1960, p. 142).

There is much more here than petty squabbles over precedence or methodology, or personality clashes, or nationalistic insularity. There is the possibility that the Austrians, or at the very least Menger, were not part of the fledgling movement of neoclassical economic theory. This possibility has already been suggested by some Austrian economists, notably by Erich Streissler in a centenary collection of essays on the marginalist revolution (Black, Coats and Goodwin, 1973, pp. 160–175). Streissler points out that Menger's scales of successive marginal satisfaction, introduced in the middle of his *Grundsätze* (Menger, 1981, p. 127), were not at all central to his conception of economic theory. This contention is indirectly supported by Kauder (1965, p. 76), who reports that Menger crossed out this table in his author's copy of the book. Howey (1960, p. 40) notes that Menger's 'importance of satisfactions' cannot easily be translated into the language of utility because it did not vary in *quantity*. 'Satisfaction' never varied, but its subjective importance could be altered in a regular manner. Streissler maintains that Menger's major concerns uncertainty, changes in the quality of goods, the absence of a notion of equilibrium, and hostility to the 'law of one price'—were motivated so fundamentally by his radical subjectivism that he could not be considered as promoting the same theory as Jevons and Walras. From our present perspective, we can find support for Streissler's thesis by examining Menger's relationship to physical theory.

After a personal visit, Bortkiewicz wrote to Walras that Menger did not have the least idea of mathematical analysis (Walras, 1965, II, p. 519). Perusal of his major works indicates that he was also unfamiliar with the physics of his time. Yet despite these inadequacies, Menger launched a scathing attack upon the German historicist school in his *Untersuchungen über die Methode*, mainly consisting of the contention that his opponents did not understand the nature of 'exact science' (Menger, 1963). In sharp contrast with Jevons' *Principles of Science*, Menger's weak and unconvincing claims that he was promoting the methods of 'exact research of a Newton, Lavoisier or Helmholtz' reveal an ignorance hastily camouflaged by bombast. He attempted to extend his radical subjectivism to physics without giving a single example from the physical sciences. He denigrated empiricism without being specific about the practices to which he objected. His conception of science was severely Aristotelian and he never addressed the fact that the scientists of his day had rejected this. He rather appropriated their names for credibility.

Menger cannot be considered a neoclassical economist because he rejected two basic pillars of that theory: the law of one price, which states that all generic goods in a market (however defined) must trade at the same price in equilibrium (see Dennis, 1982); and the concept that traded goods in some sense are related as equivalents in equilibrium (Menger, 1981, pp. 191–194). Absence of the first subverts any deterministic notion of equilibrium. Absence of the second explains Menger's hostility towards quantification. Absence of both effectively prevented the introduction of the physics analogy into economic theory. The mere postulation of a diminishing marginal utility is not sufficient to generate a neoclassical theory of price. In this respect Menger is no different from Dupuit (1952), who also recognised diminishing marginal utility, but also repudiated a single equilibrium price. Were it not for three historical accidents—first, the *Grundsätze* was first published in 1871; second, Menger's illustrious student Wieser promoted his claim to be a founder of neoclassical theory (and himself *did* adopt the new marginalist techniques from Laundhardt and Auspitz and Lieben); and third, Menger's works were largely unavailable outside the German-speaking world—Menger would not today be considered as one of the marginalist revolutionaries.

There has been much disagreement as to what constitutes the 'hard core' of neoclassical economic theory: the fundamental basis of the research programme which, if altered, would signal the substantive development of a non-neoclassical economic theory (Latsis, 1976; Boland, 1982). The core is not simply methodological individualism, nor is it utilitarianism, because both were active research strategies in social theory well before the rise of neoclassical theory, and because the Austrian and certain sociological research programmes also hold them as tenets. It is the second thesis of this paper that the hard core of neoclassical economic theory is the adoption of mid-nineteenth century physics as a rigid paradigm, a hard core it has preserved and nourished throughout the twentieth century, even after physics has moved onwards to new metaphors and new techniques. This thesis explains a number of issues which have eluded other attempts at locating the hard core of neoclassical theory.

First, it explains why neoclassical theory and mathematical formalism have been indissolubly wedded since the 1870s, even though a cogent defence of the necessity of the link has been notable by its absence. Second, it explains the success of neoclassicism in pre-empting other research programmes in economics by means of the forceful claim that it is scientific, even though standards of scientific discourse in the larger culture have changed periodically during the last hundred years. Third, it explains the preference for techniques of constrained maximisation over any other analytical techniques, which include input–output matrices, game theory, Markov chains, and a myriad of other techniques proposed over the last century (Samuelson, 1972). Fourth, it explains the persistent use of an unobservable and unmeasurable value determinant—utility—in textbooks and in applied research, despite protestations that utility is not 'needed' for neoclassical results (Wong, 1978). Fifth, it explains the modern controversy over the necessity for a 'microfoundation for macroeconomics', which can be interpreted as a complaint that Keynesian economics has not conformed to the hard core research strategy, and is therefore somehow illegitimate (Weintraub, 1979; Lucas, 1981). Sixth, it explains why neoclassicism links certain economic variables to particular exogenous variables, which are themselves 'naturally' determined and therefore analytically immutable and outside of the scope of economic theory. All these characteristics are borrowed from nineteenth century energetics.

5. Physical metaphors, organic metaphors and the role of Marshall

It is not unusual for a science to adopt the metaphors and/or analytical techniques of another discipline. The story of Darwin's appropriation of the concept of population pressure on resources from Malthus's *Essay on Population* is but one example of a pervasive phenomenon. Indeed, some historians of science attempt to explain the rise of energetics by the influence of German *Naturphilosophie* in mid-nineteenth century culture (Kuhn, 1977). What is unusual and noteworthy about the rise to preeminence of neoclassical economic theory is the lack of consciousness, and therefore the concomitant lack of any assessment or critique, of the sources of its analytical and technical inspiration. Newtonian action-at-a-distance came under severe scrutiny and criticism from philosophical perspectives in the eighteenth and nineteenth centuries. Darwinian natural selection has repeatedly been reconsidered at the level of the fundamental organising metaphor. The list could be extended indefinitely: many of the basic organising principles of physics have undergone criticism and revision over the past two hundred years. All these episodes reveal a willingness to reconsider theory at the level of the 'hard core', as opposed to revision of the 'protective belt'. In effect, the strength of physics lies in its openness to fundamental revision, and not, as the naïve conception has it, in its unwavering preservation of eternal verities.

Neoclassical economists, on the other hand, have often appealed to the dignity of the scientific endeavour, without understanding what it entails, or why they felt justified in claiming privileged scientific status for their paradigm. Until Georgescu-Roegen (1971), the extent of the dependence of modern neoclassical theory upon the physical metaphor had not even been surveyed seriously. What is still missing is a preliminary balance sheet of the gains and losses from adherence to this research strategy.

For early neoclassical theory, one can compile a condensed set of accounts. On the credit side, the main object of the early marginalists has been achieved: the abolition of the *anomie* and the lack of systematic theory of mid-nineteenth century political economy, and the creation in its place of a shared research programme with shared goals, as well as a well-defined set of research techniques. Attention moved away from broad and ill-defined growth and development issues to a much narrower set of concerns tethered to the notion of short-period equilibrium price (Garegnani, 1976). Systematic empiricism was encouraged by a shift in focus to certain easily quantifiable variables. The discipline of economics was divided up into a set of subfields, both theoretical and applied, which could provide researchers with a clearly defined expertise and thus identity. This played an important part in the growing professionalisation of economics in the later nineteenth century, guaranteeing it a secure place in the academic environment (Checkland, 1951). In other words, the appropriation of the physical metaphor effectively appropriated credibility for economics as a respected science.

The debit side of the account is more subtle, and so more contentious. Perhaps the major debit entry is the fact that the early neoclassicals themselves did not adequately understand the physical metaphor and the constraints which it imposed upon social theory. For example, Jevons did not explicitly derive the equilibrium of the lever from energetics principles in his *Theory of Political Economy,* thus leaving him open to ridicule by Marshall, who jeeringly suggested in a book review that he try to integrate his equation of exchange (Jevons, 1981, VII, p. 145). With the single exception of Marshall, all the early neoclassicals used the energetics metaphor; no other economists understood enough physics to discuss its implications and flaws.

Yet consider a short impressionistic list of these flaws. First, all energetics before the second law of thermodynamics (the entropy law) presumed that all phenomena were perfectly reversible, and thus equilibrium could not be time-dependent. In pre-entropy physics, history does not matter. The conservation principle is crucial in this respect, because it defines identity through time. When this metaphor is imported into the social sphere, it implies that in equilibrium byegones are byegones; thus one could practically ignore how a market actually functions in real time, paying attention only to putative 'eventual' outcomes. Hicks (1979) and Shackle (1967) are the latest in a long line of illustrious figures to complain about this issue; but their complaints have not made any substantive headway because they have not seen how deeply rooted this principle is in neoclassical techniques. Second, something must be conserved in order to apply the techniques of constrained extrema, the 'maximum principle'. When the physical metaphor is imported into the social sphere, neoclassicists were not at all precise about what the conserved entity was, and they have not yet been able to settle this issue (Mirowski, 1984C). If utility is conserved, then surprise and regret as psychological phenomena have analytically been ruled out of court. If income or endowments are conserved, then Say's Law is implicitly invoked, and there is no theory of output other than a psychological notion of 'virtual' production (Clower, 1970). Third, in energetics, all physical phenomena are fully and reversibly transformable into any other phenomena. When this idea is transported into the context of the economy, then all goods become fully and reversibly transformable into all other goods through trades. There is no requirement for a specific money commodity or set of financial institutions, because they would be redundant. The analogue of energetics is the barter economy. Fourth, equilibrium is identified with extremum principles in physics because they provide a concise method of summarising the actual path of particles in empirical experience. When the metaphor is imported into economics, the use of extremum principles is claimed to 'prove' the superior efficacy of a particular kind of economic organisation. Physics long ago renounced this teleological interpretation; economics has come to embrace it.

If contemporaries had understood what kind of economy the energetics metaphor described, then neoclassicism would have met substantial logical opposition. We may infer this from the fact that when the physics metaphor was explicitly introduced into the social sphere in other contexts, it met with strenuous opposition (Sorokin, 1956, ch. 1). But this is where economics is the anomaly in the history of social theory: because the 'inventors' did not understand energetics or the social metaphor with any great depth or subtlety, they rarely discussed the merits or demerits of the application of physical techniques and metaphors to social theory. No other economists understood enough physics to see its implications; nor were they induced to study physics by any of the writings of the early marginalists. Effectively, neoclassical economic theory was a *fait accompli* whose origins and fundamental bases were buried by historical accident, to the extent that the sources of inspiration of Jevons, Walras, Pareto, *et al.* could appear as a puzzle to their posterity.

It should not appear from my summary that the entire economics profession were sleepwalkers, stumbling unwittingly into a maze of energetics. Alfred Marshall, for one, certainly discussed some aspects of the adoption of physical metaphors (Marshall, 1898); and he clearly had some reservations. However, the case of Marshall is actually illuminated by an understanding of energetics.

Marshall's place in the history of economic thought has always been a curious one. He hinted, both privately and in print, that many of Jevons' ideas had been 'familiar truths' to him when they were published, thus intimating that somehow he also deserved 'discoverer' status. Since much of what appears in introductory and intermediate microeconomics texts as the theory of supply and demand is, in fact, the handiwork of Marshall, there is a grain of truth in his claim. However, once the actual sequence of events is uncovered, it appears that Marshall's major service in the marginalist revolution was as a populariser; and, like other popularisers, he altered the material which he promoted.

Recent study of Marshall's early unpublished writings, especially by Bharadwaj (1978), reveals that his early work was on the equilibrium of a supply curve with a phenomenological demand curve: he did not much care what lay behind his demand schedule. Implicitly, movements along the demand curve came from variations in the number of buyers, rather than a posited constrained maximisation by an individual buyer. 'The word "utility" itself was used only once in relation to Adam Smith, and not approvingly' (Bharadwaj, 1978, p. 367).

The saga of the journey between Marshall's early *Essay* and his *Principles* is the story of a decision to incorporate the innovations of the marginalist revolutionaries in order to shore up the foundations of the demand blade of the 'scissors', while preserving his original concerns with the underlying theories of the supply schedule. Unhappily, the superficial parallels between diminishing returns and diminishing marginal utility could not obscure the fact that the result was more like paper and stone rather than scissors. For example, much of Marshall's typology of markets involved altering of the timeframe of analysis and deriving its resulting effects upon the supply schedule. This method produced some embarrassment when applied to the demand side, either because the underlying demand determinants remained constant over time, revealing that the fundamental cause of price was an exogenous posited psychology, as Jevons had maintained, or because the demand curve would also be shifted in relatively arbitrary ways, undermining any claim that an equilibrium of demand and supply had been identified. Perhaps it was predictable that the attack would be pressed against the part of the system which Marshall originated (Sraffa, 1926), and that the ensuing retreat would vindicate Jevon's position.

Marshall sensed that his concerns could be overwhelmed by the zeal of his marginalist allies, and this partly explains why he does not conform in style to the characteristics of the marginalist cadre identified above. His defence of Ricardo *vis-à-vis* Jevons; his soft-pedalling of the mathematical method; his insistence on the basic continuity of economics from Adam Smith to his time; his persistent praise of organic metaphors: all these activities are attempts to incorporate energetics into economics while controlling or perhaps altering some of its more objectionable aspects. Many wave as a banner Marshall's claim that, 'The Mecca of the economist lies in economic biology', but few bother to quote the next sentence: 'But biological conceptions are more complex than those of mechanics; a volume on Foundations must therefore give a relatively large place to mechanical analogies . . .' (Marshall, 1920, p. xiv). However much he might protest, the fact remains that Marshall did render the energetics metaphor palatable for an English audience which would probably have resisted the brash revolution of a Jevons. Further, he fostered the illusion that 'The new doctrines have supplanted the older . . . but very seldom have subverted them' (Marshall, 1920, p. v).

It is important to appreciate that Marshall thought that the physical interpretation could be separated from the mathematical technique, and that his reservations lay in the interpretation rather than the technique. Those who happily quote Marshall's dictum to 'burn the mathematics' should read carefully the preface to the eighth edition of the *Principles:*

The new analysis is endeavouring gradually and tentatively to bring over into economics, as far as the widely different nature of the material will allow, those methods of the science of small increments (commonly called the differential calculus) to which man owes directly or indirectly the greater part of the control that he has obtained in recent times over physical nature. It is still in its infancy; it has no dogmas, and no standard of orthodoxy ... there is a remarkable harmony and agreement on essentials among those who are working constructively by the new method; and especially among such of them as have served an apprenticeship in the simpler and more definite, and therefore more advanced, problems of physics (Marshall, 1920, pp. xvi–xvii).

But of course there was dogma and a standard of orthodoxy: that was why agreement had been achieved relatively quickly by the mathematical workers; the standards and ideas had been appropriated during their apprenticeship in physics. The *Principles* is a book that touts the mathematical method while attempting to deny that the method could influence the content of what was being expressed. The clearest manifestation of this tension occurs in the Appendix to the *Principles*, where, in the midst of a series of abstruse notes concerning the application of constrained maximisation to utility, there is an incongruous discussion of the applications of Taylor's Theorem to the webbing between a duck's appendages (Marshall, 1920, pp. 841–842). The purpose of the digression is to suggest that the calculus was being borrowed from an organic evolutionary metaphor. Not only did Taylor's Theorem have nothing to do with the duck's webbing in Marshall's actual example; but the calculus of constrained maximisation was not employed by evolutionary theorists in Marshall's day.

6. The history of economic thought as an active generator of research programmes

The energetics metaphor can be found in every major neoclassical theorist of the nineteenth century and can be used to explain some controversies in the history of economic thought. It is a very neat pattern; perhaps too neat. Is it being too wise after the event in defining neoclassicism tautologically as coextensive with the introduction of the physics metaphor into social theory, and then brushing other authors aside? I do not think so. This article merely points out what has been there for all to see in published writings, biographies, and the history of science.

This paper has *not* specified why the energetics metaphor was so attractive to nineteenth century economic theorists, or discussed why the economics tail still is or is not wagged by the physics dog. Such omissions are due in part to prosaic reasons of space limitation, but also to the fact that such a discussion requires a much larger original content and a grounding in the philosophies of science and theory choice. The philosophy of science is so important because it indicates where to begin searching for acceptable explanations of the adoption of the physics metaphor. Should we look to the level of personal motivation or structural tendencies? Should we look to empirical inadequacies or logical flaws, or some less rigid intellectual influences? These questions give rise to a research project, which could be carried out at many different levels: the level of individual desires (e.g., Jevons' personal motivations (Mirowski, 1984A), that of individual influences (e.g. Edgeworth's family were friends of Hamilton), that of class interests, that of the sociology of professions (here the location of economists in universities), that of the cannons of empiricism (the rise of quantification as a preferred empirical technique), that of the status of alternative competing research programmes (say, the dilution of the Ricardian programme by Mill and the retreat of the labour theory of value), and that of metaphysical predispositions in the larger culture [e.g., the western tendency to see social relations as rooted in 'natural' processes (Levine, 1977)].

Another reason why modern philosophy of science is important is that it has highlighted the significance of the history of science. Discussion of the above issue can be cogently prosecuted only in conjunction with the study of the actual (as opposed to mythical) history of mathematics, physics, etc. Only then would we be able to extend the inquiries into the twentieth century with questions like: what is the relation between the penetration of input–output methods into economics and the preceding rise of matrix methods in quantum mechanics? What is the link between Niels Bohr's 'Correspondence Principle' and that of Paul Samuelson? Another question of interest concerns the relation of mathematical technique to model content. Did mathematical economic theorists before 1870 'fail' because they were inept, or for other more profound reasons (Mirowski, 1984B)?

Finally, we can clarify the issues broached at the outset. The antiquarian question has been settled: neoclassical economic theory is bowdlerised nineteenth century physics. The epistemological issue has been illuminated: present research techniques may be favoured *because* they were appropriated from physics. The ontological issue has been reinterpreted: neoclassicism was not 'simultaneously discovered' because it was 'true', as Jevons and others would have it; instead, the timing of its genesis is explained by the timing of the energetics revolution in physics, and by the fact that scientifically trained individuals in different Western European countries at that time had access to the same body of knowledge and techniques. The practical issue, however, has scarcely been addressed. One cannot predict where new theories will come from, but one can venture a broad inductive generalisation from past patterns: that a substantial non-neoclassical economic theory will distinguish itself by consciously repudiating the energetics metaphor.

Bibliography

Agassi, J. 1971. *Faraday as a Natural Philosopher,* Chicago, University of Chicago Press

Agassi, J. 1981. *Science and Society,* Boston, Reidel

Antonelli, G. B. 1886. *Sulla theoria mathematica della economia politica,* trans. in Chipman, J., Hurwicz, L., Richter, M. and Sonnenschein, H. (eds) 1971, *Preferences, Utility and Demand,* New York, Harcourt Brace Jovanovich

Auspitz, R. and Lieben, R. 1889. *Untersuchungen über die Theorie des Preises,* Leipzig, Duncker and Humblot

Bharadwaj, K. 1978. The subversion of classical analysis: Alfred Marshall's early writing on value, *Cambridge Journal of Economics,* vol. 2, no. 3, September

Black, R., Coats, A. and Goodwin, C. (eds) 1973. *The Marginal Revolution in Economics,* Durham, N.C., Duke University Press

Blaug, M. 1978. *Economic Theory in Retrospect,* 3rd edn, Cambridge, CUP

Blaug, M. 1980. *The Methodology of Economics,* Cambridge, CUP

Bloor, D. 1976. *Knowledge and Social Imagery,* Boston, Routledge and Kegan Paul

Boland, L. 1982. *The Foundations of Economic Method,* Boston, Allen and Unwin

Bos, H. 1980. Mathematics and rational mechanics, in Rousseau, G. and Porter, R. (eds), *The Ferment of Knowledge,* Cambridge, CUP

Bowley, M. 1973. *Studies in the History of Economic Thought Before 1870,* London, Macmillan

Brannigan, A. 1981. *The Social Basis of Scientific Discoveries,* Cambridge, CUP

Bukharin, N. 1927. *Economic Theory of the Leisure Class,* New York, International

Cannon, S. 1978. *Science in Culture,* New York, Dawson

Checkland, S. 1951. The advent of academic economics in England, *Manchester School,* January

Clower, R. 1970. The Keynesian counterrevolution, in Clower, R. (ed.), *Monetary Theory,* Baltimore, Penguin

378 P. Mirowski

Crowe, M. 1967. *A History of Vector Analysis,* Notre Dame University Press
Dennis, K. 1982. Economic theory and mathematical translation, *Journal of Economic Issues,* September
Dupuit, J. 1952. On the measurement of utility of public works, Barbach (trans.), *International Economic Papers,* no. 2
Edgeworth, F. Y. 1881. *Mathematical Psychics,* London, Kegan Paul
Farmer, M. 1983. Some thoughts on the past, present and future of the rational actor in economics, paper presented to History of Thought Conference, University of Manchester, September
Fisher, I. 1892. *Mathematical Investigations into the Theory of Value and Prices,* Transactions of the Connecticut Academy, vol. 9
Garegnani, P. 1976. On a change in the Notion of Equilibrium, in Brown, M. *et al.* (eds), *Essays in Modern Capital Theory,* Amsterdam, North Holland
Georgescu-Roegen, N. 1971. *The Entropy Law and the Economic Process,* Harvard University Press
Hankins, T. 1980. *Sir William Rowan Hamilton,* Baltimore, Johns Hopkins University Press
Harding, S. (ed.) 1976. *Can Theories be Refuted?* Boston, Reidel
Harman, P. M. 1982. *Energy, Force and Matter,* Cambridge, CUP
Hicks, J. R. 1979. *Causality in Economics,* New York, Basic Books
Howey, R. S. 1960. *The Rise of the Marginal Utility School,* Lawrence, University of Kansas Press
Jahnke, H. and Otte, M. (eds) 1981, *Epistemological and Social Problems of the Sciences in the Early 19th Century,* Boston, Reidel
Jevons, W. S. 1905. *The Principles of Science,* 2nd edn, London, Macmillan
Jevons, W. S. 1970. *The Theory of Political Economy,* Black, R. (ed.) Baltimore, Penguin
Jevons, W. S. 1972–81. *The Papers and Correspondence of W. S. Jevons,* 7 vols, Black, R. (ed.), London, Macmillan
Kahl, R. (ed.) 1971. *Selected Writings of Hermann von Helmholtz,* Middletown, Connecticut, Wesleyan University Press
Kauder, E. 1965. *A History of Marginal Utility Theory,* Princeton University Press
Kline, M. 1972. *Mathematical Thought from Ancient to Modern Times,* Oxford, OUP.
Knight, F. 1956. Statics and dynamics, in *On the History and Methodology of Economics,* University of Chicago Press
Knorr-Cetina, K. and Mulkay, M. 1983. *Science Observed: Perspectives on the Social Study of Science,* London, Sage
Kuhn, T. 1977. *The Essential Tension,* University of Chicago Press
Latsis, S. 1976. *Method and Appraisal in Economics,* Cambridge, CUP
Laundhardt, W. 1885. *Mathematische Begrundung der Volkswirtschaftslehre,* Leipzig, Engelmann
Levine, D. 1977. *Economic Studies: Contribution to the Critique of Economic Theory,* Boston, Routledge and Kegan Paul
Lisman, J. H. C. 1949. Economics and thermodynamics, *Econometrica,* January
Lowe, A. 1951. On the mechanistic approach in economics, *Social Research,* vol. 18
Lucas, R. 1981. *Essays in Business Cycle Theory,* London, MIT Press
Marshall, A. 1898, Mechanical and biological analogies in economics, reprinted in Pigou, A. C. (ed.), *Memorials of Alfred Marshall,* London, Macmillan
Marshall, A. 1920. *Principles of Economics,* 8th edn, London, Macmillan
McCloskey, D. 1983. The rhetoric of economics, *Journal of Economic Literature*
Menard, C. 1980. Three forms of resistance to statistics: Say, Cournot, Walras, *History of Political Economy,* Winter
Menger, C. 1963. *Problems of Economics and Sociology,* Nock, (trans.), Urbana, University Illinois Press
Menger, C. 1981. *Principles of Economics,* Dingwell and Hoselitz (trans.), New York University Press
Meyerson, E. 1962. *Identity and Reality,* New York, Dover
Mirowski, P. 1981. Is there a mathematical neoinstitutional economics?, *Journal of Economic Issues,* September
Mirowski, P. 1983. Review of Nelson and Winter's evolutionary theory of economic change, *Journal of Economic Issues,* September
Mirowski, P. 1984A. Macroeconomic fluctuations and 'natural' processes in early neoclassical economics, *Journal of Economic History,* June

Mirowski, P. 1984B. Whewell, Cournot, and the abortive penetration of mathematics into political economy, Tufts University Discussion Paper

Mirowski, P. 1984C. The role of conservation principles in 20th century economic theory, *Philosophy of the Social Sciences*, December

Nelson, R. and Winter, S. 1982. *An Evolutionary Theory of Economic Change*, Harvard University Press

O'Hear, A. 1980. *Karl Popper*, London, Routledge and Kegan Paul

Pareto, V. 1953. On the economic principle, *International Economic Papers*, no. 3

Pareto, V. 1971A. Ophelimity in nonclosed cycles, in Chipman, J., Hurwicz, L., Richter, M. and Sonnenschein, H. (eds), *Preferences, Utility and Demand*, New York, Harcourt Brace Jovanovich

Pareto, V. 1971B. *Manual of Political Economy*, Schwier, A. (trans.), New York, Kelley

Popper, K. 1957. *The Poverty of Historicism*, London, Routledge and Kegan Paul

Popper, K. 1965. *Conjectures and Refutations*, New York, Harper and Row

Samuelson, P. 1950. On the problem of integrability in utility theory, *Economica*, November

Samuelson, P. 1952. Economic theory and mathematics—an appraisal, *American Economic Review*, May

Samuelson, P. (ed.) 1954. Symposium on mathematics in economics, *Review of Economics and Statistics*, November

Samuelson, P. 1972. Maximum principles in analytical economics, *American Economic Review*, June

Sebba, G. 1953. The development of the concepts of mechanism and model in physical science and economic thought, *American Economic Review*, March

Shackle, G. L. S. 1967. *Time in Economics*, Amsterdam, North Holland

Sorokin, P. 1956. *Contemporary Sociological Theories*, New York, Harper and Row

Sraffa, P. 1926. The laws of returns under competitive conditions, *Economic Journal*, December

Stark, W. 1944. *The History of Economics in Relation to its Social Development*, London, Routledge and Kegan Paul

Sussmann, M. 1972. *Elementary General Thermodynamics*, Reading, Addison-Wesley

Theobald, D. W. 1966. *The Concept of Energy*, London, Spon

Thoben, H. 1982. Mechanistic and organistic analogies in Economics reconsidered, *Kyklos*, vol. 35

Volterra, V. 1971. in Chipman, J., Hurwicz, L., Richter, M. and Sonnenschein, H. (eds), *Preferences, Utility and Demand*, New York, Harcourt Brace Jovanovich

Walras, L. 1960. Économique et Mécanique, *Metroeconomica*, pp. 1–13

Walras, L. 1965. *Collected Papers and Correspondence*, Jaffee, W. (ed.), 3 vols, Amsterdam, North Holland

Walras, L. 1969. *Elements of Pure Economics*, Jaffee, W. (trans.), New York, Kelley

Weinberger, O. 1931. Rudolf Auspitz und Richard Lieben: Ein Beitrag zur Geschichte der Mathematischen Methode in der Volkswirtschaftlehre, *Zeitschrift für die gesamte Staatwissenschaft*, vol. 91, pp. 457–492

Weintraub, E. R. 1979. *Microfoundations*, Cambridge, CUP

Weisskopf, W. 1979. The method is the ideology, *Journal of Economic Issues*, September

Westfall, R. S. 1980. *Never at Rest: a Biography of Issac Newton*, Cambridge, CUP

Wittgenstein, L. 1978. *Remarks on the Foundations of Mathematics*, rev. edn, London, MIT Press

Wong, S. 1978. *The Foundation of Paul Samuelson's Revealed Preference Theory*, Boston, Routledge and Kegan Paul

Wright, C. 1980. *Wittgenstein on the Foundations of Mathematics*, Harvard University Press

Zowadzki, W. 1914. *Les Mathématiques Appliquées à L'Économie Politique*, Paris, Marcel Rivière

[22]

Robert Giffen and the Irish Potato: Note

By ULRICH KOHLI*

In their paper in this *Review* (1984), Gerald Dwyer and Cotton Lindsay express serious doubts about the existence of a Giffen-good paradox during the 1845–49 Irish potato famine. While many of their arguments and their main conclusion are convincing, one important step in their demonstration needs to be qualified.

Dwyer and Lindsay argue that nineteenth-century Ireland was essentially a closed economy, and hence that the supply of potatoes was exogenous. The sharp drop in the supply of potatoes in 1845–49 must therefore be viewed as a market experiment, rather than an individual experiment, with the price of potatoes an endogenous variable. Dwyer and Lindsay consider the following as a major problem with the common view that potatoes are a Giffen good: "...With an upward-sloping demand curve, a decrease in supply results in a lower, not a higher, price....This possibility is ludicrous: a large part of a country on the brink of starvation, and the market price of potatoes falls?" (p. 189). Dwyer and Lindsay then present some indirect evidence that the price of potatoes, far from falling, actually increased. This outcome seems inconsistent with the Giffen-good hypothesis.

The purpose of this note is to show with the help of a simple general equilibrium model that evidence of a price increase is not necessarily incompatible with the Giffen-good hypothesis, although the hypothesis must nevertheless be rejected in the Irish case on the basis of additional evidence presented (but not fully exploited) by Dwyer and Lindsay regarding the movement of prices of potato substitutes. This exercise proves instructive, for it reveals an interesting property of the Giffen-good model that seems to have gone unnoticed in the past.

The analysis presented by Dwyer and Lindsay is in terms of the inverse of the Marshallian demand curve. That is, they implicitly treat nominal income and the prices of all goods other than potatoes as given. For simplicity, assume that there are only two goods, and let the Marshallian demand for potatoes be given by

$$q_P = d(p_P, p_M, Y), \tag{1}$$

where q_P is the quantity of potatoes, p_P is the price of potatoes, p_M is the price of the other good (say meat), and Y is nominal income. The inverse of the Marshallian demand function expresses the price of potatoes as a function of the quantity available, and is defined as

$$p_P = g(q_P, p_M, Y). \tag{2}$$

One can easily see that $\partial g(.)/\partial q_P = [\partial d(.)/\partial p_P]^{-1}$. It is well known that $\partial d(.)/\partial p_P > 0$ if potatoes are a Giffen good, hence $\partial g(.)/\partial q_P > 0$ as well. That is, a decrease in the available supply of potatoes must lead to a reduction in the price of potatoes. As noted by Dwyer-Lindsay, any evidence to the contrary should lead to the rejection of the Giffen-good hypothesis.

Crucial in the above argument is the assumption that p_M is given. While Ireland was a closed economy in potatoes, it was not isolated economically, and it may well be that other goods were available at given international prices. This is possibly the view implicitly held by Dwyer and Lindsay. However, there is a certain ambiguity in this regard, for they explicitly argue that Ireland was a peasant economy that was closed in food. Furthermore, they present evidence that the prices of potato substitutes increased substantially during the famine. This last

*Professor of Economics, University of Geneva, 2 Rue de Candolle, CH-1211 Geneva 4, Switzerland. I am grateful to W. Erwin Diewert, Philip Graves, Edward Morey, and an anonymous referee for their comments on an earlier version of this note.

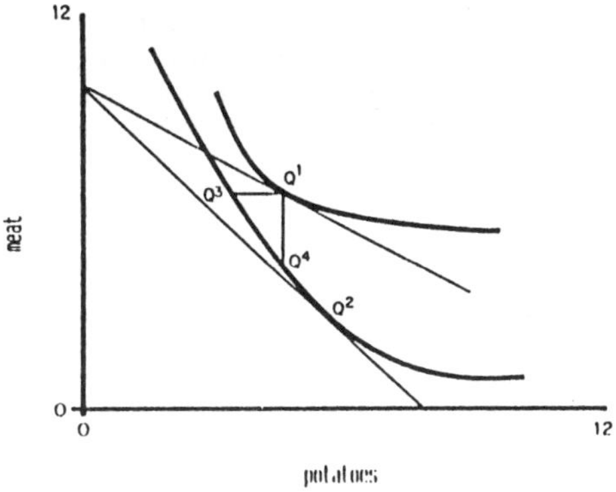

FIGURE 1

observation is inconsistent with the assumption of a perfectly elastic supply.

Let us assume therefore that rural Ireland was indeed a closed economy, that is, that the supplies of potatoes as well as of meat were given. The price effect of an exogenous reduction in the supply of potatoes can then be analyzed with the help of the inverse demand for potatoes. Inverse demand schedules express prices as functions of quantities.[1] In this example, the inverse demand for potatoes is defined as

$$p_P = h(q_P, q_M, Y), \tag{3}$$

where q_M is the available quantity of meat. Note the difference between (2) and (3).[2] In the former, the price of meat is considered exogenous and the quantity demanded is implicitly treated as endogenous, while the reverse is true in the latter.

Inverse demand functions are generally downward sloping (for example, see Ronald Anderson), that is, $\partial h(.)/\partial q_P < 0$, and it turns out that this is also true for Giffen goods. This can be shown graphically with Figure 1 that depicts a pair of indifference curves in the quantity (potatoes, meat) space. The graph is drawn under the assumption that potatoes are a Giffen good at point Q^1. (An increase in the price of potatoes, as depicted by the steeper budget line, would indeed raise the demand for potatoes, with equilibrium moving from Q^1 to Q^2.)

Figure 1 can easily be used for market experiments. Once the supply of goods is given, the marginal rate of substitution at that point determines the market-clearing price ratio. Knowing nominal income, absolute prices can be determined as well. Consider now the effect of a drop in the supply of potatoes, for a given quantity of meat. This change, described in Figure 1 by a movement from Q^1 to Q^3, is accompanied by an increase in the marginal rate of substitution between meat and potatoes; that is, the relative price of potatoes increases. This result is hardly surprising: a drop in the supply of potatoes, by reducing real income, raises the demand for potatoes and lowers the demand for meat. Moreover, it is visible from Figure 1 that, compared to the original situation, the vertical intercept of the price line (new position not drawn) moves upwards, while the horizontal intercept shifts to the left. Hence, for given money income, the price of potatoes increases and the price of meat falls in absolute terms.[3]

The analysis can also be conducted in terms of the Marshallian demand curve. Figure 2 is similar to Dwyer and Lindsay's graph (lower panel). Dwyer and Lindsay argue that a decrease in the supply of potatoes, from q_P^1 to q_P^2, leads to a price fall, from p_P^1 to p_P^2, under the Giffen-good hypothesis. Implicit in their analysis is the assumption that the price of meat remains unchanged. Yet if the supply of meat is given, its price must fall as the result of the reduction in the supply of potatoes. Hence the Marshallian demand curve must shift

[1] I use the terminology of Ronald Anderson (1980), W. Erwin Diewert (1980), and John Weymark (1980).

[2] Many authors, when discussing inverse demand, do so in a one-good context, in which case the distinction between (2) and (3) vanishes. See Hal Varian (1978), and James Henderson and Richard Quandt (1971, p. 134), for instance.

[3] See my 1985 paper for a mathematical proof of the same proposition.

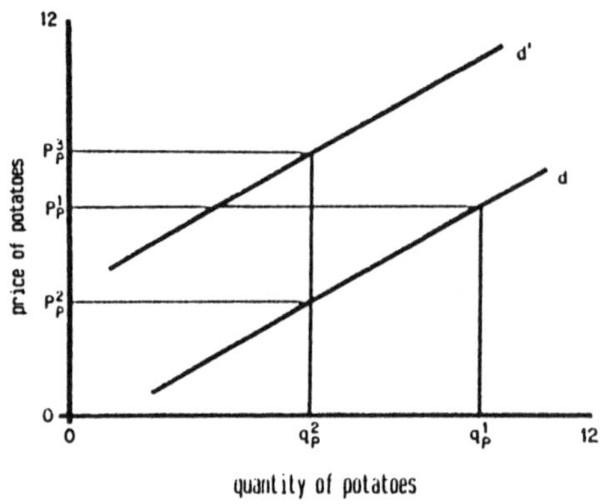

FIGURE 2

leftwards, from d to d'. The earlier discussion points out that the shift must be large enough to result in an increase in the price of potatoes, from p_P^1 to, say, p_P^3.

In these circumstances, an increase in the price of potatoes is not inconsistent with the Giffen-good hypothesis. What contradicts the hypothesis, however, is the evidence of an increase in the price of potato substitutes. Indeed, the model predicts that, for given q_M and Y, a reduction in q_P results in a fall in p_M if potatoes are a Giffen good. Although nominal income almost certainly did not remain constant during the 1845–49 events, it is hard to imagine that it actually increased. Hence a rise in p_M is incompatible with the Giffen-good hypothesis. Thus, Dwyer and Lindsay's conclusion remains intact, but the relevant piece of evidence is the increase in the price of potato substitutes, not the increase in the price of potatoes.

Dwyer and Lindsay conclude their discussion by arguing that the Giffen-good concept has no application in closed economies where the supplies of goods are given. This is not necessarily true. Giffen goods may exist in open as well as in closed economies, but it simply turns out that Giffen goods do not display any spectacular property with respect to inverse demands. This is not so for meat, however. It is worthwhile noting that a decrease in the supply of meat (for example, resulting from an outbreak of foot-and-mouth disease, depicted by the movement from Q^1 to Q^4 in Figure 1) would actually result in a *lower* price of meat. This is visible from the upward movement of the intercept of the price line when the endowments point shifts from Q^1 to Q^4. Hence, for given nominal income, the price of meat must fall. That is, the uncompensated inverse demand for meat is positively sloped,[4] and meat could therefore be termed an *anti-Giffen* good.[5] This property of the potatoes-meat model seems to have gone unnoticed in the past, for attention is generally focused on potatoes, yet is is meat that behaves abnormally when it comes to inverse demand.

[4] The uncompensated inverse price elasticity can be decomposed into two parts: a pure substitution term and a scale effect (Anderson). Although scale effects are normally negative, it is positive in the case of meat; moreover, it is large enough to dominate the negative substitution effect. Put another way, the income elasticity of meat is so large that a drop in its supply, by lowering real income, results *ceteris paribus* in a fall in demand that actually exceeds the reduction in supply.

[5] This name is inspired by I. F. Pearce's (1964) use of the term antidemand to designate inverse demand analysis. Jack Hirshleifer (1980) uses the term ultrasuperior to refer, in the two-dimensional case, to the partner of an inferior good. Anti-Giffen goods are ultrasuperior, but the reverse is not necessarily true.

REFERENCES

Anderson, Ronald W., "Some Theory of Inverse Demand for Applied Demand Analysis," *European Economic Review*, November 1980, *14*, 281–90.

Diewert, W. Erwin, "Duality Approaches to Microeconomic Theory," in K. F. Arrow and M. D. Intriligator, eds., *Handbook of Mathematical Economics*, Vol 2, Amsterdam: North-Holland, 1980.

Dwyer, Gerald P., Jr. and Lindsay, Cotton M., "Robert Giffen and the Irish Potato," *American Economic Review*, March 1984, *74*, 188–92.

Henderson, James M. and Quandt, Richard E., *Microeconomic Theory*, 2nd ed., New York: McGraw-Hill, 1971.

Hirshleifer, Jack, *Price Theory and Applications*, Englewood Cliffs: Prentice-Hall, 1980.

Kohli, Ulrich, "Inverse Demand and Anti-Giffen Goods," *European Economic Review*, April 1985, *27*, 397–404.

Pearce, Ivor F., *A Contribution to Demand Analysis*, Oxford: Oxford University Press, 1964.

Varian, Hal., *Microeconomic Analysis*, New York: W. W. Norton, 1978.

Weymark, John A., "Duality Results in Demand Theory," *European Economic Review*, November 1980, *14*, 377–95.

[23]

History of Political Economy 19:3

CCC 0018-2702/87/$1.50

Edgeworth, Samuelson, and operationally meaningful theorems

Bruce Larson

I. *Introduction*

Paul Samuelson has described an operationally meaningful theorem as "a hypothesis about empirical data which could conceivably be refuted, if only under ideal conditions."[1] The methods that he developed for deriving such theorems—optimization conditions, stability conditions, and a priori information—have found their way into the toolbox of every economist.[2]

The methodological aspects of operationally meaningful theorems have received much attention,[3] as have the methods for deriving such theorems,[4] but nothing has been said about Samuelson's priority regarding these methods. This article shows that F. Y. Edgeworth had, by 1909, employed optimization conditions, stability conditions, and a variant of a priori information to derive operationally meaningful theorems. This being the case, Edgeworth's work is found to have a significance not previously noticed and Samuelson's achievement is viewed anew.

II. *Background*

Edgeworth's first major publication was *New and old methods of ethics*, published in 1877.[5] Writing under the influence of neo-contractarianism,[6] he sought to give mathematical precision to utilitarianism, and in so doing employed the calculus of variations and what he would later call "loose quantitative relations," i.e., general functions whose derivatives are restricted only by sign. This work, which drew substantially upon the work

Correspondence may be addressed to the author, Dept. of Economics, University of North Carolina at Asheville, One University Heights, Asheville NC 28804-3299.

1. Paul Samuelson, *Foundations of economic analysis* (Cambridge, Mass., 1947), 4.
2. See ibid. 5 and 22–23.
3. See Mark Blaug, *The methodology of economics* (Cambridge, 1980); Bruce Caldwell, *Beyond positive economics* (London, 1982); and Johannes J. Klant, *The rules of the game*, trans. Ina Swart (Cambridge, 1984).
4. See Gilbert Ritschard, *Contributions à l'analyse des structures qualitatives des modèles économiques* (Berne, 1980).
5. See F. Y. Edgeworth, *New and old methods of ethics* (Oxford, 1877). For a discussion of *Methods*, see John Creedy, 'The early use of Lagrange multipliers in economics,' *Economic Journal* 90 (June 1980): 371–76.
6. See John Creedy, 'Edgeworth: utilitarianism and arbitration,' *History of Political Economy* 16 (Winter 1984): 609–18.

of Todhunter, is marked by a clear appreciation of the first- and second-order conditions for a maximum, and some familiarity with the work of Laplace; Laplace's work is well-known for the view that, a priori, unknown probabilities are uniformly distributed.[7]

Between 1877 and 1881, but no sooner than 1879, Edgeworth's interest in economics was stimulated by Jevons,[8] who undoubtedly led him to the writings of Cournot and Marshall.[9] Cournot's work emphasized the use of loose quantitative relations, employed the calculus, gave some attention to probability, as Jevons had, and derived an operationally meaningful theorem using second-order maximization conditions.[10] In addition, Cournot and Marshall paid close attention to the stability of equilibrium—Cournot in the context of duopoly theory and Marshall in the context of international trade.[11] But neither Cournot nor Marshall used stability conditions to derive an operationally meaningful theorem.

In *Mathematical psychics* Edgeworth sought to draw a parallel between mathematical physics, in which the maximum principles of Hamilton and Lagrange had served so well, and mathematical psychics. He held that physics and psychics differed in the type of data with which they had to deal, but that both could be analyzed by the same methods, i.e., the calculus of variations as applied to loose quantitative relations.[12] In developing his argument he used the second-order conditions for a maximum to examine the curvature properties of an indifference curve, thereby deriving an operationally meaningful theorem. At this date Edgeworth was already using a priori probabilities as a means of argument.[13]

7. See Isaac Todhunter, *Researches in the calculus of variations, principally on the theory of discontinuous solutions* (London, 1871), and the discussion of Laplace in Karl Henrik Borch, *The economics of uncertainty* (Princeton, N.J., 1968), 78. On Edgeworth's mathematical background, see John Creedy, 'F. Y. Edgeworth's mathematical training,' *Journal of the Royal Statistical Society*, Series A, 146 (1983): 158–62.

8. See John Creedy, 'F. Y. Edgeworth, 1845–1926,' in *Pioneers of modern economics in Britain*, ed. D. P. O'Brien and John R. Presley (Totowa, N.J., 1981), 72–104.

9. See John Hicks, 'Francis Ysidro Edgeworth,' *Hermathena* 135 (1983): 157–74.

10. On loose quantitative relations, see Augustin Cournot, *Researches into the mathematical principles of the theory of wealth*, trans. Nathaniel T. Bacon (1927; reprint, New York, 1971), 3–4. The use of the calculus and the derivation of an operationally meaningful theorem can be found at ibid. 52–62, and brief references to the probabilistic side of things can be found at ibid. 18–22. For Jevons' discussion of the probabilistic side of things, see W. Stanley Jevons, *The theory of political economy* (London, 1871), 72–74.

11. See Cournot, *Researches*, 81, and Maffeo Pantaleoni, *Pure economics* (1889; reprint, New York: 1957), 197–209. Pantaleoni's work employed Alfred Marshall's 1879 'Pure theory of foreign trade,' a reprint of which appears in John K. Whitaker, *The early economic writings of Alfred Marshall, 1867–1890*, 2 vols. (New York, 1975). For Edgeworth's familiarity with Marshall's work, see Creedy, 'Edgeworth: utilitarianism.'

12. See F. Y. Edgeworth, *Mathematical psychics* (1881: reprint, New York, 1967), 1–15 and 83–93.

13. For the indifference analysis, see ibid. 34–36 and 91. Some of this material duplicated earlier work in Edgeworth, 'The hedonical calculus,' *Mind* 4 (1879): 394–408. For a brief discussion of the role of a priori probabilities in Edgeworth's work, see Creedy, 'Edgeworth: utilitarianism,' 614–17.

Shortly after the publication of *Mathematical psychics*, Edgeworth's attention turned to statistics. His first publication in this area appeared in 1883, and in an 1884 paper he is seen discussing the notion of a priori probabilities in connection with the work of Bayes and Laplace.[14] Edgeworth went on to be a productive and fruitful statistical researcher.[15]

III. *Operationally Meaningful Theorems*

By 1884, then, Edgeworth had been exposed to the essential ideas that would enable him to derive operationally meaningful theorems, i.e., optimization conditions, stability conditions, and a priori probabilities. These ideas will now be seen in action.

Maximum conditions

Edgeworth's most recognizable operationally meaningful theorems appear in his 1897 restatement and extension of Cournot's monopoly theory.[16] The theorems were derived by using the second-order conditions for a maximum.

Edgeworth first derived Cournot's result that a per unit tax imposed upon a single-product monopolist would lead to an increase in the product's price,[17] but then he extended Cournot's work to the two-product case. He wrote:

> let the cost of producing x together with y be $\varphi(x,y)$ where $d^2\varphi/dx^2$, $d^2\varphi/dy^2$ (the law of increasing cost being assumed) and $d^2\varphi/dxdy$ are each positive. Let $f_1(x)$ be the price at which the quantity x is demanded in one market and $f_2(y)$ the price at which the quantity y is demanded in another market; then if V is the net advantage of the monopolist, $V = xf_1(x) + yf_2(y) - \varphi(x,y)$.
>
> Now suppose a small tax of u per unit is imposed on the first commodity. If dx and dy are the consequent variations in the quantities furnished we have, since $(dV/dx) = 0$, and $(dV/dy) = 0$,
>
> $$dx\, d^2V/dx^2 + dy\, d^2V/dxdy = u,$$
> $$dx\, d^2V/dxdy + dy\, d^2V/dy^2 = 0;$$
>
> whence $dx = ud^2V/dy^2 \div \Delta$; $dy = -ud^2V/dxdy \div \Delta$; where Δ is the determinant $d^2V/dx^2\, d^2V/dy^2 - (d^2V/dxdy)^2$, a quantity which must

14. See F. Y. Edgeworth, 'The philosophy of chance,' *Mind* 9 (April 1884): 223–35.

15. On Edgeworth's statistical work, see A. L. Bowley, *F. Y. Edgeworth's contributions to mathematical statistics* (1928; reprint, Clifton, N.J., 1972), and Stephen M. Stigler, 'Francis Ysidro Edgeworth, statistician,' *Journal of the Royal Statistical Society*, Series A, 141 (1978): 287–322.

16. The series was first published as 'Teoria pura del monopolio' in the *Giornale degli Economisti* and is used here in translation. See F. Y. Edgeworth, 'The theory of monopoly,' in *Papers relating to political economy*, 3 vols., ed. F. Y. Edgeworth (1925; reprint, New York, 1970), 1:111–42.

17. See ibid. 112–13. For the original statement, see Cournot, *Researches*, 71–73.

be positive in order that V should be a maximum. For the same reason d^2V/dx^2 must be negative. Also $d^2V/dxdy = -d^2\varphi/dxdy$ must be negative. Accordingly dx is negative, dy is positive; the purchasers of the taxed article are damnified, while the purchasers of the tax-free article are benefitted.[18]

As the quotation shows, Edgeworth used second-order maximum conditions to derive operationally meaningful theorems.[19] By continuing to generalize Cournot's monopoly theory, Edgeworth showed that operationally meaningful theorems could also be derived using a priori probabilities.

A priori probabilities

What are a priori probabilities? Presently such probabilities are closely associated with Bayesian ideas, an instance of which is Edgeworth's assumption that when a variable is known to take on two values with unknown frequency, the variables are uniformly distributed.[20] But Edgeworth's usage was still broader, as he also held that if two variables took on different values at different times, one always positive and the other sometimes positive and sometimes negative, then it was probable that their sum was positive.[21]

A third use of a priori probabilities assumed that the unknown value of a variable was zero, as will now be seen. Continuing to extend Cournot's monopoly theory, Edgeworth considered the case where the demand prices of the monopolist's goods depended upon the quantity of each good.[22] In such a case the pre-tax net advantage of the monopolist is

$$V = xf_1(x,y) + yf_2(x,y) - \varphi(x,y)$$

from which it can be inferred that the effect on x and y of a small per-unit tax τ on the quantity of good x is

$$\Delta x d^2V/dx^2 + \Delta y d^2V/dxdy = \tau$$
$$\Delta x d^2V/dxdy + \Delta y d^2V/dy^2 = 0$$

18. See Edgeworth, 'Monopoly,' 127–28, from which some commas between differentials have been omitted. Edgeworth's approach is what would now be called the method of total differentials, except that he wrote u where present usage would write du; similarly he often used parentheses to indicate partial derivatives. Edgeworth did not write the after-tax net advantage of the monopolist, which is $V = xf_1(x) + yf_2(y) - \varphi(x,y) - ux$.

19. Second-order maximum conditions were later used to define diminishing returns in Edgeworth, 'Contributions to the theory of railway rates,' *Economic Journal* 21 (Sept. 1911): 346–70.

20. See Edgeworth, 'Appreciations of mathematical theories,' *Economic Journal* 17 (June 1907): 221–31.

21. See Edgeworth, 'Contributions to the theory of railway rates: III,' *Economic Journal* 22 (June 1912): 198–218.

22. See Edgeworth, 'Theory of monopoly,' 134.

The second-order conditions being $d^2V/dx^2 < 0$, $d^2V/dy^2 < 0$, and $D = (d^2V/dx^2)(d^2V/dy^2) - (d^2V/dxdy)^2 > 0$, it follows that $\Delta x = (\tau d^2V/dy^2)/D < 0$ and $\Delta y = (-\tau d^2V/dxdy)/D$. Regarding Δy, "All that can be said with certainty about its sign is that it will be contrary to the sign of $d^2V/dxdy$."[23]

The possibility that Δy could be negative, i.e., that a tax on x could lower the price of y, has come to be known as Edgeworth's taxation paradox.[24] Through further analysis Edgeworth showed that

$$\frac{d^2V}{dxdy} = \left[\frac{df_1}{dy} + \frac{df_2}{dx}\right] + \left[\frac{xd^2f_1}{dxdy} + \frac{yd^2f_2}{dxdy}\right] - \left[\frac{d^2\varphi}{dxdy}\right]$$

of which he said:

> Of the three parts or terms of this expression (distinguished by square brackets), we know that the first is positive or negative according as the demand is complementary or rival; and that the third (with its sign) is positive or negative according as the production is complementary or rival. But we do not know the sign of the second term; and are therefore perhaps justified in ignoring it; especially when the sum of the two other terms is considerable, as may well be if production and consumption are either both rival or both complementary.[25]

Employing, then, the a priori assumption that the second term can be ignored, and the assumption that either production and consumption are both rival or both complementary, an operationally meaningful theorem results. Edgeworth's a priori assumption is discomforting to the present-day economist, but it does result in an operationally meaningful theorem.[26]

Stability

Economists may never be comfortable with Edgeworth's use of a priori probabilities, but there was a time when they were comfortable using stability conditions.[27] These conditions were employed in an analysis of Bickerdike's trade model.[28]

23. See ibid. 132. For more details, see 131–35.

24. For the classic exposition, see Harold Hotelling, 'Edgeworth's taxation paradox and the nature of demand and supply functions,' *Journal of Political Economy* 40 (Oct. 1932): 577–616.

25. See Edgeworth, 'Theory of monopoly,' 135.

26. For a work which parallels Edgeworth's use of a priori probabilities, see G. Polya, *Patterns of plausible inference* (Princeton, N.J., 1968).

27. For an example of the use of stability conditions, see Arthur Benavie, 'Monetary and fiscal policy in a two-sector Keynesian model,' *Journal of Money, Credit and Banking* 7 (Feb. 1976): 63–84. For a critique of stability conditions, see F. H. Hahn, 'On general equilibrium and stability,' in *Paul Samuelson and modern economic theory*, ed. E. C. Brown and R. M. Solow (New York, 1983), 31–55.

28. See C. F. Bickerdike, 'The theory of incipient taxes,' *Economic Journal* 16 (Dec.

Bickerdike's model showed that a country could, under particular conditions, benefit from a tariff, and gave rise to the elasticity approach to international trade.[29] Central to the model was a surplus-based measure of net advantage, with which he showed that the rate at which the net advantage (u) varied with the exchange rate (r) was

$$-\frac{du}{dr} = \frac{\left(\frac{1}{n_\delta} - \frac{1}{n_\sigma}\right)}{\left(1 - \frac{1}{n_\sigma}\right)\left(1 - \frac{1}{e_s}\right) - \left(1 - \frac{1}{n_\delta}\right)\left(1 - \frac{1}{e_d}\right)}$$

Bickerdike argued, implicitly using a priori probabilities, that $-du/dr$ "is positive, unless both demands are inelastic in a certain degree."[30] Given that the tariff is an *ad valorem* tax p and that the exchange rate is $r = 100/(100 + p)$, it follows that du/dp, i.e., the net advantage of the tariff, varies directly with the tax. In a 1908 paper Edgeworth indicated the a priori basis of Bickerdike's conclusion, and then showed that it could also be derived "by the condition that the equilibrium of trade with which we are concerned is stable."[31]

Edgeworth argued that a stable equilibrium was assured when the slope of the home country's reciprocal demand curve was greater in absolute value than that of the foreign country's. This condition implied that the denominator of Bickerdike's $-du/dr$ must be positive.[32] Edgeworth also developed an argument which implied that the numerator of $-du/dr$ is positive.[33]

Edgeworth, then, used the conditions for a stable equilibrium to show that a country could benefit from a tariff, an operationally meaningful theorem. As Bickerdike's version of the theorem relied on a priori probabilities, stability conditions may be viewed as a means of narrowing the range of theorems which must be justified on the basis of a priori probabilities.

IV. *Summary and Observations*

It has been seen that F. Y. Edgeworth, writing under the influence of Jevons, Cournot, Marshall, Todhunter, Hamilton, Laplace, and Lagrange,

1906): 529–35; idem, Review of *Protective and preferential import duties*, by A. C. Pigou, *Economic Journal* 17 (March 1907): 98–102; and F. Y. Edgeworth, 'Appreciations of mathematical theories [IV],' *Economic Journal* 18 (Dec. 1908): 541–56.

29. See John S. Chipman, 'A reconsideration of the "elasticity approach" to balance-of-payment adjustment problems,' in *Breadth and depth in economics*, ed. Jacob S. Dreyer (Lexington, Mass., 1978), 49–85.

30. See Bickerdike, Review, 101. Bickerdike's use of a priori probabilities is not surprising, given his close relationship to Edgeworth, on which see Bruce Larson, 'Bickerdike's life and work,' *History of Political Economy* 19.1:1–21.

31. See Edgeworth, 'Appreciations [IV],' 544.

32. For details, see ibid. 544–45.

33. See ibid. 541–43.

and probably many more, employed maximum conditions, stability conditions, and a priori probabilities to derive operationally meaningful theorems. Thus Edgeworth had used variants of Samuelson's three sources of operationally meaningful theorems by 1909. Edgeworth's priority in these methods has not been previously noticed.

Given Edgeworth's priority, what remains of Samuelson's contribution? A great deal, it would appear. First, it must be noted that Edgeworth employed 'static' rather than 'dynamic' stability to derive his meaningful theorem. As it is dynamic stability that is relevant for market processes, this is an important distinction.

Second, there is Samuelson's treatment of meaningful theorems in the *n* variable case, with regard to optimization conditions and stability conditions; theorems at higher levels of generality are more useful. Third, there is Samuelson's different view of a priori knowledge, which is more empirically oriented than Edgeworth's a priori probabilities. Samuelson's method employed existing knowledge, whereas Edgeworth's method dealt with ignorance; used with great care, Edgeworth's method could extend the scope of comparative statics.

Most significant about Samuelson's methods, however, is their conscious and deliberate use. In Samuelson's hands they became tools accessible to the average economist, whereas in Edgeworth's hands they were just used. Paul Bunyan swung a mighty axe, but who else could use it?

[24]

History of Political Economy 21:2

CCC 0018–2702/89/$1.50

Edgeworth's contribution to the theory of "Ramsey pricing"

Jun-ji Shih

I. *Introduction*

It is accepted that Ramsey's equal-percentage-cut rule was originated by Ramsey (1927) and rediscovered by Boiteux (1951, 1956).[1] However, the contribution of Edgeworth has been ignored. This article attempts to demonstrate that the very first appearance of the Ramsey rule is in Edgeworth's 1910 article 'Applications of probabilities to economics,' which appeared in the *Economic Journal*. In fact, Edgeworth discovered the theory of "Ramsey pricing" in the course of investigating the effect of third-degree price discrimination on social welfare, and then Ramsey and Boiteux independently arrived at Edgeworth's result.

II. *Edgeworth's Contribution*

Edgeworth's article was published while he was the editor of the *Economic Journal*. This article is, like almost everything he wrote, extremely elusive and allusive.[2] Perhaps because of this, his contributions to "Ramsey pricing" and the welfare implications of price discrimination have received little attention.[3]

The central question asked in the paper by Edgeworth is: Is the social welfare, defined as consumers' surplus plus that of producers, under third-degree price discrimination greater than that under simple monopoly? To answer the question, several classes of demand curves were employed by Edgeworth. They are *linear, parabola, square root, logarithm,* and *anti-*

Correspondence may be addressed to the author, Institute of the Three Principles of the People, Academia Sinica, Taipei TAIWAN.

1. See Baumol and Bradford (1970, 277–80) or Samuelson (1982).
2. All investigators of Edgeworth's work must at some point come to grips with his unique style of writing. Modern commentators will frequently use the word obscure to describe it. As Stigler (1978, 293) points out, "Edgeworth's mathematical style may be the greatest source of difficulty for most readers." Interested readers are recommended to see Stigler's discussion of Edgeworth's writing style (Stigler 1978, 292–93).
3. Ekelund (1970), Culbertson and Ekelund (1977), and Cross and Ekelund (1980) seem aware of Edgeworth's contribution to the theory of price discrimination. For example, Ekelund (1970, 268, n. 2) states that "Edgeworth—somewhat overenthusiastically—extended the same verdict on Dupuit to the area of mathematical economics."

logarithm functions. After delicate calculations, he reaches the following conclusion: "Probably the prices which the monopolist will fix in order to render his profit a maximum are such that the customers will lose through discrimination" (1925, 2:207).[4] But the opposite may occur. Thus, the welfare effect under third-degree price discrimination is indeterminate. Edgeworth went on to show that the welfare of both the monopolist and his customers can be improved by forcing the monopolist to adopt a *regulatory price* and compensating him for the resultant loss by a lump-sum transfer from those customers who gain by the imposed regulation.

Indeed, the regulatory policy proposed by Edgeworth is a second-best solution. Briefly stated, under regulation the monopoly profits are maximized subject to a fixed level of consumers' surplus that is equal to or greater than that resulting under unregulated discriminating monopoly. In fact, Edgeworth clearly recognized that a monopoly regulated in this way should practice a milder form of third-degree discrimination than an unregulated discriminating monopoly and will produce a greater amount of social welfare. Moreover, he demonstrated that the constrained discrimination "is realized by a system of prices such that the elasticity is the same for each of the demand-curves" (Ibid., 412). This is the pricing principle for regulated industries or public utilities, now referred to as the "Ramsey rule." The following is an extensive quotation from the passage in which this rule first appears.

> When a monopolist discriminates between different species of custom, subject to the conditions that the subtraction from (or addition to) the benefit of his customers as a whole should be nil, or have any other assigned value, the elasticity of demand is the same for the different species which are discriminated (cost of production being null or constant). For consider the Consumers' Surplus, say *W*, . . . , in the case of two species of commodity,[5]

4. Edgeworth's 1910 paper was later collected in his three volumes of *Papers relating to political economy* (1925, 2: 387–428). The quotations used in this article follow the 1925 version of Edgeworth's paper. Substantive variations from the 1910 paper are noted.

5. The Consumer's Surplus *W*, Lagrange multiplier λ, and dW/dy_1 were printed incorrectly as

$$W = \int_0^{x_1} y_1 dx_1 + \int_0^{x_2} y_2 dx_2 - x_1 y_1 - x_2 y_2$$

$$= + \int_{\infty}^{y_1} x_1 dy_1 + \int_{\infty}^{y_2} x_2 dy_2$$

$$\lambda = \frac{dV}{dy_1} \Big/ \frac{dW}{dy_1}$$

$$\frac{dW}{dy_1} = x_1$$

I have corrected these errata in the text.

$$W = \int_0^{x_1} y dx_1 + \int_0^{x_2} y dx_2 - x_1 y_1 - x_2 y_2$$
$$= \int_{y_1}^{\infty} x_1 dy_1 + \int_{y_2}^{\infty} x_2 dy_2$$

[where x_i is the unit sales to a customer of type i and y_i is the price charged to such a buyer]. Likewise the profit of the monopolist, say V, is, in the absence of cost of production, $x_1 y_1 + x_2 y_2$. Now the quantity which the monopolist aims at maximizing is $V + \lambda W$, where λ is the indeterminate coefficient proper to problems of relative maximum. We have accordingly

$$\frac{d}{dy_1}(V+\lambda W) = 0; \frac{d}{dy_2}(V+\lambda W) = 0$$

Whence $\lambda = -(dv/dy_1)/(dW/dy_1)$. Now $(dV/dy_1) = x_1(1-e_1)$, and $(dW/dy_1) = -x_1$. Therefore, $\lambda = (1-e_1)$ [e_i is the elasticity of demand for market i, i.e., $e_i = -(y_i/x_i)(dx_i/dy_i)$]. By parity of reasoning, $\lambda = (1-e_2)$.[6] Whence, $e_1 = 1-\lambda = e_2$. As above, e is replaced by ε [ε_i is a modified concept of elasticity, defined as $\varepsilon_i = -[(y_i - c)/x_i](dx_i/dy_i)$, where c is the marginal cost] when the cost of production per unit is a constant, but the proposition loses its simplicity when the cost (per unit) involves the variables. [Ibid., 426]

Of greater interest is his recognition of the fact that a public monopoly, in contrast to a private monopoly, may follow the same pricing technique of constrained discrimination.[7] To quote Edgeworth again,

> It may be remarked that the property of equal elasticities is also characteristic of another kind of discrimination which may seem particularly suitable for a State Monopoly to practice, namely, that regulation of prices which has for its object the maximum benefit to the purchasers as a whole, consistent with the retention by the monopolist of a fixed profit—a fixed amount, or a fixed percentage of the output, that is of the cost of production, supposing cost to be constant. [Ibid., 426]

Two points should be noted about the assertion above. First, the reasoning underlying Edgeworth's own statement comes from an application of the following "symmetry" proposition: If profits are maximized subject to

6. In the 1925 version of Edgeworth's paper e_2 was misprinted as ε_2. I have corrected this erratum in the text.

7. The emphasis on the pricing technique of public monopoly found in the writings of Edgeworth seems suggestive of Dupuit (1849). But Dupuit's own analysis was, for the most part, nonmathematical in character. Dupuit's early work has been assessed by Ekelund (1970).

a fixed level of consumer surplus, then exactly the same prices and quantities will maximize consumer surplus subject to a given level of profits, providing the constraint level in the second version is set equal to the optimal value of the maximand in the first version. Thus, Edgeworth's argument here is quite correct. Second, his pricing principle for regulated monopoly as well as state monopoly is in fact a clear statement of the condition required by what can now be called "Ramsey pricing." To appreciate this point let us consider the Ramsey rule, which follows the inverse elasticity formula, as[8]

$$\frac{R}{e_i} = \frac{y_i - c}{y_i} \tag{1}$$

where R is the "Ramsey number." Now, if the production cost is null or constant, then marginal cost equals zero ($c = 0$) and equation (1) should be

$$\frac{R}{e_i} = \frac{y_i}{y_i} = 1 \text{ or equivalently,} \qquad R = e_i \tag{2}$$

In other words, *it* requires products in any two markets, i and j, to be priced to such a level that $e_i = e_j$. Clearly, the Ramsey rule turns out to be Edgeworth's property of equal elasticities under Edgeworth's assumption of constant production cost.

In addition, as noted by Edgeworth, e_i is replaced by ε_i when the marginal cost c is a constant instead of zero. To see this, recall the definitions of e_i and ε_i, and rewrite equation (1) as

$$R = \frac{y_i - c}{y_i} e_i = -\frac{y_i - c}{x_i}\frac{dx_i}{dy_i} = \varepsilon_i \tag{3}$$

Therefore, we have $\varepsilon_i = \varepsilon_j$. It goes without saying that Edgeworth did clearly foreshadow the Ramsey-pricing results.

III. *Conclusions*

This paper has shown Edgeworth as a major, and one of the earliest, contributors to the theory of public utility pricing. It is not surprising that Edgeworth's work has not been widely appreciated because of his obscure style; indeed, few economists actually understand his discussions. As such, this provides a good example of the fact that the same scientific discovery can be realized independently by geniuses of different times. A public utility executive, Boiteux, rediscovered Ramsey some 30 years after

8. Interested readers should see the discussion of the inverse elasticity formula of the Ramsey rule in Baumol and Bradford (1970, 270–71).

the latter's breakthrough. Even a genius like Ramsey did not know that he had already been preceded by Edgeworth.

Edgeworth's place in the history of optimal public utility pricing is thus incontestable. Furthermore, his contributions to the welfare implications of third-degree price discrimination,[9] apart from their considerable historical interest, deserve fresh and careful reading.

The author would like to thank Professors C. C. Mai, J. C. Liu, S. M. Chen, and A. K. Leung for their suggestions. I have also benefited from the very helpful comments of an anonymous reader.

References

Baumol, W. J., and D. F. Bradford 1970. 'Optimal departures from marginal cost pricing.' *American Economic Review* 60: 263–85.

Boiteux, M. 1951. 'Le "Revenu distribuable" et les pertes économiques.' *Econometrica* 19: 112–33.

——— 1956. 'Sur la gestion des Monopoles Publics astreints à léquilibre budgetaire.' *Econometrica* 24: 22–40.

Cross, M., and R. B. Ekelund, Jr. 1980. 'A. T. Hadley on monopoly theory and railway regulation: an American contribution to economic analysis and policy.' *History of Political Economy* 12: 214–33.

Culbetson, W. P., Jr., and R. B. Ekelund, Jr. 1977. 'John A. Hobson and the theory of discriminating monopoly.' *History of Political Economy* 9: 273–82.

Dupuit, J. 1849. 'On tolls and transport charges.' Translated by E. Henderson in *International Economic Papers* no. 11 (London, 1962), p. 7.

Edgeworth, F. Y. 1910. 'Applications of probabilities to economics.' *Economic Journal* 20: 284–308, 441–65.

——— 1911. 'Use of differential prices in a regime of competition.' *Economic Journal* 21: 143–48.

——— 1912. 'Contribution to the theory of railway rates.' *Economic Journal* 22: 198–218; 23: 206–26.

——— 1925. *Papers relating to political economy.* London.

Ekelund, R. B., Jr. 1970. 'Price discrimination and product differentiation in economic theory: an early analysis.' *Quarterly Journal of Economics* 84: 268–78.

Ramsey, F. 1927. 'A contribution to the theory of taxation.' *Economic Journal* 37: 47–61.

Samuelson, P. A. 1982. 'A chapter in the history of Ramsey's optimal feasible taxation and optimal public utility prices.' In S. Andersen et al., eds., *Economic essays in honour of Jørgen H. Gelting.* Copenhagen.

Stigler, S. M. 1978. 'Francis Ysidro Edgeworth, statistician.' *Journal of Royal Statistical Society* Series A, 141: 287–322.

Varian, H. R. 1985. 'Price discrimination and social welfare.' *American Economic Review* 75: 870–75.

9. His contribution to price discrimination theory can be found in Edgeworth (1910, 1911, 1912) and his review of Colson (Edgeworth 1925, 3:168–75). The latter suggests a similarity between Colson's early work and Varian's (1985, 870–71) recent contribution.

Name Index

Pioneers in Economics

Section I: The Forerunners of Classical Economics

1. The Historiography of Economics
2. Aristotle (384–322 B.C.)
3. St Thomas Aquinas (1225–1274)
4. The Early Mercantilists
   Thomas Mun (1571–1641), Edward Misselden (1608–1634), Gerard de Malynes (1586–1623)
5. The Later Mercantilists
   Josiah Child (1603–1699) and John Locke (1632–1704)
6. Pre-Classical Economists Volume I
   Charles Davenant (1656–1714) and William Petty (1623–1687)
7. Pre-Classical Economists Volume II
   Pierre le Pesant Boisguilbert (1645–1714), George Berkeley (1685–1753), Baron de Montesquieu (1689–1755), Ferdinando Galiani (1727–1787), James Anderson (1739–1808), Dugald Stewart (1753–1828)
8. Pre-Classical Economists Volume III
   John Law (1671–1729) and Bernard Mandeville (1660–1733)
9. Richard Cantillon (1680–1734) and Jacques Turgot (1727–1781)
10. François Quesnay (1694–1774), Volumes I and II
11. David Hume (1711–1776) and James Steuart (1712–1780)

Section II: The Golden Age of Classical Economics

12. Adam Smith (1723–1790) Volumes I and II
13. Henry Thornton (1760–1815), Jeremy Bentham (1748–1832), James Lauderdale (1759–1839), Simonde de Sismondi (1773–1842)
14. David Ricardo (1772–1823)
15. Jean-Baptiste Say (1776–1832)
16. Thomas Robert Malthus (1766–1834) and John Stuart Mill (1806–1873)
17. Ramsay McCulloch (1789–1864), Nassau Senior (1790–1864), Robert Torrens (1780–1864)
18. Thomas Tooke (1774–1858), Mountifort Longfield (1802–1884), Richard Jones (1790–1855)

19. William Whewell (1794–1866), Dionysius Lardner (1793–1859), Charles Babbage (1792–1871)

20. George Scrope (1797–1876), Thomas Attwood (1783–1856), Edwin Chadwick (1800–1890), John Cairnes (1823–1875)

21. James Mill (1773–1836), John Rae (1796–1872), Edward West (1782–1828), Thomas Joplin (1790–1847)

22. James Wilson (1805–1860), Issac Butt (1813–1879), T. E. Cliffe Leslie (1827–1882)

23. Karl Marx (1818–1883)

Section III: Neoclassical Economics and its Critics

24. Johann von Thünen (1783–1850), Augustin Cournot (1801–1877), Jules Dupuit (1804–1866)

25. Leon Walras (1834–1910)

26. Carl Menger (1840–1921)

27. Eugen von Böhm-Bawerk (1851–1914) and Friedrich von Wieser (1851–1926)

28. Knut Wicksell (1851–1926)

29. Alfred Marshall (1842–1924) and Francis Edgeworth (1845–1926)

30. Gustav Schmoller (1838–1917) and Werner Sombart (1863–1941)

31. Dissenters
    Charles Fourier (1772–1837), Henri de St Simon (1760–1825), Pierre-Joseph Proudhon (1809–1865), John A. Hobson (1858–1940)

32. Thorstein Veblen (1857–1929)

33. Wesley Mitchell (1874–1948), John Commons (1862–1945), Clarence Ayres (1891–1972)

34. Henry George (1839–1897)

35. Vilfredo Pareto (1848–1923)

Section IV: Twentieth Century Economics

36. Arthur Pigou (1877–1959)

37. Frank Knight (1885–1972), Henry Simons (1899–1946), Joseph Schumpeter (1883–1950)

38. Edward Chamberlin (1899–1967)

39. Michael Kalecki (1899–1970)

40. Harold Hotelling (1895–1973), Lionel Robbins (1898–1984), Clark Warburton (1896–1979), John Bates Clark (1847–1938), Ludwig von Mises (1881–1973)

41. Irving Fisher (1867–1947), Arthur Hadley (1856–1930), Ragnar Frisch (1895–1973), Friedrich Hayek (1899-—), Allyn Young (1876–1929), Ugo Mazzola (1863–1899)

42. Harry Johnson (1923–1977)

43. Bertil Ohlin (1899–1979)

44. Piero Sraffa (1898–1983)

45. Joan Robinson (1903–1983) and George Shackle (1903-—)

46. John Maynard Keynes (1883–1946) Volumes I and II